ENCYCLOPEDIA OF WORLD TRADE

FROM ANCIENT TIMES TO THE PRESENT

VOLUME 2

EDITED BY CYNTHIA CLARK NORTHRUP

SHARPE REFERENCE
an imprint of M.E. Sharpe, Inc.

SHARPE REFERENCE

Sharpe Reference is an imprint of M.E. Sharpe, Inc.

M.E. Sharpe, Inc.
80 Business Park Drive
Armonk, NY 10504

© 2005 by M.E. Sharpe, Inc.

All rights reserved. No part of this publication may be reproduced, stored in a retrieval system or transmitted in any form or by any means, electronic, mechanical, photocopying, recording, or otherwise, without the prior permission of the copyright holders.

Maps on pages 76, 167, 330, 430, 509, 680, 796, 808, and 864 were adapted from Geoffrey Barraclough, ed., *The Times Atlas of World History,* 6th ed. (Maplewood, NJ: Hammond, 1982); map on page 836 was adapted from Kwame Anthony Appiah and Henry Louis Gates, Jr., eds., *Africana: The Encyclopedia of the African and African American Experience* (New York: Basic Books, 1999); maps on pages 412, 644, 712 were adapted from John P. McKay, et al., *A History of World Societies,* 6th ed. (Boston: Houghton Mifflin, 2000).

The EuroSlavic fonts used to create this work are © 1986–2002 Payne Loving Trust.
EuroSlavic is available from Linguist's Software, Inc.,
www.linguistsoftware.com, P.O. Box 580, Edmonds, WA 98020-0580 USA
tel (425) 775-1130.

Library of Congress Cataloging-in-Publication Data

Encyclopedia of world trade : from ancient times to the present / Cynthia Clark Northrup, editor.
   p. cm.
Includes bibliographical references and indexes.
ISBN 0-7656-8058-0 (hardcover : alk. paper)
 1. International trade—History—Encyclopedias. 2. Commerce—History—Encyclopedias.
I. Northrup, Cynthia Clark, 1959–

HF1373.W67 2004
382′.03—dc22
                                                2003015313

Printed and bound in the United States

The paper used in this publication meets the minimum requirements of
American National Standard for Information Sciences—Permanence of
Paper for Printed Library Materials,
ANSI Z 39.48.1984.

BM (c) 10 9 8 7 6 5 4 3 2 1

Compositors:
Nancy J. Connick and Sharon D. Ray

ENCYCLOPEDIA OF WORLD TRADE

VOLUME 2

CONTENTS

Topic Finder vii
List of Maps xi

Volume 2

East Asia 297
Economic Consequences of the Peace, The 298
Economics, Classical 299
Edison, Thomas Alva 300
Egypt 301
Egypt, Ancient 302
Electricity 304
Elizabeth I 305
Embargoes 306
Empire Building 308
Energy 319
Engels, Friedrich 321
England's Treasure by Foreign Trade 321
Entertainment 322
Etruscans 326
European-African Trade 327
European-Asian Trade 328
European Trade, Intracontinental 331
European Union 332
Exchange Rates 334
Exploration and Trade 335
Extraterritoriality 346
Fairs, International Trade 348
Fertilizer 353
Festivals and Fairs, Medieval 354
Feudalism 356
Financial Institutions 357
Flax 363
Florence (Firenze) 364
Food and Diet 365
Ford Motor Company 372
Foreign Aid 374
Frankincense and Myrrh 376
Franklin, Benjamin 377

Frederick II 379
Free Trade 380
Freemasonry 381
French Empire 382
French Revolution 385
Fruits 387
Fugger Family 388
Fur 389
Gandhi, Mohandas 391
Garamantian Empire 393
Gemstones 394
General Agreement on Tariffs and Trade 396
General Electric Company 398
*General Theory of Employment, Interest,
    and Money, The* 399
Genoa 401
German Empires 403
Ghana 406
Ghaznavids 409
Glass 410
Globalization 410
Gold 419
Gold Standard 421
Goths 422
Grain 425
Great Depression 427
Greater East Asia Co-prosperity
    Sphere 431
Greek City-States 433
Guangzhou (Canton) 434
Guano 436
Gunpowder 437
Haiti 440
Hakluyt, Richard 441
Hamburg, Germany 441
Hanseatic League 443
Hapsburgs 446
Harbors 448
Hargreaves, James 452

v

Hawley-Smoot Tariff	452
Heckscher, Eli Filip	454
Hellenistic Architecture	455
Hemp	457
Henry the Navigator	459
Hinduism	460
Hittite Empire	463
Hohenstaufen Empire	464
Hollywood	467
Hong Kong	469
Hundred Years' War	475
Illegal Trade	480
Immigration	483
Imperialism	491
Incas	499
Indentured Servants	501
Indian Ocean Trade	503
Indigo	506
Indus River	507
Industrial Revolution	509
Industrialism	514
Inflation	516
Insurance	517
Intellectual Property	521
Internal Combustion Engine	524
International Monetary Fund	526
International Trade Commission	528
Internet	530
Iron	533
Iron Law of Wages	535

Irrigation	536
Isabella of Castile	537
Islam	539
Ivory	544
Ivory Coast of Africa	545
Jade	549
Jews	550
Joint-Stock Companies	551
Judaism	553
Jute	555
Keynes, John Maynard	557
Khan, Genghis	558
Khazar Empire	559
Kilwa	559
Kipling, Rudyard	560
Knights Templars	561
Kush (Cush)	564
Labor	565
Laissez-faire	575
Law	576
Leather	584
Linear B Script	585
Linen	586
List, Georg Frederich	587
Livestock	588
Luddites	591
General Index	I-1
Biographical Index	I-45
Geographical Index	I-53

TOPIC FINDER

Banking, Finance, and Currency
  Bardi House of Banking
  Coinage
  Cowries
  Dirhams
  Disputes and Arbitration, International
  Exchange Rates
  Financial Institutions
  Gold Standard
  Insurance
  International Monetary Fund
  Money
  Rothchilds
  World Bank

Buildings and Structures
  Aswan High Dam
  Castles
  Crystal Palace
  Hellenistic Architecture
  Mesopotamian Architecture

Business and Businessmen
  British East India Company
  Carnegie, Andrew
  Clive, Robert
  Corporations
  Ford Motor Company
  Fugger Family
  General Electric Company
  Joint-Stock Companies
  Medici Family
  Multinational Enterprise
  Pegolotti, Francesco Balducci
  Pochteca
  Polo, Marco
  Singer, Issac

Cities
  Alexandria
  Amsterdam
  Athens, Ancient
  Batavia (Jakarta)
  Berenice (Berenike)
  Calcutta
  Calicut
  Cities
  Constantinople (Byzantium, Istanbul)
  Florence (Firenze)
  Genoa
  Guangzhou (Canton)
  Hamburg, Germany
  Hollywood
  Madras
  Manila
  Milan
  Mogadishu
  Nineveh
  Novgorod
  Petra
  Ragusa, Republic of (Dubrovnik)
  Shanghai
  Surat
  Venice

Commodities
  Amber
  Cacao
  Chocolate
  Coffee
  Copper
  Corn
  Cotton
  Diamonds
  Drugs
  Fertilizer
  Flax
  Frankincense and Myrrh
  Fruits
  Fur
  Gemstones
  Glass
  Gold
  Grain
  Guano
  Gunpowder
  Hemp
  Indigo
  Iron
  Ivory
  Jade
  Jute
  Leather
  Linen
  Livestock
  Molasses
  Nuts
  Oil
  Olives
  Opium
  Paper and Pulp
  Pepper
  Perfume
  Potatoes
  Pottery
  Rice
  Rum
  Salt
  Silk
  Silver
  Soybeans
  Spices
  Steel
  Sugar
  Tea
  Textiles
  Tin

Tobacco
Tortoiseshell
Water
Weapons
Whales
Wine
Wood
Wool

Communication
Alphabet, Aramaic
Alphabet, Cyrillic
Alphabet, Greek
Alphabet, Latin
Alphabet, Phoenician
Communication
Cuneiform
Internet
Linear B Script
Pony Express
Printing Press
Telegraph
Telephone

Continents
Africa
South America

Countries and Empires
Abbasid Caliphate
Argentina
Assyrian Empire
Aztecs
Babylonian Empire
Brazil
British Empire
Byzantine Empire
Carolingian Empire
China
Chinese Dynasties
Crete
Cuba
Cyprus
Egypt
Egypt, Ancient
French Empire
Garamantian Kingdom
German Empires
Ghana
Ghaznavids
Greek City-States
Haiti
Hapsburgs
Hittite Empire
Hohenstaufen Empire
Khazar Empire
Kilwa
Kush (Cush)
Mali
Manchu Dynasty
Mayan Civilization
Melaka
Ming Dynasty
Minoan Civilization
Mughal Empire
Mycenae
Netherlands
Ottomans
Portugal
Roman Empire
Sicily
Songhay Empire
Soviet Union
Spanish Empire
Srivijaya Empire
Tunisia
United States

Economics and Economic Philosophy
Comparative Advantage
Economics, Classical
Economic Consequences of the Peace
England's Treasure by Foreign Trade
General Theory of Employment, Interest and Money
Iron Law of Wages
Laissez-faire
Reciprocity
Redistribution
Transaction Costs

Economic Systems
Capitalism
Communism
Socialism

Economists
Engels, Friedrich
Heckscher, Eli Filip
Keynes, John Maynard
List, Georg Frederich
Malthus, Thomas Robert
Marx, Karl
Mill, John Stuart
Rae, John
Ricardo, David
Smith, Adam

Events
American Revolution
Black Death
Boxer Rebellion
Cold War
Colonization
Columbian Exchange
Discovery and Exploration
French Revolution
Great Depression
Industrial Revolution
Renaissance
Roman Empire, Fall of
Russian Revolution

Explorers
Columbus, Christopher
Cook, Captain James
Drake, Sir Francis
Henry the Navigator
Magellan, Ferdinand

Inventions, Inventors, and Technology
Arkwright, Richard
Astrolabe
Bell, Alexander Graham
Compass
Computers
Cotton Gin
Cross-Staff
Edison, Thomas Alva
Electricity
Energy
Hargreaves, James
Internal Combustion Engine
Irrigation
Quadrant
Steam Engine
Technology
Whitney, Eli

Legislation and Treaties
Combination Acts
Continental System
Corn Laws
Embargoes
North American Free Trade Agreement

Medicine and Disease
  Cholera
  Disease

Migrations
  Bantu Migrations
  Diasporas
  Immigration
  Migration, Human

People
  Arabs
  Armenians
  Berbers
  Bolshevism
  Bourgeoisie
  Bugis
  Dutch
  Dyula
  Etruscans
  Goths
  Incas
  Jews
  Phoenicia
  Radanites
  Vikings
  Volga Bulgaria

Politics
  Comintern
  Empire Building
  Extraterritoriality
  Foreign Aid
  Imperialism
  New Imperialism
  Open Door Notes

Politicians and Leaders
  Alexander the Great
  Bush, George Herbert Walker
  Elizabeth I
  Franklin, Benjamin
  Frederick II
  Gandhi, Mohandas
  Isabella of Castile
  Khan, Genghis
  Peter the Great

Regional Trade
  Atlantic Trade
  British-South American Trade
  Chinese-Japanese Trade
  European-African Trade
  European-Asian Trade
  European Trade, Intracontinental
  Hong Kong
  Indian Ocean Trade
  Saharan and Trans-Saharan Trade
  Soviet Union–African Trade Relations
  Triangle Trade
  U.S.-Japanese Trade Relations

Regions
  Alsace and Lorraine
  Caribbean
  Central Africa
  East Asia
  Ivory Coast of Africa
  Persian Gulf
  South Africa
  Southeast Asia
  West Africa

Religion
  Buddhism
  Christianity
  Confucius
  Hinduism
  Islam
  Missionaries
  Pilgrimages
  Protestantism
  Reformation
  Religion
  Roman Catholic Church
  Teutonic Knights

Rivers, Straits, and Canals
  Amazon River
  Dardanelles
  Danube River
  Indus River
  Nile River
  Panama Canal
  Suez Canal

Seas
  Aegean Sea
  Black Sea
  Mediterranean Sea

Tariffs
  Hawley-Smoot Tariff
  Nontariff Barriers
  Tariff Barriers
  Tariffs

Time Periods
  Baroque
  Dark Ages
  Hellenistic Architecture
  Middle Ages

Trade
  Agora
  Department Stores
  Fairs, International Trade
  Festivals and Fairs, Medieval
  Free Trade
  Illegal Trade
  Marketplaces
  Tally-Sticks
  Timber/Sorochok
  Trademarks

Trade Issues
  Advertising
  Agriculture
  Archaeology
  Art
  Barter
  Bioterrorism
  Bribery
  Cartography
  Climate
  Competition
  Consumerism
  Containment
  Copyrights
  Crop Rotation
  Entertainment
  Exploration and Trade
  Feudalism
  Financial Institutions
  Food and Diets
  Freemasonry
  Globalization
  Indentured Servants
  Industrialism
  Inflation
  Intellectual Property
  Labor
  Law
  Market Revolution
  Media
  Medicine
  Mercantilism

Mongol Invasions
Monuments
Nomads
Oases
Patents
Piracy
Population
Revolutions
Sculpture
Service Sector
Slavery
Slaves, Plantation
Terrorism
Tourism
Wealth
Weights and Measures
Women

Trade Organizations
Association of Southeast Asian Nations
British Commonwealth
Cartels
Council for Mutual Economic Assistance
Delian League
European Union
General Agreement on Tariffs and Trade
Greater East Asia Co-prosperity Sphere
Hanseatic League
International Trade Commission
Merchant Guilds
Royal Niger Company
Trade Organizations
United Nations
World Trade Organization

Trade Routes
Amber Routes
Atlantic Trade
Silk Road
Spice Route

Transportation
Aircraft
Animals
Appian Way
Automobiles
Aviation
Caravans
Harbors
Manila Galleons
Navigation
Navigation Laws
Railroads
Ships
Shipwrecks
Steamship
Trade Winds
Transportation and Trade

Unions and Labor Movements
American Federation of Labor–Congress of Industrial Organizations
Luddites

Warfare
Anglo-Dutch Wars
Crimean War
Crusades
Hundred Years' War
Knights Templars
Marshall Plan
Napoleonic Wars
Punic Wars
Seven Years' War
War of 1812
Warfare
Wars for Empire
World War I
World War II

Writers
Hakluyt, Richard
Kipling, Rudyard

LIST OF MAPS

Amber Route, 500 B.C.E. 31
Transatlantic Trade, 1700 76
Trade, Han Dynasty, Beginning of
  Common Era 167
Eurasian Trade Routes, 1450 330
European Union, 2004 333
Global Economy, 1600 412
Great Depression, United States, 1933 430
Indian Ocean Trade, 1450 504
Industrial Revolution,
  United Kingdom, 1750 509

European Trade, Middle Ages, 1300 644
Mughal Empire and Early British India,
  1805 680
Global Oil Trade, 2004 712
Roman Empire, 100 C.E. 796
Saharan Trade, 1000 C.E. 808
Silk Road, 1000 C.E. 830
African Overseas Slave Trade,
  1450–1850 836
Steamship Routes, 1900 864

ENCYCLOPEDIA OF WORLD TRADE

VOLUME 2

E

EAST ASIA

> A region that encompasses China, Japan, and Korea.

The peoples and kingdoms of East Asia have traded regionally for thousands of years. China's trade network extended as far as the Roman empire and Africa. After centuries of semi-isolation, European traders began arriving in rapidly increasing numbers. A century of exploitation and colonialism by Europeans was succeeded by the rise of Japan's colonial project. East Asia emerged from colonialism into the Cold War, with a divided China and Korea. The last half of the twentieth century witnessed the rise of Japan and South Korea and the reintegration of China into the world economy.

EARLY HISTORY

The history of trade in East Asia is largely the history of trade with and within China. Ancient China traded silk, minerals, and spices with the Roman empire and Persia through the famous Silk Road. Chinese had limited interest in expanding international trade, though, because of the low status of merchants as well as China's self-sufficiency.

Maritime trade with other kingdoms in Asia was much more consistent and important than the limited contact with kingdoms in the Middle East, especially after Arab traders stopped organizing long trips in the twelfth century. The Korean kingdoms of Paekche (350–668) and Silla (350–918) were crucial intermediaries that spread Chinese goods and culture to Japan. Trade among the Song (960–1279) in China, Koryo in Korea (918–1392), and Heian (794–1184) in Japan expanded and contracted with various rulers, and was conducted almost exclusively through specially designated ports such as Guangzhou (Canton) in China and Busan in Korea.

The most notable development in East Asia in the fifteenth and sixteenth centuries was the emergence of Japanese traders and pirates. Japanese pirates became such a problem that Shanghai and other ports built city walls to protect themselves. This period was also marked by Japan's attempted takeover of Korea in 1592. While the Ming thwarted Japan's imperial ambitions, the attack devastated the Korea Peninsula and its people. Korea became hostile to foreigners after this, earning the nickname "Hermit Kingdom."

SUSTAINED CONTACT WITH THE WEST

The Portuguese were the first European ships to travel to East Asia, putting in at Guangzhou in 1514. Tensions grew until nearby Macao was leased to the Portuguese in 1557 to serve as a trading base. The Dutch arrived in 1622, followed shortly by the British and French. A brisk trade of porcelain, silk, and tea was soon established with expanding European markets.

China was the main attraction for the European traders. While trade was liberalized in 1685, the Chinese continued their age-old custom of trading with foreigners while having as little contact as possible. The British were the dominant trader by the time the emperor decided in 1757 that the foreigners were having too much influence. He limited foreign trade to Guangzhou, starting the so-called Canton System. The Koreans were even more suspicious of foreigners, attacking any that attempted to make contact. The

Japanese, on the other hand, were the most welcoming of any East Asian country, aggressively trading with the West.

TREATY OF NANJING TO THE RISE OF JAPAN

The rapid rise in tea consumption in Great Britain led to large trade deficits with China by the late 1700s. British traders began buying opium in India and selling it to China to balance trade. The Chinese confiscated and destroyed 20,000 chests of opium in 1839. The British drug traders responded by appealing to and partially funding the British navy as it bombarded and captured several Chinese cities in the First Opium War (1839–1842). The war ended with the Treaty of Nanjing (1842), which ceded Hong Kong to the British and opened five "treaty ports," including Shanghai and Guangzhou, to foreign trade. China quickly signed treaties with other Western powers, effectively linking all the treaties together by granting each most-favored-nation status. Economic inequality and political instability would thus characterize the last fifty years of the Qing dynasty.

Korea continued to respond to the European powers with indifference and then hostility. Japan's more open policy had resulted in economic and political instability, leading to the Meiji Restoration in 1868. The Japanese then quickly assimilated Western industrial and military technology, becoming the first industrialized country in Asia. By the end of the nineteenth century, Japan had defeated both Russia and China in wars and won exclusive control over Korea, which it annexed in 1910. Japan had long dreamed of using Korea as a base to attack China, which it did in 1937. Japan colonized most of Southeast and East Asia before being defeated in 1945.

COLD WAR TO REGIONAL INTEGRATION

The fall of the Japanese empire was followed by political instability as Cold War battles left China and Korea divided nations. The Korea Peninsula and people suffered the most for this ideological divide, with the Korean War (1950–1953) costing millions of lives. The Japanese economy, however, benefited tremendously from the war, as it served as a major logistics hub and supplier for U.S. forces in the region. The Korean War laid the foundation for Japan's extraordinary economic growth from the 1950s. Similarly, the Vietnam War helped South Korea jumpstart its economy in the 1960s and 1970s. Japan and South Korea followed a similar plan of industrialization through export-led growth to record unprecedented levels of growth.

The communist and capitalist countries were almost exclusively tied into the trade networks of their respective ideological spheres until the early 1990s. China began market reform in the late 1970s under Deng Xiaoping. Since then, China has regularly recorded double-digit growth with trade increasing from $27.7 billion in 1979 to over $620 billion in 2002. South Korea reached Organization for Economic Cooperation and Development status in the mid-1990s and is becoming a technological powerhouse. Japan still has a powerful economy despite its decade-long recession. East Asian economies are becoming increasingly integrated as South Korean and Japanese capital and technology combine with Chinese labor.

W. Chad Futrell

See also: China.

BIBLIOGRAPHY
Cotterell, Arthur. *East Asia: From Chinese Predominance to the Rise of the Pacific Rim.* New York: Oxford University Press, 1994.

ECONOMIC CONSEQUENCES OF THE PEACE, THE (1919)

> John Maynard Keynes's influential and polemic *The Economic Consequences of the Peace* (1919) denounced the Versailles Peace Treaty as harsh and unworkable because of the transfer problem in international payments.

John Maynard Keynes, a Cambridge economist, was in charge of external finance at the British Treasury during World War I and represented the treasury at the Versailles Peace Conference, playing a key role in allowing Germany to use its gold to pay for food imports (over French objections). He resigned in June 1919 and published *The Economic Consequences of the Peace* in protest against the economic terms of the peace treaty. Keynes argued that by demanding excessively large reparations payments, the victorious allies would foster lasting German nationalist resentment without managing to extract the bulk of the payments. Germany's foreign securities, overseas investments, gold reserve, and remaining merchant marine (after compulsory transfers) were worth at most $3 billion, less than a tenth of the reparations demanded. To raise the foreign exchange to pay the balance of reparations payments, Germany's exports would have to exceed its imports by the full amount of the transfer payments.

Keynes pointed out that the allied countries receiving transfers would have trade deficits equal to Germany's trade surpluses, resulting from a correspondingly large shift in the terms of trade that priced producers in allied countries out of competition with German producers. He also questioned the incentive for Germans to produce goods for export, if the proceeds were to be taxed away for reparations. Keynes's analysis provided the basis for much later analysis of capital transfers. In 1929, Bertil Ohlin extended Keynes's analysis to consider the direct effect on imports of reduced income in the paying country and increased income in the receiving country.

Despite the French and Belgian occupation of the Ruhr in 1923 to punish German default, and despite the Dawes Plan of 1924 and the Young Plan of 1929, only token reparations payments were ever made, far exceeded by foreign loans to Germany that were never repaid. In 1931, President Herbert Hoover announced a one-year moratorium on reparations and interallied debts, which effectively became permanent. Resentment over reparations demands and the Ruhr occupation inflamed German nationalism. Keynes's phenomenally successful book has sometimes been credited with the U.S. Senate's refusal to ratify the Versailles Peace Treaty. However, the Senate first rejected the treaty in November 1919, before the publication of Keynes's book in London in December 1919 and New York in January 1920. Senator William Borah read large portions of the book into the record in February 1920 when the Senate reconsidered ratifying the treaty with reservations, but rejection then was due not to Keynes, but to President Woodrow Wilson's intransigence over the proposed reservations.

Robert W. Dimand

See also: Great Depression.

BIBLIOGRAPHY

Keynes, John Maynard. *The Economic Consequences of the Peace.* London: Macmillan, 1919.

Mantoux, Etienne. *The Carthaginian Peace or the Economic Consequences of Mr. Keynes.* London: Oxford University Press, 1946.

Moggridge, D.E. *Maynard Keynes: An Economist's Biography.* New York: Routledge, 1992.

Skidelsky, Robert. *John Maynard Keynes: Hopes Betrayed, 1883–1920.* London: Macmillan, 1983.

ECONOMICS, CLASSICAL

The contributions of classical economics shaped both modern mainstream and Marxian economics.

The classical school of political economy, from David Hume's *Political Discourses* (1752) and Adam Smith's *Wealth of Nations* (1776) to John Stuart Mill's *Principles of Political Economy* (1848), emphasized growth and efficient allocation through the workings of market forces, in contrast to the mercantilist belief in state direction of economic activity. They stressed the expansion of consumption possibilities rather than national power or a surplus of exports over imports.

With the exception of Jean-Baptiste Say, the leading classical economists were Scottish or English. Hume held that, as a loyal British subject, he wished France to be prosperous, viewing it as a trading partner, not a national rival. Hume showed that a lasting trade surplus was unattainable, because the resulting gold inflow would raise prices, reducing the trade balance and restoring equilibrium. Smith argued that international division of labor, like specialization and exchange between individuals or regions, permitted increased productivity (through economies of scale and learning by doing), which allowed both greater consumption and more capital accumulation. He viewed armed forces and government bureaucracy as unproductive diversions of labor from productive employments, and limited the proper functions of government to protection against foreign and domestic violence (national defense and administration of justice) and certain public works. Robert Torrens and David Ricardo expounded the principle of comparative advantage, showing that two trading partners both gain from specialization and voluntary exchange, even if one is more productive in all possible activities. John Stuart Mill analyzed the role of reciprocal demand in determining international prices and the division of the gains from trade between trading partners.

The classical economists were united in opposition to the Corn Law of 1815, which protected British agriculture against grain exports enacted during the depression following the Napoleonic Wars (except for Thomas Robert Malthus, who initially supported the Corn Laws). They objected that costlier food would squeeze profits and real wages, diminishing both consumption and capital accumulation, to the benefit only of landlords, who would receive higher rents as inferior land was brought into cultivation. The Irish potato famine was the proximate cause of the repeal of the Corn Laws in 1846, but prolonged agitation by classical economists had prepared political opinion for repeal. The Irish famine revealed the limitations of the classical laissez-faire approach to economic policy, since the famine was due not only to inadequate food supply (which could be overcome by unrestricted imports), but also to the collapse of the purchasing power of the Irish peasantry. Classical economics became so closely associated with free trade in the public mind that free-trade ideology was known in Germany as Smithianismus. The analytical contributions of classical economics shaped both modern mainstream neoclassical economics and Marxian political economy.

Robert W. Dimand

See also: Laissez-faire; Mill, John Stuart; Ricardo, David; Smith, Adam.

BIBLIOGRAPHY

Chipman, John S. "A Survey of the Theory of International Trade: Part 1, The Classical Theory." *Econometrica* 33, no. 3 (July 1965): 477–519.

Hollander, Samuel. *Classical Economics.* Oxford: Blackwell, 1987.

Hudson, Michael. *Trade, Development and Foreign Debt.* Vol. 1. London: Pluto, 1992.

O'Brien, D.P. *The Classical Economists.* Oxford: Clarendon, 1975.

EDISON, THOMAS ALVA (1847-1931)

A famous inventor and businessman, known as the "Wizard of Menlo Park," who popularized the use of electricity.

Born in Milan, Ohio, Thomas Alva Edison overcame limited formal education and severe hearing loss to patent 1,093 inventions over a career spanning almost seventy years. Edison's inventions laid the foundation for a number of industries that would emerge in the twentieth century.

Edison was a teenager working as a telegraph operator when he pioneered the first automatic "repeating" telegraph. This invention transmitted signals between unmanned stations, thus allowing anyone to translate code with ease. After moving to Boston, Edison designed an electric vote-counting machine and an improved stock ticker, the latter earning him $40,000 and allowing him the freedom to devote his energies full time to his inventions. In 1874, he opened his own laboratory in Newark, New Jersey, soon moving it to Menlo Park. In these years, Alexander Graham Bell beat Edison in the race to transmit the first human voice electronically, but Edison followed with the carbon transmitter. This helped make Bell's telephone practical and became the prototype of the modern instrument, with its separate transmitter and receiver. Edison also designed the first phonograph in 1877.

Already a respected inventor, Edison won international fame when, in 1879, he was able to get a carbon thread to stay incandescent for forty hours. Edison realized, however, that electrical appliances such as the incandescent lightbulb

Through his many inventions, including the phonograph shown here in an 1877 photo, Thomas Alva Edison virtually invented the modern electronics industry. *(Library of Congress)*

required a whole system of generators, conductors, and meters. Only with a unified electrical power system would his inventions be commercially practical. Gaining the financial banking of the banking house of J.P. Morgan, Edison formed the Edison Electric Illuminating Company to carry out the task, and in 1882 began to supply current to eighty-five customers in New York City. By the late 1880s, a number of companies making lightbulbs had merged into the Edison General Electric Company, and Edison power plants grew throughout the country. Despite launching the great electric utility industry, however, Edison still relied on direct current, which limited his systems to a radius of only several miles. Although Edison believed it too risky, his competitor, George Westinghouse of the Westinghouse Electric Company, offered an improvement in the form of alternating current, which allowed for a higher voltage with the use of new transmitters.

By the end of the nineteenth century, the alternating current had proved more practical and effectively replaced the direct current. By this point, Edison's company had merged with several other companies to form an electric conglomerate, the General Electric Corporation, which now relied on the alternating current.

A major stockholder in the new corporation, Edison devoted his time to other inventions. Patents for the Dictaphone, mimeograph, storage battery, and kinetoscope soon followed, the latter was Edison's important contribution to the first large-scale motion picture. Wealthy and respected, Edison died at the age of eighty-four, with the nation dimming its electric lights in his honor.

Brooks Flippen

See also: Bell, Alexander Graham; Electricity; General Electric Company; Telegraph; Telephone.

BIBLIOGRAPHY
Baldwin, Neil. *Edison: Inventing the Century.* Chicago: University of Chicago Press, 2001.
Collins, Theresa M., Lisa Gitelman, and Gregory Januni. *Thomas Edison and Modern America: A Brief History with Documents.* Boston: Bedford/St. Martin's Press, 2002.

EGYPT

A country that lies in the strategic bypass between two continents, Asia and Africa, and at the shores of the Mediterranean Sea.

Egypt's location has enabled it to be a center of trade and cultural exchange since the pharaonic period (thirty-second century B.C.E.). As one of three centers of the ancient period (with China and Mesopotamia), Egypt was a major contributor to world trade at that period. The pharaohs traded with nations throughout the world, as they knew it: Africa, Asia, and Europe. Even after the demise of the ancient pharaonic power (fourth century B.C.E.), Egypt continued to be a major element in world trade.

The emergence of the Islamic empire (seventh to ninth centuries C.E.) further intensified the importance of Egyptian trading traditions by satisfying the demands of religious pilgrimages to Mecca from North Africa, Andalusia (now the Iberian Peninsula), and sub-Saharan Africa, which went through Egypt. Cairo emerged as the

A major source of cotton since the nineteenth century, underdeveloped Egypt has been less effective as a manufacturer of cotton goods. Much of its weaving is still done on hand looms, as this 1991 photo of Egyptian women indicates.
(© Josef Polleross/The Image Works)

economic, administrative, and cultural center and became the center of one of the most important Islamic dynasties: the Mamluks (thirteenth to sixteenth centuries).

The Ottoman conqueror of Egypt in (1516) turned it into the center of the North African part of the Ottoman empire. The Mamluks continued to control Egypt, under Ottoman rule, maintaining the usage of the traditional trade routes. By the end of the eighteenth century, European influence in Egypt had grown. In 1798, the French, led by Napoléon Bonaparte, occupied Egypt and three years later the British occupied the territory from them. Even though Egypt remained officially under Ottoman rule, it gained independence.

Egypt's traditional markets changed because of the European infiltration. Once the U.S. Civil War began, Egypt became the world's biggest exporter of cotton, replacing the war-torn U.S. South. Egypt was also in the midst of one of its biggest construction periods, which expressed itself above all in the digging of the Suez Canal (1859–1869).

The end of the digging, however, brought Egypt to a bankrupt situation. European creditors took over Egypt and converted its economy to pay the debts. The Suez Canal made Egypt the most important country for the British empire. In 1922, Egypt gained complete independence, but only thirty-four years later did the last British troops leave the country, after a fierce war among Egypt, Israel, France, and the United Kingdom over the free movement of shipping vassals in the Suez Canal (1956).

Egypt today is a rather weak actor in global trade. Most of its exported products are expendable energy products (crude oil and petroleum products), cotton, textiles, metal products, and chemicals. It is also influenced by the rapid growth of its population (1.69 percent in 2001), which is unable to provide for all its basic needs. A second factor is the conflicts with Israel (1948, 1956, 1967, 1969, and 1973), which brought great economic losses to Egypt, including the closure of the Suez Canal. In 1979, Israel and Egypt signed a peace treaty. Nevertheless, Egypt still spends more than $4 billion on its military. Despite its weakness, Egypt will probably continue to be an important factor in the future global economy, as the world's largest Arab nation and the leader of the Arab world.

Nadav Gablinger

See also: Arabs; Ottomans.

BIBLIOGRAPHY

Central Intelligence Agency. "Egypt." In *CIA World Factbook* (www.cia.gov/cia/publications/factbook/index.html, accessed September 2002).
Lewis, Bernard. *The Middle East: A Brief History of the Last 2,000 Years.* New York: Scribner's, 1995.
Vatikiotis, P.J. *The History of Modern Egypt: From Muhammad Ali to Mubarak.* Baltimore: Johns Hopkins University Press, 1991.

EGYPT, ANCIENT

A kingdom centered along the Nile River in today's Egypt from the fourth millennium until 30 B.C.E.

The history of ancient Egypt is a continuous period of over 3,000 years, which can be roughly divided into six time periods: the Early Dynastic Period (3100–2686 B.C.E.), the Old Kingdom (2686–2040 B.C.E.), the Middle Kingdom (2040–1570 B.C.E.), the New Kingdom (1570–747 B.C.E.), the Late Dynastic Period (747–332 B.C.E.), and the Greco-Roman

Period (332 B.C.E.–30 C.E.). Pharaohs, Egyptian rulers, enjoyed supreme power, while their state achieved an impressive degree of political and economic organization, prosperity, and military power.

Ancient Egypt was not a true trading state, mostly because it had most of the resources it needed within its own territory. The fertile Nile valley provided the population with plenty of grain, which was used to make bread and beer. Bricks were made from the mud of the Nile, and various rocks, such as limestone, basalt, alabaster, and quartzite were plentiful in the surrounding desert and perfect for construction. Hemp was grown for clothes, natron and salt for embalming were found locally, and papyrus was used to make paper. However, the country had a serious shortage of wood and metals. In addition, as the Egyptian civilization developed, the demand for luxury items increased as well.

The closest neighbors of ancient Egypt were Nubia, Libya, and the people of the Sinai peninsula and Canaan (Palestine) beyond it. Egyptian merchants purchased many luxury items in Nubia, such as ebony and ivory, leopard skins, ostrich feathers, monkeys for the royal court, as well as gold and some copper. A number of other metals were procured in the Sinai and Canaan.

As its international connections grew, Egypt reached further afield to establish a long-term commercial relationship with Phoenician cities. Egypt enjoyed the closest ties with the city of Byblos, an alliance established during the Old Kingdom that lasted for two millennia. The Phoenicians exported the timber of their cedar trees to Egypt, which increasingly began to need high-quality wood for construction and maintenance of a navy that protected its coasts from invasions by the Sea Peoples. This trade was mostly controlled by the pharaohs themselves. The Phoenician and native cities of the island of Cyprus became Egypt's main source of copper, which, along with tin, was needed for the production of bronze. The pharaohs imported so much of it that Cyprus itself often experienced shortages of that metal.

Egyptian merchants did much business in Syria as well, bringing home swords, decorated helmets, and vases, many of which seem Minoan or Cretan in origin. Other Minoan objects found at excavated Egyptian sites include highly decorated skirts and curls. Pushing into the Eastern desert, the Egyptians eventually reached the Red Sea, founding the small port of Kuser from where they sailed to the land of Punt or Pwene, probably located on the African coast opposite Aden. Many expeditions, usually funded by the pharaohs, sailed there to bring back much-prized myrrh and various spices. By the fifteenth century B.C.E., Egypt was heavily engaged in trade with the Fertile Crescent, importing horses and lapis lazuli from Babylonia, turquoise from Persia, and vegetable oils and cosmetics from as far away as Afghanistan. Interestingly enough, the horses bred so rapidly in Egypt that it would eventually export them to Assyria in the Late Period.

In turn, the Egyptians exported large quantities of grain, fruit, and papyrus. The Phoenicians were paid for their copper and cedar with gold, silver, cloth, and linens. One of the main types of export were objects of art, such as scarabs, rings, beads, statues, jewelry, mirrors, and even sarcophagi. These Egyptian objects have been found all over Europe and Asia, as far apart as Britain, Malta, and India.

TRADE AND EXPANSION

Trade often imperceptibly merged into military raids or tribute gathering. For example, Egypt's frequent trading expeditions to Nubia became major military raids during the Middle Kingdom, and much of Nubia was integrated into the Egyptian empire during the New Kingdom period. This resulted in an increasing exploitation of the Nubian gold mines. Imposition of direct Egyptian authority increased the country's control over the important overland trading routes to Punt and Kush. Slaves were both purchased in the markets of the Levant and captured in Nubia and Canaan to be used for the pharaohs' massive construction projects.

Similarly, Egyptian expansion and periodic control over Canaan and parts of Syria seem to have been driven by Egypt's desire to control the trading routes leading from Asia into Europe through Syria and the Negev deserts. It is likely that the pharaohs and the local Egyptian governors enriched themselves immensely through their domination of these routes during the periods of Egyptian control in Canaan. Similar designs probably drove Egyptian attempts at ruling Libya, with its critical gold-carrying caravan road in the Western Desert.

Much of the trade took place in the form of exchange of gifts between the pharaohs and foreign rulers and was meticulously recorded by scribes or priests. Much of the private commerce seems to have been dominated by foreign merchants, who often moved to Egypt and settled there with their families. The Phoenicians and increasingly the Greeks controlled most of Egyptian commerce during the New Kingdom, essentially acting as agents of the pharaohs and even conducting trading expeditions on their behalf, the most famous of which took several Phoenician ships around the African continent. In the Late Period, the Greeks had settled in the port of Naucratis in the Nile Delta, the main port of Egypt, and soon came to control much of the national commerce, slowly edging out the Phoenicians.

Egypt lost its independence following the Persian conquest in 525 B.C.E. and was subsequently ruled by the Greeks and the Romans. It remained an important part of the Roman empire, especially as a massive grain exporter, which fed several other provinces of the Roman Mediterranean.

Mikhail S. Zeldovich

See also: Copper; Cyprus; Gold; Phoenicia; Roman Empire.

BIBLIOGRAPHY
Cameron, Rondo. *A Concise Economic History of the World*. New York: Oxford University Press, 1997.
Gardiner, Alan. *The Egyptians*. London: Folio Society, 2000.
Mark, Samuel. *From Egypt to Mesopotamia: A Study of Predynastic Trade Routes*. Austin: Texas University Press, 1997.
Moller, Astrid. *Naukratis: Trade in Archaic Greece*. Oxford: Oxford University Press, 2001.

ELECTRICITY

International borders no longer define trade in electricity, as developed nations restructure and deregulate, and developing nations sell off state monopolies to invest in infrastructure.

The Federal Energy Policy Act of 1992, which required electric utilities to permit customers' access to other utilities and to a growing number of independent power producers, signaled the beginning of a new era of trade in electricity supply in U.S. electricity markets. This policy aimed to foster competition and freer trade in the new spot markets for electricity. However, the results vary between the deregulating states. Some deregulation failed (e.g., California), while others succeeded in achieving deregulation goals.

From a global viewpoint, international borders no longer necessarily define trade in electricity. Some U.S. states, Mexican and Canadian provinces, France, and Scotland, as well as Scandinavian and other countries share varying degrees of common electricity markets and trade in electricity. The benefits are: (1) it enables participating countries to maintain lower levels of expensive electricity reserves; (2) it strengthens electricity market stability and decreases risks for participating countries; and (3) it allows for each country to optimize the pollution-investment trade-off. Some countries (e.g., United States, Australia, and so on) are too big and geographically diverse to function as a single market and actually function with multiple internal markets.

Broadly speaking, the world's electricity markets are developing along two paths. On the one hand, most of the developed world is now in some stage of restructuring, deregulation, and liberalization. Reforms usually focus on some kind of separation (either accounting or legal) of the generation and transmission-distribution segments of the market (the "wires"), introduction of competition in the generation segment and treating the "wires" as a natural monopoly, and allowing third-party access to newly entrant and incumbent competing generators and marketers. Many restructuring schemes also include establishing a spot market for electricity, in which the unregulated market price of electricity is determined. On the other hand, most of the developing world is expected to remain inefficient, lacking reserves and continuing with national (or regional) monopoly electricity supply industries, usually state owned. The problem facing both the developed and developing worlds, however, is the emergence of global monopolistic competition in the developed world and in some countries of the developing world, the latter having to sell off some or all of their state monopolies to finance infrastructure investments. Indeed, most forecasters see the future global electricity trade as being characterized by competition among a few conglomerates that will decrease capacity (an "adverse Averch-Johnson Effect"), which will increase prices and profits in a market of relatively inelastic demand.

However, one solution for expected global monopolistic competition in electricity supply, and for other generic manifestations of market power or market manipulation, is some kind of real-time pricing. The hurdle facing the implementation of real-time pricing is financial: it is tremendously costly to set up the required metering devices. Nevertheless, attempts to use real-time pricing has been made in some places in the world (e.g., England and Wales), and it has been acknowledged as a tool for achieving increasing demand responsiveness to electricity prices.

Warren Young and Eli Goldstein

See also: Industrialism.

BIBLIOGRAPHY

Newbery, David M. *Privatization, Restructuring, and Regulation of Network Utilities.* Cambridge, MA: MIT Press, 1999.

Vietor, Richard. *Contrived Competition: Regulation and Deregulation in America.* Cambridge, MA: Harvard University Press, 1994.

Young, Warren. *Atomic Energy Costing.* Norwell, MA: Kluwer, 1998.

ELIZABETH I (1533-1603)

An English monarch during the age of exploration.

Daughter of King Henry VIII and Anne Boleyn, Elizabeth was third in line to the throne behind her younger brother, Edward, and her older sister, Mary. She became the queen of England following the death of Mary in 1558. While few expected her to succeed, she proved to be a remarkable

Elizabeth I appreciated the possibilities that exploration and trade held for her nation. Under her reign in the late sixteenth and early seventeenth centuries, England began its overseas expansion. *(Library of Congress)*

ruler. Throughout her long reign, she worked tirelessly to strengthen national unity, bring prosperity to a country bankrupted by her father, and make England a maritime power on par with Spain.

The Tudor family had placed England on the road to world exploration and trade but with little enthusiasm. Elizabeth's grandfather, Henry VII, had commissioned the Italian seafarer John Cabot (Giovanni Caboto) to sail west to the New World on behalf of England. In 1497, Cabot explored along the coast of Newfoundland and claimed the region for England. Elizabeth's father, Henry VIII, sent Cabot's son, Sebastian, back to America, but showed no interest in further discoveries or colonization. Under the reign of her brother, Edward VI, more progress had been made as merchant adventurers headed east through the Baltic Sea and established trade with Russia.

In contrast to her predecessors, Elizabeth grasped the possibilities that exploration and trade held for her nation. She knew that commercial ties with northern Europe, the Middle East, Asia, Africa, and the Americas would open up markets for English goods. Exploration would lead to colonies that could serve as an outlet for England's growing population, a market for English products, and a source for raw materials useful in English manufacturing. She also realized that privateers commissioned by the Crown to attack Spanish shipping could bring much needed revenue into the royal treasury.

With this in mind, she encouraged and often funded adventurers, merchants, and explorers alike. Anthony Jenkinson traveled to Russia on behalf of the queen, and even headed to Syria, where he met with Suleiman the Magnificent. In 1576, Elizabeth granted Martin Frobisher a license to find the Northwest Passage through America to the Far East. In the following year, she secretly commissioned Sir Francis Drake to circumnavigate the globe to interfere with Spanish trade in the Far East. In 1578, she granted Sir Humphrey Gilbert a charter to found a colony in the New World. Although Gilbert died at sea following the failure of his second attempt to establish a colony in Newfoundland, Sir Walter Raleigh, his younger half-brother, continued his efforts farther to the south in a colony called Roanoke.

Elizabeth reached the height of her royal power when her navy defeated the Spanish Armada off the southern coast of England in 1588. In the last years of her reign, she continued her work to make England a major maritime nation. In 1600, she helped to lay the foundation for the British empire by granting a charter to the British East India Company. Her successor, James I, continued many of her policies and oversaw the founding of the first successful English colony in the New World.

Mary Stockwell

See also: British Empire.

BIBLIOGRAPHY

Brimacombe, Peter. *All the Queen's Men: The World of Elizabeth I.* New York: St. Martin's Press, 2000.

EMBARGOES

> Orders by governments that prohibit the movement of merchant shipping into or out of their ports, or more generally prohibit trade with, and exports to, another nation or nations.

From ancient times to the present day, nations have used the embargo as an economic weapon, refusing to trade, in order to achieve political ends. Throughout history, embargoes have had a decidedly mixed track record in achieving their goals. The most significant embargo in American history ran from December 1807 to March 1809. Britain and France had been warring almost continuously since 1793 and had raided each other's shipping. America declared neutrality and claimed the right to unrestricted trade with all countries, including Britain and France. Americans did significant business in shipping goods into and out of Europe, with shippers' earnings climbing from about $7.4 million to $42 million. While this trade helped the American economy prosper, it irked the British government, which declared in November 1807 that any neutral ships that did not stop in British ports would be liable to capture.

Napoléon Bonaparte subsequently declared in the Milan Decree that any ships that did stop in Britain would be liable to capture. President Thomas Jefferson and Congress responded by enacting an embargo, which made it illegal for American ships to sail to foreign ports and foreign ships from taking on any cargo in the United States. The aim of this "peaceable coercion" focused on punishing Britain and forcing it to drop its policy of interfering with American shipping.

EMBARGOES IN THE NINETEENTH CENTURY

Because the U.S. government did a fairly decent job of enforcing the embargo, it had a significant effect on both the American and British economies. Despite some direct and indirect smuggling, British trade statistics show that the value of goods imported from the United States fell by about 73 percent. Textile production fell by about one-third because of the severe reduction of cotton imports,

Embargoes—or the prevention of trade for political and economic ends—have been used by nations for centuries. To keep the United States out of the Napoleonic Wars of Europe, President Thomas Jefferson—shown here addressing disgruntled merchants—issued a general embargo on European trade in the first decade of the nineteenth century. *(Library of Congress)*

and overall British output fell by about 4.8 percent in 1808. Meanwhile, the prices of manufactured goods fell nearly 10 percent, since most could not be profitably exported to the United States. In the United States, the embargo proved equally harmful. The price of imported commodities rose by roughly one-third, and the average domestic price of important exports fell by about one-quarter. A recent study estimates that the overall gross domestic product in the United States fell by approximately 8 percent because of this cessation of trade.

As opposition to the embargo grew—especially in the most affected regions like New England—Congress replaced it with the Nonintercourse Act, which permitted U.S. trade with nations other than France and Britain and then removed trade restrictions altogether in 1810. The embargo and continued trade restrictions induced Americans to move their resources into the production of goods that had been imported. During the embargo period and the War of 1812, the number of factory incorporations in the United States soared, especially in the textile industry.

EMBARGOES IN THE TWENTIETH CENTURY

Many embargoes have been more selective, blocking only the export of specified goods, especially military matériel, to specific countries. During the Spanish civil war, the United States imposed an embargo in the hopes of promoting its neutrality. During the Korean War, the United Nations (UN) prohibited shipments of war goods to China and North Korea. Likewise, the UN declared an embargo on Iraq after it invaded Kuwait in 1990. Arab countries instituted an oil embargo against countries that had supported Israel in the 1973 Yom Kippur War, especially the United States and the

Netherlands. More important than the embargo, however, was a decision to reduce overall oil exports to all countries—prices soared equally for countries facing the embargo and those not explicitly targeted by it.

Embargoes work best if the target economy has a "bottleneck"—an import for which no good substitute exists and which is not available from other suppliers. One such case may have been the U.S. embargo of petroleum to Japan in 1940. Because the Japanese war machine depended crucially on imported petroleum, this embargo seems to have only accelerated the Japanese decision to attack the United States and invade the Dutch Indies and its oil fields. The United States imposed a grain embargo on the Soviet Union after it invaded Afghanistan in 1979, but it appears to have had little impact because U.S. farmers exported their grain elsewhere and the Soviet Union bought grain from other countries, especially Argentina.

In 1977, the UN adopted a mandatory international arms embargo against South Africa, with the goal of ending its racist apartheid policy. A voluntary oil embargo followed in 1987, and many nations restricted trade in other ways, including limitations on investing in South Africa and buying its exports. Many analysts credit the cumulative impact of these trade restrictions with helping accelerate the demise of apartheid, but it is difficult to know whether the international effort was decisive.

In 1960, after the new Cuban government of Fidel Castro seized property owned by Americans and sent out agents to spread the communist revolution to other Latin American countries, the United States adopted an embargo against it. The embargo has continued for over four decades. Initially, the Soviet Union subsidized Cuba, selling it oil at low prices, thus greatly mitigating the impact of the American embargo. An intense debate has arisen over the effects of the embargo and its continuation. Some maintain that the embargo has had a devastating impact on the Cuban economy, but others argue that Cuba's economic woes are due more to its own economic policies. Some argue that continuing and tightening the embargo, as was done under the Helms-Burton Act (1996), could finally drive Castro from power. Others counter that Castro has used the embargo as an excuse for Cuba's problems, stalling the move toward democracy.

As these examples show, embargoes have sometimes caused significant economic harm to both the intended target and the embargoing country. However, historically they have had only limited ability in inducing countries to change their policies.

Robert Whaples

See also: War of 1812; World War II.

BIBLIOGRAPHY
Frankel, Jeffrey. "The 1807–1809 Embargo Against Great Britain." *Journal of Economic History* 42, no. 2 (June 1982): 291–308.
Leyton-Brown, David, ed. *The Utility of International Economic Sanctions.* New York: St. Martin's Press, 1987.

EMPIRE BUILDING

The process of constructing systems of political influence.

The empire-building process permits certain polities to exercise a high and continuous degree of control over others existing outside their nominal geographical boundaries—sometimes, although far from invariably, as a prelude to full incorporation of the controlled polities into the controlling one, and often, but not invariably, through the medium of the colony. The word "empire" itself derives from "imperium," a central political concept of the Roman empire that has had many meanings in political discourse from Roman to modern times, often denoting simply the authority exercised by a sovereign and sometimes referring to the rule of a superior monarch to whom other monarchs were subject. The modern usage inherent in the term "empire building" has been closely connected to the idea of "imperialism." Both developed as concepts during the eighteenth and early nineteenth centuries, and both came to be fixed in political vocabulary during the last third of the nineteenth century. The type of historical phenomenon to which they refer is, however, very old indeed, dating back at least to the formation of the earliest extensive states in the Middle East in the third millennium B.C.E.

ANCIENT EMPIRES

Trade has almost always been implicated, sometimes very intimately, in projects of empire building. It has been theorized that the first significant empires in the ancient Middle East were constructed at least in part to control and derive income from trade connecting Mesopotamia and other areas. Most of the empires of the ancient world, regardless of whether or not they were constructed primarily for reasons relating to trade, necessarily incorporated trading systems within themselves, if only because the conduct, or at least the taxing, of trade offered a source of revenue. In almost all cases of ancient empires of which we have detailed knowledge, however, commercial factors were linked in one form or another to a great many others, so that it is often difficult to disentangle trade from politics, warfare, agriculture, public finance, and forms of economic exploitation that we would hesitate today to call "commerce." Most of the acts through which the Roman empire was constructed are reported by their ancient historians to have had little to do with trade and more with countering military threats, defending the honor of Rome, advancing the ambitions of politicians, and so forth.

And yet we discover that there was almost always a set of commercial relationships, usually of quite long standing, between the areas Rome controlled and the regions it decided to conquer, that conquering (and occasionally, as in Germany in the first century C.E., retreating) Roman armies were accompanied by merchants and traders who supplied the troops, purchased booty and slaves, and were clearly able to exploit preexisting relationships with local economies. By extending its control over the Mediterranean and the lands on all sides of it and by maintaining a naval force that reduced piracy to manageable proportions, Rome promoted an expansion of commerce larger than the region had ever seen before. And although the early Romans did not portray themselves as being a particularly commercial people, as Roman citizenship became available to persons from places throughout the empire, its advantages for merchants trading within and beyond the empire were so clear that large numbers of businessmen actively sought to acquire it. Some of the central commercial activities of the Roman empire at its height were, however, not entirely consistent with our standard notions of trade. For instance, the grain trade between Egypt and Rome was more like a state activity, a system of appropriating the bulk of the grain produced in Egypt, transporting it to Italy, and distributing it in Rome. On the other hand, around the grain system a substantial amount of market-based commercial activity of a more ordinary sort took place, headquartered in the immensely busy trading city of Alexandria in Egypt. We shall see that this kind of situation existed in some of the European empires of the sixteenth and seventeenth centuries as well.

The role of trade in the construction and operation of other great territorial empires of premodern times varied considerably, although in many cases the variation may have been due more to the ways in which commerce was valued in the prevailing moral order than to the realities of its practical role in the life of society and the state.

In China, for example, according to the Confucian worldview adopted as the conceptual framework of the imperial bureaucracy, trade was a suspect activity, sometimes useful but always dangerous to public morality because of the selfishness that lay at its motivational core. Theoretically, the place of merchants in the order of society was well below that of peasants. In reality, China was for the whole of the Common Era one of the great trading centers of the world, the key marketing area and producer of manufactured goods for all of East Asia. Chinese silks were the mainstay of trade across Central Asia and a crucial factor in China's diplomacy beyond its boundaries. Yet, except for relatively brief periods, the Chinese government declined to acknowledge the full significance of commerce, whether domestic trade between regions of China or external trade. As late as the eighteenth century, when China's public and private finances had come to be dependent on the silver imports that arose from the export of Chinese goods through Western merchants, Chinese authorities still pretended that foreign trade did not matter, that China required nothing from the outside world, and that imports into China from abroad were merely tribute paid by lesser monarchs to the emperor.

Another example is afforded by the succession of large territorial empires from the tenth century to the end of the sixteenth century in the western Sudan, just south of the Sahara in the interior of West Africa: Ghana, Mali, and Songhay. The economic basis of these empires appears on good evidence to have the trans-Saharan gold trade, the enterprise through which North Africa, Europe, and the Middle East acquired most of the gold that served as the primary medium of finance and exchange in the medieval period. The gold was mined in interior areas of the modern states of Ghana and Guinea, exchanged for salt from the edges of the desert, and transported across the Sahara along well-established routes to the cities of North Africa. The trade itself existed from Roman times until the eighteenth century, regardless of whether or not a single political entity controlled the area south of the desert through which it crossed at any particular time.

In a general sense, the empires that rose and collapsed there were not essential to the trade, although they may in some ways have facilitated it. But it is quite clear that controlling the trade was among the major objectives of the peoples who formed the empires. Nevertheless, the surviving epics and written histories that contain the consciously constructed records of the empires of Mali and Songhay make few references to the gold trade, featuring instead the feats of heroes, the imperatives of religion, and the rivalries between peoples and regions.

EARLY EUROPEAN EMPIRE BUILDING

The history of empire building as an aspect of modern imperialism begins in the early fifteenth century, and at that time trade was directly at its center. In the 1420s, a Portuguese enterprise led by Prince Henry the Navigator and backed by financial supporters that included Italian mercantile interests began exploring the coasts of western Africa, primarily to make contact with the countries from which the gold that entered the trans-Saharan trade came. It was hoped that some or all of the gold could be diverted onto Portuguese ships, which would benefit the investors, the Portuguese state, and, in a general sense, Christendom in its competition with Islam. By the time Henry died in 1460 and the enterprise fell under the control of the Portuguese government, expeditions had in fact reached areas on the West African coast where gold could be purchased. More of such areas were contacted during the next two decades as the range of Portuguese ships extended all the way to Cameroon. At no time, however, were the Portuguese able to attract more than a relatively small portion of the gold trade into routes under their control. They did, on the other hand, develop some important new forms of commerce in the region—especially the Atlantic slave trade, which Portugal pioneered partly to supply labor to the previously uninhabited Cape Verde Islands, which had been discovered and colonized as a sideline to the main African thrust of the project. Portugal also built some permanent fortifications on the coast (largely against intrusion from other Europeans, not to control African trading partners). This was not much of an "empire," but what there was of it was based on trade and on the production of commodities such as sugar in the Atlantic islands ruled by Portugal.

Circumstances changed, however, in the 1480s, when Portugal sent expeditions south along the African coast that revealed the Cape of Good Hope and the strong probability that the Atlantic was connected to the Indian Ocean. At that point, the limited resources of the Portuguese state (a very small power by contemporary European standards), backed by funds borrowed outside Portugal, were directed toward bringing Portugal into direct contact around Africa with the flourishing seaborne trade between East and Southeast Asia and the Mediterranean. This trade was conducted through a complex commercial system centered in southwestern India, a fact of which the Portuguese authorities appear to have been aware. A heavily armed fleet under Vasco da Gama was sent in 1497 around the Cape of Good Hope and into the Indian Ocean. The fleet, after contacting the edges of the Indian Ocean system in the towns of the Swahili-speaking peoples of the East African coast, sailed to southwestern India and announced the presence and intentions of Portugal. The Portuguese were not well received, both because they were Christians

The first European imperial holdings overseas were spearheaded by the Portuguese, as illustrated by this 1500 map of Portuguese explorer Vasco da Gama's voyages. *(© North Wind Picture Archives)*

in a commercial world dominated by Muslims and because they were interlopers clearly attempting to cut out the middlemen in an existing trade. Da Gama noticed, however, that his ships held a technical edge in fighting power.

In leading Portuguese fleets to India over the next few years, da Gama and his successors learned to use that edge to establish themselves by force at the center of the trading system. They stationed warships off the Indian coast, requiring coastal cities to trade with them regardless of whether they wanted to do so or not. They forced non-Portuguese merchant ships to purchase licenses to allow them to pass unmolested through the area of Portuguese maritime control. In 1510, they captured the readily defensible town of Goa on the southwest coast of India, from which they sent out military expeditions that occupied strategic positions at several constricted points along the traditional Indian Ocean trade routes. By the 1520s, they had successfully withstood naval challenges and had established a limited maritime empire built around trade—one that depended for its existence on mobility, naval strength, and heavy cannon, and therefore on the selective application of extortion and terror.

In subsequent years, the Portuguese carved out for themselves a more positive role in Asia, conducting trade between countries that did not maintain friendly relations with each other (such as China and Japan), offering transportation services between places in Asia, and developing a port of trade with China at Macao that became the primary link between China and the Western world until the end of the seventeenth century. (Portuguese from Macao exchanged Chinese goods for silver from Spanish America at the Spanish colony at Manila, thereby supplying

China with what informally became its basic currency.) The Portuguese never managed to divert more than a fraction (perhaps a third) of the European-Asian trade into their ships, but their empire in Asia nevertheless managed to subsist and to become a permanent part of the global economy, despite severe challenges that arose in the seventeenth century. The Portuguese also acquired bases in East and South Africa to protect the way to and from Europe and to provide support for their ships (and to make a profit from the part of the Indian Ocean trade that extended to Africa). In addition, they colonized Brazil, initially as an offshoot of their Asian enterprises.

Although the Portuguese state profited from its Asia–Africa–South American empire in the sixteenth century, the effects of the empire on Portugal itself were relatively small. Beyond certain limits, the tendencies toward developing a significant capitalist economy based on commerce that had been in evidence in Prince Henry's time did not progress very far, as the enterprise of the Indies became more of an operation of the state than a business undertaking. The income from the empire did not, on the whole, remain in Portugal in the form of capital investments, but was distributed (with the spices and other Asian products) to the commercial centers of northern Europe, especially the Netherlands, from which Portugal obtained the credit that permitted ships to be built and cargoes for the Asian trade to be put together. Portugal did not become a great European power. Rather, Portugal was overshadowed by its larger neighbor Spain, which created its own empire and which, after Portugal failed disastrously in an attempt to conquer Morocco in 1578, took over control of Portugal in 1580 and retained it for more than sixty years.

Spain's overseas empire became a model for the rest of Europe, in part because it was connected, unlike Portugal's, with the country that was unquestionably the most powerful in Europe (the Ottoman empire excepted) between the middle of the sixteenth and the middle of the seventeenth centuries. The founding of the Spanish overseas empire began with the voyages of Christopher Columbus in the 1490s and occurred essentially at the same time as (and in many respects as a direct result of) the formation of Spain itself out of the union of Castile and Aragon. The Spanish (actually, the Castilian) state sponsored Columbus to achieve the same aim as Portugal: finding a direct way to trade with Asia. In fact, of course, Columbus found a new continent, although he spent the rest of his life attempting to prove that he had not. Columbus established the first overseas Spanish colony in Santo Domingo in 1493, primarily to serve as a base for further exploration that would reveal the route to the mainland of East Asia and thus as a foundation for expanded intercontinental trade. But like other colonial entrepreneurs for the next two and a half centuries, Columbus attempted to make his colony pay for itself in the short run by exploiting mineral resources (especially silver and gold, if those could be found) and by establishing plantation production of consumer goods (and occasionally raw materials) demanded in Europe. It was the last that (barely) sustained the early Spanish colonies in the Caribbean until the great transformation of the Spanish empire that occurred in the middle of the sixteenth century.

The transformation was a consequence of contact by Spaniards with two major native American states: the Aztec empire of central Mexico in the late 1510s and the Incan empire of Peru in the early 1530s. In both cases, contact was made by small military forces operating under essentially autonomous leaders, not by directly appointed officials of the Spanish state or by traders. In both cases, these leaders decided that instead of trying to establish bilateral commercial and political relations (which held few advantages for them personally), they would use their possession of a more advanced military technology, surprise, and incredible ruthlessness to overcome and rule the indigenous states and to exploit them as directly as possible, and in both cases they got away with it.

In neither case, however, did the conquest in itself change the nature of Spanish imperialism, because the riches initially plundered from the Aztecs and the Incas were not replaced and the economic futures of the new colonies looked uncertain in the 1540s. What effected the change was the discovery by Spanish exploring parties in that decade of two of the richest exploitable silver veins in the world, one in what is today Bolivia and the other in north central Mexico. At this point, the

Spanish government intervened heavily in the affairs of its colonies, establishing an extensive (and expensive) system of direct rule in the New World and mustering the resources of the largest financial enterprises in Europe to provide capital for exploiting the newly discovered resources. The Spanish empire in the New World centered on silver, at least according to the official view in Spain and in the imaginations of the rulers of Spain's European rivals.

According to the official theory of the Spanish colonial empire (a theory that was the model for the legal frameworks of most European overseas empires up to the eighteenth century), the American colonies existed in an economic sense solely to benefit Spain. The key benefit was to be derived from as large and constant a flow of silver as possible from the mines in America into the Spanish state treasury, with as little diversion of the prime commodity as feasible into other pockets. The silver would be used by the Spanish government to pay the expenses of the nation's great-power standing: the costs of armies and wars, of client states, of bribes to foreign politicians, and of fleets and fortresses to keep other states from attempting to undermine Spanish control in America. In fact, Spain did manage to create and maintain a major source of revenue from the silver "trade," although not enough to match the needs of foreign policy and war, which led to frequent state bankruptcies even at the height of Spanish power in the late sixteenth and early seventeenth centuries.

To make the theory work, Spanish law restricted all commercial contacts between its colonies and Europe to ships sailing under official control in carefully regulated fleets with naval escorts. The fleets brought with them all the European (and Asian) commodities that could legally be sold in America, together with the trickle of African slaves that was officially permitted to eke out the labor resources of the colonies. The fleets, on arrival in America, took on their most important return cargoes: the state-owned silver produced in the state-owned mines. They were also supposed to carry all the products of the colonies intended for export to Europe. The intention behind the system was not only to ensure the protection of the silver supply, but also to prevent excessive expansion of the nonsilver economy of Spanish America beyond the minimum necessary to support the mines and maintain the basis of Spanish control. Spanish law theoretically forbade, or at least tried to make very difficult, the construction of an autonomous colonial economy either around internal trade in America or around exports—apart from silver—to the rest of the world.

The official theory, although seriously enforced for over two centuries, did not actually correspond well with reality and therefore could never be fully effective. It illustrates a continuing theme in the history of modern imperialism: the very great divergence that tends to exist between the relatively simplistic ways in which commerce is viewed within the ideological framework of imperialism and the complexities of actual commerce in colonial areas dynamically attached to the global economy. In fact, because Spain required a substantial Spanish population in its colonies to protect its own control and to operate a market economy in support of the silver operations, and also because in many areas it was found desirable to encourage the development of a mixed European–Mesoamerican Indian population of European culture, it could not prevent the appearance of a complex commercial, agricultural, and in some cases industrial economy that functioned parallel to the silver economy.

By the seventeenth century, this parallel economy had come to dwarf the officially recognized one, especially in areas such as central Mexico, where large cities with populations of Western culture had emerged. Intercolonial trade (which was officially forbidden) developed on a large scale, while demand for European and Asian commodities and production for export rose to a scale far beyond the capacities of the treasure fleets to accommodate. Even in the sixteenth century, demand for slave labor for work on American estates far exceeded the officially permitted limits. Between the late sixteenth and the early eighteenth centuries, Spanish America possessed one of the most dynamic economies on Earth—an economy that could be retarded by state policy, but not contained. The result was, among other things, smuggling on a large scale. In the late sixteenth and the first half of the seventeenth centuries, it was smuggling in the Spanish overseas empire and other related activities (such as piracy) that made it possible for the economies of the northwest European states to establish direct, profitable connections with the New World.

BRITISH AND FRENCH EMPIRE BUILDING

Before the early seventeenth century, French and English efforts to establish colonies in the Americas were uniformly unsuccessful. They attracted widespread public interest, and in the case of England they helped to create a kind of nationalist mystique of imperialism as England's destiny, but the actual results were less than meager. The first hints of success arose from efforts to smuggle slaves into the Spanish colonies in the 1560s and 1570s and from outright piratical raids on Spanish shipping. Even after permanent English and French colonies were established starting in 1607–1608, a significant part of the business that many of them did was involved with the smuggling trade in Spanish America. This was especially true of the formal and informal colonies established by English groups in the Caribbean in the 1620s and 1630s, but the settlements in mainland North America had some of the same character. The latter were, in any case, economically small, almost insignificant, compared to the wealth of the Spanish colonies, until near the end of the seventeenth century. When Englishmen in particular thought about their imperial future in America throughout the seventeenth century, the ideal form of that future was England's acquisition of most or all of the Spanish empire. When they attempted to rationalize their colonial administration, their first inclination was to imitate Spain.

The first major breakthrough of northwestern Europe into modern commercially based imperialism came not in America, but in Asia. In the late sixteenth century, several expeditions from the Netherlands and England sailed to the Indian Ocean to test the strength of the Portuguese presence. These first efforts were followed in the early seventeenth century by the foundation of the Dutch and the British East India Companies, which were to remain for two centuries the institutional bases for the building of European empires in Asia and the world's largest trading corporations, intimately tied to the development of modern capitalism. At the start, it appeared that the two companies would cooperate, but by the 1610s they had become serious rivals, as the Netherlands briefly rose to the status of a great power and as Dutch capital made the Dutch East India Company for the time being the larger and more successful.

The Dutch company pioneered newer, more efficient sea routes from the Atlantic into the Indian Ocean and centered its activities not in India but in Java, in modern-day Indonesia. There, often as a result of decisions taken by authorities on site as opposed to the company's directors in the Netherlands, they created the core of a substantial land empire, which eventually incorporated large parts of the Indonesian islands and a great deal of Ceylon (modern-day Sri Lanka). This empire was used as a self-supporting strategic base from which Dutch naval and military forces rapidly built up almost total control of the spice trade and a large part of the Asian pepper trade as well. Control was maintained through large expenditures on armies, fleets, fortifications, and colonial towns, all of which amounted to a heavy overhead that the company bore for the entire period of its existence. In the seventeenth century, the expense seemed to be clearly justified. Not only did the company itself obtain great profits from its direct trade with Europe, but also it supplied Dutch commerce with an array of items that were used to conduct trade throughout Europe and the rest of the world.

The Dutch also pushed aside (although they did not entirely dislodge) the Portuguese from their dominance of intra-Asian seaborne commerce, taking over, for example, the monopoly on trade between Japan and the rest of the world. The Dutch East India Company's empire was truly built around trade, but its involvement in political control over diverse peoples and political systems, its efforts to control spice production, and most of all, the large overhead that it was required to bear meant that there was always a considerable strain between the aim of conducting commerce profitably and the costs of maintaining the empire. In the eighteenth century, the strain prevented the company from responding effectively to British competition.

The British East India Company had been

Shown here is the retreat of the British from Concord, Massachusetts, at the outset of the American Revolution. The American Revolution took a large piece out of the British empire and helped to change the nature of the Atlantic economy. *(© North Wind Picture Archives)*

forced by Dutch successes in Southeast Asia to fall back on the traditional centers of Asian trade in India. More or less by accident, the English company found itself in the third quarter of the seventeenth century in a position to take advantage of a fashion that had suddenly appeared in Europe for Asian textiles, especially colored and printed cottons generically known as "calicoes" that were produced on a large scale in certain areas of India. The English company aggressively marketed calicoes in Europe and exploited the financial and industrial capabilities of India to create an immensely profitable trade, which secured the company's position in Asian commerce at the same time that it opened the company to intense criticism at home from domestic textile producers. When the latter succeeded (in 1700 and 1720) in getting Parliament to limit and then ban the sale of most types of calicoes in Britain, the company was able to move flexibly to focus on the export of cottons to other countries, and to switch its resources to the exploitation of a new commodity: tea. Although the fashion for tea had also appeared in the third quarter of the seventeenth century, it had taken the East India companies some time before they had become convinced that the custom of tea-taking (like that of coffee drinking) was permanent. In response to a growing demand for tea in the early eighteenth century, the British East India Company sought and obtained permission to conduct regular trade with Canton (Guangzhou) in China. Tea obtained by this means became the mainstay of the company throughout the first half of the eighteenth century and the source of its continuing profitability.

One of the keys to the British East India Company's success was that, until well into the eighteenth century, it remained preeminently a trading company. It did acquire direct political control over the immediate vicinity of its main commercial bases in India, especially Madras and Calcutta, the latter by agreement with the Mughal empire and the local rulers of Bengal, but that control was exercised as a convenience for commerce, not as a step toward empire. Except for a brief and unsuccessful episode in the seventeenth century, the company deliberately eschewed the more grandiose policies of its Dutch rival, thereby avoiding the overhead and the political complications that imperialism brought with it. The rewards were obvious: continual profitability, substantial capital accumulation, and the ability to move that capital flexibly into new lines of trade to meet new conditions, as happened with tea. The Dutch company also attempted to exploit the calico fashion and the demand in Europe for tea, but with much less success because it could not concentrate its resources the way the English company could.

However, by the 1740s the English (now British) East India Company found itself moving into a new, more aggressively imperialistic phase, much against the will of most of its directors. The effective collapse of the Mughal empire in the first half of the eighteenth century brought the company's officials in India into the complex politics of the empire's competing successor states, both to maintain the company's position and to take personal advantage of opportunities to make fortunes in the chaos of India's fragmentation. A serious threat from the French Company of the Indies in the 1740s and 1750s to insert itself into Indian trade and oust the British encouraged the British company to take an enhanced political role in India. During the imperial wars of the mid-eighteenth century (1740–1748 and 1756–1763), the British East India Company's forces in India, eventually backed by regular British troops and a fleet, led a coalition of Indian allies to defeat the French company and its allies. In the process, the East India company emerged as the paramount power on the Indian subcontinent, while the company's policies became a central issue of British politics. It was an uncomfortable position for a trading company. The company's commercial operations were unable to produce an income to meet its expenses in the 1760s and 1770s, while the British imperial presence in India created an opportunity for large fortunes to be made by company employees and interlopers. Through a series of changes enacted in the 1770s and 1780s, mainly in response to company insolvency and a major corruption scandal, Parliament assigned control of the company's political functions to the British government. Although the East India Company survived until 1858, it became increasingly an arm of government, losing its legal monopoly of India trade in 1813.

While the Dutch and, more spectacularly, the British succeeded in constructing substantial empires in Asia based, initially at least, on seaborne trade, the creation of empires to rival that of Spain in America arose from the establishment of an economic system in which trade was subordinated to colonial production of a consumer commodity: sugar. In the 1650s, the government of Oliver Cromwell attempted seriously to realize the English imperialist aim of conquering the Spanish colonies, starting with the Caribbean. The force sent to do so failed badly, but occupied Jamaica as a consolation prize. The English state, with English investors, moved strongly to retrieve something from the situation. It sponsored a program of promoting the rapid development of Jamaica and Barbados (which England already possessed) as plantation colonies, producing goods for the European market on a large scale. It became clear that the most promising of these commodities was sugar, already in production in Barbados using a technology and slave labor system pioneered by the Portuguese.

With strong government support and substantial investment, the sugar plantations of Barbados and Jamaica expanded greatly in the latter part of the seventeenth century. The demand for sugar also increased throughout Europe, but particularly in Britain, especially after sugar came to be taken customarily with tea, which was the case in Britain by the early eighteenth century. The success of the British sugar plantations led to efforts by France, the Netherlands, and several other countries to establish their own West Indian colonial plantation economies in the late seventeenth and throughout the eighteenth centuries. The French plantations in the country that is today Haiti, in Martinique, and in Guadeloupe became, by the middle of the eighteenth century, even more productive than the British colonies. Much of the imperial warfare of the eighteenth century centered around efforts by the British and French to dislodge each other from their Caribbean colonies, with the honors on the whole going to the British.

Around the colonial sugar economies that developed in the Caribbean, a system of trade, migration, and finance emerged that connected several areas bordering on the Atlantic together. The West African slave trade expanded enormously to meet the demand for labor in the sugar islands. English and French slave traders soon surpassed their Portuguese predecessors in the scope of their operations. The English colonies in North America, which had led a precarious economic existence up to the 1660s, now largely reoriented themselves toward the West Indies. With the partial exceptions of Virginia and Maryland, they became primarily exporters of food to the Caribbean, and the extensive economic, territorial, and demographic development that they experienced up to the time of the American Revolution continued to be based on the West Indian connection. By the third quarter of the eighteenth century, a highly complex, dynamic Atlantic economy had developed, involving the colonies of several different European countries and the satisfaction of consumer demand on both sides of the ocean. Between them, the Atlantic economy of the eighteenth century and its counterpart in Asia, by now tending to be dominated by British interests, constituted a functioning global economy, the direct ancestor of the one that now exists. That economy was held together by a complex set of trade links.

Global economies and global empires were not, however, the same thing. Every European country that engaged in the Atlantic economy attempted in one way or another to establish political control over the portion of Atlantic commerce that rested on its own colonies. The imperial systems of trade controls and economic regulations (represented in the British sphere by the Navigation Acts) by which they attempted to keep the profits derived from their colonies within their nations' own spheres required active and continuous government intervention, hence the importance of keeping colonial governments under firm central control. But the costs of maintaining such control were often high, and the costs of protecting colonies against encroachment by other empires were even higher.

Corners were frequently cut, which reduced the extent to which trade regulations could be enforced. Most of the British North American and Caribbean colonies were effectively self-governing and self-financing from their origins, which meant that until the mid-eighteenth century, the imperial policies that were regularly enforced tended to be primarily the ones in which the colonists saw benefits. Evasion of commercial regulations was widespread, largely because the realities of the Atlantic economy provided vast opportunities for profitable trade outside the legal limits of imperial systems. The French colonies were much more directly governed, but even there, the ability of trade to find its way outside imperial constrictions was quite considerable. The imperial connection was occasionally profitable to colonists, especially when it worked to reserve to them some segment of the British or French domestic market. Also, at least in the British case, the increasingly successful global aggression of the imperial state in its wars against France created significant new opportunities for trade and investment in conquered territories.

However, as is well known, the expensive success of Britain in the Seven Years' War (1756–1763), which brought British dominance in India and the practical elimination of France from imperial competition in North America, led to a concerted effort by the British government to force its American colonies into a more centralized, more coherent imperial polity, one in which the colonists' previous ability to govern themselves and to evade unwanted restrictions was to be severely limited. With other factors, this led to the American Revolution (1775–1783), which took a large piece out of the British global empire and helped to change the nature of the Atlantic economy. Although Britain strongly reasserted itself as the world's leading imperial power during its long wars against revolutionary France and Napoléon Bonaparte (1793–1815), the notion of a political empire that could control world trade and restrict it within the limits set by an imperial nation-state had effectively passed by the end of those wars.

During the years between 1815 and the 1870s, the notion of empire building lacked coherence in Britain and its colonies. The fact that Britain possessed a huge formal empire consisting of colonies around the world was recognized (and a source of pride to Britons), and that the empire was generally advantageous to trade, exports, and investment was recognized as well, despite the existence of colonies (such as those in the West Indies) that were rapidly moving toward economic marginality. But the vast expansion of British production that had occurred as a result of the Industrial Revolution, the growth of British investments across the world, and the realization that Britain's best customers resided outside its colonies all led to the conclusion that there was no necessary coincidence between a growing empire made up of colonies and a growing global economy. On the whole, the British government and the British public preferred to follow policies according to which the state acted abroad in a flexible way to protect or advance specific British interests as needed by putting pressure on foreign governments to change their tariff policies, blockading the ports of countries that defaulted on their debts, sending forces to respond to attacks on British traders, and so forth. This has been called "informal imperialism," although it does not seem to have amounted to a coherent program. It did result in the expansion of directly ruled territories abroad (especially on the borders of India, which was consolidated under British rule and greatly increased in size in the nineteenth century).

On many occasions, the British government deliberately passed up opportunities to declare new colonies, and often when it did establish them, it was a result of a slow process by which British commercial (and sometimes missionary) interests penetrated regions in which existing governments were unable or unwilling to support the kind of economic and social change the British brought with them. Colonies inhabited mainly by European settlers were regularly given self-governing status as soon as was feasible.

Other countries with rapidly developing economies but without the edge possessed by Britain tended to be more tempted to enlarge their empires deliberately before the 1870s. The United States did so by purchase and conquest, adding a large portion of North America to its holdings but eventually incorporating it all into the nation itself. France, more often motivated by domestic political considerations and by the ambitions of officials in colonial areas than by the requirements of trade, conquered Algeria, began the process of establishing a large African and Southeast Asian empire, and attempted unsuccessfully to dominate Mexico. It was not at all clear that French trade or the French economy as a whole benefited significantly from these activities, but at least they supported France's role as a great power—a matter of considerable significance in French politics.

NEW IMPERIALISM OF THE LATE NINETEENTH CENTURY

In the 1880s and 1890s, a new wave of imperialism swept across Europe, eventually involving the United States and Japan as well. The reasons for the appearance of the "new imperialism" were complex and have been heavily debated by historians. The favored explanations include changes in the diplomatic balance of power in Europe, the effects of economic modernization on European societies, the growing complexity of European politics, and class anxiety among the bourgeoisie.

One thing that is clear is that trade in itself had relatively little to do with it. Rather, areas of the world in which the merchants of particular great (and lesser) European powers had interests came to be reconstructed in public discourse as regions in which political control had to be established to secure the economic and strategic future of the country involved. The local trading and investment interest (which was as likely as not to be in some sense multinational anyway) largely provided a focus and an excuse for political action to advance national interests. Under such circumstances, trading groups naturally tried to take advantage of the situation by portraying their own concerns as appropriate ones for state support, as when Sir George Goldie obtained British government backing in the 1880s and 1890s for establishing political control of southern Nigeria and for monopolizing the palm oil trade of the region. But on the whole, it cannot be said that the intense political competition that led to the partition of Africa and to vastly heightened international tension in the years before World War I was really about trade. And the colonial empires that emerged tended, despite all the rhetoric that had led to their seizure, not to be exclusionary with regard to trade. Most had necessarily to encourage economic development for participation in world markets as well as the national markets of the imperial countries.

In the years after World War I, after France and Britain established temporary control over much of the Middle East to facilitate the development of the area's oil resources, systematic empire building by the old imperial powers essentially ceased. Attempts were made to convert imperial arrangements into economic systems beneficial both to the imperial state and to the colonies, a few of which (the British sterling area and the Commonwealth) had some positive economic effect. But the stresses of World War II and the clear failure of colonialism as a means of affording successful political and economic development in an era of globalization led to the rapid dismantling of the major surviving overseas empires after 1945. The attempt of Japan and the revived effort of Germany after 1933 to create empires, in part to protect themselves against dependency on the global economy, failed violently in World War II, and the undeclared effort of the Soviet Union to do much the same thing in defense of world communism collapsed in the late 1980s. The question of whether or not there will be a return to empire building in the twenty-first century remains open.

Woodruff D. Smith

See also: Colonization; Discovery and Exploration; Industrial Revolution; Portugal; Saharan and Trans-Saharan Trade; Tea.

BIBLIOGRAPHY

Fieldhouse, D.K. *Economics and Empire, 1830–1914.* London: Macmillan, 1984.
Louis, William Roger, ed. *The Oxford History of the British Empire.* 5 vols. Oxford: Oxford University Press, 1998–1999.
Parry, J.H. *The Spanish Seaborne Empire.* Berkeley: University of California Press, 1990.
Scammell, G.V. *The World Encompassed: The First European Maritime Empires, c. 800–1650.* Berkeley: University of California Press, 1981.
Tracy, James D., ed. *The Political Economy of Merchant Empires.* Cambridge: Cambridge University Press, 1991.
———. *The Rise of Merchant Empires.* Cambridge: Cambridge University Press, 1990.

ENERGY

New and existing energy technologies have been catalysts of changes in trade patterns since the Industrial Revolution.

Since the advent of the steam engine and the Industrial Revolution, energy technologies and the search for new fuel sources to generate energy have been one of the catalysts of changes in trade patterns, either by way of direct territorial expansion and conquest, or by way of indirect control of energy sources by the developed countries. In other words, up to the last quarter of the twentieth century, increased world trade and energy utilization grew concomitantly, at least in the developed countries. This all changed with the energy shocks of the 1970s.

Over the last decade of the twentieth century, trade in energy came to the fore. There were essentially three elements involved in this change: (1) liberalization and deregulation of energy markets; (2) increased awareness of environmental damage caused by energy production, transmission, and consumption (which is felt much more in the developed world than in the developing countries); and (3) the development of new energy production technologies.

For most of the twentieth century, public utilities in the United States as well as elsewhere were vertically integrated monopolies, either privately owned and regulated or publicly owned corporations. These monopolistic utilities supplied services and goods such as energy, communication, and transportation. The monopolistic structure of these markets was justified mainly because of the existence of economies of scale (the average cost of supplying the service/good by the utility decreases as production increases). This market structure was challenged when technological improvements reduced and even abolished the economies of scale. Thus, liberalization and deregulation of public utilities industries and markets started to shake market structures.

Environmentalists perceived the deregulation of energy markets as entailing potential danger. They traditionally saw energy production and consumption as an adverse phenomenon and aimed at curbing it. Their negative position derived from the fact that in the old regulated regime, they had political power and influence to pressure for initiatives of conservation, energy efficiency, and renewable energy investments. All these initiatives aimed at decreasing the amount of power capacity needed. The costs of these expensive programs were borne by ratepayers or taxpayers. These programs could not have been financed voluntarily in a deregulated and competitive market. Moreover, environmentalists feared that a move toward energy competition would decrease energy prices by producing and transmitting energy in more efficient ways (as well as by abolishing the environmental energy programs).

Between the oil shocks of the 1970s and 1986, "energy intensity" in the United States—as measured by energy use per dollar of gross domestic product—declined at a rate of more than 2 percent per annum. This largely derived from the emphasis given to more energy-efficient technologies in an environment of increasing and highly volatile energy prices. However, the decline in energy intensity has moderated since the mid-1980s; this is largely because of a concomitant moderation in energy price increases. The success of efficient-energy and other conservation policies in decreasing energy needs brought some to believe that by conservation and efficiency alone all energy needs could be supplied. If this were indeed the case, there would be no need to build hundreds of new power plants and upgrade transmission capacity, which besides being extremely costly has negative externalities. Unfortunately, the consequences of this school of thought were shortfalls in both transmission and available generation capacity in many electricity markets, such as in California in the summer of 2002. Moreover, the fact that the capacity crisis hit California, which was one of the world's electricity deregulation leaders, dissuaded many states from completing their deregulation plans. This infrastructure shortage has proven to be a severe constraint to competitive trade in energy and deregulation initiatives.

This trend of change in energy markets, that is, the increasing importance of trade in energy, may eventually lead to a global movement toward a cleaner and more sustainable technology: hydrogen-based energy production. Indeed, this change, for example, transformed natural gas from a power generation source that was "too valuable to use in electricity generation" to a cleaner, cheaper, and more efficient fuel input for electricity generation. Moreover, recent developments in distributed energy (small power plants located near the consumption sites, which are generally integrated with the existing electricity grid), as well as recent technological developments such as combined cycle gas turbines that rely on natural gas, have proven to be economically viable options to large-scale oil and coal-burning and nuclear power plants. However, for distributed energy to win a significant share of the market, a number of conditions must be met: (1) the new electricity metering systems should be supported by government; (2) bureaucratic barriers and adversarial regulations (taxation, standards, and so on) should be updated to sustain a new era of in-house energy production; and (3) anachronistic (indirect and direct) subsidies to older oil- and coal-burning and nuclear power plants should be abolished.

It is expected that future power plants will be much smaller than we have become used to. And this, because of innovations that not only abolish the norm in energy markets of "economies of scale," but also because the new technologies are less risky in the financial sense and more flexible. Indeed, we can now start to talk about "diseconomies of scale" in energy generation and trade.

However, even when distributed energy and other micropower technologies acquire a significant share of the energy market, the power transmission grid will not become obsolete. In the future energy market, households/businesses/factories will be both consumers and producers of power; each of them will have a small ("micro") generator, fueled with natural gas, hydrogen, or some renewable energy. The "plant" will supply all the energy needs of the economic unit, such as heating, lighting, and so on. However, it will be connected to the regional electricity grid through power meters. Thus, when the unit acquires surplus power, it will sell it through the grid at a competitive market price to other units, which are short of capacity. The existence of so many independent small potential energy producers and the real-time supply elasticity acquired through price signals from real-time energy markets will bring about a decline in the market power (ability of producers to unilaterally increase market prices above their marginal costs) of large-scale commercial power producers and "free trade in energy" may eventually emerge.

Eli Goldstein and Warren Young

See also: Electricity.

BIBLIOGRAPHY
Pindyck, Robert S. *The Structure of World Energy Demand.* Cambridge, MA: MIT Press, 1979.

ENGELS, FRIEDRICH (1820-1895)

A German revolutionary social and political philosopher, cofounder of Marxism and communism, born in Barmen in 1820.

Friedrich Engels's father was a well-to-do textile manufacturer. Early in his life, the German poet Heinrich Heine and the German philosopher G.W.F. Hegel influenced him. After serving for one year as an army volunteer in Berlin in 1842, he moved to Manchester already endorsing communism under the influence of the German socialist Moses Hess. In 1844, he published *Outlines of a Critique of Political Economy* (generally known as the *Umrisse*), in which he demonstrated that all categories of political economy presuppose competition under private property. For Engels, competition based on self-interest generates monopoly. Competition as a necessary feature of private property leads to the centralization and concentration of property. Thus, he concluded that competition is a law that produces monopoly, the elimination of private property, and social revolution, and that the capitalist system is heading toward self-destruction through forces immanent within it.

While working in his father's Manchester cotton mill, Engels was shocked by the laborers' working conditions. In 1845, he published *The Condition of the Working Class in England.* The capitalist law of competition had already set in motion the Industrial Revolution, thus creating a new revolutionary force: the propertyless working class. Engels contributed several articles to the journal *Franco-German Annals* (edited and published by Karl Marx in Paris). In 1844, Engels and Marx had their first serious meeting and realized that they truly shared the same understanding of the political economy and philosophy of capitalism. When Marx moved to Brussels after being expelled from France, Engels took Marx to London to meet several Chartist leaders including George Harney. In 1846, they went back to Brussels and set up the Communist Correspondence Committee hoping to unite all European socialists. In 1848 in London they coauthored the 12,000-word pamphlet *The Communist Manifesto* disseminated in several European languages; their goal was to explain communist theory to an international working-class audience. By the end of 1848, both Marx and Engels were expelled from Belgium. They moved to Cologne where they started publishing the radical newspaper *New Rhenish Gazette.* In less then a year, Marx and Engels were forced to leave Germany. They went to London in 1849.

Engels was the only source of financial support to the Marx family. Unable to raise enough money in London, Engels returned to Germany and worked in his father's business. After Marx's death in 1883, Engels devoted most of his time to editing his friend's drafts and eventually published the second and third volumes of *Das Kapital.* He died in London in 1895. His other major works include *Synopsis of Capital* (1868), *On Authority* (1872), *Socialism: Utopian and Scientific* (1877), *The Origin of the Family, Private Property, and the State* (1884), and *Law of Value* (1895).

Fadhel Kaboub

See also: Marx, Karl.

BIBLIOGRAPHY
McLellan, David. *Friedrich Engels.* New York: Penguin, 1978.

ENGLAND'S TREASURE BY FOREIGN TRADE

A seventeenth-century economic tract, written by Thomas Mun, that argued that England needed to establish a mercantile system based on foreign trade.

Thomas Mun was a director of the British East India Company and an important early theorist of England's mercantile system. His work, *England's Treasure by Foreign Trade,* written in the 1630s and published in the 1660s after the Restoration and as Parliament started to debate and create its navigational laws, set the basis for English mercantilism. His work sought to explain the importance of merchants and mercantile activity to England, especially as a way to increase England's wealth and power while explaining why foreign trade was so lucrative.

The tract begins by examining those qualities needed by a merchant interested in becoming involved in foreign trade. A successful merchant needed to be well educated to deal with the bookkeeping of business and knowledgeable of not only England's weights and measures but those of others. The merchant must know the customs and regulations of foreign states, be familiar with the commodities they produce and demand, and understand the system of bills of exchange. The merchant, beyond possessing the knowledge of basic business skills and the regulations and duties of his craft, must understand the shipping industry, insurance, supply and demand, prices, wages, and any other element that might affect the success of his business. All these qualities allowed the merchant to succeed at the ever-expanding and complex foreign trade. Finally, the merchant needed to learn the languages and customs of his trading partners and be a lifelong scholar.

After explaining the basic qualities of a successful merchant, the work then illustrated the importance of foreign trade to England. To succeed at foreign trade, Mun argued that England needed to ensure that it exported more than it imported, thus maintaining a favorable balance of trade and a flow of wealth into, not out of, England. Within this, because England lacked natural sources of gold and silver, wealth needed to be exported in order for England to succeed at foreign trade. If foreign trade was well managed, the outflow of specie would be minor in relation to the inflow. England would not be increasing its consumption of wares, rather, the surplus brought into England by foreign trade could then by reexported to other states in exchange for specie. The example presented in the work to support this argument concerned England's economic relationship with India. In India, little demand existed for English-produced commodities, yet England, and the rest of Europe, possessed a great demand for Indian commodities. Therefore, exportation of gold and silver allowed England to purchase large amounts of these commodities that it then could reexport to the rest of Europe in exchange for specie. One last point made by Mun, and an important one in convincing the state to support foreign trade, involved the issue of revenue. Not only could the state collect money from importation and exportation, but also the concept of reexportation created another avenue of revenue.

Ty M. Reese

See also: Heckscher, Eli Filip.

BIBLIOGRAPHY

Kammen, Michael. *Empire and Interest: The American Colonies and the Politics of Mercantilism.* Philadelphia: Lippincott, 1970.

Wallerstein, Immanuel. *Mercantilism and the Consolidation of the European World Economy, 1600–1750.* New York: Academic, 1980.

ENTERTAINMENT

Any form of performance designed to amuse.

Since ancient times people have enjoyed entertainment as a means of escape from the daily cares of their lives. Ancient Egyptians held large dinner parties during which musicians, singers, dancers, and acrobats amused the guests. Although the Egyptians engaged in a variety of leisure activities such as hunting, they did not construct large entertainment facilities. The major civilizations before the Greeks relied on the same forms of entertainment as the Egyptians.

ANCIENT AND MEDIEVAL ERAS

The ancient Greeks were the first civilization to promote entertainment on a large scale. Ancient Greeks enjoyed sports competitions, including the Olympic games. In Athens, actors performed the Greek tragedies of Euripides, Sophocles, and Aeschylus,

Mass entertainment—including gladiator combat at the Coliseum—was an important aspect of life in ancient Rome. Supplying the slaves and wild animals for the contests represented a minor, but lucrative, part of Rome's vast trading system. *(Library of Congress)*

as well as the comedies of Aristophanes. The ruins of Greek amphitheaters, where plays and other forms of entertainment were performed, can be located in most cities throughout Greece and parts of Asia Minor. People would travel from far away to enjoy these different forms of entertainment and in the process would purchase local goods, often by simply exchanging some of the products of their own region through a system of barter. This exchange of goods often developed into a long-term trading relationship between the two regions.

The ancient Romans, following the example of the Greeks, also constructed large amphitheaters for entertainment. During the first part of the Roman empire, up to the reign of Constantine, when the empire became Christian, another form of entertainment that was popular was the gladiatorial games. The Coliseum in Rome, with its subterranean tunnels where slaves, Jews, Christians, and gladiators awaited their deaths, was an expensive building project as most entertainment facilities today are. The grand scale, with 45,000 seats, indicates the widespread desire for blood sport. The Romans also enjoyed chariot races, another form of entertainment that could become deadly and was often bloody. The Circus Maximus, the largest of several circuses in Rome, could accommodate 250,000 spectators. Ordinary Roman citizens also played simple games with stones.

From ancient times through the medieval ages, all societies enjoyed annual festivals—usually connected with the worship of a deity. A statue that represented the god, goddess, or saint would be carried through the streets of the town, and a parade of people would follow. The procession usually ended with a feast where wine, beer, or delicacies could be enjoyed along with music and dancing.

During the Middle Ages, minstrels would travel from one court to another to entertain the royalty and nobility. Often, merchants would accompany these entertainers. At the larger fairs, such as the one at Champagne, entertainers would amuse the crowds while the merchants hawked their wares. Entertainment and trade had merged.

NINETEENTH CENTURY

During the nineteenth century, entertainment expanded to include actors and actresses who performed on stage. Some of these performers were musicians, some were dancers, and some were actors. Saloon owners provided entertainment as a way to entice customers to spend more time, and subsequently spend more money, in their establishments. The entertainment usually included a piano player and possibly women who sang or danced.

With the formation of professional sports teams in the late nineteenth century, sports and trade developed a symbiotic relationship. Baseball teams relied initially on the gross ticket and concession receipts to fund their organization. As sponsors began supporting the teams in exchange for advertising at the ballpark, customers began purchasing more of the listed products. Tobacco companies realized the potential of targeting the sports fans and decided in the 1870s to begin enclosing baseball cards with their cigarettes in an effort to develop brand loyalty. Later on, bubble-gum companies used the concept of combining their product with baseball cards. Eventually, baseball cards were sold separately and a whole new industry developed.

SPECTATOR SPORTS

By the 1960 and 1970s, advertisers were signing endorsement contracts with sports figures, especially after the widespread exposure of television expanded the potential target market. The first example of a sports personality endorsing a product occurred when Muhammad Ali boxed wearing Adidas shoes during the 1960s. In the 1970s, Joe Namath became the spokesman for a panty hose company, playing on his image as a sex symbol. Since then, sports personalities such as Michael Jordan, Magic Johnson, and Larry Bird have all endorsed products. By the 1990s, many sports personalities earned more through their endorsements than from their sports salaries. Sports shoe manufacturers such as Nike, Puma, and Adidas increased their market share as sports fans sought to emulate their favorite sports heroes.

Food and beverage companies also used sports figures to promote their products. The first instance of this was the endorsement of Coca-Cola by "Mean" Joe Green. Coke's competitor, Pepsi, turned to well-known entertainers such as Michael Jackson and Britney Spears to promote their product. Corporate endorsements have moved beyond the use of individual spokespeople to team sponsorship. Many sports facilities are now named after companies. The Staples Center in California and the American Airlines Center in Dallas, Texas, are two such examples. Advertisers realize that the wider the exposure of the company or product name, the greater the value of the investment. With television audiences from around the world watching sporting events, the investment helps to increase name recognition and therefore sales.

When advertisers like the tobacco industry were prohibited from purchasing ad time on national television, company executives circumvented that restriction by sponsoring big sporting events. The Winston Cup NASCAR race and the Virginia Slims Tennis Circuit are two examples of this type of sponsorship. The company name is mentioned repeatedly during the broadcast without the direct marketing of the cigarettes. It is a subtle way of advertising the product.

Besides the use of sports and entertainment personalities in advertising, both sectors have developed markets of their own. Sports teams have established clothing lines and promotional items from pennants to signed balls. Anything with a team name or logo is sold. At first, these items were sold at the stadium during games, but during the 1990s several teams began establishing retail shops in shopping centers to reach shoppers who might not attend games. Entertainers have followed the same path. Actresses such as Jaclyn Smith and models like Rachel Hunter have clothing lines named after them. Posters, dolls, and an assortment of collectibles are all marketed under their label. In most cases, none of these items has anything to do with the entertainer, but a whole market has developed from the sheer name exposure the individual receives on television and on the Internet.

HOLLYWOOD

The entertainment industry itself accounts for a substantial amount of trade. Hollywood was founded on the movie industry. Although these films are viewed across the United States, many are exported around the world as well. Filmmaking is a billion-dollar industry. According to the Motion Picture Association, domestic receipts in 2002 amounted to $9.5 billion. More than 1.6 billion people attended the movies during the year. International net revenue from the movies amounted to $9.64 billion. Half of the sales were generated in Europe, the Middle East, and Africa, while another 40 percent was generated in the Asia-Pacific region and the remaining 10 percent in Latin America. Over 7.3 million people watched the movies overseas in 2002. The profitability of the industry has attracted other countries to the industry, and they are trying to establish a position in the market. Canada, Australia, Europe, and even China are now exporting their films to other countries, but the United States still continues to dominate. The diverse music forms in the United States are also exported around the world. Everything from hip-hop to rap to country music can be found in foreign lands. The Recording Industry Association of America reported that net recording sales in 1993 was $10 billion. By 2000, that number had risen to $14 billion. The next two years showed a slight decline, but much of this was attributed to the post–September 11, 2001, slump in the economy, both domestically and internationally.

The large volume of profit generated by both the movie and music industry has attracted the greedy. The major problem that has developed in both sectors is the pirating of videos, DVDs, cassettes, and CDs. Most of these bootlegged products are produced in China and the Far East. The industry associations have worked hard to lobby Congress for assistance. Although the government is aware of the problem and has attempted to address it through a variety of means, the ease with which these items can be illegally reproduced means that it will continue to be a problem in the future until technology can be developed to prevent it.

GAMING

While sports and music concerts are examples of entertainment on a large scale, entertainment in the age of technology does not require large crowds assembled in one place. One of the largest entertainment industries today is the gaming industry. Through the use of the Internet, individuals can play other people anywhere in the world. Games such as Warcraft and Starcraft provide Web sites where a player can compete against a single opponent or join a team that plays against another team. Corporations such as AT&T sponsor most of these gaming sites. Besides Internet games, players can play on gaming hardware consoles such as PlayStation or XBox. Sales of these units exceeded $7.4 billion in 2001.

GAMBLING

Another form of entertainment that generates billions of dollars in revenue is the gambling industry. Cities such as Las Vegas, Nevada, would not exist without this industry. The Las Vegas Convention and Visitors Authority claims that 35.3 million people visited the city in 2003 and 87 percent of them gambled. With more than forty casinos on the strip that generated more than $1 million net gaming revenues that year, the average gambler spent $580 over a four-day period at the tables or slot machines. Most gamblers only spent four hours a day gambling and the rest of the time shopping, sightseeing, or watching one of the famous shows such as Wayne Newton or Siegfried and Roy. The 24,463 conventions held in 2003 account for many of the visitors, with most of the others being senior citizens. Each year visitors lose $6 billion in Las Vegas while gambling. The profitability of gambling has resulted in forty-eight states authorizing some form of gambling, either lottery or casino, but the real increase has come since the introduction of Indian gaming. The 150 Indian casinos in the United States in 1997 netted $27 bil-

Gamblers try their luck at a craps table at the Turning Stone Casino, an enterprise of the Oneida Indian Nation in Vernon, New York. Supporters of the gambling industry say it brings in revenue and jobs to impoverished rural areas; detractors argue it spreads gambling addiction and crime. (© Bob Mahoney/The Image Works)

lion in revenues. These meccas of gambling attract tourists and stimulate the local economy by providing employment for residents.

THEATER

Just as in ancient times, people still enjoy attending the theater, but instead of outdoor amphitheaters, large indoor facilities attract the crowds. Perhaps the largest theater district in the world is Broadway in New York City. In 2002–2003, more than 11.4 million people attended performances. The shows generated $721 million in gross sales. People traveled from across the United States and even the world to attend these shows and in the process generated sales for the transportation, hotel, restaurant, and other industries. In London's West End theater district, visitors attended performances in the 108 live theater and music halls. Both New York and London experienced a decline in theater receipts after the September 11, 2001, terrorist attacks, but attendance rebounded in 2003.

Since ancient times, people have sought to escape the routine of their daily lives. Entertainment has provided this outlet, especially as people enjoy more leisure time. These events and industries have generated sales on a local, regional, and international basis and will continue to do so in the future.

Cynthia Clark Northrup

See also: Greek City-States; Hollywood; Roman Empire; Tourism; United States.

BIBLIOGRAPHY

Demand, Nancy. *A History of Ancient Greece.* New York: McGraw-Hill, 1996.
Gorman, Jerry, and Kirk Calhoun. *The Name of the Game: The Business of Sports.* New York: Wiley, 1994.
Grant, Michael. *History of Rome.* Englewood Cliffs, NJ: Prentice Hall, 1978.
Motion Picture Association of America, Industry Worldwide Market Research. "MPA Snap Shot Report" (www.mpaa.org/useconomicreview/content.htm, accessed May 2004).
NYC and Company. "Broadway Statistics" (www.nycvisit.com/_uploads/docs/Broadway_Season_stats.pdf, accessed February 2005).
Schaaf, Paul. *Sports Marketing: It's Not Just a Game Anymore.* Amherst, NY: Prometheus, 1995.
Schlossberg, Howard. *Sports Marketing.* Cambridge, MA: Blackwell, 1996.
Weikel, Colby. "Sports Marketing: A Take on the History and the Future" (www.unc.edu/~andrews/ints092/weikel.html, accessed October 2003).
WGBH/Frontline. "Gambling Facts and Stats" (www.pbs.org/wgbh/pages/frontline/shows/gamble/etc/facts.html, accessed October 2003).

ETRUSCANS

A non-Indo-European ethnic group inhabiting northern Italy (Etruria) throughout the first millennium B.C.E.

According to ancient sources, the Etruscans (called Tyrhennoi by the Greeks) immigrated to Italy from Anatolia during the 1200s B.C.E. Some more recent scholars suggest that they represent the pre-Indo-European aboriginal population of the Italian peninsula, like the Basques in Spain. A distinctive Etruscan civilization began to emerge in the 800s B.C.E. The Etruscans were not politically unified, but were rather a loose confederacy of independent city-states. The most important city-states included Clusium (Chiusi), Tarquinii (Tarquinia), Caere (Cerveteri), Veii (Veio), Volterra, Vetulonia, Perusia (Perugia), and Volsinii (Orvieto).

During the seventh and sixth centuries B.C.E., the Etruscan civilization reached its peak. Etruscan society was composed of an Etruscan-speaking nobility and a subject (though probably not slave) class of native laborers. The Etruscan states were initially kingdoms but gradually became oligarchic republics. The Etruscans dominated the Umbrian states of northern Italy as well as the Latin tribes and Rome (the Tarquin dynasty of Rome was Etruscan in origin). They also developed a maritime trade network, with colonies in Corsica, Elba, Sardinia, and the Balearic Islands. They allied with Carthage in an attempt to drive Greek traders out of the western Mediterranean. However, by the beginning of the 400s B.C.E. Etruscan sea power had all but vanished.

Etruscan power continued to decline in the face of attacks by the Gauls. In 396 B.C.E., the first Etruscan state, Veii, fell to the Romans (who had asserted their independence around 510 B.C.E.); within two centuries, all of Etruria was under Roman domination. During the civil war between Gaius Marius and Lucius Cornelius Sulla (90–88 B.C.E.), the Etruscans allied with Marius; following his victory, Sulla eliminated their independence. Their language was suppressed and their distinct culture and folkways outlawed. A century later, the future Emperor Claudius compiled an Etruscan dictionary (now lost), but they vanished as a distinct ethnic group soon after. Nevertheless, many old Roman families retained a memory of Etruscan roots.

Etruscan were expert ironworkers, which allowed them to make superior weapons. Etruscans made extensive use of the chariot in both war and recreation and may have introduced the wheel to Italy. They also built and maintained a network of paved roads throughout the territories under their control, allowing trade to flow freely throughout northern Italy.

They were renowned for their pottery (which was their main export besides wine) and complex artwork, including highly lifelike statutes of bronze and other metals. They kept up extensive trade and cultural contacts with the ancient Near East, and much of their artwork reflects this influence.

Etruscan religion involved complex rituals designed to maintain the balance between humans and nature. Unlike the ancient Romans, the Etruscans believed strongly in an afterlife; one's disposition in it depended on one's behavior in this world. Many Roman deities are based on Etruscan originals.

While the Etruscan language can be easily read (it is written in a variant Greek alphabet), the vocabulary is, with few exceptions, unknown today. It seems to contain both Indo-European and non-Indo-European terms, but cannot be classified into any other language family.

Brian M. Gottesman

See also: Mediterranean Sea; Roman Empire

BIBLIOGRAPHY
Barker, Graeme, and Tom Rasmussen. *The Etruscans*. Malden, MA: Blackwell, 1998.
Heurgon, Jacques. *Daily Life of the Etruscans*. London: Phoenix, 2002.

The Etruscans, the dominant people of northern Italy in pre-Roman times, were expert artisans, as these vases from the Hermitage Museum in Saint Petersburg, Russia, indicate. Many of their creations were traded widely through the Mediterranean world in the first millennium B.C.E. *(Library of Congress)*

EUROPEAN-AFRICAN TRADE

A long-standing economic exchange that saw, over time, the dominance of Europe over the African economy.

Contact and trade between Europe and Africa is of long standing, especially among the regions that border the Mediterranean Sea, but sustained and more widespread contact was established following the Portuguese voyages down the West African coast in the fifteenth century. The Portuguese, in search of a sea route to the Far East and the source of West African gold, soon started trading with the various peoples, states, and societies they found there, which led to the establishment of their Elmina trading fort in 1482. The Portuguese soon discovered that they desired what the Africans had to offer, while the Africans desired what the Portuguese possessed. The establishment of trade in this period, combined with Christopher Columbus's discovery of the Americas, set the stage for the most infamous trading relationship between Europe and Africa: the transatlantic slave trade.

The transatlantic slave trade witnessed European and American slavers carry approximately 15 million human commodities across the Atlantic to labor in the Americas. The coastal slave trade that developed had widespread consequences for Europe and Africa and throughout the 300-year period of the trade the Africans dictated its nature. Europeans purchased most slaves from coastal African merchants and states, who acquired slaves in a variety of ways, to perform an assortment of labor in textiles, alcohol, tobacco, firearms, and various other commodities, thus making West Africa an important market for European manufacturers.

The European abolishment of the slave trade in the late eighteenth and early nineteenth centuries started the rise of legitimate trade in that if the Africans wanted to continue to receive the European goods they had become accustomed to, they needed to find legitimate, nonslave, trade items. Because of the Industrial Revolution, the trading relationship between Africa and Europe changed in the nineteenth century as Europe came to see Africa as a supplier of raw materials and a market for manufactured products. A flow of West African cocoa, Congo region rubber, East African cloves, and South African mineral resources poured into Europe, expanding the European economy and power. This meant that new parts of Africa started to experience an expanding European presence, especially in East Africa, until the increasing competition, coupled with many other factors, saw the introduction of European imperialism into Africa. By this point, the African economy was becoming secondary to that of the European and during the colonial period of Africa's history the various European imperial powers extracted great wealth from the continent.

The changes caused by the two world wars started the process of decolonization where the European powers relinquished control back to the Africans. Within this process, multinational corporations started to play a larger role within Africa as they sought to continue to profit through the one-sided trade. This set the stage for neoimperialism, where wealth continued to flow out of Africa through a variety of corporations and arrangements within a modern global economy, which widened the discrepancies between rich and poor.

Ty M. Reese

See also: Portugal; Slavery; World War I; World War II.

BIBLIOGRAPHY
Brown, Michael B., and P. Tiffen. *Short Changed, Africa and World Trade.* Boulder: Trans-National Institute, 1992.
Klein, Herbert. *The Atlantic Slave Trade.* Cambridge: Cambridge University Press, 1999.

EUROPEAN-ASIAN TRADE

A lucrative trade relationship between Europe and Asia has continued to evolve since the Roman empire.

Regular commercial activities between Asia and Europe, which invigorate the current global economy, date back to the pre-Christian era. For centuries until the late 1400s, Asian commodities—silk, porcelain, jewels, precious metals, spices, textiles, and other luxury items from China, Japan, India, and Southeast Asia—found their way to Europe through the Middle East and the Mediterranean involving a multifaceted web of trade contacts. The Silk Road (the English equivalent for the term *seidenstrafe* coined in 1877 by Ferdinand von Richthofen, a German explorer) represented a major transcontinental trade route linking East Asia with the Mediterranean. A complex network of caravan transportation that joined East and West, the Silk Road had its starting point in northwest China, traversed across Central and

West Asia, and linked up with trade trails spurring into south Iran, the northern Eurasian steppe, and the Indian subcontinent. Goods originated from East or Southeast Asian countries also arrived in Europe by way of the sea routes that connected the south and west coasts of India with the ports in the Red Sea and Persian Gulf. Central Asian and Indian merchants served as pivotal intermediaries for the land or sea traffic of Asian products to the Mideast or Mediterranean hubs of distribution for the European markets.

EARLY MODERN ERA

The structure of the European-Asian commercial nexus changed following the Portuguese discovery of a direct sea route from Europe to India by way of the Cape of Good Hope in the late fifteenth century. The sixteenth century witnessed the rise of European maritime commerce with Asia. Portugal, as a global naval power, took the lead in a European effort to dominate all seaborne access to the Asian trade. The Portuguese merchants aspired to monopolize the lucrative trade of pepper and other spices with Southeast Asia. For more sources of profits and new Asian commodities, they also sought direct commercial contacts with East Asia, China, and Japan in particular. At the turn of the seventeenth century, the Netherlands and Britain started to challenge the Portuguese control of all-water routes from the Atlantic to Asia. Each country established its own East India company as the novel trading institution in a quest for a superior status in the East-West commerce.

As a state-chartered association of merchants and bankers, the Dutch East India Company represented both a national desire for mercantilist gains and private commercial interests. By armed conquests, the company took Taiwan (or Formosa), Melaka (Malacca), Ceylon, and the Indonesian archipelago as convenient footholds and trading posts for commercial expansion in East and Southeast Asia. While losing Taiwan to the Chinese empire in the mid-1600s, the Dutch became dominant in the European trade with Southeast Asia. The Dutch East India Company, as a trading monopoly, not only helped increase the volume and value of European-Asian commercial exchange, but also adjusted the variety of Asian commodity exports for the European market. Since Asia had little demand for European products, the Dutch East India Company competed with Asian countries and won a principal role in the multilateral intra-Asian transshipping business and used the profits earned to finance the purchase of Asian goods for the European market.

BRITISH EAST INDIA COMPANY

Though less successful than the Dutch counterpart during the seventeenth century, the British East India Company represented a joint-stock venture rather than a loose alliance of merchants and had potential for a systematic operation. When Britain achieved the status of a hegemonic world power in the eighteenth century, the company conquered the Indian subcontinent as a central base for the British political and economic advance in Asia. By 1800, Britain had become the leading European dealer of Asian merchandise but, as the predominant industrial country in the West, the nation also desired Asia as a market for its own manufactured products. Using military prowess, the British government forced Imperial China to open its domestic market for British goods in 1842.

In addition, the British acquired an emporium of colonies in Asia as sources of raw materials and labor, entrepôt posts, and markets, thereby shaping a new pattern of European-Asian trade. Other European powers—France, Germany, Italy, and Russia, for example—joined the rivalry for colonial concessions and spheres of influence in Asia during the rest of the nineteenth and the early twentieth centuries. Japan, the only Asian modern military and naval power that had emerged by the first decade of the twentieth century, also joined the zero-sum struggle for colonial rule and challenged the European presence in Asia as a major hurdle for its own imperialist expansion. Nationalism also gradually gained momentum across Asia. Nonetheless, the European-dominant status (as represented by the British, French, and Dutch colonial empires) in Asia remained basically unchanged until World War II.

POST–WORLD WAR II ERA

The postwar European-Asian commercial relations evolved with the vicissitudes of national politics

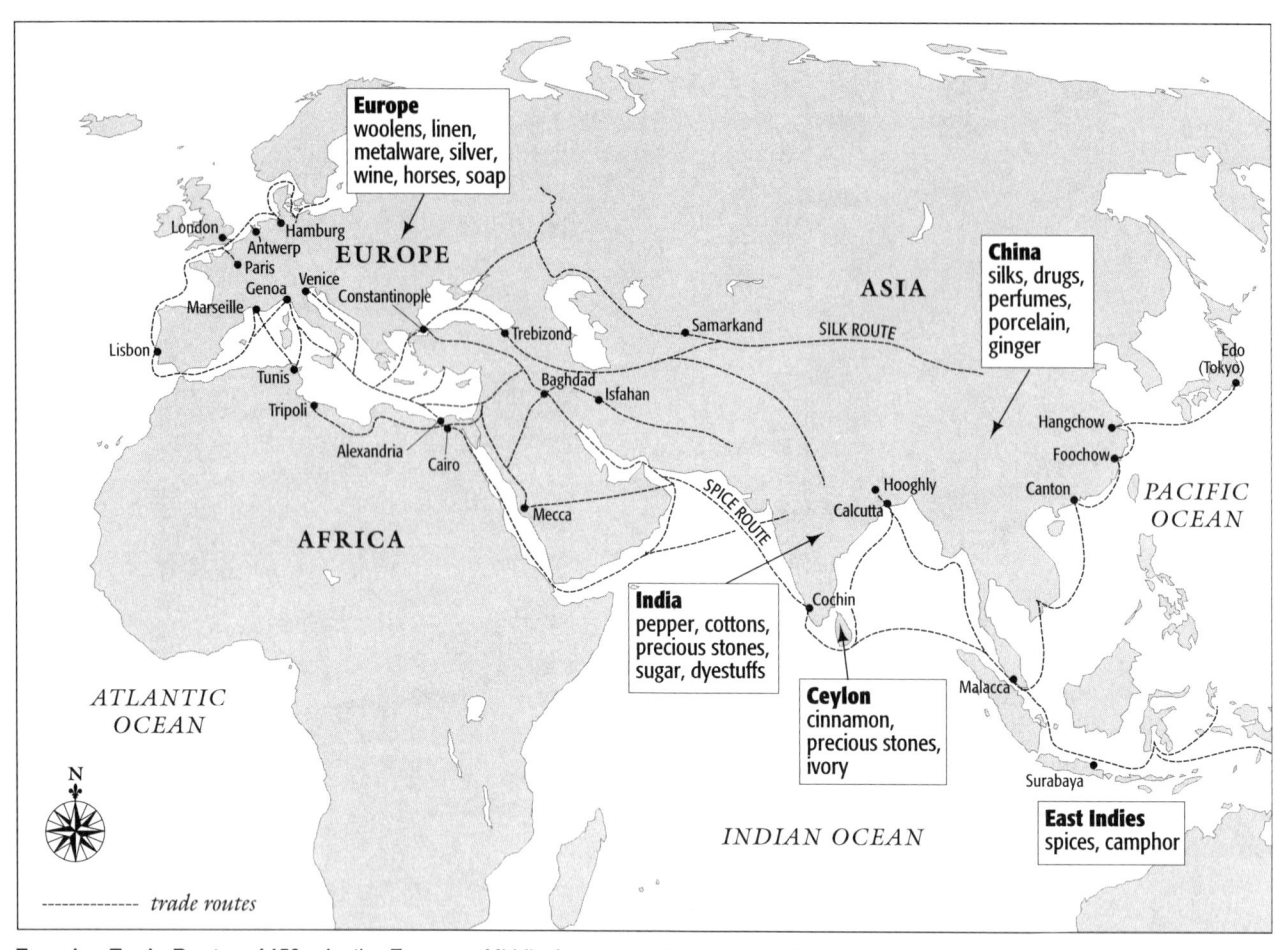

Eurasian Trade Routes, 1450 As the European Middle Ages came to a close in the late fifteenth century, overland and sea-and-land trade routes between Europe and East and South Asia were extensive. The fall of the Byzantine Christian city of Constantinople to the Muslim Turks in 1453 cut Europe off from its overland routes to Asia, forcing countries and entrepreneurs to seek all-sea routes to the East. *(Mark Stein Studios)*

and ideology in various Asian countries. China, where the Chinese Communist Party came to power in 1949 and took an anti-Western position in its foreign policy, elected to be exclusivist toward those West European industrial countries. The Chinese communist government conducted international trade (on a barter basis) essentially with the Soviet Union and its East European communist bloc until an ideological split induced a hostile Sino-Soviet relationship in the early 1960s. The colonial Asian nations won their national independence. Most of them, in trying to develop the modern economies of their own, kept active commerce with their former rulers in Western Europe. Meanwhile, a new democratic Japan gradually developed into one of the world's major manufacturing and trading countries and a principal trade partner with Western Europe. In the 1970s, the new Asian economic powers—South Korea, Taiwan, Hong Kong, and Singapore—followed suit as prominent importers and exporters in trading with Europe. During the 1980s and 1990s, China broke away from the archetype of a state-planned economy and embraced a capitalist market economy for modernization. By reopening its market to the outside world, diversifying its production, and developing new industries, China ascended to the position of a fast-growing producer and consumer in the world. European—especially west European—trade with this largest East Asian nation experienced a quantum leap. With these new developments continuing, the European-Asian commercial relations were generally moving toward a type of market-oriented interdependence as the twenty-first century dawned.

Guoqiang Zheng

See also: British Empire; China; Silk Road.

BIBLIOGRAPHY

Prakash, Om, ed. *European Commercial Expansion in Early Modern Asia.* Hampshire, UK: Variorum, 1997.

Teichova, Alice, ed. *Banking, Trade and Industry: Europe, America and Asia from the Thirteenth to the Twentieth Century.* New York: Cambridge University Press, 1997.

EUROPEAN TRADE, INTRACONTINENTAL

> Diverse and plentiful resources stimulated trade in Europe from earliest times.

The hiking trails of modern Europe follow the pathways of ancient traders, herders, and pilgrims, while the continent's waterways and seas have borne traders and adventurers over great distances since ancient times. A transalpine trade has existed for 5,000 years. In 700 B.C.E., the Celts exchanged products with the Greeks and later with the Romans. The Roman empire had a lively trade with all its provinces around the Mediterranean.

The village economies of medieval Europe were largely self-sufficient, but luxury items were traded over the continent. A northern trade route to Asia went through Russia. Scandinavian Vikings controlled this route from 1000 to 1300, when the Hanseatic League took over. Venetian traders had a monopoly on the southern trade route, which went through the Arab world, until seafaring nations, first Portugal, then Holland, and finally England, secured direct access by sailing around Africa. Large parts of the Iberian Peninsula belonged to the Arab world from the seventh century to the end of the fourteenth century. Agriculture was central for trade here, as profit was reinvested into new crops: rice, fruits, and vegetables were brought from Asia, while new irrigation technology increased production.

Luxury products from the Orient and the New World moved on trade routes connecting the continents. Grain would be shipped from Baltic seaports to Amsterdam or Antwerp and from there would be redistributed to western Europe. International trade fairs were held several times a year such as in Champagne near Paris. Merchants from the Mediterranean met traders from northern Europe to exchange perfume and spices for wool, linen, and fur. The master of a trade would participate in making a product as well as in selling it. The states, still weak, granted letters of privileges to cities. Guilds protected the interests of traders in a city and made it easier for merchants to travel through different jurisdictions. Northern Europe had successful national leagues. The mostly German Hanseatic League achieved a monopoly on almost all trade in Scandinavia, around the Baltic Sea and the North Sea. The merchant of the staple (an English merchant who traded wool) had a monopoly on wool export from England. In southern Europe, the national guilds were less important.

After the fifteenth century, the effects of intercontinental trade rattled the economical pattern of medieval feudalism. Portugal, Spain, Holland, and in turn England led the trade and exploitation with distant countries. The increased population and arrival of precious metals led to inflation.

Northern Europe focused on products for the masses, such as light and cheap textiles. An emerging merchant class took over mediating between the producer and the buyer. The effective textile manufacturing concentrated in Flanders had Europe and the colonies as markets. The second half of the sixteenth century brought production to the countryside where wages were low. The nations promoted trade through infrastructure such as roads and canals, gained control over trade under the ideology of mercantilism, and supported and financed companies for long-distance trading.

In the seventeenth century, development in southern Europe had fallen behind. Seafaring nations of the north took over the spice trade. Transatlantic trade and grain import from eastern Europe was mainly in Dutch and German hands. The Protestant ethic encouraged hard work, a frugal lifestyle, and reinvestment of profit.

Russia had a scattered population in self-sufficient villages. International trade was limited to furs and to grain that landowners sold to finance their lifestyle. Beginning in the thirteenth century large parts of southeastern Europe had fallen under Ottoman rule. The Muslim rulers would consume the surplus from agriculture instead of reinvesting it and the bureaucracy undermined commerce—any sector doing well could be put under state monopoly or preyed upon through the extraction of taxes. The Ottomans would successively lose control over the region until their empire finally collapsed in World War I.

England became a world power when the invention of the steam engine led to the Industrial Revolution. Industry became independent of wind and water as power sources. As a seafaring nation England promoted free trade, an ideology especially favorable for itself in the markets it dominated for the next century.

In the first half of the twentieth century, two world wars and the Great Depression were hardly compatible with free trade and a laissez-faire ideology. Instead, states protected their industries with tariffs and policies designed to improve one country's economic situation at the expense of others. The result was a severe contraction of trade and an exacerbation of international tensions as countries sought to gain access to resources through conquest. During World War II, occupied countries were incorporated to the German economy by being forced to deliver raw materials and labor to Germany and to buy back what the militarized economy could offer.

Russia's participation in the world economy was constrained. Once the Soviet Union came into existence, the country was put under a regime of central planning instead of a market economy, and state ownership instead of private enterprise. After the massive industrialization drive of the 1930s state enterprises showed impressive output, but always in accordance with state dictates rather than in response to the marketplace. A buyer had to take whatever the state had planned the seller to offer, regardless of price or quality.

After World War II, politicians of Western Europe started looking at trade as a means to prevent future wars. The coal and steel union of 1953 made this clear in its preamble, and cooperation over time would lead to the creation of the European Union, today a free-trade area for 400 million people. For consumer goods, there are no restrictions. In many European countries, services, especially within health care and with insurances for health and retirement, are protected with state monopolies.

Tommy Tobiassen

See also: Council for Mutual Economic Assistance; European Union; World War I; World War II.

BIBLIOGRAPHY

Dudley, Dillard. "Economic Development of the North Atlantic Community." In *Historical Introduction to Modern Economics.* Englewood Cliffs, NJ: Prentice-Hall, 1967.

Kriedte. Peter. *Peasants, Landlords and Merchant Capitalists: Europe and the World Economy 1500–1800.* Providence: Berg, 1990.

EUROPEAN UNION

A regional trade organization made up of twenty-five European countries.

Created in 1992 by the Maastricht Treaty, the European Union (EU) incorporated and expanded earlier regional economic agreements. In 1951, the Treaty of Paris created the European Coal and Steel Community, while the Rome Treaties of 1957 created the European Economic Community and the European Atomic Energy Community. These early regional economic agreements all established organizations, including ministerial councils, assemblies, courts, and executive agencies known as commissions.

In 1967, all these communities were merged into the European Communities (EC) and administered by the Council of Ministers, the European Commission, the European Assembly, and the European Court (Europa). At its inception, the EC included six countries: Belgium, the Netherlands, Luxembourg, France, Germany, and Italy. In 1972, the United Kingdom, Denmark, and Ireland joined the EC, which grew to twelve members with the accession of Greece in 1981, and Spain and Portugal in 1986.

The twelve-member EC was a customs union within which goods were traded relatively freely. The EC had a common external tariff and before the 1992 Maastricht Treaty, a program aimed at eliminating all remaining trade barriers and creating a common market through the freeing up of factor movements, had been initiated. The Maastricht Treaty added economic and monetary union to the regional economic integration realized by the EC and set out objectives related to common internal security and external defense arrangements for the union.

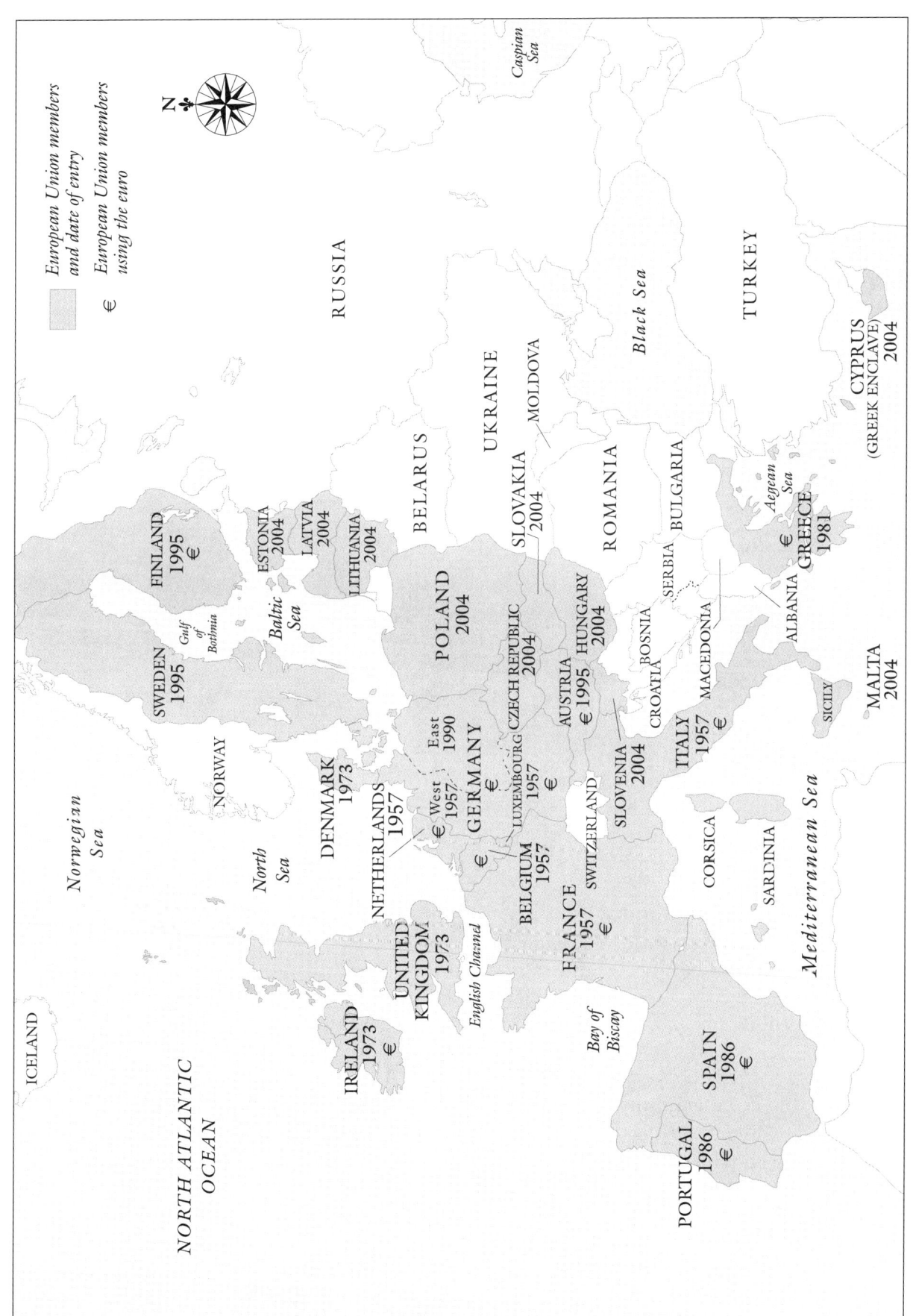

European Union, 2004 Arguably the most successful and certainly the most integrated trade bloc in modern history, the European Union began modestly in 1957 as a collection of six countries working together to lower tariffs between them. By 2004, the Union included twenty-five states, twelve sharing a common currency in the euro. *(Mark Stein Studios)*

While the European Union (EU) has been touted by leaders as a means to expand intra-European trade and European economic influence in the world, many Europeans opposed it and for various reasons. "The EU eventually pokes its nose into everything," says this Danish poster. (© Francis J. Dean/The Image Works)

The EU grew to fifteen with the addition of Sweden, Finland, and Austria and, in 1998, became a monetary union with a common currency and a common central bank. England, Denmark, and Sweden opted out of the monetary union, but the common currency, the euro, was placed in circulation in 2002 in the other countries. The EU has welcomed a number of new members from the former Soviet bloc and elsewhere, but not without adherence to strict requirements. The Czech Republic, Cyprus, Estonia, Hungary, Latvia, Lithuania, Malta, Poland, Slovakia, and Slovenia all became members in 2004. Romania, Bulgaria, and Croatia have been accepted and are likely to be admitted in 2007. Turkey's admission has been made conditional on improvements in human rights.

The members of the EU have benefited from increased trade and economic growth. The EU is the world's largest trading bloc, accounting for 36 percent of world merchandise exports and imports in 2000 if trade within the EU is included. If intra-EU trade is excluded, the EU accounts for 17.3 percent of world merchandise exports and 18.3 percent of world merchandise imports, compared to figures of 15.7 percent and 23.9 percent, respectively, for the United States. A similar pattern holds for the services trade, with the EU accounting for about 40 percent of the total including intra-EU trade. Of total exports valued at $2.25 trillion in 2000, about 62 percent were exported from one EU member to another.

E. Wesley F. Peterson

See also: Trade Organizations.

BIBLIOGRAPHY
Europa. "Europe in Ten Points: A Brief History of European Integration" (http://europa.eu.int/comm/dg10/publications/brochure/docu/101econs/text_en.html#1, accessed September 2002).
World Trade Organization. *International Trade Statistics 2001*. Washington, DC: World Trade Organization, 2001.

EXCHANGE RATES

> The rate at which one state's currency can be exchanged for the currency of another; the rules and procedures by which currencies can be exchanged make up the international monetary system.

The first modern international monetary system operated during the late nineteenth and early twentieth centuries; it was the gold standard, which established fixed exchange rates. In a fixed exchange rate system, the value of currency is fixed against the value of another currency or commodity. The gold standard was a commitment by participating countries to fix the prices of their domestic currencies in terms of a specified amount of gold. The benefit of that gold standard was that central banks could print only as much currency as their gold reserves were worth. However, central banks could not respond to economic downturns with a more expansionary monetary policy, and the money supply and trade could expand only with new discoveries of gold. World War I effectively ended the first gold standard. While there were attempts during the interwar period to create a new gold standard, these attempts were not successful. The Great Depression caused the new gold standard to crumble by 1931.

Exchange rates have a major influence on trade of all kinds, whether corporate trade involving billions of dollars or the shopping habits of individual consumers, like these El Paso, Texas, shoppers seeking bargains over the border in Juárez, Mexico. *(Library of Congress)*

In 1944, a new system of fixed exchange rates was adopted at the Bretton Woods international conference, which formed the International Monetary Fund (IMF) to maintain stable exchange rates on a global level. In the Bretton Woods gold-exchange system, gold was the official reserve asset, while the dollar became the de facto reserve asset. A country could exchange dollars for gold at any time at the fixed price of $35 to the ounce. However, persistent U.S. balance-of-payment deficits steadily reduced U.S. gold reserves, further reducing confidence in the ability of the United States to redeem its currency in gold. In 1971, the United States was forced to abandon gold convertibility.

Since 1973, countries have chosen among a currency board, a managed float, or a free float. A currency board is a monetary authority that issues notes convertible into a foreign currency at a truly fixed rate and on demand. A currency board's reserves are equal to 100 percent or slightly more of its notes in circulation. Some countries that have used currency boards include Estonia, Bulgaria, and Argentina. National governments periodically intervene in financial markets, buying and selling currencies to manipulate their value. A system in which governments intervene to manage the otherwise free-floating currency rates is called a managed-float system.

Floating exchange rates are determined by people buying and selling currencies in the foreign-exchange markets. The main perceived advantage is that nations can pursue independent monetary policies and adjust easily to eliminate payment imbalances and offset changes in their international competitiveness. However, one of the disadvantages has been exchange rate instability, which has been attributed both to differences in national inflation rates and market speculation. While many economic forces influence exchange rates and the tradability of currency, the two most important are inflation and interest rates. All things being equal, a currency appreciates if the interest rates are high and depreciates when inflation is high.

Lilian A. Barria

See also: Money.

BIBLIOGRAPHY

Eichengreen, Barry. *Globalizing Capital: A History of the International Monetary System.* Princeton: Princeton University Press. 1996.

Gilpin, Robert. *The Political Economy of International Relations.* Princeton: Princeton University Press, 1987.

EXPLORATION AND TRADE

A joint endeavor through 4,000 years of human history.

In the modern world, so many benefits have come to us from science and technology that it is hard to imagine that people once explored the world for anything but intellectual purposes. Most educated Americans are still taught that Christopher Columbus sailed west in 1492 to prove that the world was round and not flat. From the heroic quests of the age of discovery until the scientific achievements of the modern space race, historians have told the story of humanity's drive to explore the world primarily from a scientific point of view. However, a closer look at the past reveals a different reality altogether. From the time that humanity's exploration of unknown territory was first recorded, more often than not, the adventurers who took to the seas and highways of the world did so in search of new opportunities for trade.

ANCIENT EGYPT

"I left the Nile with 3,000 men," recalled an Egyptian named Hennu in 2007 B.C.E., and so begins the first recorded tale of exploration and trade in human history. Hennu and his men headed for a land called Punt somewhere south of Egypt on the eastern coast of Africa. In Punt, they hoped to find the myrrh trees that were so highly valued in their own country. The Egyptians planted the fragrant trees in the gardens near their temples and burned the wood as incense in ceremonies to their many gods. Hennu remembered that he marched his men, most of whom were slaves, through the desert north of the Red Sea. He had them dig fifteen wells on the way and gave each one of them a few jars of water and several small loaves of bread for rations each day. When they reached the Red Sea, Hennu ordered them to build a ship, probably a flat-bottomed wooden boat with a single mast for sailing and wooden oars for rowing. Soon, they were off in search of Punt and its fabled myrrh trees. When they finally arrived in Punt, they found the people to be friendly and generous. They offered the Egyptians not only myrrh trees and incense, but also gold and ivory. Hennu and his men returned home in their ship loaded down with the treasure that had come from their expedition to Punt.

While the Egyptians proudly recorded the tale of Hennu, they soon lost interest in exploring beyond their own borders. They eventually forgot the exact location of the fabled land of Punt, and most even came to believe that the story of Hennu was only a legend. The Egyptians preferred instead to trade in the familiar waters of the Mediterranean. They exchanged wheat, flax, and papyrus for gold and silver from Nubia and Syria, copper, turquoise, and a green mineral called malachite from the Sinai peninsula, tin from Spain, granite from a region past the first cataract of the Nile to the south, and precious woods like cedar and pine from Phoenicia. Exploration for trading purposes did not begin again until the reign of Egypt's first queen more than 500 years later. In 1493 B.C.E., Hatshepsut began the construction of a magnificent new temple for the god Amon-Ra at Thebes on the banks of the Nile. She planned a terraced garden of myrrh trees that would lead up from the Nile to the temple. Remembering the legendary story of Hennu, Hatshepsut sent an expedition to find Punt once again. When her men returned with boats loaded with myrrh trees as well as gold, ivory, and precious jewels, she ordered her builders to carve the story into the walls of her new temple. "Such a treasure was never brought for any king who has ruled since the beginning," can be read on the walls of Thebes to this day.

Thutmose III, the stepson and successor of Hatshepsut, pushed the borders of Egypt to their greatest extent through wars in Syria and Palestine, but he sent no further expeditions in search of trade goods. Instead, he relied on the Minoans, who lived on the island of Crete, to carry Egypt's rich import and export trade. For over 1,500 years, the adventurous Minoans had explored the entire Mediterranean in boats so small that the sailors had to beach them to eat, sleep, or gather supplies. But within only a generation after the death of Thutmose in 1436 B.C.E., the Minoan civilization came to an end in a series of catastrophes. An earthquake wrecked Crete and the neighboring island of Santorini, while soldiers from the Greek city of Mycenae invaded and conquered around 1400 B.C.E. In the next 400 years, Egypt also declined in wealth and power, which opened the way for the Phoenicians to dominate the Mediterranean. When an Egyptian ambassador named Wen-Amun arrived in Phoenicia to trade for cedar, the prince of Byblos ordered him to "Get out of my harbor!" unless he could trade goods equal in value to the precious wood needed to repair Hatshepsut's temple of Amon-Ra at Thebes.

PHOENICIANS AND CARTHAGINIANS

Unlike the Egyptians, who preferred to remain within the borders of their own fertile country, the Phoenicians understood that wealth and power could come to a people who headed out into the world through exploration and trade. The country of the Phoenicians stretched for 200 miles on the eastern edge of the Mediterranean, and included the important cities of Tyre, Sidon, and Byblos. Unable to expand eastward because of hostile neighbors, they took to the sea in boats made from the cedars of Lebanon. They traded cedar and other precious woods, along with a reddish purple dye made from shellfish found along the shores of Syria. Heading out into the Mediterranean Sea just as the Minoan civilization collapsed, the Phoenicians became fearless in their drive to explore, trade, and colonize along the shores of Europe and Africa and even sailed beyond the Pillars of Hercules into the Atlantic.

Learning to guide their ships by the North Star, the Phoenicians carried their own goods as well as the goods of other nations throughout the Mediterranean. They were the first to use keels, decks, and anchors on their boats. They also built ships with two rows of oars called biremes and three rows called triremes. Many rulers found it more profitable to have the Phoenicians trade goods for them rather than build navies of their own. In the tenth century B.C.E., King Solomon hired a Phoenician fleet to bring back gold and silver from Ophir in southern Arabia. According to the Greek historian Herodotus, the Phoenicians attempted to circumnavigate Africa on behalf of the Egyptian King Necho. They also established colonies along the southern coast of France, on the island of Sicily, and in North Africa. Their most important colony, which was called Kart-Hadasht, or Carthage, meaning "New City," was founded near the modern site of Tunis in 814 B.C.E. The new capital became the center of their civilization after Assyria attacked Phoenicia in the ninth century B.C.E., and the Babylonian empire finally absorbed Phoenicia in the seventh century B.C.E.

For the next 200 years, the Carthaginians continued to explore the western Mediterranean and the Atlantic, which they called the "Outer Sea." They discovered the Canary Islands and Madeira, and probably even sailed as far west as the Azores. They learned of a place called the Tin Islands from the Tartessians, a people who brought the metal from somewhere in the Atlantic back to their own country in southern Spain. For a time, the Carthaginians were content to carry the important metal necessary in the production of bronze tools and weapons from Spain to the eastern Mediterranean. But around the year 500 B.C.E., they conquered the Tartessians and set up a new city called Gades, or Cadiz, in southwestern Spain. About fifty years later, a Carthaginian king named Himlico led an expedition along the west coast of Europe in search of the Tin Islands. After sailing for more than four months, Himlico finally arrived at the center of the tin trade in the Scilly Islands off the coast of Cornwall in England. Another Carthaginian explorer named Hanno set out fifty years later with 30,000 settlers to explore western Africa and found colonies along the coast. He established at least nine colonies between Carthage and the island of Cerne, which remained an important port for the next 400 years. Hanno continued south and may have gone as far as the Senegal and Gambia Rivers in search of gold before turning back for Carthage.

ANCIENT GREEKS AND HELLENISTIC EMPIRES

By the time Carthaginian leaders like Himlico and Hanno were exploring the Atlantic out past the Pillars of Hercules, another adventurous people, the Greeks, had also taken to the seas to explore and trade. They had established more than a hundred colonies from city-states along the Black Sea, to Cyrene in North Africa, then on to Massilia, later Marseilles, in southern France, and eventually as far west as a port called Malaga in Spain. Twelve more Greek city-states, including important trading centers like Ephesus, stretched south and east through Asia Minor. Greek merchants had even established a trading center along the Nile Delta. Sometime in the seventh century B.C.E., a legendary sea captain named Colaeus had been on his way to trade in Egypt when a storm swept him through the Strait of Gibraltar. He landed in Spain, where he began a rich trade in silver on behalf of the Greeks.

While Colaeus had explored the Atlantic by chance, it was almost impossible for other Greeks to make it through the Carthaginian blockade of the Strait of Gibraltar. They had greater success heading east toward Asia and India, especially from the sixth century B.C.E. onward. In 510 B.C.E., a sailor named Scylax set off on the first exploration ever recorded in Greek history. He was hired by the Persian king Darius I to explore the Indus River. It took him more than two years to sail down the Indus, round the southern coast of Arabia, and return north by way of the Red Sea. Two centuries later, Alexander the Great headed east as part of his attempt to conquer the known world and explore to the very edges of the earth. After subduing the Greek peninsula under his rule in 332 B.C.E., he headed to Asia Minor and began a 10,000-mile quest that brought Egypt, the entire Middle East, and the Persian empire under his control. He explored as far to the east as Pakistan and India, and might have discovered China if his men had not refused to go any farther. He died in his capital at Babylon in 323 B.C.E. still dreaming of new explorations that would colonize the Arabian Peninsula and take Greek sailors around the continent of Africa.

Although Alexander had failed to fulfill his dreams of exploring and conquering the world, he had discovered a fact that would help later Greek adventurers as they headed east to trade with India and Ceylon for their rich supply of jewels and spices. On his return trip from the Indus River to the valley of the Tigris and the Euphrates, he and his men had learned about the effects that monsoons had on sailing in the Indian Ocean. A lieutenant of Alexander named Nearchus was the first to grasp the importance of the seasonal winds. From January until July, the winds in the Indian Ocean blew from the northeast, but in the second half of the year, they blew from the southwest. Merchants from India and Arabia had used these winds for centuries to sail back and forth on the open sea. Unlike the Greek sailors, they did not need to cling to the Arabian shore, but instead moved their cargo swiftly across the Indian Ocean in time with the monsoon winds.

Two centuries later, a Greek merchant named Eudoxus used the monsoons to guide him to India. In 120 B.C.E., he had sailed to Egypt from his homeport of Cyzicus on the Sea of Marmara in Asia Minor. At the court of the Greek king Euergetes II in Alexandria, he learned of an Indian sailor who had been shipwrecked on the Arabian Peninsula. On behalf of Euergetes, the merchant Eudoxus led an expedition eastward with the Indian sailor as his pilot. He returned with a cargo full of gems and perfume, and was later sent back to India on a second expedition by the widow of King Euergetes. During his second trip to India, he had become more fascinated with the possibilities of sailing west around Africa than in returning to the east. He had been blown off course on his way back to Egypt and had landed on the western side of Africa. There, he discovered a ship's prow shaped like a horse's head that was beached in the sand along the coast. Ship builders in Alexandria later told him that the ship's prow was from a boat that had sailed from the Carthaginian city of Gades on the southwestern coast of Spain. Determined to win greater profits by sailing for his own gain, he led an expedition around the western side of Africa. His first attempt failed when his ships ran aground on the coast of Morocco. But in 105 B.C.E., he sailed west past the Pillars of Hercules never to be heard from again.

Although Eudoxus was lost somewhere in the western sea, the memory of his earlier travels inspired other Greek traders to head east to India. In 45 B.C.E., a merchant named Hippalus used the monsoon winds to guide his ship from the Red Sea to the Malabar Coast on the western side of India. For sometime thereafter, sailors in the Indian Ocean called the southwestern monsoon winds the "Hippalus" after the Greek adventurer. By the time of Christ, at least 120 ships headed each year from the Red Sea to India and Ceylon. Within the next century, sailors learned to follow a more southerly route through the Indian Ocean that took them to the Bay of Bengal on the eastern side of the subcontinent. In 120 C.E., a Greek merchant named Alexander reportedly sailed all the way from the Bay of Bengal to the Malay Peninsula. He may have even rounded the coast of modern-day Vietnam and made it as far north as China.

While sea captains who brought treasure from the East were renowned in the Greek world, explorers who sailed the oceans to seek knowledge alone were often condemned as liars by later commentators. During the same time that Alexander the Great made his way eastward through Asia, a Greek scholar named Pytheas either sailed past the Carthaginian fleet in the western Mediterranean or traveled overland to the west coast of France and then headed north into the Atlantic. He later wrote a book called *About the Ocean* detailing his travels and discoveries. He reported how tin was mined and extracted into ingots in Britain and described the frozen sea that he had witnessed most probably off the coast of Norway or Iceland. No copy of the book detailing his 7,000-mile journey has survived. However, the Greek historian Polybius recorded much of the work in his own writings where he dismissed Pytheas as an "arch-falsifier."

ANCIENT ROME

But whether they explored to trade as merchants or to discover as scholars, both the Greeks and the Carthaginians were soon to lose their dominance of the Mediterranean to the rising power of Rome. After Carthage fell to the Romans in 146 B.C.E. following a three-year siege, the city-state on the Italian peninsula sent legions of soldiers throughout Europe, North Africa, Asia Minor, and the Middle East to establish the greatest empire that the Western world had ever seen. The frontiers of the empire stretched for over 6,000 miles from the island of Britain in the west, south through Gaul and the Iberian Peninsula, across the entire Mediterranean coast from Italy and Greece in the north to Numidia and Egypt in the south, and finally ending past Asia Minor in the ancient kingdom of Persia.

While the Romans did not link exploration and trade together in the same way that the Greeks and Carthaginians once did, they were dedicated to military conquest and the wealth that it could bring to the citizens and rulers of Rome. They sent their legions to the ends of the known world and beyond in search of lands whose goods could be brought back to their capital in Italy. In the process, they explored and settled countries that other peoples had only known in passing. They pushed their settlements away from the coastlines known to the Egyptians, Minoans, Greeks, and Carthaginians, and built forts and cities in the interior of new provinces such as Gaul, Britain, and Iberia. In their desire for power and wealth, they brought law and government to every place they conquered. They continued to use the sea routes discovered by their predecessors, but they also built roads that allowed goods to be traded by land. The Romans made it easier for merchants to carry on trade in their empire than had any people before them in the West. By the reign of Julius Caesar and later his nephew Augustus, goods from the entire empire traveled on the new roads built for the Roman soldiers and the older sea routes laid out by the people they had conquered. Merchants brought gold and tin from Britain, silver from Spain, fruit and livestock from Gaul, amber and salt from Germany, and wheat and papyrus from Egypt to cities throughout the empire. Greek ship captains continued sailing around the Arabian Peninsula to bring back rice and cotton from India and spices and pearls from Ceylon.

While the Roman legions moved out to conquer first and foremost, they often explored with an eye to future trading opportunities. In the second century B.C.E., Roman armies crossed the Taurus Mountains in the center of modern Turkey, and then headed over the Caucasus Mountains farther to the east in a drive to reach the Caspian Sea, where many caravans began the long trek to the interior of Asia. In the following century, General Pompey the Great led his men down the Cyrus or Kura River near the Black Sea. He kept detailed notes of more than seventy tribes who lived in the region to determine what goods they might someday trade with Rome. He also recommended possible overland routes to India that later Roman merchants would use. At the same time, Roman soldiers crossed the Atlas Mountains in North Africa. They headed deep into the interior of the African continent and established a trade in wild animals such as lions, elephants, and leopards that were used in gladiatorial combats in the Colosseum in Rome. The army also tried several times to mount expeditions that would find the source of the Nile River. While they were unsuccessful, a Greek merchant named Diogenes claimed to have discovered where the Nile began sometime between 60 and 70 C.E. According to the geographer Ptolemy, the merchant Diogenes was blown off course on a return trip from India and landed on the coast of modern-day Tanzania. After marching inland for twenty-five days, he came across two lakes, possibly Lake Victoria and Lake Albert, where the Nile began its long course northward.

There were other Roman expeditions that combined exploration and trade that were also failures for the empire. The most notable one came when Emperor Caesar Augustus decided to conquer the Arabian Peninsula. He was determined to find the city of Marib in present-day Yemen and bring back its riches to Rome. For centuries, Arab merchants had led caravans out of Marib loaded down with gold, precious gems, frankincense, myrrh, and cinnamon. Marib may even have been the land known as Sheba whose fabled queen made a journey to visit King Solomon nearly a thousand years before the reign of Augustus. Determined to transform Arabia into an imperial province and thereby control the trade of Marib for Rome alone, Augustus sent a general named Aelius Gallus on an expedition out of Egypt in 24 B.C.E. Gallus led an army of 10,000 Roman soldiers, along with troops from Judea, Egypt, and the Nabataean city of Petra. They sailed from the port of Cleopatris on the Gulf of Suez and headed south along the Arabian Peninsula. The fleet was shipwrecked on the coral reefs some 300 miles down the Arabian coast. General Gallus led his men on a 900-mile-long trek into the Arabian desert, where they fought and defeated many tribes along the way but never found the fabled city of Marib.

CHINA

At the same time that the Roman emperors were pushing their armies toward the East, the rulers of the Han dynasty in China were seeking greater ties with the West. Under the Han, China reached new frontiers in Asia that exceeded the size of the Roman empire. Under the leadership of Emperor Wu Di in the second century B.C.E., the Chinese looked beyond their borders to the West to find allies against the Huns (Xiongnü) in the north and trading partners for exotic goods, especially in silk. In 138 B.C.E., Wu Di sent a general named Zhang Qian into the unknown lands to the West in search of new diplomatic alliances and new trade routes. Zhang left northern China and headed west across the Gobi Desert to the city of Barkol in the Tian mountains. From Barkol, he traveled overland to Bactria in modern-day Iran. There, he met a people who claimed to be the descendants of Alexander the Great. While these blue-eyed and redheaded people refused to ally themselves with China, they did explain to Zhang that Europe lay to the northwest and India to the southeast. He returned to the court of Emperor Wu Di, who promptly sent him back on a second expedition to find the best trade routes to the West. In 105 B.C.E., Zhang opened the Silk Road from China to the Roman empire.

Chinese traders eventually laid out three routes to the West. The northern one was called the Great Silk Road, headed from China west through Central Asia to the Caspian and Black Seas, and ended at the Greek port of Byzantium. Since this route covered several mountain ranges, many merchants decided that it was too expensive to transport goods along it. A more popular middle route opened up from China to the Persian Gulf, and then up the valley of the Euphrates River to either the Black Sea or the Syrian city of Damascus. Another silk road to the south went completely by water from China, around modern-day Vietnam and the Malay Peninsula, and finally to the southern tip of India. From there, the goods continued by water into the Red Sea and then traveled overland to the Nile and northern Egypt. Silk was soon the most highly prized good in the late Roman empire. Men and women alike paid any price for the soft and brightly colored cloth. The Silk Road eventually led to a dangerous drain of gold coins from the empire to the East. When the Parthians cut off the trade with the East, the flow of silk came to a halt in the fourth century B.C.E., but it began again after 226 C.E., when the Persians conquered the Parthians and reopened the Silk Road. By the sixth century, the secret of making silk was learned in the West and Syria became an important center for silk production in the Middle East.

EUROPEAN DARK AND MIDDLE AGES

While silk and other oriental goods continued to flow in the eastern Mediterranean, few in the West could take advantage of the trade. The slow but steady collapse of the Roman empire had cut much of western Europe off from the routes that

Norsemen celebrating their discovery of the New World. The Vikings saw themselves primarily as explorers and traders.
(© North Wind Picture Archives)

had once linked it to the Middle East and Asia. The legions had taken Rome to the farthest edges of the Western world, and the wealth of Britain, Gaul, and Iberia had poured back into the empire and then out to the East to purchase goods like silk and spices. However, the cost of maintaining the empire was high, and heavy taxes were required to pay for the army, the roads, and the imperial administration. Many wealthy citizens fled from the cities to avoid paying the ever-higher taxes. Rome was further weakened by a lack of clear imperial succession, which led to a brutal competition among leading generals for control of the army and thus control of the empire. The assassination of emperors and the rebellion of the legions became more common as the empire dissolved in the West. The attacks of Germanic tribes including the Vandals, Ostrogoths, Franks, Visigoths, Angles, and Saxons further weakened the Western Roman empire. By the time that the Byzantine or the Eastern Roman empire had established itself in the new capital city of Constantinople, the older provinces of Britain, Gaul, Iberia, Germany, Italy, and North Africa were firmly under the control of barbarian kings and their nobility.

While the new barbarian kingdoms tried to reestablish trading ties with the East, the rise of Islam and its dominance of the Mediterranean brought these efforts to a swift end. Founded by an Arab merchant named Mohammed, Islam captured the allegiance of tribes throughout the Arabian Peninsula and united them as a political and military force in the seventh century C.E. The Muslim conquerors established their capital at Baghdad and eventually controlled most of Asia Minor to the north, then south through Lebanon and Palestine, and west through Egypt, North Africa, and Iberia. The new Islamic empire pressed ever closer to the gates of Constantinople and took control of the many trade routes that once linked the Atlantic Ocean, the Mediterranean, the Red Sea, the Persian Gulf, and the Indian Ocean together. Arab merchants now dominated the paths across the seas that Phoenician, Greek, and Roman traders had developed for almost 2,000 years. They also controlled most of the cities at the end of the long overland caravan routes from Asia. In turn, Arab merchants went even farther east through the Indian Ocean, bringing trade and Islam to the Malay Peninsula and Indonesia. They also headed by caravan through the Sahara and into the interior of Africa to trade with tribal peoples along the Gambia and Senegal Rivers for gold, ivory, and slaves.

Despite the chaos that had come into western Europe and much of the rest of the world with the fall of Rome and the rise of Islam, exploration into unknown regions continued. However, many of the new adventurers who set out on land and sea were men of faith rather than merchants or traders. In Europe, Catholic missionaries headed bravely into barbarian lands to spread their faith in Christ. Important figures like Saints Patrick, Augustine of Canterbury, Boniface, and Anskar helped convert the Irish, the English, many of the Germans, and even some of the Scandinavians. The legendary Saint Brendan may even have made it from Ireland to North America. Benedictine monks often founded their communities on the edges of settled areas throughout western Europe. Their monasteries became centers of pilgrimage and trade for many of the faithful. In China, the same kind of exploration on behalf of faith took place as young men left the chaos of their war-torn country and headed to

India to learn more about Buddhism. In the seventh century, a nineteen-year-old scholar named Xuanzang left China on an epic journey to the south. He traveled through the Gobi Desert, along the Great Silk Road to Samarkand, and finally through the Hindu Kush and the Khyber Pass. He spent sixteen years learning about Siddhartha Gautama and returned home to China with knowledge of the land routes to India and a precious cargo of more than 700 Buddhist texts.

As exploration on behalf of faith continued in both the East and the West, a new quest for political order was reawakened in Europe. In the eighth century, a royal family known as the Carolingians came to power in the Kingdom of the Franks. Charles Martel, the founder of the dynasty, helped to establish the new order by defeating the Muslims at the Battle of Poitiers in 732. His grandson, Charlemagne, went on to build a kingdom that stretched from the Pyrenees Mountains to the Danube River. For a time, Charlemagne was able to link the government, culture, and trade of his vast empire. However, the attempt to rebuild a united western Europe collapsed in the civil wars of Charlemagne's grandsons and in the invasions from the Vikings to the north, the Saracens to the south, and the Magyars to the east. A new political, social, and economic system later known as feudalism was developed to bring stability to the West. There was little time for exploration or the search for new goods as men swore allegiance to one another to protect themselves in the growing chaos.

As difficult as it may have been for the West to understand, the most ruthless of the new invaders, the Vikings, saw themselves primarily as explorers and traders. Also called the Norsemen, or Northmen, they came from Norway, Denmark, and Sweden and had ventured out of Scandinavia many other times in the previous centuries. In fact, their attack on the Carolingian empire was the last of three great waves of people who had come from the north to explore and raid, but also to trade and settle. Sometime during the Bronze Age, the first Vikings left Scandinavia in search of new lands and goods to trade. They were merchants who traveled in small round boats made of wood and animal skins. Each trader carried with him imported scales to weigh goods, a sword for defense, and a ladder to raid the upper stories of isolated houses along the way. These lone Viking merchants set up trading posts throughout the Baltic and established routes on the open sea from Scandinavia to as far west as Britain and Ireland. They traded wood for whale meat, oil, and bones, walrus tusks, fur, rope, eider duck feathers, and slaves.

Beginning in the seventh century, a people known as the Varaginians were the second group of Vikings to leave their home in Sweden and head south and east into the Baltic. They built sturdy wooden longboats called *drakkars*, and headed down the Volga, Dnepr, and Don Rivers. They established their capital city at Kiev. Raiders at first, they learned to carry on a more civilized trade with the Byzantine Christians in Constantinople and along the Black Sea, and with the Muslim cities on the Caspian Sea at the western end of the caravan routes from Asia. The Varaginians traded fur, wax, and slaves in exchange for gold and silver coins, silk, jewels, and spices.

The Carolingian empire felt the brunt of the third and last wave of Viking invaders, who came south from Norway. These raiders in their long ships headed through the North Sea and rounded the Shetland, Orkney, and Hebrides Islands. They raided the Irish coast and then turned southeast for Brittany before heading inland up rivers like the Thames and the Seine. They attacked and pillaged towns, churches, and monasteries along the way. Many eventually settled in Normandy, which was named for them, and from there, they went on to conquer England and Sicily. Their attacks on Europe came to an end when they converted to Christianity around 1000. However, their exploration and trade in the Atlantic continued. They explored and settled Iceland. Under leaders like Eric the Red and his son Leif, they went on to discover Greenland and the eastern coast of North America. Along the way, they traded grain, fish, lumber, fur, whale meat, and walrus tusks. But while Iceland remained a Viking stronghold for centuries to come, the settlements on Greenland survived for just 400 years, while those in North America were abandoned within only a generation of their founding.

Just as the Viking invasions came to an end in

the West, the Christian East found itself under attack from a new Muslim enemy, the Seljuk Turks. By the eleventh century, the Turks had conquered much of the Middle East once controlled by the caliph of Baghdad, as well as most of Asia Minor long ruled by Constantinople. The Byzantine emperor Alexius I Comnenus asked the pope and other Western leaders to send mercenary soldiers to help defend Constantinople from the Turks and retake Asia Minor. In 1095, Pope Urban II preached the First Crusade, calling on all Christians to protect Constantinople and to retake the Holy Land from the Muslims. The outpouring of support from king, nobleman, and commoner alike reawakened the drive for exploration and renewed the interest in long-distance trade in a manner that had not been seen in western Europe since the days of the Roman empire.

As they headed for the "Outremer," the French word for the Holy Land, the Christian knights followed nearly forgotten land and sea routes to the East. While their efforts to free the Holy Land from the Muslims ultimately failed, the crusaders of the High Middle Ages gave western Europe a taste for the silks, tapestries, porcelains, jewels, and spices of the Orient that would never be surrendered.

EUROPEAN AGE OF EXPLORATION

For a time, the Western nations were willing to rely on Italian traders in the cities of Genoa, Pisa, and especially Venice to act as the middlemen in trade with the East. From the opening years of the First Crusade, the Venetians held a monopoly on most sea routes to the Middle East and Africa. Their galleys dominated the Adriatic and much of the eastern Mediterranean. They carried trade between Constantinople, Tripoli, Beirut, and Sidon, and much of North Africa and Egypt. However, by the thirteenth century, various individuals in the West decided to explore possible ties with the Far East on their own. When news spread that the Mongols were sweeping through Asia on their way west to Europe, Pope Innocent IV sent emissaries to China in an attempt to convert Kuyuk Khan and his followers to Christianity. A Franciscan friar named Carpini and a Dominican priest called Ascelin both journeyed overland to Kuyuk's court on behalf of the Catholic Church. Another Franciscan from France, named William Rubrek, made a similar trip of behalf of his crusading king, Louis IX. Rubrek discussed a possible alliance between the Christians and the Mongols to defeat the Muslims in the Middle East once and for all.

Even some Venetian merchants themselves sought more direct ties to the Far East in the thirteenth century. Two brothers, named Niccolò and Maffeo Polo, grew tired of dealing with Arab middlemen in their own merchant trade and decided to head for Asia, where they could buy goods directly. They made the journey overland from Constantinople to China, and stayed at the imperial court for ten years. When the Polo brothers made a return trip to China, Niccolò took his young son, Marco, along with them. Marco Polo became a trusted advisor to Kublai Khan himself and traveled throughout the empire on his behalf. He later wrote a memoir of his stay in China published under the title *The Adventures of Marco Polo*. Many who read the book in western Europe became convinced that the Asian continent was much larger than previously thought and could be reached by sea more easily than anyone had ever before imagined.

The determination of kings, adventurers, and merchants in western Europe to find a route to Asia by sea launched the age of discovery in the fifteenth century. Prince Henry the Navigator of Portugal led the drive for exploration by dedicating his life to finding a way to circumnavigate Africa. In the city of Sagres, he gathered together scholars, traders, and sailors who prepared accurate maps of the known world. They helped him design a new ship called a "caravel" that could move swiftly across the ocean even when carrying heavy loads of supplies and trade goods. Henry's court at Sagres worked tirelessly to improve navigational methods and equipment so that ship captains could accurately determine their position on the latitudes of the globes. Urged on by their dedicated prince, the Portuguese explored and settled Madeira, the Canary Islands, and the Azores, long forgotten since the Phoenicians had first discovered them. Soon, a profitable trade in lumber, fruit, and wine was under way between the colonies and Europe.

Portuguese sailors continued on past the new colonies down the western coast of Africa, reaching Cape Verde in 1445. The drive to round Africa became more intense after 1453 when the long beleaguered city of Constantinople fell to the Ottoman Turks. With trade routes in the eastern Mediterranean now controlled by the Muslims, the Portuguese pressed on for their prince, their faith, and the profits that came from trading in gold, ivory, and slaves on the African coast. Although Prince Henry died before his sailors could circumnavigate Africa, his successor King John II sent even more caravels south to the equator, Angola, and beyond. The Portuguese knew if they could reach the fabled Spice Islands, also called the Moluccas, the profits would be enormous for themselves and their nation.

In 1492, Spain, Portugal's greatest rival, joined in the age of discovery when Queen Isabella and her husband, Ferdinand, commissioned the Genoese sailor Christopher Columbus to head west across the Atlantic to Asia. Columbus sailed with the royal promise that he would receive 10 percent of the profits from all the trade between Spain and the Far East. When his fleet sighted land in the Caribbean, he was convinced that he had found the Indies, which was another name for the many islands that lay off the coast of Asia between India, Japan, and China. He made three more trips west on behalf of Spain, discovering more islands in the Caribbean and exploring the shorelines of Honduras and later Venezuela. Although Columbus came to believe that he had found an "Other World" just off the coast of Asia, he had in fact discovered the New World of the Americas.

Within fifty years of Columbus's discovery of San Salvador in the Caribbean, Spain had established an empire that ran from California and Florida in the north to Chile and Argentina in the south. Wealth poured into Spain from the gold mines of the conquered Aztecs in Mexico and the silver mines of the defeated Incas in Peru. Spanish conquistadors continued to explore farther north into the Great Plains and deeper into the Amazon jungle looking for more legendary cities of gold, but they were never found. Instead, Spanish colonists produced even more wealth through the establishment of sugar, rice, and tobacco plantations worked by slaves brought from the west coast of Africa. While the Portuguese continued to head toward Asia by way of Africa with Vasco da Gama finally reaching India in 1498, other nations in western Europe now launched out into the Atlantic. The wealth that the Spanish had achieved in so short a time through exploration, colonization, and trade inspired the English, French, and Dutch to follow them west.

Shown here are European merchants in a Mediterranean port in the 1400s. With Turkey's increasing dominance of the Mediterranean, such traders sought overseas routes to Asia.
(© North Wind Picture Archives)

With the support of kings and merchants, a steady stream of explorers left western Europe to claim territory in the Americas and to continue the search for a route by sea to Asia. In 1497, the Italian sea captain John Cabot (Giovanni Caboto) headed west and sailed along the eastern coast of North America on behalf of England. His trip began a long search for the Northwest Passage through the American wilderness to Asia. Another Italian adventurer named Giovanni da Verrazano made a similar trip along the eastern coast of North America for France in 1524. Ten years later, the French explorer Jacques Cartier headed down the Saint Lawrence River into the Canadian interior on behalf of his nation. In 1609, the Englishman Henry Hudson, sailing for the Dutch, discovered and explored another important river that was later named after him.

The adventurous ship captains who sailed west on behalf of England, France, and Holland learned much about the coastline of North America, but continued to regard it primarily as an obstacle that barred their way to Asia. Slowly, they came to realize that a profitable fur trade could be established with the many native tribes who dwelled in the Americas. Called the Indians by Christopher Columbus, they lived as more than 500 separate tribes from the Atlantic westward to the Pacific. Their ancestors had crossed from Asia to Alaska sometime before the end of the last Ice Age, and then spread out across the Americas. They followed rivers, valleys, and animal trails in their migrations to the south and east. As they moved across North America, some tribes settled in villages, while others continued as nomadic hunters. The Indians had established trade routes among themselves to exchange shells, pearls, flint, and precious metals like copper and silver. Many were eager to trade fur with the Europeans for iron pots and pans, woolen blankets, and especially guns.

The nations of western Europe eventually realized that even more trade could come through the establishment of colonies in North America and the Caribbean. The colonies could produce cash crops and exotic goods like sugar, silk, and glass for export to the mother country. In turn, the colonies could purchase manufactured goods from Europe. After failures in Newfoundland and at Roanoke, the English established the first permanent colony in North America at Jamestown in 1607. The Virginia colony survived and prospered through growing and exporting tobacco. More English colonies were established along the eastern coast of North America and in the Caribbean. They produced tobacco, sugar, and rice in the tropical south, and wheat, corn, and livestock in the more temperate north. Colonies established in New England soon built merchant fleets of their own to carry trade goods between North America and the entire Atlantic. The French also established colonies in Canada from 1608 onward that exported lumber and fish to Europe. However, they relied even more heavily on the fur trade that trappers, priests, and adventurers established with the Indians on the rivers and lakes of North America. The Dutch had similar successes with farming and the fur trade in the Hudson River valley.

While explorers, traders, and colonists alike eventually discovered the value of the Americas, the drive to fulfill the dream of Columbus and sail west to the riches of Asia remained alive. In 1513, the Spanish explorer Vasco Núñez de Balboa crossed the Isthmus of Panama and discovered another ocean west of the New World. Seven years later, the Portuguese captain Ferdinand Magellan sailing on behalf of Spain found a strait around South America that led into the other ocean, which he named the Pacific. As he traveled north and west, he met the Polynesians, whose ancestors had explored and settled most of the islands of the Pacific. The Polynesians had established an extensive trade network for exchanging goods like food, boats, and knives from the Philippines to Easter Island. Magellan claimed the Philippines for Spain shortly before he met his death at the hands of natives on the island of Mactan in 1521. A few of his original crew members made it back to Europe in a ship loaded down with spices, proving at last that Asia and its riches could be reached by sailing west on the oceans of the world.

During the next 250 years, English, French, and Dutch adventurers followed the first Portuguese and Spanish explorers east around Africa and west into the Pacific. England, France, and Holland joined Portugal and Spain in establishing colonies in Asia and in Africa, and ultimately fought for control of trade in items such as silk, spices, porcelain, tea, coffee, sugar, rice, opium, and tobacco. From the late eighteenth century on to the early twentieth century, Great Britain led the world in the final exploration of the Pacific islands, Australia, and Africa not only to increase humanity's knowledge of the globe, but also to complete the building of a mercantile and manufacturing empire with colonies on every continent. Britain finally lost its dominance in the world to the United States, a former British colony in North America, which had grown west from the Atlantic to the Pacific in a national enterprise of exploration, settlement, and trade.

By the twentieth century, all the continents of the world had been discovered and mapped. The drive to explore for the sake of knowledge continued as adventurers headed to the poles and up the peaks of the highest mountains. Exploration on behalf of trade went on below the ground as companies searched for materials necessary in manufacturing like coal, iron ore, and oil. Commercial airline routes were also laid out from the 1920s onward. The recent space race helped international trade through the development of communication satellites and led many to dream of one day traveling to other worlds where the drive to explore and trade could begin once again.

Mary Stockwell

See also: Greek City-States; Roman Empire; Spanish Empire.

BIBLIOGRAPHY

Barker, Felix, with Anthea Barker. *The Glorious Age of Exploration: The Encyclopedia of Discovery and Exploration.* Garden City, NY: Doubleday, 1971.

Tavernier, Bruno. *Great Maritime Routes: An Illustrated History.* New York: Viking, 1970.

EXTRATERRITORIALITY

A legal concept applied in international law for explaining the immunity of the subjects of a state during their sojourn in other states.

Extraterritoriality designates both the privilege of immunity from local law enforcement enjoyed by certain aliens and the procedure by which a person is permitted to enter or leave a jurisdiction in which he or she would normally be subject to arrest, detention, or other deprivation. In recent times, the extraterritoriality still functions because there are diplomats, troops in passage, war vessels, official representatives of foreign states, and international organizations excepted from the jurisdiction of the country in which they are present. The legal sources for the principle of extraterritoriality were customary international law or treaty. Generally, it is about a bilateral and reciprocal legal exemption between states.

Until World War II, there was a unilateral extraterritoriality promoted in the relationships between Western powers and certain Asian and African states, like the Ottoman empire (Turkey), Egypt, Morocco, China, Japan, India, Iran, Syria, and Libya. As a result of several wars and more capitulations by China, since 1842 foreign powers, like Great Britain, France, Germany, the United States, Russia, and Japan, had acquired commercial and legal privileges for their nationals. In 1855, Siam (present-day Thailand) and Britain concluded an unequal agreement that opened up Siam to Western influence and trade. Besides more commercial privileges, for example, a 3 percent duty on all imports and free access and trade in all Siamese ports, the agreement included more stipulations concerning the immunity of jurisdiction for British subjects in all Siamese ports.

The Ottoman empire, as well as the states from the Far East and North Africa, granted the regime of extraterritoriality in their territories in the form of the most-favored-nation clause. The subjects of Venice, France, England, the Dutch republic, and Poland enjoyed a similar extraterritoriality in Ottoman territories. At the same time, the "mutuality" was one of the main features of the treaties concluded between the Ottoman empire and boundary states, for example, Venice, Hungary, Poland, Austria, and Russia. The sultans bestowed free access and commerce, safety of person and merchandise, or individual responsibility to foreign merchants, provided that the Ottomans had the same rights in the mentioned states.

THE OTTOMAN EMPIRE

The Ottoman Empire had long practiced extraterritoriality toward the Western powers, usually invoked on behalf of ambassadors, consuls, and other visiting diplomats. But the unilateral and unequal character of the system again reflected the capitulation of a Middle Eastern or Asian regime to the West. For under this arrangement, the European nations obtained immunity of jurisdiction not only for their subjects who held diplomatic positions, but also for their merchants and virtually any national who wanted to settle in the Ottoman territories.

The legal status of foreign merchants constituted an important question for commerce in the Ottoman empire. The Muslim holy law and imperial charters (in Turkish, "'ahdnâmes"; in Western languages, "Capitulations") established this legal condition. According to Islamic law, a temporary safe-conduct could protect the life and goods of an infidel who came from Abode of War and entered Abode of Islam. He became a beneficiary of protection (in Turkish, "müste'min").

Historically, extraterritoriality was originally practiced by princes who bestowed safe-conducts to foreigners who, as aliens, did not ordinarily enjoy the full protection of the host-country's law. The Ottomans took over this medieval custom, called personality of laws, which held that a foreigner was in any place subject to his own sovereignty.

Even if according to the classical Islamic law an enemy infidel could stay within the Abode of Islam for one year only, the foreign merchants received the privilege to remain for an unlimited time in the Ottoman empire without paying a poll-tax (*djizye*) and became non-Muslim tributaries (*dhimmîs*) by a clause included in the Capitulations. In this time, the Ottoman official could not violate their property and residences, or collect personal and property taxes specific to Ottoman subjects. Also, in the case of death, the Public Treasury did not confiscate the foreigners' goods; the head of their community (or caravan) had to hand them over to the legal inheritors.

The most significant aspect of extraterritoriality was the exemption of foreigners from both civil and criminal action by local authorities. Two categories of legal disputes appeared in the Ottoman Capitulations: conflicts between Ottoman subjects and foreign merchants, and conflicts within the foreign merchant communities. The clauses concerning the Ottoman-foreigner disputes stipulated that the judge did not have to consider unwritten testimony or documents in deciding when a party was absent or to accept false witness. In this manner, one tried to avoid any abuse committed by the Ottoman authorities.

The Capitulations clearly emphasized the extraterritoriality granted to foreign subjects, when the legal disputes occurred inside a foreigner community. Although physically present on the territory of another state, the foreigners continued to be considered under their ruler's protection and under the legal jurisdiction of their home country. Consequently, ambassadors or consuls, who represented their Western sovereigns in the Ottoman empire, had the right to handle all civil and criminal cases involving their countrymen, without any interference of the Ottoman officials. Due the fact that in central and southeastern Europe merchants were part of wagon trading caravans, the immunity of jurisdiction had local specificity. The judgment of the disputes between merchants of the same group by the caravan's head was a customary practice, also confirmed by the peace and commerce treaties.

The states that bestowed unilateral extraterritoriality resented it as an infringement of sovereignty. Consequently, they fought for abolishing it and, earlier or later, succeeded (Japan in 1899, Turkey in 1923, China in 1946, and Egypt in 1949).

Viorel Panaite

See also: Ottomans.

BIBLIOGRAPHY

Heyking, Alphonse. "L'exterritorialité et ses applications en Extrême-Orient." *Recueil des cours. Académie de Droit International* (Paris) 7, no. 2 (1924): 241–335.

Kahn-Freund, O. "General Problems of Private International Law." *Recueil des cours. Académie de Droit International* (Paris) 143, no. 3 (1974): 141–474.

Khadduri, M., and H.J. Liebesny, eds. *Law in the Middle East*. Vol. 1, *Origin and Development of Islamic Law*. Washington, DC: Middle East Institute, 1955.

Pélissié du Rausas, G. *Le régime des capitulations dans l'Empire Ottoman*. Vols. 1–2. Paris: n.p., 1902–1905.

F

FAIRS, INTERNATIONAL TRADE

> A temporary market or commercial enterprise organized to promote trade, where buyers and sellers gather, that has assumed an increasingly important role in international trade during the twentieth century.

Trade fairs are organized at regular intervals, generally at the same location and time of year, and usually last for several weeks. In Europe and in Asia, especially, they are popular, but almost every country has at least one major annual international exposition, from one industry or branch of industrial production to general exhibits of goods and merchandise.

By definition, fairs are large organized gatherings, occurring at regularly spaced intervals, to which merchants come from distant regions. The modern fair stems from the periodic gatherings of merchants that were a prominent economic institution of Europe in the Middle Ages. To wit, the word "fair" (*foire* in French) is derived from the Latin *feriae*, meaning "feast," indicating the close relation between medieval fairs and feasts of the early Christian church, while the German word for fair, *Messe*, is derived from the Latin *missa*, meaning "mass."

Exhibitions, which can encompass a variety of uses, are sometimes called expositions; these are large extravaganzas sometimes called "world fairs" or "international expositions," a term frequently applied to an organized public fair or display of industrial and artistic productions that is designed to promote trade and to reflect cultural progress. During the nineteenth and twentieth centuries, some fairs have been called expositions and some expositions have been called fairs, but the general distinction is that fairs traditionally are gatherings for immediate trade, and expositions are a form of advertisement.

Expositions are usually considered a product of the nineteenth century and are held at greater intervals than fairs or only on certain occasions, such as the Genoa and Seville Expositions of 1992 that celebrated the discovery of the New World; Christopher Columbus was born in Genoa, and he left for his great voyage in 1492 from the Spanish seaport.

While expositions are not trade fairs per se, where goods or services are sold directly, one of the major functions is the promotion of tourism and trade among countries. They last longer than fairs, usually no more than six months, and serve primarily to introduce businesspeople and interested spectators to new technical and industrial developments and to the arts. International expositions began in 1851 with the Crystal Palace in London.

BEGINNINGS

Evidence of the existence of fairs is sparse until the Middle Ages, which suggests that fairs historically have been a European phenomenon. In the preclassical world, it seems likely that gatherings similar to fairs were held in connection with religious feasts in the Mesopotamian valley, Syria, Palestine, and Arabia. Caravans of Phoenicians whose trade contacts extended westward around the Mediterranean visited some of these primitive fairs.

In ancient China, fairs were held only in periods of political disunity, for example, the Market of the Currents of the Four Cardinal Points held about 500 C.E. at Luoyang and the periodic fairs for medicines and silkworms held at Sichuan between the ninth and twelfth centuries.

In classical Greece, besides markets held along the boundaries of the city-states and protected by special market gods, annual fairs were held in conjunction with feasts of principal gods. Spring and autumn fairs were held at Tithorea during the feasts honoring Isis; at dawn of the second day, merchants opened their stalls for trade in slaves, cattle, clothes, silver, and gold. Similar fairs were held along with the Olympian and Isthmian feasts, with special protection granted to merchants.

Roman commerce was not centralized enough to be conducive to fairs, but some were held on the eastern frontiers of the Roman empire along the caravan routes. The fall of the empire during the third century was due, partly, to the decline of trade, industry, and towns and of the merchants and artisans.

The only reliable evidence regarding the existence of fairs in western Europe before the eleventh century pertains to one at the abbey of Saint Denis near Paris. Four documents, written between 629 and 759, describe a fair granted in 629 to the monks of this abbey by Dagobert I, the Merovingian king of the Franks. Held annually to honor Saint Denis, the fair began on October 9 and lasted four weeks.

When the fair was in session, all trade in the area had to be transacted there, and the monks received all the tolls and dues levied on the trade. Well located along a route to Paris, the Saint Denis fair was the only one to flourish in this period. It became a noted center for trade in wine, honey, grain, wood, salt, and dyes. English, Spanish, Provençal, Saxon, Frisian, Lombard, and Frankish traders frequented it. But during a period when Europe was filled with large agrarian estates, this fair served mostly as a periodic exchange center for natural products.

MEDIEVAL FAIRS

With the economic revival of western Europe, fairs became a prominent economic institution. The revival, in the late tenth and eleventh centuries, produced a merchant class, towns, trade, and industry. Fairs appeared at strategically located sites along overland routes that connected southern and northern Europe, along rivers, and at some maritime ports. Every area of Europe affected by the economic revival had fairs, but the most significant were those of Champagne, located halfway between Italy and Provence in the south and Flanders. Other important fairs included Provins and Troyes, each of which lasted about six weeks.

CHAMPAGNE FAIRS

The success of the Champagne fairs was because of their excellent location and the enlightened economic policies of the counts of Champagne. Aware of the potential economic benefits, the counts gave protection, assessed minimal taxes, and prescribed regulations for the collection of debts and the fulfillment of contracts. They also established special courts, where merchants could have their differences settled rapidly and equitably according to a sort of international "law of merchants" (*jus mercatorum*), and initiated an efficient system of administration of the law.

At the peak of the Champagne fairs in the twelfth and thirteenth centuries, merchants came from the Middle East and Africa as well as from all over Europe. The most prominent merchants were the Flemish, who dealt in wool cloth; the Italians, who introduced advanced financial techniques into northern Europe; and those from the Hanseatic League in Germany. A thirteenth-century document lists all the products sold and the place of origin. Among these products, from over forty areas and towns, were several varieties of wool cloth, silk, linen, cotton, gold, and silver-threaded cloths, along with leather goods, medicines, condiments, dyes, cereals, vegetables, livestock, fish, fruit, oils, cheese, beer, wine, precious metals and stones, jewelry, and raw materials such as wood.

ECONOMIC CHANGES

To facilitate credit, the Italian merchants in the twelfth century introduced what became the bill of exchange (letter of fair), a written promise to pay a sum of money in a place other than that in which the debt was contracted. By the thirteenth century, the fairs became a place where debts were settled and loans were contracted—the financial practices that facilitated the economic development of Europe in the twelfth and thirteenth centuries—and the great age of the fairs took form.

Fairs began to decline at the beginning of the fourteenth century as merchants ceased to travel and concentrated their efforts at one site and transportation was turned over to specialists. When direct shipping opened up between Italy, southern France, and the Flemish and English ports in the fourteenth century, overland trade slumped and there was no need for a midway meeting place. In 1285, after Champagne was annexed to France, increased taxation drove trade to other fairs, which were disrupted further by the Franco-Flemish wars at the beginning of the fourteenth century and later by the Hundred Years' War. But as fairs declined, the French kings granted special trading privileges to other areas of France to stimulate the economy of the surrounding regions, most notably Lyon, which emerged in the fifteenth century as a most important French fair.

Although the fair remained an essential economic institution as late as the nineteenth century, changes in the techniques of trade and industry contributed to its decline in the intervening centuries. Permanent trading centers developed as the result of the construction of canals, the improvement of roads, and the initiation of regular posts. In the eighteenth century, the fair suffered further when business competed with wandering peddlers in the countryside and with commercial travelers who exhibited sample wares to merchants in villages and towns and took orders for future delivery, an early type of mail-order catalog. By the end of the nineteenth century, the traditional fair was mostly found in countries such as Russia, India, Egypt, and Saudi Arabia.

The fairs that continued into the second half of the nineteenth century provided the opportunity for merchants to inspect sample products and to order in bulk for subsequent distribution at retail outlets. The best known of such fairs was that at Leipzig, which became a showplace for the products of imperial Germany in the pre–World War I era. After the war, the Leipzig fair was revived and joined by another at Königsberg, whose primary purpose was to stimulate German trade in eastern Europe.

PRESENT SITUATION

More than 700 trade fairs are held each year, especially in Europe, and provide American corporations access to a market of over $3 trillion that buys roughly over $80 billion in U.S. goods and services annually. Among the most familiar are the Paris Air Show, which displays the latest in aviation technology; the Hannover Fair (Germany), perhaps the world's largest industrial show; and the International Spring Gift Fair at Birmingham, England, which is England's largest consumer products trade show. Other well-known commercial fairs, along with the Leipzig Fair, are the Swiss Industries Fair, the Pakistan International Fair, the International Trade Fair of Thessaloníki (Greece), the Zagreb International Trade Fair (Croatia), and the Paris International Fair. Some popular specialized fairs include the International Textile and Clothing Industry Exhibition (Ghent, Belgium), the Canadian Chemical and Process Equipment Exhibition (Toronto, Canada), the International Furniture Fair (Cologne, Germany), as well as fairs in Frankfurt (books), in Nuremberg (toys), and in Berlin (tourism and travel). The most recent addition took place in Havana, Cuba, in September 2002, at the first trade show of U.S. food and agricultural products since Fidel Castro's 1959 revolution, an event made possible only after President Bill Clinton approved the easing of the forty-year trade embargo against Cuba in 2000. This development allowed American food to be sold to Cuba for humanitarian purposes, providing the country with paid cash up front.

HISTORY

The first manufacturers' fair was held in the Masonic Hall in New York City in the late 1820s under the auspices of the American Institute in the City of New York to encourage and to promote domestic industry in agriculture, commerce, manufacturing, and the arts in the United States. There are, however, rudiments of fairs in ancient times with biblical references to great feasts held at important population centers that included markets, athletic games, and visiting dignitaries. During medieval times, great fairs were held at major crossroads of trade as a mixture of commerce, entertainment, and theater. They were basically international to the extent that they involved several regions, principalities, and kingdoms. In England, the fairs were national and a blend of trade show and public entertainment. From these fairs, the industrial exhibitions were developed in France and then spread to England, where they were sponsored by mechanics institutes to teach scientific principles to the working class. The mechanics institute exhibitions included scientific, mechanical, as well as exotic and fine arts sections that merged into the 1851 Crystal Palace Exhibition and then into the international expositions that followed.

PARTICIPATION DIFFICULTIES

These fairs moved beyond being mere showcases of industrial progress to involve such things as the inclusion of special themes and more nonindustrial features, such as fine art and amusements. All demonstrated a strong streak of nationalism, boasting the national image and the people's pride in it. Fair managers, often with strong government support, strived to heighten nationalistic features on behalf of the host country to make it look better than its rivals. In the United States, the Smithsonian Institution and its National Museum had major responsibility for American participation in mid-nineteenth- and early twentieth-century expositions. Congress appropriated funds, sometimes right before the exposition was to open, which was a standard procedure until World War I. With no control or regulation of fairs, the latter part of the 1800s and the early 1900s saw several expositions, some major events, like Chicago's 1893 extravaganza. Others were celebrations of colonial empire, for example, those fairs held in Australia and in New Zealand.

In other countries, there was more substantive support from the federal government. In 1928, the Bureau of International Exhibitions (BIE) was established to regulate the fairs industry, including the number of fairs to be held at a given time and the levels of participation (universal or specialized). The BIE has been consistent in certifying expositions and fairs, with the result that these events are better planned and held at more regular intervals.

LONDON'S CRYSTAL PALACE

The first international exposition was held in London in 1851 at the urging of Queen Victoria's consort, Prince Albert, who believed that such a function would introduce the world to British goods and manufacturing processes, stimulating demand as visitors from the Continent and the rest of the world became acutely aware of the superiority of British goods, machinery, and production techniques. Immediately, orders for British goods showed a sharp increase. The exposition was a tremendous success, housed in the magnificent Crystal Palace, which had been built for the occasion in Hyde Park. The United States was represented by over 500 of its products, among which were such industrial innovations as the McCormick reaper, the Colt revolver, and Goodyear India rubber products, as well as a display of chewing tobacco.

OTHER COUNTRIES

Not to be outdone by the British, the French sponsored a number of international expositions in the nineteenth century. Napoléon III, like Prince Albert, was determined for Paris to present an even more beautiful and amazing spectacle than the one at the Crystal Palace. In 1855, the Paris exposition was unfolded in a huge building, the Palais de l'Industrie, generally called the "cathedral of commerce" on the Avenue des Champs-Elysées. Its model was the Crystal Palace.

Belgium has consistently excelled in expositions. Because the nation had been a center of international trade and finance since the Middle Ages, the presentation of expositions has come naturally to Belgian businessmen and industrialists, as indicated by such successful expositions at Liege (1930), Brussels (1935), and the controversial Brussels Universal and International Exhibition of 1958, which presented the vast panorama of international humanistic development and hosted the Cold War propaganda rivalry between the United States and the Soviet Union.

The first American exposition to draw large

numbers of people and promote American goods, although it did not generate a profit, was the Philadelphia Centennial of 1876, which was planned to celebrate a century of American independence and to promote national unity after the Civil War. The 8 million visitors not only saw the products and arts of the world, but also recognized that the United States had become a powerful industrial nation with a genius for invention and production, as indicated by Alexander Graham Bell's telephone, Thomas A. Edison's duplex telegraph, Isaac Singer's sewing machine, and the typewriter. Then the twentieth century began with the Pan-American Exposition in Buffalo (1901), which promoted the social and commercial interests of the states of the Western Hemisphere.

EXPOSITIONS SINCE WORLD WAR II

In the United States, two agencies took over responsibility from the Smithsonian Institution for expositions: the U.S. Department of Commerce for fairs held in the United States and the U.S. Information Agency (USIA) for those held outside the country. The USIA derives this authority from the Mutual Educational and Cultural Exchange Act of 1961, which was popularly known as the Fulbright-Hays Act (Public Law 87–256).

Between 1958, when the first major post–World War II exposition was held, to the present date, several expositions have been held with mixed success. One of the most controversial was the Exposition Universelle et Internationale de Bruxelles (Brussels, Expo '58), the first universal exposition held after the war, which is best remembered for the standoff in Cold War propaganda between the American and Soviet pavilions as they promoted their ideologies and products amid international tension.

In 1962, the Century 21 Exposition, or Seattle World's Fair, drew 48 countries as exhibitors and 9.7 million visitors, and was considered the first financially successful U.S. fair. It presented a preview of the type of life promised for the twenty-first century through scientific advances. The main symbol was the 607-foot steel and glass Space Needle that was topped by a revolving, glass-enclosed restaurant. The Space Needle and other structures were retained for a new, permanent civic center.

The Universal and International Exhibition (Montreal, Expo '67), held on two man-made islands in the Saint Lawrence River, boosted tourism and trade and commemorated Canada's Centennial of Confederation in a six-month period that attracted over 50 million persons to its 166 pavilions (62 of them built by participating nations), more than 200 boutiques, and 76 restaurants. The general theme of "Man and His World" unified the displays.

The Okinawa Ocean Exposition (1975) was the first and largest forum of its kind devoted entirely to the seas, and it drew most Japanese government and private-sector managers of oceanic enterprises to Okinawa with conferences, trade shows, and conventions that concentrated on special aspects of oceanography.

The World Exposition held at Vancouver, British Columbia, under the theme "World in Motion, World in Touch" (Expo '86), emphasized advances in transportation and communication. This fair was a commercial success; it enhanced U.S.-Canadian relations, and it benefited from the terrorism scare in Europe that caused many Americans to stay home that summer. Instead, they traveled to Vancouver to the world's fair.

Australia's World Exposition (Expo '88), held in Brisbane, took place in the same year Australia celebrated its bicentennial. Despite its distance, it was another financial success with its theme of recreation and leisure. The U.S. Pavilion, with its artifacts from several American halls of fame and the continual demonstrations by athletes in the pavilion's courtyard, was one of the most popular attractions at the fair, but other countries benefited as well. The theme and the presentations combined to bring visitors to a city that was not that easy to reach, and this, in turn, sparked big sales in the gift shops and restaurants. Most important, it strengthened trade relations between the host country and its participating countries, including the United States—one of its major trading partners.

The Columbus Quincentennial Exposition in Seville (Expo '92) was supposed to be Spain's international emergence as a democracy in its final year before full integration into the European Community, but it presented many problems for the United States, beginning with a presentation budget that the U.S. Congress slashed considerably, resulting in a limited American presence.

At Genoa (1992), the USIA worked with Amway officials, who provided some major funding, but the next year, at Taejon (1993), Amway administered American participation, this time with advice only from USIA officials. Even though this was the first time the private sector took responsibility for U.S. participation at an exposition, corporations were allowed to promote their brands and to stimulate sale of their products. This was to be the pattern at all future fairs in which the United States participated, but it ended at the next fair, Lisbon (1998). After this, the U.S. Department of State decided that the United States would no longer participate at international expositions. This was a blow to U.S. trade relations and caused ill will, which the United States experienced at Hannover, Germany (2000). The U.S. withdrawal from the exposition was considered an insult to U.S.-German relations. Ironically, the American withdrawal came after the designated U.S. commissioner general displayed the floor plans for the U.S. Pavilion.

Martin J. Manning

See also: Crystal Palace.

BIBLIOGRAPHY

Allwood, John. *The Great Expositions*. New York: Macmillan, 1978.
Auger, Hugh A. *Trade Fairs and Exhibitions*. London: Business Publications, 1967.
Cartwright, Gillian. *Making the Most of Trade Exhibitions*. Boston: Butterworth Heinemann, 1995.
Findling, John E., and Kimberly D. Pelle, eds. *Historical Dictionary of World's Fairs and Expositions, 1851–1988*. Westport: Greenwood, 1990.
Landers, Robert K. "World's Fairs: How They Are Faring." *Editorial Research Reports* (April 18, 1986): 291–308.
Rydell, Robert, and Nancy E. Gwinn, eds. *Fairs Representation: World's Fairs and the Modern World*. Amsterdam: University of Amsterdam Press, 1994.
Shemenski, Frances. *A Guide to Fairs and Festivals in the United States*. Westport: Greenwood, 1984.
———. *A Guide to World Fairs and Festivals*. Westport: Greenwood, 1985.
U.S. Department of Commerce, Bureau of Foreign Commerce. *U.S. Business Participation in Trade Fairs Abroad*. Washington, DC: U.S. Government Printing Office, 1957.

FERTILIZER

Organic matter, manure, or synthetic chemicals that are added to soil to increase plant growth.

Fertilizers have been used for thousands of years to improve crop production. Egyptian and Mesopotamian civilizations first recognized the value of silt deposits over 5,000 years ago. Over 3,000 years ago, Chinese farmers began mixing human and animal wastes, grasses, and plant ashes, applying this organic manure to various soils and recording how different plants responded. Trade of fertilizer did not become globally significant until the twentieth century.

Nitrogen, phosphorus, and potassium are the most important of the thirteen mineral nutrients plants need to grow. Over two centuries of rapid technological innovation has enabled the extraction of these nutrients from an increasing number and variety of sources. The United States and Germany have traditionally led the world in discovering new extraction and processing methods, but many countries have discovered processes and sources that enabled them to use domestic sources.

The history of phosphorus (phosphate, P_2O_5) is an illustrative example of how commercial fertilizers have developed. Chinese farmers began using lime-treated bones for fertilizer over 2,000 years ago. By 1815, the British were importing as much as 30,000 tons of bones annually. The British applied sulfuric acid to the bones to improve the solubility of the phosphorous, creating what came to be known as superphosphate. England had fourteen superphosphate manufacturing plants in 1853, and the United States was producing 140,000 tons by the mid-1880s. While superphosphate was the world's dominant phosphate fertilizer for almost a hundred years, several other sources and methods were also used. The mining of phosphate rock began in the 1840s in Europe, spreading to the United States in 1867. Phosphate rock deposits have now been discovered in many countries, shifting production and trade throughout the twentieth century. Finally, Germans discovered the phosphoric acid production process in 1870.

The development of more potent fertilizers

drove the huge increases in agricultural productivity commonly referred to as the Green Revolution. The consumption of commercial fertilizer exploded during the twentieth century, rising from less than 2 million tons of nutrients in 1920 to almost 140 million tons at the turn of the twenty-first century. Nitrogen experienced the largest gain, going from negligible consumption in 1920 to over 80 million tons consumed annually in 2000. Potassium and phosphate also rose dramatically during the twentieth century, but annual world consumption peaked at around 25 million and 35 million tons, respectively, in the 1980s.

Fertilizer production is also shifting from developed to developing countries. Developing countries produced 31 percent of the world's nitrogen fertilizer in 1980, increasing their share to 57 percent by 2000. Developing countries are also consuming more, accounting for 63 percent of the 138 million tons consumed in 2000, up from 12 percent of the 30 million tons consumed in 1960. China alone accounts for a quarter of fertilizer consumption, while it and India account for a third of global production. Fertilizer is now behind only coal, iron ore, and grain in terms of world dry bulk trade.

W. Chad Futrell

See also: Guano.

BIBLIOGRAPHY
Nelson, Lewis B. *History of the U.S. Fertilizer Industry.* Muscle Shoals, AL: Tennessee Valley Authority, 1990.

FESTIVALS AND FAIRS, MEDIEVAL

Open-air markets held by traveling merchants during the Medieval period.

In the twelfth century, merchants traveled with their goods to different villages, where for a few days or even a few weeks a year an open-air market would be held. At this time, permanent markets were nonexistent, so this was the primary exhibition of goods and services. Buyers and sellers would gather to transact business. Although a fair could be the product of religious, secular, and economic activities, the primary function remained the promotion of trade. Many fairs originated in religious events that required many people for extended periods of time. Among ancient Greek and Roman times, fairs or public markets were used to announce new public laws. In early Christian times, religious events were used as special occasions for marketing. During the thirteenth century, every German town held at least one annual cattle and horse market or fair where local traders competed with one another. The most prosperous one—which survives as a successful trading event today—was held in Hochheim am Main, near Frankfurt, beginning in 1483.

Many of the villages near major rivers hosted fairs. For example, the various towns of Champagne, lying where the Saône, Rhone, and Seine Rivers meet, held various fairs year round. Before people were able to travel easily, fairs furnished the primary opportunity for the exchange of goods and served as a community social activity. They also brought people together from different villages, and thus were places where one might find a marriage partner. Fairs are ancient and universal mechanisms for regional and even international interaction. Fairs were held generally at the same location and time of year and would last between a few days and a few weeks. During the sixteenth century, fairs occurred on an annual or semiannual basis. These fairs were commonly a gathering of local producers, both agricultural and artisan, petty merchants, and local consumers. In pursuing economic goals, the merchants also reflected their own backgrounds and interests throughout such gatherings. In the seventeenth century, pleasure fairs emerged. These fairs were dominated by entertainments such as plays and became popular.

One of the first known successful fairs began in Britain around 1125. It was known as the Boston Fair and was the most popular in Europe. Commercial life revolved around this fair, which was a privilege granted to the town by the Crown. There were exhibitions by monks, natives, and foreigners. The main commodities from England at this time included wool, iron, and lead, which were exchanged for furs and falcons from Norway, wine from France and Italy, cloth from the

Festivals have brought together peoples for trade and entertainment since ancient times. In more recent times, such festivals—like this 1941 Vermont carnival—have lost much of their trading dimension. *(Library of Congress)*

Low Countries, and spices and other exotic items from the eastern Mediterranean. The king's servants were allowed to purchase goods at this fair.

Many new trade routes were developed because of such fairs. Producers, traders, and consumers traveled from long distances to take part in these exhibitions. The major trade routes that developed throughout this time directly affected the growth of individual trade fairs; among the most prominent were Geneva, Madrid, Antwerp, Burgundy, and Bartholomew Fair in England. Of the variety of goods traded at such fairs, cloth was probably the most important. An alliance was also created between 1250 and 1450 that united northern Europe as one economic unit. This consisted of many port cities joined together for a more effective way to travel. The alliance, known as the Hanseatic League ("hansa" means guild or company), ensured the security of the merchants and the goods being transported. This league developed a more organized and secure method for traveling to and from the long-distance ventures. The Hanseatic League had its own flag, developed its own laws, and engaged in diplomacy with foreign governments.

Fairs have always been one of people's most enjoyable experiences, a universal part of cultural life around the world. In Eltville, Germany, the locals have celebrated the Festival of Sparkling Wine since 1811, which focuses on their most precious local product. This not only boosts the local economy, but creates an artificial demand for the product. No fewer than 200,000 join the community for the celebration every June. Another enduring example is the Hochheim Market, which began as a cattle and horse trading fair in the fifteenth century and now attracts some 300,000 visitors every November with its arts and crafts displays, livestock shows, auctions, food and wine stands, and other features.

Fairs have adapted to many changes throughout the centuries, including changes in consumer demand for what is bought and sold. However, three major factors concerning the success of fairs have not changed: concept, location, and date. To this day, fairs continue to display many different kinds of products in specific commodity or industrial groupings. The fairs also support the local economies.

Danielle Poole

See also: Fairs, International Trade.

BIBLIOGRAPHY
Augur, Helen. *The Book of Fairs*. Detroit: Omnigraphics, 1992.
Walford, Cornelius. *Fairs, Past and Present: A Chapter in the History of Commerce*. New York: Augustus M. Kelley, 1968.

Feudalism, a political order that dominated Europe in the Middle Ages, included the limited political sovereignty of centralized states, making long-distance trade difficult. Feudalism also involved hierarchical relations between masters, or lords, and their servants, or vassals. Shown here is the investiture of a vassal from a 1492 Italian miniature. *(The Art Archive/Bibliothèque National Paris/Dagli Orti [A])*

FEUDALISM

An economic, political, and social system of medieval Europe.

Historians in the eighteenth century coined the term "feudalism" to describe the political, social, and economic system of much of western Europe during the Middle Ages. The name derives from a grant of land known as a fief (*feudum*) that a lord gave to his vassal in exchange for performing military duties. The origins of the feudal system can be traced to practices of the late Roman empire and to the customs of the Germanic tribes. Roman aristocrats who lived in the provinces granted a tenure (*precaria*) of land to retainers in exchange for a variety of services. Roman law called the relationship *commendatio* since the retainers commended themselves to their aristocratic patrons. The Germanic tribes had a similar practice that the Romans called *comitatus*, whereby a group of followers attached themselves through deep bonds of loyalty to a powerful leader. The Anglo-Saxons called such a leader a *hlaford*, from which the English word "lord" is derived. The Carolingians used the term "vassal" (*vassus*) to describe a man who served his lord through military service.

Beginning in the eighth century, Carolingian leaders granted tracts of land to vassals to strengthen their rule. This reversed the more traditional practice whereby a vassal first promised service to a lord and then received a grant of land in return. Now vassals performed services because they had been granted land. The process remained a fluid one for some time as younger sons of the nobility and even freemen were able to win land for themselves by promising to serve the royal family. However, the many invasions of the ninth and tenth centuries made feudalism a more rigid system. With Europe under steady attacks from Viking, Saracen, and Magyar invaders, lords and vassals swore oaths of fealty to one another. In a formal ceremony known as *homage*, vassals pledged to be faithful to their lord and to serve him in war, while the lord promised to protect his vassals and grant them the use of fiefs. The lord and vassals in turn were to protect the freemen and peasants who lived on their land. Under these new conditions, feudalism strengthened the power of local lords over the rule of kings. It also made the development of trade difficult since fiefs were economically self-sufficient. Trade was further discouraged by the tolls and fees that lords could charge merchants who passed through their land.

The institution of feudalism took hold in northern France during the tenth century and spread to the rest of western Europe by the twelfth century.

Ironically, at the moment that feudalism triumphed, changes were already under way that would bring it to an end as a viable economic system by the fourteenth century. The rise of cities, improved trade routes, and the financial effects of the Crusades laid the foundations for capitalism that made feudalism obsolete. However, it would continue to influence the political and social life of Europe until the democratic revolutions and world wars of modern times.

Mary Stockwell

See also: Crusades.

BIBLIOGRAPHY

Hoyt, Robert S., and Stanley Chodorow. *Europe in the Middle Ages.* New York: Harcourt, Brace, Jovanovich, 1976.

FINANCIAL INSTITUTIONS

> Any form of formal organization operating under government regulations for the purpose of exchanging money or business securities.

The most common financial institutions are banks, stock exchanges, and saving and loan associations, but other companies that handle mortgages, consumer finance, insurance, and credit also fall under this classification. The definition of banking in the modern sense encompasses a wide range of functions performed by a single company—functions such as issuing bank notes, clearing checks, maintaining cash accounts, and discounting commercial paper.

BANKS

A prerequisite for lending money is the existence and usage of coin. During prehistoric and early recorded history, barter was the only form of exchange. Under this type of economic system, the lending of money was not possible. With the coinage of money, however, individuals who acquired and saved enough coin could lend it to those in need. Interest was charged, and if payment was not rendered, the borrower could have his possessions or freedom taken from him. The first known attempt to regulate the interest charged was during the reign of Solon, who passed laws establishing the maximum rate allowed under the law. The law applied to individuals or even partners who lent money.

From the time of the Babylonian empire through the Roman empire, governments required some form of institution to store and distribute coins. Instead of banks, these civilizations developed treasuries where money would be amassed, and when funds were needed money was withdrawn. The treasuries could include items other than coin—for instance, gold or silver objects or even gems might be stored in the treasury. The Delian League formed a treasury for the purpose of funding defense efforts to protect cities and trade. Treasury houses were placed in prominent places within the city as evidenced by their location in ancient caravan centers like Petra.

Although governments might regulate the amount of interest that could be charged by individuals throughout ancient times, it was not until the medieval period that the foundations of the modern banking system developed as contact with the Middle East, beginning with the First Crusade in 1095, renewed interest in luxury items from the Far East throughout Europe. In 1118, a new religious order, the Knights Templar, formed to protect the holy sites and the Kingdom of Jerusalem. The order attracted many adherents throughout Europe who, on becoming knights, renounced their worldly possessions. The Templars received land and wealth from the local rulers and population and their estates provided goods for the crusading members of the order.

With fortresses across Europe, many kings and princes deposited their wealth with the Templars before departing on the Crusades. Although prohibited from charging interest, the Knights Templar did issue a loan as early as 1149 to King Louis VII of France. Instead of interest, the Templars charged transaction fees. They also levied fees for the storage and protection of the wealth deposited in their fortresses. With the order covering most of Europe and the Middle East, a system of credit developed. Through the use of receipts, an individual who deposited money in London could collect the funds in Jerusalem without having to physically transport the gold or other items.

The wealth amassed by the order would be its downfall. The king of France, Philip IV, resented the economic power of the Templars, especially because of the desperate straits that the French treasury was in. He accused the Templars of a number of charges including heresy. The pope ordered an investigation that revealed the charges unfounded but in the mean time the king of France ordered the confiscation of all Templar lands under French control and the death of the Templars, including the grand master. Although the pope would eventually dissolve the order and transfer its possessions to the Knights Hospitallers, the Templars had provided the foundation for the modern banking system with the introduction of concepts like the charging of fees. While the order was founded for religious reasons during the Crusades, it also engaged in commercial activities. In London, the Templars would come to control the wool trade. In other areas, they provided merchants with the funds to conduct trade.

During a conflict with Emperor Manuel Comnenus in 1171, the city of Venice needed financing to fight the war, so city officials implemented a forced loan. Money was collected, and a 4 percent interest rate was promised to the lender. A corporation, the Chamber of Loans, was established to handle the payment of interest at regular intervals. The reputation of the institution resulted in the acceptance of bills of exchange under the corporate name. The chamber engaged in the practice of discounting commercial paper. Merchants began depositing their wealth in the institution, and transfers between the accounts of two customers could be made without the physical movement of gold. The practice of deposit and circulation (or at least one step removed from actual circulation of bank notes) evolved from the Venetian bank. Before long, similar banks, like the Chamber of Saint George in Genoa and the Table of Exchange in Barcelona, were established.

The Venetian, Genoese, and Barcelonan banks charged transaction and deposit fees but were prohibited from lending money at interest no matter how low. During the Second Lateran Council of the Roman Catholic Church in 1139, the pope decreed that usury, defined as the charging of interest, was forbidden. Forty years later, at the Third Lateran Council, the pope denied usurers the right to participate in communion or to receive a Christian burial. Christian merchants were restricted to trade only. Since European rulers prohibited Jews from engaging in most trades, because of the pope's edicts, one of the few occupations left open to them was money lending. Jewish and Syrian merchants traveled throughout Europe from the twelfth to the fourteenth centuries selling their wares at annual fairs such as the one held at Champagne. The role of the moneylender was central to the expansion of trade and commerce, but like the Knights Templar before them, Jews who settled in Europe soon found that when a ruler could not, or would not, repay the loan, entire communities of Jews were often persecuted and sometimes executed for their religious beliefs, while the ruler would reap the benefit of no longer having to repay the loan. While they dealt in money, these Jews could not be called bankers in the true sense of the word.

Throughout much of the Middle Ages, the Italian city-states controlled trade. After the Crusades, the Germanic cities of Lübeck and Hamburg joined in a mutual trade arrangement that would eventually become known as the Hanseatic League. The league dominated the commerce of the Baltic region for several centuries, but with the age of discovery came a shift in the prominence of the Germanic towns to the Atlantic seaports—especially Amsterdam. The Dutch city became the most prominent trading center in northern Europe with goods being exchanged from all parts of Europe. Most of the larger mercantile firms had established branches in the city. The cosmopolitan nature of the town resulted in the acceptance of coin from neighboring countries. However, the Dutch soon discovered that coin, over time, becomes worn and the original weight of the metal is reduced. While the amount of wear was not important for small dominations, larger transactions would have resulted in a loss to the Dutch since the value of the coin was still based on its weight, rendering its real value less than its nominal value. The Dutch decided to remedy the problem by establishing the Bank of Amsterdam. Depositors would place their original deposits in the bank and receive credit on the bank's books for the value of their deposit—these credits were known as bank money. Bank money was also sold to noncustomers at a premium price. Depositors received a receipt for the value of their deposit that they, or any other bearer, could redeem within six months, after which the coin became the property of the bank. Fees were levied for storage and transactions. Besides issuing bank money, the Bank of Amsterdam helped establish a uniform currency that made trade easier.

Throughout the seventeenth century, England experienced many changes—politically and economically. At the beginning of the century, Queen Elizabeth I received Spanish treasure from Sir Francis Drake after he captured it from the Spanish on the high seas. The English treasury was never full, and when Charles I called Parliament into session, the conflict between king and Parliament resulted in a civil war and the beheading of the king. During the period known as the Interregnum, navigation laws were passed to strengthen the British navy and encourage trade between the mother country and its colonies in the New World. By 1660, when the monarchy was restored under Charles II, trade had increased substantially and the country appeared on the road to prosperity when another political interruption occurred. In 1688, after the appointment of Catholics to high-ranking positions, James's acceptance of the Catholic faith, and the birth of King James II's son by a Catholic wife, Parliament offered the kingdom to Mary, the Protestant daughter of James II and his wife, Anne Hyde, and her husband, William III of Orange. Together, they reigned as co-rulers.

William recognized the need for an institution similar to the one in his native Holland that could administer the funds of the government. Chartered in 1694, the capitalization of the Bank of England was based on 1.2 million pounds in government stock. The subscribers lent that amount to the government at an 8 percent annual interest rate (interest being legal in Protestant countries) and an annual payment of an additional 4,000 pounds. The bank received a twelve-year charter and could buy and sell bills of exchange. Soon, the bank began distributing its own notes that the merchants used as a substitute for legal tender. Initially, the bank notes were all backed by the deposits, but as the notes circulated continuously, the bank was able to increase the amount of notes in circulation while feeling secure in the knowledge that not all the note holders would demand payment in coin at once. The effect of the bank notes on commerce was to expand the money supply and increase circulation, thereby allowing merchants to conduct their business in a more efficient manner. The charter of the bank was renewed several times, but as the British government became more powerful, the interest rate charged by the bank was reduced.

The Bank of England operated as a central bank in that all loans were issued to the government only; the bank managed the public debt including the payment of interest to the subscribers; advances were given on future tax receipts; it issued exchequer notes (bonds); and discounted commercial paper for the merchants. The last of these functions was important since merchants who held receivables for long periods had their capital tied up and could not reinvest in their business. The discounting of mercantile paper allowed merchants to have the funds available when they needed money. As the Bank of England realized increased profits, private bankers attempted to capitalize on the sale of bank notes, but the bank was able to pressure Parliament into passing legislation that required banks that issued notes to have a minimum of six partners. Through this act, the bank was able to eliminate competition from destroying its prominent position.

To the north of England, the Scots developed another aspect of banking. The Bank of Scotland, founded in 1695, and the Royal Bank of Scotland, established in 1727, faced competition from private banks. These two banks pioneered the use of cash accounts where depositors could open an account with the initial deposit being used as a bond against the repayment of a larger loan that had been signed and guaranteed by three people. The advance credit could be drawn on in amounts as needed, and the interest did not accrue until the withdrawal of the funds. Deposits into the bank by the borrowers would be credited against the loan. The availability of funds on such a flexible arrangement allowed Scottish merchants to maximize the use of their loan money while reducing the cost of the interest.

In the British colonies, the economy was restricted because of the lack of specie and bank notes. Colonial legislatures issued currency to ease the restriction on trade, but wild fluctuations in the value of the notes and continued fraud and corruption resulted in Parliament passing the Currency Act, which forbade the issuance of bank notes without the approval of Parliament. After the United States declared its independence, the first banking institution established in 1781 was the Bank of North America located in Philadelphia. Congress chartered the bank in an effort to handle the financial problems associated with the cost of the American Revolution and the operation of the new government. The United States owned one-fourth of the bank, and subscribers, both foreign and American, purchased the remaining shares. The responsible management of the bank resulted in its bank notes being widely accepted throughout the states. Investors received handsome profits, and Congress was pleased with the way the bank handled the government affairs. The popularity of the bank led to the creation of two additional banks: the Massachusetts Bank and the Bank of New York.

The Bank of North America operated under the Articles of Confederation government. When the United States adopted the Constitution, the question of whether or not the country needed a national bank was raised. Alexander Hamilton, the first secretary of the treasury, argued that under the "necessary and proper" (Article 1, Section 8) clause of the Constitution that the federal government had the right to establish a central bank that would act as a clearinghouse for government receipts and expenditures. Although Thomas Jefferson, then secretary of state under President George Washington, opposed the plan, a bank would be established in 1791. The First Bank of the United States was successful in its mission of managing the public debt. Soon, other banks would be established in various states. The number of banks continued to multiply as merchants expanded their trade.

Unfortunately, when the twenty-year charter of the First Bank of the United States expired in 1811, Congress failed to renew it. For the next five years, while the nation was at war with Great Britain, state banks filled the need for banking services. During this period, state notes circulated in larger numbers than the bank could possibly redeem. Bank directors persuaded the government that they must suspend redemption of notes in species. Since the government relied on loans from the state banks to finance the war, tacit approval was granted. At the conclusion of the war, Congress passed an act that required the resumption of species payments and then chartered the Second Bank of the United States for a twenty-year period. Although the Second Bank of the United States was responsibly managed, one of its presidents, Nicholas Biddle, used the issue of the bank's recharter as a political tool against sitting President Andrew Jackson in the election of 1832. Jackson was reelected and instructed the secretary of the treasury to withdraw government funds from the central bank and place the money in state banks. Although the charter did not expire for another four years, the bank was forced to start calling in its loans to settle the accounts before the doors shut in 1836. The following year, the United States was plunged into a panic that lasted for four years. State banks would eventually rebound and the economy stabilized, but many farmers and merchants were forced into bankruptcy as a result of the bank's closure.

During the last half of the nineteenth century, the United States experienced panics in 1873 and 1893. After another panic in 1907, advocates of banking reforms took up one of the Populist Party platform issues—government control of the monetary supply and an increase in circulating medium—and searched for ways to improve the banking system. In 1913, Congress approved the Federal Reserve Act, which created twelve equal branches with the ability to create elasticity in the money supply through the adjustment of interest rates. Since the opening of the Federal Reserve Bank, with the exception of the Great Depression when outside forces precipitated a worldwide crisis, the U.S. economy has escaped a major economic calamity.

The stability of the U.S. economy has allowed business to expand around the world with a distinct advantage. Other countries followed the example of the United States in establishing central banks and consequently witnessed an increase in trade. Since the Great Depression, banks have operated under increased regulation. The funds of depositors are guaranteed by the Federal Deposit Insurance Corporation, which renewed confidence in the banking system. Banking activities have been separated from other financial functions since the depression in an attempt to minimize speculation and corruption.

INTERNATIONAL BANKS

The causes of the Great Depression can be directly linked to the outcome of World War I. The Treaty of Versailles divided three great European empires —the German, Austro-Hungarian, and Ottoman— into many smaller independent nations. Attempting to protect their own industries, these new countries erected high tariff barriers that disrupted normal trade patterns. The requirement that Germany accept responsibility for the war and pay an outrageous amount in reparations fueled inflation and led to the collapse of the German economy, which allowed Adolf Hitler to assume control of the country in 1931. While World War II was still being fought, the United States and other nations discussed the future of the world economic system. Meeting at Bretton Woods in 1944, participants established two postwar institutions that continue to operate into the twenty-first century: the World Bank and the International Monetary Fund, which assist developing nations as they attempt to compete in the global economy.

Throughout human history, the process of refining banking procedures have developed as a means of assisting governments as well as merchants in the exchange of goods. Concepts ranged from the depositing of funds to lines of credit and discounting of commercial paper. Banks play an integral role in trade every day. Companies, like countries, need financial flexibility, which banks provide. The transfer of funds by check or electronic transfer allows businesses to conduct trade without the risk of losing their assets through theft.

STOCK EXCHANGES

While banks were initially formed to assist governments and then merchants, the formation of the stock exchange was purely for the purpose of increasing trade. During the age of discovery, the Dutch competed with the Portuguese and Spanish for control over trade with the Far East. Instead of individuals assuming the entire risk of a voyage, which could result in a large debt, the Dutch developed joint-stock companies that limited the liability of the stockholder much like the modern corporation. One of these joint-stock companies was the Dutch East India Company. This large trading company required additional funds for its operations and raised the money by selling shares. The strength of this company resulted in its shares being traded regularly by the early seventeenth century along Damrak Street in Amsterdam. City officials recognized the need for an indoor trading facility and commissioned the construction of the first stock exchange building that opened in 1611. Soon, many companies were trading shares and investors were buying options as well. The Amsterdam exchange, the oldest in the world, continued to operate for the next 400 years until it merged with the Brussels and Paris exchanges in 2000 to form Euronext, NV.

The British, like the Dutch, formed joint-stock companies to promote trade with the East. The British East India Company and other companies sold shares to investors. In 1698, John Castaing began selling shares in his coffee shop in London. He developed a list of stocks and commodities that became known as "the Course of the Exchange and other things." By the 1720s, the wild speculation in the stock market resulted in a financial panic when the South Sea Bubble collapsed and the market fell. Brokers continued to sell shares in London and by 1773 the brokers had changed the name of their trading organization from the "New Jonathan's" to the Stock Exchange. In 1801, the exchange required that only members could buy and sell directly on the exchange floor. The following year, the exchange moved to a new facility and within the next decade a code was written to govern trading activities.

While the British and the Dutch were successful in creating thriving stock exchanges, the French were more reluctant. As early as 1250, brokers had been selling bills of exchange throughout France, but the French proved less willing to risk their limited capital. When John Law attempted to persuade the French to use bank notes, his experiment resulted in bankruptcy, which further alienated the French from such activities. Finally, in 1724 the king authorized the creation of an exchange in Paris. In 1793, during the crises of the French Revolution, the exchange closed, but Napoléon Bonaparte would later reopen it and initiate changes that would place the French stock exchange on a solid footing. From the early 1800s until 2000, when it merged to form Euronext, NV, the exchange served the needs of business and investors.

In the United States, the New York Stock Market was established by a group of brokers who met under a tree at 68 Wall Street in 1792. Brokers traded stocks on a commission basis. Until 1869 when Jay Gould and Jim Fish attempted to corner the gold market, the stock exchange operated relatively smoothly. The crisis of 1869, followed by the panic of 1873, shook the market. During the panic of 1893, the directors of the exchange advocated the publishing of financial reports that would allow investors the opportunity to know the condition of the companies on the exchange. Except for brief periods during World War I and the Great Depression, the exchange has remained in operation.

The New York Stock Exchange, as well as the other exchanges within the United States, operates under the supervision of the Securities and Exchange Commission. The second oldest U.S. exchange, the American Exchange, began operations in the mid-1800s. Both exchanges were computerized during the 1970s. A third exchange, the NASDAQ, formed in 1971 for the exchange of over-the-counter stocks. During the 1990s, the exchange expanded with the sale of computer and dot-com companies, but since 2000 the volume of trade has declined significantly.

During the post–World War II period, countries around the world have established stock exchanges to facilitate the investment of capital in business. Since the fall of the Soviet Union and communism, the capitalist system has dominated the world's economy and the stock exchange is the pump that primes that system. The number of exchanges within a region is a good indicator of its wealth. For instance, there are thirty-four exchanges in Europe, while Africa has only three, two of which are located in South Africa. The United States, Canada, and Mexico have twenty exchanges, while the entire Middle East has only five, all of which are located on the eastern Mediterranean, and none can be found in countries such as Saudi Arabia, Syria, Iraq, Iran, or the Persian Gulf states, where wealth is held by the ruling families.

OTHER FINANCIAL INSTITUTIONS

There are many other companies and industries that service financial needs. Savings and loan associations allow individuals to deposit savings and obtain loans for mortgages or other purchases. Credit agencies provide loans to individuals for the purchase of automobiles or other consumer items. These types of financial institutions have less of a direct impact on trade and therefore will not be discussed in depth. Insurance companies have also assisted business and trade, and are discussed in a separate entry.

As a global economy developed after the discovery of the New World, financial institutions played a large role in developing trade. Central banks combined various functions that had developed since the twelfth century to form the modern bank. Stock exchanges were a natural outgrowth of the new joint-stock company. Without these institutions, trade would have remained restricted. The free flow of money and the ability of the investor to shift capital from one firm to another with ease is the key to the global market.

Cynthia Clark Northrup

See also: British Empire; Dutch; Greek City-States; Medici Family; United States; Venice.

BIBLIOGRAPHY

Bisschop, W.R. *The Rise of the London Money Market, 1640–1826.* New York: Augustus M. Kelley, 1968.
Geisst, Charles R. *100 Years of Wall Street.* New York: McGraw-Hill, 2000.
Giuseppi, John. *The Bank of England: A History from Its Foundation in 1694.* Chicago: Henry Regnery, 1966.
Hildreth, Richard. *The History of Banks.* New York: Augustus M. Kelley, 1968.
Michie, Ranald C. *The London Stock Exchange: A History.* New York: Oxford University Press, 1999.
Sobel, Robert. *The Big Board: A History of the New York Stock Market.* New York: Free Press, 1965.
"Stock Exchanges Worldwide Links" (www.tdd.lt/slnews/stock_exchanges/stock.exchanges.html, accessed February 2004).

FLAX

> An annual plant used as a source of fiber and the source of linseed oil.

Flax (*Linum usitatissimum*) was domesticated early in human history, probably in the Mediterranean region. Flax is best known for its use in making linen cloth. The fibrous stems are scutched (beaten to separate the fiber) and hackled (combed) to obtain the textile fibers that are woven into linen fabrics. Linen was used to wrap many of the Egyptian mummies. Besides its fiber, flax is cultivated for the oil that can be extracted from the plant's seeds. Linseed oil is used in paints, varnishes, and inks. After the oil is extracted from the flax seeds, the seed pulp byproduct is turned into a high-protein cake for livestock feed. The varieties of flax used for fiber are different from those used for oil. Flax seed can also be used as human food and is often sold in health food stores for its alleged cholesterol-lowering properties. Flax seed included in the diet of hens appears to reduce the amount of cholesterol in their eggs.

The cultivation and use of flax have declined substantially since the nineteenth century. Flax fibers have been replaced first with cheaper cotton and more recently with a wide array of synthetic fibers. Linseed oil is not as widely used today because of the development of synthetic substitutes. Although linseed cake is high in protein, there are many other oilseeds, particularly soybeans, that are much more widely used in livestock feed. Since 1961, the area planted with flax has fallen from around 4.9 million acres for the world as a whole to around 1.2 million acres. Total production has also declined, although only slightly. Similar patterns are seen for linseed oil and cake. Oil production was around 900,000 to 1 million metric tons in the early 1960s and fell to less than 700,000 metric tons in 2000 and 2001. Cake production fell from around 1.8 million metric tons in the early 1960s to 1.2 million at

While flax has lost out to cotton in recent centuries as the most widely traded plant-based fiber, it was still grown and traded throughout the world in the twentieth century. Shown here are flax pickers harvesting a crop on a collective in the former Soviet Union. *(Library of Congress)*

the end of the century. The leading producers are the former Soviet republics and China.

Flax products were widely traded until the twentieth century when synthetic fibers and alternatives to linseed oil were developed. Flax fiber exports have increased slightly in recent years from averages around 110,000 metric tons in the 1960s to 180,491 metric tons in 2000. These exports represent about 30 percent of world flax production. Linseed oil exports have not changed greatly over the past forty years and cake exports appear to be declining. Linseed oil exports represent about a third of total production, and cake exports amount to around 27 percent of production. France is the leading exporter, accounting for some 42 percent of world exports.

E. Wesley F. Peterson

See also: Food and Diet; Linen.

BIBLIOGRAPHY

Food and Agriculture Organization of the United Nations. "FAOSTAT: Agricultural Data" (http://faostat.fao.org/faostat/collections?subset=agriculture/, accessed September 2002).

Oplinger, E.S., et al. "Alternative Field Crops Manual: Flax." University of Wisconsin and University of Minnesota Cooperative Extension Services (www.hort.purdue.edu/newcrop/afcm/flax.html, accessed September 2002).

FLORENCE (FIRENZE)

A city in central Italy and the capital of Tuscany that served as a major trade center during the Renaissance.

Located on the Arno River at the foot of the Apennines, Florence today is a center of tourism, glassware, metalwork, leatherwork, ceramics, clothing, and art. The city is adorned with the painting and sculptures created by famous artists such as Giotto di Bondone, Lorenzo Ghiberti, Donatello, Michelangelo, and Sandro Botticelli. The glassworks of the city cater to tourists by manufacturing a wide variety of objects in all price ranges.

Originally an Etruscan village, Florence became a Roman city located on the Caspian Way during the Roman Republic. After the fall of the Western Roman empire in 476 C.E., the Goths, Byzantines, and Lombards controlled the city. By the twelfth century, the town had become autonomous. During the thirteenth century, two factions within the town, the Guelphs and the Ghibellines, fought for control of the city. After the Guelphs succeeded, divisions within the group led to two additional factions: the Blacks and the Whites. Dante Alighieri was one of many Whites who were banished from the city in 1302. By the early fourteenth century, Florence began to prosper as the guilds of the city banded together to promote Florentine goods such as silks and tapestries. But the landlocked city needed a port through which to ship its goods.

When Pisa and Lucca engaged in a feud, the Florentines assisted Pisa. Located on the coast, Pisa offered a share in the profits from its silver mints, trade concessions, and a promise to carry Florentine goods and people on its ships in exchange for help against its rival. Trade of Florentine goods occurred with Constantinople and farther east as well as with northern Europe. The increase in trade resulted in the strengthening of the guilds. But in 1348 the Black Death decimated the city—60 percent of the population died.

After the city recovered from the Black Death, power came to rest in the hands of one particular family: the Medici. Although craftsmen had traded with England and Iberia for coarse wool that they transformed into superior textiles, it was the Medici family and its extensive banking connections that made Florence wealthy and ushered in an era of patronage of the arts. Although the pope had forbidden the lending of money and the charging of interest, the Medici family circumvented the prohibition by negotiating contracts that included a variety of fees in lieu of charging interest. Branch offices of the Medici banks were established in London, Geneva, and Bruges in Belgium. Other important banking houses included Acciaiuoli and Bardi och Peruzzi. The reputation of Florence and the gold florin, known for its gold purity, added to the prestige of the city. However, in an age of kings and nobility, the Medici family, one of many wealthy merchant families who happened to rise to power in Florence and other Renaissance cities, realized that it needed to legitimize its power. Part of that process involved sponsoring public projects, from building to sculpture and paintings that would persuade the population that its rule was legitimate. The Medicis supported the construction of a cathedral and adorned it and other public buildings and piazzas with the work of famous Renaissance artists, and the public acquiesced. Humanists such as Leonardo Bruni promoted public works as a civic responsibility that provided food and shelter for Florentines.

As long as times remained prosperous, the citizens were content, but by 1494 the city experienced its first revolt against the Medici rule. Savonarola, a religious reformer, seized power from 1494 to 1498, a period when Niccolò Machiavelli served as a diplomatic representative. The Medici family regained power in 1512, but another revolution occurred in 1527 and ended when Emperor Charles V took Tuscany. Florence would eventually become part of the newly formed kingdom of Italy in 1865. Florence managed to escape much of the devastation that occurred during the two world wars. Although flooding of the Arno River in 1966 caused harm to many treasures, restoration has repaired much of the damage.

Cynthia Clark Northrup

See also: Medici Family; Roman Empire.

BIBLIOGRAPHY

Goldthwaite, Richard A. *The Building of Renaissance Florence: An Economic and Social History.* Baltimore: Johns Hopkins University Press, 1980.
Hibbert, Christopher. *Florence: The Biography of a City.* New York: Norton, 1993.

FOOD AND DIET

> The aspect of everyday life affected the most by trade since globalization.

The nature of food, as an absolute necessity for the survival of humans, gives it a unique role in world economics and trading patterns. The ability of a people to produce, acquire, or steal foodstuffs in quantities large enough to sustain population levels has been the measuring rod of the continuation or decline of a society. Throughout history and geography, how a society feeds itself has been as manifestly varied as the societies themselves. Yet, this process of securing sufficient amounts of food invariably involved and continues to involve trading and commerce with other societies. From nearby neighbors to cultures around the world, people and nations have continually sought out new, often exotic, food resources. To this end, nations have engaged in some of the most cruel and inhumane behaviors such as fighting wars and enslaving other human beings. Conversely, the desire to feed their people had led nations to make scientific discoveries, not only in agriculture, but also in navigation, medicine, and nutrition. The history of food and trade is the story of humanity's initial struggle for survival. Food is the most basic of human necessities. Little else can develop if that need is not satisfied.

ANCIENT ERA

The history of food and trade began in Sumer, the earliest known locus of civilization, in approximately 3800 B.C.E. The Sumerians resided in the Fertile Crescent of Mesopotamia in the land between the Tigris and Euphrates Rivers, in modern-day Iraq. The Sumerians were the first to develop a system of writing, known as cuneiform. Writing was developed not for literary or religious purposes but to keep track of business transactions, to write down laws, tax records, and contracts.

The transactions of food and livestock merchants were of prime importance. The typical food items known to the Sumerians were barley cakes, onions, beans, barley ale, barley, wheat, millet, lentils, garlic, cucumbers, mustard and lettuce greens, pork, and mutton or lamb. Particularly common were the many fish vendors who sold not only fresh fish from the rivers and sea but fried fish (foreshadowing the famous English fish and chips).

The brewing of ale and the baking of bread seem to have appeared simultaneously in Sumer, although it may be that bread was made as a by-product of beer or ale. There were eight types of barley ale, eight types of wheat ale, and three types of mixed grain ale. Ale was so prominent that not only did approximately 40 percent of the barley harvested go to the brewing of ales, but ale was also valuable enough to be used as currency. In fact, the use of alcohol as currency was common in many cultures, particularly in a barter economy. Rum was a common currency in colonial American society, as well as whiskey among many rural farmers, which ultimately resulted in the famous Whiskey Rebellion in Pennsylvania.

Throughout the history of the ancient Near East, societies that could produce surplus foodstuffs were in stronger bargaining positions than societies that could not. For example, King Solomon, the most renowned king of the Hebrews, who ruled from 970 to 935 B.C.E., was able to establish vast trading networks from distant lands like Egypt, North Africa, and Yemen because his kindgom had large food surpluses. Of particular importance to Solomon was the trading relationship with the Phoenicians, who inhabited present-day Lebanon. The Phoenicians were the master seafaring peoples of the ancient Mediterranean, who colonized and explored along the North African coast and as far away as Cornwall in Britain. Yet, because the Phoenicians lived mostly along the coast, they could not produce enough food to feed their people, so they were forced to trade. Solomon traded grains like wheat, along with olive oil, in exchange for the famous cedar trees of Lebanon as well as bronze and iron tools and weapons.

Solomon and the Phoenicians demonstrate that despite advances in technology and exploration, societies that cannot produce enough food have to trade with those societies that can. Similarly, those societies or lands that can produce food are also subject to invasion and conquest by those societies that have superior technology and weapons.

The Greeks were perhaps the most influential society of the ancient world. The introduction of coined currency dramatically altered how all levels of business were conducted. Peasant farmers, who previously had taken out loans in the form of sacks of seed grain, were now forced to borrow money to buy seed grain. When peasants borrowed money to buy seed, they did so at the time of greatest scarcity, the planting season, when prices were at their peak because of low supply. When these same peasants repaid their loans, they sold their grain at harvest when prices were at their lowest because of low demand. This introduction of minted currency had a psychological as well as economic effect on society. Coined currency changed everything. In many respects, it standardized and systematized a previously chaotic system of exchange, but those people, particularly peasants, who were caught in the transition, often suffered terribly.

In the sixth century B.C.E., Solon, an Athenian oligarch, banned the export of all agricultural products except for olive oil. The result was to drive commercial farmers into focusing on olive oil production at the cost of neglecting other vital agricultural products. Athens became a leading producer and exporter of olive oil in the Mediterranean. At the same time, Athens and the surrounding Greek countryside was denuded of all trees and plants except for the olive tree. Also, Greece became heavily dependent on other people for its food supply because of the focus on a single crop. Over the next few centuries, olive oil as a primary commodity was slowly replaced by wine. Greece became a leading center of wine making in the Mediterranean from the fifth century to the first century B.C.E.

Eventually, however, Italian or Roman wine began to dominate the Mediterranean, replacing the previously superior Greek wine, a phenomenon that mirrored the supplanting of Greek culture generally. By the first century B.C.E., the Romans produced over 1,600 gallons of wine per acre. The Greeks were simply unable to compete with that level of efficiency. As shown throughout history, those societies or nations that can produce food more efficiently will dominate and even control the vast majority of an economy.

The Romans were also one of the first people to implement food-related government assistance, known as the *annona*. The Roman government offset the cost of food distribution, particularly bread, to alleviate poverty and to prevent famine. It included the distribution of free bread and the purchasing of grain from public granaries at below market value. The growing numbers of people taking advantage of the annona concerned the Roman government such that by the time of Julius Caesar's reign, the numbers had increased so dramatically that Caesar was proud that he was able to reduce the number to a mere 150,000 persons. The overall effect was a tremendous drain on the Roman treasury. By the time of Augustus Caesar, 14 million bushels of wheat were required to feed the people for one year.

Of particular importance to the history of food and trade was the spice trade of the late fifteenth and sixteenth centuries. However, the Romans were no strangers to the exotic and enticing delicacies of the Far East. Of the eighty-six classifications of imported agricultural goods to the Mediterranean from Asia and East Africa, forty-four were spices. Rome imported huge quantities of spices, particularly cinnamon. Arab merchants of the Middle East were the facilitators of trade between Rome and Asia until the end of the second century C.E. To protect this monopoly on the spice trade, Arabs spread legends and mythical stories about the origins and locations of the valuable spices to frighten would-be adventurers and merchants from Rome. Whether this worked or not, these legends would filter back to the rest of Europe and become part of the mythology about the Far East.

This trade with China, or Cathay, as it was known, was only possible once the Han emperors were able to establish peace among warring nomads in central Asia in the first century C.E. Once peace was established, the famous overland trading route known as the Silk Road could be opened. By the second century C.E., the Romans were trading with China at such an unfavorable rate that Pliny estimated that Rome was losing approximately $35 to $40 million in today's money per year. This unfavorable balance of trade caused inflation in the Roman empire to skyrocket. A measure of wheat in the first century cost an estimated 6 drachmae, but by the fourth century, the price of that same measure of wheat had risen to 2 million drachmae. The result, in many parts of the Roman empire, was a return to a barter economy. It is important to realize that an unfavorable balance of trade, particularly of food items, can directly contribute to the fall of an empire. Rome's collapse was because of economic crisis as much as from barbarian invaders from the north.

Furthermore, it is important to keep in mind that China, India, Southeast Asia, Africa, and the Middle East all conducted vast and extensive trading relationships of food items that never involved Rome or Europe at all. The impact of the European involvement in the spice trade in the late fifteenth and sixteenth centuries was minimal at best to the local markets and economy. It would not be until the Portuguese and the Dutch took control of the spice trade through military force and violence that the Europeans had any significant impact on the spice trade.

India and China imported cumin from Arabia and nutmeg, mace, and cloves from the Spice Islands off the coast of Southeast Asia. Indian styles of food are so diverse that to speak of an "Indian cuisine" would be like speaking about a "European cuisine." India exported pepper, cardamom, and ginger, yet it would not be until chilies from the New World were discovered and brought to India that the famous "hot" curries would be created. China, during the Han period (206 B.C.E.–220 C.E.) increased the consumption of tea such that it became a taxable food item. During this same period, China imported pomegranates, sesame, caraway, and coriander.

MIDDLE AGES

The Arabs of the Middle East constantly struggled against the Byzantine empire. After the fall of Rome in 476, the Roman empire was divided into two empires, west and east. Constantinople, present-day Istanbul, became the capital city of the eastern empire, known as Byzantium. The Byzantine empire would last for a thousand years, until the fall of Constantinople in 1453 brought about by the Ottoman Turks. During this period, the Byzantines and the Arabs were engaged in constant conflict, each vying for control of the eastern Mediterranean. With the rise and spread of Islam, the Arabs conquered North Africa and thus gained control of Egyptian wheat production. As a result, the Byzantines were forced to find wheat elsewhere. They turned north toward the Balkans and ultimately to southern Russia. Therefore, the conflict between the Arabs and the Byzantines acted as a catalyst for wheat production and economic growth in northern territories.

Europe developed and implemented technological advances in farming and food production that could be considered agricultural revolutions several times throughout the late medieval and early modern periods. Europe from about 1000 to 1492 (the eve of the discovery of or contact with the New World) experienced population growth because of new agricultural technology and practices. The scratch plow, which was basically a single piece of wood or metal that was dragged through the ground behind oxen to create furrows in the soil, had been around since the time of the Sumerians. This was replaced by the moldboard plow, which consisted of three parts that cut deep into the soil both vertically and horizontally. This new plow made it possible to clear and cultivate larger extents of land. Yet, like most technology, the new plow had social consequences. These new plows were expensive to maintain, and it took six to eight oxen to pull them. Therefore, farmers had to work together and formed cooperatives in which plows and oxen were shared. The result was a strengthening of communal bonds and lands, the benchmark of medieval peasant society.

Other farming techniques were the implementation of crop rotation, in which fields were planted with different crops from year to year to prevent soil deterioration. The two-field system of the Roman empire was replaced with the three-field system. This meant that fields that normally would lie fallow for one out of two years were now productive two out of three years. Not only did farmers produce more food, but it was also more nutritious. The result was an increase in population throughout much of Europe.

In the twelfth century, German grain merchants organized to form the Hanseatic League. The Hanseatic League acted as grain broker, dealing especially in wheat. It bought up the entire surplus in times of plenty and distributed the surplus in times of famine. This process created a stable market for grain and bread prices. Yet, the league was so successful at managing the grain trade, particularly the huge grain harvests from the Baltic region, that many grain farmers in other parts of Europe found it hard to compete and eventually turned to other occupations like wine making and cattle or sheep herding.

EARLY MODERN ERA

With a return to a monetary economy in much of Europe, vendors of ready-cooked food, particularly meat and fish, a practice that dates back to the Sumerians, began to thrive in many towns and cities. Yet, the Crusades of the eleventh and twelfth centuries brought Europe back into contact with that most alluring of exotic foods: spices of the East. In the later Middle Ages, spices were so valuable that, like alcohol, they were used as currency. A pound of pepper was equal to two or three weeks' labor of fieldwork. Venice controlled the flow of spices from the East to the rest of Europe.

The quest for spices would ultimately be one of the most influential and world-changing events in human history. Europeans desired spices such as pepper, cinnamon, mace, cloves, and many others from the Spice Islands, Southeast Asia, and India. Some spices were used as food preservatives and were therefore sought after. It is a common though incorrect myth that spices were desired to mask the rancid and rotten odors and tastes of European foods, particularly meat products. Spices were a luxury item that enhanced and changed the local fare. Those people that could afford them demonstrated their wealth and status through the consumption of spices. It was the elite status of Eastern spices that motivated Europeans such as the Portuguese, the Dutch, the Spanish, and the English to venture out into the Atlantic Ocean. Staple foods are rarely a catalyst for long-distance trade because most societies produce their own. Fortunes were made and lost over spices. Wars were fought to secure the spice trade. And ultimately, the New World was discovered as a result of trying to find a quick and easy route to Asia and the Spice Islands.

Because the Venetians controlled the Mediterranean access to the overland trade routes to Asia, other European nations decided to go by sea to the Spice Islands and thereby cut out the middleman. This desire to sidestep the Venetian monopoly led to new discoveries and inventions in navigation and ship design. The old medieval cogs were not able to venture out into the deep ocean. New technologies had to be developed and implemented if transoceanic voyages were to become a reality.

The Portuguese were the first to begin exploration under Prince Henry the Navigator, who founded navigational schools. Portuguese navigators began charting the west coast of Africa in the late fifteenth century. Bartolomeu Dias rounded the Cape of Good Hope in 1488. Soon after, the Portuguese reached India and then Southeast Asia and the much sought-after Spice Islands of Ternate and Tidore. The Portuguese established their first trading post in 1511 in present-day Indonesia. Yet, the Portuguese empire was never more than a string of trading centers scattered throughout the world. Portugal was a small nation with few people. Ultimately, the Portuguese were defeated by the Dutch in the sixteenth century and their control of the Spice Islands transferred to the Dutch. Yet, the Portuguese maintained a strong presence in parts of India and significantly in Brazil.

Of the important spices that Europeans sought, pepper comprised nearly 70 percent of the total spice trade in the sixteenth and seventeenth centuries. Pepper was commonly available because it was grown in a variety of countries; cinnamon, nutmeg, and mace were only grown in certain places so they were more limited in supply and more valued than pepper—literally worth their weight in gold.

Real change in world trade did not occur until the Portuguese, and then later the Dutch began to take over areas of spice production by force. Through military intervention, rather than trade and competition, the West dominated the spice trade and profits that had filled Eastern coffers now went to the investors in the Dutch East India Company. However, production of spices was never replicated with much success. The "spice islands" and "pepper coasts" remained locally or regionally specific. Efforts to transplant spices to other parts of the world never amounted to much. What is significant about the spice trade is that it was demonstrative of an emerging trend in world history. Power and wealth, and thus influence, were shifting from the East to the West.

While the Portuguese had concentrated on the eastern route to the Spice Islands, the Spanish took an alternate route. Under the Spanish flag of Isabella and Ferdinand, a Genoese navigator believed he could get to the East by sailing west. Ultimately, Christopher Columbus, in 1492, landed somewhere in the Bahamas and the subsequent result would change the world forever. While the Spanish did not find great spices in the New World, the impact and significance of what they did find was staggering. The interaction and exchange of New World foods and Old World foods (as well as diseases) is known as the Columbian exchange.

The list of new food products from the Americas is often overwhelming and surprising. Many commonly recognized European foods and cuisines are in fact American in origin. The Irish owe a debt of gratitude to the Incas for the cultivation of the potato. Italian cooking would not be what it is today without the tomato. The "hot" curry dishes of Indian cuisine come from chilies from the Americas, and the peanut made famous in Chinese food is also an American food product. Other New World food items are maize or corn, squash, beans, manioc, sweet potatoes, and avocados.

Maize comes from the Taino word *mahiz*. Maize was known as Indian corn, but to the English, corn was a generic term for any grain. The English Corn Laws do not apply specifically to corn but to grain in general. The Portuguese took corn to Africa, where it became a hugely successful staple crop. In fact, corn was so successful that its cultivation led to an increase in West African populations. The tragedy is that the increase in population among West Africans provided a supply of slaves who were then transported to work in Brazilian sugar plantations.

The potato was a product of the Andean region. Dried and preserved, it was commonly known as *chuñu*. Spanish investors in the silver and gold mines bought huge quantities of *chuñu* to feed the mineworkers in places like Potosí. It thus became the main source of nourishment for those forced to work in the mines. The potato was well received in Italy, Spain, England, and Ireland. The potato, besides providing essential nutrition, was an amazingly resilient food. Unlike grains and cereals that grew above ground, the potato was well protected from marching or fighting armies that trampled wheat fields under foot. Yet, in much of central and eastern Europe, the potato would not be popular for nearly 200 years. In 1774, Frederick the Great, in an attempt to alleviate famine and hunger, sent wagonloads of potatoes to peasants, who only ate them at gunpoint.

Bananas are an Old World food item, but they would see their greatest success in the New World. Many Caribbean and Central American economies are based solely on the banana industry, giving rise to the term "Banana Republics." Bananas are the most consumed fruit in the United States and the second most consumed fruit in the world, after grapes, although much of the grape consumption is in the form of wine.

Yet, the most significant Old World food commodity brought to the New World was sugar. Originally considered a spice, sugar was the only condiment that could be produced in the Mediterranean and Atlantic world that could rival the spice trade of the East. Sugar production, from cane rather than sugar beets, began in the twelfth century by Venetian merchants in the Kingdom of Jerusalem. In the fifteenth century, sugar production became an extremely profitable business endeavor on the recently colonized islands of the eastern Atlantic, namely Madeira, the Canaries, and the Cape Verde Islands.

Intricately connected to the production of sugar was slave labor. In Brazil, the Portuguese focused on sugar plantations. As part of the Columbian exchange, Europeans brought many diseases with them against which Native Americans had no immunity. The result was the death of perhaps millions of indigenous peoples. With the decline in native populations, the Portuguese turned to Africa for slave labor. Pope Nicholas V not only endorsed this, but also commanded the Portuguese to "attack, subject and reduce to perpetual slavery the Saracens, pagans and other enemies of Christ southward from Capes Badajir and Non, including all the coast of Guinea." Along with this, merchants and rulers along the African Gold Coast were willing and happy to trade African people that they did not want for commodities such as textiles, firearms, and alcohol.

Brazil and many West Indian islands focused so intently on a single cash crop—sugar—that they neglected to grow other food items that were necessities of life. As a result, these countries had to import almost all their food. For example, in 1783 Jamaica imported from England 16,576 tons of salt pork and beef, 5,188 flitches of bacon, and 2,559 tons of tripe. Brazil was dependent on dried cod from New England to feed its slaves. This set up the commonly known triangle trade between Europe, Africa, and the Americas. New England, that great champion of liberty, had been critical of the institution of slavery. Yet, New England merchants and society were ever increasing their profit margins by selling cheap cod to Caribbean and Brazilian planters to feed their slaves. By the early 1700s, Boston alone was sending 300 ships a year to the West Indies.

Sugar became so economically important because of its high demand that in the 1670s the Dutch yielded New York to England in return for the sugar plantations of Surinam and after defeat in the French and Indian War, the French agreed to relinquish all of Canada to focus on sugar production of Guadeloupe.

Sugar became even more highly sought after with the introduction of coffee, tea, and chocolate. Coffee had originated in Ethiopia, tea in China, and chocolate in the Americas. All three were consumed as hot drinks and as their popularity increased, so, too, did the demand for sugar to sweeten them. Today, sugar is the world's most-consumed food product with the English accounting for 86 pounds of sugar per person a year, while Americans consume 120 pounds of sugar per person per year.

Salt, like sugar, was another important food item. The word "salary" is from the Latin for salt rations. Salt is essential for life. It was and still is used as a preservative and must be imported if population use exceeds local supply. Salt is one of the world's oldest items of bulk trade. It was so important to French society that a lucrative salt tax, the *gabelle,* was created to generate revenue. Because of an increase in population in northern Europe in the sixteenth century, a crisis arose because of low salt supplies in food production. The desire for salt was a principal reason for the creation of the Dutch West India Company in 1621. The Dutch needed access to salt reserves that Spain controlled. As with many other food items, the quest for salt would be a catalyst for war between Spain and the Netherlands in the Caribbean. Salt was essential to the salt herring and salted butter and cheese industry of the Netherlands. After two decades of fighting, a rapprochement between Spain and the Netherlands was reached in 1648.

The rise of scientific agriculture and the Industrial Revolution dramatically changed the quantity and quality of food and the techniques of food production. The early modern period saw an agricultural revolution that eclipsed previous advances in agriculture. This process began in the Low Countries (modern-day Belgium and the Netherlands), as well as in England. The prime motivator was a scarcity of land. In light of the limited amount of available land and the ever-increasing populations, efficiency was of utmost importance. The Dutch developed a seven-course crop rotation system, but this proved to be too complex for the rest of Europe, where land was not as scarce. In most of western Europe, a four-crop rotation system was implemented: (1) wheat and barley for human consumption, (2) clover and soybeans to fertilize and revive the soil, (3) turnips for the green tops (onions), which killed weeds by depriving them of sunlight and which provided roots for animal feed (4).

Jethro Tull's seed-planting drill (1782) eliminated waste in planting and created higher yields during harvesting because of the uniform spread of seeds. In addition, there were vast improvements made in the casting of iron, allowing for mass production that made farm tools more widely available and less expensive than goods made by the local blacksmith.

The dependence on a single food crop created a demographic and human holocaust during the Irish Potato Famine of 1846–1848. The potato, which proved to be so valuable in supplying the nutritional requirements of the vast majority of the Irish population, ironically dealt a devastating and deadly hand to over 1 million Irish when it succumbed to a fungus that made it inedible. Another million Irish left to seek better fortunes in England and primarily in the United States. The British government, guilty of acting too late, repealed a high tariff on grains to Ireland. While this was seen as an attempt to alleviate the famine in Ireland, it ultimately created a precedent for free trade that would have serious consequences later in the nineteenth century.

INDUSTRIAL REVOLUTION AND BEYOND

The Industrial Revolution affected every aspect of life in nations directly involved, especially those in Europe and North America, but the changes that occurred in those places would influence the course of world history. Discoveries and the development of new technologies often have unintended effects on many different and unrelated industries. The growth of the railroad was perhaps the most influential development of the Industrial Revolution. The railroad transformed the food industry in terms of the quality and quantity of food production. Cattle no longer had to be herded into towns and cities, which produced lanky and tough meat. Cattle could be slaughtered and butchered, and then shipped in refrigerated railcars directly to the cities. Milk from cows kept under controlled conditions could also be transported in refrigerated cars. Before the advent of the railroad, people got milk from cows that were kept in unsanitary local milking sheds.

By the middle of the nineteenth century, industrial nations understood that they had to provide larger quantities of food at lower prices to satisfy the growing numbers of factory workers. Railroads were able to link farms and plantations, not only to cities, but also to seaports from which food products could be transported around the world. Tea from India and wheat from the United States could be shipped by rail to ports and then transported across the ocean to Europe more economically than European nations could produce these goods locally.

U.S. wheat production in the second half of the nineteenth century became so productive and efficient that it dominated and replaced traditional local sources of European wheat. America had always been labor poor and land rich. This motivated Americans to create and develop labor-saving technologies, especially in the nineteenth century. These technologies included the McCormick reaper (1834), the Pitts mechanical thresher (1837), the Marsh harvester

(1858), and the Appleby binder and knotter for sheaves of grain (1878). These developments in horse-drawn machinery led to an increase in draft horses in America from 6.2 million in 1860 to 15.5 million horses by 1900. The lasting effect of American wheat production on Europe's economy was twofold. It provided a cheap source of grain, and thus bread, to urban factory workers, while at the same time it had a devastating effect on those European farmers who could not compete. Some, like many Norwegian farmers, migrated to America, while other nations like Denmark were forced to develop other food industries such as bacon for English consumers. Other technological developments that dramatically increased the food supply were canning, freezing, and refrigeration.

If the nineteenth century saw vast quantitative improvements in increasing food supply, then the opposite can be said of the qualitative changes. The nutritional value of much of the food supply had declined because of efficient mass processing and preservation techniques. While Gail Borden's patent on sweetened condensed milk created huge profits in the 1850s, this type of milk was made from skim milk, not whole milk, which lacked fats and vitamin A and D (vitamins were unknown at the time). The result was an increase in the cases of rickets and other malnutrition-related diseases in infants.

The same nutritional deficiencies occurred in the mass production of flour. New roller mills made of iron and then porcelain did such a magnificent job of processing wheat that they separated the nutritionally valuable endosperm from the husk. While this improved the color of flour to a marketable white (previously flour was a dull yellow) and increased the shelf life, the result was bread that had few nutrients. The very people who needed cheap nutrition the most, the working poor, were being deprived of any nutrients in the bread they were eating.

These types of problems were highly scrutinized in the early twentieth century. In England in 1917 and 1918, 41 percent of the 2.5 million young men who were supposedly in the prime of their lives were deemed unfit for military service due to malnutrition. This kind of scrutiny led to the development of and advancements in the field of nutrition and diet. In the late twentieth century, agribusiness, implementing and developing patents related to genetic engineering of foods, would see profits of $50 billion to $100 billion per year.

Mike Downs

See also: Discovery and Exploration; Grain; Roman Empire.

BIBLIOGRAPHY

Corn, Charles. *The Scents of Eden: A Narrative of the Spice Trade.* New York: Kodansha International, 1998.
Crosby, Alfred W., Jr. *The Columbian Exchange: Biological and Cultural Consequences of 1492.* Westport: Praeger, 2003.
Davidson, Alan. *The Oxford Companion to Food.* New York: Oxford University Press, 1999.
Fernández-Armesto, Felipe. *Near a Thousand Tables: A History of Food.* New York: Free Press, 2004.
Foster, Nelson, and Linda S. Cordell, eds. *Chilies to Chocolate: Food the Americas Gave the World.* Tucson: University of Arizona Press, 1996.
Jenkins, Virginia Scott. *Bananas: An American History.* Washington, DC: Smithsonian Institute, 2000.
Kiple, Kenneth F., and Kriemhild Coneè Ornelas. *The Cambridge World History of Food.* Vols. 1–2. New York: Cambridge University Press, 2000.
Kurlansky, Mark. *Cod: A Biography of the Fish That Changed the World.* New York: Penguin, 1997.
———. *Salt: A World History.* New York: Walker, 2002.
Mintz, Sidney W. *Sweetness and Power: The Place of Sugar in Modern History.* New York: Viking, 1985.
Schivelbusch, Wolfgang. *Tastes of Paradise: A Social History of Spices, Stimulants, and Intoxicants,* trans. David Jacobson. New York: Vintage, 1993.
Stoll, Steven. *Larding the Lean Earth: Soil and Society in Nineteenth-Century America.* New York: Hill and Wang, 2002.
Tannahill, Reay. *Food in History: The New, Fully Revised, and Updated Edition of the Classic Gastronomic Epic.* New York: Crown, 1989.
Toussaint-Samat, Maguelonne. *History of Food,* trans. Anthea Bell. New York: Barnes and Noble, 2003.

FORD MOTOR COMPANY

A leading automotive maker for almost a century.

Eight years after the motorcar was first offered for sale in 1895, Henry Ford and eleven other investors founded the Ford Motor Company with less than $30,000 in capital. Within years, employing mass-production techniques such as gravity

Henry Ford, founder of the Ford Motor Company, whose workers are shown here assembling cars in the late 1940s, pioneered the mass production of automobiles. Mass production lowered the cost of cars, making them affordable to ordinary people and turning them into the world's most valuable internationally traded manufactured product of the twentieth century. *(Library of Congress)*

slides and chain conveyors, Ford had revolutionized the industry. Today, Ford ranks as one of the largest automotive companies in the world, with 2001 sales surpassing $131.5 billion.

From the outset, Ford sought to expand internationally, exporting its first cars to England in the year of its incorporation. In 1905, production of the company's first foreign-made cars began at a Canadian plant, and within eleven years assembly plants operated in Europe and Latin America. Plants in Asia soon followed. It was the 1908 Model T, however, the famous "tin lizzie," that appealed to customers worldwide. Uniformly black, the Model T was cheap and dependable, its plain design spanning different cultures. Ford sold over 15 million between 1908 and 1927, and by the end of the period the Model T made up half of all automotive sales worldwide. Faced with strong competition from the General Motors Corporation and its efforts to provide different cars for specialized markets, however, Ford unveiled his Model A at the end of this period. To better manage the company's growing business in Europe, the Ford Motor Company Ltd. was formed in 1928, a reorganization that helped keep the company at the forefront of the industry. Three years later, Ford opened the largest automotive plant in Europe, at Dagenham, England.

Strong management extended to labor relations and contributed to Ford's success. As World War I began, Ford employed revolutionary corporate welfare techniques. Besides establishing regular medical inspections, sanitary conditions, and recreational facilities, the company allowed employees a shorter, eight-hour day. In 1914, it unveiled its "Five Dollar Day," an early incentive plan.

In the years after World War II, Ford answered periods of declining profits with new models. In the 1950s, it was the Falcon; in the 1960s in Europe, the Cortina; in the 1980s, the Taurus; and, most recently, the Explorer. The company also sought to acquire smaller companies, for example, in 1987 the automaker Aston Martin and the rental company Hertz. Most notably, Ford acquired Volvo in 1999. In the 1950s, the company went public, at the time the largest initial public offering in the history. Not every endeavor proved successful, however. In the late 1960s, Ford rushed into production of the Pinto, aware that a design flaw caused the gas tank to explode easily. Rather than incur the cost to repair the tank, the company sought to hide the problem. Lawsuits, bad publicity, and the inevitable recall resulted. Battling to maintain its market share, Ford recently has undertaken a new restructuring plan, merging its European and American divisions under a unified management. To date, the company remains a force in the international economy, operating 110 factories worldwide and selling cars in 125 countries.

Brooks Flippen

See also: Automobiles; Corporations.

BIBLIOGRAPHY

Banham, Russ. *The Ford Century: Ford Motor Company and the Innovations that Shaped the World.* New York: Artisan, 2002.

Studer-Noguez, Isabel. *Ford and the Global Strategies of the Multinationals: The North American Auto Industry.* New York: Routledge, 2001.

FOREIGN AID

> Refers to an explicit as well as implicit transfer of resources at concessionary terms from developed to developing countries at the governmental level.

Foreign aid is distinct from such transactions as flow of private foreign capital, which involves private entities motivated by profit to undertake transactions that take place at fair market prices. Explicit aid is given in the form of loans and grants, while implicit grants involve favorable treatment of imports coming from less-developed countries. Foreign aid can be for military or developmental purposes and is commonly labeled official development assistance.

Grants refer to a transfer of resources without any need for repayment. Loans require repayment with interest within a specified period, but the terms are more liberal than those of the commercial type. Thus, loans involve three financial elements: maturity date, interest rate, and the grace period. Loans may be "soft" or "hard": soft loans have the longest maturity period, lowest interest rate, and the maximum grace period, while hard loans have the opposite characteristics.

Other than the financial terms, grants or loans can be subjected to nonfinancial conditions, in particular involving some form of "tying." Tying can be project based, requiring the grants or loan proceeds to be spent on specific projects, or procurement based, restricting the procurement from a specific source, commonly the donor country. Because of tying, the aid value of grants or loans can be lower than its nominal value, as the procurement prices from the specified source may be higher than that from alternative sources. Moreover, from the recipients' perspective the project grants or loans may have lower development value than their nominal value would indicate.

The rationale for giving aid can stem from the concern for international equity and human solidarity, realizing political and strategic advantage, or even a donor's pure commercial objective. But giving foreign aid is essentially a political decision, especially in the case of bilateral aid.

Foreign aid can be bilateral or multilateral. In the latter case, it is channeled through such multinational organizations as the International Bank for Reconstruction and Development (World Bank), or its affiliates like the International Financial Corporation, International Monetary Fund (IMF), or some form of consortia set up by the donors for a specific recipient country.

FOREIGN AID AS A POST–WORLD WAR II PHENOMENON

Historically, foreign aid is a post–World War II phenomenon, initiated for the reconstruction of postwar Europe. While the war was still raging in Europe and the Far East, representatives from forty countries met at Bretton Woods in 1944 to establish the institutional framework for a postwar multilateral economic order. Two new organizations, the World Bank and the IMF, were set up to provide the institutional framework for reconstruction of a new international economic order.

But by mid-1947, the United States abandoned institutional multinationalism and adopted the European Recovery Program, also known as Marshall Plan, in 1948. During the next four years, the program disbursed over $13 billion to the West European countries. More than 90 percent of this aid was in grants. Besides contributing to the reconstruction of Western Europe, this program was aimed at the continuation of U.S. export flows to Europe, thereby maintaining its domestic prosperity and preventing the European Left from winning political power.

The Marshall Plan was a success story of U.S. foreign policy. As such, it led United States to extend a similar policy to Third World countries in order to help raise the standard of living in these countries, and thereby reducing income inequality between the developed and the developing nations. The objective was also to foster U.S. hegemony over these nations and thwart a foothold by the communist bloc. During the Cold War, foreign aid, especially the bilateral type, was more often used as a tool of foreign policy than of development assistance.

The evolution of foreign aid can be divided into four stages during the four and a half decades following the Marshall Plan. The 1950s were a period of dominance of bilateral aid, given by the developed countries. The United States was the highest contributor, with 67.6 percent of the total official development assistance in 1956 and 60.5 percent in 1960. The program called PL480, which distributed surplus food from the United States, started in this period. The Soviet Union made its first commitment of economic aid (to Afghanistan) in 1954. By 1960, the total contribution of the communist bloc amounted to less than 5 percent of total official development aid. Even this small contribution affected the foreign aid strategy of the Western world significantly, guiding the level of disbursement among the recipient countries. In this era, distinction between military and development aid became blurred.

While the bilateral aid by the Western countries was still dominant in the 1960s, contributing more than 50 percent of the official development assistance, aid given by multilateral institutions was growing at a significantly faster rate. This occurred in response to concern by the Third World countries about the efficacy of the bilateral, especially the tied, aid. Most of the aid in this period was for development purposes because major donor countries realized that long-term peace is best supported not through from military buildup but by economic development.

OIL REVENUES AND FOREIGN AID

The 1970s saw emergence of a new donor group: the Middle Eastern members of the Organization of the Petroleum Exporting Countries (OPEC). Following the rise in oil prices in the early 1970s, which created significant surplus in these countries, a portion of the reserve was invested in Third World countries at a concessionary rate. Their contribution to the total official development aid increased from 5 percent in 1972 to 25 percent in 1976, and most of it as bilateral aid to other Arab countries. While the share of the Organization for Economic Cooperation and Development countries' official development aid was declining and stood at 0.33 percent of their combined gross national product (GNP) in 1976, OPEC's contribution was 2.29 percent of their combined GNP.

The next two decades saw a basic shift in the foreign aid regime for the following reasons: First, the private sector, not the government, was viewed as the engine for economic development. Since official development assistance involved governments, the role of foreign aid also lost priority; private foreign capital was considered to be more important than foreign aid. At the same time, innovations in international banking and availability of foreign private capital made the shift easier. Second, unobstructed trade, not foreign aid, was believed to be essential for the development of Third World countries. Therefore, these nations campaigned, through the United Nations Conference on Trade, Aid, and Development (UNCTAD), for free access to Western markets and sustained price increases for primary commodities. While the Western world was sympathetic in the beginning, persistent political pressure in the UN adversely affected the attitude of the rich donors. These governments were also facing budgetary problems at home. Above all, the era of the Cold War was coming to an end, removing the foreign policy incentive for the aid.

These factors contributed to the decline of foreign aid during the 1980s and 1990s. As a percentage of GNP, official development assistance stood around 0.26 percent of the UN member states' combined GNP in 1997, which is less than half of the target of 0.7 percent. This decline was largely a result of the decline in U.S. aid, whose contribution was 0.21 percent of its GNP in 1990, but fell to about 0.08 percent in 1997.

While the foreign aid movement started with great optimism and goodwill, the mood has significantly changed over the past five decades. Over this period, public opinion in major donor countries has changed from optimism to pessimism, the role of foreign aid as a development policy has been questioned in both the donor and the recipient countries, and the geopolitical atmosphere in the world has changed. The combination of weak economic arguments and the lack of political incentives in donor countries could drive foreign aid to oblivion.

M. Hasan Imam

See also: Council for Mutual Economic Assistance; Marshall Plan.

BIBLIOGRAPHY

Bhagwati, J.N., and R.S. Eckaus, eds. *Foreign Aid.* New York: Penguin, 1970.
Freedman, J., ed. *Transforming Development: Foreign Aid for a Changing World.* Toronto: University of Toronto Press, 2000.
Hawkins, E.K. *The Principles of Foreign Aid.* New York: Penguin, 1970.
Healy, J.M. *Economics of Aid.* London: Routledge and Kegan Paul, 1971.
Ryrie, W. *First World, Third World.* New York: St. Martin's Press, 1995.

Wood, R. *From Marshall Plan to Debt Crisis: Foreign Aid and Development Choice in the World Economy.* Los Angeles: University of California Press, 1986.

FRANKINCENSE AND MYRRH

> Key ancient trade items in the Mediterranean Sea and Indian Ocean areas derived from the resins of several species of trees belonging to the Burseraceae, or Balsam, family of plants, native to the southern Arabian Peninsula and the adjoining Horn of Africa.

The three species of Boswellia (Boswellia sacra, or *B. carterii*) native to the mountainous areas of Yemen and the Hadramawt (western Oman), are the principal historic source for high-quality frankincense. Myrrh trees (from the Arabic word for "bitter") are more common than frankincense trees and belong to the Commiphora genus—Commiphora myrrha is the preferred source—that grow in southern Arabia, Ethiopia, and Somalia. East African myrrh has historically outweighed Arabian myrrh in exports.

Famous attempts were made in pharaonic Egypt to import the trees, as evidenced in the sculptures on Queen Hatshepsut's tomb in the Valley of the Kings depicting an expedition to the land of Punt that returned with samples of plants, animals, and trees—including potted myrrh trees for her mortuary temple. Although the ancient Greek doctor Theophrastus records around 295 B.C.E. that a frankincense tree was successfully transplanted in the city of Sardes in Asia Minor—where he himself saw it growing—neither frankincense nor myrrh have been produced commercially outside of their native range. The cities of Yemen have traditionally been the seat of wholesale production and Egypt the center of worldwide distribution—in ancient times, this was apparently true of trade even to the East. Although the Red Sea and the Indian Ocean were common transport routes, inland Arabian kingdoms kept a stranglehold on supply in the ancient world through a network of land routes circumventing the Arabian Peninsula's central deserts.

The ancient cultures of the Fertile Crescent

Frankincense and myrrh were aromatics highly prized and traded in ancient times. Shown here is a third-century B.C.E. bronze incense burner from Marib (in modern-day Yemen).
(© The British Museum/Topham-HIP/The Image Works)

used frankincense primarily as incense; myrrh was employed more extensively in ointments, unguents, perfumes, and medicines and in embalming Egyptian mummies. There is scholarly debate, however, whether Ethiopia or Arabia was the ancient source of Egyptian myrrh. The most accurate and firsthand description of the collection, production, and distribution of these two items in ancient times comes from the periplus of the Erythraean Sea, a Greek merchant's description of Arabian and Indian Ocean trade written in the first or second century C.E. Pliny's description of importation into Rome suggests production reached up to 3,000 tons of frankincense and 600 tons of myrrh in the first and second centuries C.E., coinciding with the introduction of epidemic diseases by way of the same trade network.

Frankincense's value equaled that of gold in the markets of Rome, and the heavy transportation costs fueled economic development along the main trade arteries to the Mediterranean basin. Increasing demand during the Roman empire's heyday encouraged Arabians to overcrop frankincense and myrrh trees, degrading the sources. Early Christians, however, rejected the use of incense in worship because of its association with Greek and Roman polytheism, despite the famous gift of the Magi to the baby Jesus in the New Testament of frankincense, myrrh, and gold. Trade consequently decreased between the fifth and the seventh centuries, but picked up again when Muslim commerce expanded from the Atlantic to Asia and market demand increased as the Christian church accommodated ancient religious practices like incense burning into its rituals. Profuse amounts of frankincense were used in the medieval cathedrals, and myrrh continued to be a key ingredient in unguents, ointments, and medicines throughout the medieval period.

Commerce in frankincense and myrrh declined in the modern period as other plant materials and the development of synthetic sources supplanted the need for the original tree resins, though even at the beginning of World War I the city of Aden in Yemen was still annually exporting 1,000 tons of myrrh and substantial amounts of frankincense. Both substances have remained liturgically important in many faiths and are used in the perfume industry.

Fabio Lopez-Lazaro

See also: Perfume; Religion.

BIBLIOGRAPHY
Groom, Nigel. *Frankincense and Myrrh: A Study of the Arabian Incense Trade*. New York: Longman, 1981.

FRANKLIN, BENJAMIN (1706-1790)

An internationally known figure of eighteenth-century British North America, who contributed much to the development of North America, the printing trade, science, and industry, while promoting the colonies within the British empire.

FRANKLIN, BENJAMIN (1706-1790)

Shown here at the court of France in the late eighteenth century, Benjamin Franklin was, among other things, a self-made entrepreneur who helped promote business values in early America. *(National Archives at College Park)*

Benjamin Franklin was born in Boston to a large family whose father toiled as a soap and candle maker. At the age of eight, he entered grammar school and, while he excelled, his father removed him from school because the family could not afford it. He then started to work as an apprentice to his father, but he did not care for his father's trade; thus when Franklin was eleven, he was apprenticed out to his brother, who operated a printing business. Franklin's inquisitive and intellectual mind was well suited for the printing trade, and he soon became skilled at his job, even though he had continual problems with his brother. At the age of seventeen, Franklin, who had always romanticized the maritime life, ran away, but instead of sailing the open ocean he ended up in Philadelphia, where he soon found work in a print shop. As he established himself in Philadelphia by being industrious and bright, he journeyed to London in the hopes of financing his own print shop. When this fell through, he found work in a London print shop, where he refined his skills and his work ethic. During this early period, he saved money by not drinking beer and earned money by lending money, at interest, to his fellow workers who were short on cash. At one point, he ate only vegetables to save money and developed a list of thirteen virtues that he strived to maintain.

When he finally opened his own printing house, he quickly achieved business success because of his reputation as a hard worker. In his autobiography, Franklin admitted that often he left a candle lit in his shop to make it look like he was working late. With his business established, Franklin began financing printing houses in other colonies and devoted more of his time to his other interests. Franklin was not interested in becoming rich; he was more concerned with his reputation and having enough money to explore his other interests.

The middle part of his life saw him creating his newspaper and almanac, his library, a fire brigade, an intellectual circle in Philadelphia, the invention of his stove, his experiments in electricity, his attempt to organize the Pennsylvania militia, and his growing international reputation. In 1757, he traveled to London to represent the Pennsylvania legislature against the Penn family over the legislature's ability to tax Penn family land, and he soon returned to London as a colonial agent. His return marked the beginnings of the American Crisis, and Franklin was soon writing many letters to the *London Chronicle,* in which he explained colonialist views on taxation and representation. Franklin led a life where his initial economic success allowed him to dedicate himself to public improvement.

Ty M. Reese

See also: American Revolution.

BIBLIOGRAPHY

Brands, H.W. *The First American: The Life and Times of Benjamin Franklin.* New York: Doubleday, 2000.

Morgan, Edmund S. *Benjamin Franklin.* New Haven: Yale University Press, 2002.

FREDERICK II (1712–1786)

Frederick II of Prussia's brilliant strategy and enlightened despotism vaulted a middling German state to the level of a major eighteenth-century European power.

Frederick II became king in 1740 following the death of his father, Frederick William I. He rapidly increased the size of the Prussian military and expanded his nation's borders. The new king took advantage of the War of Austrian Succession when the Austrian king and Holy Roman Emperor Charles VI died, leaving his daughter Maria Theresa to inherit the Hapsburg holdings. While Maria Theresa fought off various claimants to the Hapsburg lands, including Philip V of Spain, Frederick quickly invaded and then captured

Frederick II of Prussia, a brilliant strategist and enlightened despot, vaulted a middling German state to the level of a major eighteenth-century European military and trading power. *(Library of Congress)*

Silesia in a mere seven weeks. The War of Austrian Succession ended with the election of Maria Theresa's husband, Francis, as the Holy Roman emperor and then king of Austria, while Frederick retained control of Silesia. Frederick again used the element of surprise, quickly attacking and adding portions of Saxony to his kingdom. The Prussian king later fought Russia under Catherine the Great and Peter III without winning any great victories, but by maintaining his borders against Russia's colossal armies he established himself as a great military leader of the eighteenth century.

Frederick was the essential enlightened despot. As a young prince, he respected everything French and adopted French mannerisms, including a healthy respect for its monarchy and military, shaping his own after the Gaelic model, after ascending the throne. Frederick befriended the greatest philosopher of the age, Voltaire, who tutored the young prince in philosophy and gave him the moniker Frederick the Great for abolishing torture and reopening the academies his father had closed in his quest for frugality.

Frederick wrote essays attacking the Germany of Frederick William I as fatally divided into small independent states. In these essays, many of which were written before he ascended the throne, he declared that Austria was dangerous to the hegemony of Prussia, but provided both a necessary barrier against the militant Turks and a neighbor friendly to trade.

Frederick built a healthy Prussian economy based on military might. He believed that people became exceedingly lazy and prone to decadence in time of peace and stated that a policy of war provided gainful employment for those who would otherwise burden the state. When not involved in large-scale war, Frederick fueled the economy with massive building projects, including elaborate road and canal systems. When the combined might of the Austrian and Russian armies defeated Prussia in the Seven Years' War, Frederick returned to his homeland defeated, but with his empire intact. Because of Frederick's leadership and economic planning, Prussia emerged the best equipped of all continental European countries to rebuild. Frederick began a public assistance program to rebuild Prussia and ushered in an era of industrialization. Frederick II is remembered by the world as a military genius and by his own people as a caring sovereign and a hero of the poor.

Michael J. Alberts

See also: Wars for Empire.

BIBLIOGRAPHY
Van Cleve, Thomas Curtis. *The Emperor Frederick II of Hohenstaufen, Immutator Mundi.* Oxford: Clarendon, 1972.

FREE TRADE

> The absence of government intervention aimed at influencing the international exchange of goods and services.

Free trade might be thought of as the opposite of autarky, a state in which no international trade occurs because of circumstances that remove all gains that might be realized by international exchange. In the case of autarky, however, the conditions that prevent trade from occurring include such nongovernmental factors as high transportation costs or product perishability, as well as barriers created by governments. In contrast, free trade may exist even if transportation costs are prohibitively high, as long as there are no government interventions that interfere with the voluntary exchanges of rational producers and consumers.

International trade has never been perfectly free of all government interventions. In fact, the laissez-faire anarchy often thought to characterize free markets and free trade would not be a recipe for prosperity. In the absence of such institutions as the law of contract, markets would fail to achieve the optimal allocations of resources and consumer well-being suggested by models of the perfectly competitive economy. Only government can provide many of the institutions needed for markets to function. This suggests that some form of government intervention is needed for market exchange to take place. Advocates of free trade generally recognize the need for some government regulations but argue for the benefits of policies that allow the free exchange of goods and services within an institutional framework designed to prevent fraud, monopolies, and other forms of market failure. The specific targets of those favoring free trade are protectionist policies based on tariffs, nontariff trade barriers, subsidies, and a wide range of rules and regulations designed to favor domestic over foreign economic interests.

Among practicing economists, the notion that free trade is the best policy for national governments to follow receives almost unanimous support. It can be shown that an international regime of free trade in the context of fair and transparent legal institutions will maximize world social welfare. In contrast, protectionism always lowers someone's welfare. Protectionism is widespread because politicians find that it is safer to implement policies that protect powerful special interests from foreign competition than to pursue policies that increase overall welfare when changes in overall welfare may be difficult to discern. Protectionism is costly because it leads to efficiency losses, resource misallocation because of lack of competition, limited internal markets in which scale economies are sacrificed, retaliation by foreign suppliers, and many other economic costs. Besides

While promoted by politicians and business leaders as a source of prosperity, free trade has been criticized by workers around the world—including these at a Free Trade Area of the Americas summit in Miami, Florida—as a source of job loss in the developed world and of labor exploitation in the developing world.
(© Jeff Greenberg/The Image Works)

these direct costs, protectionism is likely to have a negative impact on the distribution of wealth and income within a country because the wealthy are usually more effective rent seekers than the poor and, thus, better able to lobby the government to distort markets in their favor. Since the inception of capitalism, there have been many arguments against free trade, and opposition to this doctrine is likely to remain strong despite the theoretical and empirical evidence marshaled by economists in its favor.

E. Wesley F. Peterson

See also: Nontariff Barriers; Tariffs; Trade Organizations.

BIBLIOGRAPHY

Irwin, Douglas A. *Against the Tide: An Intellectual History of Free Trade.* Princeton: Princeton University Press, 1996.

FREEMASONRY

A set of moral teachings, rituals, and symbolism practiced by groups of fraternal organizations with origins traced back to the stonemasons who built the churches and cathedrals of England.

Manuscripts dating from the late fourteenth century trace the legendary origin of the Freemasons to the biblical flood story, the Egyptian pyramids, and Solomon's Temple, but Freemasonry as an institution is dated at June 24, 1717, when the Grand Lodge of England, the first national Masonic organization, was formed. There is no central organizational authority; autonomous national grand lodges determine local rules and customs.

In the early eighteenth century, Freemasonry spread into France and became identified with the Enlightenment. The Freemasons also incorporated the legends of other groups, such as the Knights Templar and Teutonic Knights, into their rites and became staunch advocates of political and social reform. By the late eighteenth century, Freemasonry experienced a schism between the "Ancients" and the "Moderns," signifying class distinction. During the nineteenth and twentieth centuries, Freemasonry continued to develop into two groups: the English and French.

The teachings of the Freemasons have remained stable over time. The main concept is the transformation of humans from a primitive personality to that of a higher consciousness. Freemasonry's stress on the improvement of moral character rather than redemption placed it at odds with other religions. Despite its secrecy and radical social beliefs, Freemasonry has a worldwide membership governed by independent grand lodges. The organizations are racially mixed, but independent black lodges do exist.

Lisa A. Ennis

See also: Religion.

BIBLIOGRAPHY

Stemper, William H., Jr. "Freemasons." In *The Encyclopedia of Religion,* editor in chief Mircea Eliade. New York: Macmillan, 1987.

Freemasonry, a movement founded by builders in medieval Europe, has long advocated the benefits of trade and economic enterprise. Shown here is President Calvin Coolidge greeting an international delegation from the Scottish Rite of Freemasonry, including John Henry Cowles, the sovereign grand commander, to the president's right. *(Library of Congress)*

FRENCH EMPIRE

Seventeenth- through twentieth-century rule of colonial possessions by France, first in North America and the Caribbean and then in Africa and Southeast Asia.

AMERICAN COLONIES

After the discovery of the New World by Christopher Columbus for Spain in 1492, other European countries sent expeditions along the North American coast in search of gold. The French voyages of Giovanni da Verrazano and Jacques Cartier resulted in the discovery and claiming of the Grand Banks off Newfoundland in the sixteenth century. French exploration and settlement of the new lands were delayed throughout the rest of the century as the country struggled through the Wars of Religion brought on by the Reformation. At the beginning of the seventeenth century, the French established two important posts in Canada: one at Port Royal in the colony of Acadia (present-day Nova Scotia) and the second at Quebec (in present-day Montreal). These posts operated as fur-trading centers between the French and the indigenous peoples, who exchanged furs for glass trinkets and other European goods. The French did not start a massive migration and settlement movement, which would have created hostilities with the native peoples. Instead, the French left the native peoples to their own lifestyle except for a few Jesuit priests who attempted to convert them. The French restricted the area of their settlement to the Saint Lawrence valley until the end of the century, when France established another colony in Louisiana in 1699. French exploration from the source of the Mississippi River down to the Gulf of Mexico resulted in their claim to the navigation rights for the continent's largest river. Since overland trade was cost prohibitive, the control of the Mississippi was important for the movement of goods from the interior of North America to other destinations such as the Caribbean and Europe. The French established port cities at Mobile and New Orleans (1719).

While the French were expanding their empire in North America, they were also establishing colonies in the Caribbean and the northern tip of South America. In 1624, French Guiana was founded, followed by Saint Kitts in 1627. The French Compagnie des Îles de l'Amerique founded Guadeloupe and Martinique in 1635 and Saint Lucia in 1650. In 1664, the French established the colony of Saint Domingue on the western half of the Spanish island of Hispaniola (present-day Haiti and the Dominican Republic). Saint Domingue developed into the leading sugar-producing colony for the French. Every inch of available land was planted with sugarcane, the most lucrative commodity of the eighteenth century. Slave quarters were limited in size, and food production was restricted. Instead, the French imported wheat, grain, salt, and other food items from Louisiana to feed the slave population.

COLONIES IN AFRICA AND INDIA

Throughout the seventeenth century, French colonies were also established in Africa and India. The lucrative slave trade attracted the French to the West African region of Senegal in 1624. Portuguese and British colonies in India and Asia enticed the French to also establish trading posts in India at Chandernagore in Bengal (1673), Pondicherry (1674), Yanam (1723), Mahé (1725), and Kirikkale (1739). Three additional colonies were established in the Indian Ocean on the Île de Bourbon (Réunion) in 1664, the Île Royale (Mauritius) in 1718, and on the Seychelles in 1756.

During the eighteenth-century wars for empire, the map of the French empire changed dramatically. As a result of the French king's involvement in attempting to restore King James II of England to his throne, King William II declared war on France in the War of the League of Augsburg (also known as King William's War). Although at the end of the war all former possessions were restored, the hostilities between the two countries led to three additional wars. At the conclusion of the War of Spanish Succession, the French lost control of Acadia to the British as well as the island of Saint Kitts under the terms of the Treaty of Utrecht in 1713. The third war for empire, the War of Austrian Succession, ended with a status quo antebellum and no change of territory, although the French achieved some success in India. The last of the wars, known as the Seven Years' War, or the French and Indian War in North America, ended with British dominance around the world. The French were forced out of India and lost much of the profits from the lucrative pepper and cotton cloth trade. The French also lost their possessions in North America. Canada was ceded to the British empire, as was the part of Louisiana east of the Mississippi River, Saint Lucia, and Grenada. The Spanish, who had joined the French late in the war, lost Florida temporarily to the British. The French, to compensate Spain for the loss of Florida and to prevent the British from gaining control of Louisiana, ceded the territory of Louisiana to Spain, who ruled the colony until 1800, when it was ceded back to France.

FRENCH-BRITISH COMPETITION

The animosity of the French toward the British led to French involvement in the American Revolution. Although initially reluctant to enter the conflict, after several unconventional victories and one major European-style victory at Saratoga, the French agreed to provide supplies, men, and ships to the Americans. The Treaty of Paris (1783) that ended the American Revolution resulted in France regaining Saint Lucia. However, war plagued the French colonial empire again during the French Revolution as a slave rebellion in Saint Domingue resulted in the formation of an independent country of Haiti in 1804. During this period, Great Britain captured most of the French overseas colonies, which would be returned to them in 1802 under the Peace of Amiens. After 1802, Napoléon Bonaparte began preparations for another campaign to control the European continent. He hoped to fund the cost of the war through the sale of sugar from Saint Domingue, but after the slave insurrection of 1803 and the loss of 25,000 of his trained soldiers in attempting to recapture the island, he decided on an alternative plan to finance the campaigns. When approached by an emissary of the administration of Thomas Jefferson, who hoped to negotiate a right-of-deposit in New Orleans for $10 million, Napoléon offered to sell all the Louisiana territory to the United States in exchange for $15 million. Since Napoléon no longer needed the territory as a breadbasket for the slaves on Haiti, the sale became a means to fund his army.

During the remaining Napoleonic Wars (1804–1814), trade became an important issue. Great Britain reasserted the Rule of 1756, which prohibited countries that had not traded with France in that year for trading with them then. Since the United States had been part of the British empire in 1756, it had not traded with France and therefore the rule was aimed at preventing trade between France and a neutral country. The Orders in Council then placed a blockade on continental Europe in an attempt to deprive Napoléon and his army of food, medicines, and much needed supplies.

Napoléon responded by passing the Berlin and Milan decrees, both of which countered the Rule of 1756 and imposed a blockade on the British Isles. The United States was drawn into the conflict as both countries attempted to strangle its ability to engage in vital trade. After implementing a number of measures, including non-importation and an embargo, the French responded to an offer by the United States to only trade with the country that respected its neutrality. The United States then declared war on Great Britain, resulting in the War of 1812. The consequence of the war included the establishment of a protective tariff by the United States.

SECOND FRENCH EMPIRE

The end of the first French colonial empire forced France to seek colonies elsewhere to compete with the strong European empires. Although the British returned many of the captured French colonies in the Caribbean and West Africa, the French sought to expand their empire. Algeria was invaded in 1830 and took seventeen years to conquer. From there, the French moved into Tunisia (1881) and then dominated most of North, West, and Central Africa, including the modern-day countries of Mauritania, Senegal, Guinea, Mali, Ivory Coast, Benin, Mali, Niger, Chad, the Central African Republic, Republic of the Congo, and Djibouti. Morocco became a protectorate in 1911. The French also established control over present-day Syria, Lebanon, Togo, and Cameroon. In 1883, the French moved into Cochin China (southern Vietnam), Tonkin, and Annam and later into Cambodia and Laos. These regions were known as French Indochina.

After World War II, the French attempted to regain control over Vietnam but were defeated by the forces of Ho Chi Minh and his nationalist fighters, who had defeated the Japanese during the war. The primary product that the French exported from Vietnam had been rubber, a vital commodity in the age of the automobile.

The end of World War II witnessed the beginning of a worldwide movement for self-determination. Vietnam gained its independence from France in the 1950s, and by 1960 most of the African countries under French control were also recognized as sovereign states. Like the British, the French sought to retain economic ties with their former colonies through the French Community (an organization that links France and its former colonies). Much of this trade has diminished over the last several decades as the French have opted for trade within the industrialized European Union. Few colonial possessions remain from the French empire in the Caribbean, the Indian Ocean, and Antarctica and those that do remain are administered through its Overseas Department.

Cynthia Clark Northrup

See also: British Empire; Napoleonic Wars; Southeast Asia; Wars for Empire.

BIBLIOGRAPHY

Anderson, Fred. *Crucible of War: The Seven Years' War and the Fate of Empire in British North America, 1754–1766.* New York: Vintage, 2003.

Eccles, William John. *The French in North America, 1500–1783.* East Lansing: Michigan State University Press, 1998.

Pocock, Tom. *Battle for Empire: The Very First World War, 1756–63.* London: Michael O'Mara, 1998.

FRENCH REVOLUTION

A volatile period causing much disruption in trade.

France had emerged as a major trading nation by the time of the French Revolution (1789–1791) and was surpassed only by Great Britain, its major rival. France's foundations in trade remained weaker than Britain's. Most of this trade involved its colonial possessions in the Caribbean, with external trade only accounting for about one-third of the total trading activity. During the seventeenth and eighteenth centuries, mercantilism remained the primary economic policy followed by governments. With respect to trade, mercantilism meant the exclusiveness of trade and the reliance on duties. A movement toward more freedom in trade began in France with the philosophical views of the economists (Vincent de Gournay) and the Physiocratic School. In 1774, Jacques Turgot, the prerevolutionary comptroller-general of finances, attempted, with his Six Edicts, to establish the free circulation of grain within the kingdom of France. The French signed a commercial treaty with the newly formed nation of the United States in 1778. It contained a most-favored-nation clause.

In spite of these measures, protectionism remained a salient feature of French trade policy until the Eden-Reyneval Treaty of 1786 between England and France. It brought to a close a century of trade wars between the two nations. Conrad de Reyneval's statement, "We should move closer to England, as hereafter there would no longer be any goods in which trade is prohibited between the two nations," marked a departure from the traditional policy that would later be restored by the revolutionaries and Napoléon Bonaparte. The 1786 treaty tended to favor the British and is often blamed for a serious industrial decline in French industries such as cotton, crockery, hardware, and leather goods. The French market became saturated with cheap British goods. The treaty gave rise to unemployment and thus prompted a strong reaction against free trade during the revolutionary period.

Liberalism, the end of privilege, and equality became the hallmarks of the early years of the French Revolution. These principles extended to the realm of trade in the sense that the members of the Constituent Assembly declared free trade in grain on August 29, 1789, again on September 18, 1789, and continued this policy throughout 1789 and 1790. However, exports in grain were banned. France became a free trading nation within its own boundaries by abolishing the prerevolutionary custom duties between provinces with a decree providing for a uniform tariff on October 31, 1790. The tariff repealed the Anglo-French Treaty of 1786. The revolutionaries recognized the importance of trade to a strong economy, "The National Assembly, considering that commerce is the source of all agricultural and industrial development and strength . . . decrees as follows." As a result of the growth in trade within and without France, the French introduced a metric system during this period. Charles Talleyrand introduced the change in the assembly's debates in 1790. A standard and common system of weights and measures become a necessity. The metric system did not became compulsory until 1840.

As an attempt to continue the ending of privilege status, the revolutionaries withdrew from the commercial port of Marseille its prerevolutionary monopoly of trade to the Levant. Commercial companies such as the French East India Company, which had been reconstituted in 1785, suffered the same fate, as the Constituent Assembly abolished its monopoly of trade to East Africa. The Senegal Company suffered the same fate on January 18, 1791.

The revolutionary motto of liberty did not extend to colonial trade policy during the years of the liberal revolution. Despite the efforts of some radical agitators, the revolutionaries practiced a policy of protectionism. The interests of plantation owners were protected by a system known as the *exclusif*, passed on March 18, 1791, which obliged the colonies to trade only with the mother country. The law of June 22, 1791, opened trade with the colonies to all French ports. The

The French Revolution overturned the political order of early modern France, helping to pave the way for the rise of France as a modern democratic and capitalist state. Shown here are lower-class Parisians invading the National Assembly during the revolution. *(© North Wind Picture Archives)*

Navigation Act of September 21, 1793, reinforced this commercial nationalism: all boats claiming to be French had to be constructed in France, owned by Frenchmen, and captained by Frenchmen, and the crew had to be 75 percent French. The system of the ancien régime was maintained in maritime and colonial trade.

WARS OF THE FRENCH REVOLUTION

The declaration of war on April 20, 1792, by the French on the king of Bohemia and Hungary had serious consequences for the French economy in general and trade specifically. Any liberal policies of the early years of the revolution were reversed because of the dire circumstances in which France found itself over the next few years. Measures taken by the revolutionaries during this period were affected by war, assignat depreciation (this was the French revolutionary paper currency), and inflation. The French National Convention established a number of committees during the Reign of Terror (1793–1794) to deal with trade and the food supply. These included agriculture, trade, navigation, and communications. The French moved to a controlled economy. In fact, at the height of the Terror, the government's control over the economy far exceeded what it had been before the revolution. The grain trade that had been freed up during the liberal revolution was closely monitored. A maximum price for grain was established on May 4, 1793. Manufactured goods from Great Britain, its colonies, and other allied powers were prohibited entry into France (October 9, 1793). The British, for their part, declared that they would seize any ships trading with France, including American ones. The United States passed the Jay Treaty in 1794 to avert war with Britain. But the French viewed it as an alliance with Britain and by 1796 they began harassing American ships and threatening the Americans with punitive measures.

The extreme measures taken during the period of the Terror continued until the end of 1794, when French ports opened to trade once again with neutral powers and the Navigation Act of September 1793 was repealed. The maximum law was repealed in December 1794 with the opening of foreign trade. French trade did not improve until 1795–1796, when France concluded peace treaties with Spain, Holland, and Prussia. In general, the revolutionary period saw a turbulent and destructive time for French trade.

Leigh Whaley

See also: Mercantilism; Navigation Laws.

BIBLIOGRAPHY

Aftalion, Florin. *The French Revolution: An Economic Interpretation*, trans. Martin Thom. Cambridge: Cambridge University Press, 1990.

Braudel, Fernand, and Ernest Labrousse. *Histoire économique et sociale de la France*. Vol. 3, *L'avènement de l'ère industrielle (1789–années 1880)*. Paris: Presses Universitaires de France, 1976.

Jones, Colin. *The Longman Companion to the French Revolution*. London: Longman, 1988.

Pollard, S., and C. Holmes, eds. *Documents of European Economic History*. Vol. 1, *The Process of Industrialization*. London: Edward Arnold, 1968.

FRUITS

Edible products derived from the ripened reproductive body of certain plants.

Fruits constitute a desirable food for people and for many species of animals. Fruit usually contains seeds that are protected and nourished by the pulp surrounding them. The use of a plant's fruit as food serves the plant because animals that eat the fruit disperse the seeds over wide areas in the process of consuming and digesting it. A great variety of fruits are produced and traded around the world. Citrus fruits, including oranges, grapefruits, and lemons, are the most widely traded, often in the form of frozen concentrate used for juice. Most citrus fruits as well as bananas, pineapples, and mangoes can be grown only in tropical or subtropical zones, and there has long been active trading between the main production centers in Africa, Asia, and Latin America and the main consumption areas in Europe and North America.

Other types of fruit grow well in temperate climate zones and have historically been less widely traded because of their perishability. Temperate-zone fruits include apples, pears, peaches, nectarines, grapes, avocados, strawberries, blueberries, and raspberries. World exports of all types of fruit (excluding melons) in 2000 totaled 88.7 million metric tons, or 19 percent of world fruit production. World production of oranges and mandarins in 2000 totaled 78.7 million metric tons, or about 17 percent of world fruit production in that year. Other important fruit crops included bananas (14.3 percent of world fruit production), grapes (13.8 percent), and apples (12.7 percent). In 2000, 40 percent of world orange production was traded, while the figures for bananas, grapes, and apples were 22 percent, 10 percent, and 19 percent, respectively. These four types of fruit accounted for about 72 percent of world fruit exports.

Ecuador is the leading banana producer and exporter, accounting for about 10 percent of world production and 29 percent of world exports. Costa Rica, Colombia, and the Philippines are other significant banana exporters. The primary producer and exporter of oranges and mandarins is Brazil, which accounts for around 26 percent of world production and almost half of world exports. Spain and the United States are other important orange exporters. For both grapes and apples, the leading exporter is the European Union (EU). Including intra-EU trade, in 2000 the EU accounted for 40 percent and 33 percent of world apple and grape trade, respec-

Bananas became a major commodity of international trade in the late nineteenth and early twentieth centuries, as this photo of a banana-packing warehouse indicates. *(Library of Congress)*

tively. China is the leading apple producer, but exports limited amounts. The United States is a significant exporter of both apples and grapes, while Chile and Turkey are leading grape exporters.

Most temperate-zone fruits are perishable and available only seasonally. Recent advances in transportation technology have allowed countries such as Chile to take advantage of the fact that growing seasons in the Southern Hemisphere coincide with winters in the North. Chile is a major exporter of grapes, peaches, and nectarines destined for markets in North America during the winter. Because of its perishability, much fruit is processed into jams, jellies, juices, and other preserved products. These processed fruit products are also widely traded.

E. Wesley F. Peterson

See also: Food and Diet.

BIBLIOGRAPHY

Food and Agriculture Organization of the United Nations. "FAOSTAT: Agricultural Data" (http://faostat.fao.org/faostat/collections?subset=agriculture/, accessed September 2002).

FUGGER FAMILY

A financially powerful family in the fifteenth and sixteenth centuries.

The Fugger family began accumulating its fortune during the lifetime of Hans Fugger, a master weaver, who settled in Augsburg in 1367. His descendants took advantage of Augsburg's strategic trade location at the Brenner Pass to build a financial dynasty based on banking and offering loans, a situation made possible by the increasing willingness of the Catholic Church to ignore loopholes that allowed interest to be charged on moneylending.

Under Jacob Fugger II "the Rich," the family achieved such influence on the Hapsburg family that Augsburg was made an imperial free city, independent of the control of regional aristocrats, and the Fuggers were given mining concessions that gave them control of large stores of mercury, copper, gold, and silver. The Hapsburgs, the ruling dynasty of Spain and the Holy Roman empire, desperately needed money to control the elections for the papacy, their own empire, and to finance explorations of the New World, so they looked to the Fuggers for support. In return, the family became the Vatican's bankers for much of the sixteenth century and received noble titles (count, then prince) from the Hapsburgs. As the Spanish reaped huge quantities of precious metals from Mexico and South America, the Fuggers advanced them such enormous sums of money every year in anticipation of the arrival of the treasure fleet that, including high interest, much of the proceeds went directly into the Fugger coffers.

As patrons, the Fuggers sponsored palaces, a family chapel, and portraits and statuary of Renaissance princes, but they also used their wealth to address the increasing overcrowding of Augsburg, which, as a free city, attracted refugees from all over central Europe. The Fuggeri, a complex of living quarters for the workers of Augsburg, was available at reasonable rent through the wishes of Jacob Fugger II, who also specified that the residents offer prayers for the family daily, a tradition that continues in the surviving units today.

Fugger power, however, declined in tandem with that of its greatest debtor, the Spanish monarchy, which declared bankruptcy in 1557, 1575, and 1607, each time defaulting on its increasingly high-interest and high-risk loans. The subsequent Thirty Years' War and its depredations to Germany further damaged the Fuggers' business. The Fuggers were not crushed by this failure because of their diversity of other investments, but they ceased to act as the bankers of emperors and kings, instead concentrating on regional trade and manufacturing. Three branches of the Fugger family, bearing the titles "count" and "prince," still exist today.

Margaret Sankey

See also: Renaissance.

BIBLIOGRAPHY

Ehrenberg, Richard. *Capital and Finance in the Age of the Renaissance: A Study of the Fuggers and Their Connections*, trans. H.M. Lucas. New York: Augustus M. Kelley, 1963.

Mathews, George Tennyson, ed. *The Fugger Newsletters.* New York: Capricorn, 1970.

Streider, Jacob. *Jacob Fugger the Rich: Merchant and Banker of Augsburg, 1459–1525*, ed. Norman Scott Brien Gras, trans. Mildred S. Hartsough. New York: Adelphi, 1931.

FUR

A trade item that became vital to the European settlement of North America while changing the way many indigenous tribes survived.

As the Puritans of New England and the French of Canada arrived and developed their colonies in the seventeenth century, both understood that no matter what constituted their major reason for traveling to the New World, they needed to find a way first to survive and then to prosper. Unlike the Chesapeake colonies of British North America, and the fertile sugar-producing islands of the West Indies, the land of New England and Canada was not suited for the production of cash crops or for large-scale staples production. What both found was a heavily forested wilderness teeming with native peoples and animals, and, as the Europeans and indigenous tribes worked to establish a relationship, trade served an important role in this early cultural interaction.

As the Europeans traded with the Native

The fur trade was a major impetus for the European exploration and conquest of North America between the seventeenth and twentieth centuries. Shown here is an Inuit fur trapper of the early twentieth century with his load of pelts, the raw product from which furs are derived. *(Library of Congress)*

Americans, they noticed that they were skillful hunters willing to exchange furs for a variety of goods. After acquiring furs through trade with these hunters, Canadian and New England merchants sent the furs back to Europe, where, because the wearing of fur was becoming a vital part of elite fashion, increasing demand meant increasing profits. At the same time, colonists used the furs to clothe themselves and protect themselves from the harsh winters.

The realization of the profits available through the fur trade created a quick expansion of the trade and at the same time increased government regulation. In New France (Canada), fur traders were expected to give one-quarter of the value of their furs to the king. Some traders quickly discovered that Native Americans had a weakness for alcohol, and they plied them with drinks until they were willing to give up all their furs. At the same time, some Europeans, especially the French coureurs de bois (unlicensed traders), decided to cut out the middlemen and trap the furs themselves. The fur trade quickly became responsible for the rapid movement of Europeans throughout North America as the coureurs de bois became highly efficient through their adaptation of native ways.

While the fur trade was profitable for some, it also had many negative consequences. Furs are a natural resource and the increasing demand for fur quickly caused areas to be overtrapped, often eliminating local populations of animals such as beaver. The fur trade created many problems for the Native Americans. At first, they exchanged their small surplus of furs for European commodities but, as the Europeans demanded more, they started to change their ways to meet this demand. As some tribes began focusing entirely on fur trapping, the Native Americans gradually became more dependent on the Europeans and, as areas became depopulated, they needed to move ever farther away from their traditional tribal lands. This brought them onto the tribal lands of others, thereby initiating conflicts between native groups seeking to profit from the fur trade.

Ty M. Reese

See also: Columbian Exchange.

BIBLIOGRAPHY

Hafen, Le Roy, ed. *French Fur Traders and Voyageurs in the American West.* Lincoln: University of Nebraska Press, 1997.

Van Kirk, Sylvia. *Many Tender Ties: Women in Fur-Trade Society, 1670–1870.* Norman: University of Oklahoma Press, 1983.

G

GANDHI, MOHANDAS (1869-1948)

> An attorney, social activist for Indian rights in the late nineteenth- and early twentieth-century South Africa, and the most prominent leader of Indian independence and social justice movements from 1915 to 1948.

Mohandas Gandhi became the leading theorist and practitioner of active nonviolent resistance in the twentieth century. In 1885, Gandhi traveled to London to study at the Inner Temple, one of the four Inns of Court around the Royal Courts of Justice there. In 1891, he completed his studies and became a barrister. As a student in London he was exposed to a wide array of ideological views, including those of Indian nationalists, vegetarian reformers, and theological activists espousing a direct relation between the individual soul and the divine principle through personal contemplation.

In May 1893, Gandhi moved to South Africa after having received an offer from a Porbandar Muslim firm to settle a lawsuit involving Indian laborers. He remained in South Africa until 1914. Financially successful, he also became concerned about the treatment of Indians by the white South African government. In 1894, he formed the Natal Indian Congress. As spokesman for the Indian community, he wrote letters and pamphlets espousing Indian rights while encouraging his brethren to adopt a program of English education, English sanitary habits, and community responsibility. During the Boer War of 1899 and the Zulu Rebellion of 1906, Gandhi formed an Indian volunteer ambulance corps and did volunteer nursing in a hospital.

The imposition of new restrictions on Indian residence and trading rights in the Transvaal Colony led Gandhi to establish a newspaper, the *Indian Opinion*, in 1903. Increasing restrictive legislation against the minority Indian population resulted in a mass declaration on September 6, 1906. Johannesburg Indians announced their intention to, according to Judith Brown, refuse to "obey a new registration law, inaugurating the nonviolent civil disobedience for which Gandhi soon invented the name *Satyagraha* (truth-force)." Because of his political activities, Gandhi was jailed three times in 1908 and 1909, the last time at hard labor. While debating Indian terrorists in London in 1909 and communicating with Count Leo Tolstoy, the Russian pacifist, Gandhi published his fundamental essay on nonviolent nationalism, "Hind Swaraj" (Indian Home Rule). When he returned to South Africa, he conducted experiments in labor, food, and health to promote his views on nonviolent action. In 1913, the South African government instituted a new series of anti-Indian acts that, according to James Hunt, resulted "in a large-scale strike of Indian sugar and coal workers in Natal, and a march of over 2,000 Indians led by Gandhi into the Transvaal." The employment of Satyagraha concluded in the Indians Relief Act of 1914. Gandhi's strategy involved attacking the economic base of unjust racial policies through a policy of nonviolence. Boycotting South African production and trade policies produced a measure of victory and enabled Gandhi to return to his native land.

GANDHI AND INDIAN INDEPENDENCE

In 1915, at age forty-five, Gandhi arrived in Bombay. Considered a national hero, he was given the title Mahatma (Great Soul). In the in-

GANDHI, MOHANDAS (1869-1948)

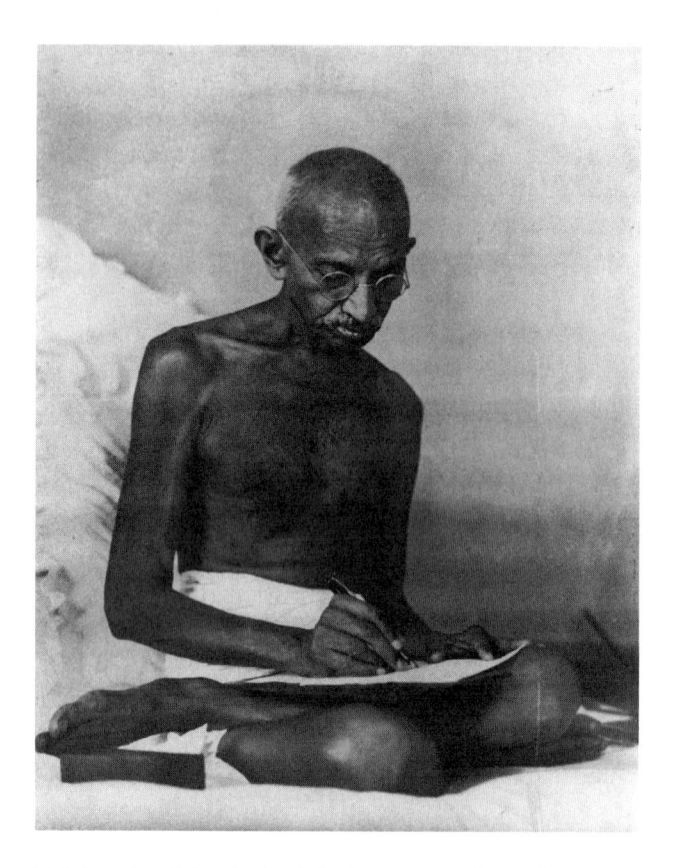

Mahatma Gandhi understood the importance of trade for empire and used the boycott of British goods as a method for driving India's imperial rulers out of the subcontinent. *(Library of Congress)*

dustrial city of Ahmedabad in his native Gujarat, Gandhi established an *ashram* (community), where he continued training his core of disciplined followers. In 1917, he led a strike of mill workers in Ahmedabad and a peasant strike in the district of Kheda. After World War I (Gandhi supported military service during the conflict as a claim for full partnership), the continuation of wartime antiterrorist legislation under the Rowlett Act thrust Gandhi into the national limelight when he called for a nationwide one-day work stoppage in April 1919. According to Hunt, the unforeseen disturbances accompanying the protest "led to a brutal repression in Amristsar, where 379 unarmed civilians were killed." Gandhi received an appointment to the investigation committee of the Indian National Congress (INC) and constructed a report that contradicted the official account presented by the ruling British government.

By 1920, Gandhi had accumulated significant political power within the INC. He organized an effective campaign that reached into the villages to begin his first mass noncooperation campaign, calling for the boycott of the schools, law courts, polls, legislative councils, and perhaps eventually taxes, as well as the renunciation of foreign goods. His movement for Indian independence from British rule advocated Indian self-reliance. In 1922, British judges sentenced him to six years in prison, but he was released in 1924 because of ill health. In 1929, he called for complete independence. Throughout the 1920s, according to Judith Brown, Gandhi had experimented "with a whole range of symbolic and small-scale modes of *Satyagraha*, such as refusing to wear foreign cloth, selling banned books and papers, [and] making salt illegally." On March 12, 1930, in one of his most daring acts of civil disobedience, later called the Gandhi Salt March, he walked 240 miles to the sea at Dandi, where, as Hunt describes, he intentionally made salt "and launched a national wave of protest resulting in the jailing of over 60,000 men and women." Again, British officials sentenced him to jail. In 1931, he won his release after negotiating the "Gandhi-Irwin Pact" with the viceroy, thus ending the protests with a compromise on the salt issue.

The coming of war in 1939 led to further calls for independence. In these struggles, Gandhi's "constructive program" focused on three functions of civil disobedience: to redress a local wrong; to rouse consciousness of a particular wrong; and in the struggle for political freedom, to concentrate on a particular issue like freedom of speech. He expressly warned that "civil disobedience can never be directed for a general cause such as independence. The issue must be definite and capable of being clearly understood within the power of the opponent to yield." In October 1940, he conducted a number of "individual satyagrahas" aimed at opposing Britain's refusal to let Indians decide their own participation in the Indian army. In 1942, Gandhi declared a "Quit India" campaign; he and other INC leaders remained jailed until 1944. His nonviolent campaigns netted him a total of 2,338 days in the prisons of South Africa and India.

India finally achieved independence in 1947. Independence occurred at the same time as the partitioning of the subcontinent as Muslim Pakistan separated from predominantly Hindu India. For years, Gandhi sought to ease tensions between the Hindus and Muslims, arguing that they belonged to one nation. On January 30, 1848, in New Delhi, a Hindu assassinated him, blaming Gandhi for the partition because of his sensitivity to India's Muslim minority.

Gandhi became the first person to demonstrate effectively the strength of nonviolent civil disobedience. Many of his protests focused on economic and trade issues. His "constructive program" concentrated on social and economic uplift for India's millions. More than any other person in the twentieth century, with the possible exception of Martin Luther King Jr., Gandhi dedicated his life to peace and economic justice. For him, no distinction existed between one's public and private life. He insisted that "the public and political domain, as much as the life of the individual, must be seen as a moral enterprise, as the arena in which men and women must seek after ultimate truth and love according to it."

Charles F. Howlett

See also: British Empire; Salt.

BIBLIOGRAPHY

Brown, Judith M. *Gandhi: Prisoner of Hope*. New Haven: Yale University Press, 1989.
Copley, A. *Gandhi: Against the Tide*. Oxford: Basil Blackwell, 1983.
Erikson, Erik. *Gandhi's Truth: On the Origins of Nonviolent Action*. New York: Norton, 1969.
Gandhi, M.K. *An Autobiography: The Story of My Experiments with Truth*. London: Jonathan Cape, 1966.
Hunt, James D. "Mohandas Karamchand Gandhi." In *Biographical Dictionary of Modern Peace Leaders*, ed. Harold Josephson. Westport: Greenwood, 1985.
Nanda, B.R. *Gandhi and His Critics*. Delhi: Oxford University Press, 1985.
Parekh, B. *Colonialism, Tradition and Reform: An Analysis of Gandhi's Political Discourse*. New Delhi: Sage, 1989.
Sharp, Gene. *Gandhi as a Political Strategist*. Boston: Porter Sargent, 1979.

GARAMANTIAN EMPIRE

An ancient civilization located in the southwestern region of present-day Libya.

The Garamantian empire existed during the Greco-Roman period from approximately 500 B.C.E. to 500 C.E. Roman sources indicate that the Garamantes were nomadic people who frequently raided the coastal cities of the southern Mediterranean Sea. Living on the edge of the Sahara between sand and rock, the citizens of the empire relied on the small amount of annual rainfall to replenish their water source each year. A complex irrigation system stretched for thousands of miles into the desert from the capital oasis of Garama (present-day Germa). Agricultural production provided for the needs of the local population, while income from trade was obtained by selling animals such as lions to the Romans for their gladiatorial games.

Evidence of trade between the two civilizations is also indicated by recent archaeological finds that reveal the existence of hypocaust tiles and flue tiles used for the construction of Roman baths. If the evidence proves to be substantiated, the Roman bath at Germa will be the southernmost bath ever located. The distance the tiles would have been transported would have exceeded 620 miles. Garamantian burial tombs also indicate exposure to Greek, Roman, and Egyptian burial sites. Of the 10,000 sites discovered so far, some have been styled after the Greco-Roman mausolea, while others are 6- to 13-feet-high pyramids that each contain over 100 monuments. Unfortunately, most of the tombs were raided centuries ago, removing all evidence of imported goods that might have been considered luxury items at the time.

Besides exchanging live animals with the Romans, the Garamantes also produced quite a bit of jewelry made from ostrich eggshells and carnelian stone beads. They engaged in textile production and metalworking as well. During the formation of the Garamantian empire, the rainfall in the region remained sufficient to maintain an irrigation system after the shift of the southwest monsoons from the region. When the rainfall started to decline again, the Garamantes attempted to compensate for the inadequate water supplies necessary to sustain their irrigation systems by digging deep wells and reducing the number of acres under cultivation. This period corresponds with the development of walled citadels, a reorganization of society, and the reliance on long-distance trade across the Sahara. Located on the north-south route between the Mediterranean and the sub-Saharan region, the Garamantian empire sought to capitalize on the trade between the two regions.

Interestingly, ancient sources indicate that the Romans sought to conquer the empire but failed, even though the indigenous population lacked the weapons to defeat the Roman army. The empire continued to exist, although in a weakened state, as a result of a reduction in annual rainfall. Eventually, the civilization declined and disappeared. In the nineteenth century, archaeologists discovered its ancient ruins.

Cynthia Clark Northrup

See also: Roman Empire.

BIBLIOGRAPHY

"Administration: Lost Cities of the Sahara" (www.le.ac.uk/press/press/sahara.html, accessed December 2003).
Cremaschi, Mauro. "The Late Desertification in the Central Sahara: Rise and Decline of the Kingdom of the Garamantes" (http://atlas-conferences.com/cgi-bon/abstract/caji/, accessed December 2003).
"Lost Kingdom of the Sahara" (http://news.bbc.co.uk/1/hi/world/middle_east/845160.stm, accessed December 2003).

GEMSTONES

Minerals or stones that are used in jewelry after being cut or polished.

There are many varieties of gemstones, including agate, alexandrite, amethyst, ametrine, aquamarine, chalcedony, citrine, diamond, emerald, garnet, iolite, jade, lapis lazuli, onyx, opal, pearl, peridot, ruby, sapphire, spinel, tanzanite, topaz, tourmaline, turquoise, and zircon.

Gems have been traded and treasured since ancient times. The ancient Persians believed that the world rested on a giant sapphire and the reflection of the stone created the brilliant blue sky. Some believed that Moses received the Ten Commandments from God carved on tablets of sapphire. The association of sapphire with the heavens meant that kings and priests often used the stone in their crowns or ornaments. Ancient sources for sapphire were Sri Lanka and Thailand as well as the African continent, in areas such as

Gemstones, which are both valuable and portable, have been a major source of licit and illicit trade since ancient times. Here, a Pakistani roadside gem seller displays his wares.
(© Akhtar Soomro/Dean Pictures/The Image Works)

present-day Nigeria and Kenya. The demand for sapphire by the ruling elites helped to maintain the price of the gem at a relatively high level. It is one of the most sought-after gemstones and the deepness of the blue color, along with cut and clarity, determines its value.

Another gemstone that has been prized since ancient times is the ruby. The stone's red color denotes blood and romance. Ancient legend states that God placed a ruby around the neck of Aaron, the high priest of the Israelites. The ancient mines at Myanmar and Mogok produced rubies with the most brilliant color of red, which were the most expensive. Emperors and kings purchased rubies from India during the Middle Ages and later. Rubies were one of the most expensive luxury items traded between the Far East and the West.

Another important gemstone was the emerald. Believed to represent love and rebirth as well as giving the gift of intelligence and eloquence to the wearer, the ancient Egyptians used this gemstone in their burial tombs. During the reign of Cleopatra, emeralds were mined from the area of the Red Sea. The ancient Romans, including the emperor Nero, wore emeralds. According to the ancient historian Pliny, nothing soothed the eyes like the color green, and the emerald was the greenest green. Highly prized by royalty, the gemstone was discovered in the Americas and brought back for the use of kings and queens during the age of discovery. The Mughal emperors of India also prized the stone so much that they had their names carved on the face of one stone in particular, which is now part of the British Imperial Crown.

The ancient Mesopotamians, Egyptians, Persians, Greeks, and Romans traded for lapis lazuli, which is brilliant blue in color. Although the stone has a low degree of hardness and therefore scratches easily, it was thought to possess aphrodisiac powers and protected the soul. The stone was ground into a powder used during the Middle Ages to produce the brilliant blue tones used in paintings of both the sea and the sky. Modern sources of the stone are located in Afghanistan, Colorado, and Chile.

Turquoise is a gemstone that is often thought to possess powerful metaphysical powers. In the Aztec culture, it was reserved for the gods. In the Americas, most turquoise was mined in the Southwestern portion of the United States. The Native American cultures believed that warriors who wore the stone would be protected or would be able to aim a weapon more accurately. In the Middle East, most turquoise was mined in Iran, Tibet, or China, and was not as sought after by the upper classes as were sapphires, rubies, or emeralds.

Many gemstones have been traded over time and across great distances, but it is the diamond that has emerged as the most marketed gemstone in the modern world. Diamonds are formed from carbon that has been highly pressurized under extremely high temperatures. With a melting point of 7,232 degrees Fahrenheit, a diamond is valuable because of its rarity. The most expensive diamonds are colorless. Clarity and cut also determine the price of the diamond. The diamond trade followed the established trade routes from the Far East through Venice, the city that controlled the diamond trade throughout the thirteenth century. By the fourteenth century, Lisbon had emerged as the diamond center of Europe after the discovery of a direct route to the East. The Jewish merchants, who had to move frequently from one place to another throughout much of history, transported their wealth in diamonds—the stones were lighter than the equivalent in gold and easier to conceal. As Jewish merchants were forced from eastern Europe to more liberal countries, the diamond trade followed with them. During the thirteenth century, the Belgium city of Bruges became the center of the diamond trade. During the fourteenth century, Amsterdam, with its religious tolerance, was a safe haven for the Jews, so the city developed into the largest diamond-trading center of the world until after World War II. The diamond exchange continues to function there, and the diamond-cutting capital of the world is now in Antwerp.

During the late nineteenth century, Cecil Rhodes founded the De Beers mining company in South Africa. Although a competitor threatened his monopoly on the mining industry, the two companies were united under the leadership of Ernest Oppenheimer in 1929. The marketing strategy of the firm was to limit the number of diamonds on the market and thereby ensure a high price for the gemstones. In addition, extensive marketing campaigns made the diamond the gem of choice for engagement and wedding rings. Known for its endurance and strength, the diamond remains one of the most desired gems today. The image helps to sustain the value of the gemstones, even though other stones, such as rubies, are even more rare.

Cynthia Clark Northrup

See also: Amsterdam; Diamonds; South Africa.

BIBLIOGRAPHY

Dickinson, Joan Younger. *The Book of Diamonds: Their History and Romance from Ancient India to Modern Times.* Mineola, NY: Dover, 2001.

Hall, Cally. *Gemstones.* New York: Dorling Kindersley, 1994.

Kanfer, Stefan. *The Last Empire: De Beers, Diamonds, and the World.* New York: Farrar Straus Giroux, 1993.

Seidler, Ned. *Gems and Jewels.* New York: Odyssey, 1964.

GENERAL AGREEMENT ON TARIFFS AND TRADE

> A set of multilateral agreements signed in 1947 by twenty-three countries in Geneva, Switzerland, aimed at eliminating obstacles to world trade in manufactured and agricultural goods.

In addition to the goal of eliminating impediments on trade, the General Agreement on Tariffs and Trade (GATT) also represents a code of conduct and procedures for resolving trade-related disputes among nations. The name GATT, however, has been more commonly used to refer to the international forum with a secretariat in Geneva that provided the framework for the negotiation of these trade agreements. On January 1, 1995, the GATT ceased to exist as an institution when the World Trade Organization (WTO) went into effect. At the time of the termination, 111 countries subscribed to GATT as full-contracting parties and 22 nations held limited membership. Together, these countries conducted about 90 percent of world trade.

ORIGINS OF GATT

GATT is widely credited with facilitating the robust growth of world trade in the latter half of the twentieth century. The agreements negotiated under the auspices of GATT cumulatively reduced average tariffs on the world's industrial goods from 40 percent of their market value in 1947 to less than 5 percent in 1993. The GATT agreements did not govern diplomatic relations between contracting parties. During the Cold War, most of the world's communist states were excluded from GATT membership. Neither did GATT deal with embargoes and other trade-denying measures taken for national security reasons. Trade accords signed at GATT conferences were subject to ratification by each national government in accordance with its constitutional process.

The emergence of GATT as a sustained forum for discussing international trade matters in the post–World War II period owes much to American commercial policy since the 1930s. As the world searched for ways out of the economic dislocations caused by the Great Depression, officials in the U.S. State Department, most notably President Franklin D. Roosevelt's secretary of state, Cordell Hull, pushed for orderly reductions of trade barriers as the basis for a lasting world peace. Their vision and policy initiatives culminated in the passage of the Reciprocal Trade Agreement Act (RTAA) of 1934, in which Congress shared its authority to set the nation's tariff rates with the president by allowing him to enter into bilateral tariff-cutting negotiations with foreign countries. The RTAA was renewed and modified periodically thereafter and provided the domestic legal basis for U.S. negotiations of reciprocal trade agreements with foreign governments. Congress's most important remaining tool for controlling negotiations at GATT conferences was its deliberations over the extension of this enabling legislation.

In the early postwar period, the U.S. government sought to expand its trade liberalization efforts, which had been limited mostly to bilateral meetings with Latin American countries and wartime allies, into a multilateral framework. It proposed a multilateral institution called the International Trade Organization (ITO) to preside over an orderly elimination of trade barriers and provide a common mechanism for addressing trade-related disputes. The ITO was also expected to function as a multilateral institution parallel to the International Monetary Fund and the International Bank for Reconstruction and Development (the World Bank), both created at a United Nations conference in Bretton Woods, New Hampshire, in July 1944. In 1948, an international meeting in Havana, Cuba, produced the Havana Charter, which spelled out the terms of the proposed ITO. The General Agreement on Tariffs and Trade had been drawn up the previous October to record the results of an ongoing multilateral tariff conference in Geneva. GATT thus incorporated many of the commercial policy provisions of the ITO draft charter.

When it became clear that the U.S. Senate would not ratify the Havana Charter and the ITO would not materialize, the General Agreement, with minor modifications, was adopted as the foundational document for a new international trade forum. It also set the ground rules for conducting future multilateral trade negotiations and conflict resolution.

One of the key principles informing GATT as an international trading regime was the rule of nondiscrimination. This notion was embedded in GATT's unconditional most-favored-nation (MFN) provisions. It requires that a trade benefit given to a contracting party must be shared by all other GATT member nations. For example, once a GATT contracting party and its leading trade partner have agreed to a tariff reduction on an item, the concession extends automatically to others. Also implicit in this principle was the notion of procedural transparency. Tariffs, because of their visibility and universal applicability to all imports passing through national borders, were considered the best means for ensuring transparency. An escape clause (Article 35), however, permitted contracting parties to withhold MFN treatment from new GATT members under certain circumstances.

Multilateralism was also a basic GATT principle. GATT member nations were not to engage in the bilateral deal making and exclusionary bloc transactions that had characterized world trade in the 1930s and during World War II. This principle stemmed from the U.S. trade policy planners' belief that bilateral negotiations under the prewar RTAAs had been innately limiting and had, in some cases, contributed to the contraction of trade. In GATT's early years, the enforcement of the multilateral principle was fiercely resisted by Great Britain and most of its Commonwealth partners, who regarded it as an assault on the British Imperial Preference System. Contracting parties, including the United States, made many back-channel bilateral arrangements, such as voluntary export restrictions, to circumvent this principle.

Finally, the principle of reciprocity was at the foundation of GATT. No contracting party was required to grant unilateral concessions or concessions without adequate "mutually advantageous" concessions. GATT made a basic distinction between tariffs and other trade-restricting measures. Only tariffs and surcharges, and not import quotas or other quantitative restrictions, were considered legitimate means of protecting domestic industry within the GATT system. GATT, however, contained exemption clauses (notably Articles 12 and 19) that permitted contracting parties to resort to nontariff, numerical controls as a temporary measure in stipulated circumstances, such as balance-of-payments difficulties and acute distress experienced by domestic industry because of a recent tariff concession.

GATT MEETINGS

During its forty-seven-year-long existence, GATT sponsored eight major multilateral tariff meetings ("rounds"), beginning with the one held in Geneva in October 1947, where the drafting and signing of the General Agreement took place concurrently. The two ensuing conferences in Annecy, France (1949), and Torquay, England (1951), were held primarily to handle the accession of countries that had not taken part in the inaugural Geneva Round, and the tariff concessions produced there were limited in scope. Beginning with the next round (1956), all subsequent negotiations, each multiyear in duration, took place mainly in Geneva. The rounds held between 1960 and 1962 and between 1964 and 1967 bore the names of their organizers (e.g., U.S. Undersecretary of State Douglas Dillon and President John F. Kennedy). The convening of the 1960 to 1962 round reflected the American intention to harness Western Europe's drive for regional integration, which was then embodied in the establishment of the European Economic Community (EEC).

The 1964 to 1967 negotiations, popularly known as the Kennedy Round, produced the greatest number and scope of concessions up to that point in GATT's history. Nearly fifty nations participated and an average cut in tariff rates of one-third was achieved, but a great number of agricultural commodities were exempted from the negotiations and left for future discussions. The seventh meeting, the Tokyo Round (1973–1979), involved ninety-nine contracting parties and gave special attention to various nontariff barriers, such as internal administrative requirements, and the needs of the developing world. The eighth and final GATT tariff conference, known as the Uruguay Round, lasted the longest, from 1986 to 1994. The resulting documents called for global tariff reductions on manufactured goods by an average of 40 percent, major cuts in agricultural subsidies, and trade liberalization in the service sectors, such as banking, insurance, and securities.

The Uruguay Round was also notable for its engagement with emerging concerns in international trade, such as the protection of intellectual property rights and the impact of trade on the natural environment. A GATT committee on environment, which had been organized in 1971 but remained inactive, met for the first time in 1991 as part of Uruguay Round discussions. During that round, GATT contracting parties also voted to establish a new organization, the WTO. This institution monitors and regulates international trade and reduces barriers to trade in services and other areas not affected by the GATT agreements. The WTO's secretariat is located in Geneva, Switzerland, and the organization now embraces more than 140 countries, including countries of the former Soviet bloc and China, making it a more broadly global institution than was GATT.

Sayuri Guthrie-Shimizu

See also: World Trade Organization.

BIBLIOGRAPHY
Zeiler, Thomas W. *Free Trade, Free World: The Advent of GATT.* Chapel Hill: University of North Carolina Press, 1999.

GENERAL ELECTRIC COMPANY

A leading diversified technology, manufacturing, and services company, with sales of approximately $145 billion in 2003.

A century old, the General Electric Company today employs over 300,000 people worldwide. It operates in over 100 countries, with 250 manufacturing plants in 26 nations. The company traces its history to the famous inventor Thomas Alva Edison, who designed the first incandescent lightbulb in 1879. His company, the Edison Electric Illuminating Company, attracted the interest of banking tycoon J.P. Morgan, who helped finance an early electrical distribution system based on direct current. At the end of the 1880s, Morgan and railroad magnate Henry Villard helped Edison consolidate a number of electrical companies into the Edison General Electric Company.

In 1892, Morgan and Villard chartered the General Electric Company by combining Edison's company with the Thomson-Houston Company, which employed different electrical systems. General Electric (GE), therefore, brought together in a single concern manufacturers of alternating and direct-current equipment, of arc and incandescent lighting, and of electric equipment for transportation purposes. With an expanded research staff and the superior managerial talents of the Thomson-Houston officials, GE was in a position possibly to dominate a growing industry. It still faced, however, stiff competition from the Westinghouse Corporation, and for several years the two competitors launched extensive patent litigation. Finally, in 1896 the two pooled their patents and agreed to pay royalties to the other if either exceeded sales quotas.

In the years that followed, GE's research lab employed many scientists to create electrical products for daily use. Their record was impressive, including over the decades advances in such areas as air conditioning, radio, medical equipment, and air travel. Around their homes, Americans enjoyed improvements in such products as the electric fan, toaster, electric range, and refrigerator. The company prospered, rapidly extending its operations globally. Throughout the 1920s, GE invested heavily in Europe and even in the Soviet Union, which the United States had not yet recognized. With Westinghouse, GE formed the Radio Corporation of America. During the Great Depression, GE formed its own financing company, GE Capital, to assist people to purchase company products. By the 1960s, GE Capital had expanded into broader markets.

During World War II, GE played a pivotal role in supplying needed electrical equipment, but chaffed at federal regulations demanding that war industries bargain collectively with their employees. Worried that this regulation might encourage the American Federation of Labor to establish itself in its factories, GE established its own union, a tact that over 100 other large corporations soon adopted.

After the war, GE was an integral part of what President Dwight D. Eisenhower termed the "military-industrial complex." The company's innovations were important as each side struggled for

Since its founding in the early twentieth century, the General Electric Company has been one of America's leading manufacturers and exporters. Shown here are early twentieth-century workers receiving the technological training critical to the company's innovations. *(Library of Congress)*

technological advantage and, therefore, the company received much of its income from defense contracts. It even employed future president Ronald Reagan as its spokesman. In recent years, GE has sought to further diversify and globalize its operations, in terms of both raw materials and products.

Brooks Flippen

See also: Electricity; Edison, Thomas Alva.

BIBLIOGRAPHY

Aris, Stephen. *Arnold Weinstock and the Making of GEC.* London: Aurum, 1998.

Carlson, W. Bernard. *Innovation as a Social Process: Elihu Thomson and the Rise of General Electric, 1870–1900.* New York: Cambridge University Press, 1991.

GENERAL THEORY OF EMPLOYMENT, INTEREST, AND MONEY, THE

> A work by the British economist John Maynard Keynes of King's College, Cambridge, which founded Keynesian macroeconomics, an analytical framework in which public and private spending decisions affect output and employment.

John Maynard Keynes's *The General Theory of Employment, Interest, and Money* analyzed the determination of aggregate output and employment. Written during the Great Depression, the *General Theory* argued that governments could

John Maynard Keynes took a leading role in the Bretton Woods monetary settlement that established the International Monetary Fund and the World Bank at the end of World War II. Keynesian ideas shaped macroeconomic policymaking in the industrial countries for a quarter-century after the war. *(AP/Wide World Photos)*

use expansionary fiscal and monetary policy, stimulating aggregate demand, to reduce unemployment and increase national income. Keynes denied that market forces would automatically restore full employment in a monetary economy after demand shocks in the absence of active government stabilization policy. Keynes took a leading role in the Bretton Woods monetary settlement that established the International Monetary Fund and the World Bank at the end of World War II, and Keynesian ideas shaped macroeconomic policymaking in the industrial countries for a quarter-century after the war. In the Bretton Woods negotiations and in his "Notes on Mercantilism" in the *General Theory*, Keynes held that maintaining the autonomous ability of national policies to stabilize employment is more important than the unrestricted international movement of goods and funds.

In the 1920s, Keynes had pioneered analysis of the forward market for foreign exchange and had warned that Britain's 1925 return to the gold standard at an overvalued exchange rate would necessitate domestic deflation and unemployment. At the beginning of the Great Depression, Keynes advocated a protective tariff as a politically acceptable substitute for devaluation, dropping his tariff proposal in 1931 when Britain left the gold standard and allowed the pound to depreciate against other currencies. The analysis of the *General Theory* dealt formally only with a closed economy. Keynesian macroeconomics was extended to open economies by Keynes's associate James Meade and, most influentially, by Robert Mundell and J. Marcus Fleming. The Mundell-Fleming or IS-LM-BP (where IS is the investment-saving equilibrium curve for the goods market, LM is the liquidity-money equilibrium curve for the money market, and BP the balance-of-payment equilibrium curve for the foreign exchange market) model is an open-economy extension of the interpretation of Keynes's *General Theory* presented in John Hicks's IS-LM diagram.

This framework for analyzing the simultaneous determination of aggregate income, interest rates, and exchange rates continues to be widely used. Post-Keynesian economists criticize the IS-LM-BP framework for neglecting Keynes's insight that private investment is volatile because of limited knowledge of the future. In contrast, New Classical economists claim that Keynes underestimated private-sector stability and that government attempts at stabilization cause instability and inflation.

Robert W. Dimand

See also: *Economic Consequences of the Peace, The*; Great Depression; Keynes, John Maynard.

BIBLIOGRAPHY

Clarke, P. *The Keynesian Revolution in the Making, 1924–36.* Oxford: Clarendon, 1988.

Dimand, R.W. *The Origins of the Keynesian Revolution.* Stanford: Stanford University Press, 1988.

Harcourt, G.C., and P.A. Riach, eds. *A "Second Edition" of the General Theory.* New York: Routledge, 1997.

Moggridge, D.E., and E.A.G. Robinson, eds. *Collected Writings of John Maynard Keynes.* New York: Cambridge University Press for the Royal Economic Society, 1971–1989.

GENOA

A major port city located on Italy's Ligurian coast.

Genoa's fine natural harbor attracted native Ligurian people and seafaring ancient merchants since at least the fifth century B.C.E. Trade-minded Etruscans also settled there, and Rome had strong contacts with the city by the outbreak of the Second Punic War (218 B.C.E.). Hannibal sacked Genoa in 205 for cooperating with Rome, but the Romans quickly rebuilt it as a base from which to control Liguria.

Little is mentioned in Roman historical sources about Genoa (*Genua*), though the geographer Strabo mentions the major goods that flowed through the city: local timber (especially good for shipbuilding), hides, honey, wool fells, and amber, exchanged for olive oil and wine. A minor outpost on the Roman Aemilian Way, in the later empire it became a major seaport for western Lombardy, including Milan and Pavia.

As the Roman empire disintegrated, like much of Italy, Genoa fell under Ostrogothic, then Byzantine, then Lombard, and then Frankish rule from the fifth through the ninth centuries. With few natural resources at its disposal, Genoa relied on maritime trade, which had all but disappeared. North African Muslims sacked the city in 934–935, and there is some indication it was a local center of the cloth trade. Apparently abandoned for some years, by the eleventh century the Genoese were counterraiding Muslim holdings in Sardinia and Corsica and trading in North Africa. By at least 1065, Genoese ships were found in Syrian ports, having gained leverage that would make them extremely valuable to the crusader armies. During this time, Genoa emerged as an independent-minded city that ran most of its own affairs.

The revival of the northern Italian economy in the High Middle Ages meant both a supply of goods to ship out and a demand for goods from all over the Mediterranean and beyond. The landed aristocracy of the early Middle Ages became the merchant aristocracy of the twelfth and thirteenth

A bird's-eye view of the harbor and city of Genoa, Italy, circa mid-nineteenth century. Genoa's natural harbor attracted native Ligurian people and ancient seafaring merchants since at least the fifth century B.C.E. *(Library of Congress)*

centuries. *Genuense ergo mercator*—Genoese therefore a merchant—was a valid cliché. War, especially at sea, went hand in hand with the development of markets. Genoese aid to the Castilian *reconquista* against the Moors was exchanged for a near monopoly on Spanish seaborne trade before Catalonia's rise in the 1300s. Genoese merchants held a privileged place in Constantinople from 1155 until being evicted by the victorious Venetians in the wake of its capture and sack in 1205. After 1261, the restored Greek monarchy cut off the Venetians and reinstated the Genoese. The Genoese empire also supported the Genoese control of the eastern Aegean region. Rivalry with nearby Pisa ended in 1284 with the naval victory of Meloria. Venice proved more resilient, and Genoese power had clearly waned after four wars (1255–1381). In this struggle, control of trade in the eastern Mediterranean was at stake. In the years before the fourth war ended, trade with Alexandria alone amounted to well over half of the total value of its overseas commerce. The Genoese had colonies in the Black Sea, through which they gathered goods from the Silk Road and the Golden Horde, and slaves for Muslim and Christian markets, and through one of which, Caffa, they supposedly imported the Black Death into the Mediterranean and Europe.

The rulers of Cyprus relied on Genoese ships, and the Genoese used Cypriot ports as bases for Levantine and Armenian trade. Beginning in 1277, Genoese ships sailed into the Atlantic, directly trading with London and continental ports as far north as Bruges. Its merchants also penetrated inland trade routes, from Milan to central Europe and through the Aquitaine to thirteenth-century French fairs. With such far-flung offices, colonies, and customers, medieval Genoese were in the forefront of developing instruments of commercial credit, new forms of commercial partnership, and insurance. Genoese shipbuilders were also instrumental in developing both round ships and galleys into more spacious and reliable conveyances, and in advancing navigation tools and techniques.

GENOA AND THE AGE OF EXPLORATION

The fifteenth century saw the rise of the important Banco San Giorgio, which dominated Genoese finance until the eighteenth century. Genoa fell under foreign domination by Milan (1421–1436) and Milan and France (1463–1499). Genoa's fortunes declined further with the fall of Constantinople, the shift of economic activity from the Mediterranean to the Atlantic seaboard, the rebellions along the Ligurian coast, and the continuation of traditional interfamily strife. In 1522, the Spaniards sacked the city in the midst of the Hapsburg-Valois Wars. Nonetheless, Genoa survived as a republic until Napoléon Bonaparte's arrival in 1797. During the sixteenth and seventeenth centuries, Genoa enjoyed some economic recovery, and many local fortunes were made through foreign investment and foreign exchange speculation. The Genoese chartered their vessels and made loans to foreign merchants. Napoléon's Continental System and the British blockade diminished Genoa's role as a major port, but the Genoese regained it after the French defeat when Piedmont annexed Genoa. From this point on, Genoa has served first Piedmont and then united Italy as the country's major commercial port, with only Marseilles as a peer in the Mediterranean.

Genoa's extensive harbor area (seventeen square miles) was badly damaged by Allied action during World War II, and storms ravaged the area again in 1954 and 1955. Genoa, with a population of about 650,000 in 2000, is the main outlet for northern Italian bulk goods such as olive oil, wine, macaroni, cheese, fruits, rice, and textiles. Fuel of all kinds, grain, and industrial raw materials lead the list of imports. Genoa also leads all other Italian ports in the volume of passenger traffic. Genoa's industrial base remains important, though declining and well behind the port and its activities. Iron and steel, cement, chemicals, ships, airplanes, rolling stock, paper, textiles, and sugar are among the area's major products. Banking and finance are increasing in importance, and as a land, sea, and air transportation hub, Genoa is without peer in contemporary Italy.

Joseph P. Byrne

See also: Crusades; Mediterranean Sea; Napoleonic Wars; Roman Empire; World War II.

BIBLIOGRAPHY

Day, Gerald. *Genoa's Response to Byzantium, 1155–1204: Commercial Expansion and Factionalism in a Medieval City.* Urbana: University of Illinois Press, 1988.

Epstein, Steven. *Genoa and the Genoese, 958–1528.* Chapel Hill: University of North Carolina Press, 1996.

Quintieri, Beniamino, ed. *Patterns of Trade, Competition, and Trade Policies.* Brookfield, VT: Avebury, 1995.

GERMAN EMPIRES

> Germany's economic and political strength has waxed and waned in step with Europe's wars.

The first German empire lasted for eight and a half centuries. Otto "the Great" was crowned German king in 936 and Holy Roman emperor in 961. Before the Thirty Years' War (1618–1648), the Holy Roman empire had virtually ceased to exist and Germany had become a loose confederation of territories and states. Germany emerged from the war considerably weakened. Its population fell from 20 million to 6 million, economic activity suffered enormously, and trade was so badly affected that the Hanseatic League almost ceased to exist.

During Otto's reign, the widespread use of the word "deutsch" indicated a growing sense of national identity, but for several generations after the Thirty Years' War, German ruling classes preferred not to identify themselves as German. Status was achieved by traveling to France and by building German imitations of Versailles. Louis XIV of France both fostered and profited by this weakness and division: the French annexed several German towns and territories, including Strasbourg, Alsace, and Lorraine.

Prussia, an independent German state, emerged from the Seven Years' War (1756–1763) as the leading European military power and a strident sense of national identity began to emerge. However, in the early nineteenth century, a further assertion of French imperial power weakened Germany: Napoléon Bonaparte annexed a large part of the north German coast and banned all trade with England.

The first German empire was formally dissolved between 1804 and 1806, as Napoléon consolidated the French empire. The Napoleonic domination of Germany revived the spirit of German nationalism; but the War of Liberation, which culminated in the 1814 Treaty of Paris and the 1815 Congress of Vienna, did not liberate Germany from its fractious past. The 300 or so territorial remnants of the Holy Roman empire were consolidated into 39 sovereignties, but the post-Napoleonic peace treaty was designed by Klemens Metternich of Austria to ensure that Germany would remain a loose confederation of states, with Austria exerting a dominant influence.

In the early nineteenth century, Germany was economically backward in comparison with some of its European rivals, especially Great Britain. German agriculture was still largely based on feudal principles, and its industry was nascent. Trade and commerce were highly regulated, and German territories were rigidly protectionist against each other. German manufacturers had to navigate their way through many tariff and exchange regimes and had great difficulty competing with their English and French competitors. In 1815, Prussia had 60 different tariffs and 2,800 classes of taxable goods. Prussia also had a long and porous border, with thirteen enclaves.

Baron Heinrich von Bulow, the Prussian minister responsible for commerce and shipping, and Georg Maassen, the Prussian minister of finance, sought and achieved a system of comparative free trade. Raw materials were tariff-free, 10 percent was levied on manufactures and 20 percent on "colonial wares." By January 1834, the greater part of Germany (although not Austria) was linked by a Customs Union (the Zollverein). Initially, the Zollverein had a low external tariff, although part of the business community sought increased protection.

Both France and Austria had a common interest in keeping Germany backward and divided. But Prussia was now economically and militarily strong enough to confront these divisive forces. Otto von Bismarck, the prime minister and foreign minister of Prussia, declared "the great questions of the day will be settled not by resolutions and majorities... but by blood and iron." Austria was defeated in 1866. These divisive forces were further confronted—through a common war against a common enemy: France.

Napoléon III of France declared war on Prussia on July 14, 1870. Within six months, the second French empire had fallen and the second German empire was created. William I, the king of Prussia, was proclaimed German emperor and Alsace and the greater part of Lorraine were "returned" to Germany, acquisitions that soured international relations for a generation.

UNIFICATION AND THE SECOND GERMAN EMPIRE

Germany had experienced extraordinary economic growth before 1871, but the establishment of the German empire made it unquestionably a new world power. This power was firmly based on industrial and demographic factors; its improved capacity for trade had important military and geopolitical ramifications.

The 1871 Treaty of Versailles added to the North German Confederation the kingdoms of Bavaria and Württemberg, the grand duchy of Baden, and the southern provinces of the grand duchy of Hesse. Rapid population growth provided the manpower requirements of the new German empire. In the 1840s, both France and Germany had populations of approximately 35 million. From the midcentury on, German population growth had begun to outstrip that of France. In the 1890s, emigration from Germany almost ceased. By 1911, the French population was less than 40 million, while the German population exceeded 65 million. In 1870, one-third of Germans were urban; by 1914, this proportion had risen to two-thirds.

Before World War I, the economic "greatness" of a country tended to be measured by its output of coal and iron. In 1871, German production of coal exceeded that of France and Belgium combined; by 1913, German production almost matched that of Britain, the world's leading coal-producing country. German iron and steel production increased fivefold between 1850 and 1874; the annexation of Lorraine made Germany the world's second-largest iron-producing country.

Germany also pioneered the development of new techniques and products. The electrical and chemical industries soon became dynamic sectors of the German economy; by the end of the nineteenth century, Germany produced about 90 percent of the world's dyestuffs. In the first decade of the twentieth century, Germany's cotton textile industry grew faster than that of any others.

The unification of Germany also removed the last barriers to internal trade and established a common banking and currency system. Germany's first steam line railway was opened in 1835. In June 1873, an imperial railway office was established, which facilitated an improvement in intra-German trade. By 1920, the German railway system exceeded 35,000 miles (5.3 percent of the world's total). Several reforms improved the environment for trade. A common system of weights and measures had been introduced in 1868. In 1870, joint-stock companies with limited liability were recognized under Prussian law.

In 1871, Germany still had seven different currency systems, each state had its own paper money, and there were over 100 banks with the right to issue bank notes. In 1871, a common imperial system was adopted, a gold currency was introduced, and the use of silver was restricted. States still had the right of coinage, but the only acceptable paper currency was that issued by the Prussian bank (which became the Imperial Bank in 1873). In the mid-nineteenth century, German foreign lending had been almost nonexistent; by 1914, German's had invested $5.8 billion abroad, almost one-third of the British level and 13 percent of the world's total.

In 1866, universal male suffrage was introduced for elections to the Diet of the North German Confederation; in 1871, this was extended to elections to the Imperial Parliament (Reichstag). The unification of Germany was strongly supported by the National Liberal Party, which could legitimately claim to have established a quasi-liberal regime: a strong united Germany, free trade, universal suffrage, and a parliamentary system. The National Liberal Party proposed that by 1877 many foreign manufactured goods should enter Germany without a tariff. However, liberal optimism began to wane in the last quarter-century before 1914: the 1879 German Tariff Act was one of several reversals that left only Britain and Holland as free-trade countries.

Germany remained primarily focused economically and militarily on Europe; its overseas possessions were never as extensive as those of the French or the British. However, at the outset of the German empire, commercial groups sought to include Saigon, Cochin China, Martinique, Saint Pierre, and Miquelon as transfers from France to Germany in the 1871 Franco-Prussian Treaty of Frankfurt.

After 1876, commercial interests began to exert increasing influence over Bismarck and his policy. Between 1884 and 1914, Germany acquired 1.03 million square miles of colonial territory (the British, 4.75 million, and the French, 3.58 million). But by 1914, German overseas territory contained only about 5,000 permanent German inhabitants. Ninety-five percent of all the overseas territory that Germany ever held was acquired between 1883 and 1885.

German companies sought to control the copra (dried coconut) trade and other trading stations throughout the South Seas. (In 1879, the Samoan Subsidy Bill rescued some of these German trading companies in the South Seas). In 1883, Australian officials became alarmed by German interest in New Guinea. In 1884, the British established a protectorate on the southeastern coast of New Guinea but declined to oppose German expansion to the northeast of the island.

F.E. Lüderitz, the head of a Bremen mercantile house, spearheaded German trade with southwest Africa. In 1883, the German government requested that the British government protect a small German coastal settlement at Angra Pequena on the northwestern border of Cape Colony. Having received no reply, Bismarck proclaimed German authority over Angra Pequena plus a large chunk of its hinterland in the Kalahari Desert.

German companies were more active in Zanzibar than their British counterparts; companies from Hamburg and Bremen were also involved in extensive trade with Togoland and the Cameroons. All three territories were subsequently secured for the German empire. Neither Germany nor Britain sought conflict with the other over colonial possessions and in 1890 an Anglo-German agreement resolved some minor outstanding problems.

In 1888, Britain and France effectively monopolized Turkish trade and finance. All the European powers sought railway concessions, but it was German companies that built and financed the Turkish railway network. By 1900, the most active commercial groups in Constantinople and Asia Minor were German. Support was provided for the modernizing groups who were gaining power in Turkey and in 1914 Turkey entered World War I on Germany's side.

In 1914, shortly after the outbreak of hostilities, Germany lost control of the Caroline, Mariana, and Marshall Islands (to Japan), German New Guinea (to Australia), and Western Samoa (to New Zealand). After the war, the disintegration of the German empire continued, but the victors were reluctant to simply expropriate these territories. Instead, the League of Nations divided Germany's African empire as "mandates" or "trusts" among the victorious powers: the Cameroons and Togoland were shared by the British and French and German East Africa was shared between the British, the Belgians, and the Portuguese.

The dissolution of the second German empire was enforced by French politicians, some of whom had bitter personal memories of the humiliation of the German incursion into France in 1870–1871. In 1919, the German delegation reluctantly signed the humiliating Treaty of Versailles, concluding what contemporaries called the "Great War," but later renamed "World War I."

In 1919, German rivers were internationalized and the Kiel Canal was opened to the military and merchant ships of all nations; the German navy scuttled itself. Other aspects of the peace treaty were disastrous both for German trade and for the world. Germany had to surrender all its large merchant ships, half of its medium-sized ships, and a quarter of its fishing fleet and build 200,000 tons of shipping for the victors annually for five years. Large quantities of coal had to be delivered to France, Belgium, and Italy for a decade. Several territorial concessions were imposed on Germany (including Alsace and Lorraine, which were "returned" to France).

In 1871, the French were obliged to provide a financial indemnity (which had important monetary consequences for German unity, allowing a gold currency to be introduced; it also fueled an investment boom). The reparations imposed on Germany as its second empire ended had important monetary consequences: its currency collapsed and Germany became engulfed in hyperinflation. The 1919 peace treaty turned out to be a prelude (or an invitation) for the German invasion and occupation of France two decades later.

Robert Leeson

See also: European Union; World War I; World War II.

BIBLIOGRAPHY

Barraclough, G. *The Origins of Modern Germany.* Oxford: Basil Blackwell, 1972.
Cipolla, C., ed. *The Fontana Economic History of Europe: The Emergence of Industrial Societies 2.* London: Collins-Fontana, 1973.
Phillips, W.A., J.W. Headlam, and A.W. Holland. *A Short History of Germany and Her Colonies.* London: Encyclopedia Britannica, 1914.
Pollard, S. *European Economic Integration, 1815–1970.* London: Thames and Hudson, 1974.
Roll, E. *A History of Economic Thought.* London: Faber and Faber, 1973.

GHANA

> One of fifty-one countries in Africa; as a British colony, it was known as the Gold Coast.

Ghana is located in western sub-Saharan Africa. Côte d'Ivoire, Burkina Faso, Togo, and the Gulf of Guinea in the Atlantic Ocean border this equatorial country. As of 2000, Ghana's economy had stabilized. The average growth rate of Ghana's economy is 4.3 percent per year, and gross domestic product (GDP) totals $5.2 billion, or $270 per capita. Ghana is a significant exporter of gold, cacao, lumber, and electricity; the United States is one of its major trading partners. Having suffered the disruption and destruction of its economy at the hands of the European imperial nations, Ghana is experiencing an economic recovery.

ANCIENT GHANA

Ghana has a rich cultural history. Before coming under British dominion, the Ghana empire had existed until 1076. The highly advanced society included many Muslims but most Ghanaians were followers of traditional African religions. At the height of its power, Ghana controlled the southwestern section of the trans-Saharan trade route, in particular the gold regions. Economically, this empire was prosperous.

The Ghana empire was weakened and destroyed by drought and outside invaders, and from the ruins arose the Mali empire in the thirteenth century. Within a century, three of Mali's kings, Sundiata, Mansa Uli, and Mansa Musa, expanded its borders and reestablished its greatness. Primarily a Muslim state, the reputation of Mali spread around the world, attracting many scholars to live and work in the country. The establishment of a mosque and learning center at Timbuktu brought heightened economic prosperity under Mansa Musa.

Despite its return to greatness, the Mali empire was built on a weak foundation, and the Songhay empire overtook it in the mid-fifteenth century. The empire reached its height under Askia the Great (Askia Muhammad), who worked to establish the Islamic code of law in the Sudan area. He granted special status to Muslim scholars, providing them with access to his patronage and land. In this way, Timbuktu flourished as a learning center and was unrivaled in its day. Askia also divided the empire into regional provinces and the government into functional units that enabled him to have better control. These changes restored the empire to economic heights. Askia was dethroned by his own sons, and over the next three years the empire declined politically at a rapid pace. In 1591, the country was invaded and crushed by the Moors from North Africa.

ARRIVAL OF THE EUROPEANS

Over the next 300 years, no formal empire existed, though there was fairly frequent contact with Europeans. During the fifteenth century, the Portuguese were involved in active trade with the peoples along the west coast of Africa. It was the Portuguese who named the area the "Gold Coast" because of the profits they made from gold dust. Recognizing the importance of this find, the Portuguese established a trading port stronghold. They arranged for a lease of land from the local leader, Elmina, built San Jorge Castle (also known as Elmina Castle), and traded profitably there until the mid-seventeenth century.

Word of the profits from gold attracted other merchants and adventurers. By 1800, over forty different forts and castles were built along the Gold Coast as the different European nations tried to control their holdings. Bitter fights and rivalries broke out and simmered among the various groups.

During this period, the slave trade also developed in this part of West Africa. Originally, Europeans came to West Africa to trade gold, ivory, and pepper, but as they established cotton, tobacco, and sugar plantations in the American colonies, the demand for laborers to work on the plantations began to increase. Local rulers began trading West African natives—mostly prisoners of war—to Europeans for guns and commodities; the Europeans would then trade the prisoners to the American plantation owners as slaves, in exchange for raw materials that were shipped back to Europe. Great Britain established its economic and political control in the Gold Coast as a direct result of its success in the slave trade competition among European nations. The British Royal African Company, a group chartered and funded by King Charles II to develop African trade (specifically including the slave trade), had established ten forts along the Gold Coast and easily overtook the efforts of the Dutch East India Company. The Ashanti people, the dominant West African power at this time, were also profiting from trade. They ran a regional operation in gold, ivory, and slaves and occasionally worked to aid the Dutch against the British.

African traders were most interested in purchasing guns, gunpowder, tobacco, cloth, alcohol, and luxury goods. Trading between Europeans and African merchants became routine. The introduction of foreign goods to the West African economy had far-reaching implications. The Ashanti developed rapidly into a large powerful organization. The power and weapons fostered war among the African tribes. From the European traders came new foods: cassava, maize, and sweet potatoes grew especially well in the sub-Saharan humidity.

The slave trade continued until the early nineteenth century, with British and local slave traders cooperating. By the 1820s, British merchants handed their forts over to the British government, which by this time had abolished slavery and was intent on ending the slave trade in West Africa. These efforts to halt the slave trade led to conflict with the Ashanti.

In January 1824, the British governor led an expeditionary force inland, penetrating the Ashanti empire. The Ashanti were waiting with superior forces and won a decisive victory against the British, who were heavily outnumbered. Later that year, the Ashanti raided and defeated the British again before withdrawing from the coast to regroup. By 1828, the British government withdrew its forces from the Gold Coast and turned the management and protection of the forts, still British territory, over to the London Committee of Merchants in an effort to reestablish peaceful trade relations with the locals. In 1831, peace was negotiated between the British and the Ashanti by the president of the London Committee. By the late 1800s, the other European powers along the Gold Coast had either closed their forts or relinquished them to Britain.

BRITISH COLONIAL ERA

The start of British rule in West Africa came in 1874, when Britain sacked the Ashanti capital and annexed the region as a colony, reestablishing its claim to the Gold Coast. Around 1880, the "Great Scramble for Africa" began among the European powers. At the Berlin Conference of 1884–1885, the European powers carved up Africa into spheres of influence. In 1896, the British declared Kumasi, the Ashanti capital city, a British protectorate. Then in 1900, the British declared ownership of the Northern Territories around Kumasi. Sporadic wars broke out between the British and the ever-resisting Ashanti tribe. At the Versailles peace conference after World War I, Britain was granted one-third of Togoland, a former German province; the acquisition made up the Gold Coast colony (modern-day Ghana).

The British established a centralized government that consisted only of Europeans. Traditional tribes were dissatisfied with this arrangement and began to form resistance groups. Discontent grew steadily throughout Africa until after World War II. At this time, the United Gold Coast Convention (UGCC) was formed to speak out against the government's failure to deal with the country's issues and demand self-rule. The secretary of the UGCC was a young man named Kwame Nkrumah. He left this post in 1949 to form the Convention People's Party (CPP), whose platform called for immediate self-government.

INDEPENDENT MODERN GHANA

The road to independence for Ghana was long and slow. Nkrumah's CPP spread the call for self-rule throughout Ghana. When the British government failed to comply, the CPP ordered all workers to stage a general strike. Nkrumah and other CPP leaders were arrested and jailed. He was released in 1951, after he won a seat in the Legislative Council of the CPP. By 1954, Ghanaians were running their own domestic affairs while the British handled foreign policy, defense, and the police. Until 1957, there was great conflict between the African leaders themselves. Political differences and old ethnic rivalries surfaced and made it difficult for African leaders to act in concert.

In 1957, Britain agreed to Prime Minister Kwame Nkrumah's appeal for independence and changing the country's name to Ghana. On March 6, 1957, Ghana became an independent country and was admitted into the United Nations a few days later.

Nkrumah was instrumental in establishing the new republic during the first decade after independence. He established models for Ghana's economy, focusing on industrialization of the country and an end to foreign interference. He was the founder of "Pan-Africanism," the philosophy that unites all African groups to work together and aid each other in gaining independence.

By ten years after independence, internal opposition had arisen in reaction to revelations of corruption, mismanagement, and excesses in Nkrumah's government. Worse, his government had failed to stem poverty. A military coup followed in 1966, and the National Liberation Council was installed to lead the government. Several military coups, none of which served to improve the economy or stabilize the government, followed. In 1978, Jerry John Rawlings took power in a military coup. A year later, he relinquished control of the country to a civilian leader, Hilla Limann. When the economy worsened, Rawlings deposed Limann. In 1983, Rawlings initiated serious economic reform and agreed to a structural adjustment plan with the International Monetary Fund. As the economy began to recover, Rawlings began to initiate democratic reforms. A multiparty constitution was adopted, and in 1992 Rawlings became the first democratically elected president of Ghana. He was constitutionally limited to two terms as president. In 2000, John Kufor of the opposition New Patriotic Party was elected president, and for the first time Ghana experienced a peaceful and democratic transfer of power.

Ghana's economy has stabilized as the country's political structure has become more secure. Between 1990 and 2000, Ghana's economy grew an average of 4.3 percent a year and had a gross domestic product of $5.2 billion, or $270 per capita. Ghana is active in exporting gold, cacao, lumber, and electricity, and its total exports were valued at $1.4 billion with imports of $3.4 billion. Its major trading partners are the United Kingdom, the United States, Germany, Nigeria, and Japan.

Jeannine Loftus

See also: Africa.

BIBLIOGRAPHY

Ahiakpor, James C.W. "Rawlings, Economic Policy Reform, and the Poor: Consistency or Betrayal?" *Journal of Modern African Studies* 29, no. 4 (December 1991): 583–600.

Apter, David E. *The Gold Coast in Transition.* Princeton: Princeton University Press, 1972.

Berry, La Verle, ed. *Ghana: A Country Study.* Washington, DC: U.S. Government Printing Office, 1994 (http://lcweb2.10c.gov/frd/cs/ghtoc.html, accessed August 2003).

Fage, J.D. *A History of West Africa: An Introductory Survey.* 4th ed. London: Cambridge University Press, 1969.

Forde, Daniel, and P.M. Kaberry, eds. *West African Kingdoms in the Nineteenth Century.* London: Oxford University Press, 1967.

International Monetary Fund. *Ghana: Adjustment and Growth, 1983–1991.* Washington, DC: International Monetary Fund, 1991.

Killick, Tony. *Development Economics in Action: A Study of Economic Policies in Ghana.* London: Heinemann, 1978.

Rimmer, Douglas. *Ghana: 2000 and Beyond: Setting the Stage for Accelerated Growth and Poverty Reduction.* New York: Pergamon, 1992.

GHAZNAVIDS

> One of the Turkic Muslim peoples who periodically invaded and pillaged Persian Islamic lands.

In the tenth century, the caliphate in Baghdad lost control of its outlying regions due, in the West, to the Crusades and, in the East, to a large influx of Turkish nomads from the steppes of Central Asia. The shifted balance of power in the eastern Islamic world brought down the Persian Sassanian empire and brought about the rise of Ghazna, home of the Ghaznavids, in eastern Iran.

After breaking away from Baghdad, a former Turkish slave in Ghazna founded a kingdom in 962. Eventually, under his son Mahmud, the city's empire encompassed a large part of present-day Afghanistan, Iran, northwest Pakistan, and India. Mahmud came to the throne at the age of twenty-seven in 998, already reputed to be an able administrator and statesman. To satisfy his ambitions to build his small kingdom into a great one, Mahmud turned his attention to Kashmir, the Punjab, and eventually Iran.

In 1000, Mahmud invaded India and returned sixteen times before 1026. Consistently victorious, Mahmud brought the wealth of Indian cities to the Ghaznavid empire. Mahmud annexed the Punjab, and used its booty to create in Ghazna a center of culture and art surpassed only by Constantinople and Baghdad. He established colleges, brought in scholars, built gardens, mosques, palaces, and caravansaries, and encouraged his court to emulate him. The Ghaznavid period also saw the shift from the pre-Muslim hill forts to cities on the plains.

More important, the Ghaznavids established themselves as an intermediary for the Mediterranean-Chinese trade. Also, the Ghaznavids opened new military and commercial routes, tying to the other cities of Afghanistan and central Asia. Their central location on what would later be the Silk Road and the wealth they looted were fuel for a major involvement of the Muslim kingdoms in regional trade.

Mahmud spent his last few years fighting the invading Turkic Seljuk hordes. He died in 1030. By 1040, his empire had fallen to the Seljuk. As did the Ghaznavids, the Seljuk spoke Persian and contributed to the development of modern Persian. Ghazna was destroyed by yet another group, the Ghorids, who defeated both the Seljuk and Ghaznavids and ruled from central Afghanistan between 1150 and 1217. By the thirteenth century, the Mongols had taken the entire region into their empire. Subsequent waves of invaders made Afghanistan peripheral by the sixteenth century.

The Ghaznavids were Sunni Muslims, and their presence stalled the progress of Iranian Shiite Islam, leading to the spread of Sunni rather than Shiite Islam into Afghanistan and South Asia. The Ghaznavids probably introduced Islam into India, which was then dominated by the Hindus. They were the first to give Afghanistan a prominent political and cultural role in the area's Islamic civilization. In 1010, the poet Firdawsi dedicated to the Ghaznavid ruler the great Iranian epic *Shāhnāmeh* (Book of Kings).

In the 1990s, Ghazna, long renamed Ghazni, remained on a trade route between Kabul and Kandahar. Victim to periodic incursions and general decline for a millennium, the town was a market for corn, fruit, camel-hair cloth, wool, and sheep. It is recognized for the manufacture of the highly renowned Afghan sheepskin coat.

John Barnhill

See also: Mongol Invasions; Silk Road.

BIBLIOGRAPHY

Bosworth, Clifford Edmund. *The Ghaznavids: Their Empire in Afghanistan and Eastern Iran, 994–1040*. Edinburgh: Edinburgh University Press, 1963.

———. *The Medieval History of Iran, Afghanistan, and Central Asia*. London: Variorum Reprints, 1977.

"Ghazni, Afghanistan." Columbia University Press, 1993 (www.afghan-network.net/Culture/ghazni.html, accessed October 2002).

"The History of Afghanistan." 2000 (http://hinduwebsite.com/history/afghan.htm, accessed August 2002).

"Mahmud of Ghazni 971 A.D.–1030 A.D." Afghan-network (www.afghan-network.net/Rulers/mahmud-ghazni.html, accessed August 2002).

Pugachenkova, G.A., A.H. Dani, and Liu Yingshen. "Urban Development and Architecture, History of Civilizations of Central Asia" (www.unesco.org/culture/asia/html_eng/chapitre4218/chapitre4.htm, accessed June 2002).

GLASS

> Objects made of glass, from utilitarian to luxury items, have been traded since ancient times.

The earliest glassmaking technologies probably emerged along with early metallurgy within river civilizations that could combine fine sands, ash (soda), and lime with high heat to create opaque glass. Both Sumerian and Egyptian archaeological sites have yielded small beads that date to the early third century B.C.E. No doubt these brilliant objects were traded from the first, and widespread trade was likely in the hands of Phoenician merchants. By the mid-second millennium B.C.E., Near Eastern glassmakers were producing much more sophisticated hollow ware, such as bowls, cups, and vases. Over the next centuries, the technology spread around the Mediterranean and developed in China, but sand types, recipes for additives, and forms of objects differed among the cultures, and markets remained active.

Around the turn of the common millennium, glassblowing was discovered in the eastern Roman empire, creating an even wider variety of forms for sale. In about 100 C.E., Alexandrians—the finest glass artisans of the Roman period—developed the technology for producing clear glass, and archaeological evidence shows its limited use in Roman window enclosures. As with other technologies, with the fall of the Roman empire the East retained a high level of production quality and trade circulation, while the Germanic-controlled West produced pedestrian works for the localized luxury trade.

The early medieval Byzantine and Islamic worlds thus inherited a tradition of fine glassmaking and active trading, while the Latin West had to await a revival of trade and technology. Venice played a key role in this, serving as a linchpin between the Eastern and Western worlds, and northern Europe eventually developed its own recipes and forms. Self-reliance led to innovation and invention, and eventually to the great stained glass windows of the Gothic north. By the later Middle Ages, the clear-glass windowpanes, often round or diamond shaped, were not uncommon in wealthy homes north and south. The particulars of Venetian fine glass production were considered state secrets, and their products—many simply utilitarian objects like mirrors, beads, and cups—were widely traded, dominating Mediterranean markets. The association of Venetian glass with the island of Murano has been of long standing, but the official relegation of the industry to that center dates from 1291.

The material revolution that began in the European Renaissance called forth ever-new demands for glass objects, and craftsmen met these with vigor and genius. In the seventeenth century, Moravian craftsmanship and French mercantilism shifted the center of European production away from the Mediterranean. Advances in optical science created demands for finely ground lenses for spectacles, telescopes, and microscopes. In 1674, Englishman George Ravenscroft patented lead crystal, whose brilliance and clarity eclipsed Venetian wares. In Jamestown, Virginia, the production of windowpanes and bottles was the settlement's first industry. The New Amsterdam Dutch, from the beginning of their colony, marketed stained and painted glass products and traded glass beads to Native Americans.

The Industrial Revolution and modern industry have continued the tradition of innovation in both production and products, though in the twentieth century an increasingly wider range of plastics and other synthetic materials have come to play many of the past roles of glass.

Joseph P. Byrne

See also: Genoa.

BIBLIOGRAPHY
Macfarlane, Alan. *Glass: A World History.* Chicago: University of Chicago Press, 2002.

GLOBALIZATION

> Typically referring to the greater integration of economic activities around the world, globalization is a historical process driven primarily by human innovation and technological change.

People around the world are more closely and unexpectedly interconnected than ever before. People travel across national boundaries and over greater geographical distances more often, much faster, and under fewer restrictions now than only half a century ago. Advances in communications and transportation technologies make it possible for information and money to flow quickly and more freely through avenues hardly imaginable a quarter-century ago. New technologies enable people to organize themselves and relate to each other in novel ways. Goods and services produced in one part of the world are increasingly and more reliably available elsewhere. These are some of the key facets of a phenomenon, or a historical process, commonly referred to as "globalization." In popular parlance, the age of globalization is also synonymous with the contemporary era. It is a historical period ushered in by the advent of satellite and electronic communications, punctuated by the end of the Cold War, and characterized by the collapse of time and space and the standardization of experience around the globe.

ORIGINS OF GLOBALIZATION

Globalization, by its nature, is a vastly complex and multifaceted subject. There is no single definition of globalization agreed on among scholars, activists, and policy practitioners. Nor is there any consensus among students of globalization as to when the process began as a distinct long-term pattern in the ways individuals, groups, and societies have conducted themselves and interacted with each other. World-systems theorists, most notably Immanuel Wallerstein, argue that the processes typically meant in current commentaries by the term "globalization" are not new, as they have existed for some 500 years. The present global situation is a transition in which the capitalist world-system, which had emerged first in Europe by the sixteenth century, is evolving into something that has yet to be determined. Scholars who study the globalization of popular culture tend to locate the emergence of globalization in the latter part of the twentieth century. By focusing on a mass media–generated homogenizing world culture or by questioning its existence, their debate has loosely evolved around the notion of what anthropologist Marshall McLuhan calls "the Global Village" in his *Gutenberg Galaxy* (1962).

Thomas L. Friedman, an American journalist considered by some the guru of globalization, sets forth a slightly different timeframe in his agenda-setting *The Lexus and the Olive Tree* (2000). He argues that globalization hit the world in two waves. Round I lasted from the mid-1800s to the late 1900s, with Round II opening with the end of the Cold War and the collapse of the Soviet Union. The roughly seventy-five-year period from the start of World War I to the end of the Cold War can be seen as "a long time-out between one era of globalization and another." The post–Cold War phase of globalization is clearly central to Friedman's concept of globalization. The world in this period is driven by free-market capitalism characterized by "opening, deregulating, and privatizing," creating an increasingly uniform global culture, and defined by new technologies: computerization, digitization, satellite communications, fiber optics, and the Internet.

In a similar vein, the globalization literature produced by global society theorists such as Anthony Giddens and Roland Robertson holds that the concept of global society has become a viable notion only in the modern age, more specifically, in the twentieth century. Sociologist Leslie Sklair sees globalization as a consequence of post-1960s capitalism powered by transnational practices in three interconnected spheres: economic, political, and cultural-ideological.

DEFINITION OF TERM

The term "globalization" has also become a heavily coded word, having acquired a powerful emotive force when invoked by opinion leaders across the ideological spectrum. The concept's celebrants tout it as a process that is highly beneficial and fundamentally benign. Less enthusiastic adherents regard it more neutrally as a key to the future, a pathway to continuous world economic development and social change. It follows from these positive views that globalization is both inevitable and irreversible. Many in this loosely aligned ideological camp tend to use globalization and Americanization interchangeably. Globalization's detractors counter that the pro-

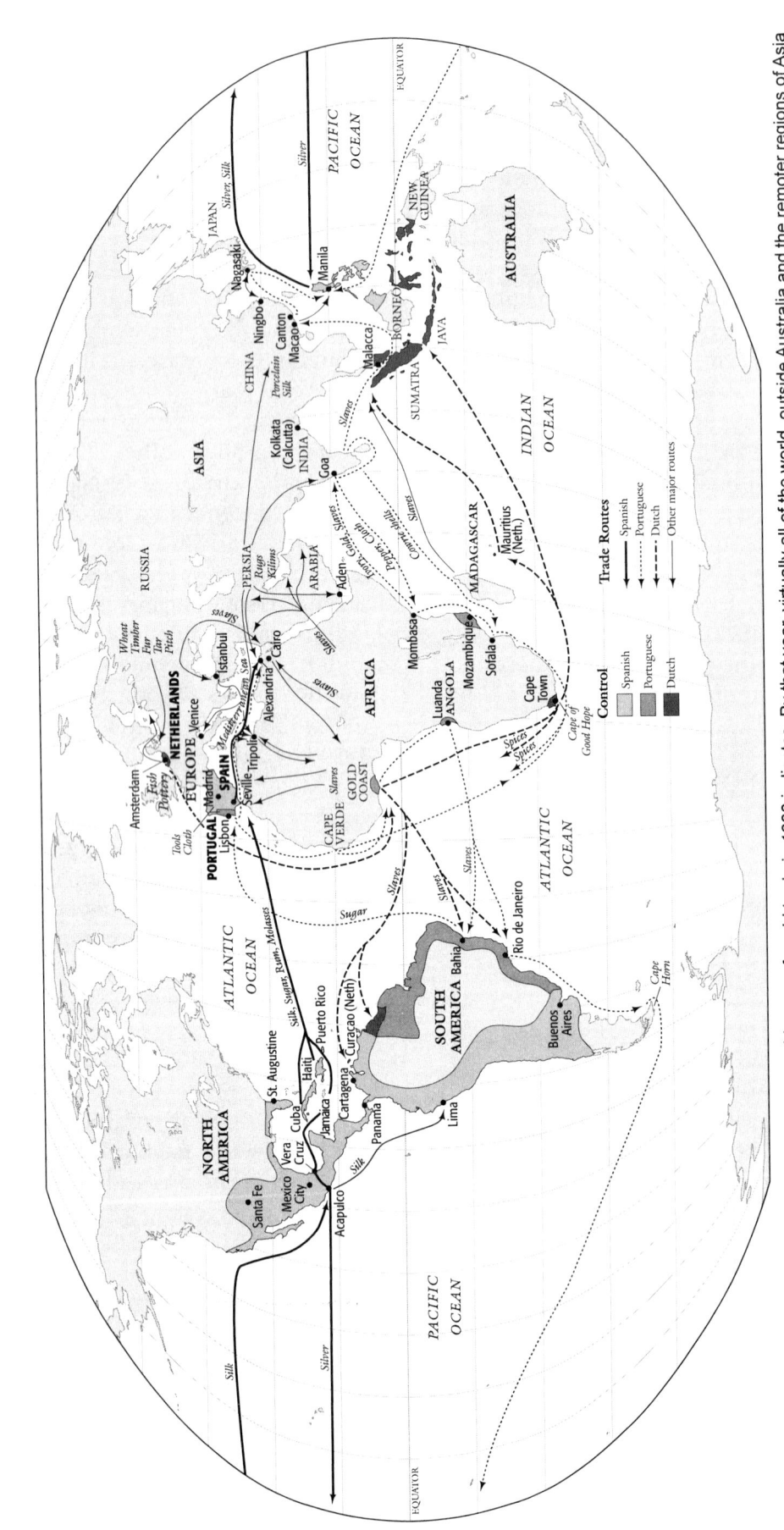

Global Economy, 1600 Globalization is nothing new, as this map of world trade in 1600 indicates. By that year, virtually all of the world, outside Australia and the remoter regions of Asia and North America, were part of the global trading network. (*Mark Stein Studios*)

cess is inherently detrimental. It widens inequality within and among nation-states. It exacerbates existing social injustices. Globalization, the critics argue, may create more opportunities for some people but threatens jobs and lowers living standards for others. Furthermore, globalization has corrosive effects on local ways of life and threatens to homogenize and vulgarize regional cultures.

The dissenters share a tendency to believe that globalization is neither inevitable nor a condition to which there is no alternative. Such skepticism is not the exclusive province of academicians such as Wallerstein. It encompasses former operators of institutions popularly associated with globalization, such as Joseph Stiglitz, the former chief economist of the World Bank. With these varied visions of globalization in mind, this survey highlights some aspects of globalization defined as an evolving socioeconomic system that achieved significant coherence in the latter half of the twentieth century. It also examines globalization as a cluster of cultural phenomena that have unfolded in roughly the same period.

Globalization, as the term has come into common usage since the 1980s, is a historical process driven primarily by human innovation and technological change. It typically refers to the greater integration of economic activities around the world, particularly through increased, faster-paced, and more variegated trade and capital flows made possible by advances in communications technologies, such as cheaper international telephone rates, cell phones, faxes, the Internet, and other means of electronic transactions. Globalization also means the accelerated movement of labor and information across international borders. More people now migrate across existing national boundaries aided by a greater range of affordable means and sprawling networks of transportation. In doing so, these workers carry knowledge, skills, and ideas with them. An increasing number of people now produce and deliver goods and services in and from locations farther removed from points of consumption. These human dimensions of worldwide interconnectedness create broader cultural, political, and environmental effects. In short, globalization refers to a projection beyond the borders of the modern nation-states policed by complex governing mechanisms of the type of market forces that have operated for centuries at all levels and units of human economic activity.

Since the advent of capitalism, markets have promoted efficiency through competition and the division of labor among people and their various aggregates, including national economies. Globally connected markets offer more ways for some people to tap into more and larger markets around the world and to gain access to more capital flows, technology, and labor. But markets have not necessarily guaranteed that all participants in this process equally share the benefits of improved efficiency. Nor have markets been the most reliable purveyors of social justice. This basic limitation of markets remains intact and in some cases becomes magnified in the global marketplace.

GLOBALIZATION AND POST–WORLD WAR II ORDER

The twentieth century was a period of unparalleled economic growth, and global per capita gross domestic product (GDP) during this time increased almost fivefold. The strongest expansion came during the second half of the century. The United States became the engine of that massive growth because the nation came out of World War II with its economy unscathed. Buttressed by political and military alliances with this unrivaled economic superpower, many countries in Western Europe and Japan underwent a period of relatively smooth and orderly postwar reconstruction in the midcentury and embarked on a sustained economic growth after the 1960s. Nations in East Asia, most notably Taiwan and South Korea, also underwent a period of rapid economic expansion in the 1980s and thereafter. Liberalization of trade within the capitalist world took place under the auspices of the Bretton Woods institutions such as the General Agreement on Tariffs and Trade during this period. This was typically followed by financial liberalization that gathered momentum in the industrial world in the 1970s.

Even those analysts who argue that the world economy was just as globalized 100 years ago as it is today generally agree that financial services are far more developed and the transactions are more extensively intertwined today than they were in the early twentieth century. The single most important driving force of the integration of financial markets is modern electronic communications. But the bulk of the developing countries have been largely left out of this financial integrative process until the last two decades of the twentieth century. When capital accumulated through the worldwide increase in oil prices in the 1970s was recycled to many of the developing countries, they became integrated into the global financial system as large-scale debtors. During the Cold War, nations in the communist bloc remained largely left out of the rapidly integrating global financial markets.

The twentieth century witnessed remarkable average income growth in the industrialized world, but the progress in aggregate and/or personal incomes was not evenly dispersed around the globe. The gaps between rich and poor countries, and rich and poor people within countries, grew further in the latter half of the twentieth century. The richest quarter of the world's population comprising members of the Organization for Economic Cooperation and Development saw its per capita gross national product (GNP) increase nearly sixfold during the century. The poorest quarter, mostly non-oil-producing nations in Africa and Latin America, experienced less than a threefold increase. Per capita incomes in Africa have, in particular, declined relative to the industrial countries and in some countries have declined in absolute terms.

GLOBALIZATION IN THE LAST QUARTER OF THE TWENTIETH CENTURY

In the last quarter of the twentieth century, this polarizing trend became more pronounced. Developing countries as a whole increased their share of world trade from 19 percent in 1971 to 29 percent in 1999. There were significant variations among the world's major regions as well. The newly industrialized economies of East Asia and Southeast Asia did well, while Africa as a whole lagged behind other regional units. Among other variables, the composition of export factored into the widening gap. Countries that export manufactured goods recorded the greatest rise in per capita GNP. The share of primary commodities in world exports declined in the post–World War II period. This category of exports, comprising foodstuffs and raw materials, were often produced and exported by the poorest countries in the world, most of them former colonies of European empires. Various forums sponsored by the United Nations and other multilateral institutions began to address problems unique to commodity-producing countries in the 1960s. Liberalization of agricultural trade, however, remains one of the most intractable challenges today.

As political scientist Linda Weiss notes, as of 1991, 81 percent of the world stock of foreign direct investment was still concentrated in high-wage countries of the North. In a phenomenon popularly associated with the term "globalization," a sharp increase in private capital flows to developing countries took place in the 1990s. But these private capital transfers to the developing countries have not taken place on equal terms. Critics of financial globalization argue that intergovernmental financial institutions have participated in the inequitable terms of capital transactions between the net capital exporter countries and the developing world. This typically occurs when the developing countries or nations shifting from command to free-market economies are required to privatize certain economic sectors or open them up to foreign investment as a condition for receiving loans. Assets in the newly privatized or deregulated sectors are then quickly taken over by foreign capital moving in from the industrial North, particularly the United States. United Kingdom–based American muckraking journalist Greg Palast elaborates on the mechanics of such "privatization" programs as Bolivia's water supply systems in 2000. He charges that these cases reveal a dark side of global financial "cooperation" that is not frequently reported in the U.S. mass media.

While conversion to the free-market system has been generally arduous, not all former communist states have traveled on a rocky path to integration into the global economy. Given the diversity of experience among former communist states, some observers note that the term "transition economy" is losing its conceptual usefulness.

Countries such as Poland and Hungary are converging relatively smoothly toward performance approaching that of advanced industrial economies. Others, particularly most of the former Soviet republics, confront long-term structural and institutional challenges similar to those faced by developing countries. China also constitutes a unique case, reporting strong growth but demonstrating dramatic gaps between the vibrant and rapidly expanding state-sanctioned free-market zones and the laggard rural areas.

The composition of private capital flows from the industrial world to developing countries changed dramatically in the 1990s as well. Direct foreign investment has become the most important category of cross-border capital movement. Portfolio investment and bank credit among relatively capital-rich countries rose, but they have been extremely volatile and have fallen sharply in the wake of the financial crisis of the late 1990s. The string of financial crises that shook Mexico, Thailand, Indonesia, Korea, Russia, and Brazil suggested to some that financial crises and disruptive volatility are a direct and inevitable result of globalization. Net flows of public capital in the form of official government aid or development assistance have fallen significantly since the early 1980s. Among industrial countries, official development assistance fell to 0.24 percent of GDP in 1998 in advanced countries in contrast to the United Nations' announced target of 0.7 percent. The overall picture thus points to the increased influence and unpredictability of private financial forces in the global capital markets, the type of relatively unregulated mass of economic force labeled by Thomas Friedman as "the electronic herd."

GLOBALIZATION AND LABOR

Since time immemorial, people have been moving from one place to another to find better employment opportunities and to pursue intangible values such as political and religious freedoms. The last half of the twentieth century saw an accelerated pace of the cross-border labor migration. In the period between 1965 and 1990, the proportion of the labor force around the world that was foreign born increased by about half.

This trend has been particularly conspicuous in the United States, where the changes in immigration law since 1965 have made it easier for the immediate family members of legal immigrants to move to the country. Although not commonly known, most migration still occurs between developing countries. At the same time, the increasing flow of migrants from developing countries to industrial economies in the past few decades carries several implications. First, certain economic sectors of industrialized countries will grow more dependent on continual flows of labor migration from overseas, resulting in a sharper segmentation of labor markets. Second, it may provide a way for global wages and living standards to converge. Remittances by workers to their home countries will likely play an important role in the process.

Another important implication is the sharing of skills and technical knowledge upon return to the country of origin or among fellow workers in the host country; in either venue, such sharing is facilitated by electronic communications media. Such information exchange is an integral aspect of globalization, and various agents of globalization other than individual workers and their personal networks partake in this process. For example, increased direct foreign investment means not only an expansion in the physical capital stock but also a movement of technical innovation, patent privileges, and licensing arrangements. Knowledge about production methods, marketing and advertising information, and management techniques is also dispersed to the developing countries as a result of direct foreign investment.

The ubiquity of antiglobalization sentiments in the industrialized world shows that a significant number of workers feel threatened by "low-wage economies." The competition, either perceived or real, comes from two main sources. Laborers migrating from low-wage countries may displace workers holding less-skilled jobs in higher-wage countries. Manufacturers and producers of certain goods and services may ship their facilities wholesale to overseas locations where wages are lower, labor is not unionized, and regulatory regimes are less rigid and encompassing. This greater mobility of globalization affords private economic players to create a profound public policy dilemma. In a trend shared among industrial countries, as national economies mature, they become more service-oriented to meet the changing demands and rising expectations of their populace. While globalization alone is by no means responsible for this general trend, it quickens the speed of the shift and different socioeconomic groups within a country feel the reverberations unevenly. The concept of globalization thus generates starkly varied responses from different segments of society.

The globalization debate in the industrialized world has largely hinged on what constitutes the appropriate response to this policy conundrum. Is it the responsibility of government to try to protect particular groups, such as low-skilled workers or those employed in "sunset" industries, by controlling international trade and capital flows or adopting restrictive immigration policy? Or should governments pursue policies that encourage further integration into the global economy by accepting international division of labor but institute safety nets to soften the blow to those adversely affected by the changes? If so, what are the parameters of politically acceptable and practically feasible adjustment assistance?

GLOBALIZATION AND NATIONAL SOVEREIGNTY

Another focus of policy debate and scholarly inquiry has been whether or not globalization reduces national sovereignty in policy making. International relations theorist Kenneth Waltz argued in his 1999 James Madison Lecture before the American Political Science Association that the nation-states will continue to display a great deal of resilience and adaptability in this regard. As a mechanism of governance, national systems still possess a range of options accompanied by coercive enforcement and, in that respect, the nation-states are unmatched by any other political entity. But does increased global integration, notably in the financial sphere, make it more difficult for individual governments to manage their domestic economic activities? Some observers emphasize, for example, the international financial market's ability to limit governments' options in setting domestic tax rates and designing internal tax structures. The freedom of action of each nation regarding monetary policy, too, has often been curtailed. While globalization does not necessarily reduce national sovereignty per se, it does create a strong mandate for national governments to pursue certain types of economic policies. In a world of highly integrated financial markets characterized by great short-term volatility, national governments will find it all the more imprudent to adopt policies that may threaten the nation's financial and monetary stability and thus invite a flight of international capital. The "electronic herd" is extremely fickle and footloose.

Many students of international political economy nonetheless maintain that the nation-state will remain central to any efforts to manage the international financial markets, even though the task of stabilizing short-term capital movements must be shared with the international financial institutions, most importantly the International Monetary Fund (IMF). Some apostles of free market have expressed concern that such supranational entities place excessive constraints on private-sector business activities. Others hold different kinds of apprehension about the international institutions' role in managing the vagaries of cross-border capital flows.

As Waltz reiterates in the aforementioned lecture, the world is fundamentally a system without centralized governance. In such a sphere, the influence of the members who possess greater capacity is disproportionately powerful since there are no effective laws or ultimate authorities to dictate or constrain them. Influential nations, particularly the all-powerful United States, can also work multilateral mechanisms to their advantage. They are capable of creating and sustaining a set of rules governing the international political economy that primarily serve their national interests. That some critics think of the IMF as another enforcement arm of the U.S. Treasury stems from those realities of power in international relations, and hence, anti-Americanism's great appeal and resonance among antiglobalists everywhere in the world.

The question of national sovereignty is also germane to an examination of globalization's cultural fallout. Is globalization creating a homogenizing global culture and undermining the national state's role as the gatekeeper of culture? Is an emergent global culture incubated in the global village eroding the basis of national and local identities? Some observers argue that a standardized world culture already exists for educated cosmopolitan individuals and privileged socioeconomic groups across the globe. Embracing similar worldviews and lifestyles, these cosmopolitans putatively form a coherent elite class united across national boundaries. They identify with one another far more than with their less sophisticated compatriots with a parochial worldview. Political scientist Samuel Huntington refers to such a transnational elite class in *The Clash of Civilizations and the Remaking of World Order* (1997). It is a disparate functional group, comprising people with careers in international finance, media, technology, and diplomacy.

Some sociologists include another type of cosmopolitan elite in this class: a global web of academicians and researchers, espousing similar ideals, curiosities, and attitudes toward political participation. They exercise influence through their affiliation with educational institutions, think tanks, international scholarly networks, and multidirectional circulation of study-abroad students and visiting scholars. Many of them are involved in the activities of nongovernmental organizations and thus project their values and agendas to the international arena by bringing to the fore such issues as environmentalism, health and food safety, the regulation of multinational corporate behaviors, and universal human rights. Antiglobalism draws much of its strength from this group as well. Most of these individuals and organizations situate themselves on the right side of the global "digital divide" and mobilize and fund-raise aggressively through the Internet.

Another type of transnational subgroups has also formed out of migrating workforces. Anthropologist Arjun Appadurai examines in detail such forces in his *Modernity at Large* (1996). This cadre includes not only low-skill laborers moving across national borders in search of better pay and a haven from various forms of social oppression. It also encompasses highly educated and skilled professionals who participate in the emerging transnational service sector that is relatively untethered by geographical constraints on production and delivery. For example, Appadurai's study highlights English-speaking East Indian nationals who moved to California's Silicon Valley and contributed to the area's entrepreneurial energies in software engineering and e-commerce in the 1990s. A growing portion of telemarketing and billing services for U.S. corporations is now performed from locations outside the United States. Unlike transnational migrant workers of earlier times, these digital-age foreign workers tend to retain multiple home bases and remain embedded in several social networks extending over national borders. Inexpensive international telephone rates, air travel, and, most recently, e-mail make it possible for these expatriates to retain multiple allegiances.

"GLOBAL VILLAGE"

The broadening domain of shared experiences and sensual stimulation among people inhabiting the "wired" part of the world also causes national borders to thin out in matters of cultural formation. The rapid integration of visual media, particularly the worldwide diffusion of television, was a key element in McLuhan's vaunted notion of the global village. The spread of American-style television programming and news reportage began in the early postwar period. The American television network pioneered production techniques in this new medium, and other media outlets in the industrial West largely emulated the know-how until the 1960s. Foreign aid programs undertaken by the U.S. Information Agency during the Cold War also deeply influenced the development trajectories of visual and print media in the noncommunist world.

What is newsworthy is being increasingly determined by a handful of media giants that dominate over the massively expensive communications infrastructure.

With the advent of cable and satellite broadcasting, the American-style media culture began to penetrate deeper into myriad nooks and crannies of the world round the clock. The global presence of CNN is a case in point. This geographical

The spread of U.S. fast-food franchises around the world has become a metaphor for cultural homogenization and has often incurred the wrath of antiglobalists. Pictured here is a McDonald's restaurant in the Santa Maria Novella train station in Florence, Italy. (© Jim West/The Image Works)

and temporal proliferation came in tandem with the emergence of global media conglomerates that control other aspects of the mass culture, including Hollywood studio films, music, and commercial publishing. Visual images disseminated worldwide through these conduits shape viewers' aspirations about material culture (food and beverages, clothing and fashion, household appliances, and means of transportation) and attitudes toward such social standards as idealized beauty, acceptable sexuality, comfort, and interpersonal relations.

The rise of global conglomerates facilitated the standardization of other facets of individual experience, creating the illusion of a global uniform culture. The spread of American fast food franchises around the world has become a metaphor for cultural homogenization and has often incurred the wrath of antiglobalists. The missionaries of American fast food and soft drinks, such as McDonald's, Coca-Cola, Kentucky Fried Chicken, and Pizza Hut, proselytized the world with a diet high in fat and sugar and a culture of throw-away packaging and utensils. The effects of the exported consumptive practices are not limited to obvious health risks. They have also yielded deleterious environmental impacts on these locales.

But culinary culture's disseminating paths have not shepherded one-way traffic either. As historians Warren Cohen and Donna Gabbaccia note, America's own foodways have gone through profound change, particularly since the late 1960s. Cultural anthropologists attribute Americans' growing acceptance of "ethnic food" to various factors, including unlikely political origins. For instance, American GIs and their dependents returning from their overseas posts are given partial credit for increasing the popularity of Asian and Middle Eastern food among Americans not fitting the traditional cosmopolitan mold. The massive family driven immigration after the 1965 immigration and reform and the recent growth in intermarriage have created more diverse ethnic communities in America and thus enlarged markets for cuisine previously dismissed as too exotic.

Since the mid-1960s, the cost of international travel has dropped significantly, and foreign travel has become affordable for many middle- and even working-class people around the world. With the growth in popular tourism came the demand for hotels, food, toiletries, and recreational services that approximate, if not completely duplicate, standard American expectations. When Americans travel to any major city or tourist destination in the world, they can assuredly expect the same kinds of experience, services, and comfort levels they take for granted back home. The benefits of global standardization also extend to the minute levels to ensure the duplication of hometown experience: thanks to the uniform thickness of credit cards, they can be used at any place in the world where merchants are equipped to handle such cashless transactions.

The increasingly similar material conditions and sensory universe surrounding people in certain parts of the world are no doubt creating greater uniformity in consumption styles. It does not mean, however, that globalization is obliterating national, regional, and local identities and creating an undifferentiated global culture. There is plenty of empirical evidence presented by anthropologists, sociologists, and historians that indicate that receivers of American-style cultural wares worldwide deftly appropriate the originals and create localized variants or distinct syntheses. They often invest their own meanings into

American artifacts and practices that have little, if any, to do with the original American contexts. In *Not Like Us* (1997), historian Richard H. Pells depicts the subtle and complex interplay between American cultural icons and institutions introduced into Europe in the postwar period and local resistance to and reconfiguration of the American intrusions.

In a collection of anthropological essays aptly titled *Remade in Japan* (1992), Joseph Tobin and other contributors to the volume show how contemporary food, clothing, household furnishings, and leisure activities in Japan can be more accurately described as a pastiche of indigenous Japanese and appropriated Western elements. It is probably safe to argue that James Cameron, when he directed *Titanic,* never intended his handiwork to be embraced enthusiastically by aging veterans of the Chinese Cultural Revolution. But they did and used the Hollywood blockbuster as a politically safe vehicle for publicly grieving over the carefree youth and romance denied to them. The "politically safe" is the operative phrase here, however. Once the state authorities decide that such a public expression of regret for lost opportunities is disruptive and threatening, they can choke off that avenue of trafficking in invested meanings. The nation-state, in that respect, remains the most powerful arbiter of cultural politics, if not the one and only.

As people's everyday life and sensory experience appear to converge inexorably under the rubric of globalization, local culture, identity, and the human networks that produce them remain irreplaceable. Place still matters to many people; it is just that they have greater freedom from the dictates of place. The breakthroughs in communications technology that are triggering the current unique phase of worldwide convergence and compression also permit people to hold multiple identities and embed themselves in multiple webs of human relationships without having to give up others.

Sayuri Guthrie-Shimizu

See also: Columbian Exchange; European Union; Trade Organizations; Wars for Empire; World War I; World War II.

BIBLIOGRAPHY

Appadurai, Arjun. *Modernity at Large: Cultural Dimensions of Globalization.* Minneapolis: University of Minnesota, 1996.

Friedman, Thomas L. *The Lexus and the Olive Tree.* New York: Farrar, Straus, Giroux, 2000.

Huntington, Samuel. *The Clash of Civilizations and the Remaking of World Order.* New York: Touchstone, 1997.

McLuhan, Marshall. *The Gutenberg Galaxy: The Making of Typographic Man.* Toronto: University of Toronto Press, 1962.

Pells, Richard H. *Not Like Us: How Europeans Have Loved, Hated, and Transformed American Culture Since World War II.* New York: Basic, 1997.

Tobin, Joseph. *Remade in Japan: Everyday Life and Consumer Taste in a Changing Society.* New Haven: Yale University Press, 1992.

Wallerstein, Immanuel. *Geopoliticas and Geoculture: Essays on the Changing World System.* New York: Cambridge University Press, 1991.

GOLD

The oldest metal used by humans as specie or in ornaments and jewelry.

Gold is abundant in many places throughout the world, but the cost of mining the metal is often prohibitive. Gold is found in the form of dust, flakes, grains, and nuggets and is often mixed with other metals such as silver when found in the ground. Since the metal is not affected by moisture or oxygen, it is ideal for jewelry worn next to the skin.

The earliest pieces of jewelry located in burial tombs in both Egypt and Ur were made of gold. The skill of the goldsmith produced intricate pieces that combined gold with gemstones such as turquoise. The ancient Israelites, under the reign of King Solomon, used gold to decorate the pillars of the temple and the ornaments used in it. But perhaps the one ancient civilization where goldsmiths excelled was the Minoan culture. Gold was pounded into thin sheets used to produce masks with filigree work. Ornate jewelry and gold objects attracted traders from other parts of the Mediterranean, and the Minoans soon dominated trade throughout the region. The Greeks and the Romans used gold for jewelry for the upper classes. Roman jewelry included cameos, earrings, headdresses, and necklaces that contained gold and sometimes precious gemstones as well.

During the Middle Ages, gold from the sub-Saharan region was traded for salt. Ancient Ghana supplied much of the precious metal that was desired for the production of coinage by civilization around the Mediterranean. By the eleventh century, the Mali empire replaced Ghana as the supplier of gold. Arab traders crossed the Sahara with their caravans of camels to trade for the gold. They were not able to locate the gold mines since the rulers insisted that the location remain secret. Europeans used the gold for coin as well as jewelry. The Catholic Church used some of the gold in its artwork and in the illuminated manuscripts. The introduction of gold into Mediterranean economies did not produce an adverse effect until 1324–1325, when Mansa Musa, the ruler of Mali, arrived in Egypt with a ton of gold. Adding that much gold into the economy created inflation and an economic crisis.

After the discovery of the New World, gold flowed into the Spanish treasury in unregulated amounts. The Spanish monarchs, who had just forced the Jewish moneylenders with their knowledge of financial management out of the country, used the gold recklessly. Between 1500 and 1650, more than 181 tons of gold and 16,000 tons of silver were transferred from the New World to Spain. Gold fueled the economy of not only Spain but also of England and Holland. English seadogs like Sir Francis Drake pirated bullion from the Spanish galleons that sailed once a year back to Spain laden with precious metals and other cargo. But in Spain the introduction of so much gold created inflation and became the downfall of its empire.

The availability of gold bullion allowed European nations to mint coin that was used as specie for the payment of goods. The use of gold allowed west European nations to expand their markets, although on a limited basis, into a global economy. However, gold was still limited in supply, and these nations turned to mercantilism to protect the wealth that they had gained.

During the seventeenth century, gold was used widely throughout the Mughal empire. In China, gold was used primarily by royalty of the various dynasties beginning in the common era. The Chinese introduced the use of gold and goldsmith skills to Korea, but the Japanese never used gold on an extensive basis.

During the nineteenth century, Americans pushed westward. While the United States was engaged in war with Mexico over the annexation of Texas, Americans declared California a free republic. In 1849, prospectors discovered gold in the hills of California and a gold rush followed. The introduction of gold into the U.S. economy helped the nation, especially since world economies had begun to adopt the gold standard, with Great Britain being the first in 1821. By the 1870s, the other European countries had agreed that a nation would not issue more currency than the amount that was backed by gold. When the United States began purchasing silver in the 1890s, foreign investors became reluctant to purchase U.S. bonds. President Grover Cleveland pushed for the repeal of the Sherman Silver Purchase Act after the panic of 1893 brought the nation close to bankruptcy. The use of the gold standard continued until World War I, when European nations suspended the redemption of currency in gold. The United States continued to honor the arrangement except during the Great Depression, when gold exports were halted. In 1971, the United States, facing stagflation, abandoned the gold standard and was the last nation to do so.

During the twentieth century, the primary producer of gold (and diamonds) was South Africa. The country operated under a system of apartheid, and the international community decided to place an embargo on South African gold until the system was abolished in 1991.

Meanwhile, the price of gold was affected by the financial crises of the 1980s. The price of gold rose to over $800 an ounce in the early 1980s. Since then, the price dropped to around $200 an ounce before rebounding in December 2003 to over $400 an ounce. Gold has been touted as a way of protecting one's investment in the uncertain times after the 2001 terrorist attacks in New York and Washington, DC.

Cynthia Clark Northrup

See also: Discovery and Exploration.

BIBLIOGRAPHY

Bordo, Michael D. *The Gold Standard, Bretton Woods and Other Monetary Regimes: A Historical Appraisal.* Cambridge, MA: National Bureau of Economic Research, 1993.

Crosby, Alfred. *The Columbian Exchange: Biological and Cultural Consequences of 1492.* Westport: Greenwood, 1972.

Pomeroy, William J. *Apartheid, Imperialism, and African Freedom.* New York: International, 1986.

GOLD STANDARD

> A monetary system in which units are defined in terms of their value to gold.

The gold standard is a monetary system in which gold coins (or other forms of money backed by a fixed quantity of gold) were used as the standard unit of currency. In the domestic context, the government would guarantee the conversion of its currency into a fixed amount of gold. At the international level, gold or a currency backed by gold is used as a means of payments between countries. In such a system, the exchange rate would be fixed, and only small fluctuations are allowed as long as they do not exceed the cost of shipping gold from one country to another.

According to classical economist David Hume's specie-flow mechanism, if the exports of a given country are greater than its imports, an inflow of gold will take place, leading to an increase in the money supply within the country. This would cause domestic prices to go up and exceed foreign prices, which would cause exports to fall and imports to rise up to the point where exports and imports become equal. Similarly, if the imports of a given country are greater than its exports, an outflow of gold will take place, leading to a decrease in the money supply within the country. This would cause domestic prices to fall, which would cause imports to fall and exports to rise up to the point where exports and imports equalize again.

HISTORY OF THE GOLD STANDARD

The gold standard was first established in 1821 by England, followed by major world economies. A bimetallic gold-silver system prevailed throughout the world until France, Germany, and the United States abandoned silver in the 1870s because of discoveries of new gold mines. The gold standard disappeared from 1914 to 1928, when countries restricted gold exports during the war period. The Great Depression also led many countries to opt out of the gold-exchange standard during the 1930s.

After World War II, the United States was able to reestablish an international gold standard by fixing the value of the U.S. dollar in terms of gold and having all other countries peg their currencies to the U.S. dollar. All central banks around the world (except the U.S. Federal Reserve Bank) used U.S. dollars and gold as reserve currencies.

In 1971, the gold standard was finally abandoned for good when the United States declared its currency no longer convertible into gold because of a lack of gold reserves and the increasingly negative U.S. balance of payments. In principle, exchange rates were allowed to float freely. Most central banks, however, have adopted a "dirty-float" policy by intervening in the foreign-exchange market to avoid large appreciations or depreciations of their national currency.

Behind the apparent convenience of the gold standard that many policy makers have admired was a misleading strong belief in its theoretical foundations that dominated the way economists formulated their theoretical positions and policy prescriptions with regard to international trade, employment, inflation, and growth. More than three decades after the demise of the gold standard, many economists still formulate theory and policy as if the world were still operating under an international gold standard.

ARGUMENTS FOR AND AGAINST

The proponents of the gold standard argue that such a system would reduce the amount of risk involved in international trade by providing a stable pattern for exchange rates. At the domestic level, a gold standard system could help in limiting the power of governments (through their central banks) to cause inflation by printing more money than warranted by their gold reserves. Critics of the gold standard, however, argue that central banks in practice have rarely reduced the level of money supply when their economy experienced an outflow of gold.

The gold standard was an inherently rigid system because of its ultimate reliance on the quantity of gold available in the system. It did not allow for the flexibility necessary to accommodate the needs of a dynamic economy. A fast-growing economy often finds itself in a liquidity crisis because of the mismatch between the quantity of money in circulation and the high demand for money required to keep the economy on a sustainable growth path.

Lack of liquidity is even worse for economies with high unemployment and slow economic growth. These economies need to increase exports to accumulate more gold and be able to expand the quantity of money domestically. But increasing exports often requires an initial expansion of the money supply through bank credit or government spending; both of which would be difficult to achieve under a gold standard system.

It could be argued that the gold standard has continued to overshadow mainstream economic thinking to this day. Many developing countries as well as economies in transition have adopted a currency board arrangement. Under such a system, a country seeks to implement a self-restraining monetary policy by fully backing its national currency by a strong foreign currency such as the U.S. dollar or the euro. The central bank can issue a national currency bill or coin only if it has its U.S. dollar or euro equivalent in reserve.

The so-called dollarization process in many Latin American countries is essentially the same thing as adopting a currency board arrangement, which means that the dollarized country cannot have any effective control over its fiscal and monetary policies. In such a case, during a recession the government cannot increase deficit spending to compensate for social and economic distress. However, many leading economists at the World Bank and the International Monetary Fund do not understand that these policies are remnants from the gold standard system and therefore do not apply to the modern monetary system.

L. Randall Wray has written that, in a nongold standard system, tax payments *do not* and *cannot* finance government spending; at the aggregate level, only the government can be the "net" supplier of fiat money. As a result, after government spends (creates or supplies) fiat money to purchase goods and services, it provides the public with the necessary amount of money to meet tax liabilities.

According to Wray's analysis, the government (theoretically) can have a balanced budget, meaning that the public's net money receipts are equal to tax liabilities. However, if the government attempts to run a surplus, the public's net money receipts would run behind tax liabilities. Therefore, the only way for households to pay their tax liabilities is either to use their hoarded money from previous government deficits or to present government bonds for payment. On the other hand, the government can safely run a deficit up to the point where it has provided the quantity of noninterest-earning fiat money and interest-earning bonds desired by the public.

A nongold standard monetary system with flexible exchange rates is a modern money system in which sovereign governments can issue their currency without any financial constraint. Both full employment and price stability can be achieved if economists and policy makers try to escape the theoretical baggage of the gold standard.

Fadhel Kaboub

See also: Exchange Rates.

BIBLIOGRAPHY

De Cecco, Marcello. *The International Gold Standard: Money and Empire.* London: Frances Printer, 1952.

Hume, David. "Of the Balance of Trade." In *Political Discourses.* Edinburgh: R. Fleming for A. Kincaid and A. Donaldson, 1752.

Wray, L. Randall. *Understanding Modern Money: The Key to Full Employment and Price Stability.* Northampton, MA: Edward Elgar, 1998.

GOTHS

A group of Germanic peoples who inhabited the region north of the Black Sea before being driven into the Roman empire by the Huns, after which they established several kingdoms in central and western Europe.

Like many other names denoting tribal identity, "Goth" is more convenient than it is precise. It is used to describe a variety of related peoples from Scandinavia who migrated southward through the Baltic region into what is now southern Russia and the lower Danube around 150 C.E.

EARLY HISTORY

The Roman historian Tacitus (early second century C.E.) referred to the Goths (Gutones) as living along the Baltic coast of what is now Poland. They were one of many groups associated with the Wielbark culture. Our knowledge of early Gothic history comes largely from the Getica, written by a Gothic historian in Constantinople named Jordanes. Jordanes's account is based largely on Ostrogothic court records and legends; much of it is pure myth, and it is difficult to ascertain with certainty what parts are reliable.

The Getica describes how the Goths began to migrate south under a leader called Filimer. As they crossed a great river (possibly the Dnieper), their bridge collapsed. Those who had already crossed settled in southern Ukraine, Crimea, and the Caucasus and became known as Ostrogoths. Those left behind moved southwest to the northern banks of the Danube and were known as the Visigoths.

Archaeological findings support the literary evidence, suggesting that large-scale, belligerent movements of Germanic groups through eastern Europe did in fact take place between roughly 150 and 230. This was possibly because of feuds between rival groups within the Wielbark tribes. However, there were most likely many such movements, and Jordanes's story of one migration and the subsequent division into Ostrogoths and Visigoths is pure speculation.

Beginning in 230, Gothic armies began to launch major raids into Roman territory. In an effort to control the Bosporan trade routes, the Goths invaded and eventually seized Crimea and other areas around the Black Sea. Between 267 and 269, a fleet of 2,000 Gothic ships raided cities around the Aegean. Two Roman emperors, Decius (251) and Valens (378), were killed by the Goths, while Claudius II gained the surname "Gothicus" for his stunning victory on the Danube in 269.

The Goths began to be Christianized during the mid-300s. A Gothic bishop named Ulfilas was consecrated and developed a unique Gothic script for writing. Because Arianism was the dominant sect at the moment, it was to this branch of Christianity that the Goths converted.

In 375, the Huns invaded the Pontic steppes, crushing the Ostrogothic kingdom and forcing the Visigoths west into Roman territory.

THE OSTROGOTHS

The Ostrogoths fell under Hunnic dominion (they would later form a major part of Attila's armies in his European conquests). Following the breakup of the Hunnic empire in the mid-450s, the Ostrogoths began to settle in Pannonia (modern-day Hungary and northern Yugoslavia). Under Theodoric the Great, a remarkable leader who was both king of the Goths (the Visigoths acknowledged him as their king between 511 and his death in 526) and a Roman consul, the Ostrogoths invaded Italy in 493, capturing and murdering Odovacar (the king of the Heruli, who had seized control of Italy in 476). In 497, the Byzantine emperor Anastasius officially recognized Theodoric as king of Italy.

The Ostrogoths attempted to maintain separation between a Germanic noble class and a largely Roman peasantry. Roman citizens were permitted to be judged by their own laws but were largely forbidden to bear arms or to perform military service. There was also a great deal of tension between the Arian Ostrogoths and their largely Orthodox subjects. Nonetheless, the Ostrogoths were successful at maintaining control over the Italian peninsula for half a century. After Theodoric's death in 526, his daughter Amalasuntha was regent for her son Athalric. She placed herself under the protection of the Byzantine emperor Justinian I but was murdered in 535, giving Justinian a pretext to reconquer Italy. The Byzantine general Belisarius crushed the Ostrogothic kingdom, but on his recall in 541 a warlord named Totila led an uprising and reestablished the kingdom. In 552, another Byzantine general, Narses, defeated and killed Totila. The Ostrogoths were reincorporated into the Roman empire and eventually lost their national identity. Byzantine hegemony over Italy was short lived; within a generation it had fallen to another German group, the Lombards.

Under the Ostrogothic kings, such scholars as Boethius and Cassiodorus revived the culture of late antiquity. The Catholic Church, despite the Ostrogoths' Arian leanings, flourished as well; the ecclesiastic legal theorist Dionysius Exiguus and Saint Benedict, the father of Western monasticism, both lived in Italy during this period.

THE VISIGOTHS

In the late 300s, the Visigoths were caught up in a civil war between a pro-Roman faction led by Fritigern and an anti-Roman faction led by Athanaric. Despite their victory over Emperor Valens at Adrianople (378), the Visigoths could not overcome the Eastern empire and eventually settled in Thrace and along the Danube. With the arrival of the Huns in the 390s, the terrified Visigoths swept into the Roman empire, where, after a few abortive raids, they were settled as federates in the Balkans.

In 395, the Visigoths rebelled under a leader named Alaric, the first true king of the Visigoths. Alaric was an extremely energetic leader and military genius. He led several attacks into Italy beginning in 401, but was defeated by the Roman general Stilicho. However, after Stilicho lost favor with Emperor Honorius and was murdered, Alaric had a free hand. In 410, the Visigoths sacked Rome, which sent shock waves throughout the Latin-speaking world, although in all likelihood the "barbarous" Visigoths conducted themselves with remarkable restraint for the age. After only three days, Alaric withdrew from Rome and died shortly thereafter.

In 412, under Ataulf, the Visigoths left Italy and migrated into southern Gaul and northern Spain. They pushed the Vandals out of most of Spain and conquered Aquitaine, establishing a new kingdom with Toulouse as its capital. Under Euric (466–484), the Visigoths finished their conquest of Spain (the Vandals having departed for North Africa) but began to lose control over Gaul to the rising power of the Franks during the early 500s. By 507, the Franks had taken all the Visigothic territories north of the Pyrenees, and the capital was moved to Toledo.

Like the Ostrogoths in Italy, the Visigoths were separated from their subjects by their sense of Germanic superiority and their Arian faith. They were remarkably tolerant, however, in matters of religion until their conversion to Catholicism in the late 500s. Following this conversion, Visigothic kings, beginning with Recared, issued many laws against religious minorities, particularly Jews. In 654, Roman law was abolished in favor of a common law for both Visigoth and Roman subjects. Church councils began to overshadow the power of the monarchy and civil war became a mainstay of life in Visigothic Iberia. The last king, Roderick, seized power, causing his rivals to appeal to the Muslims for aid. Tariq ibn Ziyad, a deputy of the governor of Morocco, led a token force on a scouting mission into Spain in 711. However, the country was in such a poor state by this point that its armies all but collapsed, surprising even the Arabs with the rapidity of their conquest. Tariq did not have enough soldiers to garrison his conquest, so he was forced to rely on previously disenfranchised peoples, such as the Jews, to aid him in holding the cities he had won.

With the Moorish conquest the Visigothic period came to an end. The Visigoths maintained only a narrow strip along Spain's northern coast, which became the kingdom of Asturias (the progenitor of all the Christian kingdoms of the Iberian Peninsula). The distinctive Visigothic culture, however, was quickly lost in favor of the post-Roman culture we know today as Spanish.

THE GOTHS IN THE EAST

The least powerful, the least known, and paradoxically the longest-lived Gothic communities were those that remained in the ancestral homelands around the Black Sea, especially in Crimea. A Gothic principality around the strongholds of Mangkup and Doros continued to exist through various periods of vassalage to the Byzantines, Khazars, Kipchaks, Mongols, Genoese, and other empires until well into the 1500s, when the Girai Khanate finally incorporated it.

Gothic texts from this region exist as late as the late 1500s and Gothic communities appear to have survived intact until the late 1700s, when

Catherine the Great deported many. Their language vanished by the 1800s. The so-called Volga Germans who could be found in southern Russia as late as World War II were not Goths. Rather, they were a distinct people who spoke a West German language akin to modern German, as opposed to the East Germanic Gothic language.

Brian M. Gottesman

See also: Roman Empire.

BIBLIOGRAPHY

Burns, T.S. *History of the Ostrogoths*. Bloomington: Indiana University Press, 1984.
Christian, David. *A History of Russia, Central Asia and Mongolia*. Vol. 1. Oxford: Blackwell, 1998.
Jordanes. *Getica: The Gothic History of Jordanes in English*. 2nd ed. Cambridge: Speculum Historiale, 1966.
Vasiliev, Aleksandr A. *The Goths in the Crimea*. Cambridge, MA: Medieval Academy of America, 1936.
Wolfram, Herwig. *History of the Goths*. Los Angeles: University of California Press, 1979.

GRAIN

An important food commodity that is traded globally.

During ancient times, wheat grown in Sicily, North Africa, and Egypt provided food for the Romans. Certain areas of Europe, primarily eastern Europe and Poland, had greater success in growing wheat and other grains than did western Europe. Trade developed between the two regions beginning in the sixteenth century. The importance of the grain trade increased as England and the Netherlands began the process of industrialization. Instead of growing foodstuffs, these countries concentrated on producing manufactured goods.

The global grain trade began in 1846 when Great Britain repealed its Corn Laws and permitted the free trade of grain. Almost immediately after repealing the Corn Laws, Britain negotiated the first modern multinational trade agreement: the Anglo-French Cobden-Chevalier Treaty of 1860, which included a most-favored-nation (MFN) clause.

During the following decade, Europeans concluded a series of MFN treaties. The treaties reduced tariff barriers between countries and thereby stimulated trade. But until World War I, the grain trade remained largely regional: as Black Sea grain to Athens, Baltic grain to Amsterdam, and Egyptian grain to Rome.

After World War I, the grain trade expanded along with the industrialization of agriculture in the United States. In addition to having fertile land and a favorable climate, the United States developed a system for producing, financing, and transporting grain, which allowed the industry to attain a truly global reach. This system of production, sometimes called the "Chicago system," included converting bagged grain to bulk containers, adopting inspection standards for minimum grades of grain, constructing large grain elevators for storage, building railroads from grain-producing areas to coastal ports, constructing 10,000-ton-plus ocean cargo ships, and developing a futures market to manage investment risk.

A huge private American company, Cargill, Inc., became the focal point of the world grain trade. By 1960, Cargill had emerged as the world's largest grain distribution company. It first expanded eastward, successfully challenging all the major non-American grain traders, including Continental, Bunge-Born, and Dreyfus. In 1998, Cargill bought the grain-handling business of Continental Grain, its second-largest rival after the U.S.-owned Archer Daniels Midland (ADM). Cargill and ADM now control about 80 percent of the world's grain supplies.

Cargill is the largest privately owned corporation in the world. With headquarters in Minnesota, about eighty members of the Cargill and MacMillan families own the company. Annual sales exceed $50 billion. The company maintains production facilities in 59 countries and operates in 130 other countries, giving it enormous economic and political power.

Cargill and a handful of other companies control more than 60 percent of the world's food supply, including the purchase and sale of grain, seed, fertilizers, pesticides, processing, and shipment of food. For example, Cargill and three other companies control 87 percent of U.S. beef supplies and the world's supply of corn, wheat, to-

A Cargill Superior Elevator. Cargill and a handful of other companies control more than 60 percent of the world's food supply, including the purchase and sale of grain, seed, fertilizers, and pesticides and the processing and shipment of food. *(Library of Congress)*

bacco, tea, rice, pineapple, jute, timber, and many other commodities.

Cargill, the other large grain companies, and their home-country governments advocate the globalization of the grain trade. They estimate that world population will grow by about 75 million people annually between 1995 and 2020, when it is projected to total 7.5 billion. Most of this growth will occur in the urban areas of the so-called developing countries. China alone is expected to account for 233 million more people, or 12.7 percent, of total population growth.

FUTURE OF THE GRAIN TRADE

Economists predict that the per capita income of this population will also increase. With higher household income, families will demand higher-quality food, with the focus on protein. To meet the needs of the additional population, agribusinesses must produce 40 percent more grain by 2020. China alone accounts for one-fourth of the increased requirement for cereals.

To minimize the risk of food shortages and famine, developing countries must double their cereal imports. Farmers in North America, Europe, and Australia must also produce 40 percent more wheat, rice, and other grains. Investment in biotechnology (genetically modified crops) must also occur to make food grains more nutritious and to combat widespread nutrient deficiencies among the poor.

The opponents of the world grain trade argue that the movement of capital, technology, and labor across national borders, along with the location of industrial plants, determines the balance of power and wealth in the world. Grain trade also determines the share of the wealth available to countries and their citizens. In the case of the world grain trade, critics argue that instead of feeding the poor, the system in effect erodes the food security of developing countries. The grain companies buy, trade, and sell food worldwide. They create surpluses and manipulate supply, demand, and commodity prices to guarantee profits. For example, because of crop failures in the United States in 1995 and 1996, Cargill and Continental Grain bought wheat from India at a price of $60 to $100 per metric ton and then sold it at $230 to $240 on the international market, thus making a profit of 170 percent per ton. Indeed, if India experienced a shortage of grain supplies, its government would be forced to buy back the country's own grain at a higher price than Indian producers received from Cargill.

An increasing demand for grains worldwide translates into higher prices that could easily mean increased hunger in many countries that depend on grain imports. The Food and Agriculture Organization estimates that importing grains adds $3 billion to the food bill of developing countries every year.

The world grain system could assist developing countries by enabling them to buy what they need and sell what they make. But trade rules, as reflected in the World Trade Organization, favor rich countries and large companies such as Cargill. The grain trade benefits rich and powerful nations often at the expense of poor countries.

Ronald T. Libby

See also: Amsterdam; Athens, Ancient; Black Sea; Corn Laws; Egypt; Population; World Trade Organization.

BIBLIOGRAPHY

Gunilla, Andrae, and Bjorn Beckman. *Bread and Underdevelopment in Nigeria.* New York: St. Martin's Press, 1985.
Kneen, Brewster. *The Invisible Giant and Its Transnational Strategies.* London: Pluto, 1995.
Libby, Ronald T. *Protecting Markets: U.S. Policy and the World Grain Trade.* Ithaca: Cornell University Press, 1992.
Morgan, Dan. *Merchants of Grain.* New York: Penguin, 1980.

GREAT DEPRESSION

A worldwide economic downturn that began in 1929, hit bottom in 1933, and lasted throughout much of the 1930s.

The Great Depression was an economic event of unprecedented dimensions. There had been no downturn of its magnitude or duration before, and there has been none of its like since.

In the United States, the value of economic output (real gross domestic product) fell by 27 percent from 1929 to 1933. Simultaneously, prices fell about one-quarter. The unemployment rate, which had averaged 5 percent in the 1920s, soared from 3.2 percent in 1929 to 25.2 percent in 1933 and averaged 14 percent in the 1930s. Gross investment plummeted by 98 percent. The impact of the depression was not confined to the United States, although it took the brunt of the effects. Table 1 shows that industrial output fell substantially in many of the world's economically developed countries, with the United States the hardest hit, followed by Canada and Germany. Some states avoided outright collapse, but every country listed in Table 1 suffered a decline in industrial output of at least 10 percent between 1929 and 1932. In addition, the Great Depression also hurt most less-developed countries.

This economic implosion triggered a drop in trade of an even greater magnitude (see Table 2).

CAUSES

The causes of the Great Depression remain complex and have been the subject of much debate among economic historians. Most explanations point to weaknesses in credit markets, both internationally and within the United States.

At the time of the depression, many argued that the U.S. economy had become too productive. Rapid technological gains, because of innovations such as electricity and the internal combustion engine, had brought unprecedented productivity gains in agriculture and industry during the 1920s. Some felt that these gains made the economy so productive that consumers could not buy as much as was being produced, causing unsold inventory and widespread layoffs. Subsequent history has shown, however, that increases in productivity have been accompanied almost automatically by increased demand by consumers and that technological unemployment has not been a problem.

Aggregate demand did drop after 1929, but the causes of this must be sought elsewhere. The crash in the stock market contributed to this decline. Stock prices surged upward from 1926 to September 1929 and then crashed downward, losing 36 percent of their value in the next year

Table 1

Industrial Production as a Percentage of the Total, Peak Pre–World War II Years, 1927 to 1935 (1929 = 100)

	1927	1928	1929	1930	1931	1932	1933	1934	1935
Britain	95	94	100	94	86	89	95	105	114
Canada	85	94	100	91	78	68	69	82	90
France	84	94	100	99	85	74	83	79	77
Germany	95	100	100	86	72	59	68	83	96
Italy	87	99	100	93	84	77	83	85	99
Netherlands	87	94	100	109	101	90	90	93	95
Sweden	85	88	100	102	97	89	93	111	125
United States	85	90	100	83	69	55	63	69	79

Source: Organization for European Economic Cooperation, *Industrial Statistics, 1900–1957* (Paris: Organization for European Economic Cooperation, 1958).

Note: 100 represents industrial production in the peak year of 1929. The figures for before and after 1929 are percentages of that industrial output.

and 84 percent of their value when they hit bottom in June 1932. Many argue that the run-up in stock prices had been part of a speculative frenzy spurred by financial manipulation and overextended financing and that this played a role in the market's rise and fall. Much wealth disappeared in the collapse, and this helped reduce consumer spending, but most historians argue that the stock market mostly reflected investors' outlooks rather than driving the economy.

It appears that a collapse of consumer spending in 1930 turned a minor recession into the Great Depression. Households shouldered an unprecedented amount of debt, which had doubled as a share of income during the 1920s. Much of this involved installment debt linked to the booming automobile market, with large down payments and short contracts. Missed installment payments triggered repossession and the forfeiture of the down payment and any subsequent payments. Rather than defaulting on these loans when the recession brought falling incomes and uncertainty, consumers responded by cutting back other expenditures, with overall real consumption expenditures falling over 6 percent. Unfortunately, this caused a snowball effect, with firms forced to lay off additional workers. The drop in demand also caused prices to fall, and this deflation further crippled the economy by making it harder for businesses to earn a profit and by increasing the real value of business and household debts.

The collapse in spending was then abetted by weaknesses in the banking system. Most banks in the United States remained small ventures, with only a single branch and loans tied almost completely to the local economy. When low prices meant that many cotton farmers could not repay their loans, this led to a series of bank failures in the South in late 1930. Along with the failure of New York City's Bank of the United States, these failures began to make depositors wary of keeping their funds in banks. Bank failures mounted during 1931 and peaked after Britain went off the gold standard in September. The Federal Reserve reacted to Britain's decision by trying to convince international investors that the United States would not abandon gold. It responded by increasing interest rates, which made the dollar more attractive to international investors, but which also made it harder for troubled banks to borrow funds needed to respond to their depositors' withdrawals.

Finally, the entire banking system froze up in early 1933. When negotiations to save a large Detroit bank failed, the governor of Michigan declared a statewide bank "holiday" in February 1933. Michigan depositors rushed to banks in nearby states to withdraw needed funds, but this

Table 2

Decline in Import and Export Dollar Values from 1929 to 1932 (%)

	Imports	Exports
Argentina	74	64
Australia	74	55
Britain	58	64
France	49	61
Germany	65	58
United States	69	69

Source: League of Nations, *World Economic Survey, 1932–1933* (Geneva: League of Nations, 1933).

precipitated mandatory shutdowns in neighboring states, until most of the banks in the nation closed. The erosion of confidence in the banking system proved critical because it caused depositors to withdraw their funds, leaving banks with few resources to lend. Reduced lending meant reduced spending. In addition, the withdrawals caused the overall money supply in circulation to shrink, which spurred deflation and its negative consequences.

These events in the United States reduced its lending to the rest of the world. In addition, American demand for imports from the rest of the world declined, and the United States began to experience a surplus in its balance of payments. Europe paid for this trade imbalance by shipping gold to the United States, which normally would have pushed up American prices. But the Federal Reserve "sterilized" these gold inflows by not allowing them to increase the money supply and prices. As Europe was drained of gold, America's trading partners were pushed off the gold standard. This financial shock and the reduction of exports to the United States helped spread the depression abroad.

One of the responses of the United States to the depression was the passage of the Hawley-Smoot Tariff in June 1930, which raised taxes on imports (largely because the tariffs were in dollar terms and the deflation of the era pushed up the effective tax rate). America's largest trading partner, Canada, immediately retaliated by increasing its tariffs on U.S. imports. While the Hawley-Smoot Tariff was not a major cause of the Great Depression, it became part of a response to the depression in which countries turned inward and tried to reduce imports while increasing exports—in an effort to put their unemployed populations back to work. This "beggar-thy-neighbor" strategy of tariff increases and currency devaluations helped spread the depression and helps explain the tremendous reduction in world trade seen in Table 2.

ROOSEVELT AND THE NEW DEAL

The larger response to the Great Depression came with the election of 1932. Herbert Hoover had taken unprecedented actions to dampen the depression, including the creation of the Reconstruction Finance Corporation to assist failing banks and businesses, but this clearly was not enough in the eyes of the electorate, which elected Franklin D. Roosevelt president in a landslide victory. Roosevelt and the Democratic Party responded to the depression with a blizzard of new programs, most of which substantially increased the role of the federal government in the economy. These responses included government building projects, income supports to farmers, bank deposit insurance, laws promoting unions and collective bargaining, the creation of an agency to oversee the stock market, and the establishment of the Social Security system, unemployment insurance, and the minimum wage.

Congress also decided that tariffs had become too high and granted the president powers to negotiate lower tariffs with individual countries under the Reciprocal Trade Agreements Act of 1934. Unfortunately, because the damage done by the depression (especially to the banking system) proved so severe or because some of the new policies remained deeply flawed (especially the National Recovery Act), the recovery from the depression was slow and painful, with a second recession (the "Roosevelt Recession") hitting in 1937 and the unemployment rate remaining at or above 10 percent until the end of the decade.

Robert Whaples

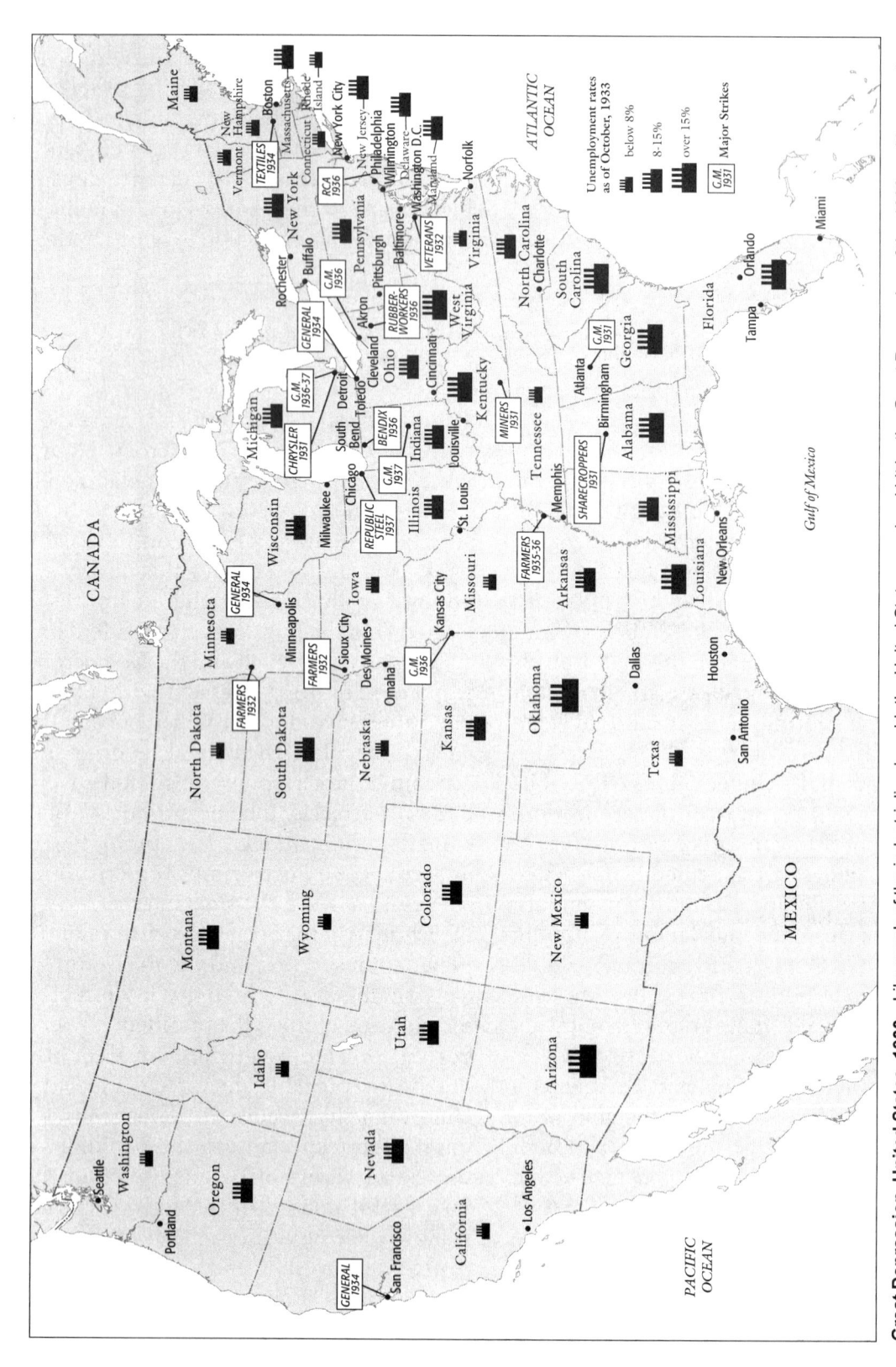

Great Depression, United States, 1933 Like much of the industrialized world, the United States was hard hit by the Great Depression of the 1930s, with unemployment rates up to ten times higher than they had been in the previous and succeeding decades. As the map indicates, the hardship was felt all over, notably in the South. *(Mark Stein Studios)*

Unemployed men queue up outside a soup kitchen opened in Chicago by Al Capone in February 1931. The Great Depression was an economic event of unprecedented dimensions. In the United States, the value of economic output (real gross domestic product) fell by 27 percent from 1929 to 1933. *(National Archives at College Park)*

See also: Gold Standard; Keynes, John Maynard.

BIBLIOGRAPHY

Eichengreen, Barry J. *Golden Fetters: The Gold Standard and the Great Depression, 1919–1939.* New York: Oxford University Press, 1992.

Fearon, Peter. *War, Prosperity and Depression: The U.S. Economy, 1917–1945.* Lawrence: University Press of Kansas, 1987.

Hall, Thomas E., and J. David Ferguson. *The Great Depression: An International Disaster of Perverse Economic Policies.* Ann Arbor: University of Michigan Press. 1998.

Kindleberger, Charles. *The World in Depression, 1929–1939.* London: Allen Lane, 1973.

Rothermund, Dietmar. *The Global Impact of the Great Depression.* New York: Routledge, 1996.

GREATER EAST ASIA CO-PROSPERITY SPHERE

In 1940, the Greater East Asia Co-Prosperity Sphere was declared by Japan, which envisioned an independent pan-Asian alliance free of Western influence and based on strategic and economic interests.

When Prime Minister Matsuoka Yōsuke laid out the plan for the Greater East Asia Co-Prosperity Sphere in August 1940, he asserted a pan-Asianism that dated back to at least the 1880s. The tradition included romantic idealism, an aware-

A struggle partly over trade in East Asia, the Russo-Japanese War of 1904–1905 was the first major conflict to result in the victory of a non-European power over a European one. Shown here are Russian sailors loading torpedoes. (© Topham/The Image Works)

ness of a common cultural heritage, and a view of Asian spirituality as superior to the materialism of the West. By the 1930s, pan-Asianism was more pragmatic and realistic, based on strategic and economic considerations. The sphere also served as an expression of Japanese "manifest destiny," its mission to become Asia's leader. This sentiment had been growing since the turn of the twentieth century.

Japan had established a presence in China and in Korea and in 1905 had won the Russo-Japanese War. Still, it perceived that the West had not shown Japan the respect it was due. In 1919, the West rejected Japan's request for inclusion of a racial equality provision in the League of Nations charter. The Washington Naval Conference of 1921 defined a battleship ratio of 5:5:3 for the United States, Great Britain, and Japan. And in 1924 the United States enacted the Japanese Exclusion Act.

Japanese militarism found an outlet in China, a source of raw material and a market for Japanese industries and investments. Japanese aggression in China led the United States to embargo oil from the Dutch East Indies and rubber from Indochina, and the other colonial Westerners restricted other resources. Japan needed Asian raw materials for economic self-sufficiency. As a neomercantilist venture, the co-prosperity sphere was to provide Japan markets for its finished goods in return for a secure source of raw materials. It was also hoped that Japanese expansion would help relieve population pressures mounting in Japan.

The popular projection of the plan did not stress aspects that highlighted Japan's expansive designs on its neighbors. Rather, it stressed "Asia for the Asians," liberated and prosperous Asian nations working together without the West. Rhetoric of coexistence and co-prosperity was designed to increase cooperation. Burma and Indonesia remained more susceptible to the rhetoric than other Asian countries. But the reception in Asian countries did not matter to the Japanese government, which established puppet governments, notably in the Manchurian region of China. The program of "Japanization" disregarded local customs and mores. The Japanese also practiced torture, execution, and forced labor, causing local populations great suffering.

Some Japanese wanted the sphere to include India, Australia, and New Zealand. When attempts to include part of India failed, military considerations limited the western extent to Burma. Japan occupied Indonesia, North Sumatra, Malaya, Vietnam, Burma, the Philippines, Papua New Guinea, and Siam (renamed Thailand in 1939), though its control varied by location. Generally, local elites worked with the Japanese to preserve or enhance their power. Most conquered nations experienced armed violence and political disruption. A disruption of commercial links with Europe followed. In Indonesia and Malaya, the sphere promoted local nationalism, but the rest of Southeast Asia changed little. Japan's defeat in World War II ended its pursuit of the Greater East Asia Co-Prosperity Sphere.

John Barnhill

See also: World War II.

BIBLIOGRAPHY

Gordon, Bill. "Greater East Asia Co-prosperity Sphere" (http://wgordon.web.wesleyan.edu/papers/coprospr.htm, accessed March 2000).

Lebra, Joyce C., ed. *Japan's Greater East Asia Co-prosperity Sphere in World War II: Selected Readings and Documents.* Kuala Lumpur: Oxford University Press, 1975.

McCoy, Alfred W., ed. *Southeast Asia Under Japanese Occupation.* New Haven: Yale University, Southeast Asia Studies, 1980.

GREEK CITY-STATES

> City-states that dominated the mainland and islands off of Greece from 700 to 332 B.C.E.

During the sixth century B.C.E., a shift in the political and economic structure throughout Greece occurred. Several cities consolidated their control over the surrounding countryside, with Sparta, Athens, Corinth, and Thebes emerging as the most prominent. Citizens were no longer identified by their village affiliation but by the city-state under whose control they resided. Walled fortifications were erected around each of the dominant cities. Inside the walls stood the temples, the public meeting places, and the marketplaces (agoras). Agricultural goods from the surrounding countryside were sold in the city.

POLITICAL AND MILITARY BACKGROUND

By the sixth century B.C.E., Sparta had emerged as the strongest city-state. Located in the Peloponnesus region of Greece (the southwestern portion of the country), Sparta developed a thriving culture based on the arts. The fertile valley along the Eurotas River produced sufficient agricultural produce for the population, but the Spartans relied on Messenians, a group of people that they had conquered, to work the land. When the Messenians revolted in 640 B.C.E. (a revolt that lasted for two decades), the Spartan society was transformed into a military state. Although the political structure continued to be controlled by two kings, ordinary Spartans were extended the right to vote to ensure their loyalty to the state during these difficult times. Once the Messenian wars were over, Sparta used its military power to dominate the rest of the Peloponnesus. The Spartans did not subjugate the other city-states, but instead negotiated alliances with them. The Spartan army offered protection from outside forces while it eradicated tyrants and established oligarchies throughout the region. The overall effect was a more stable region.

While Sparta continued to control the south and west of Greece, the city-state of Athens was consolidating control over Attica along the eastern coast of Greece. The Athenian political system was based on democracy, with each man receiving one vote. The city was located near a natural harbor, and the Athenians gradually expanded their navy and influence over the Greek islands. At the beginning of the fifth century B.C.E., the Persian king turned his attention on Athens.

The Persian empire had emerged out of the fragmented Near East in the late sixth century B.C.E. under King Cyrus. The empire grew rapidly and by the beginning of the fifth century B.C.E. had expanded to the borders of Greece. The Persian army first landed in Attica in 490 B.C.E. at a place called Marathon. The Athenian army, some 20,000 strong, marched to Marathon to engage the Persian forces. Greatly outnumbered, the Athenians dispatched a runner to Sparta asking for assistance. The messenger made the 140-mile run and reached Sparta the following day. The Spartans could not assist the Athenians because they were in the middle of a festival. After the conclusion of the festival, however, they did march toward Marathon but arrived the day after the battle.

The Athenians, under the leadership of Miltiades, were vastly outnumbered. For days, they waited to launch their attack. When news arrived that the Persian cavalry had boarded the ships and was planning on heading directly to Athens, the Athenian forces struck. The Persians suffered a devastating defeat—one that would result in the arrival of larger Persian forces in the future and one that also boosted Greek confidence in their ability to defend their home against the mighty Persian forces.

The next time the Persians attacked, their army was so large that it had to march overland within sight of the coast where ships resupplied the forces. The Spartans, Athenians, and twenty-nine other city-states joined together in an effort to defeat the approaching army. Xerxes, the Persian king, ordered a simultaneous naval and land assault. The Athenians, with their large navy, were responsible for preventing a Persian naval victory, which they were able to achieve after two separate storms wiped out a large portion of the Persian ships. The remaining ships were tricked into attacking the Athenians and were defeated at Salamis.

Meanwhile, the Spartan commander chose a fifty-foot-wide passage through the mountains at Thermopylae to engage the Persian land forces. The Spartans held the ground for a long time, killing thousands of Persian soldiers, before finally being overcome. All the captured Spartans were executed. Although central Greece now lay open to the Persians, the arrival of winter forced a break in the campaign. Several Persian defeats in the following years forced them to withdraw toward the Hellespont. At that point, in 478 B.C.E., the Greeks began to actively pursue the Persians. They formed the Delian League to coordinate their efforts. The Athenians, now the dominant power in Greece, used the league to expand their empire. After the final defeat of the Persians, problems arose between the Athenians and the Spartans. The defeat of the Athenians by the Spartans signaled the decline of the golden age of the city-state.

ECONOMIC HISTORY

The rise of the city-states resulted in the stimulation of political and economic contacts with the eastern Mediterranean. Greek olive oil and wine were traded with Phoenicia, where goods from points farther east were available for exchange. Trade between the mother city-state and its colonies also occurred with each major city-state establishing several colonies. One of the regions settled by the Greeks was Sicily. Agricultural goods were routinely transported back to Greece from the fertile portions of the island. It was the abundance of food on Sicily, as well as its strategic location, that attracted the attention of the Carthaginians as well as the Romans. The success of the Greek traders in the Ionian Sea helped usher in the decline of the Phoenician dominance of trade. The Carthaginians, once a colony of Phoenicia, attempted to secure control of trade in the central and western portions of the Mediterranean resulting in the clash over Sicily. While the Greek city-states had to deal with outside forces from the east (Persia) and the west (Carthage and Rome), a larger threat developed to the north (Macedonia). King Philip II of Macedonia decided to expand his control over Greece before turning his attention eastward toward Persia. After consolidating Greece under his rule, Philip II made plans to conquer the greatest empire of the day but was murdered before he could implement them. Instead, his son Alexander the Great would lead his forces to the borders of India and down into Egypt.

During the height of the Greek city-states and after, Greece exported agricultural goods. In addition, Greece exported its culture as well. The Romans prized Greek bronze sculptures. Architectural forms were replicated in the temples of Rome until the Romans perfected the construction of the arch, after the development of concrete, which replaced the Greek post-and-lintel structure. Greek political systems were also used as an example in the formation of the Roman republic. With the decline of the Greek empire and the rise of the Roman empire, control of the trade throughout the known world shifted to Rome.

Cynthia Clark Northrup

See also: Olives; Phoenicia; Roman Empire.

BIBLIOGRAPHY

Demand, Nancy. *A History of Ancient Greece.* New York: McGraw-Hill, 1996.
Starr, Chester G. *A History of the Ancient World.* New York: Oxford University Press, 1991.

GUANGZHOU (CANTON)

The historical gateway to China, Guangzhou is a thriving metropolitan city at the heart of national and global economic processes.

Located just north of Hong Kong in the southeastern province of Guangdong, Guangzhou, or "Canton" (based on the Portuguese *Coutco*), is a wealthy and modern city. It has deep historical roots and is at the center of China's rapid industrial development.

Guangzhou was already an important river and seaport by 214 B.C.E., when the emperor Qin Shihuang made the city the administrative seat of the Nanhai (South Sea) prefecture. Roman traders arrived soon after, followed by Arab and Southeast Asian traders during the Tang dynasty (618–907). Once Arab traders lost the ability to organize long journeys, however, Guangzhou's international trade declined until the arrival of Europeans in the sixteenth century.

The Portuguese were the first Europeans to arrive, coming to Guangzhou in 1514. Tensions between the Chinese and the Portuguese grew until the Chinese leased Macao to them in 1557. Allowing foreigners to set up a trading base away from the city was in keeping with China's long-held custom of sustaining substantial trade while minimizing cultural and personal contacts. The Dutch came shortly thereafter, followed quickly by the British. Trade in silk, tea, porcelain, and cotton was brisk despite the controls of the Ming dynasty. After consolidating power, the emperor Kangxi of the Qing dynasty (1644–1911) opened the nation's ports to foreign trade in 1685, just as Britain was becoming the dominant Western trading power in the region.

The emperor Qianlong sought to limit foreign influences in 1757, restricting all foreign trade to Guangzhou. Foreign traders were not allowed to enter the walled city; instead, they were relegated to specially designated "factories." They were prevented from learning Chinese, could work only through assigned interpreters, could not bring women or weapons, and could only stay in Guangzhou during the trading season. Also, all transactions had to go through the cohong, a monopolistic guild organized by thirteen government officials.

Despite burgeoning trade, the British sent successive trade missions near the turn of the eighteenth century seeking access to other ports. The dramatic emergence of tea consumption in Britain led to a considerable trade deficit. British traders responded by promoting opium consumption in China, reversing the trade flow by the 1830s. While the Chinese emperor had passed several laws and had appealed to the British to curb the opium trade, opium consumption rose unabated, wreaking havoc on China's society and economy. The opium trade increased even more after the British East India Company lost its monopoly on British trade to China in 1833.

Lin Zexu, a government official sent to stop the opium trade, confiscated and destroyed 20,000 chests of opium in 1839. The drug traders appealed to and then partly funded the British navy, which responded by bombarding and subjugating several cities. The First Opium War (1839–1942) ended when the Chinese capitulated to the Treaty of Nanjing, which ceded Hong Kong to the British. The treaty also ended the Canton System by opening five so-called treaty ports to foreign trade, including Shanghai. The foreign settlements were considered to be extraterritorial space, with each site governed by the laws and customs of the foreign nation. Foreigners not only had their own police force and justice system, but also controlled trade, taxes, and tariffs. China quickly entered into similar treaties with other Western powers, granting all foreign traders the same advantages through linked most-favored-nation clauses.

Guangzhou's economy and population quickly declined as Hong Kong and other ports took its role in foreign trade. Nonetheless, Guangzhou was at the center of several political movements, including the pseudo-Christian, anti-Qing "Taiping Rebellion" of the 1850s. Later, Sun Yatsen, the founder of the Nationalist Party, organized several coup attempts from Guangzhou. One of the first communist communes in China was set up in Guangzhou in 1927. Guangzhou became a major industrial center in the 1930s before being taken over by the Japanese in 1938. Finally, the communist takeover of Guangzhou in 1949 signaled the defeat of Chiang Kaishek's Nationalist forces.

While Guangzhou's development was not one of Chairman Mao Zedong's priorities, Deng Xiaoping chose it for the first market reforms of the late 1970s. Located near the Shenzhen and Zhuhai Special Economic Zones, Guangzhou has reestablished itself as a vital gateway to China and as the fifth-largest city in China.

W. Chad Futrell

See also: China.

BIBLIOGRAPHY
Garrett, Valery M. *The Heaven Is High, the Emperor Is Far Away: Merchants and Mandarins in Old Canton.* New York: Oxford University Press, 2002.

GUANO

> Bird droppings accumulated over hundreds of years that gained popularity as a fertilizer in the nineteenth century and became a leading trade item in both Europe and America.

The native populations of South America used guano, originally called *huano,* a Spanish word for the dried excrement of seafowl, as a fertilizer for thousands of years. The rocky barren islands off the coast of Peru proved the richest source for guano. Coastal Peru's climate—of cold water flowing from the equator and meeting Peru's warm air, which inhibited rainfall—allowed guano to solidify in a dry climate while preserving its nutrients. The coastal waters drew huge numbers of migratory birds, including the guanay cormorant, gannets, gulls, and pelicans that rested on the islands free from predators. Over time, these birds produced guano as deep as 150 feet.

The Peruvian government recognized the value of guano and kept tight control of the commodity with high prices. In 1830, the Peruvians exempted guano from taxation, since it was important to Peruvian agriculture, fostering a local market, but an international market did not develop until 1840, when it was introduced in England on a large scale. As journals, newspapers, and almanacs praised guano as a fertilizer and as its popularity grew, English farmers found that their yields increased between 30 and 300 percent. Unlike other fertilizers, guano was more soluble, performed well in heavy and light soils, and was rich in both nitrogen and phosphate. It was also versatile and had positive effects on a broader range of crops than other fertilizers.

Extracting guano was no easy task. During the day, guano baked into a solid mass that required picks and shovels to break it loose. Most of the miners were indentured servants, convicts, military deserters, kidnapped Peruvians, and slaves who worked twenty-plus hours a day digging trenches 60 to 100 feet deep. The chunks of guano were then hauled by wheelbarrow to a canvas chute that went directly into a ship's hold. The working conditions often made the workers ill. Also, the dust produced by guano was inhaled by workers and caused many respiratory and gastrointestinal problems.

As the English market grew, prices declined and the English merchants began to look to the United States as a potential customer. American farmers were eager to try the fertilizer, and when they did, their yields increased as did the demand for guano. American farmers became increasingly unhappy with the high prices and began to petition the U.S. government to help keep prices down. In response, the United States tried to negotiate a free-trade agreement with Peru, but was unsuccessful.

In the absence of a free-trade agreement, the United States drafted and passed the Guano Island Act of 1856, which allowed American citizens to take possession of areas not under the lawful jurisdiction of other nations. As a result, American entrepreneurs claimed any piece of land with guano. Approximately ninety-four islands, rocks, and keys were claimed under the Guano Island Act, and sixty-six of them were recognized by the U.S. State Department as American acquisitions, including the islands of Howland, Baker, and Jarvis, as well as some Caribbean islands. As artificial fertilizers were developed in the late 1800s, the demand for guano lessened. In Peru during the height of demand for guano (1840–1880), an estimated 20 million pounds was excavated for export and generated $2 billion in profit. As the guano market declined, the United States returned most of the acquisitions.

By 1910, Peru's guano islands were severely depleted and the economy was suffering. In an effort to conserve the remaining guano reserves, the Peruvians established the Guano Administration to preserve the guano, the birds, and the environment. Islands were designated off limits for six months to allow birds to raise young and replenish the reserves without interference from humans. Steps were also taken to manage the fishing industry so the guano-producing birds would remain attracted to the area, and bird preserves were established on the mainland.

Lisa A. Ennis

See also: Fertilizer.

BIBLIOGRAPHY

Mathew, W.M. "Peru and the British Guano Market, 1840–1870." *Economic History Review* (New Series) 23, no. 1 (April 1970): 112–128.

Skaggs, Jimmy M. *The Great Guano Rush: Entrepreneurs and American Overseas Expansion*. New York: St. Martin's Press, Griffin, 1994.

"TED Case Studies: Guano Trade." Trade and Environment Database (www.american.edu/TED/guano.htm, accessed April 2004).

GUNPOWDER

> A chemical explosive mixture that transformed warfare and global trade patterns in the early modern period.

Gunpowder seems to have been first invented by alchemists in ninth-century China, where the explosive began to be used in ceremonies and for limited military purposes. Thirteenth-century trade along the famous Silk Road then brought gunpowder to Europe and the Middle East, where it began to impact military practices significantly.

Gunpowder was quickly adopted by designers of late medieval European war machines, and armies fighting in the Hundred Years' War soon employed early gunpowder cannon in sieges. European bell-founding techniques and processes probably influenced the early techniques of founding artillery pieces, which tended to be shaped like church bells. By the early fifteenth century, heavy bombards were being built that could shoot immense stone shot of 700 pounds or more against city walls. Gunpowder artillery strengthened the offensive capabilities of armies that could employ cannon in large numbers. Aragon and Castile employed a huge artillery train to accomplish a rapid "cannon conquest" of Granada in the fifteenth century and complete the *reconquista*. Extensive use of siege artillery allowed French armies to seize many castles during the latter stages of the Hundred Years' War, contributing significantly to the ultimate French victory. The Ottoman imperial army used over seventy guns to batter the walls of Constantinople in 1453.

The awesome power of gunpowder siege artillery prompted cities and states to develop new defensive techniques. Attempts to adapt existing castles or to modify fortification techniques for gunpowder technologies resulted in fifteenth-century artillery towers. In the early sixteenth century, Italian Renaissance engineers began to design bastioned fortifications, also known as "star forts" for their appearance. These fortifications were built to sustain heavy fire from besieging artillery, while using mutually supporting artillery batteries sited in bastions to create a murderous zone of cross fire that attackers would have to cross to assail the defenses. The costs of building these bastioned fortifications and arming them with sufficient artillery became astronomical. Yet, the ongoing Italian wars demanded that even small city-states, such as Mantova, attempt to refortify their defenses according to the new designs or risk capture. Larger states used bastioned fortifications to protect strategic towns and market towns that were centers of trade and protoindustry. Well-defended cities employing bastioned fortifications could sustain long sieges even by immense armies, as Vienna's defenses showed several times during the sixteenth and seventeenth centuries.

Gunpowder began also to transform infantry weaponry in the fifteenth century, as hand-cannon began to be used alongside longbows and crossbows. In the sixteenth century, infantry increasingly turned to the harquebus, a matchlock weapon that could be effectively employed in conjunction with squares of pikemen that could protect the harquebusiers.

Experimentation in weapons production and gunpowder manufacture produced a burgeoning arms protoindustry. Renaissance scholars studied projectiles and ballistics, while alchemists experimented with chemical mixtures of saltpeter, sulfur, and charcoal to create ideal formulas for gunpowder. Corning processes were invented to manufacture gunpowder with grains resistant to humidity so that powder could be effectively conserved and transported. Complex, labor-intensive cannon foundries cast huge bronze siege guns, as well as smaller field artillery pieces. Transporting guns and supplying gunpowder for them required the extensive use of logistic services.

An international arms trade in gunpowder and firearms emerged in the sixteenth century and led to a proliferation of firearms. When cavalry began to use pistols in addition to their swords or lances, sixteenth-century pistol makers quickly responded with new lightweight com-

Gunpowder—shown here being turned into weapons at Woolwich Arsenal in England in 1750—enabled Europeans to manage vast colonial enterprises using small arms, artillery, fortifications, and ships without fear of serious challenge to their maritime connections and trade. *(The Art Archive/Eileen Tweedy)*

ponents and elegant designs. Nobles and rulers, such as Louis XIII of France, invested in extensive collections of both military and hunting weapons. Arms experts, military engineers, and technical specialists found employment throughout Europe and the Middle East.

Military enterprisers and mercenary leaders embraced gunpowder weapons and offered their specialized military services to princes and rulers who were engaged in the Italian wars of the sixteenth century. Groups of religious militants, often composed of dedicated freebooters, armed themselves with firearms to fight for their faith during the European wars of religion of the sixteenth and seventeenth centuries. Military enterprisers such as the Strozzi from Firenze and Albrecht von Wallenstein were able to build considerable fortunes through their military activities. Mercenaries and religious militants devastated war-torn areas: taking contributions from towns and villages, stealing food, and destroying crops, leaving peasants destitute.

Larger and more extensive military forces developed during the late sixteenth and seventeenth centuries, partly because of the pressures of gunpowder warfare. States began to use permanent units of soldiers armed in part with gunpowder weapons and led by military elites. By the early seventeenth century, infantry were using heavier, more powerful matchlock muskets. These firearms required soldiers to carry forked rests to support the weight of muskets when aiming them, while new forms of military drill and discipline were developed to use them effectively. Seventeenth-century armies, such as Gustavus Adolphus's Swedish army in the Thirty Years' War, also used significant amounts of field artillery. States sometimes used their larger armies to man lines of fortifications, as in the Netherlands, where Calvinist Dutch forces mounted a largely successful defense of their towns against Spanish armies during the Dutch Revolt.

Gunpowder radically transformed naval warfare in this period, as shipbuilders adapted naval vessels to the possibilities of firearm technologies. Although attempts had been made to use naval artillery for centuries, shipborne artillery only became really effective in the sixteenth century. New heavily armed sailing ships, known as galleons, resembled floating fortresses brimming with artillery. European states began to build up extensive naval forces in the late sixteenth and seventeenth centuries to assert power and to protect shipping on key trading routes.

The combination of galleons with the bastioned fortifications to control ports gave Europeans the key tools to build and sustain powerful maritime empires in the Americas and coastal trading posts in Africa, India, and Southeast Asia. Galleons could easily withstand attack by other forms of naval vessels, giving European maritime power a great advantage over non-Western powers, even on seas far from home. There was little fear of retaliation from non-Europeans, except in port. European ships could even dismantle hostile port fortifications, if necessary. The Portuguese achieved dominance in the Indian Ocean spice trade by the early sixteenth century. Armed ships in the Atlantic could connect with these Indian Ocean trade networks, supplanting overland trade routes from China to the Middle East.

Naval power and gunpowder technologies helped produce an economic shift from Mediterranean trade to Atlantic trade as the most important economic zone. While Spain's conquest of Central and South America was made possible largely by epidemic diseases that ravaged Native American populations during the Columbian exchange, galleons were key to the Spanish imperial system in the Americas. Spanish naval forces supported large-scale Spanish colonization in Mexico and portions of South America and helped bring large numbers of West African slaves to work in the Americas. Galleons also transported the silver and gold shipments from South American mines to Europe, creating a price revolution—a period of rapid worldwide inflation caused by the influx of large amounts of precious metals from New Spain onto the world market during the sixteenth century. Following the Spanish lead, the English developed sugar plantation colonies in the Caribbean and tobacco plantation colonies in North America. French and Dutch shipping also became involved in the Atlantic Ocean triangle trade networks. Rivalries developed between European imperial powers, leading to the development of mercantilism.

States that were able to develop military systems and administrations to use gunpowder more effectively had a distinct advantage in the early modern period. Japanese daimyo fought a series of civil wars in the sixteenth and early seventeenth centuries, but the leaders who used gunpowder most successfully—Oda Nobunaga, Toyotomi Hideyoshi, and Tokugawa Ieyasu—emerged as Japan's unifiers. Japanese state development and subsequent arms control policies ensured stability in Japan and a closed market system. Korean naval artillery design helped stop Japanese attempts to take over the Korean Peninsula. Mughal armies used firearms to maintain their control of northern India, while the Ottomans controlled much of the Middle East with their Janissary musketeers and artillery. These Muslim "gunpowder empires" were successful in preventing European domination or colonization of North Africa, the Middle East, and northern India during the early modern period.

Brian Sandberg

See also: Baroque; Castles; Mercantilism.

BIBLIOGRAPHY

Hall, Bert S. *Weapons and Warfare in Renaissance Europe: Gunpowder, Technology, and Tactics.* Baltimore: Johns Hopkins University Press, 1997.

McNeill, William H. *The Pursuit of Power: Technology, Armed Force, and Society since A.D. 1000.* Chicago: University of Chicago Press, 1982.

Parker, Geoffrey. *The Military Revolution: Military Innovation and the Rise of the West, 1500–1800.* 2nd ed. Cambridge: Cambridge University Press, 1996.

Rogers, Clifford J., ed. *The Military Revolution Debate: Readings on the Military Transformation of Early Modern Europe.* Boulder: Westview, 1995.

H

HAITI

> A relatively minor actor in today's global economy, Haiti played a central role as an exporter of tropical products and an importer of African slaves during the eighteenth century.

Little is known of the native population of Haiti, the Tainos, most of whom died during the decades following Christopher Columbus's first voyage to the New World (1492). The Spaniards exported small amounts of gold and Mesoamerican Indian slaves, but Haiti did not become a major trade partner until the French took over the western third of Hispaniola, which they renamed Saint Domingue, following the Treaty of Ryswick (1697).

The French imported a total of 1.7 million African slaves to their various Caribbean possessions between the 1650s and the 1830s. By 1790, 500,000 slaves of African origin lived in Saint Domingue alone. Slaves not employed as house servants worked as field hands producing tropical products for the European market, most notably sugar, cotton, coffee, cocoa, and indigo. So large were the colony's exports that they represented two-thirds of France's foreign trade; half of Europe's consumption of tropical products originated in Saint Domingue.

In keeping with the then-dominant mercantilism, the French strictly controlled trade to and from Saint Domingue under a system known as the *exclusif*. Saint Domingue specialized in raw materials and foodstuffs, exported all its production to France, and imported all its needs, including slaves, foodstuffs, luxury products, and manufactured goods from France or from French merchants. Despite these trade restrictions and the scarcity of cash, smugglers traded with non-French ports, particularly Boston, to which planters sent molasses in exchange for the dried fish they fed their slaves.

The many contacts involved in the slave trade and the production of export crops had a great political and cultural impact on Haitian history. Deeply resentful of the exclusif, white slave owners initially viewed breaking away from the French colony, along the lines of the American Revolution, with interest. Inspired by the ideals of the French Revolution, free men of mixed black and white ancestry, known as *mulâtres* (mulattoes), also supported independence, hoping that the revolutionary call for equality and fraternity would put an end to the legal racial discrimination under which they suffered. Slaves forcibly imported from Africa, who outnumbered free whites and mulattoes ten to one, eventually launched a revolt in August 1791. After twelve years of fighting, slaves gained their freedom and Saint Domingue, renamed Haiti, became independent in 1804.

Postindependence trade rapidly dwindled, as former slaves shunned plantation work and opted for small-scale subsistence farming instead. Political instability and land erosion further diminished Haitian exports, while slave imports disappeared. As of 2000, Haiti's imports, a mere $1 billion, were four times as large as its exports.

The cultural and racial legacy of eighteenth-century trade proved more lasting, and the mixing of African and French traditions is a characteristic of contemporary Haitian society. The main religions are Catholicism and Voodoo (a religion incorporating gods and saints from the Catholic and African pantheons). The main languages are French and Creole (a language based on French and African dialects). Racially, Haiti remains divided between a black majority (90 percent) and a mulatto minority of mixed European and African ancestry (10 percent).

Philippe R. Girard

See also: French Empire; French Revolution; Slavery.

BIBLIOGRAPHY

Heinl, Robert, Nancy Heinl, and Michael Heinl. *Written in Blood: The Story of the Haitian People, 1492–1995*. Lanham, MD: University Press of America, 1996.

HAKLUYT, RICHARD (1552-1616)

An Elizabethan chronicler of exploration.

Trained as an Anglican priest at Westminster and Oxford, Richard Hakluyt is better known as the most important chronicler of English exploration, trade, and colonization during the reign of Queen Elizabeth I. He was inspired to pursue his studies of navigation when just a boy by his older cousin and namesake. Richard Hakluyt the elder was a lawyer in London who collected maps and globes that showed the latest discoveries of the Spanish, French, and Portuguese. The younger Hakluyt soon went far beyond his cousin by collecting letters, government documents, business reports, logs of ship captains, and eyewitness accounts of explorers and seamen. He titled his collection *The Principal Navigations, Voyages, Traffiques and Discoveries of the English Nation* and published the first edition in 1589 and the second edition between 1598 and 1600.

Nearly one-tenth of the first edition of Hakluyt's *Voyages* was dedicated to medieval accounts of exploration before Christopher Columbus. The largest part of this section covered the legendary trip of Sir John Mandeville to the Far East. The remainder of the work dealt with eyewitness accounts of English voyages, including those undertaken by traders with Russia and the attempts of John Davis to find the Northwest Passage. The efforts of Sir John Hawkins to establish a triangle trade between England, Africa, and the West Indies along with accounts of Sir Francis Drake's circumnavigation of the globe were also included.

The second edition of Hakluyt's *Voyages* clearly showed how much England had changed in only one decade. The small island nation just learning about the wider world beyond its shores was now a rising imperial power. Legendary accounts of exploration were removed, while a greater emphasis was placed on trade with Russia and Scandinavia along with the colonization of the New World. The efforts of both Sir Walter Raleigh and his half-brother Sir Humphrey Gilbert to found colonies in North America were included. Eyewitness accounts of important naval battles between England and Spain in the Atlantic, Caribbean, and Pacific were added, along with detailed information about the defeat of the Spanish Armada in 1588.

While Hakluyt was not an official member of the English government, he worked closely with Queen Elizabeth's top advisors. Lord Burghley, Sir Robert Cecil, and Francis Walsingham relied on the documents he had collected when determining the economic and foreign policy of the nation. He also provided valuable information to traders and explorers on the best routes to take to the New World and beyond. Since maps were hard to come by in the late sixteenth century, his *Voyages* often provided the only directions available on sailing. He included "ruttiers," or sailing instructions that outlined specific routes to take on the high seas, along with descriptions of the land and people who would be met along the way. Hakluyt also participated in trade and colonization himself. He helped to organize the British East India Company in 1599 and the Second Virginia Company in 1609. He died a hero to his nation and was buried in Westminster.

Mary Stockwell

See also: Discovery and Exploration.

BIBLIOGRAPHY

Blacker, Irwin R., ed. *Hakluyt's Voyages*. New York: Viking, 1965.

HAMBURG, GERMANY

The largest port city in Germany, founded in 825 C.E.

In 825, the castle of Hammaburg was constructed between the Alster and Elbe Rivers. After the Archbishop Ansgar began using the castle as a

Since its days as a member of the German Hanseatic League of trading cities, Hamburg has been a major port of northern Europe. *(Library of Congress)*

base from which to convert the barbarian Germanic tribes, the importance of the city increased, but it was not until the founding of Lübeck on the coast of the Baltic Sea that Hamburg emerged as an important port city. In 1189, Emperor Frederick I (Barbarossa) issued a charter to the merchants of Hamburg to build a new town beside the former city and extended the right of toll exemptions from the Elbe River to the North Sea, navigational privileges, and special trading rights. Hamburg developed into Germany's largest port city after the founding of the Hanseatic League in Lübeck in 1321. After the decline of the Hanseatic League, the city of Hamburg was declared a free imperial city (1510), established its own stock exchange (1558), founded the Bank of Hamburg (1619), and devised a protective convoy system for its ships (1662). During the Napoleonic Wars, Hamburg fell under French control.

In 1819, the city once again became a free and independent town. Shipping began from Hamburg to Australia and across the Atlantic Ocean during the mid-1800s. By 1912, the city had become the most important port in Europe, and second only to London and New York in the world. Just before World War I, the harbor area was expanded with the construction of the oil harbor, the Walterhofer harbor, the park harbor, the Maakwerder harbor, and the Ruegenberger harbor. During both world wars, the city sustained heavy losses. After World War II, more than 50 percent of the city's facilities and 80 percent of the harbor had been destroyed and would not be rebuilt for another twenty years or more.

During the period of the Hanseatic League, the city of Hamburg was a transshipment site for products such as grain, cloth, fur, herring, spices, timber, and metals. Its primary export was beer. By the nineteenth century, Hamburg had also become a storage area for products shipped into

Europe such as coffee, cocoa, spices, and carpets. After the reconstruction of the harbors and facilities following World War II, Hamburg attracted many foreign firms. By the beginning of the twenty-first century, more than 185 Chinese and 135 Japanese firms had established offices in the city. Today more than 3,000 import-export companies operate in Germany's second-largest city. Each year more than 12,000 ships depart from the harbor to all points around the world. Hamburg continues to be a banking center for northern Europe as well as one of the country's largest insurance centers. Besides the port, Hamburg is also home to many service industries, famous entertainment districts, and opera houses. Although more than 3 million people live in the city, more than 40 percent of the land is reserved for nature parks or landscape reserves.

Cynthia Clark Northrup

See also: German Empires; Hanseatic League.

BIBLIOGRAPHY

Raff, Diether. *A History of Germany: From the Medieval Empire to the Present,* trans. Bruce Little. New York: St. Martin's Press, 1988.

Tuck, Eleanor L. *The History of Germany.* Westport: Greenwood, 1999.

HANSEATIC LEAGUE

> A loose association of northern Germanic towns that promoted and protected their mutual commercial activity throughout the Baltic region.

During the twelfth century, as the Crusades were being fought, German peasants began migrating eastward into Slavic lands. Local rulers encouraged the immigration for a number of reasons, including the Christianizing of the Slavs, cultivating the land for the production of food, and extending their power. Initially, the Brethren of the Sword, a crusading order, was active in the Slavic lands, but the group was evidently absorbed by the Order of the Teutonic Knights whose grand master controlled the region. The Rhineland was also being linked commercially during this period with Cologne as the center of the alliance.

Meanwhile, trade between Hamburg and Kiel along the salt road had developed in the west. In 1143, the count of Holstein founded Lübeck, and fifteen years later the duke of Saxony acquired the city and conferred on it the rights of an imperial free town. He offered peace terms to leaders in Norway, Sweden, Denmark, and Russia if they traded with the merchants of the city. A canal was constructed that linked Hamburg with Lübeck, which replaced the overland route formerly used to transport the salt mined in Kiel. Merchants from the two towns agreed that it was in their best interest to cooperate in matters of trade. The two cities enjoyed trading privileges in London and Flanders as early as 1270. From Lübeck, trading centers were established at Visby on the Swedish coast of Jutland, Riga, Revel (present-day Tallinn), Danzig (present-day Gdansk), and Dorpat (present-day Tartu). These cities linked Lübeck with the trade of Novgorod and the eastern Baltic Sea.

EARLY YEARS

Trade was initially focused on Novgorod, where furs were exchanged for grain. Amber, honey, tar, and flax were also shipped from Russia throughout the Baltic. The forests around Novgorod would later yield the timber, masts, and naval stores highly desired by the Spanish, French, and English in the fifteenth and sixteenth centuries. Grain from Poland was shipped to England and Flanders, where it was exchanged for cloth and other guild-manufactured goods. Trade from the north included copper and iron ore from Sweden as well as herring. Fish was a vital commodity during the Middle Ages because it was a source of protein and was eaten throughout Europe on fast days, during lent, and on Friday because of a papal prohibition on the consumption of meat on that day. Shipping fish over long distances presented a problem until the merchants of Hamburg supplied Lübeck with salt to preserve the herring.

During the 1280s, the three groups—the Lübeck-Hamburg merchants, the Order of the

Founded as a mercantile association of north European towns for the purposes of promoting mutual security and exclusive trading privileges, the Hanseatic League came to dominate the trade of northern Europe by the fourteenth century. Here, league judges try a rule-breaking merchant. *(Mary Evans Picture Library)*

Teutonic Knights, and the Rhineland merchants—joined to form the Hanseatic League. To facilitate trade in foreign countries, the Hansa established counters (Kontore) in Bruges in Flanders, Bergen in Norway, Novgorod in Russia, and the Steel Yard in London. These counters were three-story buildings staffed by young, unmarried men who committed to a minimum of one-year's service (required since the Hansa ships completed their journey once a year). The first floor of the building was used for buying and selling, the second as a warehouse, and the third for living quarters. The employees were required to live on the premises and were locked in at night. The counters operated as the equivalent of an early stock exchange.

Cities involved in the Hanseatic trade could apply for membership, which would either be accepted or rejected. Those accepted into the league were extended the same privileges as other members. One of the benefits of belonging to the Hansa was that merchants could ship their goods on a number of vessels also being used by other merchants. By dividing their goods among several vessels, the risk of losing a large amount of goods at one time because of a shipwreck or to pirates was reduced. In a period when no insurance was available, this option was vital for the merchants. Hansa ships would also travel in convoys and thereby offered added protection to the merchants and their cargo.

The success of the Hansa merchants was secured by the development of the cog, a flat-bottomed boat with one mast and a square sail that had the capacity to carry as much as 200 lasts, with the average ship holding 100 lasts (200 metric tons per last). This technological development replaced the Viking ships that were faster but could carry only 20 lasts. The cogs moved like barges in the shallow waters along the coasts of northern Europe carrying bulk items such as grain to their destinations. Without the use of advanced navigational tools, the ships relied on the astrolabe and a Book of the Seas that listed landmarks along the coast that would indicate their location. Churches, inlets, and the depth of the water would often be the only useful indicators for where the ships were on their journey. The use of the square sail meant that the ships could not sail into the wind but the seasonal wind directional changes allowed the vessels to travel one way and then back within a one-year cycle.

Although it is generally agreed that the roots of the Hanseatic League can be traced back to the original cooperation of merchants between Hamburg and Lübeck in 1241, no exact date exists that marks the formal start of the league. Members did not operate under a formal constitution but did meet occasionally to discuss policies involving mutual defense and trade agreements. Attendance was sporadic and the results nonbinding. Members could voluntarily leave the association or could be removed if they failed to follow the policies of the league in matters involving foreign trade. Representatives would negotiate favorable trade agreements with foreign leaders, yet each city would receive its own copy of the agreement. During the thirteenth and fourteenth centuries, the Hanseatic League secured favorable, and in some cases, monopolistic agreements with foreign rulers and maintained their position through gifts and bribes. When the situation required more serious measures, the league could threaten to withdraw its trade or start an embargo as in 1358 against Flanders. Rarely would a threat of force be used.

A conflict did occur between the western third of the Hanseatic League, controlled by Lübeck, Hamburg, and Waldemar IV of Denmark. The Danish king, who controlled the southern tip of

Sweden (Scania) at the time, believed that he should control the revenues generated by the sale of herring caught in the waters off the coast of his territory. In 1361, representatives had just returned to Lübeck after renegotiating the herring rights when the king attacked and sacked Visby. An appeal for help from the other two portions of the league was ignored since the Rhineland did not see any benefit in the war and the grand master of the Teutonic Knights was a close friend of the Danish king and forbade any involvement in the conflict. Lübeck sent 52 cogs, each with 100 armed men, along with auxiliary ships to Copenhagen, where they sacked the city and then preceded to the Danish fortress on Scania. The plan was to join the army of the king of Sweden, but the army did not arrive. Instead, the Hanseatic forces disembarked in preparation for the attack and were on land when the Danish navy arrived in the harbor with their ships. The Hanseatic ships were either destroyed or captured, and the vanquished Hansa forces made their way home on foot. The leader of the expedition, Johann Wittenborg, was hanged in the public square on the insistence of the angry merchants who had not only lost their ships, but also their trading privileges for herring.

The Danish king concluded a peace agreement with Lübeck, but since the Rhineland portion of the league had not been involved in the conflict he decided that attacks on the center portion of the league was not prohibited by the treaty. Subsequent attacks went unanswered initially by both the western portion of the league that had just lost much to the Crown and the eastern portion under the grand master until the raids began inflicting losses on the Order of the Teutonic Knights. The Prussian cities were allowed to defend the league against the Danish attacks. Meanwhile, the king faced a revolt led by his nobles who wanted to recoup some of the privileges wrested from them by the king in his effort to consolidate power. Waldemar sought refuge with the grand master, who persuaded him that it was in his best interest to sue for peace with the league. The terms of the Peace of Stralsund (1370) granted Lübeck the revenues generated from the herring trade control over the Danish fortress and even allowed the league to veto the ascension of any new king to the Danish throne for the next fifteen years. One of the consequences of the war was that the privateers who had received letters of marque, authorizing them to seize Danish ships as prizes, continued to ply the Baltic waters as pirates seeking easy wealth by attacking Hanseatic ships.

DECLINE OF THE LEAGUE

During the next century, the power of the league declined. Losses caused by piracy were compounded by the sudden movement of herring spawning from the southern tip of Sweden to the North Sea, which was controlled by the Dutch. Pressures also mounted as the neighboring region consolidated into nation-states. In 1386, Lithuania and Poland were united, followed by the formation of a union between Norway, Sweden, and Denmark in 1397. These new nations and unions refused to grant the same trading privileges as before and in many instances insisted, for the first time, on the collection of duties on items imported by the league. In 1494, Tsar Ivan III cancelled the rights of the league to transact business in Novgorod. At the same time, the discovery of the New World shifted the emphasis of trade from the Baltic region to the Atlantic seaports. Amsterdam replaced Lübeck as the busiest port.

The peasant revolts that followed the Reformation resulted in the need of the German princes to consolidate control over the population. Many of the privileges enjoyed by the merchants were withdrawn. At the same time, the Hansa merchants found themselves unable to compete against the new large commercial firms such as the Fuggers. Member cities, which no longer perceived the benefit of participating, withdrew from the Hansa, further weakening the league. Trade between the league and the Atlantic countries continued until the 1600s with the Hanseatic merchants supplying timber, naval stores, and grain to the unified nation-states of Spain, France, and England, but the glory days of the German merchants were over.

Since the Hansa was not a formal institution, its membership remained fluid and ambiguous. Membership estimates varied over time between 200 at the height of the league's influence to 70 cities as the power of the merchants declined in the seventeenth century. The last meeting of its members occurred in 1669. Few members attended, and no decisions were made. Although the league was never formally dissolved, the cities of Hamburg, Lübeck, and Bremen continued to be referred to as Hanseatic cities through the nineteenth century.

Cynthia Clark Northrup

See also: Discovery and Exploration; Fugger Family, Novgorod; Ships.

BIBLIOGRAPHY

Dollinger, Philippe. *The German Hansa,* trans. and ed. D.S. Ault and S.H. Steinberg. Stanford: Stanford University Press, 1970.

Scammell, G.V. *The World Encompassed: The First European Maritime Empires, c. 800–1650.* Los Angeles: University of California Press, 1981.

HAPSBURGS

The Hapsburg family of Europe is one of the oldest and most distinguished of the royal houses.

The Hapsburgs reigned in one form or another from the fifteenth to the twentieth centuries. Guntram the Rich, who lived in the mid-tenth century, is considered by scholars to be the earliest traceable ancestor of the House of Hapsburg. However, it was Werner, who died in 1096, who became the first count of Hapsburg. Otto was the count of Hapsburg to actually use this designation. He died in 1111.

The Hapsburg name comes from the family castle built in 1020. The castle was named Habichtsburg meaning Hawk's Castle. It was located on the Aare River in the canton of Aargau in Switzerland. In 1173, Otto's grandson Count Albert III inherited large estates in Alsace, Baden, and Switzerland. In turn, Rudolf II, who died in 1232, and Albert IV inherited these lands. The Hapsburgs acquired more lands when the Houses of Lenzburg, Zähringen, and Kyburg became extinct. The rise of the Hapsburgs to European prominence had begun.

The Hapsburgs became prominent in Europe in 1273 after the election of Count Rudolf IV as the German king and as Holy Roman Emperor Rudolf I. A war with King Ottocar, or Ottokar, II of Bohemia precipitated this election. However, King Ottocar's defeat and subsequent death at Marchfeld in 1278 allowed the Hapsburgs to take possession of the duchies of Austria, Carniola, Styria, and, in 1335, Carinthia. In 1282, Emperor Rudolf I declared these lands and the title itself hereditary.

Rudolf's son, Holy Roman Emperor Albert I, was assassinated in 1308. This led to the suppression of the imperial title for more than a century. In the early fifteenth century, Albert V of Austria married a daughter of Holy Roman Emperor Sigismund. After Sigismund's death, Albert succeeded him as king of Bohemia and Hungary. In 1438, Albert became the German king as Albert II. From this time on, except for the short period from 1742 to 1745, the head of the House of Hapsburg was elected both the German king and the Holy Roman emperor.

In 1453, Holy Roman Emperor Frederick III elevated Austria to an archduchy. In 1471, Frederick acquired Fiume. During this time, he was in constant warfare against Matthias Corvinus, king of Bohemia and Hungary. The task of consolidating the empire would fall on the shoulders of his son, Maximilian. After becoming emperor in 1493, Maximilian I, through his shrewd diplomacy, was in a large measure responsible for the establishment of Hapsburg domination of Europe and its politics until the beginning of the twentieth century. Maximilian's marriage to Mary of Burgundy brought the family the Bourguignon inheritance in the Low Countries. His son Philip's marriage to Joanna of Castile brought Aragon and Castile in Spain into the empire. His successor, Charles V, inherited Spain and its overseas empire, parts of Italy, the Netherlands, and the Hapsburg German and Austrian possessions. The Hapsburgs were at the zenith of their power, control, and prestige. After his abdication in 1556, Charles V left all his holdings to his son Philip II of Spain. This meant that Philip II ruled Spain, the Netherlands, the Italian provinces, and the overseas empire. At the same time, Charles's brother, Emperor Ferdinand I, ruled Austria, Bohemia, and Hungary.

During the reign of Charles V, the king of Spain and emperor of Germany, the Hapsburgs ruled over much of Europe in the first half of the sixteenth century, a time when the continent was beginning to establish itself as the dominant trading region of the world. *(Library of Congress)*

After the death of Charles, the House of Hapsburg was divided in two. The Austrian branch retained the imperial title. However, even with this division the Spanish and Austrian branches fought together during the Thirty Years' War (1618–1648). Additionally, they fought the French in the Third Dutch War (1672–1678) as well as in the War of the Grand Alliance (1688–1697). This much warfare led to a major decline in resources for the Hapsburgs.

The extinction of the Spanish Hapsburg line in 1700 led to the War of the Spanish Succession at the beginning of the eighteenth century. After the Peace of Utrecht in 1713 and the Treaty of Rastatt in 1714, Spain was no longer part of the Hapsburg empire. The family holdings had been reduced significantly. The war shifted economic power to Great Britain, which received the asiento from Spain granting the British the exclusive monopoly on the importation of slaves into the Spanish New World. The French lost their lucrative fishing rights along the North Atlantic seaboard. The Austrian Hapsburgs received the Italian provinces, except for Sicily, and the southern Netherlands. Shortly, the male line of the Austrian Hapsburgs would cease to exist, thereby creating more hereditary complications.

By the Pragmatic Sanction of 1713, Charles attained the constant indivisibility of the Hapsburg lands as well as the right of succession of his daughter Maria Theresa. When Charles VI died in 1740, the male line of the Austrian Hapsburgs ended. On the death of Charles Albert of Bavaria, Holy Roman emperor as Charles VII, and the only non-Hapsburg to rule since 1438, the imperial title was bestowed on Archduchess Maria Theresa's husband, Francis. He was the grand duke of Tuscany and the former duke of Lorraine, and became Emperor Francis I. Their marriage in 1736 had created the House of Hapsburg-Lorraine. In 1740, the Prussians invaded Austria, a move that resulted in the War of Austrian Succession. During the conflict, which was also known as King George's War, territory changed hands, but at the conclusion of the war most of the gains were returned in the Treaty of Aix-la-Chapelle in 1748, except for some Austrian lands that the Prussians retained.

Maria Theresa, unhappy with the outcome of the war, attacked Prussia in 1756, thus precipitating the Seven Years' War, also known as the French and Indian War. This conflict affected trade worldwide. As a result of the fighting, the European nations verged on bankruptcy. Increased taxation and the imposition of taxes by the British on their American colonies led to the American Revolution. French attempts to force the British out of India resulted in British control over the subcontinent and its pepper and cotton trade in the postwar period. Britain emerged as the dominant world power as a result of its victory in this conflict.

At this point, the Hapsburgs again split into two lines. One carried on the main Hapsburg heritage, and the other was the Hapsburg-Lorraine line. Maria Theresa's grandson, Francis II, was the last Holy Roman emperor. During his reign, the Hapsburg empire played a leading role in the defense of Europe against Napoléon Bonaparte. In 1804, sensing the end for the Holy Roman empire, Francis II assumed the title of Francis I, emperor of Austria.

At the Congress of Vienna (1815), Francis was one of the most powerful European monarchs, even with Napoléon at the height of his power. Ferdinand I, Francis's infirm son, proved unable to hold his office. During the Revolution of 1848, Ferdinand was compelled to abdicate in favor of his nephew, Francis Joseph (Franz Josef). Francis Joseph ruled from 1848 until 1916. In 1859, Austria lost its possessions in Italy. The Prussians assumed the role of leaders even as that of the German Hapsburgs declined.

The Hapsburg realm was restructured in 1867 as the Dual Monarchy of Austria-Hungary. The assassination of heir apparent Francis Ferdinand in 1914 brought about World War I. This along with the death of Francis Joseph in 1916 left his grandnephew, Emperor Charles I, to witness the defeat of Austria-Hungary.

The Austro-Hungarian empire was dissolved after Charles's abdication in 1918. The Hapsburgs were the ruling house of Austria from 1218 until the end of World War I in 1918. The new Austrian republic banished the Hapsburgs in 1919. Charles attempted to regain his Hungarian throne in 1921, but his efforts proved unsuccessful. He died in exile. Charles's son, Archduke Otto, succeeded him as head of the Hapsburgs. In 1961, Archduke Otto petitioned the government to allow him to return to Austria as a private citizen. Otto's request was granted in 1963. He became a resident of West Germany.

Peter E. Carr

See also: World War I.

BIBLIOGRAPHY

Evans, R.J.W. *The Making of the Hapsburg Monarchy, 1550–1700: An Interpretation.* Oxford: Oxford University Press, 1979.

Kann, R.A. *A History of the Habsburg Empire, 1526–1918.* Berkeley: University of California Press, 1977.

HARBORS

Part of a body of water along a coast—either naturally formed or man-made—that is safe and offers protection for ships.

Harbors have been centers of trade since ancient times and continue to be so today. Ancient harbors were locations where traders, merchants, and sailors congregated and cities developed. Since overland travel was traditionally expensive and dangerous, merchants transported their goods by water. Rivers from the interior regions flowed to larger seas. If the mouth of the river included a safe harbor for ships, a commercial center would develop with storehouses and marketplaces. Traders would congregate there to conduct their business. Cultural exchanges also occurred at these harbor cities, with multiple languages commonly spoken. Items from faraway places could be exchanged for local goods or products from other parts of the world.

Most harbor cities operated under the protection of the local ruler who collected taxes on the sale of items. Trade brought wealth to the ruler who could then use the profits to construct a navy to protect the harbor or to conquer other people. On many occasions throughout history, the formation of a navy signaled the beginning of a period of colonization, such as with the Phoenicians, Greeks, Romans, Spanish, and British. Harbors became important for military purposes as well as for trade. The military power of the country or empire was increasingly required to protect trade. The British were among the first to realize the connection and began passing a series of navigation laws in the 1660s that required English goods to be carried on English ships with English crews. In the late nineteenth century, the United States, having already expanded from coast to coast, searched for harbors in the Pacific Ocean (Hawaii, the Philippines, Guam, and Midway) for their merchant and military ships. Harbors remain vital for the projection of both economic and military power throughout the world.

MEDITERRANEAN WORLD

One of the most ancient harbors is that of Sidon in present-day Lebanon, which was in use during Phoenician times. The natural harbor was located at the end of the Lebanon Mountains at a point where the cedar forests were not very dense. Goods from Damascus to other parts of the Mediterranean Sea were shipped through Sidon during the fifteenth and fourteenth centuries B.C.E. Local goods such as cedar were shipped to Egypt in exchange for grain and wheat. After 1253 B.C.E., when the Philistines attacked and destroyed the city, power passed to a second harbor city of Tyre, which was a colony of Sidon. Tyre remained dominant until the Babylonians destroyed much of the region after a revolt by Egypt, Syria, Sidon, and Phoenicia in 606 B.C.E. Sidon surrendered before the Babylonians arrived and was spared. Tyre was destroyed, thereby allowing Sidon to once again emerge as the leading harbor of the Levant. Sidon prospered by trading its unique purple dye and textiles as far away as Spain. Cedar and the city's transparent glass were also important exports. During the Roman empire, Sidon operated a mint and was the point of transshipment for goods moving from Damascus to Rome. The harbor was later used by the crusaders and others until the seventeenth century, when Fakhr ad-Din II ordered its entrance filled to prevent invasion by the Turkish fleet.

When Alexander the Great conquered the Persians, he gained control over Egypt. In 332 B.C.E., he founded the city of Alexandria, which had a double harbor. When Alexander died, his dominions were divided among his generals, with Egypt going to Ptolemy. The city of Alexandria became the largest city in the Mediterranean region by 250 B.C.E. A lighthouse, one of the seven ancient wonders of the world, guided ships into the harbor, where exotic spices from India arrived by sea and where goods were shipped to all parts of Europe. Alexandria continued to operate as a major harbor city with businessmen establishing offices from many different countries in the city itself. Fragments of contracts reveal the sale of goods from Punt (present-day Somalia) and even the southern tip of the Arabian Peninsula (present-day Yemen) being received for merchants from Greece, Macedonia, Rome, and Carthage. Alexandria declined in importance after the Arabs moved the capital of Egypt to Cairo in 969 C.E., and by the fourteenth century the harbor had silted up. In 1819, a canal to the Nile was constructed and the importance of the city was acknowledged once again as a deep-water port. In the twentieth century, Alexandria operated as an industrial center that produced refined petroleum, cotton textiles, paper, plastics, and processed food.

Another important Mediterranean harbor was located at Ostia, an ancient city at the mouth of the Tiber River just south of Rome. The founders of Rome used the harbor as a source of protection as well as for the shipment of goods. Under the empire, Augustus, Claudius I, Trajan, and Hadrian all expanded the harbor and the city. The harbor had many storehouses where goods would be held until they were put on barges that oxen would then pull up the Tiber to Rome. One of the largest commodities shipped to Ostia were slaves from North Africa and the Middle East. Most Roman families had at least one slave, and many slaves also worked in the storehouses and on the docks. By the third century C.E., the importance of the city began to decline as the wealth of the Roman empire shifted to Constantinople.

Ancient ports reflected the wealth and importance of the empires in which they were located. During the reign of Athens over much of the Mediterranean, Athenians constructed and fortified the harbor at Piraeus located about four miles south of the city. The port continues to operate as a transshipment point for Greek exports such as olive oil and for the importation of goods from throughout the world. Ancient Carthage also had a major port on the Lake of Tunis. The harbor offered both protection and food, as a variety of fish lived in these waters. Founded as a colony of Tyre, Carthage became one of the largest trading centers in the Mediterranean as the ancient harbors experienced a series of conquests. Goods from North Africa, Sicily, and Spain were traded regularly. Items such as cloth, ceramics, glassware, arms, and woodworks were exported from Carthage. After the Greeks consolidated their control over the eastern Mediterranean, they faced the Carthaginians at Sicily, where the Romans began their ascent over both cultures. The Romans, at the conclusion of the Punic wars, destroyed the city of Carthage, and salt was sown into the soil to prevent the growing of crops.

EAST ASIA

Outside of the Mediterranean world, other important harbors existed. In the Spice Islands, the port at Melaka (Malacca) offered safety to ships plying the dangerous waters of the region. Melaka continued to dominate trade in the area until the British took control of Singapore in 1824. Under

The harbor in Hong Kong, one of the finest in East Asia, became the leading opium port in the world in the mid-nineteenth century. *(Library of Congress)*

the British rule, Chinese and Malay merchants began trading at Singapore. With the development of the harbor, trade flourished. Tin and rubber became the primary commodities. The construction of a railroad from the Malay Peninsula to Bangkok and the construction of an airport helped to increase trade further.

Another important harbor in the Far East is located at Hong Kong. The rocky, barren island off the coast of southeast China, already occupied by the British since the First Opium War (1839–1842), was leased to the British by the Chinese government in 1898 for ninety-nine years. Hong Kong has many natural harbors, but the Victoria harbor is one of the finest harbors in the world. Operating as a free port, Hong Kong became a point of transshipment for goods exported from China to the rest of the world. A booming trade center developed along with a large banking and shipping industry. The textile industry is one of the world's largest, primarily because of the availability of cheap labor. Other products manufactured in Hong Kong include plastics, electrical and electronic devices, watches, jewelry, and toys. Food is imported from China, except for fish that are abundant in the waters around Hong Kong.

In 1997, Hong Kong reverted to Chinese rule and operates as a conduit for most of the trade between China and the rest of the world. Other major deep-water harbors throughout the South Pacific and the Far East include Sydney, Australia; Manila, Philippines; and Auckland, New Zealand.

AMERICAS

Cities in the New World developed around harbors as major cities from the seventeenth through the twentieth centuries. Boston has a natural harbor that protected the early immigrants as well as the shipping industry that developed in New England. Philadelphia also boasted a natural harbor, as did Baltimore. All these cities relied on the transatlantic trade for their livelihood during the colonial and early republic period. Goods such as salted fish, foodstuffs, lumber, and naval stores were shipped either to Great Britain or were exchanged for slaves along the west coast of Africa. The slaves would be sold or exchanged in the Caribbean for sugar and molasses, which were used for the production of rum in New England. Goods shipped from these ports to Great Britain would be exchanged for manufactured items not available in the colonies. The lucrative trade from these harbor cities ensured the growth of the colonies, and when this trade was disrupted by various acts of Parliament in an attempt to raise tax revenues, these harbor cities were the first to resist this new form of direct British taxation, resistance that led to the American Revolution. Other colonial port cities included Charleston, South Carolina, from where rice and tobacco were sent to England, and Providence, Rhode Island, which exported salted fish.

The two major harbors in the Gulf of Mexico that became part of the United States were New Orleans, Louisiana, and Galveston, Texas. New Orleans, located at the mouth of the Mississippi River, operated as a port for the French, the Spanish, and then the French again before the United States purchased Louisiana for $15 million from France. As Americans moved further west after the American Revolution, the right to navigate the Mississippi River became vital since shipping goods over land was too expensive. In 1795, Thomas Pinckney, envoy extraordinaire to Spain, negotiated a treaty for free access to the Mississippi River and the right of deposit at New Orleans. Without such access, American settlers in the then western portion of the United States would have been prohibited from trading with the rest of the country. Great Britain recognized the importance of the harbor at New Orleans and attempted to capture the city to win the War of 1812.

The other major port was located at Galveston. Galveston was the port city through which much of the cotton from Texas was shipped during the nineteenth century. Unfortunately, in 1900 the island was decimated by a hurricane with a great loss of life and property. Plans were then made to dig a deep-water ship channel to Houston so that ships would be better protected. Since the channel's completion in 1914, Houston has developed into the fourth-largest city in the United States, with trade centered on petroleum, chemical, natural gas, salt, and limestone products.

On the U.S. West Coast, harbors at Los Angeles, Seattle, and San Francisco developed during the mid-1800s, especially after the gold rush of 1849. The British recognized the importance of a deep-water harbor when negotiating with the United States over the Oregon Territory. Instead of risking that the United States would gain control of all the territory, the British agreed to the present-day borders that gave them Vancouver, British Columbia. Primary goods from the region included lumber, iron, copper, gold, fish, and agricultural products.

To the south of the United States a major harbor is located at Panama City (important because of its location vis-à-vis the Panama Canal). Mexican harbors include Acapulco and Cancun, both known for their tourist industries. South American harbors include several in Argentina, including Buenos Aires, Bahia, Exolgan Terminal, Quequin, and Río de la Plata; Brazil, including the Imbituba, Itajaí, Itaqui, Maceio, Para, Recife, Rio Grande, Santos, and Vitoria, as well as the Amazon Authority and Terminal 1 Rio; Chile, including Antofagasta, Chacabuco, Puerto Montt, San Antonio, Valparaiso, and Ventanas; Columbia, including Buenaventura, Cartagena, and Santa Marta; Equador, including Guayaquil; Uruguay, including the Ports Authority; and Venezuela, including Cabello and Maracaibo. Products from minerals and metals to foodstuffs are shipped out of these harbors, linking South America to trade networks around the world.

Although Africa has a long coastline, there are few major ports and harbors. Some of the major ports include Algiers, Annaba, Bejaïa, and Skikda in Algeria; Lobito in Angola; Djibouti harbor in Djibouti; Banjul in Gambia; the Namibian Ports Authority in Namibia; Nigerian Ports Authority in Nigeria; and Portnet in South Africa.

EUROPE

The major ports of Europe contributed to the rise of trade, especially from medieval times to the present. Antwerp in Belgium; Copenhagen in Denmark; Marseilles and Paris in France; Hamburg in Germany; Genoa and Venice in Italy; Amsterdam in the Netherlands; Cadiz and Barcelona in Spain; and London, Liverpool, and Cardiff in England have operated as harbors of trade for centuries. As these harbors developed, the adjacent cities prospered from trade and the economy expanded.

Even after the advent of the railroad and the airplane, a majority of goods were shipped from one harbor to another, both internationally and domestically. The ability of ships to load and unload their cargo under the protection and safety a harbor was necessary for the conduct of trade. Many countries have worked to increase the depth of their harbors to accommodate the larger modern supertankers. In some instances, such as in Manhattan and Brooklyn, larger ships can no longer reach the docks, so trade has shifted to the New Jersey side of the harbor, where goods are off-loaded and trucked into New York City. As the size of ships increases, some harbors will become obsolete while others will be developed to take advantage of the opportunities. Harbors will continue to play an important role in trade in the future.

Cynthia Clark Northrup

See also: British Empire; Greek City-States; Roman Empire; United States.

BIBLIOGRAPHY

"Overseas Maritime Ports of the World" (www.overseasmaritime.com/ports/samer.htm, accessed November 2003).

"Sidon" (www.ancientroute.com/cities/sidon.htm, accessed November 2003).

Smith, Robert H. *The Complete Guide to Harbors, Anchorages, and Marinas.* Del Mar, CA: C Books, 1981.

HARGREAVES, JAMES (1720-1777)

British inventor of the spinning jenny.

Born in 1720 to a rural agricultural family in Oswaldwistle, England, James Hargreaves was not an educated person, but he did have experience in weaving cloth (during the eighteenth century, English families in the countryside produced their own food and weaved their own cloth) and as a carpenter. John Kay's invention of the flying shuttle when Hargreaves was just thirteen years old reduced the time needed to weave cloth, however, it also created a shortage of thread. Hargreaves married Elizabeth Grimshaw in 1740, and the couple went on to have a large family. Two years later, several inventors developed a machine for spinning thread, but the required investment included the building of a small factory. The complex process failed to catch on, and the shortage of thread continued.

In 1761, the Society for the Encouragement of Arts, Commerce, and Manufacturers offered a 50-pound prize for the best machine designed to alleviate the shortage. Hargreaves won the prize with his spinning jenny. The machine consisted of a moving carriage, designed to stretch the thread, which was attached to a large wheel with six spinning-wheel mechanisms. The device was easy enough for a small child to operate and was small enough to fit into the average cottage kitchen. The original spinning jenny could spin 8 threads at a time, while later models were capable of producing 120 threads at a time. The original model was capable of producing the same amount of thread as eight people. Since fewer workers were required, many feared that they would lose their livelihood.

Although initial reaction to the new machine aroused suspicion and resulted in the destruction of Hargreaves's machines by angry workers, by 1770, when he received his patent, more than 20,000 spinning jennies were in operation, all constructed by those who had used his original design or improved on it. But the spinning jenny was only capable of producing coarse thread. In 1771, Richard Arkwright created the water frame. In 1775, Samuel Crompton combined the water frame and the spinning jenny into a device called the spinning mule, which perfected the process begun by Hargreaves. With the invention of the spinning jenny, the water frame, and the mule, the shortage of thread was resolved and English textile mills boomed.

Hargreaves died in his Nottingham factory in 1777.

Cynthia Clark Northrup

See also: Textiles.

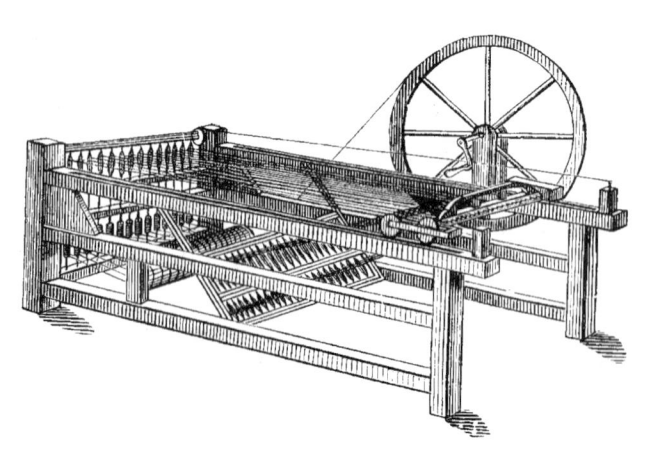

James Hargreaves's spinning jenny, invented in the 1760s, revolutionized weaving in England and helped establish the country as the world's greatest exporter of woolen cloth.
(© North Wind Picture Archives)

BIBLIOGRAPHY

Aspin, Christopher. *James Hargreaves and the Spinning Jenny.* Helmshore, UK: Helmshore Local History Society, 1964.

HAWLEY-SMOOT TARIFF

The Hawley-Smoot Tariff culminated a forty-year period of protectionism in the United States. From Benjamin Harrison's defeat of free trading Grover Cleveland in the election of 1888, protection remained the Republican program.

Among the highest tariffs in U.S. history, the 1929 Hawley-Smoot Tariff, named after its sponsors, Representative W.C. Hawley (left) and Senator Reed Smoot, hampered trade and, say some historians, contributed to the onset of the Great Depression. *(Library of Congress)*

As early as the McKinley Tariff of 1890, Republicans advocated protection of not just infant industries, but even mature industries. They understood that a high tariff would discourage imports. As a bonus, because it would shrink revenues it would also reduce the national surplus. Republicans remained so committed to protection that they willingly accepted the Sixteenth Amendment, the federal income tax, in exchange for the Payne-Aldrich Tariff of 1909. For forty years, the only exception to the consistent increases in rates was the Underwood Tariff of 1913, passed under the Democrat Woodrow Wilson.

Back in power, Republicans enacted the Emergency Tariff Act of 1921, which, with the Fordney-McCumber Tariff of 1922, reflected the desire to protect the "war babies," the new industries such as chemicals and dyes that produced products formerly imported from Germany. Fordney-McCumber raised average duties to about 33 percent.

Although American sales were possible primarily because of American overseas lending, the prosperity of the 1920s occurred because of the high protective tariff. Logically, once the economy turned sour in 1929, conservatives thought to avoid depression by raising tariffs still higher. Congress debated for a year and in 1930 passed the tariff, over protests from foreign countries and American economists.

After the end of World War I, agriculture experienced a depression. Herbert Hoover, hoping to give farmers some relief through protection from foreign competition, signed the bill. In fact, although the tariff provided farmers minimal protection from foreign competition (it dropped from the free list hides, leather, shoes, timber, cement, long-staple cotton, and brick), the tariff protected industry while hurting agriculture. It led other nations, in self-defense, to establish high tariff walls against American products, including agriculture.

Hawley-Smoot raised rates to the highest levels in more than a century. Increases of 50 percent were not unusual, and some rates doubled. With an average rate of 42 percent, Hawley-Smoot rates doubled those of the Underwood-Simmons Tariff of 1913.

Debate continues about whether or not Hawley-Smoot caused or exacerbated the Great Depression. World trade nearly collapsed coincident with the tariff war. Between 1929 and 1932, national income fell by half, and exports dropped from $5.4 billion to $1.6 billion. Unquestionably, high tariffs and retaliatory measures did not encourage revival of trade.

In the election of 1932, the Republicans campaigned on a platform of even higher tariffs. The Democrats ran on promises of reciprocal trade agreements, whereby the president could negotiate tariff reductions of up to 50 percent with countries agreeing to reduce their tariffs in turn. Between 1934 and 1947, reciprocity reduced average tariff rates by 25 percent.

John Barnhill

See also: Great Depression; Tariff Barriers; Tariffs; World War I.

BIBLIOGRAPHY

Bartlett, Bruce. "The Truth About Trade in History" (www.freetrade.org/new/buch1.html, accessed September 2002).

Dobson, John M. *Two Centuries of Tariffs*. Washington, DC: U.S. Government Printing Office, 1976.

Irwin, Douglas A., and Randall S. Kroszner. *Log-Rolling and Economic Interests in the Passage of the Smoot-Hawley Tariff*. Chicago: Center for the Study of the Economy and the State, University of Chicago, 1996.

Kaplan, Edward S. *American Trade Policy, 1923–1995*. Westport: Greenwood, 1996.

O'Brien, Anthony. "Smoot-Hawley Tariff." In *EH.Net Encyclopedia*, ed. Robert Whaples (www.eh.net/encyclopedia/contents/obrien.hawley-smoot.tariff.php, accessed August 2001).

HECKSCHER, ELI FILIP (1879-1952)

A Swedish economist and economic historian who was considered a groundbreaker in both economic history and trade theory.

Eli Filip Heckscher is known for his article "The Effect of Foreign Trade on the Distribution of Income" (1919), which maintained that the types of commodities that a nation exports depends entirely on the nation's endowment of resources. This scholarly masterpiece broke from classical international trade theory and introduced what became the Heckscher-Ohlin model of international trade. Born in Stockholm, Sweden, he studied at Uppsala University where he was a student of David Davidson. He did his doctoral work at Stockholm University under Gustav Cassel.

Heckscher's doctoral dissertation was entitled "On the Importance of Railroads to Sweden's Economic Development." After finishing his doctorate, he served with a Swedish government committee as permanent secretary. In 1909, he was appointed professor of economics and statistics at the Stockholm School of Economics. Heckscher's academic interests were in both history and economics. His scholarship became largely focused on economic history, where he broke new ground. In 1929, Heckscher was appointed to a research professorship in economic history at the Stockholm School of Economics and was made chair of the Economic History Institute (now called the Institute for Research in Economic History).

Heckscher's opus "The Effect of Foreign Trade in the Distribution of Income," which was translated into English in 1949 in *Readings in Theory of International Trade*, broke from the classical international trade theory of predecessors like Adam Smith and David Ricardo. In this article, Heckscher developed the rudiments of the factor endowment theory of international trade by predicting the pattern of trade between nations centered on the characteristics of those countries. The Heckscher-Ohlin theorem states that a relatively capital-abundant country will export a relatively capital-intensive commodity. The theory is expressed in terms of factor intensity and factor abundance. Not only natural resources such as water, land, and minerals were considered, but also supplies of labor and capital. Simply stated, Heckscher-Ohlin claims that a nation will export the commodity whose production requires the intensive use of the nation's relatively abundant and cheap factor and import the commodity whose production requires the intensive use of the nation's relatively scarce and expensive factor. Therefore, the capital-abundant country will have a comparative advantage in the production of goods that are capital intensive. The country in which labor is plentiful will have a relative advantage in the production of goods that are labor intensive. Under this model, the opening of trade implies a movement toward factor-price equalization. The theorem connotes that free trade will result in the equalization of factor prices internationally. So then, the basis of trade is the difference in prices because of differences in factor abundance. Trade may then happen because of these differences. Heckscher's student Bertil Ohlin developed and elaborated the factor of endowment theory and went on to prominence in the field of economics. He received the Nobel Memorial Prize in economic sciences in 1979 for his work on international trade theory. There have since been many enlargements of the Heckscher-Ohlin theorem, most notably those of Paul Samuelson and Jaroslav Vanek.

Heckscher was a prolific writer, with over 1,000 works to his credit. His two-volume tome *Mercantilism* (1931) is considered a landmark work of twentieth-century economic history. The work appeared first in Heckscher's native Swedish, then in German in 1932, and in English in 1934. In it, he details the genesis, expansion, and workings of mercantilism over the sixteenth through the eighteenth centuries, covering every major European country. Heckscher viewed the mercantile system as embodying the political and economic values of competitive young nation-states. He refuted the arguments of Adam Smith for saving and investment and questioned the validity of mercantile theory that held that the way for a nation to become rich was to export more than it imported. Heckscher was successful in identifying a set of mercantilism's significant characteristics, the pursuit of power being the most important.

Mercantilism was regarded the first contemporary fusion of mercantile theory and practice and drew much criticism from his contemporaries in the field of economic history. Heckscher's other major works include *Ekonomisk historia: nara antydningar* (1904), *The Continental System: An Economic Interpretation* (1918), *A Plea for a Theory in Economic History* (1929), *Monetary History from 1914 to 1925* (1930), and *An Economic History of Sweden* (1954), which covers 400 years of Sweden up to the early twentieth century. He died at the age of seventy-three in 1952.

Arthur Holst

See also: Ricardo, David; Smith, Adam.

BIBLIOGRAPHY

"Eli F. Heckscher." EHF Institute for Research in Economic History (www.hhs.se/EHF/Html/DefHeckscher1b.htm, accessed November 2002).

Irwin, Douglas A. *Against the Tide: An Intellectual History of Free Trade.* Princeton: Princeton University Press, 1996.

McCusker, John J. "Review of Eli F. Heckscher *Mercantilism*." Economic History Services (www.eh.net/bookreviews/library/mccusker.shtml, accessed December 2002).

Sandmo, Agnar. *Globalisation and the Welfare State: More Inequality–Less Redistribution?* Bergen: Norwegian School of Economics and Business Administration, 2002.

HELLENISTIC ARCHITECTURE

> The design and construction of buildings around the Mediterranean and across Asia Minor from the death of Alexander the Great in 323 B.C.E. to the fall of Egypt to Rome in 30 B.C.E.

Hellenistic architecture combined Greek (Hellenic) forms with those of other cultures brought into contact through trade, hence its name. Tending toward a monumentality and lavish ornamentation unknown to Greek architecture of the preceding Archaic and Classical periods, Hellenistic architecture has long been labeled a corrupt and degenerate style. Its origins are often linked to Athens's fall from power as the center of Greek cultural, political, and economic life after its defeat by Sparta in the Peloponnesian War (from 431 B.C.E.). The fragile balance of power between the Greek city-states, disturbed by Sparta's victory,

Monumental and highly ornamented, Hellenistic architecture—as represented in the Athenian Temple of Zeus of the fourth century B.C.E.—manifested the wealth flowing into Greece as a result of conquests by Alexander the Great. *(Library of Congress)*

ended when Alexander conquered the Hellenic world during the next century. His rise to power is often considered emblematic of decades of a basic cultural shift, wherein the Hellenic peoples shifted their primary loyalties from the city-state to the self. This shift—from social to individual consciousness—is central to the Hellenistic age and its architecture.

This period also came after the greatest accomplishment of Classical Greek architecture, the Parthenon, built on the Athenian Acropolis between 447 and 432. The culmination of centuries of Doric temple building in stone, the perceived perfection of the Parthenon led Hellenistic architects to believe that only increasingly baroque manipulations of traditional temple forms were possible. The oversized Temple of Zeus Olympus in Athens (ca. 170)—borne on fifty-seven-foot Corinthian columns (the Parthenon's were just over thirty-four feet)—is often cited as a prime example of Hellenistic architecture. But while temples grew ever larger, secular buildings, such as marketplaces, theaters, and administrative buildings like the bouleterion (council meeting hall), were innovative and showed a new, dynamic sense of experimentation.

The most vigorous expression of Hellenistic architecture is not to be found in the traditional centers of mainland Greece—Athens and Sparta, by now suffering from declining wealth and few exportable goods—but in the new centers of imperial power such as Alexandria, Antioch, and Pergamon. Enmity and uneasy peace connected the fragments of Alexander's empire after 323, but so too did trade routes, which facilitated trade not only in grain and olive oil, but also in architectural style. Greek architectural style was disseminated along these trade routes to outlying regions, where architects often mixed more traditional Greek forms with native architectural practices. Architectural theory also benefited from these trade ties, which spread the work of the major Greek theorists Pytheos (fourth century B.C.E.) and Hermogenes (second century B.C.E.).

As a powerful center of trade and wealth, Alexandria was perhaps the greatest of Hellenistic cities. Grand buildings proliferated amid the broad streets organized in a Hellenic grid pattern, including the Ptolemies' massive royal palace, Alexander's tomb, and the temple of the Muses. The city's lighthouse, built on the island of Pharos and dedicated in 279, drew the most awe: its massive size—440 feet tall—technical mastery, and eclectic style (though primarily pharaonic) mark it as Hellenistic. Likewise, it was an example of monumental architecture built in service of trade: its flame directed ships to the city's two harbors.

While important to the development of the Corinthian order, Antioch, the capital of Seleucid Syria built on a major trade route, did not rival Alexandria's grandiosity. But Pergamon did between 200 and 150, its Attalid rulers transformed a hilltop fortress into a visually stunning city that was a center of art and culture. Its steeply sloped theater and its sanctuary of Athena Ploias Nikephoros are notable, but the Great Altar of Zeus (ca. 180–160)—with its massive, elaborate frieze in high relief ambitiously depicting the battle between the gods and the giants—remains one of the most imposing examples of Hellenistic architecture.

Hellenistic civic life was centered on the city's agora, the open space that served primarily as a marketplace. It was usually bounded by one of the most important structures in Greek public life: the stoa. Resembling a modern porch or arcade—at the front a row of columns, at the back a wall, between an open space; often, especially during the Hellenistic period, of two stories and with several rows of columns—the stoa facilitated the political and educational aspects of urban life. But it was most often used for commerce. Rooms along the rear wall of the elaborate stoa of Attalos II in Athens (second century B.C.E.), for example, housed shops. Stoas were often placed in "L" or "U" shapes around an agora and achieved a massive, imposing scale during this period.

Hellenistic architecture spurred limited trade in materials, although architects and builders used primarily local stone and some timber. Evidence of imported stone does exist, however, in some structures: the Temple of Zeus at Olympia, for example, incorporates sculpture made from imported marble.

J.E. Luebering

See also: Agora; Alexandria.

BIBLIOGRAPHY
Chamoux, François. *Hellenistic Civilization*, trans. Michel Roussel. Oxford: Blackwell, 2003.

Havelock, Christine Mitchell. *Hellenistic Art*. 2nd ed. New York: Norton, 1981.
Steele, James. *Hellenistic Architecture in Asia Minor*. London: Academy, 1992.
Walbank, F.W. *The Hellenistic World*. Rev. ed. Cambridge, MA: Harvard University Press, 1993.

HEMP

> Hemp has played a role in world commerce for at least 6,000 years, beginning in China as early as 4500 B.C.E., where it was fashioned into rope, fishnets, and scrolls.

Hemp made its way from China to Korea and Japan around 3000 B.C.E. and was used to create clothing, rope, and paper. It later spread to the Mediterranean and Germanic regions along ancient trade routes. During the sixteenth through the eighteenth centuries, hemp and flax dominated Asian, European, and North American fiber crops. The first explorers to the Americas—the French, Dutch, Spanish, and British—had fashioned and depended on ropes and sails made from hemp.

England needed great amounts of hemp during the 1600s and expected colonies to supply its naval needs. Hemp was a recommended crop from Jamestown, and the British government continued to offer bounties for American hemp, yet hemp was not a profitable American crop and remained mostly imported.

Hemp grew all over the world, but Russia maintained superior quality during the 1700s and 1800s. The hemp plant (*Cannabis sativa*) was usually dew-rotted in America, an easier process, but one that did not produce an adequately waterproofed rope. The Russian water-rotted process was slow and meticulous, often taking up to two years, but produced rope of exceptional quality and strength for naval purposes. Hemp became Russia's largest agricultural export during the 1700s, and its prominence in world trade during this century created the "age of hemp."

By the 1800s, the United States imported 3,400 tons of its hemp with a peak importation of 5,000 tons annually during the 1820s and 1830s. American hemp planters did grow the crop

Once a major internationally traded agricultural commodity, hemp—used for rope and other purposes—was banned in the United States and elsewhere in the twentieth century because of its association with marijuana. Shown here, government officials inspect a hemp shipment in Manila, Philippines, in the early twentieth century. *(Library of Congress)*

mainly in Kentucky and Missouri, areas that relied on the expanding cotton culture market to keep their prices high, as cotton bales required hemp rope and bagging, for which dew-rooted hemp sufficed.

By the mid-1800s, hemp's vital role in world commerce declined with the rise of two inventions: the steam engine, which powered ships not requiring extensive ropes and sails from hemp; and the cotton gin, which slashed cotton clothing production costs. Renewed interest in hemp developed slightly in 1916 with a scientific paper noting that hemp hurds, a plant waste product previously burned in fields, could be used to produce quality paper.

Hemp was promoted as a war crop during World War II as U.S. propaganda encouraged its cultivation on the grounds of both patriotism and profits. The United States had imported its hemp from the Philippines until the Japanese occupation in 1942, and six states (Iowa, Illinois, Wisconsin, Minnesota, Indiana, and Kentucky) were encouraged to grow industrial hemp. Production in 1943 and 1944 was so successful, at 100 million pounds annually, that enough straw tonnage was produced for the next two years. National production was then discouraged despite farmers' desire for hemp as a mechanized and profitable crop.

Despite the current amount of creative and environmentally safe products that can be produced from the entire plant, industrial hemp still suffers from governmental policies that confuse it with marijuana. Manila hemp, or abaca, is manufactured from a different plant entirely (a Philippine plant from the banana family [*Musa textilis*]) and has also been used to make high-quality rope, paper, and clothing.

Lisa Ossian

See also: Agriculture.

BIBLIOGRAPHY

Crosby, Alfred W., Jr. *America, Russia, Hemp, and Napoleon: American Trade with Russia and the Baltic, 1783–1812.* Columbus: Ohio State University Press, 1965.

Hurt, R. Douglas. *American Agriculture: A Brief History.* Ames: Iowa State University Press, 1994.

Ossian, Lisa Lynn. "The Home Fronts of Iowa, 1940–1945." Ph.D. diss., Iowa State University, 1998.

Roulac, John W., and Hemptech. *Hemp Horizons: The Comeback of the World's Most Promising Plant.* White River Junction, VT: Chelsea Green, 1997.

HENRY THE NAVIGATOR (1394-1460)

The leader of early Portuguese exploration.

The son of King Joao I of Portugal and Princess Philippa of Lancaster, England, Prince Henry spent his life winning wealth and glory for his country and a treasure of knowledge related to sailing and geography for the rest of the world. Trained in the best traditions of medieval chivalry as a boy, he spent most of his adult life as a member of the Military Order of Christ, the successor of the Knights Templar in Portugal. At the age of nineteen, he participated in his first expedition against the city of Ceuta across the Strait of Gibraltar in Morocco. In Ceuta, Prince Henry learned of caravans that brought gold across the Sahara from tropical regions along the Gambia and Senegal Rivers farther to the south. He returned to Sagres, a town on a promontory in southern Portugal that jutted out into the Atlantic, where he spent much of the rest of his life planning expeditions to find this fabled land on the western coast of Africa.

Between 1415 and 1425, adventurers sent out from Portugal to explore Africa discovered the islands of Porto Santo and Madeira just northeast of the Canary Islands in the Atlantic. While settlement of Porto Santo failed, the colonization of Madeira was an immediate success. Prince Henry directed the settlement himself and ordered prisoners from the jails of Lisbon to be the island's first colonists. He sent cattle and seed for the settlers to use on the small farms he laid out for them on the island. He also imported sugarcane plants from Sicily and grapevines from Crete and Cyprus. Soon, Madeira was exporting lumber, honey, fruits, vegetables, sugar, and a wine named for the island to Portugal. As Madeira was being settled, Portuguese sailors also discovered a 400-mile-long chain of islands in the Atlantic farther to the west that they named the Azores, the Portuguese word for "hawks," in honor of the many birds that flew there. Along with Madeira, the islands of Santa Maria and Sao Miguel in the Azores soon became important Portuguese colonies in the Atlantic.

Throughout the discovery and settlement of Madeira and the Azores, Prince Henry continued to urge his men to explore the western coast of Africa. He ordered his sailors to head past Cape Bojador just 100 miles south of the Canary Islands. The cape was the farthest point to which any Portuguese ship had ever sailed. Many of his men feared heading past Cape Bojador since legend said that the ocean turned thick and murky beyond this point. Others believed that the sea would boil and set on fire those ships that dared to pass through it. Still others believed that mountains in the Southern Hemisphere were magnetic and would tear the metal bolts right out from ships as they approached. Ignoring these superstitions, Prince Henry sent more than fifteen expeditions along the western coast of Africa before his captain Gil Eannes finally rounded Cape Bojador in 1534.

As his men struggled with the high winds, treacherous currents, and shallow inlets along the African coast, Prince Henry realized that the traditional Portuguese sailing ship known as a *barca* was not suited for the task of exploration. The square-rigged vessel was difficult to maneuver in the wind. It was also too heavy to carry the many supplies necessary on a long ocean trip. The deep bottom of the ship made it too dangerous to sail along the African shore without running aground. Working with the best craftsmen in Europe and the Mediterranean, Prince Henry constructed a new ship called a *caravel.* It was smaller, lighter, and swifter than a barca, and was also capable of carrying the heavier loads necessary on a long sea voyage. He soon made the Portuguese city of Lagos one of the most important shipbuilding centers in all of Europe.

Sailing in one of Prince Henry's new caravels, Nuno Tristao made it past Cape Bojador to Cape Blanco at the entrance of the Argium Bay in 1441. When Tristao returned to the bay two years later,

Prince Henry the Navigator helped spur the Portuguese toward overseas exploration and trade in the fifteenth century. This statue of Henry stands near New Bedford, Massachusetts, home to many Portuguese immigrants. *(Library of Congress)*

he captured more than 200 natives and returned them to Portugal. Prince Henry oversaw the sale of the men, women, and children into slavery, and so began the modern Atlantic slave trade. Soon, other adventurers followed in Tristao's wake down the western coast of Africa, claiming new territory for Portugal and capturing more slaves. They discovered Cape Verde and the Cape of Masts, which was named for the palm trees on shore that had been stripped of their leaves in a storm. Tristao himself made it to the mouth of the Gambia River, where natives killed him in 1446.

Back in Sagres, Prince Henry assembled the best minds of his day to help with his nation's discoveries. Arab scholars and Jewish merchants along with sailors from Genoa, Venice, Germany, and Scandinavia worked together to create maps that reflected the best geographical knowledge of the time rather than the myths and legends of the past. He also encouraged his sailors to use a simplified astrolabe called a *balesilha* for a more accurate calculation of latitude. He promoted the study of the stars as a way to determine a ship's position. He was as admired throughout Europe for his learning as he was for his explorations.

While he never joined an expedition to West Africa, he participated in two more campaigns against Moroccan towns. In 1437, he and his younger brother Fernando led an attack on Tangiers. The Portuguese were forced to surrender and leave Fernando behind as a hostage. Fernando's death while still in prison in 1443 was the greatest sorrow experienced by Prince Henry. It was said that the prince never smiled again. Some twenty years later, the now elderly Prince Henry led a successful campaign against the Moroccan town of Alcacer Ceguer in 1458. He died in November 1460 convinced that someday his sailors would circumnavigate Africa and go on to dominate the trade routes to the Indies on behalf of Portugal.

Mary Stockwell

See also: Exploration and Trade.

BIBLIOGRAPHY

Ure, John. *Prince Henry the Navigator.* London: Constable, 1977.

HINDUISM

> Throughout its history, Hinduism has been tightly correlated with the structure of the Indian society and its economic system.

Hinduism is generally regarded as the oldest world religion still practiced today. As a normative system, Hinduism encompasses all aspects of life, and the regulations of trade (and sometimes also the general attitude toward trade and worldly possessions) play a central part of the social attitude toward trade. Hinduism forbids the consumption of meat and alcohol. However, unlike most other major religions of the world, Hinduism represents more of a cultural and geographic identification than a strict ideological dogma. It is defined more by a common ritual, stemming from a particular culture, than by a common belief or doctrinal base. Hindus share few common practices or beliefs.

The caste system is inherent to the Hindu society. Preservation of the caste system served to contain social conflict between different classes and helped maintain the highly inegalitarian social structure. The caste system provided believers with a systematic rationale for everyone's place in the world.

INFLUENCE OF TRADE ON THE PROLIFERATION OF HINDUISM

Unlike many other religions, Hinduism did not spread significantly because of trade links with other regions. It spread to Malaya and Indonesia, but not to other regions outside South and Southeast Asia. Archaeological findings indicate that, by the fourth century C.E., maritime trade had brought Hinduism to Java and other areas of modern-day Indonesia, where Buddhism was already established. Hindu traders might have reached the area two centuries earlier, as shown by some indications of Hindu presence in Malaya in the second century C.E.

One of the chief reasons that Hinduism did not spread as widely as Buddhism did was its nonproselytizing character. Hindu religious identity, unlike that of Buddhists, depends on the Hindu culture and ethnicity. In contrast to Buddhism or Islam, Hinduism did not spread significantly in consequence of the presence of Hindu traders along the Silk Road and other trade routes.

The weakening of the Silk Road trade in the fifth century, with the decline in trade with the Roman empire and Persia, had affected the economy of several Indian cities. By this period, Hinduism as a religious power began to be shaped. This included the codification of sacred laws, the building of the great temples, and the accumulation of the myths and rituals in the *Puranas*.

The economic problems and the loss of unity by the end of the fifth century were two of the causes of the growth of mystical sects in Hinduism, many of which survived until the modern period. Between the seventh and eighth centuries, a movement of missionaries, wandering around and singing praises for Vishnu, grew.

TRADE AND HINDUISM IN THE MIDDLE AGES

It was during this period that the *bhakti* movements developed. They mobilized the followers of Hinduism to move away from their traditional association with the Indian aristocracy to coalesce into a movement, one that helped focus the frustrations of the poor toward devotion.

Beginning in the tenth century, the wealthy in Indian society were the landowners. By this time, the caste system developed to include peasants forbidden to leave the land where they worked. Furthermore, the Hindu institution discouraged landowners from being involved in trade or investment. The Brahmin elite considered association with trade beneath them and even forbidden for their class. They also disapproved of interactions with strangers through trade and declined to travel overseas. Religious contemplation was privileged over interest in material matters.

Consequently, in tenth-century India trade routes deteriorated. The lack of use and of trade also affected communication and social interaction. But trade with foreign groups continued even as internal trade in India declined. During this period, India exported rice, grains, coconuts, spices, sugar, wood, dyes, and precious stones and imported perfume, finished cloth, silk, precious stones, gold, medicinal herbs, tools, and metalware. The discouragement of trade by the Hindu religious institution and the objection to trade by the Brahmins left some of the trade to other religious groups, mainly Muslims.

This religiously based disinterest and scorn for the merchant had an effect on agriculture, as the Brahmins declined to investigate newer technologies. Merchants faced both social and practical obstacles, as they lacked respect or legitimacy for their profession and at the same time had to work in an environment with limited infrastructure and outdated methods.

This caused a gradual decline in trade. Trade guilds began to vanish by the end of the thirteenth century, and many of the trade routes fell into disuse from lack of traffic. Muslims held control over almost all of India's overseas trade, especially maritime trade. The expansion of Hinduism was

Three high-caste Hindu children pose for the camera in Bombay, India, in 1922. While caste is not exclusively related to income level, higher-caste families tend to be better educated and have more wealth. *(Library of Congress)*

also affected, as Muslim influence broadened in Southeast Asia (especially Indonesia) through Gujarati traders. By the end of the fifteenth century, Islam had become widespread in Indonesia.

Over the years, the Muslim hegemony over maritime trade faded and Hindu merchants once more entered the field; the two groups developed a modus operandi regarding different tasks within the maritime trade. This agreement was breached with the arrival of the Portuguese, who used force to attain control of the maritime trade in the Indian Ocean. In the fifteenth century, more Hindus were involved in the Southeast Asian maritime trade (although most the merchants continued to be Muslim).

Under the Islamic Mughal empire (from the eleventh to the eighteenth centuries), Hindus usually enjoyed liberal and pragmatic religious policy, even though Islam generally viewed Hindus as "heathens," because they are not among the "people of the book." However, by the end of the seventeenth century, with the reign of Aurangzeb, conditions had deteriorated. Aurangzeb levied taxes on Hindu merchants at twice the amount levied on Muslims. He also imposed *jiziya* (graduated property tax) on the Hindus. Many ascribe this policy to the disintegration of the Mughal empire. During the seventeenth century, Indian trade with Europe in textiles grew, especially with the closing of Japan to European trade in 1640. Trade with Europe, which was to become a critical power in the region, played a major role in the shaping of Hinduism from this point onward.

TRADE WITH EUROPE AND ITS IMPACT ON HINDUISM

The Portuguese tried to infiltrate the lucrative fifteenth-century trade in India, but had difficulty because their attitude toward trade and disrespect for local trade customs created ruptures with the Indian rajas. This was especially apparent in the Portuguese disrespect for Hindu shrines, which led India to refuse further trade with them.

In the nineteenth century, several Hindu sects became prominent for their attempts to bridge the gulf between modernity and the structure of the Hindu society. Ramakrishna and Vivekenanda and the sects of Arya Samaj and Brahmo Samaj were among those working to integrate Hindu philosophy with political and social ideals to address the need for social reform.

The creation of Hindu diasporas is a by-product of trade activity. Some evidence indicates that Indian merchants reached the eastern coasts of Africa before the establishment of Hinduism (the seventh to the first centuries B.C.E.), as well as the Middle East, Central Asia, and other trade ports. In the modern period, the reach of the British empire spread Hindu diasporas far and wide, to South Africa, the Caribbean, and Great Britain itself. Trade or global economic forces shaped these communities outside India, whose ethnic identity is integrally connected with Hinduism.

Hinduism has continued to affect Indian policy in the modern era. The British attitude toward India originated in trade interests. During the colonial period, the British manipulated the caste system to maximize their control. Even Western-educated Indians such as Mohandas Gandhi have drawn on Hindu philosophy in formulating their political philosophy. Hinduism was, therefore, affected twice by the colonial experience, which both transformed it in the land of its birth and allowed it to thrive outside India as the Hindu diaspora community has spread throughout the world.

Tamar Gablinger

See also: Buddhism; Indian Ocean Trade; Islam.

BIBLIOGRAPHY

Dirks, Nicholas B. *Castes of Mind: Colonialism and the Making of Modern India.* Princeton: Princeton University Press, 2001.

Metcalf, Barbara D., and Thomas Metcalf. *A Concise History of India.* Cambridge: Cambridge University Press, 2001.

Richards, John F. *The Mughal Empire.* Cambridge: Cambridge University Press, 1993.

Thapar, Romila. *A History of India.* London: Penguin, 1966.

Van Der Veer, Peter. *Imperial Encounters: Religion and Modernity in India and Britain.* Princeton: Princeton University Press, 2001.

Wolpert, Stanley A. *A New History of India.* Oxford: Oxford University Press, 1997.

HITTITE EMPIRE

An ancient empire located in the region of Anatolia, Syria, and ancient Phoenicia that controlled the trade routes between Greece, Egypt, and Babylon.

The land of the Hittites is surrounded by a deep gorge formed by the Halys River. The gorge, encompassing all the region except for one portion of the northwest, offered protection for the Hittites against possible invaders. The Hittites, a warlike group of people with yellow skin and black hair, moved into the region and established rule over the indigenous population around 1900 B.C.E. They did not disrupt the agricultural way of life that had existed for centuries. The high plateaus of the region were ideally suited for the cultivation of wheat and barley crops. In the lower elevations, vineyards and orchards were cultivated. Animals such as cattle and sheep were also raised.

The peasants attended to the agricultural needs of their new rulers, while the Hittites themselves focused on expanding the empire through a series of wars. After securing a large portion of Anatolia (present-day Turkey), the Hittites turned their attention to the region along the Tigris and Euphrates Rivers. They conquered the Babylonians and in the process co-opted many of their laws and customs. The Code of Hammurabi that the Babylonians had lived under was modified with most crimes being punished through the imposition of fines and compensation only. Few crimes, such as murder, were punished by death. Women enjoyed greater legal rights, as did slaves. Instead of establishing a direct administration over Babylon or any of their other conquered regions, the Hittites relied on loyal satraps, or governors, who collected the tribute required of the people. Tribute from the Troad, Lydia, Babylon, the cities south of the Black Sea, and even northern Canaan was usually in the form of a few gold coins. The tribute money funded additional campaigns and helped support the warrior ruling class.

Although the Hittites were warriors, their society also relied on skilled craftsmen such as potters, cobblers, and smiths. The smiths developed the first iron tools and weapons from the iron ore obtained from the region of present-day Armenia. The use of this stronger metal gave the Hittites a distinct advantage over their enemies in battle and in the process changed the way battles were fought. The secret of iron smelting was maintained until the end of the Hittite empire, at which time other civilizations began using iron as well. Some scholars argue that the spread of iron technology led to the demise of the empire.

Along with iron weapons, the Hittites also developed the horse-drawn chariot that they used effectively against the predominately infantry armies of their neighbors. These chariots were used against the Egyptian army around 1300 B.C.E. at the Battle of Kadesh. Muwatallis, the Hittite king, had pushed into Syria and Phoenicia in search of further wealth and control of the lucrative trade of the Levant. The Egyptians, under the rule of Rameses II, assembled more than 20,000 men and 2,000 chariots and marched from Egypt to Kadesh, where they captured two Hittite spies who informed them that the Hittite army was still some distance away from Kadesh. The Hittites, with more than 40,000 men, sent out 500 chariots that attacked 5,000 Egyptian soldiers as they marched. Many Egyptians were slaughtered, but some escaped and fled back to relay the news to Rameses II. Confident in their victory, the Hittite charioteers began looting the Egyptian camp. Rameses II ordered 500 of his chariots to attack the Hittites, who could not maneuver their own chariots because they were too close to each other. Only with the assistance of the rest of the Hittite forces were the Egyptians defeated. The Hittites continued to control the trade between Greece and Egypt to the south.

Throughout the Hittite empire a single law code helped to unify people from diverse cultures. Many languages were spoken. Although the Hittites were warriors, not traders, they protected traveling merchants who then paid tribute to the Hittites. International trade remained limited since the Hittites simply conquered areas that produced goods that they wanted. However, several cities, such as Carchemish, held regular markets for foreign goods. Artifacts, including many seals, indicate that an extensive trade network existed throughout the empire. Diplomatic relations were established with other countries, often with the queen in charge of correspondence with other queens. Cuneiform writing on clay tablets was adopted from the Babylonians and passed on to the civilizations of Crete. These tablets were useful in the keeping of inventories and the recording of business transactions.

The demise of the Hittite empire occurred around 1200 B.C.E. Scholars argue that a number of factors, including the spread of iron technology, contributed to its end. Continuous warfare with Egypt proved costly in terms of both resources and men. About the same time, the Assyrian empire gained strength and challenged the Hittite power. Meanwhile, the Sea Peoples were attacking along the coast of Anatolia, Crete, Syria, and Palestine, even reaching as far south as Egypt before being stopped. After the sacking of the Hittite capital at Hattushash, the empire declined rapidly. Many Hittites migrated down into the region of Canaan just as Abraham was moving into the area. The mixing of Semites and Hittites is thought to have resulted in the development of a distinctive facial feature—the aquiline nose. Biblical references to the Hittites refer to them as the descendants of Heth, the second son of Canaan.

Cynthia Clark Northrup

See also: Assyrian Empire; Babylonian Empire.

BIBLIOGRAPHY
Gurney, Oliver Robert. *The Hittites*. 2nd ed. New York: Penguin, 1990.
"Hittite Empire" (www.ancientroute.com/empire/hittite.htm, accessed January 2004).
Troy, Fox. "Who Were the Hittites?" (www.touregypt.net/featurestories/hittites.htm, accessed January 2004).

HOHENSTAUFEN EMPIRE

A German empire lasting from 1138 to 1272 under which German territory was expanded, wars were fought, and trade was developed.

In 1079, Frederick, count of Swabia, married Agnes, the daughter of Holy Roman Emperor Henry IV, who changed Frederick's title to duke. The couple had two sons, Frederick and Conrad. Frederick was defeated for the election as Holy Roman emperor with the title passing to Lothair of Saxony (Lothair II). Conrad became an antiking to Lothair and traveled to Milan, where he was crowned. After Pope Honorius II excommunicated him, Conrad failed to take the crown from Lothair and finally swore allegiance to him. After Lothair's death, the German princes elected Conrad as king in 1138 to prevent Lothair's son-in-law, Henry the Proud, from gaining too much power. Conrad took away Henry's duchy, and a civil war broke out between the Guelfs (supporters of Henry) and the Ghibellines (supporters of the Hohenstaufens). The war continued after the death of Henry the Proud under his son Henry the Lion.

In 1147, Saint Bernard of Clairvaux persuaded Conrad III to join the Second Crusade. He and his armies laid siege to Damascus but the campaign resulted in failure and he returned home two years later. Conrad III sought to conquer Sicily, a strategically located, rich island off the southern coast of Italy, but failed when the Guelf faction assisted Roger II of Sicily.

Frederick I became the second Hohenstaufen

king in 1152 and reigned until 1190. Known as Frederick Barbarossa because he had a red beard, he was forced to deal with challenges to the power of the monarchy in Germany. His wife was a Guelf, and Frederick often found himself negotiating between his mother's family and his uncle Conrad III, who named Frederick as his successor in an attempt to end the rivalry between the two families. After his coronation, Frederick restored the duchy of Bavaria to Henry the Lion but offset Henry's power by creating a separate duchy of Austria. He sought support in Italy, where he was crowned emperor in 1155 by agreeing to assist the pope in his efforts to protect papal lands from the Normans of Sicily. When his army forced him to withdraw from Italy before fighting on the side of the pope, the new pope, Adrian IV, formed an alliance with the Normans.

Frederick would return to northern Italy and claim Lombard lands as part of his imperial rights. Italian city-states throughout the region revolted and Frederick withdrew until 1166 when he returned and conquered Rome. The pope was in a desperate situation until an epidemic spread through Frederick's forces, causing them to abandon their attempts to conquer papal lands. The city-states banded together to form the Lombard League against Frederick, whom they defeated at Legnano, partially because of a lack of support from Henry the Lion. When Frederick returned to Germany, he took away Henry's duchy and partitioned Germany.

Years of fighting against an alliance that included the Italian city-states and the pope produced negligible results for the power of the German monarchy. German princes capitalized on Frederick's absence to start a policy of expansion and settlement into the eastern Slavic lands, including Pomerania, Silesia, Bohemia, and Moravia. Frederick died while on a crusade in 1190.

Henry VI was crowned Holy Roman emperor in Rome after his father's death. Through his wife, Constance, Henry inherited Sicily. He marched south to Rome, where he was crowned Holy Roman emperor, and then to Sicily, where he attempted to secure control of the island for his wife but failed to oust Tancred of Lecce, who

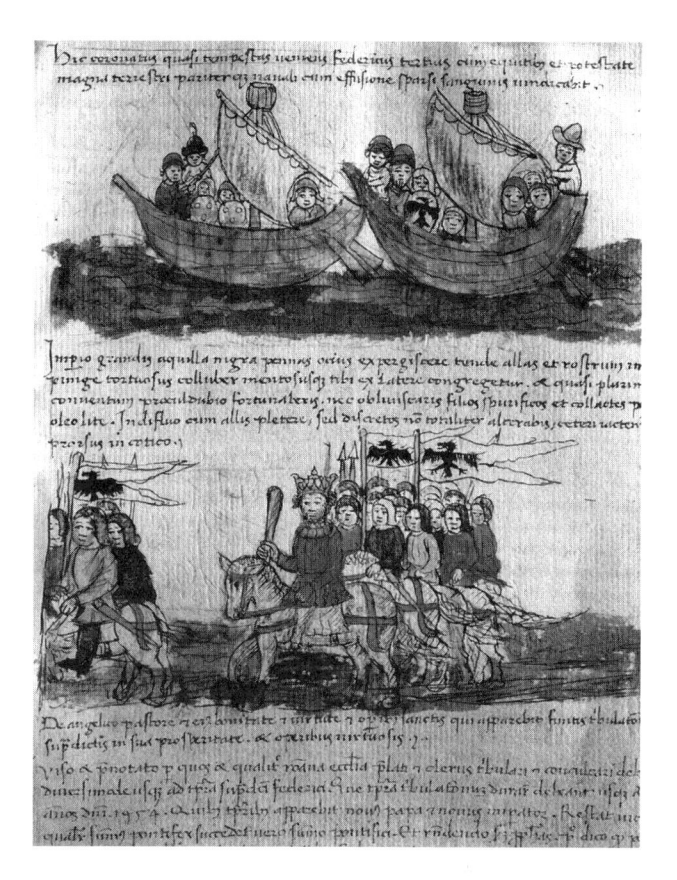

Under Frederick Barbarossa (King Frederick I of Germany, 1123–1190), in this fifteenth-century manuscript shown invading Italy, the Hohenstaufen empire grew in size and importance, with trade being a major source of its wealth. *(The Art Archive/Biblioteca Nazionale Marciana Venice/Dagli Orti [A])*

had assumed the crown. Unrest in Germany between the Guelfs and the Ghibellines forced him to return north. After Tancred's death, Henry marched south a second time and secured Sicily in 1194. The following year, he proposed another crusade to the Holy Land while pressuring the emperor in Constantinople to pay him tribute. Henry died of natural causes in Sicily just as he was about to leave on crusade. Since Henry's son, Frederick II, was only a toddler, his uncle, Philip of Swabia, became king of Germany while Frederick was invested as the king of Sicily through the efforts of his mother and the pope. Warring factions between the Hohenstaufens and the Guelfs resulted in the appointment of a rival king, Otto IV, who received the support of the pope. Frederick II captured Cologne in 1206, and the war between Otto IV and Frederick II ended. Philip was murdered over a personal matter in 1208. The French killed Otto IV during battle six years later.

FREDERICK II

Frederick II, the son of Henry VI and grandson of Frederick Barbarossa, was born on December 26, 1194. His mother was Constance, daughter of Roger II of Sicily. When Frederick was two years old, Henry VI died. Frederick became emperor at the age of two and king of Sicily at age three. Frederick II was placed under the guardianship of Pope Innocent III and raised in Palermo until the age of fourteen, when he assumed control over the government.

Frederick II was elected to the German throne in 1212 while Otto VI was still alive but had become an enemy of the pope. After Otto's death, Frederick was crowned a second time in 1215 and promised to participate in a crusade. At the time, Sicily was in debt. Frederick initiated a series of changes including an increase in taxes to address the problem. Government was highly centralized with all power being held closely by either Frederick II or his wife, Constance of Aragon, whom he left in charge as he traveled to Germany or waged wars in Italy. Although his administration demanded much from the people, including men to help him fight his wars, the island kingdom flourished economically and culturally during his reign.

Although Frederick II had made a vow to lead a crusade, matters in Germany, Sicily, and the Lombard region required his attention. When Frederick moved against the Lombard towns, the pope perceived the move as a preemptive strike aimed at positioning Frederick for an attack on papal lands. He excommunicated Frederick on the grounds that he had failed to fulfill his vow. The conflict between the Holy Roman emperor and the pope spread throughout Italy and then Europe. Meanwhile, after Constance's death Frederick II married Yolanda of Brienne, who was in line to inherit the Kingdom of Jerusalem. Frederick decided to fulfill his crusading vow after the marriage and managed to negotiate a treaty with the sultan of Egypt that gave him control over the Holy Land without the shedding of one drop of blood. Frederick could then claim to have honored his vow. In 1229, he was crowned king of Jerusalem. Wars between Frederick II and the pope continued until his death in 1250 in Palermo. The papacy focused on the destruction of the family's power after his death, a move that fostered resentment against the Catholic Church for waging a war against fellow Christians.

During the reign of Frederick II, attention was focused on Italy instead of Germany. Centralized power eroded as the German princes were granted control over their own territories through a statute signed in 1232. After Frederick's death and, especially after the death of his last rightful heirs Conrad IV (1254) and his son Conradin (1268), Germany fragmented.

During the reign of Frederick II, many German towns developed into trading centers and achieved a level of autonomy, and merchants prospered. Lübeck became the center of the Hanseatic League. Without a strong central government to protect trade routes from London and throughout the Baltic Sea region, other northern German cities soon joined together in mutual defense pacts and trade agreements. Colonization of Slavic lands occurred, and products were shipped throughout the Baltic Sea and as far away as Novgorod. Cities received tax concessions and enjoyed greater autonomy, which contributed to the desire for merchants to increase their profits. Individuals or voluntary associations of cities controlled the trade of the north, while the Hohenstaufen kings focused on developing trade in the south. Under Frederick II, trade developed between Sicily and other parts of the Mediterranean. Frederick II encouraged trade in agricultural goods as well as other items and established a trade network with Spain, Morocco, and Egypt.

The Hohenstaufen dynasty ended with the death of Frederick II's two illegitimate sons, Manfred (1258) and Enzio (1272).

Cynthia Clark Northrup

See also: Crusades; Hanseatic League; Sicily

BIBLIOGRAPHY

Barraclough, Geoffrey. *The Origins of Modern Germany.* New York: Paragon, 1979.

Thompson, James W. *Feudal Germany.* New York: F. Ungar, 1962.

Tout, Thomas F. *The Empire and the Papacy, 918–1273.* Westport: Greenwood, 1980.

HOLLYWOOD

The center of U.S. film making.

Film making is a multibillion-dollar industry that helped shape modern Los Angeles, California, and the United States. For better or worse, the world sees the United States through the lens of films made in Hollywood. American films also disseminate American culture throughout the globe. The films are spread in theaters and through television, the Internet, cable, and rentals. Emerging markets, in China, Russia, and India, provide new opportunities for the industry as well as increasing the markets in which to fight the massive struggle against piracy.

PIRACY

The film industry is struggling against piracy around the globe. The Motion Picture Association (MPA), the parent association of the Motion Picture Association of America (MPAA), estimates that the U.S. motion picture industry loses over $3 billion in potential worldwide revenue because of piracy. This does not include the incalculable losses owing to Internet piracy. The MPA launched over 60,000 investigations into suspected pirate activities worldwide (roughly 1 percent in the United States) with over 18,000 raids in 2000. Piracy takes many forms. Broadcast piracy, signal theft, videocassette piracy, Internet piracy, and optical disc piracy are each different categories of such theft.

Signal theft and broadcast piracy are different sides of the same coin. Signal theft involves illegally receiving cable and satellite signals. Broadcast piracy involves the broadcasting of copyrighted material, bootleg or legitimate, without permission from the copyright holder. Videocassette piracy is the oldest of the modern forms of piracy and is closely related to optical disc piracy. Both involve the duplication of a videocassette or DVD to another videocassette or DVD in a method called "back-to-back" copying. Either the original video is copied to a blank cassette or a DVD is copied to a computer and then copied to blank DVDs. Copies of first-run movies recorded by a camcorder in the theater are often distributed in the same method. Most "camcording" is done in the New York City area.

Internet piracy is the newest and most difficult form to trace. "Hard goods" piracy is the illegal sale and distribution of actual copies through the Internet. Streaming media is the transmission of data to an online user in real time. Downloadable media is the most common form of Internet piracy. It also is a great challenge to the music industry. This form involves the illegal uploading of digital files that a user may download to a personal computer at a nominal fee or no cost.

Many laws to fight piracy exist. The U.S. Copyright Act of 1976 contains some of the strongest antipiracy legislation in the world. A 1982 amendment increased penalties to the felony level and was later confirmed by the U.S. Sentencing Commission. The U.S. Communications Act of 1984 established similar penalties for piracy of cable television and satellite. The original all-encompassing federal law protecting copyright is the Communications Act of 1934. It is sufficiently broad enough in scope to include the then-unimagined videocassette, DVD, and Internet piracy issues. Furthermore, U.S. laws to address Internet piracy include the Digital Millennium Copyright Act and the No Electronic Theft Act. In 2003, more than eighty nations had copyright laws. Several treaties and trade agreements further protect intellectual property. These include the Berne Convention for the Protection of Literary and Artistic Works, the Universal Copyright Convention, the Geneva Phonograms Convention, the Patent Cooperation Treaty, the World Intellectual Property Organization treaties, the Paris Convention for Protection of Industry Property, the Madrid Convention for the International Registration of Marks, and the Agreement on Trade-Related Aspects of Intellectual Property Rights.

The MPA identifies Asia as the greatest source of piracy in the world. Although the MPA names Malaysia and Taiwan as the centers of piracy in the region, China is the greatest producer of pirated material with rates as high as 90 percent. This includes movies, music, and software. India, Japan, and the Philippines also have high rates of piracy. Russia is quickly replacing China as the global capital of piracy. Germany has a high level of Internet piracy, while the United Kingdom struggles against cable piracy. Turkey has a high rate of CD and DVD piracy. In 1999, Brazil topped the piracy market in Latin America, causing an estimated loss for Hollywood of $120 million.

The MPAA avoids all mention of piracy in relation to China for purely business reasons. The film industry lobbied the U.S. Congress successfully to pass permanent normal trade relations for China in 2000. This cleared the way for China's entry to the World Trade Organization. This gave the MPAA the right to increase the number of movie releases in China from ten to fifty per year. It also gave foreign firms the ability to invest up to 49 percent in joint ventures to build, own, and operate cinemas and to distribute video and sound recordings.

Antipiracy technologies vary by medium and have limited success. Videocassette, DVD, pay-per-view cable, and satellite systems use forms of Macrovision, which blocks reproduction using a Content Scrambling System. This is an encryption system, introduced in 1996 and updated in 1999, that relies on an authentication system programmed into DVD players. Macrovision is a system that prevents copying of copyrighted material at a rate greater than 95 percent of original clarity. Cable and satellite companies also protect their signals by requiring clients to use an apparatus to interpret and clarify the signal.

DOMESTIC AND OVERSEAS MARKETS

Hollywood's primary market focus is the United States. Although it exports entertainment to the entire world, it creates product for the American audience. The domestic industry is massive and rarely profitable. Domestically, only 10 percent of films break even on the investment from the initial release. Worldwide, four out of ten movies never recoup the original investment. Nevertheless, the industry has seen phenomenal growth. The box-office gross revenue in 2002 was over $9 billion, almost triple the gross in 1982. The average ticket price only doubled during this timeframe. The average cost to create a movie increased over 6.5 times during this period. At the same time marketing costs increased almost fivefold to an average of $31 million per film.

The demographics of movie goers also changed greatly. The number of screens doubled between 1980 and 2003 to total 35,786. The old-fashioned drive-in screens comprised only 18 percent of the total in 1980. According to Texas Instruments, digital cinema screens now number 124 only four years after the technology was first introduced. In 2003, the total number of theaters has dropped to 6,066. Two- to seven-screen theaters still occupy 40 percent of the market, but the number of all types of theaters is falling except megaplexes with sixteen or more screens.

The highest-grossing film in history is *Titanic,* which had total receipts of $601 million. This surpassed the previous top grosser, *Star Wars,* by $140 million. *E.T., Star Wars: Phantom Menace,* and *Spider-Man* round out the top five, with each grossing over $400 million at the box office. The trend for movies in the twenty-first century is a high-grossing opening weekend, with a 50 percent, or more, drop-off in revenues the following weekend. There were 467 films released in the United States in 2002. Although the production of movies, especially television movies, is moving to Canada and Mexico, the U.S. motion picture industry employs 583,000 people. That is 242,000 more jobs than in 1988, but the number of U.S. positions has declined steadily since 1999.

Entertainment technology supported by Hollywood has an astounding penetration rate in American homes. In 2002 televisions were in 97.6 percent of households in the United States. Basic cable was in 67.7 percent of households with televisions, up from 22.6 percent in 1980. And 21.1 million of those cable subscribers had digital cable. Pay cable was in 32.2 percent of households with televisions. There were 17.6 million households with satellite connections in 2002, up from 3.3 million in 1995. Even more significant, the number of cable and satellite channels had increased 345 percent since 1990, to 267 channels. VCRs were in 97.6 percent of households with televisions, up from 1.9 percent in 1980. Introduced only in 1997, DVD players were in 43.1 percent of households by 2003. The decrease in price of DVD players by 65 percent and the increase in the number of titles to over 20,000 have aided in the adoption of DVD technology. In 2003, personal computers were in almost 61 percent of homes, up from 23 percent in 1990; 61 percent of homes had Internet access, 15 percent of those broadband, compared to 9.5 percent of homes with access in 1995.

INDUSTRY FINANCES

Television advertising expenditures in 2002 reached almost $29 billion. Television reaches a wide audience. In that year the average American watched 1,661 hours of television and was exposed to 3,622 total hours of media. This included cable, satellite, and broadcast television, the Internet, home video, movies at the theater, radio, recorded music, daily newspapers, magazines, books, and video games. This averages 9.9 hours per day, which is entirely plausible considering that Americans are exposed to media almost everywhere they go.

The entertainment industry is a huge part of American life, culture, industry, and export. It defines American culture internally and externally, is the primary export of the United States, and influences the whole world.

Ryan Matthew Evans

See also: Entertainment.

BIBLIOGRAPHY

Chynoweth, Graham J. "Reality Bites: How the Biting Reality of Piracy in China Is Working to Strengthen Its Copyright Laws." *Duke Law and Technology Review* (February 2003).

Duke, Paul F. "Trade Bills OK Clears Hollywood's Path into China." *World Tibet Network News*, 25 May 2000.

Macrovision.com. "Copy Protection" (www.macrovision.com/solutions/video/copyprotect/index.php3, accessed August 2003).

Motion Picture Association of America. "Anti-Piracy" (www.mpaa.org/anti-piracy/, accessed December 2003).

Motion Picture Association of America, Industry Worldwide Market Research. "U.S. Entertainment Industry: 2002 MPA Market Statistics" (www.mpaa.org/useconomicreview/2002/02%20Economic%20Review%20w-cover_files/frame.htm, accessed December 2003).

Tolkacheva, Julie. "Russia Seen Overtaking China in Music Piracy" Forbes.com, June 5, 2003 (www.forbes.com/home_asia/newswire/2003/06/05/rtr991570.html, accessed December 2003).

HONG KONG

A major port city and trade hub, officially recognized as the Hong Kong Special Administrative Region, People's Republic of China.

With a land area of 427 square miles, the Hong Kong Special Administrative Region embraces the island of Hong Kong, the Kowloon Peninsula, the New Territories (a portion of mainland China extending to the Shenzhen River, which is now the boundary between Hong Kong and Guangdong Province), and more than 230 small islands. Hong Kong has a tropical monsoon climate and a hilly-to-mountainous topography with natural deep-water harbors. With a population of approximately 7 million (95 percent Chinese and 5 percent other nationalities), Hong Kong represents one of the most densely inhabited areas in the world. Based on a market economy, Hong Kong thrives on diverse industries: textile, clothing, electronics, toys, watches, and tourism. It also holds primary status in both regional and international finance and commerce. Hong Kong enjoys principal partnership in import-export trade with major economic powers in the world: mainland China, the United States, Japan, Germany, United Kingdom, Taiwan, Singapore, and South Korea.

FOUNDING

The founding of Hong Kong, a British Crown Colony until its return to China on July 1, 1997, resulted from the First Anglo-Chinese War (1839–1842). Also known as the First Opium War, this conflict stemmed from intensified clashes of economic-political interests and cultural values between the Qing dynasty of China (1644–1911) and the West, Britain in particular. Following the loss of its American colonies in the late eighteenth century, Britain turned its attention to Asia, soon

Since its founding by the British in the early nineteenth century, Hong Kong has served as a key trading port for southern China. Here, laborers pull a loaded cart on the city's docks sometime around the turn of the twentieth century. *(Library of Congress)*

imposing political and commercial domination over India. With India as its foothold, Britain became the most powerful Western imperialist in Asia, leading other Western countries in trade with China. Chinese tea and silk enjoyed high demand in Britain, but the British also saw China—the most populous and expansive East Asian empire—as a potential market for its own manufactured products.

The Qing court, however, held an ambivalent stance toward commercial contacts with the outside. While it viewed the exportation of profitable Chinese commodities as a source of additional state income, the Qing government, based on a self-centered outlook of China's superiority, remained xenophobic toward foreign influence and sought to keep foreign imports from entering the Chinese domestic market. Historically, the Qing administration had established and practiced the Guangzhou (Canton) system, an arrangement that restricted commercial contact with the outside world to the single port of Guangzhou, used cohong (an officially certified Chinese merchants' guild) as the monopolistic intermediary for foreign traders, and demanded payments in bullion (gold or silver) for Chinese goods. Only during the trading season from October to May were foreign merchants allowed to live in the Guangzhou district, though only in their "factories" outside the city. In addition, foreigners had to abide by the imperial protocols, legal or ritualistic, as subjects to the Qing throne.

To break those trading barriers and end what the West regarded as undignified Chinese etiquette, Britain sought to negotiate a diplomatic relationship on equal footing and open trade with the Qing dynasty. Two British diplomatic missions, one led by the Earl George Macartney and another by the Lord William Pitt Amherst in 1793 and 1816, respectively, went to Beijing in vain. Meanwhile, the British East India Company, which monopolized all British commercial activities with China, intensified its reliance on India's opium as a profitable export to China. Solely responsible since 1763 for all aspects of the opium economy—including plantation, production, and overseas sale—the company from the beginning licensed only noncompany ships to carry opium to China in an effort to disguise public connection with the trade. By so doing, the company also superficially complied with the British-Indian policy of respecting the Qing court's prohibition on the importation of opium. Yet huge profits from trafficking and smuggling the drug into China became the foundation for the British East India Company's increasing surpluses in trade with China.

Complying with rising demands for free trade, the British government officially terminated the British East India Company's monopoly over China commerce in 1834. Eyeing economic gains, free traders expressed an urgent desire to force the Qing dynasty to alter its restrictive Guangzhou trade practices, to yield a Chinese port as a foothold for British commerce in China, and to legalize the opium trade. Also driven by the need for imperialist competition with other Western powers, the British government recharged its challenge to the Qing closed-door policy by sending a diplomatic embassy headed by Lord William John Napier, British chief superintendent of trade in China, to Guangzhou in 1834. But the Napier mission failed and instead caused the Chinese boycott of the British merchants to persist. This failure of diplomacy only worked to whet the British appetite for some Chinese offshore islands to use as a British forefront venue to China, as a base for the British Royal Navy, and as a link for a British emporium of trade in Asia. Lord Napier (before his death in Macao in 1835) suggested the island of Hong Kong as ideal for such purposes, and Captain Charles Elliot, deputy chief superintendent of trade in China, formally recommended this site in 1836.

Simultaneously, the Qing authorities grew frightened by the widening scope of opium sale and its grave consequences in China: drug addiction among the Chinese produced an uncontrolled outflow of silver currency that imperiled the Qing dynasty's political, social, and fiscal stability. After a heated court debate in 1838, the Qing government chose to eradicate the sale and consumption of opium, and in January 1839 the Qing emperor promulgated *Regulations Concerning the Absolute and Final Suppression of Opium by Imperial Order*. At Guangzhou, Lin Zexu, imperial plenipotentiary commissioner for suppressing opium, enforced the ban by taking such extreme measures as detaining the British and Western merchants in their warehouses and forcing them to surrender all opium stock. Eventually, Commissioner Lin confiscated and publicly destroyed 21,000 chests (over 2.6 million pounds) of the forbidden drug.

The loss of opium and the harsh manner in which the Chinese treated British citizens (even though many were opium traders) provided a convenient and necessary excuse for Great Britain to declare war on the Qing dynasty and force China open. The First Anglo-Chinese Conflict, or the First Opium War, was well under way in June 1840 when the British expeditionary fleet under Admiral George Elliot's command reached China. Intimidated by Britain's naval prowess, the Qing court dismissed Lin Zexu from office and agreed to negotiate peace. In January 1841, British envoy Charles Elliot and the Qing representative reached the Chuanbi (Bogue) Convention, a pact that gave Britain several concessions: the transfer of Hong Kong Island and its harbor to Britain; Chinese payment of 6 million taels of silver for the British losses; establishment of trade relations on the basis of mutual equality; and the opening of Guangzhou as a free-trade port. But the Qing monarch considered the pact humiliating and refused to recognize it. Meantime, London judged the convention insufficient to reflect Britain's demands and rejected it, sacking Elliot.

Subsequent British military campaigns forced the Qing dynasty to concede total defeat and give in to all British demands. In August 1842, Sir Henry Pottinger—who replaced Elliot as British plenipotentiary—and the Qing government's envoy concluded the Treaty of Nanjing. This treaty and its ensuing supplementary articles opened five Chinese ports (Guangzhou; Fuzhou; Xiamen, or Amoy; Ningbo; and Shanghai) to British trade and residence; granted British extraterritorial authority in China; paid 21 million taels of silver as the Qing court's compensation for British economic losses and military costs; and gave favorable tariff rates for British commodities. Aside from that, the Treaty of Nanjing ceded the island of Hong Kong (already under British military occupation since January 1841) to be possessed "in perpetuity" by the British monarch and subsequent heirs.

The founding—and territorial expansion—of Hong Kong as a British Crown Colony officially began with the British-Chinese exchange of ratification instruments for the Treaty of Nanjing on June 26, 1843. A royal charter issued simultaneously set up the basic frame of the colonial government for Hong Kong: it consisted of a governor, a Legislative Council, and an Executive Council. The governor of Hong Kong, who also served as the British plenipotentiary and superintendent of British trade in China, answered directly to the British Crown and held wide discretionary legislative and executive power. The Executive Council, appointed by and subordinate to the governor, only had consultative tasks. The Legislative Council, whose members the governor had the authority to appoint and dismiss, held responsibility for passing laws and regulations for the colony (and for all English subjects in China until 1854, when the governor of Hong Kong no longer acted as Britain's chief diplomatic and commercial representative in China). The governor was to administer Hong Kong with the Legislative Council's advice and consent but had the right to pass laws independently of his Legislative Council whenever necessary. High-ranking British officials occupied all seats on the legislative body.

Only after 1850 were nonofficial British—and later European—members appointed, and not until 1880 were citizens from the elite of the Chinese community permitted to participate in the Legislative Council, though Chinese constituted an overwhelming majority of Hong Kong's population. Such restrictive colonial rule (which remained basically unchanged until the 1980s) aimed to secure Hong Kong as a permanent principal center of dynamic commerce for Britain.

Hong Kong, as a trade hub, had a difficult beginning because British commercial ships and merchants directly dealt with the newly opened Chinese treaty ports. Nonetheless, Hong Kong's trade did grow steadily, thanks to its fine deep-water harbor and strategic location for major sea routes connecting Southeast Asia, East Asia, Europe, and America. Before long, Hong Kong became a major entrepôt for international trade in Asia. It became a hub for the shipbuilding industry and a stopping point for ships coming from Europe, America, or India for repairs, or for storing supplies or commodities temporarily. Hong Kong's population kept pace with business activity, particularly because more and more Chinese immigrants arrived in pursuit of profit and employment or to escape China's domestic political turbulence.

The number of Western residents, mainly British, also swelled. Local demands for food and other supplies boosted commercial growth in Hong Kong, causing an upsurge in insurance service and banking. In 1845, the Oriental Bank opened a branch in Hong Kong, specializing in the exchange of currency. The Chartered Mercantile Bank of India, London, and China followed suit in 1857, and the Chartered Bank of India, Australia, and China established an outlet there in 1859. Meanwhile, Hong Kong emerged as an administrative center for trade since the island, as a British naval and military base, afforded safety to some of the principal British merchant houses in China trade: for example, Jardine, Matheson and Company and Dent and Company.

As a burgeoning British colony, Hong Kong benefited from the Second Opium War (or Second Anglo-Chinese Conflict) that unfolded from 1856 through 1860 and, in consequence, forced China to conclude the Treaty of Tianjin in 1858 and the Treaty of Beijing in 1860. Taken together, the two treaties obliged China to open up more ports and grant the British rights to an embassy in the Qing capital, to "spheres of influence" and consular jurisdiction, to travel and religious missions in China's interior, and to a most-favored-nation status in terms of tariff as well as trade.

Moreover, the Qing government had to pay 8 million taels of silver of indemnity to the British and surrender the Kowloon Peninsula to permanent British possession as part of the British Crown Colony of Hong Kong.

ACQUISITION OF KOWLOON

The acquisition of Kowloon, a three-square-mile territory on mainland China located opposite Hong Kong Island, allowed the British to control the whole harbor area to enforce Hong Kong's status as a naval and military center from a strategic angle and to expand its capacity for residence, industry, and business. A rural backwater at the time of takeover, the peninsula experienced rapid and well-planned development and by the late 1880s became a busy harbor, an emerging center for ship-building industries, an industrial village for manufacturing, and a residential-business region.

At the same time, as more Chinese ports opened to foreign commerce, Hong Kong's position as a crucial entrepôt in China trade escalated in volume and value. In 1880, for instance, Hong Kong handled 20 percent of China's total export trade and 37 percent of its import trade. The legalization of opium enhanced Hong Kong as the main distribution center for the drug, which generally accounted for 45 percent of China's total import value. As well, Hong Kong played a key role in the China coast trade. Along with commerce, banking and insurance kept growing. The Hong Kong and Shanghai Bank, founded by local capital for profit in 1864, engaged itself actively in overseas investment and, by the late 1870s, had expanded into a major locally based international bank, opening branches in China, India, Indochina, Japan, Malaysia, and the United States. In the meantime, Hong Kong's manufacturing sector began to diversify gradually. New industries emerged that included match making, soap making, rattan work, food processing, sugar refining, salt manufacturing, and cement production.

Hong Kong's population saw steady growth following the expansion of its territorial perimeters in 1860. The number of residents in Kowloon alone, for example, increased from about 3,000 at the time of takeover to 25,000 in 1897. At the same time, Hong Kong hosted more than 240,000 people of diverse ethnic and national origins. Land reclamation of the sea advanced urban construction and the development of the infrastructure to meet the colony's social and economic needs. Educational initiatives involved the birth and growth of Chinese private academies, Protestant and Catholic missionary institutions, government schools, and, in the 1880s, a college of medicine and a technical institute. Hospital care accompanied Hong Kong's expansion, as did interest in sanitation with the founding of a sanitary board to promote public hygiene in 1879.

Despite its boom, Hong Kong remained vulnerable as a British naval base and trade nucleus in East Asia after the Second Opium War as other Western imperialist powers—mainly France, Germany, Russia, and Japan (a latecomer)—intensified their own quest for markets, spheres of influence, and territorial concessions in China. Hong Kong's security especially concerned the British government when, following the Sino-French War (1884–1885), France sought control over China's southern provinces and Japan took possession of Taiwan (with other special rights secured from the Qing government) by defeating the Qing empire in the Sino-Japanese War (1894–1895). For reasons of defense, but also for the further development of Hong Kong, the British government looked to even more territorial exactions from China and concluded the Convention on the Border Extension of Hong Kong with the Qing authorities on June 9, 1898.

According to this agreement, Britain leased the New Territories—a large piece of mainland and hundreds of offshore islands—from China for ninety-nine years. This new territorial acquisition of more than 365 square miles provided a buffer zone for the proper protection of Hong Kong, increased Hong Kong's total area by 89 percent, and added more than 100,000 people to its population. Rural in nature, this extension to the Chinese mainland also made a major agricultural base available for the support of the colony and, more important, afforded freshwater supplies needed for the continued development of Hong Kong as the number of its inhabitants grew. By expanding its border on Chinese mainland, moreover, the colony gained room for the growth of commerce and manufacturing as well as space for preparing a potential terminal connection with railroads planned for construction in Qing China's southern provinces. Thus, Hong Kong would have direct land-transportation access to the mainland Chinese market, thereby further enhancing its position as an entrepôt in China and East Asia trade.

With the New Territories under its jurisdiction, the British Crown Colony of Hong Kong had taken new shape in terms of size, government, and economy. Throughout the whole period from 1842 to 1898, London generally implemented a laissez-faire policy toward Hong Kong and, by treating it as a British free-trade port, nourished the underpinnings of a free-market economy and stimulated the colony's prosperity. However, London's stance toward Hong Kong became gradually mercantilist starting in the early twentieth century, especially after World War I, as Britain's share of the world—and China—trade declined compared to other industrial countries. (By 1931, Britain had abandoned the principle of free trade for Hong Kong and adopted protectionism.) As British exports to China dwindled in the 1920s and 1930s, Hong Kong compensated by shifting its transshipping focus toward Southeast Asia and the western Pacific. Meanwhile, Hong Kong maintained its economic progress by moving increasingly toward manufacturing diversification, including expansion into light industries. Its political stability as a British colony further attracted capital and labor from mainland China, which was torn by chronic political disorder and war.

Hong Kong suffered dire economic circumstances under the Japanese occupation between December 1942 and August 1945. After the defeat of Japan in 1945 and until 1946, Hong Kong's prospect as a British colony appeared uncertain because of mounting nationalism in China and an anticolonialist zeal in postwar Asia. The British government, nonetheless, stood fast and determined to recover and continue its possession of Hong Kong for its symbolic, economic, and strategic importance to the British empire. Simultaneously, Britain faced a demographic challenge as the Chinese settlers returned to Hong Kong in large numbers, and the civil war (1946–1949) between the Nationalists and the communists in China, especially the communist rise to power in 1949, further swelled the influx of Chinese immigrants to the colony. By 1950, the population of Hong Kong had climbed to over 2 million, but the immigrants had brought with them capital, skills, and expertise, necessary assets for Hong Kong's economic revival and takeoff.

DECLINE OF BRITISH INFLUENCE

But Hong Kong's entrepôt-oriented economy was affected by the decline of British influence in the Pacific region. Hong Kong also had to contend with a sharp decrease in trade with mainland China because of an economic embargo that the United Nations and United States imposed on the Chinese communist government following its participation in the Korean War in 1950. Still, Hong Kong bounced back to sustain and elevate its status as a trade center. The 1950s witnessed Hong Kong's rapid maturity in labor-intensive export-oriented industrialism with textile and garment making industries taking the lead. By the early 1960s, Hong Kong had advanced its trading status on the international market, especially its exports to Britain and the United States. With increasing capital accumulation, Hong Kong further expanded its export trade and became a world economic center by enlarging its banking service worldwide and improving its infrastructure to world-class standards.

In the 1970s and early 1980s, with its growing competitiveness in the world market, Hong Kong achieved high industrial productivity by developing high-value technology-oriented industries such as electronics as well as economic sophistication through its efficient banking, telecommunications, tourism, and transportation services. Hong Kong also revived its position as entrepôt in East Asian commerce when China reopened itself to the outside world beginning in 1979. By the late 1980s, Hong Kong had become a major international financial and trade center and has maintained such a status in the world economy (even after China regained its sovereignty over Hong Kong in 1997).

Guoqiang Zheng

See also: British Empire.

BIBLIOGRAPHY

Lo, C.P. *Hong Kong*. London: Belhaven, 1992.

Shipp, Steve. *A Political History of the British Crown Colony's Transfer to Chinese Rule*. Jefferson, NC: McFarland, 1995.

HUNDRED YEARS' WAR

> A military conflict between England and France from 1337 to 1453 that had domestic and international origins.

During the thirteenth century, Flanders operated as the industrial center of northern Europe. Wool cloth from Flanders was in demand, but Flanders was forced to import wool from England to meet increasing demand. A triangle trade developed wherein wool from England was sold to Flemish manufacturers, who then sold the cloth to the English-controlled portion of southern France, which then sold wine to England. Since the count of Flanders was a vassal of the French king, it was not long before the French monarchy attempted to exert control over Flanders, a move that the English could not allow because of its potential for disrupting their source of foreign exchange. A civil war in Flanders ensued. Meanwhile, the English, through Edward III, who was the son of the British king Edward II and his French wife, Isabelle, became heir to the French throne. The French reinstated the Salic Law, which prohibited the inheritance of property through the female line. The ensuing Hundred Years' War encouraged nationalism in England and France, and its outcome brought an end to English landholding in France and led Britain to become a naval power.

During the war's early years, the conflict was fought over the feudal obligations of the English king in France, the claims of the English king to the French throne, and the ambitions that both England and France had to control the wealthy wine-growing area of Gascony and the prosperous industrial cities in Flanders. Wines were a popular import for the English nobility. People in general saw the war in France as the fulfillment of English expansionist policy, which that country had committed itself to since the time of Edward I.

The English and the French fought over disputed territory in France. The king of England possessed land in France, but he held it as a vassal of the French king. English kings since the eleventh century had presided over territories in France. They were English fiefs, or lands that England owned in return for pledge and loyalty to the king of France. The English king had to pay homage to the French king. The war began in 1337 when Philip VI of France took over the English-held Duchy of Guyenne in France from Edward III of England. Edward III had claims to the duchy and to the French throne. Since the rules of succession to the French throne were unclear, the kings of England could make a reasonable claim to the monarchy. The English answered the French takeover by invading France from the north and then, in 1340, by destroying a French fleet to remove the threat of a possible French invasion of England. There were three major phases that comprise the Hundred Years' War: the Edwardian (1340–1360), the Caroline (1369–1389), and the Lancastrian (1415–1435). The first and second phases were dominated by Edward III of England and Charles V of France, respectively.

There were several significant effects of the war. It revolutionized military technology as the prowess of the English longbow and the French cannon became evident. Some of the battles that were fought are legendary in history: Crécy, Poitiers, and Agincourt are the most well known. There were sieges, ransoms, lootings, as well as the burning and killing of many people. Militarily, it was hard to find effective leaders who could lead a large group of men in the French countryside. France had a harder time finding leaders than did England.

The war changed English and French society and created wealth and misfortune for many. The conflict produced regular standing armies and effective systems of taxation. Since the war was so long, the number of men at arms and the funds raised via taxation varied. The Catholic Church also made financial demands on the peasants by instituting the collection of tithes, or one-tenth of one's income. Tithes were also an income tax on all personal earnings.

One of the more important lands in English possession during the early 1300s was Gascony

The Hundred Years' War between France and England had a debilitating effect on trade between the two countries in the fourteenth and fifteenth centuries. Shown here are English longbowmen resisting a charge of French knights at the Battle of Crécy, France, in 1346. *(© North Wind Picture Archives)*

in southwestern France, an area known for its wine production. The French had been aggressive in trying to influence the region and gain control of it. Edward I of England had a son, Edward II, who married the daughter of the French king, Philip IV. The result of their union was a son, Edward III, who eventually laid claim to the French throne after Philip IV's son died in the 1320s. The French were not pleased, believing that the throne should belong to someone whose claim to it could be substantiated through male lineage. Edward III invaded France in 1337 with an army of about 15,000 men. He had mostly soldiers who were archers or mobile light-armored infantry. The archers carried the deadly and accurate longbow with them. Edward realized that heavily armored knights and their horses were too weighty to transport across the unpredictable English Channel.

Both sides faced the burdensome task of raising an army during the Middle Ages. Armies were ruinous to pay, impossible to feed, and hard to command. They lived off the land, while destroying it at the same time. Disease ran rampant in campaigns and killed many soldiers. Leaders recruited armies mainly through contract, also called indenture, and paid soldiers at agreed-on rates of pay. Mercenaries, or hired soldiers, were part of the armies as well. A typical army during the Hundred Years' War included armored men, knights, squires, sergeants, and many archers. The lower ranks of England's royal armies were often recruited from the lesser gentry, since there seemed to be an emphasis on highly trained and well-equipped mounted archers. It was unlikely that more than 10 percent of the adult male population of England ever fought in the conflict at any one time. In the war's early years, the English Crown recruited troops through compulsory methods. Since money and supplies were acquired through the noncombatant population, that section of society did acquire some sense of a vested interest in the army and war. The war created a special relationship between the people and the state. Political propaganda included the English monarch's attempts to instill the idea that the wars were intended to protect the interests of the king, the aristocracy, and the nation as a whole.

Financially, England raised over 9.5 million pounds throughout the war. In the years before the war, it was common for people like the Italians to lend money to governments in times of conflict. Fiscal reform relied on borrowing from English nobles and merchants. There was also the indirect taxation of overseas trade. Both of these methods gave England much-needed revenue. The English were faced with royal agents coming into towns and villages to collect money and supplies for the war. English monarchs continued to overspend throughout the war. Richard II in the 1380s and Henry VI in the 1440s overspent to the verge of bankruptcy. They were unable to match increased expenditures with increased revenues. The population of England had been pushed to the limit with regard to taxation. This was especially true in the 1340s, the 1370s, and the 1410s. During the end of the war, there was a decrease in taxation, as the community became less willing to pay.

The English king and his council needed an effective propaganda machine to get the population to side with their wartime objectives. The sheriffs and the church were the backbone of this machine. The sheriffs made public proclamations in the cities, villages, and courts. The church was also asked to support the war during masses, processions, sermons, and prayers.

France had a larger population than England, and it mustered more men than its enemy throughout the war. Still, it is not likely that the French army ever had more than 30,000 men at any major campaign, even during the major battles at Crécy, Poitiers, and Agincourt. The English armies were much smaller, somewhere between one-half and one-third of the French armies. The English had the disadvantage of having to transport their army to the continent. They could only hope to receive reinforcements from their allies in Gascony or Burgundy. The English king also had to man English forts in France and leave an adequate number of men to guard England against possible French raids and Scottish invasions. These distractions faced the English throughout the war.

The French suffered even more directly from the war. English invasions in northeastern and southwestern France meant that the towns there witnessed the conflict firsthand. Big cities with adequate defenses were less likely to suffer the misfortunes of war than small cities with little or no defenses. Fighting destroyed much of the farmland and countryside, which hit the French economy hard. Many in France starved because of the lost farmland or succumbed to diseases like the Black Death, which ravaged Europe during this time. Looters and ne'er-do-wells traveled throughout the French countryside in search of food, material goods, money, and trouble. They contributed to the economic and social chaos in that country during and after the war. France did not have the money, skilled workers, or incentive to build or repair the devastation.

The first two decades of the conflict witnessed significant English victories. The longbow was able to pierce chain mail armor and inflicted heavy casualties on the enemy. The English used this weapon to their advantage, and it helped them win at Crécy, Poitiers, and Agincourt. In the Battle of Crécy in 1346, the English captured Normandy, and in the following year they captured Calais, a significant port. This battle also signaled the beginning of the end of the calvary charge and the introduction of the use of explosives in warfare. The use of mechanical weapons like the longbow and the cannon made hand-to-hand combat insignificant and futile. It also signaled the end of the noble knight. The knight was replaced by the professional soldier. In the 1350s, Edward III's son, the Black Prince, defeated the French in the west at the Battle of Poitiers. He captured the French king, John II, and held him for ransom. Because of the French defeat in these two battles, they were forced to give up the southwestern region of Aquitaine in the subsequent Peace of Bretigny. The English received a large ransom for the captured king, and the treaty also made Edward III the nominal sovereign of a third of France. This ended the Edwardian phase of the war.

From 1369 to the beginning of the 1400s, known as the Carolinian phase of the war, the French fared much better. One reason was because of superb leadership on the battlefield and at home. France also gained a valuable ally in Spain. Lastly, the French were able to maintain a regular army with an adequate taxation system to fund that army. France was now under the leadership of Charles V (1364–1380), and he found the right nobles to lead his army. The French were able to recapture much of the territory that they had lost, though England still controlled some coastal cities. It was Charles who established the system of taxation and a regular army for the first time. Spain defeated the English in the 1370s, and the rebuilt French fleet was able to raid the southern English coast. But Charles V died in 1380, and this brought French momentum to a halt.

Henry V of England invaded France in 1415. The English and French troops fought one another near Agincourt in northern France. The English archers with their longbows and foot soldiers proved to be too much for the feeble French cavalry charges. The arrows penetrated chain mail armor, and there were heavy casualties on the French side, especially among the French nobles. The Battle of Agincourt was a decisive English victory. Even though the English were outnumbered, the longbows and incompetent French tactics negated that disadvantage. The French leadership was not as effective as it had been under Charles V. Henry V was able to conquer Normandy and other areas in northwestern France.

France underwent political turmoil in the 1420s, as there was doubt as to who was the heir to the French throne. It was a similar situation to the one that plagued France in the 1330s. Support grew for the dauphin, Charles VII. It was Charles VII who was visited in 1429 by a French peasant girl who said she had visions of saintly people who told her that she was to lead a French army against the English. After some doubt, Charles VII arranged for this to happen. This girl, Joan of Arc, led a French army that defeated the English at Orléans and Patay. Orléans was on the northern bank of the Loire River. It had been under English siege as they had built a series of small forts around it and were waiting for the inhabitants of the city to starve. Joan was able to enter the city without much opposition and brought with her a wealth of supplies. She attacked the English forts one by one and defeated the English. It was the greatest possible morale-builder for the French. She became a heroine and helped Charles VII become the king of France. She was, however, captured by enemies and executed in the early 1430s, when she was only nineteen years old.

The tide of war began to turn against the English in the 1430s, during the Lancastrian phase of the conflict. The French again had a regular army and an effective tax system that produced money to fund the war. They also improved their field artillery using mobile cannons that inflicted heavy casualties and destruction on the English. The deployment of the mobile cannon spurred French successes and helped them regain lost territories and eventually drive the English out of France altogether. The English signed a truce in the 1440s, and by the 1450s the French recovered all the possessions that England had in France, except Calais. The war ended in 1453 but it was not until the 1560s that the French would get Calais back.

New developments during the war and the effects of the fighting continued to impact Europe long after its end. The face of warfare had changed with the introduction of the longbow and mobile cannon. Taxation provided the means to fund the war, and governments created a highly effective propaganda machine to convert the populaces to their causes. The age of chivalry ended because the war signaled the end of the knight, who was killed by the introduction of technology. The French nobility was virtually eliminated, either cut down by the English longbows or by diseases. But, as one often sees in times of war, there were heroes and heroines who demonstrated capable leadership. The French monarchy after Charles VII had no rivals, and he was better able to handle the rest of the social class, mainly the lower class and the emerging middle class. In the end, both countries were exhausted by taxation and the French countryside was devastated because of English raids. England was defeated and would never again mount an attack on the Continent for territorial gain.

David Treviño

See also: British Empire.

BIBLIOGRAPHY

Bishop, Morris. *The Middle Ages.* Boston: Houghton Mifflin, 2001.

Cantor, Norman F. *The Civilization of the Middle Ages.* New York: HarperCollins, 1993.

Curry, Anne, and Michael Hughes, eds. *Arms, Armies, and Fortifications in the Hundred Years' War.* Woodbridge, UK: Boydell, 1994.

Fowler, Kenneth, ed. *The Hundred Years' War.* London: Macmillan, 1971.

"Hundred Years' War." Microsoft Encarta Online Encyclopedia 2003 (http://encarta.msn.com, accessed May 2003).

Neillands, Robin. *The Hundred Years' War.* London: Routledge, 1990.

Perroy, Édouard. *The Hundred Years' War.* Bloomington: Indiana University Press, 1962.

Seward, Desmond. *The Hundred Years' War: The English in France, 1337–1453.* London: Constable, 1978.

ILLEGAL TRADE

Goods and services prohibited by governments for various reasons.

Trade that national governments refuse to condone, license, or tax is illegal trade, including the unauthorized domestic and international distribution of that which governments claim a monopoly or on which governments collect taxes. The range of commodities exchanged illegally on international markets includes narcotic and nonnarcotic drugs, illegally mined precious stones (such as those extracted to pay for illegally purchased weapons), illegally harvested animal products, stolen vehicles, illegally exported antiquities, and even human smuggling or the illegal transport of migrants. The legal status of certain transactions varies from one jurisdiction to another.

Trade in narcotics, weapons, and antiquities are the world's leading illicit markets. More than 200 million people are estimated to participate in illegal markets for drugs worldwide, and Asia is the most seriously affected by heroin traffic and abuse. According to Interpol, which counts 181 nation-states as members and coordinates individual states' investigations of drug cases, of the 36 tons of heroin seized worldwide, about 19 tons were seized in Asia and 15 tons in Europe. Most heroin consumed in Asian countries is produced in Afghanistan and Myanmar. While heroin production in the "golden triangle" at the borders of Myanmar, Thailand, and Laos seems to have remained stable since 1997, an immense stockpile continues to supply markets in Australia, New Zealand, and North America. Illegal export from Ho Chi Minh City reaches Sydney, which is then distributed to other Australian cities by road. While Asian heroin remains strong in international illegal trade, Interpol reports a dramatic shift in origin of the heroin consumed in North America within recent years. Until 1994, about 68 percent of that seized by authorities was produced in Southwest Asia; and after 1995, 62 percent originated in South America.

ARMS TRADE

The United Nations Conference on the Illicit Trade in Small Arms and Light Weapons in All Its Aspects convened during the summer of 2001. Representatives of more than 140 nation-states and over 170 international nongovernmental organizations (NGOs) estimated that 500 million small arms and other light weapons are currently in illegal circulation. Methods continue to be implemented by which national laws could better regulate national arms brokers, effectively criminalizing illicit production and restricting unauthorized trade of weapons.

In an attempt to curtail this trade, the conference recommended that licensed arms manufacturers "appropriately and reliably" mark each weapon during the manufacturing processes, which would allow weapons to be traced through resale, meaning accurate records of weapons distribution could be created. The conference recommended that surplus stocks of small arms lacking such identifying marks be destroyed to prevent their potential illegal distribution. Speaking for the European Union, Belgian officials stated the need for stringent export controls and careful stockpiling management with supervised destruction in support of the conference's measures. Representing one of the world's largest weapons exporting nations, U.S. officials opposed measures to constrain legal manufacture and trade of small arms and light weapons and resisted the activities of nongovernmental organizations.

CULTURAL OBJECTS

Interpol and the United Nations Educational, Scientific, and Cultural Organization (UNESCO) rank stolen art and cultural objects as the world's third largest illegal market, behind drugs and the arms trade. Interpol has been tracking illicit trade in cultural objects since 1947. This trade came under regulation by a 1970 UNESCO convention that regulates cultural objects' transfer among the ninety-four signatory nations. An international agreement, the Convention on Stolen or Illegally Exported Cultural Objects, was signed at a 1995 convention of the United Nations International Institute for the Unification of Private Law. Widely recognized as the world's fourth largest art market, Switzerland represents one of the few countries not to have signed the UNESCO convention. As Andrea Raschèr, of the Swiss Federal Culture Office, explains, "It's easier to import an ancient vase [into the country] than a tomato." Neil Brodie, the Illicit Antiquities Research Center (Cambridge, UK) coordinator, explains, "the fact that [Switzerland] hasn't signed up to the UNESCO convention is certainly linked to the fact that it is a thriving center for antiquities." A recently proposed draft law would extend the period after which cultural goods of unidentified origin could legally enter Swiss markets from five to thirty years.

That weapons, drugs, and antiquities are the illegal goods trading at comparable levels of value is not a coincidence: most of the world's illegal transactions are nonstate actors purchasing weapons, with the proceeds from illegal sale of drugs and antiquities.

STATES AND ILLEGAL TRADE

During times of war, state institutions are at their most modern. In times of political emergencies, such as afforded by a declaration of war, much local and almost all foreign trade in consumer and producer goods becomes subject to government control. As historian John Singleton points out, "During peacetime a nation has no generally accepted economic objective, and what counts is the satisfaction of the subjective wants of individuals. But when a major war breaks out the national objective becomes victory or, at the very least, survival. Hence in wartime, it is the function of the government to deploy the country's resources in those activities which will maximize the chances of the country's military success." Consumers' trading habits are subject to disruption, in the form of rationing. Goods freely traded in peacetime, including items of clothing, meats and animal fats, dairy goods, and sugar, are subject to controlled distribution or rationing during wartime. Officials also restrict trade in labor (employment of draft-eligible individuals) and trade in industrial commodities (including metals, fuel, lubricants, fabric, rubber, plastics, and paper) to defense contractors.

This is not to say that governments leave trade to markets during peacetime. In peace, as in war, modern states adopt policies to control trade in national currencies. The national currency continues to circulate within the nation's boundaries: local residents' domestic trade may remain undisturbed by such controls. It is only international trade in goods and services that is affected, as the state administration seeks to prioritize access to "reserve currencies" for such autarkic measures as the national defense or an industrialization drive. Officially set local exchange rates for "soft currencies" then deviate from international market values that are governed by impressions of political or economic uncertainty, and a black (or illegal) market becomes the location for unauthorized exchange of domestic and international currencies. The classic illustration is the Soviet Union's currency controls, which anthropologist Alaina Lemon describes as "currency apartheid." The value of the Soviet ruble was strongly controlled through a state monopoly on foreign trade; in 1988, toward the end of the Soviet state, the official exchange rate was 0.61 ruble for one U.S. dollar, while a dollar traded for four to six rubles on various Soviet black markets. This is not to say that the U.S. dollar was the only reserve currency to trade in illegal Soviet currency markets: Canadian dollars circulated along with sterling pounds and deutsche marks.

Economist Case Sprenkle describes the way in which reserve, or "hard," currencies trade in the world. Sprenkle suggests most U.S. currency circulates among nations in the developing world, as about $300 billion was in the hands of the public during 1992. Domestic households and business demands account for a bare 16 percent of dollar bills: the remainder was distributed among children, illegal enterprises, and foreigners. While the Federal Reserve is reluctant to attribute a large share of the missing currency to foreigners, residents of foreign countries circulate U.S. currencies abroad, without receiving goods and services from the United States equal in value to those initially purchased by U.S. citizens abroad. What Sprenkle describes includes unequal exchanges between industrialized nations and the rest of the globe.

Within sovereign states, legal trade in labor—employment—like currency is subject to restrictions governing the employee's age, hours of labor, and payment of taxes and social benefits, as well as other factors. Employment of children and young persons subject to compulsory school attendance is severely limited during school hours, which ensures their presence in school. In New Brunswick, a minor must attend school until graduation from high school or until he or she reaches the age of eighteen. In the United States, a sixteen-year-old must present proof of school attendance before receiving a driver's license. Other industrialized countries have similar rules and restrictions.

ALCOHOL AND TOBACCO

Trade in goods is no less subject to modern states' restrictions than labor, even in peacetime. Trade in goods, including alcoholic beverages and tobacco products, is legal in many jurisdictions only if the transaction is registered and/or taxed. According to the World Bank, different tax rates are as important as variations in socioeconomic conditions and geographical proximities to various markets in contributing to illegal trade in tobacco.

Now, European Union (EU) representatives accuse a leading U.S. tobacco manufacturer of systematic illegal distribution of its products within EU jurisdiction. It must be noted that consumers of smuggled tobacco products may or may not be aware of the legal status of the cigarettes they consume. Few smokers stop to examine the excise stamp on the package, although they may notice the discounted price. In such a price-sensitive market as that for tobacco, consumers respond to lower prices by buying more. This contributes to a widely held perception that contraband trade in tobacco is victimless. Law enforcement officials complain that, based on this perception, convictions for evasion of tobacco taxes are accompanied by comparatively lenient penalties.

While private firms produce tobacco goods, and public authorities tax these goods, public authorities control production, distribution, and sale of alcoholic beverages in many jurisdictions. While many consider contraband trade in tobacco to be relatively harmless, the first wave of feminists identified and enumerated the victims of trade in and consumption of alcoholic beverages. During the mid-nineteenth century, the Women's Christian Temperance Union (WCTU) linked anti-alcohol sentiment with feminist principles and identified working men's renunciation of alcohol with women's increased economic security. In the WCTU, Frances Willard lined an anti-alcohol campaign with women's suffrage, equal pay for equal work, and the eight-hour day.

Sociologist Harry Levine attributes Scandinavians' warm reception to nineteenth-century temperance movements to Sweden's Christian revival movement. Responding to public anti-alcohol sentiments, Sweden became one of several nineteenth-century imperial states to institute monopolies over the trade in alcohol to restrict its retail trade. The Swedish state's monopoly dates from 1865; a controlled distribution network and high taxes were intended to keep Swedes from high-proof beverages. System Bogalet, the Swedish retail monopoly for beverage alcohol, compares the taxes levied on low-proof beverages with those levied on high-proof beverages: "[A] bottle of French wine that costs SEK 900 is taxed at just over 20 percent," while "a bottle of unflavored vodka is taxed at 80 percent of the retail price, including a value-added tax." Distribution of both is limited to certain hours and certain days of the week.

In contemporary Finland, another successor state to the territories formerly governed by Imperial Sweden, officials transformed these historical restrictions to contemporary trade in advertising media by banning all advertisements for alcohol. However, these restrictions have recently relaxed, permitting distribution of images containing beer and wine consumption in national media. Social science research alerts contemporary Finnish legislators to the effects of alcohol trade, suggesting that Finns' increased access through either price/taxation reductions or extending an alcohol retail network contributes both to higher rates of consumption and drinking-related damage. In 1969, Finland's distribution system was dramatically liberalized through changes in the places licensed to sell alcoholic beverages, increasing the density of retail outlets in the rural areas. A 50 percent per capita increase in alcohol sales in one year contributed to substantially higher rates of drinking-related deaths and other complications in following years.

The Russian empire's monopoly over trade in alcoholic beverages was revived by the Soviet Union in 1937, which extended the production chain as a monopoly in legal manufacture as well as trade in these beverages. The Soviet Ministry of Agriculture was responsible for coordinating production and internal sales of all alcoholic beverages (including wines) in each of the fifteen constituent Soviet republics. International trade in alcohol was the monopoly of the all-Soviet foreign economic association Soyuzplodoimport, which controlled legal distribution of all foods and beverages produced in the Soviet Union, including branded vodkas, worldwide. Until the end of the Soviet state, all other beverage trade was illegal.

Elizabeth Bishop

See also: Drugs.

BIBLIOGRAPHY

Lader, Malcom, Griffith Edwards, and D. Colin Drummon, eds. *Nature of Alcohol and Drug-Related Problems.* New York: Oxford University Press, 1992.

Lemon, Alaina. "Your Eyes Are Green Like Dollars: Counterfeit Cash, National Substance, and Currency Apartheid in 1990s' Russia." *Cultural Anthropology* 13, no. 1 (1998): 22–55.

Singleton, John. "The Cotton Industry and the British War Effort, 1914–1918." *Economic History Review* 47, no. 3 (1994): 601–618.

Swissinfo. "Iraqi Artifacts Find Easy Route via Switzerland." March 5, 2003 (www.swissinfo.org/sen/swissinfo.html?sitesect=111&sid=1668784/, accessed September 2003).

United Nations Office on Drugs and Crime, Mission Statement (www.unodc.org/unodc/en/about.html, accessed March 2003).

World Bank. *Curbing the Epidemic. Economics of Tobacco Control.* Washington, DC: World Bank, June 1999.

IMMIGRATION

> Throughout history, trade required people to leave home, willingly or under duress, as immigrants or sojourners, and make a new home elsewhere.

Migrants carried not only goods but also culture —new foods, new customs, and new ideas. Societies that welcomed immigrants and trade generally flourished. When the Egyptians sailed the Nile to Nubia, they carried their Egyptian customs and traditions with them; likewise, when merchants traveled the trade roads to Egypt, they brought their Asian customs and traditions. The exchange of ideas and goods—and sometimes people—held Egypt intact for two and half millennia.

In 800 B.C.E., the Phoenicians sailed the Atlantic and Mediterranean, from the British Isles to Argos and Assyria, a distance of 2,400 miles, spreading goods and ideas. Before the first century, Greeks and Arabs were sailing yearly to India and China, bringing back pearls, pepper, jewelry, perfume, as well as ideas. The Romans built roads, copied Phoenician styles of ships, and adapted long-distance mail from Egyptian and Persian models. Migration, on at least a small scale, occurred along these trade routes. Jews, forced to settle in widely scattered settlements after the Diaspora, established vital trading communities virtually everywhere they went over the centuries. As late as the mercantile era (and afterward), Jewish migration to the Netherlands and then to the Americas established a network of traders from San Francisco to Singapore, New York, Paris, and London. The Netherlands' free commerce and trade boom came about because of the infusion of Jews, Huguenots, and others not tolerated elsewhere in the world.

Iberia's decline began after the expulsion of the Jews in 1492, the Inquisition, and the removal of the Moors between 1609 and 1614. In the ages of imperialism, vibrant growth in trade followed English immigration to the Western Hemisphere, Oceania, and South Africa. In the twenty-first century, trading cities are cities made up of immigrants.

EARLY EMPIRES

The first civilization was that of the Sumerians, traders who intermingled with their neighbors and left with them more than just trade goods. They influenced Babylon, Egypt, and India. Similarly, the Hittites of Turkey changed Egypt, and the Minoans on Crete influenced their successors, the Mycenaeans. On the other side of the world, the Chinese exchanged goods and ideas with India and Southeast Asia.

When European society was still primitive, urbanized India, Egypt, and Mesopotamia interacted through trade and immigration. Trade attracted immigrants and changed the demography of the trading center. Merchants traveled long distances, vulnerable to bandits and other adversity. The trip carried many risks, so a secure destination with a guaranteed sale was desirable. Resident sojourner merchants drew immigrants—business partners, employees, and families—to foreign cities. These immigrants served as unofficial ambassadors for their place of origin. They kept communication open between the societies at each end of the trade route. The merchants became leaders of immigrant communities adjusting to a new culture. Trade tied the world together, and immigrants ran trade.

Egypt was stable for three millennia. Still, it conquered Nubia for its gold mines and the land routes to Kush and Punt; entered the Sinai for metal and gems and for trade routes to Arabia, the Horn of Africa, Persia, and India; and took Canaan and Syria as buffer zones and as a crossroads of trading routes. And Egyptian ventures in Libya controlled the trade between Africa and Europe. Egyptian trade became the preserve of Phoenician and Greek merchants who settled on the Nile Delta. Merchants from Egypt's many trading partners commonly brought their families for extended stays in Palestine and Egypt. The Greeks founded Alexandria as a center of knowledge and trade for the Middle East.

Mediterranean trading civilization arose around 3000 B.C.E. The earliest Mediterranean traders were Cretan sailor merchants. They flourished for 2,000 years, and their culture influenced other great trading civilizations, including the Phoenicians, who distributed the goods of Babylonia and Egypt from ports such as Sidon, Tyre, and Carthage. Phoenicians were not military seafarers, and they fell successively under the Egyptians, Assyrians, Babylonians, Persians, Greeks, and Romans. By paying tribute, they kept their sea trade with the West and caravan trade with the East. Phoenicia traded with Arabia for gold, agate, onyx, incense, and myrrh; with India for pearls, spices, ivory, ebony, and ostrich plumes; with Mesopotamia for cotton and linen clothes; with Palestine and Egypt for grain, wheat, and barley; and with the regions of the Black Sea for horses, slaves, and copper. By sea, they traded with Syria, North Africa, Asia Minor, the Aegean Sea region, Spain, France, and England. Phoenicians colonized and mingled with the people of Cyprus, Egypt, Crete, Sicily, Africa, Malta, Sardinia, Spain, Asia Minor, and Greece. Phoenicia influenced all Mediterranean civilizations until it fell to Rome after the Punic Wars.

A typical Phoenician trading city was Ugarit. After the Hittites defeated the Egyptians in the thirteenth century B.C.E., the resultant peace brought prosperity to Ugarit as a terminus for trade with Anatolia, Syria, Mesopotamia, Greece, and Egypt. Merchants traded for the king and themselves. Immigrants and sojourners who flocked to Ugarit included Hittites, Hurrians, Cretans, Cypriots, and Assyrians. Prosperity and cultural exchange lasted until the city lost its agricultural base. Then trade passed to the maritime cities, and Ugarit disappeared.

GREECE AND ROME

After the collapse of Mycenae, the Greek islands declined, but in the ninth to eighth centuries B.C.E., the Greek island culture expanded as a growing population and a lack of arable land forced a revival of the old cities and the old sea trade. The Greek culture was spread through trade and migration. Greek culture peaked in Athens during what is known as the "Golden Age" of Greece during the 400s B.C.E. With the rise and conquests of Alexander the Great, Greek culture and influence was spread throughout the Mediterranean world and east, into Persia. With the collapse of Alexander's empire upon his death and the Roman conquest of Greece a few centuries later, Greek culture and presence was carried over to Rome, and bringing significant change to central and western Europe.

Rome's 400,000-man army bestowed Roman citizenship on the peoples it conquered. Citizenship gave the conquered and occupied peoples a stake in the empire. After pacification in Britain and elsewhere, Rome retired whole units and established several thousand soldiers at a time in *coloniae* around their old fortifications. Rome involved the locals in government and the market economy. Former Roman soldiers, now immigrants to the far reaches of the empire, brought with them their goods and beliefs, changing the societies they joined and changing as they joined these societies. Rome's military presence also provided a source of profit and access for local merchants to the vast Roman trade road system. Roman roads moved people and goods throughout the empire. The roads also featured post stations for the courier service as well as mansions where traders could stay—these mansions housed riders, drivers, conductors, blacksmiths, wheelwrights, doctors, and animals.

Roman traders also dominated the Mare Nostrum—the Mediterranean. Merchant ships carried passengers and freight. Roman trade extended to Denmark, up the Amber Road, from the Danube to the Baltic, and across the sea to Sweden. From the far reaches, Italian traders brought furs and slaves. In Africa, Greek and Roman traders penetrated past Somaliland and Abyssinia. Trade covered Arabia Felix, India, and China. Each year, up to 120 vessels left Alexandria for the route through the Red Sea and Indian Ocean to India and China. But the Roman empire crumbled because of the onslaughts of Huns, Goths, Visigoths, and Vandals; by the fifth century the empire had fallen.

SILK ROAD

The major trading route in Central Asia tied Mesopotamia and China to trading partners in Europe and Asia. The Silk Road was a network of routes around the rim of the dry, sandstorm-prone Taklimakan and Gobi Deserts and through the least inhospitable parts of high and icy mountains. Mesopotamia began trading along the Fertile Crescent. China, with its mountainous terrain, was much more difficult for traders to reach. Beginning in 138 B.C.E., Zhang Qian spent thirteen years trying to expand what was a small-scale trade, in the process learning of a new breed of horse and unknown peoples in the west. Subsequent expeditions for horses and objects of beauty opened the route significantly.

More than just silk was carried along the road. Metals, stones, ivory, and glass were brought to China, and ceramics, gunpowder, jade, bronzes, lacquer, and iron were brought to the west. Caravans of 100 to 1,000 camels, each carrying around 500 pounds, were easy targets for bandits, making security essential. The Chinese established forts and walls, but not until local government stabilized the Taklimakan did settlement occur. Settlers prospered from trade and incorporated both local cultures and the cultures of those who traded along the route. Buddhism and Islam traveled to China along this route, as did Christianity. At the Silk Road's peak, Chang'an was a massive city of millions, with thousands of emigrants from the communities along the road as well as others including Malays, Koreans, and Japanese. After the thirteenth-century conquest by Genghis Khan and his Mongols, the Silk Road became a path of communication as well as a trade route. The Mongols kept the road open and safe, and the thirteenth century saw the beginnings of European travel to East Asia.

The road declined as the Chinese empire turned inward under Ming nationalist isolationism in the fourteenth century. Political and religious barriers proved more insurmountable than the deserts and mountains. Once the road closed, the traders shifted to sea routes. Europeans learned how to produce their own silk and otherwise get by without the East. Lessened maintenance, increased banditry, declining trade, and religious conflict meant the demise of the Silk Road.

During its life, the Silk Road was the most important of the trade routes that joined East and West, making possible the exchange of technology, art, and knowledge of the great civilizations. As were all trade routes, the road was a vital carrier of ideas, as shown by the transport of Buddhism from India to China by itinerant and immigrant monks (100–600 C.E.). The road itself shifted with time, climate, and drought—and the "road" also included sea travel on the Mediterranean. The Silk Road was more of a network of exchange using various routes, rather than a physical road.

The sea was neutral, an avenue for the exchange of information, goods, and human resources. The Japanese sailed to Korea and China, and by the sixth century Chinese and Korean immigrants were entering Japan, which in return sent students, monks and officials to China for training. The Sea of Japan and the Yellow and Eastern Seas were in effect an extension of the Silk Road and from the sixth century, Osaka, at the road's end, was Japan's portal to the West.

EUROPE

After Islam split the East from the West, trade and migration continued in the East. The West went into the shell of feudalism, shunting its immigrant merchants into the Jewish quarter and other ghettoes. European societies were not hospitable to trade and immigration anyway.

While the Eastern civilizations thrived, Europe was tribal, mostly a hunter-gatherer society. Emigrants from outside Europe introduced agriculture in the fifth millennium B.C.E., and the Minoan culture reinforced the cultural change when it entered mainland Greece in the first part of the second millennium B.C.E. By late in the third millennium B.C.E., Europeans practiced subsistence agriculture and cattle raising—and rustling. Agricultural surpluses were uncommon, unlike in the Eastern civilizations. This, in combination with the Europeans' fondness for cattle raids against their neighbors and the Eastern immigrants, prevented the rise of urban centers and the associated culture that characterized Egypt, Mesopotamia, the Indus Valley, and the Yellow Valley of China.

There was an effect on European warrior civilizations from the Mesopotamians and Egyptians, whose civilizations had metalworkers without adequate supplies of raw materials, especially tin. The search for tin and other metals and amber led the great states to establish trade routes to Europe. The presence in Europe of more advanced Egyptians and Mesopotamians allowed Europe to enter the Bronze Age with greater speed and fewer false starts than were experienced by earlier world cultures. As far west as England and as far north as Scandinavia, third- and second-millennium B.C.E. Europeans were pushed into cultural growth in exchange for tin, amber, bronze, faience, gold luxury items, and copper. Even as trade and Eastern influence continued, central Europe became more entrenched as a warrior society, letting immigrants of other cultures handle trade. In place by 700 B.C.E., this pattern persisted through the Middle Ages.

In southern Europe, the Roman empire was primarily a Mediterranean empire, but it had frontiers in the woods of northern Europe and in the deserts of the Middle East and the Sahara. Syrians and Jews dominated Roman trade, which allowed the various regions of the empire to specialize. Under the empire, the Romans and the Germanic tribes influenced each other. On the other hand, Roman defeats in the east resulted in barriers to trade that were not negotiable. The fall of Rome to the Goths in 410 C.E. cut off the Mediterranean grain trade from Egypt and the importation of tin from Cornwall. Also slowing trade and immigration was the spread of Islam between the seventh and eleventh centuries across the Middle East, North Africa, and Spain.

As early as 500, Cushite and Bantu immigrants forced the Bushmen from coastal East Africa. As part of the expansion of Islam around 700, Arabs, Persians, and Indians migrated to the area. They were active traders with Arabia, Egypt, and Rome. Benefiting from the monsoon winds, traders came in dhows to barter with the coastal middlemen, preferring not to enter the dry zone inland, or encounter hostility and disease farther west. Cowrie shells sometimes served as currency in this trade that peaked between 1300 and 1500. Principal exports were gold, ivory, and slaves. Also exported were skins, rhinoceros horns, along with other raw materials. Imports included Chinese silk and porcelain, Maldive cowries, Persian rugs, Burmese jars and pots, and Arabian weapons and ironware.

In a time of unrest, Europe lost contact with the East for 700 years. Slowly, stability was reestablished, and from 1000, Europe began to recover. Helping the process were the Vikings. From their Scandinavian homelands, they traded Baltic amber and Russian slaves in Constantinople for silk and spices. They also traded furs, skins, and walrus-tusk ivory from Greenland and northern Europe with the trading towns of western Europe. They settled where they traded. Viking cities include Birka, Skiringsal, Ribe, and Hedeby in Scandinavia. York, England, and Dublin, Ireland, were also Viking trading cities. From Kievan Russia, Vikings kept trade with Byzantium open when the Mediterranean routes were closed or unsafe. They also brought to Europe Arab silver, Byzantine silk, and the rudiments of a still-viable civilization, perhaps even economic growth.

European trade was mostly local, with itinerant peddlers traveling from one place to another. Sometimes peddlers would settle, but cultural interchange was minimal. Another group of immigrant traders, dating from at least the mid-thirteenth century, the Hansa or Hanseatic League was a medieval combination of German cities trading in the Baltic Sea. The merchants commonly had special quarters in the cities with which they traded, leading to a natural association with the locals. In the absence of a strong central state, the Hansa combined for defense against pirates and built lighthouses for safety. At their peak, Hansa enclaves in Belgium, Norway, Russia, and England had the power to demand and receive special privileges, including monopolies. Hansa power peaked in the mid-fourteenth century when the league exceeded 100 cities, some of which were not German. The league's army and navy defeated the Danes in 1386, but the world was changing, and merchants working through centralizing states were becoming more powerful than merchant cities and the traders in immigrant ghettoes.

In the twelfth century, the old roads came back into partial use, but they were risky and inconvenient. By the fifteenth century, Europe was awakening, consolidating, and looking for a way to trade without going through Asia Minor or the Magyar- and Saracen-controlled areas. Merchant-influenced governments were sending explorers, priests, and immigrants in search of trade, preferably a monopoly.

MERCANTILISM AND EUROPEAN MIGRATION

After unifying and funding Christopher Columbus's voyage to the New World in 1492, Spain was present in the Philippines by 1565, Christianizing the natives, settling among them, and dominating the spice trade. Spain kept its Asian colonies for three centuries and its American ones into the eighteenth and nineteenth centuries. Spain's immigrants altered world trade patterns in the East and West.

Spanish immigrant landowners extracted money and labor from the natives. Under government auspices, the Philippines controlled the trade between Mexico and China from the sixteenth through the nineteenth centuries. Mexican silver in Manila bought Chinese silk and porcelain. Heavily controlled by the Spanish government until the 1820s, the Philippines were opened to free trade by the Spanish Crown in 1834. Manila quickly became an international center for the United States and Europe looking to establish trade relations in Asia.

Not all immigrants had landholdings, or opportunities. As early as 1503, African slaves filled the Caribbean labor shortage as involuntary immigrants to Spanish Cuba, Haiti, Puerto Rico, and elsewhere. Ships and crews in the trade were Spanish, Genoese, Portuguese, Dutch, French, Flemish, and English.

Portuguese from Lisbon and Oporto sailed around Africa in search of the East Indies and established a lucrative trade in West Africa for gold, pepper, ivory, and slaves, and in the Atlantic islands for honey, timber, and other raw products. Having a population of only 1.25 million people at the beginning of the fifteenth century, Portugal failed to establish political control over its territories as Spain did. By the end of the sixteenth century, the overseas population was too great for the home population to support; Portugal compounded its population shortage when it expelled the Jews and Muslims, and suffered a disastrous plague.

The Dutch had their own republic, along with religious tolerance and liberal views toward innovation in trade and financial arrangements. These factors attracted educated and well-connected immigrant bankers and merchants from northern Italy and Jews and Huguenots, among others, from elsewhere in Europe. Amsterdam became the commercial center of the seventeenth century. Its stock market, the world's first, was a venue for French, Venetians, Florentines, Genoese, Germans, Poles, Hungarians, Spaniards, Russians, Turks, and Armenians. Educated, ambitious, and welcome, immigrants used Amsterdam as the center of their world trading networks. Dutch trade colonies existed from Batavia, Java, to New Amsterdam in the West. Immigrants founded the financial trade networks.

The English entered the world picture late, establishing colonies in a world where they had to establish their own cities first. The American colonial populations grew as a result of trade. Once they figured out that gold was not a realistic route to wealth, the middle and southern colonies traded tobacco and naval stores. English mercantilism gave New England a protected shipping industry. Protected trade promoted colonial growth through natural increase and through immigration. When the European homelands tightened colonial trade restrictions, immigrants in the colonies resorted to smuggling to continue trade.

Western colonists sent raw material to Europe, which sent back finished goods, sometimes brought from the East. Liverpool, Lisbon, Bordeaux, Cadiz, and other port cities prospered. One of the principal moneymakers was the involuntary immigrant: the slave. Slavers from England, Portugal, and the other mercantile states traded cheap finished goods on the coast of West Africa for slaves, who furnished the labor that produced the tobacco, cotton, and other crops that made more fortunate immigrants rich and independent.

Sometimes, immigrants took over the work of slaves. In the French territories of Martinique and Guadeloupe, planters imported contract workers from the Indian subcontinent after emancipation of the slaves in 1848.

ASIA UNDER IMPERIALISM

In Asia, European immigrants were not as able to eliminate the indigenous populations as they were elsewhere. They established trading companies such as the British and Dutch East India Companies, and they did influence governments, as when the British company held large segments of India as a virtual fiefdom. But the older Asian countries managed to resist, wanting nothing but European silver and gold, and they held the upper hand through most of the mercantile era. The cultural exchange centered on Manila, where the Chinese traders met the Spanish galleons filled with Mexico's silver.

In the South China Sea, the Chinese traded silk and porcelain for rice, medicinal plants, aphrodisiacs, and birds' nests, luxury items for Chinese consumption. This network also linked to other regional trade routes through Batavia and the Strait of Melaka (Malacca). Besides the South China Sea network, the Dutch East India Company in Batavia marginalized the Javanese traders, as it became the dominant organization from Aceh to the Moluccas. The company traded cloves, nutmeg, tin, and pepper. Although focused on Indonesia, the company had links to Asia and Africa, from the China Sea and the Indian Ocean to Cape Town, Arabia, Persia, India, Burma (Myanmar), Siam (now Thailand), Vietnam, Formosa (Taiwan), and Nagasaki.

The British East India Company sailed from South Asia to Burma, Siam, and Malaya up to Sumatra. This trade consisted of Indian cloth, rice, teak ships from Burma, pepper and tin from Malaysia, and spices from around the area of the Strait of Melaka. The company employed not only English, but also Gujaratis, Muslims, and Chulias from India, Persians, Arabs, and Syrians. Significantly, although the Europeans dominated these trade and cultural exchanges, the most important group remained the overseas Chinese.

China entered the overseas trade between 1405 and 1433. Fleets entered the Indian Ocean seven times, sailing as far as Africa. The largest junks in these fleets had nine masts and a length of 400 feet. Supply ships and patrol boats escorted trading vessels. Crews totaled nearly 30,000. But after this period, China withdrew from overseas commerce, its fleet wasted away, and its navigation charts were burned by the minister of war.

In the sixteenth century, overseas Chinese merchants became important as immigrant traders in the present-day Indonesia, Thailand, and Malaysia. The most important of Chinese immigrant traders where the Hakkas, who migrated to central China then on to the rest of Asia. The Hakkas comprised a significant proportion of Chinese in Taiwan and elsewhere outside China.

By the eighteenth century, the overseas Chinese trading network tied Asia to the West. This network included Vietnam, Siam, and Malaya to the west and the Philippines and Indonesia to the east. The overseas Chinese in Siam had a fleet consisting of 136 junks, 82 of which sailed between China and Malaya, Java, and Vietnam. Others traded from South China to Vietnam.

Most of the 60 million overseas Chinese lived in Southeast Asia, being the majority in Singapore and making up significant minorities in Indonesia, Siam, and Malaya. Overseas Chinese in the nineteenth and twentieth centuries migrated to North America, especially Canada and the United States, initially to work on the railroads and in the mines. Once this work ended or they were forced out, they established small shops and restaurants and an overseas trade with their home country. These immigrants concentrated in "Chinatowns" in the Western states, for example in San Francisco. The Chinese Exclusion Act of 1883 banned Chinese immigration. After the act was repealed in 1943, Taiwanese professionals immigrated on student visas. This influx discontinued after the Taiwanese economy improved in the 1970s, but mainland Chinese began immigrating after restrictions eased in 1977.

Overseas Chinese were vital in Sir Stanford Raffles's colonial Singapore. Raffles developed an economic, legal, and social system open to all the diverse peoples of the port city. This openness led to emigration from Indonesia and China. Hong Kong and Taiwan were open as well and benefited from the arrival of Shanghai merchants and financiers, much as the Netherlands had benefited from skilled refugees from Iberia and Europe centuries before. The open cities of Asia were hubs of networks modeled after the historical use of Jews, Armenians, and Parsees, all the unwanted but not the untalented of the world.

COLONIALISM AND AFTER

In the late nineteenth century, the European nations engaged in vigorous colonialism that made much of Asia and Africa a provider of raw materials and slaves for the home nations. The degree of exploitation varied, as did willingness to accept emigrants from the colonies, but the presence of Asian and African colonials in the European countries led to some cultural exchange. After World War II, immigration occurred on a massive scale, and failure or success depended on how the immigrants were treated. Postcolonial France attempted to preserve the influence it had in Asia, Africa, and the Americas. It had, after all, given citizenship (under certain conditions) to all members of its empire. As the dislocations of independence produced hardship, many emigrants from the former colonial areas entered France, as did the Europeans abandoning now hostile former territories. Still, trade had been established with the original immigration, and nothing in the new immigration shifted the trade priorities the immigrants had set.

Germany's loss in World War I cost it the empire it had acquired earlier, but its final colonial venture came later in the twentieth century, when it forced millions of Germans to move to conquered territory and non-Germans to move from there. After World War II, the relocation of displaced persons was an immense undertaking. Between 1945 and 1961, 12 million immigrants, mostly skilled, entered Germany. Three-fourths were Germans from Poland and Czechoslovakia. Others were refugees from East Germany. As a result, West Germany in the 1950s and 1960s had a higher ratio of workers to total population than other states: 50 percent versus 45 percent in France, 40 percent in the United Kingdom, 42 percent in the United States, and 36 percent in Canada. When the European influx slowed, new skilled workers flowed in, first from the Mediterranean states, then from the edge of Asia. But when the economy slowed in the late 1990s, there was pressure to deport immigrants.

In the United States, immigrants continued to flourish. Trading cities in early twenty-first-century United States shared the characteristic growth of earlier trading cities. Approximately three-fourths of the 10 million immigrants that arrived in the United States during the 1980s settled in a few urban states. New York and California absorbed half the immigration. Eight of the ten most ethnically diverse counties were in New

Immigrants to the United States—like these on Ellis Island in 1930—have long served as a major source of cheap labor for manufacturers, giving U.S. industry a great competitive advantage in world trade through much of the nineteenth and twentieth centuries. *(Library of Congress)*

York, Los Angeles, or the San Francisco area. Southern California became attractive in the 1980s to new immigrants from Asia, the Middle East, and Latin America. Los Angeles was especially attractive for those with business and financial skills.

Los Angeles once had a decaying warehouse/factory district east of downtown. A Hong Kong immigrant, Charlie Woo, revitalized the neighborhood and attracted more than 500 toy importers, warehouses, and distributors who employed 6,000 people in a $1 billion business. Most of the owners and workers emigrated from the Middle East, Asia, or Latin America. Most of the customers were immigrants as well, bringing the world's toy buyers and consumers together. Similar successes occurred in the flower, fish, vegetable, trucking, and textile industries. Occupancy rates exceeded 95 percent in the once-decaying district.

Another success was New York's trade in services—media, advertising, and finance. New York's combined Latino and Asian populations in 2000 approached 3 million. New York immigrant-owned companies dealt throughout the world. New York's immigrant base—including Russian Jews, Koreans, and Asians—gave the city's companies a better grasp of foreign and domestic market demographics.

In Miami, the high crime and out-migration in the 1970s and 1980s gave way in the 1990s to a thriving Latino culture fueled by Miami's 650,000 Cubans, 75,000 Nicaraguans, and 65,000 Colombians. In 1994, Miami had one-fourth of America's South American trade, almost 40 percent of the export business, 40 percent of Caribbean trade, and nearly 60 percent of Central American trade. Miami was home to Univision and Telemundo, broadcasters to Spanish speakers in the United States and Latin America. Other southern cities from Jacksonville to Houston are seeking the same access to international markets using their immigrant populations.

Between 1870 and 1910, 60 million Europeans migrated, mostly from underdeveloped areas, to the United States, Canada, and Latin America. Additional migrations occurred between less-developed countries and from rural to urban areas of the same country. About 10 percent of the world population emigrated, and more than that migrated. But the migrations slowed as opportunity arose at home, and at the end of the millennium, only about 2 percent of the world's population lived outside its country of citizenship.

At century's end, trade became a potential route to globalization because trade policy affected employment, patterns of consumption, production, and distribution, cultural and social values, and the environment, all of which were global issues. Trade, especially in services, grew drastically in a world without borders. Between 1970 and 2000, the share of manufactured goods created by developing countries rose from 3 to 18 percent. In the 1990s, the economies of the thirteen largest poor countries grew an average of 7.3 percent a year. Women as well as men benefited from the worldwide growth of professional services (law, banking, and computing), tourism, and information services from offshore airline booking and credit card distribution to word processing for publishers and others regardless of geographical location.

After thousands of years, immigration peaked in the nineteenth century. Twenty-first-century globalization allows those who would have emigrated to trade at home. The trade-immigrant nexus is weaker than it has been because the would-be immigrant now travels the Web instead of the roads and seas.

John Barnhill

See also: Barter; British Empire; Chinese Dynasties; Crusades; Dutch; European Trade, Intracontinental; Food and Diet; French Empire; German Empires; Jews; Polo, Marco; Slavery; United States; Vikings; Warfare.

BIBLIOGRAPHY

Abdelnour, Farras. "Trade at Ugarit in the 13th Century B.C." (www.escape.com/~farras/ugarit.htm, accessed November 2002).
AfricanMecca Inc. "Trade and Immigration to the East Coast of Africa, 2001–2002" (www.africanmeccasafaris.com/africa/history/tradeimmigrationeastafrica.asp, accessed July 2002).
Baird, Rod. "Ancient Routes." 2002 (www.ancientroute.com, accessed August 2002).
Boardman, John. *The Greeks Overseas: Their Early Colonies and Trade.* London: Thames and Hudson, 1980.
Cargill, Jack. *Athenian Settlements of the Fourth Century B.C.* Leiden: E.J. Brill, 1995.
Cohat, Yves. *The Vikings: Lords of the Seas.* New York: Abrams, 1992.
Dollinger, André. "Ancient Egyptian Overseas Trade: A Short History of Ancient Egypt" (www.reshafim.org.il/ad/egypt/trade/, accessed July 2002).
Figueira, Thomas J. *Athens and Aigina in the Age of Imperial Colonization.* Baltimore: Johns Hopkins University Press, 1991.
Fontaine, Laurence. *A History of Pedlars in Europe,* trans. Vicki Whittaker. Durham: Duke University Press, 1996.
Gonzales, Ray. "The Geography of the Silk Road" (www.humboldt.edu/~geog309i/ideas/raysilk.html, accessed August 2002).
Hooker, Richard. "World Civilizations: European Middle Ages, the Peoples." 1996 (www.wsu.edu/~dee/ma/peoples.htm, accessed August 2002).
Kammen, Michael. *Empire and Interest: The American Colonies and the Politics of Mercantilism.* Philadelphia: J.B. Lippincott, 1970.
Kotkin, Joel. "Free Trade: Salvation for Cities" (www.freetrade.org/pubs/freetotrade/chap9.html, accessed September 2002).
Liu, Xinru. *Ancient India and Ancient China: Trade and Religious Exchanges.* Delhi: Oxford University Press, 1994.
Magnusson, Lars. *Mercantilism: The Shaping of an Economic Language.* London: Routledge, 1994.
McCusker, John J. *Mercantilism and the Economic History of the Early Modern Atlantic World.* Cambridge: Cambridge University Press, 2001.
Rempel, Gerhard. "Rome: From Republic to Empire" (http://mars.acnet.wnec.edu/~grempel/courses/wc1/lectures/11republic.html, accessed September 2002).
Rothermund, Dietmar. *Asian Trade and European Expansion in the Age of Mercantilism.* New Delhi: Manohar, 1981.
Russell-Wood, A.J.R. *The Portuguese Empire, 1415–1808: A World on the Move.* Baltimore: Johns Hopkins University Press, 1998.
"The Viking Network." 2000 (http://viking.no/e/travels/etrade.htm, accessed August 2002).
Wacher, John. *The Coming of Rome.* London: Routledge and Kegan Paul, 1979.
Watkins, Thayer. "Economic History of Europe" (www.sjsu.edu/faculty/Watkins/econ110.htm, accessed August 2002).
World Bank Group Transition Newsletter. "Globalization and Migration." July–September 2001 (www.worldbank.org/transitionnewsletter/JulAugSep01/boxpg7.htm, accessed August 2002).

IMPERIALISM

> A policy of extending the rule of one country over another country or colonies that began with the establishment of empires in the sixteenth century and lasted until the twentieth century.

From 1492 to 1776, mercantile imperialism spread European influence around the world. Portugal, Spain, Holland, France, and England all attempted to exploit parts of the world that were new to them and seemingly undeveloped and uninhabited. The powers competed with each other in Africa, the Americas, and in Asia, each trying to establish trade arrangements that secured its own interest while it excluded the others. Because of the need for control, the indigenous populations were quickly subordinated to colonists —traders, merchants, and agriculturalists—from the home country. These colonists had different roles. Initially, they were to produce the massive stocks of gold and silver for the Spanish. The gold flowed through piracy to the English and through commercial services such as insurance and banking to the Dutch. Mercantilists without gold and silver mines found trade assets in other raw materials: furs, ships, stores, tobacco, rice, and sugar.

Commodore Matthew Perry, shown here being received by the Japanese emperor in 1854, helped open up the island kingdom to U.S. and world trade. *(Library of Congress)*

Settlers provided markets for the finished goods the European states—England, then the others—began producing. Integral to mercantilism was the migration of Europeans to the areas to be exploited.

During the initial settlements, the Europeans were at a disadvantage because they were the intruders and because they came long distances with limited technology that allowed them to come only in small numbers. The initial European toeholds in the Americas, for instance, mostly failed. Successful efforts relied on the aid of the indigenes, whether in Mexico, Virginia, or Canada. Where the natives resisted, as in Asia and India, the European presence was tenuous. In the Americas, the slight European edge in technology, the inability of the indigenous groups to band together, and the major impact of European diseases allowed the Europeans to conquer. Within relatively short periods, they began to take full possession and create mines and plantations to supply the home country with wealth and resources for the mercantile competition of the European states. In Asia, the Europeans were supplicants to a more sophisticated market, wanting more of the Asians' goods than the Asians wanted of theirs; the Europeans remained dependent on local trading patterns and indigenous elites.

The characteristic "old imperialism" had involved the movement of people to establish primarily coastal agricultural colonies in areas previously unexplored. The Europeans attempted to replicate their home countries in the new areas and named them accordingly: New England, New France, New Spain, New Sweden, and New Netherlands. Success came to those in the most heavily populated settlements. There was a false belief that the expansion was occurring into unsettled and unpopulated lands.

The British success came because trade and empire reinforced each other. As colonies grew, trade between the colonies and the home country increased. Increased trade encouraged merchants to expand their fleets and the volume and variety of goods they shipped to the growing colonial market. The demand for raw materials increased, promoting the slave system in the Caribbean and, once the indentured system faded on the mainland, in the southern colonies of North America as well. Accelerating population growth continued as the colonies became more attractive as sources of economic opportunity or religious refuge, and the expanding population of eighteenth-century North America provided more raw products in return for more finished British goods. At the same time, the larger population led to a greater diversity and sophistication of demand, and British industry such as textiles diversified in response. Linen, cotton, and new hardware and metalware grew in demand in the second half of the eighteenth century. The ideal colonial arrangement was a closed system with large volume, which is what the British had during the quarter century preceding the American Revolution.

But this ideal situation was an anomaly. More typical were the power struggles that characterized the mercantile competition. The frequent wars of the rival imperialists during the sixteenth through the eighteenth centuries diverted attention from economic well-being and drained national treasuries. The slow loss of trade wealth eliminated the weaker nations, which were already hampered by the absence of colonies anywhere near as robust as the British Americas. Over time, the competition won over Portugal, Spain, and Holland, leaving the field to France and Britain who fought four wars in less than a century. By 1763, Britain was the last empire to remain standing. But the British perceived a need for colonial assistance in financing the war debts, and the effort to impose taxes and other revenue-enhancers on colonial trade led to the loss of the colonies. The death of mercantilism occurred about the same time as the rise of Adam Smith's ideas on free trade. As some colonies became independent, others became economically less significant. Therefore, the imperial impulse lessened for a time.

NEW IMPERIALISM

The old style of imperialism was largely abandoned by 1776, and for 80 to 100 years imperialism waned. However, there was a period of lighter activity—the British taking of the Cape Colony (1815), Hong Kong (1842), and New Zealand (1840), the French expansion into Algiers, and perhaps the misadventure of Maximilian in Mexico. But this activity was sporadic, and the trading system was what came to be known as free-trade imperialism, with colonial outposts serving a competitive edge but not necessarily competing with one another. A major contributor was the protective tariff barriers imposed by the Europeans against the British, who consequently looked elsewhere for markets. And because the British had the edge industrially, they had no fear of the competition. The new imperialism was ratified by trade agreement rather than by war: the term of choice was free-trade imperialism.

The first European venture into the greater world, during the age of exploration and discovery after Christopher Columbus, was at least initially a major leap into the unknown, and they had extremely limited assets. By the time the second age of imperialism occurred, the process was more precise, discovered areas had been controlled, and the advantages lay overwhelmingly with the Europeans. The reasons for exploration had changed from the intent to civilize, Christianize, and exploit easy wealth, such as gold and silver. The age of imperialism, from 1850 to 1914, was better characterized as a race by the European powers to possess what was available—the world was being divided quickly, and national prestige, geopolitical influence, and military advantage were all on the line. But more important, in a time when Europe and the United States were fueling their Industrial Revolutions, there was a need for access to reliable markets and sources of raw material.

Initially, the imperial impulse was a political and economic rivalry, with Russia entering Persia, Austria-Hungary entering the Balkans, Italy entering North Africa, Germany entering Baghdad and southwest Africa, and Britain entering North and South Africa as well as western North America. The United States took the spoils of the

Spanish-American War, but also entered Canada, Mexico, and the Panama Canal region. Technology penetrated the continent and allowed links back home: railroads and steam engines, telegraphs and weapons far beyond those of the indigenes. There was also quinine, used to treat malaria, and the preferred approach of divide and conquer.

As the pace of "new imperialism" accelerated mid-century, the Europeans used their advanced weapons and technology (transportation and communication) to move into the interiors of the continents. They built railways, dams, roads, and industry to better exploit the raw materials found in the interior. To an extent, the expansion occurred because technology made it possible; to a greater extent, it occurred because the technological advantage at home had created surplus output and a system that needed more raw materials to maintain itself, and perhaps free itself of the economic cycle that featured periodic depressions due to surplus capacity and insufficient consumption. The trade was in European-finished goods for native raw materials, a disadvantage to the natives in Africa, the Near and Middle East, China, Southeast Asia, and North America, including Mexico and Canada.

AFRICA

The societies of West Africa had well-developed and extensive trade arrangements that extended across the Sahara to the north and east. The East African societies traded from Somalia to Mozambique. They traded with the inland Great Zimbabwe and Mwene Matapa. From the fifteenth century on, these traditional economic and cultural links came under pressure from the intrusion of foreign cultural and commercial elements along the coasts. But until the nineteenth century, the impact remained predominantly on the edges of the continent because the interior was inhospitable to the Europeans, limiting the extent of their disruption of interior Africa. Then, late in the nineteenth century the Europeans had the technology, the spirit, and the immunity through new medicines—and their presence quickly became an occupation of virtually the entire continent. In the mid-nineteenth century, they finally did away with the slave trade that they had abetted and profited from, if not coerced. In the late nineteenth century they extended their moral crusade to the source, Africa.

The British, with a vast empire left over from the old imperialism, had no need for Africa. They had moral qualms about the slave trade, but their qualms were not sufficiently strong to put troops on the ground. Although the Atlantic slave trade ended before the resurgence of imperialism, there continued to be a trade across the Sahara and around the Indian Ocean. This trade affected the British experience as the British penetrated Africa. In their pursuit of African products, such as palm oil and groundnuts for margarine, soap, and machines, they interfered with local politics, backing those who at least purported to be abolitionist and were willing to become capitalist. They won over the slave interests in Zanzibar by imposing a naval embargo, resulting in a quick, rewarding, and symbolically uplifting victory. When it came to economic interests, in Africa, the Suez Canal and South Africa were most appealing to the British empire.

The Suez Canal shortened the trip to India by 6,000 miles. The subcontinent was even more an asset than before. The French built the canal on land belonging to the Khedive of Egypt. In return, he received stock in the company. When he ran into financial difficulties in the 1870s, the British bought his stock and thus the controlling interest in the canal.

With the canal open, African ports became moot. South Africa was of interest for other reasons. In 1871, the British annexed the Kimberley field after the discovery of diamonds in 1870. In 1877, they annexed the Boer Transvaal, which led to the Boer uprising of 1881 and defeat for the British—until the discovery of gold in the Transvaal. In 1895, Cecil Rhodes tried to overthrow the Boer government, but he failed and only the second Anglo-Boer War (1899–1902) ended hostilities between the Boers and the British. The British granted home rule within the British empire in 1906, allowing local legislatures to decide domestic issues.

As Spanish gold brought the Americas to the attention of European mercantilists in the sixteenth century, the discovery of gold and diamonds accelerated the race for Africa. Quickly, the competition for African territory became so fierce that the Europeans met to stabilize the situation. The Berlin Agreement of 1884–1885 specified that no nation would compete for another's claim. By 1914, Ethiopia and Liberia were the only African nations free of European control.

Having established hegemony, the Europeans began exploiting both the land and the people. The plantation was the preferred arrangement for producing peanuts, rubber, cocoa, and palm oil. Mines were needed to collect South Africa's gold and diamonds and the Congo's copper and tin. The Europeans opposed indigenous rulers who resisted their attempt to control the trade, who maintained slave labor or trade, or who attempted to impose tariffs and taxes. The internal slave trade and associated wars persisted despite the European efforts to quell them.

By disrupting the old power arrangements and erasing tribal boundaries, the European intrusion opened the export business to new producers. Tied to the world economy, prices became unstable. Where the imperialists controlled the traditional male activity of slave trading, their actions encouraged the displaced slave traders to take over other economic sectors. For instance, displaced slavers took over palm oil production, traditional women's work, which led to the loss of women's economic power and social standing.

OTTOMAN EMPIRE

By the late nineteenth century, the Ottoman empire grew weak, letting Greece become independent in 1830 and giving Serbia autonomy within the empire in 1806. By 1914, the empire was on the verge of collapse. Within the empire, modernizers broke Egypt away from the Ottomans and convinced the Egyptian peasants to grow cotton instead of food because cotton was in demand in Europe. Further modernization in Egypt led to the creation of the Suez Canal, which speeded trade immensely. When Egypt ran into financial hard times (as was generally to happen to the colonized end of this trade arrangement), the British took the canal and the country.

Britain and Russia competed in Persia as well. Persia would have given Russia an outlet to the Indian Ocean. Britain wanted Persia as a buffer between Russia and India. Then, at the turn of the twentieth century, oil was discovered and the British agreed to develop the fields. After local forces deposed their ruler because he was pro-European and corrupt, Russia and Britain took Persia for their own benefit.

INDIA

The British presence in India dated to the mercantile age, and the British East India Company dominated until it finally gave control over India to the British government. The indigenous Mughal empire in India began declining in the early eighteenth century. By mid-century, the British East India Company had almost all the subcontinent under its control. By law, India had to provide Britain with tea, indigo, cotton, and coffee. The law also prevented the development of Indian manufacturing. After the East India Company built the rail lines that linked the agricultural interior with coastal ports, India became even more valuable. India did benefit in that the British railway system built there was the third largest in the world, and the British built schools, dams, canals, bridges, telephone and telegraph networks, and roads. They also improved literacy, sanitation, and public health. Negative effects of the British presence in India included substituting commercial production for self-sufficient agriculture, leaving the populace vulnerable to famine and death. British racism delegitimated and weakened Indian culture, leading to protests against the company that led the government to take over in the mid-nineteenth century. Unrest persisted through the period, as did British exploitation of India.

ASIA

The European system of exploitation unfolded similarly in Southeast Asia. The region was valuable for its proximity to China and the legendary Chinese market. It also had the climate and soil to grow commercial crops, some imported and some native, such as sugar, rubber, cocoa, and coffee. Traders initially established an outpost and negotiated with the local leaders. As trade grew, the European investment increased, and dependence on local rulers, who were sometimes unstable, became less desirable. The need for political stability led to increased control by the European powers, including the taking of territory. The Dutch took Indonesia. The British took Singapore, Malaya, and Burma (Myanmar). The British also promoted the spread of skilled Chinese merchants throughout their empire. France took Indochina, coercing farmers to grow rice commercially and thus reducing the amount of rice the growers had for themselves. Siam avoided the colonial rush through skilled political maneuvering during this entire period. Colonialism brought improved schools, sanitation, and health. It also brought outsiders to work on the colonial plantations and mines, thereby producing a mix of cultures.

In China, American and European merchants had traded for tea and silk since the 1780s. The Europeans had an insatiable desire for Chinese tea and porcelain, but they did not have anything they could sell in adequate volume to hold a reasonable trade balance. When the Qing rulers of China sought to rejuvenate their society by eradicating the opium stored in Guangzhou, the British Parliament declared that open trade was the foundation of civilization and progress, affirmed that God would replace the Chinese evil with good, and declared war. The war ended with concessions to the British in Hong Kong and Shanghai and the general opening of China to British trade, including opium. After China lost the First Opium War (1839–1842), the United States, Britain, and France won concessions and trading privileges in five ports under the 1844 Treaty of Wangxia. Merchants, missionaries, and diplomats set the pattern for the Open Door Policy in the aftermath of the Boxer Rebellion, which gave the powers unfettered access to all of China.

That the war forced an unwanted drug trade on the Chinese mattered little compared to its aftermath, a continuing loss of Chinese autonomy. The revived imperialism expanded geographically as Europeans began racing to take their own parts of Asia between 1850 and 1880. The Dutch expanded in Indonesia, the French in Indochina, and the United States and Britain in Japan.

But that route to the great China market was a long-term project. In the middle of the pursuit was Japan, which was closed off to the West. Japan came under pressure to open its doors when Commodore Matthew C. Perry intruded in 1854, in pursuit of the American desire to link Asia with the western United States in trade. For the moment, the opening of Asia remained a casual impulse, diverted by the U.S. Civil War and Reconstruction. Then postwar industrialization demanded new sources of raw materials and new outlets for American agricultural and manufactured products (maybe broader markets would stabilize an economy characterized by periodic economic depressions). This demand coincided with missionary and military interests: the need to spread Anglo-Saxon Protestant civilization through the world and the closing of the frontier. Early imperial ventures included the purchase of Alaska, the annexation of the Midway Islands, Samoa (the building of a U.S. naval base on Pago Pago in 1878 and then the formal partition in 1899), and Hawaii (annexed 1898). Samoa had the benefit of being on the trade route to Australia, and Hawaii was on the route to the broad Asian market. Although the United States fought two wars to acquire it, the Philippines lacked the significance for trade that it had enjoyed during the centuries of the Manila-Acapulco trade. For the United States, the Philippines was a stepping-stone to greater Asia. It was not even considered a trading partner until the Jones Act of 1914, which established free trade for the United States. With the Philippines, Hawaii, Guam, Wake, and Johnston Atoll, the United States had a strong military posture to protect its trade routes in the Pacific to China.

AMERICAS

Latin America began industrializing late, as it was in a position of dependency on Europe. The sympathetic countries were Britain and the United States, both of which advocated free trade at the time. Latin America had to cooperate as Britain took Spain's place as its leading partner. Britain continued its export of finished goods in return for raw materials from Latin America. Ports and agricultural interests flourished, but nascent regional industry languished as the old economy and class structure strengthened, maintaining Latin America's backwardness and animus toward equality for mestizos, women, and others, and its refusal to reform land distribution.

In Latin America, most of the countries won independence early in the nineteenth century, and their original leaders were enlightenment figures with a dislike of colonial government. The colonial legacy also discouraged participatory government in favor of class leadership. The colonial parochialism persisted, with class and regional divisions and wide disparities in wealth.

In the late nineteenth century, the economies began to grow, as liberal reformers took office and established the infrastructure and government needed to bring economies up to date. Population and demand soared. Foreign capital and merchants tied the Latin American economy to that of the West, but the growth excluded the peasants. Landowners, still resistant, incorporated new forms of peonage, servitude, and tenancy, and women remained subordinate. The market economy became volatile, especially as outside conditions, mostly European, affected markets. Open trade allowed Germany and the United States to enter the Latin economies by offering financing and incentives. Eventually key industries became foreign controlled, which led to foreign influence on governments. Foreign business people preferred stability, so they allowed or promoted the old elites, maintaining the economic and social status quo.

American interest in Latin America dated from 1855, when William Walker, the filibusterer, assembled his own army and invaded Nicaragua, declaring himself president. Walker's term lasted two years before he was ousted by hostile Central American states. Similarly, in Panama an isthmian railroad was built in 1855, but the greater effort was the building of the canal. American interest in the canal zone dated from 1814. After Spain opened Cuba to world trade in 1818, it came under strong commercial influence from the United States due to its proximity—interest that led to periodic talk of annexation. In 1848, the United States offered $100 million to buy sugar and cotton slaves and markets, but Spain refused. After Spain lost the war of 1898, the United States kept bases in Cuba and controlled internal affairs, foreign policy, and the economy until 1934 under the Platt Amendment. Cuba was a de facto protectorate.

Elsewhere in the Americas, the Pan-American Union of 1889 promoted U.S. trade and cultural exchanges with Latin America. At one point, the United States owned 80 percent of Mexican railroads and 70 percent of Mexican oil.

JAPAN

Before Commodore Perry's arrival in 1854, Japanese society was highly structured, with commercial elements—merchants and bankers—looked down upon. Perry's ships challenged Japanese independence and isolation and its ability to resist the pressure to Westernize. While China succumbed and allowed itself to be divided into spheres, Japan learned the potential of Western military strength, established a nationalist resistance, and began borrowing from the West the ideas and skills that would make Japan strong, rich, and able to resist cultural domination. The Japanese acquiesced when resistance was either hopeless or self-defeating. They channeled nationalism from xenophobia to a disciplined and organized strength for long-term resistance to Western institutions, and they held their basic values while incorporating Western ideas and technology.

Japan incorporated Western science and an imperialism of its own; loosened the caste structure to develop a leadership of merit; began strengthening the state, economy, and military; imposed national taxes, a national education system, and a state-sponsored industry; reformed currency; and established conscription. They did away with the samurai and other obsolete elements. And while developing industry, infrastructure, and exports, Japan managed to avoid provoking the Europeans.

COSTS

The nineteenth-century expansion of European interests into the rest of the world was an expensive process as the Europeans invested in ports, mines, factories, utilities, plantations, and railroads. They wanted internal improvements good enough to handle the trade they envisioned. Trade did increase, and the economies of both sides developed as a result. The West became much more prosperous than the rest of the world. And the European effort, although it might have begun peacefully enough, reverted to force when faced with obstacles, whether in Africa or in Asia.

CONCLUSION

The late nineteenth-century imperialism was the final wave of European expansion and the culmination of the free-trade imperialism that had replaced the mercantilist empires in the late eighteenth century. Between 1870 and 1925, there was a general scramble for increased control in Asia and new control in Africa. Factors included power politics, racism, and Darwinian survival of the fittest. It happened because the imperialists had the overpowering industrial and technological advantage. During this period, there grew an increasing disparity in income and population. Also, there were the battles such as the one in Omdurman (1898), where the machine gun caused thousands of deaths for those who did not have it compared to dozens for those who did. Those who resisted militarily lost, those who accommodated survived (elites and masses alike), and those who incorporated the Western tools prospered. Japan learned all too well, becoming imperialist in its own right.

The European claims met with resistance—the Afrikaans tried and failed to keep the British out. And in Africa the colonial map ignored the preexisting pattern of states, kingdoms, and ethnic groups. The European effort undid old empires—the Ottoman empire became history, with Europeans taking parts. And in some cases, as in India, the Europeans took the rest of what they had earlier occupied, and in the process they remade the local economy into something to fit the colonial power's interests, not those of the colony. Southeast Asia was a popular arena, where even the United States entered the race. Early in the nineteenth century, the European presence in Africa was negligible, restricted to only the coast. The imperial impulse and improved tropical medicine fueled the race to control the raw materials that made Europe's industrial economies strong. Strong industrial output meant that they wanted guaranteed markets—and the colonies provided just that.

In the thirty years before the turn of the twentieth century, Great Britain, France, and Germany colonized 8.75 million square miles, home to 105 million people. The empires were global rather than limited, as were those of the first imperial era. Technology made this possible: the steamship that cut a two-month voyage to two weeks; the telegraph that made communication and commerce immeasurably more immediate and efficient; medicine such as quinine, which allowed Europeans to penetrate areas where they would have previously succumbed to disease; and, most important perhaps, the machine gun, which safeguarded European property and resources.

The European powers had entered fully into the industrial age, and their attention was fixed on developing industry and enhancing the growth of their economies. The rapid industrialization and growth generated shortages of raw materials and an oversupply of finished goods that required new markets, either at home or abroad—the latter being preferred because the new market could also become the new supplier of raw materials. Because the Europeans had the technological edge, they managed to venture deeper into areas where their presence had been mostly peripheral, almost dependent on the indigenous leaders for access. They leveraged their initial advantage into an ever-larger disparity in power and wealth as they used the less industrialized areas of the world to their own material advantage.

John Barnhill

See also: British Empire; French Empire; German Empires.

BIBLIOGRAPHY

Carlisle, E. Fred. "Colonialism in America." Lecture notes (http://athena.english.vt.edu/~carlisle/Postcolonial/Colonialism_Africa.html, accessed September 2003).

Forgotten History Foundation. "The Age of Imperialism: Africa and Asia, 1800–1914" (www.forgottenhistory.org/imperialism_files/frame.htm, accessed September 2003).

Johnson, G. Wesley. *Double Impact: France and Africa in the Age of Imperialism.* Westport: Greenwood, 1986.

Kwok, Alexander. "How Extensive Were United States Overseas Activities and Interests up to 1900?" 1999 (www.geocities.com/CollegePark/Square/7961/Hist/USexp.htm, accessed August 2003).

Lairson, Thomas D. "East Asia: Nineteenth Century Imperialism." Lecture outline, POL 384 (http://fox.rollins.edu/~tlairson/asia/lecimp.html, accessed August 2003).

Magdoff, Harry. *The Age of Imperialism: The Economics of U.S. Foreign Policy.* New York: New York University Press, 1969.

Morgan, Kenneth. "Trade before Empire or Empire before Trade?" King David High School, 2002 (www.kdhs.org.uk/history/a/as_unit5/reasons_trade.htm, accessed August 2003).

Neill, Robin. "The Second National Policy" (www.upei.ca/~rneill/canechist/topic_15.html, accessed September 2003).

Schaffer Library of Drug Policy. "A Short History of the Opium Wars." (www.druglibrary.org/schaffer/heroin/opiwar1.htm, accessed September 2003).

"Telescoping the Times: The Age of Imperialism, 1850–1914." In *Modern World History: Patterns of Interaction.* McDougal-Littell, 1999 (http://mclane.fresno.k12.ca.us/wilson98/Assigments/ImpCH11.html, accessed August 2003).

INCAS

The Incas ruled one of the largest empires ever established by Native Americans in the Western Hemisphere.

The Incas called their empire Tahuantinsuyu (Land of Four Quarters). It stretched for 2,500 miles along the western coast of South America, from the northern border of present-day Ecuador to the middle of modern Chile. Half of Bolivia and much of northwest Argentina were also within its borders. The empire included the arid deserts of the Pacific coast, the fertile highlands of the Andes, and dense tropical jungles on the eastern slope of the mountains. The Incas were the last of several peoples who had dominated the same region in succession for thousands of years before the coming of the Spanish conquistadors in the sixteenth century. At the time of the conquest, the Incas ruled as many as 10 million subjects under a highly organized social, political, and economic system.

The most ancient people known to have lived in the Andes were called the Chavin. They lived in the highlands and were expert stonemasons and engineers. After the Chavin disappeared, another people known as the Moche appeared in the desert regions along the Pacific coast. They developed an extensive irrigation system that allowed them to cultivate the arid land for nearly 500 years. Their civilization collapsed sometime between 700 and 800 C.E. A new people called the Tiwanaku flour-

The Spanish conquest of Peru, including the burning of Inca leader Atahualpa by conquistador Francisco Pizarro, provided vast mineral wealth to Spain, making the Iberian country the wealthiest in Europe in the early sixteenth century. Ultimately, the vast influx of precious metals produced inflation, undermining the competitiveness of Spanish products. (© *North Wind Picture Archives*)

ished high in the central Andes from 600 to 1000. They built their capital city along the shores of Lake Titicaca. It was filled with temples and palaces made of enormous stone blocks that were pieced together without the use of any mortar.

ORIGINS

According to legend, the first Incas were four brothers and four sisters who emerged from caves in the Cuzco valley just north of the Tiwanaku capital on Lake Titicaca. The eldest brother, Manco Capac, became the first king of the Incas. He taught his own people and the tribes he conquered how to live in villages and raise crops by farming. His eldest sister who was also his wife taught the women how to spin thread and weave beautiful cloth. The next six legendary kings were each remembered for performing some great feat on behalf of their people. Sinchi Roca, the second king, filled in the marshes around the capital city of Cuzco and gave the land to his people for farming. Llonque Yupanqui, the next king, established a class of local officials called the *curacas*. Subsequent rulers led the Incas beyond the Cuzco valley and helped them conquer tribes along the Pacific coast. They also established a school for royal princes and the nobility and coined the term "Inca," meaning leader or ruler.

The Incas left the realm of legend and entered the world of history under the reign of their eighth king, who called himself Viracocha after the Incan Sun god. Viracocha was a powerful military leader who conquered a vast territory of more than 150,000 square miles for his people. His son Pachacuti fought an important battle against a tribe known as the Chanca in 1438 and went on to transform the Incan domain into an empire. He rebuilt Cuzco into a magnificent capital with over 4,000 buildings in the main city and another 20,000 in the surrounding area. The most important structure was known as the Coricancha (Enclosure of God). This walled sanctuary housed many temples including the Temple of the Sun, which was covered in gold and precious gems. A huge stone fortress called the Sacsahuaman guarded the entrance to the capital city of Cuzco.

Pachacuti's son, Topa Inca, was the tenth Incan king. He ruled the empire at the height of its power from 1471 to 1493. He oversaw an administrative system that tied every person from the lowest commoner to the highest member of the royal family to the state. His son, Huayna Capac, reigned from 1493 to 1525 and pushed the empire north into Equador, where he established a second capital at a place called Tumibamba. Shortly before his death, he divided the Incan empire between two of his sons. Huáscar was to rule the southern half of the empire from the capital of Cuzco, while Atahuallpa was to rule the northern half from the city of Quito.

CLASS SYSTEM

Every Incan ruler stood at the top of a rigid class system. He was given the official title of "Sapa" or "Unique" Inca. He made all laws for the empire, and he controlled the army. The emperor was more than just a powerful earthly ruler; he was also considered to be a descendant of the Sun god. Despite the power and glory granted to him, the emperor was expected to travel through his realm every few years to discover any problems the common people might be experiencing. When an emperor died, his oldest son did not automatically inherit the kingdom. Instead, the nobility voted for the next emperor from among the most worthy sons of the last emperor. Since inheritance laws considered the empire to remain in the possession of the dead emperor, the new ruler was required to conquer more territory for his own support. He was also expected to take his eldest sister as his wife and empress of the realm.

The nobility was the class immediately below the emperor and his family. They were known as the *orejones* and were themselves divided into two groups. The first group was called the "Nobles of the Royal Blood" and could trace their ancestors back to the legendary early kings of the Incas. Members of the second group were known as "Inca by Privilege." They were descendants of conquered peoples who accepted Incan rule and later served as *curacas*. While the latter group could pass their noble titles down to their children, they were always considered lower in the social hierarchy than the Nobles of the Royal Blood. The sons of both groups attended the royal academy called the Yachahuasi, where they were trained to serve in the government, the priesthood, and the military.

Artisans stood below the nobility in the Incan hierarchy. They created religious objects along with luxury items of gold and silver for the emperor and the nobility. They were exempt from all taxation and relied on the commoners to support them. The common people were the largest group in the Incan society. They were farmers who grew food and raised livestock for themselves and all other classes. In the dry coastal regions, they built canals and ditches that irrigated large fields of corn, squash, peppers, beans, peanuts, tomatoes, cotton, avocados, and sweet potatoes. In the highlands of the Andes, they built terraces into the hills to increase the amount of arable land and prevent the runoff of soil down the mountains. Their main crops were the white potato and quinoa, a cereal grain. They raised alpacas and llamas primarily for their wool.

Incan society was also divided into clans called *ayllus*. Every clan had a specific function to perform in the empire. The people were further subdivided into groups of ten each. Each group of ten had its own leader, who reported in a chain of command all the way up to a provincial governor known as the *tocricoc apu*. Each governor was responsible for 40,000 people below him and in turn reported to one of the four *apus* who administered the four main regions of the Incan empire. The four apus reported directly to the Incan emperor himself. The emperor and his many imperial officials oversaw the daily administration of the realm and frequently put people to work in a compulsory labor service known as the *mita*. The commoners were required to serve in the army, build palaces, temples, and other fortifications, and maintain the *Capac Nan*, the great system of stone highways that connected every part of the Incan empire. They also built the storehouses set up every few miles along the roads to support the army as it moved through the empire. Runners could travel up to 150 miles each day carrying messages back and forth between Cuzco and the provinces.

The well-organized Incan empire collapsed soon after the arrival of the Spanish conquistadors under Francisco Pizarro in 1532. Atahuallpa, the last Incan king, had recently defeated his brother Huáscar in a civil war, but had not taken complete control of the empire. The Spanish took Atahuallpa prisoner and refused to release him even after the Incas paid a ransom in gold and silver that filled one of the rooms in the royal palace to the height of a man. Atahuallpa was tried and executed. Helped by smallpox and the measles, and aided by their guns and horses, the Spanish completely conquered the Incas by 1569. They taxed the Incas heavily and put many to work digging in the silver mines. Despite the hardships, millions of descendants of the Incas and their conquered subjects still live in Peru, Ecuador, and Bolivia.

Mary Stockwell

See also: South America.

BIBLIOGRAPHY
D'Altroy, Terrence N. *The Incas*. Malden, MA: Blackwell, 2000.

INDENTURED SERVANTS

A system of labor that developed from traditional European agricultural husbandry, which crossed the Atlantic Ocean into the Americas as Europeans exchanged a set amount of service for passage and new opportunities.

As Europeans crossed the Atlantic to settle in the Americas, they were continually impressed by the abundance of land and its productive capabilities. This abundance of land, coupled with the need for labor to make it productive, played an important role in the colonial history of the Americas. In the early seventeenth century, in both the West Indies and British North America, the early European settlers there possessed a cash crop; in the West Indies, it was sugarcane, and in Virginia, it was tobacco. Both crops were labor intensive. The problem that plagued the settlers was not the lack of land or a way to profit but the lack of labor needed to produce a profit from the situation.

Early on, plantation owners attempted to use the local natives as a source of labor but, because of their knowledge of the local environment, their connections, and the introduction of European diseases that decimated them, the Europeans soon discovered the futility of Mesoamerican and American Indian slavery. The next possible solution involved bringing European agricultural laborers to the Americas to work. The problem was that while many Europeans were willing to travel to the Americas and start their life anew, they lacked the money needed for a transatlantic journey. The indentured servant system provided the solution to this problem. In Europe, changes in agriculture, including the process of enclosing the land and the introduction of New World crops, made European agriculture more efficient and productive. This meant that fewer people were needed to toil on the land, and therefore, increasingly larger numbers of people were forced to find new ways to survive.

Concurrently, the increase in agricultural production caused a demographic revolution in Europe, increasing the number of people looking for work. The traditional European contractual system of husbandry and apprenticeship, which allowed individuals, or families, to trade their labor for skills

In the earlier years of American colonization, many Africans were imported not as slaves but as indentured servants, including this woman pouring a beverage for her pipe-smoking mistress. Other indentured servants produced many of the major export crops of the American colonies. *(Library of Congress)*

and the means of subsistence, no longer served its purpose, and declined in Europe. The indentured servant system transferred this system of contractual labor across the Atlantic, where it changed in its new American environment and provided this surplus population with a new option.

ECONOMIC EXCHANGE

The indentured servant system was a contractual system of not only labor but also economic exchange. The process began in the Americas, in regions such as Virginia and the West Indies, but the system extended through many colonies as all required sufficient numbers of laborers to develop and prosper. In Europe, agents were hired to announce the demand for labor and the opportunities the Americas presented. Interested individuals either contacted the agent, a merchant, or a captain, where they agreed on an initial contract. If contracted to an agent or merchant, the owner of the contract usually sold the contract to the captain of a vessel heading to the Americas who, once in the Americas, would sell the contract to the landowner. The passage across the Atlantic was unpleasant for the servants, as the captain understood that the cheaper he could carry them across the Atlantic, the more money he made when he sold the contracts. The landowner and the servant then negotiated the details of the contract—this usually included the number of years of service, if any skills would be taught or education provided, the means of subsistence, the behavior of the servant, and if any freedom dues would be given on the expiration of the contract.

While different from slavery, indentured servitude was similar in that the experience of the indentured servant depended on not only the stipulation of the contract, but more importantly on the nature of their master. Not all indentured servants had the same experience. In Virginia during the tobacco boom of the 1620s, indentured servants were akin to machines and experienced a harsh life where any minor infraction could increase the length of their service. Many of the indentured servants who arrived in the first half of the seventeenth century did not survive their first-year seasoning period, as the new climate, disease, the lack of food, and endless toil decreased their ability to survive. In most areas where indentured servitude took hold in the early 1600s, again in Virginia and the West Indies, changes to the system occurred when the plantation owners gradually started to move to African slavery as the preferred system of forced labor.

While early indentured servants were predominately used as agricultural laborers, over time, especially as the colonies expanded in the eighteenth century, indentured servants provided a variety of skilled and unskilled labor. Indentured servants continued to be used as agricultural laborers, but as the plantation owner switched to using African slaves, farmers who produced staple crops, such as in Pennsylvania, continued to use indentured servants. Servants existed throughout the colonies, and their use began to expand in urban areas. Here, servants were used because of the dearth of free-wage laborers and they worked in a variety of skilled and unskilled jobs. Many became apprentices and learned a trade, while others became porters or sailors; therefore, great differences as well as similarities existed between seventeenth- and eighteenth-century indentured servitude. The eighteenth century saw the rise of the redemption system, mainly used in the migration of Germans to the Americas, where individuals or families entered into contracts. Most redemptioners could pay off their contract at any point, and many received wages. This system of contractual labor not only provided the workers who expanded the American economy, but it also helped create the process of the European settlement of the Americas.

Ty M. Reese

See also: Columbian Exchange; Labor; Slavery; Sugar; Tobacco.

BIBLIOGRAPHY

Menard, Russell R. *Migrants, Servants and Slaves: Unfree Labor in Colonial British America.* Burlington, VT: Ashgate, 2001.

Salinger, Sharon. *To Serve Well and Faithfully: Labor and Indentured Servants in Pennsylvania, 1682–1800.* New York: Cambridge University Press, 1987.

INDIAN OCEAN TRADE

> This network spans from the east coast of Africa, through the Middle East, to western and eastern India, and then on through Burma (Myanmar) to the different islands of Southeast Asia.

Indian Ocean trade is a vast network that has witnessed thriving trade since ancient times. In early times, coastal trade occurred between different regions. For example, the people of the Indus Valley had good trade relations with the Sumerian and Mesopotamian civilizations. This trade network was equally important to Europe even before the Suez Canal came into existence. Usually, the goods from the East would be carried by way of the Arab merchants either through the Red Sea route overland to the Nile or through the Persian Gulf by way of Syria and the Black Sea. The European ships that came directly to this region traveled via the Cape of Good Hope in the southern tip of Africa.

SURVEY OF KEY PORTS

The east coast ports of Africa were in the Benadir Coast, Mrima Coast, Mozambique, and Madagascar. The Benadir Coast is a desert area with trade centers like Mogadishu and Brava. The coral islands of the Lamu archipelago form the northernmost border of the Mrima Coast. Mombasa, Malindi, Pemba, and Zanzibar are located on these islands. The Mrima Coast produced food items: Pemba exported fruit, yams, and rice to Socotra, Mogadishu, and Yemen. Sofala, in southern Mozambique, was a center of gold trade with Torwa. Most of Mozambique's trade was directed toward India. Along the Eritrean shore in Ethiopia, the island of Massawa was the center of grain, salt, ivory, slaves, cloth, and firearm trade.

Some of the most important trading centers were located from the Red Sea region to the Persian Gulf: Mocha, Aden, Socotra, the Yemen coast, Muscat, Bandar Abbas, and Hormuz. Coffee trade was important for Mocha. Jidda was the port of Mecca, with which there was a regular trade with India. The westernmost port of the Persian Gulf was Basra on the mouth of Tigris River. Trade between the Levant and the Orient was conducted by way of Basra and Hormuz. *Baniya* merchants conducted the trade between Bahrain and India. Bahrain was also an entrepôt center during the ancient times. Aden was another important center that developed as a place from which to control entry into the Red Sea. In earlier times, horses were a significant export from the Arabian region. Muscat was a flourishing trade center and controlled the trade between the gulf and Makran Coast. On the eastern end of the Makran Coast, Barbaricum and later, Lahri-Bandar, was located at the mouth of Indus River. These served as the ports for the hinterland.

On the western coast of India were the centers in Gujarat, Konkan, and the Malabar Coast. Gujarat had the Gulfs of Kachchh and Khambayat (Khambhat) sharing within them the Kathiawar peninsula. The main centers of trade in Gujarat were Cambay, Bharuch (Broach), Surat, Diu, and many minor ports like Jamnagar, Porbandar,

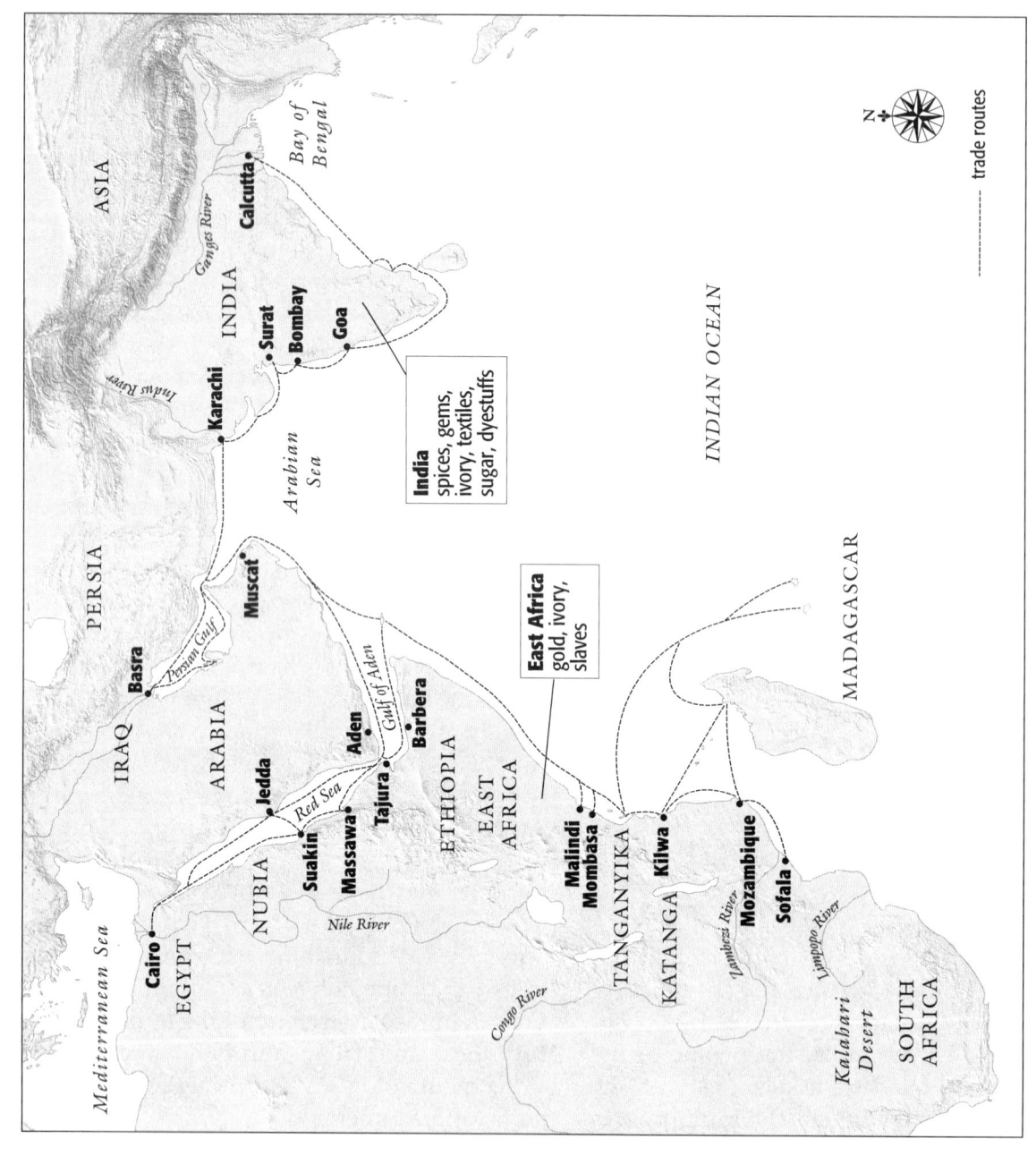

Indian Ocean Trade, 1450 On the eve of European overseas expansion in the late fourteenth century, Arabic-speaking merchants had developed an elaborate trading network connecting ports in East Africa, the Arabian Peninsula, and India. Key items of trade included precious metals, fabric, and agricultural goods, as well as slaves. (Mark Stein Studios)

Namanah, and Goga. In medieval times these areas were either under the control of local rulers or the Mughals. Textile, indigo, and grain were the main items of trade. To the south of Gujarat were the seaports of Daman, Bassein Salsette, and Chaul. On the Konkan Coast were also the ports of Janjira, Dabhul, Vengurla, and Goa among others. Dabhul was the main outlet for the Bijapuris in the seventeenth century. The established trading centers of Karwar, Cannanore, Mahé, Calicut, and Cochin were located on on the Malabar Coast. The Malabar Coast of Kerala was a frequented region since ancient times, when there were settlements of Europeans and Arab merchants. The main attraction of the Malabar Coast was spices, particularly the pepper trade.

Ceylon on the east coast of India—the Coromandel Coast, on the Bay of Bengal—had important trade centers like Masulipatnam, Pulicat, San Thome, Pondicherry, Cuddalore, Porto Novo, and Nagapatam. To its northeast was the Bengal coast, where the ancient port of Tamralipti (Tamluk) was located. Later on, important centers emerged like Chittagong and Satgaon. The coming of European East Indies trading companies led to new centers being created such as Hugli and Bandel. Important trade centers of later times, such as Calcutta, emerged because of the settlement of Europeans. This was also true of places like Bombay on the west coast or Madras on the Coromandel Coast.

In the Southeast Asian region, trading centers were situated on the coast of Burma, and thereon to the ports in Melaka (Malacca), Sumatra, Java, Aceh, and Siam. In ancient times, the Southeast Asian region had thriving trade relations with southern and eastern India and also with China. Trade in this region was also influenced by culture and there was active adoption of Indian culture as evidenced by the presence of Hinduism in this region. Southeast Asia became important in the trade network because it was a major producer of spices, which were the main attraction for traders. The Dutch had become the major player in this region after the Amboyna incident of 1623, when the Dutch seized an English factory and executed its occupants. Thereafter, the English role in Southeast Asia was marginalized.

Trading centers were generally under the control of powerful regimes, such as the the Ottomans, Safavids, and Mughals during medieval and early modern times. Most of these centers specialized in specific products that were indigenous to the area, though they would also function as entrepôts. Often, there were settlements of foreign traders from different kingdoms and regions in trade centers, and frequently the major group of traders in a particular place were not native to that area. This was particularly true of Arabs or the Baniyas, who were quite influential in different centers that they did not come from originally. There were Arab settlements in places like Calicut and Surat, while there were Baniya settlements in places like Basra. Other trading communities that dotted the various trade centers of this region included Jews, Armenians, Genoese, Tamil Chettiars, and Javanese. Most of the trade centers were well connected with the hinterland through navigation channels.

An important factor in the Arabian Sea region was the presence of monsoons, which were seasonal winds that brought rains to the different regions and that propelled the ships on the seas. The benefit of monsoons had been discovered early and was used as a facilitator of direct trade between the trading centers without needing to go through the coastal route.

ARRIVAL OF THE EUROPEANS

The Indian Ocean trade network developed into a rivalry with the entry of European trading companies, which aimed to monopolize the trade exclusively. Before the Europeans arrived, the Arabs were dominant. Among the Europeans, it was the Portuguese who first entered in the region. However, they aimed more at political control over the sea rather than trade. Among the others, the Dutch were largely involved in the cotton trade from the east coast of India and the spice trade from the islands of Southeast Asia. Among the many items of trade were salt, sugar, grain, spices, horses, silk, jewelry, slaves, calico, dates, building material, timber, glass, aromatics, and coffee.

The Indian Ocean trade network was connected to other parts of the world like Europe, America, China, and the Far East. Consequently, the market forces generated in these other regions also influenced the trade network of the Indian Ocean. A consequence of having access to other world markets was that new products like potatoes, corn, and pineapples were introduced to the region.

An important factor affecting the trade was the development of ships that were sturdy and capable of making long journeys. By the end of fifteenth century, ships could carry loads of up to 350 to 400 tons. Because timber for ships could not be found in Arabia or Persia, most of the ships were built in Gujarat or the Malabar region. The industry gradually adopted Western methods of building ships. However, technologically the Indo-Arab boom and the Chinese junk were on a par with European ships. European ships would attain superiority only by the mid-nineteenth century when they started to use the steam engine.

The Indian Ocean trade network, which had its origin in ancient times, became fully developed by the nineteenth century. The two most important influences on this trade network were the entry of monopolistic European trading companies, which arrived by way of the Cape of Good Hope, and the building of the Suez Canal, which provided a much shorter route between Europe and the Indian Ocean region.

Anup Mukherjee

See also: European Trade, Intracontinental; Mughal Empire.

BIBLIOGRAPHY

Barendse, R.J. *The Arabian Seas: The Indian Ocean Trade in the Seventeenth Century.* Armonk, NY: M.E. Sharpe, 2002.

Chaudhuri, K.N. *Trade and Civilization in the Indian Ocean.* Cambridge: Cambridge University Press, 1985.

Prakash, Om, and Denys Lombard, eds. *Commerce and Culture in the Bay of Bengal.* New Delhi: Manohar, 1999.

INDIGO

A natural plant that yields a highly prized blue dye that has been used for thousands of years.

The indigo plant of the *Indigofera* genus has over 300 varieties, but the two most often used for the production of indigo dye are the *I. tinctoria* (found in India and Asia) and the *I. suffructiosa* (found in Central and South America). The dye is extracted from the leaves of the plants through a fermentation process.

The first known use of indigo was to dye the fabric in which the mummies of the XVIII dynasty of Egypt were wrapped. Although the ancient Greeks knew of indigo and the Greek historian Herodotus mentions it around 450 B.C.E., the use of indigo remained limited until the Middle Ages. During the Crusades, Arab traders exported the dye to Egypt, Cyprus, and Asia Minor. Europeans resisted the importation of the dye since regions in Germany, England, and France were producing an inferior blue dye and the introduction of indigo would have resulted in the destruction of this agricultural industry. By the seventeenth century, the Dutch and British East India Companies began importing the dye and the demand for it exceeded the available supply. Indigo was usually used for textiles worn by royalty or for religious purposes. The British colony of South Carolina provided an additional source of indigo for Great Britain. The dye was sold to textile dyers throughout Europe. The Spanish cultivated the indigo plant in Central and South America beginning in the mid-1500s. The French indigo from Saint Domingo was of the highest quality available during the seventeenth and eighteenth centuries.

The use of indigo continued during the nineteenth century, but the dye remained relatively expensive. The wealthiest enjoyed indigo-dyed textiles with their subtle variations of shades that appeared more brilliant with age, but the average person could not afford such a luxury. Then, in 1880, Adolph von Bayer, a German, developed a synthetic indigo dye. During the last two decades of the nineteenth century, a period commonly referred to as the second Industrial Revolution, manufacturers began using chemical processes to create, improve, or substitute products. The chemical process required the transformation of naphthalene into phthalic acid and from that to phthalimide, anthranilic acid, phenylglycine carboxylic acid, and finally into indigo. Although the synthetic indigo is less expensive to produce, it lacks some of the qualities of natu-

Until the invention of chemical dyes in the late nineteenth century, agricultural crops like indigo—shown here being processed at a factory in Bengal, India—were the primary coloring agents for textiles and thus were a valuable export commodity. (© The British Museum/HIP-Topham/The Image Works)

ral indigo, such as its ability to produce subtle shading. By the late twentieth century, more than 17,000 tons of synthetic indigo was produced annually. Although some natural indigo dyes are still available, they are rare and therefore expensive.

Cynthia Clark Northrup

See also: British Empire; Mercantilism; Textiles.

BIBLIOGRAPHY
Balfour-Paul, Jenny. *Indigo.* London: British Museum Press, 2000.
"Chemistry of the Natural and Synthetic Indigo Dyes" (www.chriscooksey.demon.co.uk/indigo/index.html, accessed September 2003).
Mattson, Anne. "Indigo in the Early Modern World" (www.bell.libumn.edu/Products/Indigo.html, accessed September 2003).

INDUS RIVER

The Indus River rises in southwestern Tibet, circles around different mountains, runs a course of 1,800 miles, and finally drains into the Arabian Sea near Karachi (Sindh, Pakistan).

The main course of the Indus River now runs through Pakistan. The lower course is on a wide low-lying alluvial plain. It is an area of wheat production. The Indus is the westernmost river within the Himalayan river system. In its course, it drains glaciers and mountain slopes of important peaks like Tirich Mir (25,260 feet), Rakaposhi (25,550 feet), Masherbrum (25,660 feet), and Nanga Parbat (26,660 feet). Nearly 90 percent of the water in the Upper Indus basin comes from remote glaciers.

Since ancient times, the Indus River has been a cradle of civilization. It was the lifeline of the Harappan civilization, more popularly known as the Indus Valley civilization. Various estimates put the mature phase of this civilization at the end of third millennium B.C.E. Its most important metropolis—Mohenjo Daro—was situated on this river. For the Harappan civilization, the river had various functions. It was a source of agricultural surplus, which sustained the urban civilization. It provided a source of ritual performances, and it was the most important channel of interregional trade. The Harappan cities were connected with rural agricultural communities and mining areas through an effective trade network. The external trade link extended to Central Asia, the Arabian Sea region, and distant Mesopotamian cities, such as Susa and Ur. Persian Gulf sites like Bahrain and Failaka (near Kuwait) functioned as entrepôts. White lustrous seals made of steatite with beautiful carvings and pictographic script were used for the purpose of trade.

The main tributaries of the Indus are the five rivers of the Punjab: Jhelum, Chenab, Ravi, Beas, and Sutlej. This along with the now underground Saraswati River, together known as Sapta Sindhu, was the center of the Rig Vedic civilization. The Indus was one of the most revered rivers during the Rig Vedic period. The river was referred to many times in Rig Vedic literature and was considered sacred.

It was from this river that the name "India" was derived. When the Persians came in contact with the region around fifth century B.C.E., they had difficulty pronouncing "S." Instead, they pronounced "Sindhu" as "Hindu." Thus, anyone who was on the eastern side of Sindhu was a "Hindu." Later on, the word passed on to the Greeks, for whom the river became "Indus."

This fortified late nineteenth-century British railway bridge, spanning the Indus River—and its agriculturally wealthy hinterland—has been a source of imperial conflict for ages. *(Library of Congress)*

Barbaricum, which was situated in the middle mouth of the Indus, was an important seaport and market town of ancient India. Its imports included fine clothes, linen, precious stones, silver, gold plates, and wine, while it exported cotton clothes, silk yarn, and indigo. By the end of fifteenth century, Lahri-Bandar, situated on the mouth of the Indus, became important because of its trade with Persia.

The river has also been important as a defense against invasions from the West. It stopped Alexander the Great and brought an end to his world conquest. The river later posed a challenge to Genghis Khan in 1221 and stopped him from invading India.

Anup Mukherjee

See also: Alexander the Great; Indian Ocean Trade.

BIBLIOGRAPHY

Allchin, Bridget, and Raymond Allchin. *The Rise of Civilization in India and Pakistan.* New Delhi: Cambridge University Press. 1996.
Cunningham, Alexander. *The Ancient Geography of India.* Varanasi: Indological Book House, 1979.
Michel, Aloys A. *The Indus Rivers.* New Haven: Yale University Press, 1987.
Possehl, Gregory, ed. *Ancient Cities of the Indus.* New Delhi: Vikas, 1979.

INDUSTRIAL REVOLUTION

A spectacular and sudden transformation that occurred in a portion of the manufacturing sector of the British economy in the second half of the eighteenth century.

The term "industrial revolution" is used to refer to the spread of a process of rapid transformation to the entire British manufacturing sector and to other countries such as Belgium, France, Germany, and the United States during the first half of the nineteenth century. There are additional usages that treat "industrial revolutions" as a sequence of cycles of economic change, usually paced by significant alterations in technology, that originated with the British Industrial Revolution of the eighteenth century. Hence, there is the notion of a "second Industrial Revolution" centering around steam power and iron-producing technologies in the second quarter of the nineteenth century, and a "third

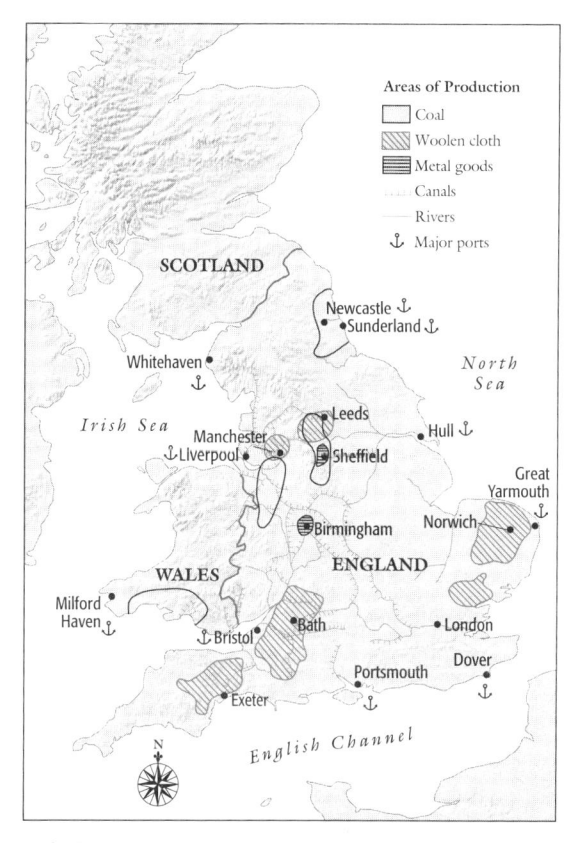

Industrial Revolution, United Kingdom, 1750 As the first country in the world to industrialize, England pioneered a pattern since imitated by countries around the world—building a transportation network, utilizing new energy sources, and developing basic industries like textiles and metalworking. *(Mark Stein Studios)*

Industrial Revolution" in the last third of the nineteenth century sparked by the development of electrical machines and internal combustion engines. Some commentators have applied the term "fourth Industrial Revolution" to changes in production associated with information and automation technologies in the contemporary world.

INNOVATION

According to the classic narratives of the British Industrial Revolution, its central feature was a set of innovations adopted in certain industries (especially cotton manufacture and pottery) starting around the 1760s, with related developments in mining, metals production, and engineering. (James Watt's invention of a new type of steam engine brought all three of the latter together.) Improvements in the productivity of the weaving side of the cotton industry in the second quarter of the eighteenth century had produced

Improvements in weaving (the power loom), dyeing, and printing helped make the cotton industry a major sector of the British economy by the early nineteenth century and the mainstay of the nation's exports. Here, a weaver tends a machine in a Lancashire cotton mill in the 1890s. *(Mary Evans Picture Library)*

pressure on the thread-spinning side, which elicited a series of spinning inventions (the jenny, the mule, and the water frame) in the 1760s and 1770s.

Most of these innovations required that machinery be centrally located where sources of power were available. Originally, cotton factories were located near water so they could be powered by water mills. Later, they were powered by stream. Together, with subsequent improvements in weaving (the power loom), dyeing, and printing, these innovations made the cotton industry a major sector of the British economy by the early nineteenth century and the mainstay of the nation's exports. Innovations in every aspect of the pottery industry of Staffordshire, such as new techniques for pro-

ducing porcelain and other ceramics on a large scale, new systems of worker discipline, and novel marketing approaches, led to a revolution in that sector as well, customarily associated with the name of Josiah Wedgwood. Other industries followed suit, and by the early nineteenth century not only had the manufacturing sector become the most dynamic part of the British economy, but also the landscape of the north and midlands of England was being transformed by the growth of industrial cities. A massive process of social and political change had begun, a process that lay at the heart of the phenomenon of modernization.

The classic description of the Industrial Revolution is highly insular, focusing on events (mostly innovations and their consequences) within Britain. Most of the traditional interpretations of the causes of the Industrial Revolution are similarly centered around factors present within the British economy and society in the early and middle years of the eighteenth century: a supposed abundance of labor in industrial areas created by earlier innovations in agricultural production that had reduced demand for workers; a stable political and fiscal system that provided scope and encouragement for technical innovation; and the availability of capital.

Typically, trade fits into the traditional interpretations in two ways. First, there is the thesis that the expansion of British trade in the late seventeenth and eighteenth centuries contributed heavily to the domestic pool of investable capital and to the erection of the organizational infrastructure within which some of that capital could be efficiently directed into the sectors central to the Industrial Revolution. The most famous of all interpretations linking trade to eighteenth-century British industrialization, the argument of Eric Williams that the Atlantic slave trade and the system of sugar production based on West Indian plantations that it supported provided the capital for the Industrial Revolution, belongs to this category. The second type of argument, not necessarily inconsistent with the first, focuses on demand: the expansion of British trade created markets for British goods abroad and income for British consumers at home, which in turn led to a large and sustained demand for British manufactured products.

Although almost no contemporary historian of industrialization claims that these two approaches are completely without merit, several difficulties have prevented them from becoming explanations for the central causes of the Industrial Revolution. In the case of the first approach, it has become clear that most of the capital for the early Industrial Revolution was generated locally in the areas in which the important innovations took place. In the second, research has shown that the largest share of the demand for the products of the early Industrial Revolution arose in Great Britain itself, not abroad, and that most of that demand came from people not closely connected with trade. If the Industrial Revolution is regarded from a classic or traditional perspective, trade can be seen to play a role in its origins, but not a decisive one.

It is, however, possible to look at the Industrial Revolution in ways more consistent with contemporary interest in the process of globalization. From these standpoints, trade performs a more central historical function. Important as the events that occurred in Britain in the second half of the eighteenth century were for revolutionizing manufacturing, it is important to realize that they were embedded in a network of events and developments that extended considerably further back in time and covered a substantial part of the world outside of Britain. Much of this network can be described as the construction of the global economy, or at least of its immediate preindustrial ancestor. The innovations that took place, for example, in the British cotton and pottery industries make little sense in any respect and would almost not have occurred outside the context of the global economy, that is, without the existence of the system of intercontinental seaborne trade relations that had developed since the latter part of the fifteenth century and without the concomitant systems of finance, manufacturing, marketing, consumption, and, to some extent, political authority that had grown up around it.

COTTON AND PORCELAIN INDUSTRIES

Both cotton textiles and the kind of pottery (porcelain or china) around which most of the initial technological development in the latter industry was centered were relatively recent additions to European society, brought into prominence, and made available on a substantial scale in the seventeenth century by the newly expanded trade between Europe and Asia. Cotton and cottons were not unknown in the Mediterranean during the Middle Ages, but it was only in the second half of the seventeenth century that a sudden fashion for using brightly colored, printed cotton textiles from India ("calicoes") swept European society, eventually at almost all status levels. The "calico craze" was made possible by the capacity of the East India companies to respond rapidly to heightened demand. This response was in turn enabled by the existence of a large and efficient, if labor-intensive, cotton manufacturing industry in India not under direct European control and by a local system of commercial finance in India with which the European companies could make satisfactory arrangements for short-term credit.

Although calicoes lost their faddish character in Europe by the end of the seventeenth century, the habit of wearing them and other cotton fabrics and of using white cottons as substitutes for linen for shirts, underclothes, napkins, tablecloths, and so forth expanded greatly, causing protests among producers of other textiles in England and France. In Britain, Parliament was persuaded in 1700 and 1720 to pass laws severely limiting the importation and use of Indian cottons. The demand for cottons was so large that this legislation did not put an end to the business, but it did drive much of it into the illegal economy of smuggling and clearly left opportunities for domestic producers to try to build a domestic, and thus (mostly) legal, cotton manufacturing industry.

The innovations in the weaving side of the industry and then the crucial innovations in spinning that constituted the core of the "revolution" in cotton production occurred in part as a response to those opportunities. English cotton manufacturers discovered that they could not produce cotton cloth of sufficiently high quality to match Indian cottons with the techniques and the skill levels of the existing English textile industry, and so they were forced to turn to technological innovation to find a solution to their problem. Thus, world trade was vitally important to the Industrial Revolution in cotton: it brought to Europe the product itself (cotton textiles) under circumstances in which its use became first fashionable and then a permanent fixture in European life. Not just the existence of trade with Asia, but also the fact that the trade was conducted by organizations such as the East India companies, which could effectively switch capital and effort into procuring large quantities of popular textiles, were essential factors in the context in which the cotton revolution occurred.

Like cotton, porcelain was a product imported in small quantities into Europe from China before the middle of the seventeenth century. Its use became fashionable, first in elite circles and then more widely, in the second half of that century. This created a demand that was partly filled by the East India companies, which persuaded the Chinese government to allow them to trade directly with China (mainly to procure tea), and partly by the Chinese porcelain industry, which was able to respond flexibly to new and changing demand patterns emanating from Europe. The demand was so large, however, that it stimulated successful efforts in Europe in the late seventeenth and early eighteenth centuries to develop reasonable European imitations of Chinese porcelain.

One of the central features of the revolution in the English pottery in the mid-eighteenth century was the creation of new forms of porcelain, which could be produced in an array of styles, in a range of prices, in sufficient quantities, and in appropriate levels of quality to satisfy a large market that had originally appeared in response to a product supplied by world trade. Again, without the prior operation of the kind of trading system that had been constructed between Europe and Asia, the context for the revolution in the pottery industry would not have existed.

GLOBAL ECONOMY

It is also useful to look at the immediate consequences of the Industrial Revolution in terms of the structure and dynamics of the global economy. Before the Industrial Revolution, European manufacturing industries had played at best a secondary role in world trade. By the middle of the eighteenth century, European-manufactured goods had found significant and growing markets only in those overseas areas that were inhabited by large numbers of people of European descent, especially in the British colonies of North America. The big manufacturing centers in the global economy were India and China. European ships all over the world brought Indian textiles and a range of products from China. The former were vital, for example, in the West African slave trade, in which they were exchanged for the labor needed to operate the Caribbean sugar plantations. With the development during the Industrial Revolution of a substantial European capacity to manufacture on a large scale many of the high- and medium-quality consumer goods that had previously been imported only in Asia, Europe's role in global trade changed markedly. The expanding industries based on new technologies became the center of world manufacturing, just as European banks and trading companies had already become the centers of global finance and commerce. European producers acquired the ability to develop markets for their products in areas of the world that had been penetrable in the past only through the use of American silver or Asian commodities.

In most regions, others emanating from a rapidly changing Europe accompanied these alterations. In West Africa, for example, Britain's abolition of the slave trade in 1807, which was followed by similar actions by other countries, joined with the beginnings of British industrialization and a relative decline of the importance of sugar in the world economy to effect a basic change in the basis of commerce in the region. West Africa lost its status as a vital segment of the Atlantic portion of the world economy by being a source of slave labor and became just another, fairly marginal place to sell Manchester cotton or Birmingham metal products. To develop such trade, it was necessary to find West African commodities saleable in Europe to exchange for European goods. The main West African export product in the nineteenth century was palm oil, used in Europe as a lubricant for machinery and as an ingredient in soap. It was also necessary to expand the market for European-manufactured goods beyond the African elites and the coastal peoples who had been the main African partners in the slave trade.

This motivated European economic interest groups to support missionary outreach beyond elite groups and to press for action to undermine or replace African states that still traded in slaves and that dominated trade with interior areas. Well before the period of the full-scale colonial partition of Africa in the last quarter of the nineteenth century, shifts in trade patterns in West Africa, most of them connected one way or another with the Industrial Revolution, had altered the region's economies and societies, linking them more comprehensively to Europe than had been the case during the height of the slave trade, even though West Africa had become a much more marginal segment of the global economy as a whole in terms of its importance.

In other places, the restructuring of world trade as a result of the Industrial Revolution was even more spectacular. Before the American Revolution, the largest export of the British North American colonies had been foodstuffs to the plantation economies of the West Indies. This trade declined to quite small proportions after the 1780s. From the early nineteenth century onward, by far the largest export of the United States was cotton—a raw material for the new cotton mills of Britain and, later in the century, France and Germany as well. The growing U.S. economy also became an immense market for European-manufactured products in the nineteenth century.

There was, of course, an American Industrial Revolution, commencing with the establishment of a British-style cotton industry in New England in the early decades of the nineteenth century and accelerating just before the time of the Civil War. That such a revolution was possible in the United States, flooded as it was with European goods, was in no small part because of the ability of the American federal government to set up a system of tariffs that allowed American manufactured products to find a market in their own country. Even so, American industrial exports were negligible. The main exports of the United States continued to be cotton and other agricultural commodities well into the twentieth century. Many other countries were not so fortunate.

Dynamic economies in the new South American republics were, throughout much of the nineteenth century, highly dependent on British and other European imports and were not able to emulate the United States in developing major industrial sectors of their own. In some cases, such as Argentina, economic dependence occurred because of direct European intervention to prevent the establishment of high tariffs, but more often because of factors such as limitations in the size of domestic markets, the existence of elite groups interested in maintaining free trade, and political instability.

The Industrial Revolution also profoundly altered previous patterns of trade in Asia. India, the center of the world's cotton textile production in the eighteenth century, experienced a disastrous decline in its manufactured exports in the first half of the nineteenth century because of its inability to compete with European cottons. This situation was exacerbated by the fact that much, and eventually almost all, of India was under British-controlled governments that did not permit the Indian cotton industry to adopt the new technologies until late in the century, and then only under conditions that limited it to the domestic Indian market. The place of cottons in Indian exports was taken by raw cotton, opium, and eventually tea. Many parts of India in which cotton production had been heavy in the eighteenth century effectively "deindustrialized" in the nineteenth century.

In the case of China, the traditional textile and porcelain industries experienced substantial competition from European producers, but even more important was the flood of European-manufactured goods that entered China after Britain, in the Opium War of 1839–1842, forced the Chinese government to reduce its restrictions on trade and on the presence of Europeans in the country. China did, in fact, develop a modern industrial sector in the course of the nineteenth century and reappeared by the early twentieth century as an important exporter of textiles. But the new Chinese industries were dependent on European investment and tended to fall under a high level of European control, which had not been the case earlier.

Japan, which had deliberately isolated itself from a high level of contact with the rest of the world between the seventeenth and the middle of the nineteenth centuries, was abruptly forced by pressure, first from the United States and then from other countries, to enter the global economy in the 1850s. The story of how the Japanese responded to these circumstances by rapidly developing a modern industrial economy and becoming a world-class industrial exporter is one of the most remarkable in the history of the modern world. As France, Belgium, and the German states had done in the first half of the nineteenth century, Japan imported the technology and techniques of modern industrial production from the current industrial centers in the latter part of the century. Unlike the Europeans during the initial period of industrialization, however, the Japanese had felt obliged to import a large part of the cultural and political apparatus of the countries from which the techniques came and to graft them onto more traditional Japanese elements. Many, but not all, of these techniques were relatively adaptable to the new circumstances of industrial production, but were nevertheless different. The result was the creation of an industrial and commercial powerhouse of the twentieth century.

Woodruff D. Smith

See also: Cotton; Discovery and Exploration; Empire Building; Tea.

BIBLIOGRAPHY

Eltis, David. *Economic Growth and the Ending of the Transatlantic Slave Trade.* New York: Oxford University Press, 1987.

Engerman, Stanley L., ed. *Trade and the Industrial Revolution.* 2 vols. Aldershot, UK: Elgar, 1996.

Fieldhouse, D.K. *Economics and Empire, 1830–1914.* London: Macmillan, 1984.

Mathias, Peter. *The First Industrial Nation: An Economic History of Britain, 1700–1914.* New York: Methuen, 1983.

Williams, Eric. *Capitalism and Slavery.* London: Deutsch, 1964.

INDUSTRIALISM

> A process of moving from labor-intensive to capital-intensive production and a top social and economic objective of the most developing countries.

The recognition of the importance of industrialization dates back to the Industrial Revolution of the 1750s. Liberal capitalism was born in west European countries in the late eighteenth and early nineteenth centuries. The most important process of this period was the integration of the various regions of the world with the capitalist world economic system centralized in western Europe. That course of action started in the sixteenth century and continued to expand until it included peripheral countries. The participation of the other regions of the world in this system occurred only after the Industrial Revolution in the nineteenth century.

The meaning of integration, at a simple economic level, is to produce for the world market. This process has converted self-sufficient countries into societies whose future is vastly dependent on the world economy. Although there are various types of integration, diverse regions of the world accepted that process in different ways. From about the fifteenth century onward, the European communities gradually moved from feudalism, to mercantilism, then through the Industrial Revolution, and currently into classical liberalism.

The Industrial Revolution brought about a big change and transformation in daily life, and England emerged as the final victor of intra-European rivalry. It is associated with the transformation from hand tools and handmade items to manufactured and mass-produced goods. The government, the arts, literature, music, architecture, and humanity's way of looking at life all changed during this period. Within a fairly short time, societies of peasants and craftsmen turned into societies of machine-tenders and bookkeepers.

These developments were the origins of the first Industrial Revolution. By the 1750s, the Industrial Revolution had begun. At first, inventions were strictly limited to cotton weaving (e.g., the power loom and the spinning jenny). These inventions helped the manufacture of cotton goods by speeding up the process. Mass-production had begun along with capitalism. Capitalists who had their own materials, money, and space, bought many machines and stored them in a factory where hired people worked the entire day manufacturing goods. The factory system had replaced the cottage industry, where workers would buy raw materials from a merchant, take it back to their cottages, and produce goods at their home. The factory system was usually owned and managed by one or more people who were relatively close to the workers. This cooperative worker-boss relationship was destroyed by capitalism.

Mass-production made expensive items, such as shoes, less expensive and easily affordable by lower-class and less-wealthy people. The quality of life improved. In the 1800s, inventions were not just limited to the cotton industry. Steam engines were invented, replacing the horse and carriage and providing a faster transportation system. With the steam engine, cities were able to exist farther away from rivers and sources of water. Other inventions like the telephone, the telegraph, and electric lighting followed.

During the period between the publication of Adam Smith's pioneer work, *Wealth of Nations*, in 1776 and 1850, the origin of the second Industrial Revolution, several events of tremendous social, political, and economic significance, occurred. The American and French Revolutions were two important upheavals. The rise of industrialism and the factory system in England, continental Europe, and the United States followed these upheavals.

The factory system ushered in major transformations in the social and economic landscape. Many contemporary writers feel that the working class bore the chief cost of these changes in the form of economic dislocation and urban congestion. Critics of the period arose to question the benefits of industrialization and the validity of an analytical system that sought to explain the consequences and momentum of the new industrial society. Thus, the nineteenth century was an intellectual battleground of sorts for literary, methodological, and, to a lesser extent, analytical skirmishes in the social sciences.

SECOND INDUSTRIAL REVOLUTION

The second Industrial Revolution involved not only inventions, but also social and government policies and reforms. Art and culture flourished. Electricity improved the quality of life by supplying people with light and power for machines. Communications also improved as a result of electricity. The telephone and telegraph became the first communication devices available for public use. With the development of technology, radio waves were discovered. Advances in science were also made. The discovery of radioactivity (by Marie Curie), the breakdown of chemical compounds (during the 1800s, over 70,000 chemical compounds were broken down), and the discovery of the nuclear bomb also occurred during this period. Petroleum began to be widely used as an alternate energy source. The internal combustion engine made transportation faster for the public. Orville and Wilbur Wright successfully completed the first airplane flight at Kitty Hawk, North Carolina, which led to the development of the aviation industry.

In seeking rapid economic development, most developing countries drew lessons from the experience of the advanced countries. The main conclusion was that industrialization was the key to economic success. Developing countries have traditionally been primary exporters. Industrialization allowed them to exploit their comparative advantage in labor-intensive goods. However, with a low world income elasticity of demand for primary products, with the development of synthetic substitutes, and with the protection of agriculture in developed countries, the demand for primary exports has grown slowly. At the same time, the demand for manufactured imports into developing countries has grown rapidly. Dissatisfaction with relying on primary exporting has led most countries to embark on a process of industrialization.

Economic development is usually viewed as the transformation of a low-income society using traditional technologies and producing mainly primary products into a high-income society using modern technologies to produce both primary products and a variety of industrial goods.

The desire to industrialize is common to the less-developed countries for various reasons. First, most of the current developed market economies themselves achieved this status through industrialization, so it may seem reasonable to assume that following this same route will lead to the same results. Second, because of the inelastic world demand for the primary products, they are considered as an unsatisfactory basis for development. Third, it is believed that economic diversification may lead to greater stability in national income and foreign currency earnings. Fourth, it is believed that industrialization may reduce the country's dependence on the rest of the world. Finally, having an industrial sector is seen as a symbol of independence.

Two issues have dominated the general debate concerning industrialization strategies and experiences. The question of strategy has largely focused on the choice between the inward-looking strategy of import-substituting industrialization (ISI) and the outward-looking strategy of export-oriented industrialization (EOI). Some countries preferred ISI, which is a strategy of restricting imports of manufactured goods and using the foreign exchange saved to build up domestic substitute industries. It is considered the best way to become industrialized, especially for countries facing the shortage of foreign currency to finance their import spending. By contrast, some countries gave priority to EOI strategy, meaning to encourage not only free trade, but also the free movement of capital, workers, enterprises, the multinational enterprise. There is still ongoing debate between the trade optimists (free traders) and trade pessimists (protectionists), and between outward- and inward-looking strategies of development.

Although different countries applied different industrialization strategies, generally, all countries have viewed industrialization as the "engine of growth."

Elfi Cepni

See also: Aviation; Communication; Industrial Revolution; Transportation and Trade.

BIBLIOGRAPHY
Ekelund, Robert. B., and Robert B. Hebert. *A History of Economic Theory and Method.* New York: McGraw-Hill, 1990.
Sodernsten, Bo, and Reed Geoffrey. *International Economics.* New York: Macmillan, 1994.

INFLATION

> The rate of inflation measures the annual percentage of increase in prices.

The most common measure of inflation is that of retail prices. The government publishes the consumer price index (CPI) each month, and the rate of inflation is the percentage of increase in that index over the previous twelve months. The CPI (or the retail price index as it is known in some countries) tends to be constructed differently from one country to another and this makes international comparison difficult. CPI measures the cost of buying a fixed basket of goods and services representative of the purchases of urban consumers. Price indices are based on consumer purchases.

The most commonly used cost-of-living indices are the Paasche and Laspeyres price indices. The Laspeyres price index answers the question: What is the amount of money at current-year prices that an individual requires to purchase the bundle of goods and services that was chosen in the base year divided by the cost of purchasing the same bundle at base-year prices? The Paasche price index shows the amount of money at current-year prices that an individual requires to purchase the bundle of goods and services chosen in the current year divided by the cost of purchasing the same bundle in the base year.

Both indices are fixed-weighted indices. The quantities of the various goods and services in each index remain unchanged. For the Laspeyres price index, however, the quantities remain unchanged at base-year levels, while for the Paasche price index they remain unchanged at current-year levels.

Fighting inflation is among the most important goals in macroeconomic policy goals. Moreover, inflation is sometimes declared public enemy number one. But why is inflation such a big problem?

Inflation redistributes incomes from the economically weak to the economically powerful, it causes uncertainty in the business community and as a result reduces investment, and it tends to lead to balance-of-payment problems and depreciation (or devaluation) of the domestic currency.

There are two different types of inflation: demand-pull inflation and cost-push inflation. Demand-pull inflation is caused by persistent rises in aggregate demand (total spending), whereas cost-push inflation is caused by the persistent rises in the cost of production. Rises in costs may origi-

Because war creates increased demand for labor and commodities, sometimes it leads to inflation. This 1942 display was part of a U.S. government effort to fight inflation or, at least, explain it to consumers. *(Library of Congress)*

nate from a number of different sources. The main types of cost-push inflation are: wage push, profit push, import price push, and tax push.

If inflation originates from the rise in aggregate demand (demand-pull inflation), both the general price level and national output (production) will increase. If inflation originates from the rise in the cost of inputs, the general price level will increase but national output will decrease, which in turn will cause a bigger unemployment problem. Cost-push inflation will cause more serious economic harm.

Expectations play a crucial role in determining the level of inflation. The higher people expect inflation to rise, the higher it will. There are different anti-inflation policies. To alter the level of total spending, demand-side policies, namely, monetary and fiscal policies, can be used, and to alter the total production through decreasing costs (such as tax incentives), supply-side policy can be used.

Elfi Cepni

See also: Money.

BIBLIOGRAPHY

Pindyck, Robert S., and Daniel Rubinfeld. *Microeconomics.* New York: Prentice Hall, 2001.
Sloman, John. *Economics.* New York: Financial Times, 2002.

INSURANCE

The process by which an individual or company can obtain financial protection against loss or harm through the payment of a premium to another individual or company.

Insurance, in one form or another, has existed since ancient times. The first mention of any form of insurance appears in the Babylonian Code of Hammurabi. Under the law, if goods were lost in transit, either by caravan or ship, the transporter was absolved of any liability unless it was proven that he was involved in the theft. The merchants then shared in the loss of the goods. The Chinese, as early as 3000 B.C.E., ordered that merchants should split up their shipment of products among several vessels to minimize any losses that they might incur. Greek sailors, who plied the waters of the Mediterranean Sea, relied on a system of average to protect their cargoes and ships against the risk of storms, pirates, or damage. Losses would be compensated on a pro rata basis from funds contributed by the merchants. One or more individuals who provided the coverage guaranteed each cargo individually. This system remained in effect under the Roman empire. There were no insurance companies, just protection on single ships. A captain was often given a loan that would be repaid if he had returned without any damage to ship or cargo. The loan would protect the shippers from debt if the merchandise was lost or destroyed in transit. This rudimentary type of insurance was known as the bottomry loan.

Beginning in the eleventh century, Italian and English merchants formed associations that operated under the Amalfi Sea Code. Under the code, members of the association would contribute funds regularly that could be used to compensate merchants for the loss of cargo. With the rise of Venice as the merchant power in the eastern Mediterranean, the first modern marine insurance policies were used. The amount of trade and the value of the cargo required some protection against the risk of loss. Portugal and France developed marine insurance as well. During the fourteenth century, the Venetians began using agreements that dictated how commerce was conducted. Most of these agreements were verbal while some were written and became official since a notary was involved. However, many of the early insurance agreements were conducted in secret, especially after the government proposed the taxation of such transactions. During the fifteenth century, the Venetians established laws governing the use of insurance policies, primarily to prevent fraud. Throughout the Middle Ages, the Catholic Church discouraged the use of insurance policies since, like loans, insurance was perceived as a wager on the outcome and was therefore equivalent to usury. Eventually, the insurance policy was separated from the risk and the charge of usury no longer applied.

During the late Middle Ages, craft guilds formed mutual aid societies. These groups functioned in much the same manner as life or disability insurance companies. Widows and children were provided for if the head of household died or was disabled. All members of the guild contributed to the fund so that the resources would be available in times of need. During the early seventeenth century, German princes employed the concept of the mutual aid society to all citizens within a particular region. Every head of household would contribute a proportion of the wealth of his assets to the fund in case an emergency occurred and one or more homes were damaged or destroyed.

During the height of the Hanseatic League, merchants in the Baltic region did not have insurance policies as we know them today. The risk of loss was again reduced through the method of spreading cargo among a number of ships. The first insurance company was finally established in Italy in the seventeenth century. Later on, Lombard traders established marine insurance policies in England while other references exist that indicate that the Dutch were also using insurance policies to protect against the loss of their cargoes during this same period. Existence of such policies continued even after the Reformation and into the reign of Elizabeth I, when the Lombard traders had left England. In 1601, a special Court of Policies of Assurance was established to resolve cases involving marine insurance policies, although few suits were actually heard. Marine insurance was accepted in France as a legitimate method of protecting merchants. Under the Ordonnance de la Marine, passed in 1681, King Louis XIV accepted the practice. Napoléon Bonaparte reinforced the use of marine insurance in the Code of Commerce passed in 1807.

Meanwhile, in 1688 Edward Lloyd issued his first insurance policy and over the centuries his company developed into the largest marine insurer in the world. With his first shop located on Tower Street, Lloyd soon moved to Lombard Street (the location of the insurance industry since the establishment of the Lombard insurers in London). Initially, the company provided shipping news to the merchants and captains, but the company soon expanded to offer marine insurance. During the next century, London developed into the center of the insurance industry with insurers copying the policies offered by Lloyd's company. This same policy served as the blueprint for the Marine Insurance Act of 1906 in Great Britain.

FIRE INSURANCE

Although marine insurance dates back to ancient times, the first instance of fire insurance policies being offered occurred after the Great Fire of London that began on September 2, 1666. The fire started in a baker's shop on Pudding Lane. High winds blew the burning embers across the city. The wooden structures quickly ignited and the situation was made worse by the fact that one of the first places to be burned was the waterwheel that supplied the city with water. The fire reached a crisis point, and King Charles II called on his brother, the duke of York, the head of the navy, to assist in fighting the fire. The duke ordered everything surrounding the fire to be pulled down and removed so that the fire no longer had fuel to continue spreading. After five days, the fire finally died out. During that short period, more than 13,200 homes and 87 churches in London spread out over more than 400 acres were destroyed. When rebuilding commenced, new structures were required to be built of brick and stone to prevent another disaster. The Great Fire of 1666 had destroyed four-fifths of the city.

Merchants lost all their property and goods, ruining their futures as well as those of their families. The following year, Nicholas Barbon founded the first fire insurance company. The company offered a policy against future fires, but to ensure that it did not sustain substantial losses in the future, the firm was forced to establish and maintain fire brigades throughout the city—the first brigade being formed in 1680. Other insurance companies formed to offer fire protection as well. Since the cost of maintaining the fire brigades was not cheap, companies would issue emblems representing their insurance company to policyholders who placed them outside of the insured buildings. When a fire broke out, men from several different companies would show up, but if the emblem was not the one for their company, many times they refused to fight the fire. Eventually, the various fire brigades were merged and the companies were relieved of their responsibility for fighting fires in 1865 when Parliament passed the Metropolitan Fire Brigade Act.

The example established in England was followed in the American colonies. Fire insurance policies were first available in Charleston, South Carolina, in 1732. Benjamin Franklin established a fire insurance company in Philadelphia in 1752. Relatively few fires occurred, and the companies managed to earn profits. The largest fire to strike the United States occurred in Chicago on October 8, 1871. The fire lasted for 29 hours and destroyed more than 17,000 structures valued at more than $2 million. Relief efforts assisted the victims of the fire, and the city slowly rebuilt, but fire struck again in 1874, destroying another 800 buildings. Although most of the damage from the initial fire occurred in the business district, fire insurance helped the merchants recoup most of their losses. After the second fire, the insurance companies threatened to refuse to sell any fire insurance in Chicago until the city improved its fire department and updated its city code to enforce the use of more fire-resistant material in the construction of the buildings.

Fire protection in the twentieth century still remains important even though most structures are constructed with fire-resistant materials and city ordinances require the availability of fire extinguishers and sprinkler systems in larger buildings. Since the number of fires remain relatively small in comparison to the value of the property insured, insurance companies continue to earn a profit. Meanwhile, business owners and individuals are covered, and if a fire does occur they will not be forced out of business or into poverty from the loss.

LIFE AND HEALTH INSURANCE

Life insurance has its roots in medieval times when guilds would provide for the widow and children of a deceased member. Contributions would be collected from all members on an equal basis. In 1693, Edmond Halley, the astronomer, devised a mortality table based on the statistical probability of mortality. Additional revisions to the table in 1756 by Joseph Dodson resulted in the payment of fees for life insurance based on the age of the insured. The first life insurance company in the United States was formed in Philadelphia in 1759. Established by the Presbyterian Synod of Philadelphia, the policies covered the lives of that denomination's ministers and their families. Although companies did not generally provide life insurance for their employees until the mid- to late twentieth century, business owners and the wealthy would often purchase such policies to cover the expenses that might occur as a result of their death. The future needs of both their businesses and their families usually determined the amount of insurance purchased. In the late twentieth century, many companies offered the employee life insurance benefits or the option to pay for such insurance at group rates.

Health insurance is another field that has developed primarily in the mid- to late twentieth century as medical advances have resulted in increased cost of services. Individuals had paid the physicians themselves or offered some form of barter arrangement to pay for their medical expenses until hospitals began investing in advanced technology. Corporations started offering health insurance benefits to their employees as the cost of medical treatment continued to escalate. By purchasing insurance at group rates, the employees, who sometimes had their own insurance paid for while having to cover the cost for dependents, could have the maximum coverage at the lowest price. Self-employed businesspeople often found that the insurance available to them was (and still is) either more expensive or did not offer the same coverage.

During the 1990s, changes in insurance resulted in the formation of health maintenance organizations, where a doctor receives a specified amount per month for each patient assigned to him or her through the insurance company. Fee schedules have been established as well. Medical professionals, bound by contracts with the insurance companies, often find that the procedures that they recommend are not covered or that some patients, those who they see frequently during the month, actually end up costing them money. These issues have opened the debate over national health care in the United States.

SOCIAL WELFARE

Governments began experimenting with public forms of insurance in the mid-twentieth century. The rising cost of medicine meant that a portion of the population could no longer afford adequate medical services. In Great Britain, Parliament passed the National Health Service Act that provided free medical treatment for everyone. A national health tax and the treasury covered the cost of the program. As prices increased, small fees were charged to cover items such as dentures, glasses, and prescriptions. Doctors are paid directly by the national system. Canada eventually adopted a similar health-care program, as did Sweden and other European countries.

Of the industrialized Western countries, the United States remains the only nation that has not adopted a national health-care program. Resistance from doctors, who would receive a lower wage under the system, and from the insurance carriers, who have built large companies with thousands of employees in the industry, has blocked several attempts to pursue this type of public health insurance. Consumers argue that the Canadian and British systems have resulted in dissatisfied patients who often have to wait months or years to receive a particular treatment. Those who can afford to travel to the United States for treatment do so, while the poor must wait.

Since the problem of income disparity has not been addressed, the U.S. Congress has not seen fit to approve such a program. Congress has authorized two programs that specifically address the health-care needs of the poor. Under Medicare, senior citizens have access to medical coverage and even some prescription drug benefits, while Medicaid covers the medical expenses of the poorest in society. American hospitals cannot refuse to treat patients who do not have the means to pay in an emergency, although the patient might later be transferred to a county hospital.

PROPERTY/CASUALTY INSURANCE

Just as the ancient and medieval mariners relied on some form of insurance to cover their losses, automobile insurance is a vital aspect of life in modern times. Motor vehicles are used to transport goods and people over short and long distances. Merchants protect their goods from loss or damage through insurance policies. Most states require that owners maintain a minimum policy of $25,000 for personal automobiles to cover damages incurred during an accident. That coverage might eventually have to be raised since the average cost of a new vehicle exceeds that amount. The failure to maintain financial responsibility comes with a stiff fine. Insurance companies support legislation requiring such coverage not only because it allows them to write more policies, but also because damage caused by uninsured motorists would have to be covered by paying customers if the law did not exist.

Insurance companies have traditionally offered other forms of coverage such as flood insurance. Since the terrorist attacks of September 11, 2001, the cost of insurance that would compensate the policyholder for damage caused by acts of terror has skyrocketed. The government has attempted to intervene since the extreme spike in premiums placed many large construction projects on hold. Continued terrorist attacks would force insurance companies out of business unless some mechanism can be implemented to prevent the destruction of high-value properties.

The insurance industry, from its rudimentary beginnings to the sophisticated policies of the twenty-first century, has allowed trade to flourish. Merchants could not have continued to ship or sell their goods if some protection against loss was not available. Economically, insurance made trade possible and profitable.

Cynthia Clark Northrup

See also: British Empire; Hanseatic League; United States; Venice.

BIBLIOGRAPHY

Ackroyd, Peter. *The Great Fire of London.* Chicago: University of Chicago Press, 1988.
Bagehot, Walter. *Lombard Street.* New York: Arno, 1979.
Barlow, Douglas, ed. *The Marine Insurance Code of France, 1681: A Translation of the Articles on Bottomry, Respondentia, and Marine Insurance, of the Ordonnance de la Marine, 1681, of France.* Toronto: n.p., 1989.
Gutner, Howard. *The Chicago Fire.* New York: Scholastic, 2002.

Harper, Robert Francis. *The Code of Hammurabi King of Babylon about 2250 B.C.E.* Holmes Beach, FL: Gaunt, 1994.
Lister, John. *By the London Post: Essays on Medicine in Britain and America.* Waltham, MA: New England Journal of Medicine, 1985.

INTELLECTUAL PROPERTY

> The protection of intangible assets such as inventions, designs, trademarks, and copyrights.

In today's "knowledge economy," intellectual property is central to Western notions of prosperity and international trade. The global agreement on intellectual property, called the Agreement on Trade-Related Aspects of Intellectual Property Rights (TRIPS), is now integral to membership in the World Trade Organization (WTO).

DEFINITION

Intellectual property rights refer to the rights given to people over their inventions or creations. The rights usually give the creator exclusive use of a creation for a certain period.

Ideas and knowledge are an increasingly important part of trade. Most of the value of new medicines and other high-technology products relate to the amount of invention, innovation, research, design, and testing involved in their development. Films, musical recordings, books, computer software, and online services are bought and sold because of the information and creativity they embody, not because of the physical resources used to make them. Many products that used to be considered low-technology goods or commodities now have a value that takes account of the effort in their creation due to invention and design, for example, brand-name clothing or new varieties of plants.

Creators can be given the right to prevent others from using their inventions, designs, or other creations. These rights take a number of forms. For example, books, paintings, and films are covered by copyright laws; inventions can be patented; brand names and product logos can be registered as trademarks; and so on.

The TRIPS Agreement covers copyright and related rights, trademarks, geographical indications (which identify a good as originating on the territory of a TRIPS member), industrial designs, patents, integrated circuit layout-designs, and protection of undisclosed information. Intellectual property rights are traditionally divided into two main categories: copyright and rights related to copyright (i.e., rights granted to authors of literary and artistic works) and the rights of performers, producers of phonograms, and broadcasting organizations. The main purpose of protection of copyright and related rights is to encourage and reward creative work.

Industrial property includes distinctive signs such as trademarks and geographical indications. Industrial property is protected primarily to stimulate innovation, design, and the creation of technology. In this category are inventions (protected by patents), industrial designs, and trade secrets.

TRIPS requires even the least-developed countries to have some minimum protection in place by 2006. Whether this is good for the poor is hotly debated. Developed countries generally preach that patents help to foster growth in poor places, since they stimulate domestic innovation, boost foreign investment, and improve access to new technologies.

Knowledge is considered an exception to the principle of diminishing marginal benefit, and it is generally believed that additional knowledge makes people more productive. And there seems no tendency for the additional productivity from additional knowledge to diminish. Because knowledge is productive and generates external benefits, it is necessary to use public policies to ensure that those who developed new ideas have incentives to encourage an efficient level of effort. It is believed that the main way of providing the right incentives is to assign intellectual property rights to creators. And the legal device for establishing intellectual property rights is the patent or copyright. These are the government-sanctioned exclusive rights granted to the inventor of a good, service, or productive process to produce, use, and sell the invention for a given number of years. A patent enables the developer of a new idea to prevent others from benefiting freely from that invention for a limited number of years.

Innovation does not happen by accident. It takes long hours and a great deal of investment—often many millions of dollars. Innovation can be defined as the application of new ideas to the products and processes of a firm's activities. Innovation is concerned with the process of commercializing or extracting value from ideas. This is in contrast with "invention," which need not be directly associated with commercialization. From this perspective, firm performance is linked to innovation. Indeed, there is widespread support for the assertion that firms must be innovative to survive and prosper in a competitive economy. Patents encourage invention and innovation and create incentives for investors to put money into risky new ideas, but it is also known that the protection provided by patents is not without cost. For example, patents are the strongest form of intellectual property right, since they give holders a claim over ideas encapsulated in a work, and not just (as copyright does) on the work's particular form. Their purpose is to reward inventors so as to encourage future invention. It is believed that society is balancing the benefits of a free exchange of ideas against future gains from further invention. And the means of striking this balance is to award a legal monopoly to a patent holder for twenty years from the date of application.

The monopoly power of the patent holder is a source of inefficiency. Moreover, monopolies create their own problems. Firms or individuals holding patents must register and defend them, risking potentially crippling lawsuits. Those without patents must license them or engage in inefficient and anticompetitive alliances.

COSTS AND BENEFITS

Economists have wrestled for decades over ways to balance these costs and benefits. Some believe that, in certain industries, strengthening intellectual property protection accomplishes nothing positive. Others think that it may actually do some harm. Many governments in poor countries show their reactions against these forms of protection. They believe Western-style intellectual property protection brings many costs and few benefits. Patent systems are expensive to implement, draining scarce money and trained manpower from other more pressing concerns. Patents hurt, rather than help, domestic industries, which are often based more on copying than on innovating. And in the process, Western patent rules prevent poor people from getting life-saving drugs, interfere with age-old farming practices, and allow foreign "pirates" to raid local biodiversity or traditional handicrafts, without getting permission or paying compensation.

This phenomenon has been dubbed the "Tragedy of the Anti-Commons"—in contrast to the classic "Tragedy of the Commons" that described how free resources such as fresh air and clean water could be overused and destroyed by selfish agents. Here, the opposite occurs: when lots of property owners have to grant permission before a resource can be used, the result is that the resource tends to be chronically underused.

The debate over this topic has not been eliminated completely, but it has lost its tension to a great extent as a result of the introduction of the TRIPS agreement, which came into effect on January 1, 1995.

Before the 1986–1994 Uruguay Round of negotiations, there was no specific agreement on intellectual property rights in the framework of the General Agreement on Tariffs and Trade (GATT) multilateral trading system. The TRIPS agreement recognizes that widely varying standards in the protection and enforcement of intellectual property rights and the lack of a multilateral framework of principles, rules, and disciplines dealing with international trade in counterfeit goods have been a growing source of tension in international economic relations. Rules and regulations were needed to cope with these tensions. To that end, the agreement addresses the applicability of basic GATT principles and those of relevant international intellectual property agreements, the provision of adequate intellectual property rights, the provision of effective enforcement measures for those rights, multilateral dispute settlement, and transitional arrangements.

The TRIPS Agreement says WTO member countries must comply with the substantive obligations of the main conventions of the World Intellectual Property Organization, the Paris Convention on industrial property, and the Berne Convention on copyright (in their most recent versions).

With respect to copyright, parties are required to comply with the substantive provisions of the Berne Convention for the protection of literary and artistic works, in its latest version (Paris 1971), though they will not be obliged to protect moral rights. It ensures that computer programs will be protected as literary works under the Berne Convention and lays down on what basis databases should be protected by copyright. Important additions to existing international rules in the area of copyright and related rights are the provisions on rental rights. The draft requires authors of computer programs and producers of sound recordings to be given the right to authorize or prohibit the commercial rental of their works to the public. A similar exclusive right applies to films where commercial rental has led to widespread copying, which is materially impairing the right of reproduction. The draft also requires performers to be given protection from unauthorized recording and broadcast of live performances (bootlegging). The protection for performers and producers of sound recordings is for no less than fifty years. Broadcasting organizations have control over the use that can be made of broadcast signals. This right lasts for at least twenty years.

With respect to geographical indications, the agreement specifies that all parties must provide means to prevent the use of any indication that misleads the consumer as to the origin of goods and any use that would constitute an act of unfair competition. A higher level of protection is provided for geographical indications for wines and spirits, which are protected even where there is no danger of the public being misled as to the true origin. Exceptions are allowed for names that have already become generic terms, but any country using such an exception must be willing to negotiate in order to protect the geographical indications in question. Furthermore, provision is made for further negotiations to establish a multilateral system of notification and registration of geographical indications for wines. Industrial designs are also protected under the agreement for a period of ten years. Owners of protected designs would be able to prevent the manufacture, sale, or importation of articles bearing or embodying a design that is a copy of the protected design.

Regarding patents, there is a general obligation

to comply with the substantive provisions of the Paris Convention (1967). In addition, the agreement requires that twenty-year patent protection be available for all inventions, whether of products or processes, in almost all fields of technology. The TRIPS Agreement also introduces additional obligations in areas not addressed in these conventions or that were thought not to be sufficiently addressed in them. The TRIPS Agreement is therefore sometimes described as a "Berne and Paris-plus" Agreement.

The text of the TRIPS Agreement also makes use of the provisions of some other international agreements on intellectual property rights. WTO members are required to protect integrated circuit layout designs in accordance with the provisions of the Treaty on Intellectual Property in Respect of Integrated Circuits together with certain additional obligations. The TRIPS Agreement refers to a number of provisions of the International Convention for the Protection of Performers, Producers of Phonograms, and Broadcasting Organizations (Rome Convention), without entailing a general requirement to comply with the substantive provisions of that convention.

Elfi Cepni

See also: Copyrights; Patents; World Trade Organization.

BIBLIOGRAPHY

"Knowledge Is Power." *Economist Survey: The New Economy*, September 21, 2000.
Parkin, Michael. *Economics*. Reading, MA: Addison Wesley, 2002.
World Trade Organization. "Standards Concerning the Availability, Scope, and Use of Intellectual Property Rights" (www.wto.org, accessed December 2004).
———. *What Are Intellectual Property Rights?* Washington, DC: World Trade Organization, September 24, 2002.

INTERNAL COMBUSTION ENGINE

A mechanical device in which he combustion of fuel in a small area produces gases that expand to generate power.

The most common types of the internal combustion engine are the reciprocating, spark-ignited, four-stroke gasoline engines (used in automobiles); jet propulsion engines; rocket engines; and gas turbine engines.

The piston-type engine used in cars has cylinders (where the combustion occurs), pistons that slide up and down inside the cylinders, connecting rods that turn the crankshaft, and a head (metal cover) where the spark plugs create the ignition. Two additional openings allow for the intake of the gasoline mixture and for the discharge of exhaust. Some vehicles use diesel engines that were invented by Rudolf Diesel in 1892. The diesel relies on the heat produced by compression for its power instead of ignition from the spark plugs. This type of engine is generally used in heavier vehicles that require large amounts of power such as trains, ships, and trucks. Both types of engines are lubricated by oil to reduce friction and overheating.

Scientists and engineers have been improving the internal combustion engine since the late seventeenth century. Dutch physicist Christiaan Huygens was the first known person to have conducted experiments with the engine in 1680. More than 150 years later, French engineer J.J. Étienne Lenoir designed a spark-ignition engine that worked on a continuous basis. In 1878, Nikolaus A. Otto built the first four-stroke engine, which was followed by the invention of the two-stroke engine by Sir Dugald Clerk that same year. But the real advances occurred with the development of the prototype of the modern engine by Gottlieb Daimler in 1885.

In the early 1880s, motorized vehicles were constructed by using small combustion engines mounted on bikes called motorcycles. Karl Benz was the first to build an automobile using an internal combustion engine, three wheels, and differential gears. His creation was first used in Mannheim, Germany, in 1885, and the following year he received a patent for it. By 1894, the Daimler Company was producing the Panhard car in France. During that same decade, automobile manufacturers like Charles Duryea and J. Frank Duryea, Elwood Haynes, Henry Ford, Ransom E. Olds, and Alexander Winton were producing basic automobiles for the American public. With so many competitors, the issuing of a patent to one individual, George Selden, complicated the situation in the United States. Ford was sued for

With its combination of power and compact size, the internal combustion engine was ideal for automobiles, the primary manufactured product of the twentieth century. Shown in this 1886 photograph is German inventor Karl Benz with the first automobile powered by an internal combustion engine. *(© National Motor Museum/Topham/The Image Works)*

violating the patent, which he refused to recognize. By 1911, the U.S. Circuit Court of Appeals ruled that the patent did not apply to four-stroke engines such as the one used by Ford. With this hurdle behind him, Ford worked on implementing the assembly line in the manufacturing process to reduce the time and cost of producing his Model T. During the 1920s, when credit was easily obtainable, average Americans purchased these new vehicles, with their internal combustion engines, in record numbers.

The internal combustion engine transformed the transportation industry and society. The automobile allowed people to travel farther away from their homes on outings and vacations. Service industries such as restaurants, motels, and gasoline stations catered to the needs of drivers and passengers. Tire stores, windshield companies, and mechanics serviced the vehicles. Trucks, also powered by the internal combustion engine, made it easier to move goods from one point to another without having to load and reload the merchandise on boxcars. The invention of the internal combustion engine helped bring about the decline of the railroad industry. Automobiles became so popular in the United States that soon other countries wanted them as well. However, high tariff barriers raised the cost of the cars to a prohibitive level. Ford was the first manufacturer to operate a plant outside the United States to circumvent these trade restrictions. The multinational corporation has since changed the way business is conducted around the world.

During World War II and the postwar period, the internal combustion engine was adapted to provide power for planes, jets, and even rockets.

From the development of these new forms of transportation, the world, and now even outer space, is becoming increasingly interconnected. People and goods can be moved from one destination to another in a matter of hours. The technology developed in the airline industry and space exploration has produced a number of consumer goods that have affected trade. Freeze-dried goods and computers are just two such items made possible by the use of transportation powered by the internal combustion engine.

During the 1960s and 1970s, individuals began speaking out about the harmful effects of manufacturing on the environment. Emissions from automobiles became a big issue during the 1980s and 1990s as California passed stricter emission standards. By the 1990s, the use of the internal combustion engine was so prevalent that to ban its use would be economically unfeasible. Instead, new devices were invented to reduce harmful emissions. Leaded gasoline was also phased out. Experimental use of alternatives to the internal combustion engine have been conducted but with little commercial success. Electric cars and hybrids that combine electric power with gasoline are also on the market, but consumers continue to favor the gasoline engine. Oil producers and their auxiliary suppliers are also resisting such a change. The impact on the world market from such a dramatic change would be tremendous.

The internal combustion engine has been romanticized throughout the decades. In 1911, the first auto race was held at Indianapolis. Since then, the Indianapolis 500 has attracted tens of thousands of fans, and an entire circuit of races is now run each year both in the United States and abroad. New improvements on the engine have resulted in the creation of the high-performance industry, with manufacturers such as Porsche and Ferrari leading the pack. While the original car ran on one cylinder, the latest engines can have up to sixteen cylinders. As speed increases and safety improves, the transition from the internal combustion engine to another form of mechanical power remains doubtful.

Cynthia Clark Northrup

See also: Automobiles.

BIBLIOGRAPHY

Ayres, Robert U., and Richard P. McKenna. *Alternatives to the Internal Combustion Engine: Impacts on Environmental Quality*. Baltimore: Published for Resources for the Future by the Johns Hopkins University Press, 1972.

Olney, Ross Robert. *The Internal Combustion Engine*. New York: Lippincott, 1982.

Urquhart, David Inglis. *The Internal Combustion Engine and How It Works*. New York: H.Z. Walck, 1973.

INTERNATIONAL MONETARY FUND

An intergovernmental organization established by treaty in December 1945 to facilitate monetary cooperation, stabilize currency exchanges, and expand international liquidity.

The International Monetary Fund (IMF) is formally a specialized agency of the United Nations and headquartered in Washington, D.C. As of December 2004, it had a global membership of 184 countries. The organization's highest authority rests with a board of governors, which meets once a year. The governors are usually member countries' finance ministers or heads of their central banks. An executive board that usually meets three times a week or more as needed administers the IMF's day-to-day operations. It consists of twenty-four executive directors. Eight of them represent five leading share-holding nations (the United States, the United Kingdom, Germany, France, and Japan), plus China, Russia, and Saudi Arabia. The remaining sixteen represent the fund's other member countries grouped by world regions.

A managing director, who is appointed for a renewable five-year term, chairs the executive board. This position traditionally goes to a European. The IMF's resources come mainly from members' quota subscriptions. These contributions are based on their wealth and economic performance measured by several agreed-on criteria and are subject to review every five years. The quotas also determine the amount members can borrow and their relative voting power. In practice, this weighted voting system permits the United States to exert a preponderant influence in the IMF's decision making.

At its inception, the IMF was designed to address the lessons learned collectively by the world's leading economic powers from economic dislocations in the preceding decades. At a United Nations conference held at Bretton Woods, New Hampshire, in July 1944, representatives of forty-five governments agreed to create a cooperative framework for avoiding a replay of the beggar-thy-neighbor economic policies many had adopted following the Great Depression. They also proposed a fund with which to maintain convertible currencies at stable exchange rates and to provide financial assistance to facilitate orderly balance-of-payments adjustments, thus obviating the need for imposing exchange controls or competitive currency devaluations or pursuing deflationary economic policies to make exports more competitive in world markets.

The IMF's activities have evolved over time to adapt to the changing realities in the international financial system. Its central mission, however, has remained the same: it seeks to maintain stable currency exchange rates, to finance members' short-term balance-of-payments deficits, and to support adjustment and reform policies targeting the internal structural problems of borrowing countries. For these purposes, the IMF also provides advice and technical assistance to the governments and central banks of borrowing countries. Recent examples of such advisory functions include the fund's work with South Korea during the 1997–1998 Asian financial crisis and its involvement in the transition of former republics of the Soviet Union to market economies following its collapse in 1991.

Between 1947 and 1971, the IMF supervised a modified gold-standard system of pegged currency exchange rates. Countries that joined the IMF during this period agreed to a value of their national currency fixed in relation to the U.S. dollar. The U.S. Treasury reciprocally agreed to buy and sell gold to other governments at the rate of $35 per ounce. These stipulated rates could be adjusted only to correct a "fundamental disequilibrium" in the balance of payments and with the IMF's concurrence. In August 1971, however, U.S. president Richard Nixon ended this arrangement unilaterally by suspending the convertibility of the U.S. dollar and, by extension, dollar reserves held by other governments into gold. Since then, each member has been free to make its own foreign exchange arrangement. For example, some members have chosen a free float; others have elected to peg their currencies to another currency or a group of currencies.

IMF members experiencing short-term balance-of-payments deficits may obtain loans in foreign currencies held by the fund by purchasing them with their own currencies. Members may borrow up to 25 percent of their quotas and must repay within a specific period with interest. They may also receive additional lending through customized programs arranged under the Extended Fund Facility. The IMF determines the amount of each loan and the macroeconomic adjustments and internal reforms it deems necessary to restore the country's balance of payments. Details of the required adjustment program are spelled out in a "letter of intent" written by the borrowing government and addressed to the IMF's managing director. The IMF typically requires borrowing governments to reduce their budget deficits; to deregulate selected aspects of the domestic economy; to remove export barriers; and, in cases rooted in structural balance-of-payments problems, to devalue their currencies.

In 1969, the IMF created a new international reserve asset called special drawing rights (SDRs, also known as "paper gold") as the first amendment to its original Articles of Agreement. Members were concerned at the time that the existing pool and future growth of its reserves, consisting of gold and currency, might not be sufficient in light of the inherent uncertainties of world gold production. Neither did they wish global reserves to depend on the continuing U.S. balance-of-payments deficits. The IMF can distribute this form of reserve asset to members as needed. It also uses SDRs as a unit of accounting. The most recent SDR allocation took place in 1981, during which SDR 21.4 billion was divided among the 141 countries then on the IMF membership roster. Countries can transfer SDRs among themselves for debt settlement. The SDRs' value is calculated daily as a weighted average of four key currencies: the U.S. dollar, the euro, the Japanese yen, and the British pound.

The IMF's lending practices have been the subject of intense debate. Critics argue that IMF loans permit member countries to pursue ill-conceived and often reckless economic policies and avoid needed internal reforms. Others contend that the IMF is all too eager to bail out powerful international bankers, many of them Americans, who have made bad loans and risky international investments. The IMF has also been charged with imposing uniform remedies and failing adequately to heed each borrower's unique needs and circumstances.

Sayuri Guthrie-Shimizu

See also: United Nations.

BIBLIOGRAPHY
De Vries, Margaret Garritsen. *The IMF in a Changing World, 1945–85.* Washington, DC: International Monetary Fund, 1986.

INTERNATIONAL TRADE COMMISSION

> An independent federal agency charged with providing data and information relative to international trade to both the legislative and executive branches of government.

The International Trade Commission (ITC) houses an extensive library of international trade resources and reference materials (the National Library of International Trade) and makes it available to the general public. A nonpartisan, quasi-judiciary body, the ITC consists of six commissioners appointed by the president of the United States and confirmed by the U.S. Senate. The commissioners serve overlapping nine-year terms. The ITC is vested with broad investigative authority and advises the president, the U.S. Trade Representative (USTR), and members of Congress as they determine the impact of imports on American domestic industries and formulate policies regarding foreign trade practices that may be considered unfair.

Public debate on national tariff rates, by its very nature, impinges on important domestic economic interests and has incited intense partisan passions throughout the nation's history. In 1916, Congress established the ITC's institutional predecessor, the U.S. Tariff Commission, in part to introduce impartial expertise and factual foundation to the innately politicized process of debating national tariff legislations. The creation of the U.S. Tariff Commission also represented an emerging faith characteristic of the Progressive Era in "scientific" management of complex public policy issues by trained experts. A controversy first arose within the federal government over the establishment of an independent tariff board in the early years of the administration of William Howard Taft. The Republican president proposed the appointment of a panel of experts to advise him on the modification of the nation's tariff schedules. His low-tariff Democratic opponents in Congress, most notably Oscar Underwood of Alabama, initially viewed Taft's proposal as a backhanded attempt to delay proposed tariff reductions. Three years after the enactment of the Underwood Tariff of 1913, which represented the first substantial tariff reductions since the mid-nineteenth century, Congress established the U.S. Tariff Commission to gather and analyze information on trade matters in a factual, nonpartisan fashion. To ensure impartial deliberation, Congress built multiple safeguards into the commission's structure. For instance, no more than three of the six commissioners could be of the same political party, and the commission's chairman and vice chairman, designated by the president from among the current commissioners for two-year terms, had to come from different parties. The chairman could not be from the same political party as his or her immediate predecessor.

The U.S. Tariff Commission enhanced its prominence in the nation's trade policy-making process after World War II, when Congress transferred jurisdiction over the Reciprocal Trade Agreement program's escape clause and peril-point investigations from an executive interagency panel to the commission. In the Trade Act of 1974, Congress renamed the U.S. Tariff Commission the U.S. International Trade Commission. This name change reflected the broader range of issues beyond import duties that came to be considered relevant to foreign trade, such as intellectual property rights. In its original enabling legislation, the ITC was empowered only to advise the president and Congress by providing data and information

Steelworkers in Merrillville, Indiana, in 2001 attempt to sway members of the International Trade Commission, a federal agency that advises the president on trade issues, to impose tariffs on imported steel and thus save U.S. jobs.
(© Scott Olson/WirePix/The Image Works)

on which U.S. trade policy was to be based. As such, it is a fact-finding agency and not a policy-making body in its own right. Nor does it negotiate trade agreements on behalf of the U.S. government, as is the case with the USTR. Recent legislation, such as the Trade and Competitiveness Act of 1988, however, has expanded the purview of the ITC's advisory authority to include quasi-enforcement functions. It is now authorized not only to investigate the effects of imports on competing domestic industry, but also to direct imports to be excluded should it find that foreign producers are engaging in unfair trade practices or violating patent or copyright laws.

The ITC's current formal mission is threefold. First, the ITC administers U.S. trade remedy laws within its mandate in a fair and objective manner. Second, it provides the president of the United States, the USTR, and Congress with independent analysis, information, and support on matters of tariffs and international trade and competitiveness.

Finally, it maintains the Harmonized Tariff Schedule of the United States. To fulfill these institutional mandates, the ITC engages in the following categories of specific activities in concert with other federal agencies involved in trade policy:

1. It conducts investigations to determine whether domestic industries suffer material injury by reason of imports priced at less than fair value or from foreign government subsidization. In such countervailing duty and antidumping investigations, the ITC shares responsibility with the U.S. Department of Commerce. It is the department's task first to determine whether the alleged subsidies or dumping are actually taking place. Then, the ITC's responsibility is to determine whether the affected U.S. industry is materially injured by reason of the dumped or subsidized imports. If the department's subsidy or dumping determination and the ITC's injury determination are both in the affirmative, the Commerce Department, as a federal executive

agency, issues an order to the U.S. Customs Service to impose additional duties.

2. The ITC may direct actions, subject to presidential approval, against unfair practices in import trade, such as patent, trademark, or copyright infringement. If the ITC determines that a violation of the law exists, it may order the exclusion of the imported product from the United States.

3. The ITC makes nonbinding recommendations to the president regarding relief for industries seriously injured by imports for the purpose of facilitating adjustment to foreign competition. Relief may take the form of tariff increases, import quotas, or temporary adjustment assistance for the affected domestic industry.

4. The ITC advises the president whether agricultural imports are interfering with domestic price-support programs administered by the U.S. Department of Agriculture.

5. The ITC undertakes studies and conducts public hearings on trade and tariff issues and monitors import levels. It furnishes the results of such investigations to the president, the Senate Committee on Finance, or the House Committee on Ways and Means.

6. The ITC participates in the development of uniform statistical data on imports, exports, and domestic production and in the establishment and modification of the International Harmonized Commodity Code, which is a list of all the items that are imported into and exported from the United States.

Sayuri Guthrie-Shimizu

See also: Tariff Barriers.

BIBLIOGRAPHY

Dobson, John M. *Two Centuries of Tariffs: The Background and Emergence of the U.S. International Trade Commission.* Washington, DC: U.S. Government Printing Office, 1976.

INTERNET

A computer network that connects military, government, educational institutions, companies, and individuals around the world.

In 1969, the U.S. Department of Defense began exploring the feasibility of creating a computer network system that could survive an attack. The plan was to link three computers in California with one in Utah and then additional links were established using the Internet Protocol (IP). The existence of ARPAnet was revealed to the American public in 1972, and by that time more than fifty universities and other research companies with defense contracts had become part of the system. In 1973, ARPAnet was linked to computers in England and Norway. The National Science Foundation's NSFnet, which used the Transmission Control Protocol (TCP), eventually replaced ARPAnet as the primary network of the Internet. By 1995, the personal computer industry had boomed and the NSFnet was turned over to the private sector. Within the next several years, millions of Americans gained access to the information through the World Wide Web, via a graphical interface browser such as Netscape, popular in the 1990s, and Explorer.

Companies wishing to set up a Web site, where customers can shop and find answers to questions, among other services, have to obtain an IP address, which consists of a series of numbers. That address is linked to a domain name, usually the name of the company followed by .com (for commercial), so users of the Web do not need to remember the IP address to access the site.

Another way to find Web sites is through a search engine, which direct an Internet user to Web sites that contain keywords selected by the user. By the early 2000s, the nearly unchallenged leader in search engines was Google. Like its competitors, such as Yahoo, Google makes its money by including advertising and paid links.

The Internet is used for a variety of purposes, of which one of the most popular is electronic mail (e-mail). Messages and files of various types, usually sent as attachments, can be sent from one user to another instantly. Newsgroups and bulletin boards offer the opportunity for individuals to discuss issues with other like-minded people. Chat groups allow online conversations. Researchers can access information from many computers linked to the Internet through the use of search engines. More important to trade is the development of sectors such as electronic business (e-business, or business-to-business) and electronic commerce (e-commerce, or business-to-consumer).

E-commerce sales have risen at a steady pace. In 1999, e-commerce sales accounted for only 0.6 percent of all retail sales in the United States. Ac-

As an engine of the so-called new economy of the late twentieth and early twenty-first centuries, the Internet has revolutionized trade, allowing businesses and consumers to seek out the best prices around the world. The global spread of the Internet is demonstrated in this 2004 photo of Kenyans surfing the Web at an Internet café in Nairobi. *(© Chet Gordon/The Image Works)*

cording to a bulletin from the U.S. Department of Commerce dated February 23, 2004, that proportion increased to 1.6 percent in 2003, which translated to $54.9 billion. E-commerce transactions have spiked each year during the third and fourth quarters. For the fourth quarter of 2003, e-commerce totaled $17.9 billion. Worldwide e-commerce reached $3.5 trillion in 2003.

Another form of e-commerce is stock trading. Stock trading in 1998 accounted for 20 percent of all stock transactions. By May 1999, Internet stock trading reached $2.7 million. According to J.D. Power and Associates, that figure rose to $3.5 million in January 2000. Stock trading, especially day trading, has remained popular among Internet users. Ordinary individuals can research the companies in which they invest and can more easily manage their portfolios with the help of stock trading software. The stock market has also responded to the changes brought about by the Internet. Over-the-counter stocks traded on the NASDAQ exchange are predominately dot.com and information technology (IT) stocks. The Internet has also allowed twenty-four-hour trading and enabled investors around the world to engage in trading on a particular stock exchange with few inconveniences.

Along with e-commerce, the Internet has allowed the development of e-business. Companies use the Internet for daily business transactions such as purchasing, notifying vendors, tracking shipments, and communicating with business associates through videoconferencing or e-mail. The Internet has allowed firms to communicate quickly and efficiently. Orders can be processed the same day that they are received. The communication revolution created by the Internet has revolutionized the way companies conduct business.

Online auction and wholesale servers are another aspect of the Internet that directly affects trade. EBay, one of the largest online auction companies in the world, announced 225 million sales, totaling $509.3 million for the second quarter of 2003. In recent years, the company has also offered fixed-price purchases and, in 2003, that business accounted for 27 percent of the sales. Net revenues for the firm amounted to $2.2 billion in 2003, compared with $1.2 billion in 2002. Other large competitors are Amazon.com, which reported $5.26 billion in revenue for 2003. Internet companies such as Yahoo have also realized high revenues. Yahoo's revenues amounted to $1.2 billion in 2002 and rose to $2.2 billion in 2003, primarily because of a more aggressive policy of advertising on Yahoo sites. Meanwhile Internet service providers that have developed into giants within the industry include American Online (AOL) and Earthlink. In addition to providing e-mail services to customers, these firms also promote their high-speed connections and other services, including pop-up blockers, which help the companies maintain their dominant position in the industry.

Internet advertising developed early with the use of pop-up or pop-under ads that appear while the user is searching the Web. Users have complained that this invasive use of the Internet to promote products and services is frustrating and annoying. Civil lawsuits brought against companies that provide the pop-up ads have led to legal decisions against this form of advertising. In the summer of 2003, pop-up ads accounted for just over 8 percent of all online sales, but by the end of that year the sales figures had dropped to 6 percent and have continued to decline since then. Advertisers realize the enormous marketing potential of the Internet and have adapted their strategy in an effort to attract Internet sales. New types of advertising include media-rich ads, which have both audio and video streaming, have begun to appear in fifteen- to thirty-second spots between Web searches. Earthlink and AOL have already offered their customers the option to block this type of advertising. However, many users will continue to see pop-up and media-rich ads for the next several years. Banner ads, which appear at the top of the screen, are less intrusive than pop-up ads but generate less revenue. Nevertheless, the banner ads help offset the cost of maintaining Web sites and will continue to exist for that reason.

The Internet has helped a wide array of companies reach new markets. By the beginning of the twenty-first century, most retail, and even service-oriented, companies had developed Web sites to attract new business. A Web site allows customers from around the world to examine goods and services and then decide whether or not to purchase from that particular company. Online suppliers of electronic and software products compete for customers on the basis of pricing, while others, such as jewelers, compete on the basis of quality.

Another industry that has taken advantage of the Internet's reach is the gaming industry, which comprises both online interactive games, where two or more players compete, and online casinos that offer gambling anywhere in the world. Software providers sell programs for players to compete and large corporations sponsor the Internet sites in exchange for advertising exposure. Many Native American nations within the borders of the United States run casino and online gambling Web sites. Ultimately, however, the most lucrative area of commerce on the Web is pornography, with thousands of sites pandering to every prurient interest. In 2003, it was estimated that pornography sites generated $57 billion in revenue worldwide, $12 billion of which came from the United States.

The Internet has, since its inception, allowed for the free flow of information among people, although some countries, most notably China, have tried to block access to politically controversial sites. In addition, trade has received a boost as companies around the world can offer their products and services to a larger market at a relatively low cost. New companies that provide services for Internet providers bring jobs to the local economies as well. The primary key issue for governments is taxation on Internet sales.

Cynthia Clark Northrup

See also: Financial Institutions; United States.

BIBLIOGRAPHY:

Buckley, Ciaran. "EBay Revenues Soar." ElectronicNewsNet, January 22, 2004 (www.enn.ie/news.html?code=9388141/, accessed March 2004).

Cassavoy, Liane. "Bye-Bye, Pop-ups. Hello . . . ? Use of Pop-ups Wanes, but Worse Intrusions May Be Coming." *PC World* (April 2004) (www.pcworld.com/news/article/0,aid,115026,00.asp, accessed March 2004).

Konrad, Rachel. "EBay Revenues, Profits Hit Record." DeseretNews.com, July 25, 2003 (http://deseretnews.com/dn/view/0,1249,510042251,00.html, accessed March 2004).

"Retail E-Commerce Sales in Fourth Quarter 2003 Were 17.2 Billion, up 25.1 Percent from Fourth Quarter 2002, Census Bureau Reports." U.S. Department of Commerce (February 23, 2004) (www.census.gov/mrts/www/current.html, accessed March 2004).

IRON

> An element first discovered over 6,000 years ago in meteorites; was referred to as the "metal of heaven."

The three oldest pieces of iron discovered so far made up a sickle blade found near Thebes in Karnak under the base of a sphinx, a 5,000-year-old blade found in one of the Egyptian pyramids, and a crosscut saw made around 920 B.C.E. found in Iraq at Nimrud.

Pure iron is white, shiny, and soft. Because the pieces of iron were mixed with nickel they were harder. People eventually discovered that they could fashion iron by using a hot fire in a process called smelting. The Chinese began using iron around 600 B.C.E. and have been using the smelting process since then.

FIRST USES

The first people to employ iron weapons were the Hittites, who were from the southern part of modern-day Turkey. With their iron weapons, they were the dominant force in Mesopotamia from about 1400 to 1200 B.C.E. They copied Babylonian ideas, though their laws were less stringent than those of the Babylonians. In the eighth century B.C.E., the Assyrians absorbed the Hittite empire, which gave them access to west Asian trade routes. The iron ore that had belonged to the Hittites now belonged to Assyrians. The Sea Peoples, invaders from the eastern Mediterranean, furthered the spread of iron weapons. Bronze had been available only to the upper class, whereas iron was common and could be obtained by anyone.

In 487 B.C.E., the Chinese began their maritime trade by exporting iron and iron tools to Southeast Asia and the Pacific islands. During the thirteenth century, the Catalan forge was invented in Spain. A major technological advancement since classical times, this forge could produce 350 pounds of metal in five hours. During the Middle Ages, European ironworks got a boost with the invention of the wolf furnace, or Stuckofen, which produced iron in Belgium, Germany, Austria, and Bohemia. The Stuckofen produced cast iron or pig iron, but not wrought iron. Cast and pig iron can be formed only by casting and machining; wrought iron is a low-carbon metal that is formed by heating and beating steel and is used for decorative purposes.

The first practical blast furnace was made in Belgium in 1340, but was not introduced to major European cities for some time. By the sixteenth century, England in particular possessed many blast furnaces, but the iron industry declined from a shortage of fuel. Charcoal derived from wood was needed to produce iron. However, this put the supply of timber at risk, and so its use was restricted and there were few alternatives. This problem was alleviated in 1709 when Abraham Darby invented coke smelting, which created high temperatures exceeding those possible with previous fuels, a huge step in the smelting and refining of iron. The 1500s saw the beginning of mineralogy and economic geology. Georgius Agricola, inspired by the mining in Saxony, Germany, wrote many books on the subject, and his explanations are the basis for modern theories about iron formation.

England turned to its American colonies for timber to be used in iron production. At this time, iron production had already started in America, though its progress had been slow. In 1622, Native Americans attacked an ironworks plant in Virginia, stopping an early attempt at establishing a facility. Among the southern colonies, Virginia as well as Maryland had ironworks. In 1714, Peter Hill came over from Germany with ten other men and their families and formed the Germana colony near Fredericksburg, Virginia. These colonists were ironworkers from Germany. George Washington's father, Augustine Washington, owned valuable ore deposits near the Rappahannock River in Virginia. He partnered with English merchants to form Principio ironworks. These ironworking groups produced guns and ammunition for the colonies during the Revolutionary War and iron for the British.

INDUSTRIAL REVOLUTION

During the Industrial Revolution, iron became a chief raw material for heavy industry. This was brought about by several inventions, notably

Shown here is the Republic Iron Mine, in upper Michigan, with a miner ascending the slope, around 1880. During the Industrial Revolution, iron became a chief raw material for heavy industry. (© North Wind Picture Archives)

James Watt's steam engine, which pumped water out of the mines, and James Nasmyth's steam hammer used for forging large iron objects. Because of these developments, transportation improved. Railroads were made possible by the improvement of iron rails. Major developments using iron took place in Europe, especially Germany. The first blast furnace in Germany was in Upper Silesia at Malapane during the reign of Frederick the Great in 1753. From 1780 to 1820, the state raised the industrial capacity by creating a bureaucracy with the Prussian industrial and mining agency. Count Fryderyk von Reden, financial adviser to Frederick the Great, helped to search Europe for industrial techniques and technologists. Because of this, the iron-puddling process was commissioned in Silesia just slightly after Britain developed it. Another major event was the French defeat by the Prussians in 1871, which cost France the province of Alsace and Lorraine, where 80 percent of the country's known iron ore reserves were located.

Tariffs were introduced in 1879 in Germany, which was the start of industrial growth that would make Germany an industrial powerhouse. Germany quickly surpassed both France and Great Britain in the production of iron. The total length of German railways tripled between 1870 and 1914. With its rich natural resources such as iron ore, Germany had an advantage. German industrialists studied the methods of other industrialized countries and learned from them.

In 1906, Sweden signed a trade agreement with Germany that gave favorable terms for Swedish woodworking industries in exchange for freer export of high-grade Lapland iron ore. In 1911, the German government indicated to France that it would not stop further inroads into Morocco unless German iron interests in West Morocco were left alone and parts of the French Congo were transferred to Germany; France complied. In 1936, Hermann Göring requested the industrialists to expand iron ore production by about 10 million tons. With this addition, Germany would have produced about half the iron ore it needed, but the industrialists declined.

Looking at the past, a key element of solving European political and social problems would be the institutionalization of Franco-German cooperation. In one view, the wars of the European past—1870–1871, 1914–1918, and 1939–1945—were struggles for integration and dominance of Europe's iron ore resources or attempts to bring together the iron ore of Alsace and Lorraine and the coalfields of the Ruhr.

Carolyn Falk

See also: Industrial Revolution; Weapons.

BIBLIOGRAPHY

Blanning, T.C.W. *The Oxford Illustrated History of Modern Europe.* New York: Oxford University Press, 1996.

Braudel, Fernand. *Memory and the Mediterranean.* New York: Knopf, 2001.

Fitzgerald, Karen. *The Story of Iron.* New York: Franklin Watts, 1997.

Grant, Neil. *Oxford Children's History of the World.* New York: Oxford University Press, 2000.

Holborn, Hajo. *A History of Modern Germany, 1840–1945.* Princeton: Princeton University Press, 1969.

IRON LAW OF WAGES

> Ricardo's Iron Law of Wages, formulated in the early nineteenth century, appealed to British capitalists who wanted to maximize profits.

In the early nineteenth century, David Ricardo wrote that it is futile to attempt to improve wages, because when wages rise beyond the subsistence level, they cause higher birthrates and a larger population of workers. The greater workforce creates a buyer's market in which too many workers vie for too few jobs. This surplus of workers forces wages to fall back to the subsistence level. Ricardo's ideas appealed to British capitalists, who wanted to maximize profit and minimize costs.

Adam Smith's *Wealth of Nations* (1776) defined the concept of laissez-faire. Thomas Robert Malthus's *Principles of Population* (1798) forecast a world population boom and catastrophe. Ricardo added the Iron Law, which helped to justify industrialists' and the British government's disinclination to listen to demands for reform of the dismal working conditions of the early Industrial Revolution, and the Poor Laws, which brought some small relief early in the nineteenth century. They combined to refute the protectionist theories that had dominated the mercantile era, replacing them with hands-off, or laissez-faire, government.

Ricardo was the son of a wealthy Dutch Jew. He entered the family stock brokerage at age fourteen and by age twenty-one had become a Unitarian and married a Quaker. Within a few years, he had made his fortune. He read Smith's *Wealth of Nations* in 1799 but did not write on his own until 1810, producing a work tying the volume of bank notes to the level of prices and, subsequently, to foreign exchange rates and the flow of gold. This work led to the repeal of British controls on gold flows.

Ricardo's associates included James Mill, the father of John Stuart Mill, Jeremy Bentham the utilitarian, and Malthus. In 1815, Ricardo published his *Essay on the Influence of a Low Price of Corn on the Profits of Stock*. He argued that grain tariffs, the Corn Laws, benefited the country gentry, while decreasing investment capital available to the rising industrial class and forcing workers' expenses—and wages—higher. He continued to develop as an economist and in 1817 published his major work, *The Principles of Political Economy and Taxation*, which contains the Iron Law. Ricardo also established the labor theory of value (cost equals labor used in creating a product) and defined the concept of comparative advantage, which explained how countries could find trade with each other mutually advantageous if trade was free, even if one could produce the goods traded more cheaply than could its partner. This theory remains a foundation of modern economics. Ricardo was less insightful than Smith, but his deductive and scientific method defined the model for economics.

The early nineteenth century saw the birth of modern economics. Malthus assumed that the human population would grow geometrically, while its food sources would grow arithmetically, leading to inevitable overpopulation and helping the field of economics to gain the epithet "the dismal science." Ricardo built on Malthus's pessimism by pointing to the inevitable fall of wages to the subsistence level. Ricardo influenced John Stuart Mill, who explored both international trade and industrial expansion. And he influenced critics of free trade such as Friedrich List of Germany and Henry C. Carey of the United States.

A variation of Ricardo's Iron Law is attributed to the German Ferdinand Lassalle, who stated that capitalism by definition barred the rise of wages. Karl Marx has been linked to this view, but his *Critique of the Gotha Programme* (1875) declared that the view was obsolete, false, and irrelevant. Marx was more concerned with exploitation, which inevitably would grow more severe regardless of whether wages rose or fell.

At the beginning of the twenty-first century, Ricardo's Iron Law of Wages reemerged as a rationale for what was increasingly a system in which global corporations accrued massive profits at the expense of social safety nets and wages. According to this argument, wages never stabilized at Ricardo's minimum subsistence level because industrializing societies stabilized population growth, defying Malthusian mathematics, and workers unionized and established political parties to protect their interests against capitalism's tendency to force wages down. These conditions changed once globalization, which emphasized free trade and unrestrained circulation of capital, created unrestrained competition among the world's workers, driving wages down to Ricardo's levels. At the same time, the safety net weakened, as did labor organizations.

John Barnhill

See also: Industrial Revolution; Marx, Karl; Ricardo, David; Smith, Adam.

BIBLIOGRAPHY
Bloy, Marjie. "The Peel Web" (http://dspace.dial.pipex.com/town/terrace/adw03/peel/peelhome.htm, accessed August 2003).
Hollander, Samuel. *The Economics of David Ricardo.* Toronto: University of Toronto Press, 1979.
"Malthus, Ricardo, and Mill" (www.infoplease.com/ce6/bus/A0857883.html, accessed September 2002).
Royal Danish Ministry of Foreign Affairs. "A Modern Version of the Iron Law of Wages" (www.um.dk/udenrigspolitik/copenhagenseminars/summary97/sum_4_2.asp, accessed September 2002).

IRRIGATION

The process of bringing water to dry areas primarily for the purpose of growing crops.

Ancient civilizations developed along rivers such as the Tigris, Euphrates, and Nile. While the population levels remained relatively low, the land close to the river yielded enough food, but as the population increased, people were forced to move away from the rivers onto the plains. They needed a source of water to grow their crops, and in ancient times this required the digging of canals that channeled water from the rivers to the fields. This form of agricultural development first appeared around 4,000 B.C.E. The civilizations that used irrigation techniques flourished as food was plentiful and merchants from other regions traded with the local inhabitants. From 4000 to 2000 B.C.E., the Mesopotamian region blossomed, cities expanded to population levels reaching 60,000 people, and farmers worked the countryside. Even with changes in rulers, the region remained prosperous. Over time, the irrigation systems became more sophisticated, especially after the advent of writing under the reign of Ur III. Then around 2000 B.C.E., the irrigation system declined from lack of maintenance. Without adequate food supplies, civilization and trade also declined until the neo-Babylonian era, when irrigation improved once again. Although many cultures dominated the region for the next thousand years, agriculture continued to yield enough for the population to grow until the Mongol invasions.

Around 1220 B.C.E., the Persians revolted against Mongol rule and Genghis Khan retaliated by burning villages, selling prisoners off as slaves to distant lands, and, most importantly, destroying the qanat (underground) irrigation system that had sustained continuous settlement in the region for thousands of years and replacing a prosperous region with isolated oases surrounded by barren land.

The ancient Egyptians could never have developed into such a powerful civilization with-

The ancient practice of irrigation has vastly expanded humanity's ability to raise crops for both consumption and trade. Shown here is an early twentieth-century irrigation canal on a Jamaican sugar plantation. *(Library of Congress)*

out the use of irrigation. Canals dug from the Nile increased the amount of land placed under cultivation. As food production increased, the Egyptians could afford to feed an army, export food items for needed materials such as wood, gold, and spices, and exert their influence over much of the Middle East. Egypt became known as the grain house of the ancient world.

In China, despite years of warfare and internal division from 1122 to 256 B.C.E., the rulers continued to expand the irrigation systems. A subsequent population boom allowed the Chinese to populate regions farther south and expand their control over a larger area. At the same time that the irrigation systems were developed, the Chinese began using the buffalo-drawn plow, minted coins, and started the silk industry. The large urban populations were supported by the increased agricultural yields produced by the irrigation of outlying fields.

Although the ancient and medieval worlds relied on irrigation on a limited basis, during the twentieth century the use of wide-scale irrigation projects placed millions of acres of semiarid and desert land under cultivation. The first country to initiate such a policy was the United States. With millions of acres of unsettled land in the West, the government enticed settlers to endure the hardships of frontier life by offering free land.

Under the Homestead Act of 1862, American citizens could claim 160 acres for free if they lived on the land for five years. Eventually, during the 1870s Americans moved slowly westward after the virtual annihilation of the buffalo, the invention of barbed wire, and the use of dry farming. Past the 100th meridian, the land became progressively drier and less desirable. The U.S. government passed the Timber and Stone Act and the Desert Act to encourage settlers into regions with minimal annual rainfall. Estimates in the 1990s indicated that of the water used in irrigation, 63 percent was surface water and 37 percent was underground water pumped by wells. Out of all the water used, only 53 percent was used for consumptive purposes with the rest becoming return flow or lost to evaporation.

The continued use of irrigation has allowed the United States to become the world's largest producer of agricultural products. Other countries have recognized the benefit of irrigating fields and have implemented their own projects. In 2000, the United States was the largest producer of wheat and corn in the world, in part because of the irrigation systems used throughout the Midwest. The United States has become the breadbasket of the world.

Cynthia Clark Northrup

See also: Agriculture; Egypt, Ancient; United States.

BIBLIOGRAPHY

Hurt, R. Douglas. *Agricultural Technology in the Twentieth Century.* Manhattan, KS: Sunflower University Press, 1991.

Snell, Daniel C. *Life in the Ancient Near East: 3100–332 B.C.E.* New Haven: Yale University Press, 1997.

Starr, Chester G. *A History of the Ancient World.* New York: Oxford University Press, 1991.

ISABELLA OF CASTILE (1451-1504)

> The Spanish queen who sponsored Christopher Columbus's voyages that resulted in the discovery of the New World.

Married to Ferdinand of Aragon, her cousin, at the age of seventeen, Isabella became queen of Castile in 1474, following the death of her older brother. She immediately went to work strengthening the Crown's hold over Spain and launching Castile on a quest for domination of trade routes in the western Mediterranean and the Atlantic Ocean. From the beginning of her reign, Isabella insisted on royal control of all Spanish trade overseas. She held a monopoly on certain products and demanded one-fifth of the profits from other items. She improved Spain's navy and completed the conquest of the Canary Islands. She also declared that all native peoples conquered by Spain must be treated as her royal subjects.

To unite the country under her rule, Isabella fought a series of wars against the Portuguese, the Spanish nobility, and the Moors of Granada. Victorious on all fronts, she believed that her triumphs would secure royal control of Spain and help throw back the rising tide of the Ottoman Turks, who in her lifetime had taken Constantinople, swept north

Christopher Columbus kneels in front of Queen Isabella I. The queen sponsored Columbus's voyages to the Americas, opening up the continents to European conquest and trade. *(Library of Congress)*

through the Balkans, and now threatened Italy. As part of her efforts to unite Spain under the Crown, she introduced the Inquisition to her country to weed out false converts, or *conversos,* to the Catholic faith from Islam and Judaism. After Granada, the last Moorish stronghold in Spain, fell to her armies in 1492, she ordered all Jews expelled from the country.

Following the conquest of Granada, Isabella set her sights on wresting control of trade with the Far East from the Portuguese. She was intrigued by Columbus's plan to take Spanish ships west across the Atlantic when he first proposed it to her in 1485. Seven years later, she again invited the Genoese sailor to make his case before her court. When most of her advisors argued that the trip was unnecessary since Portugal no longer posed a threat to Spain, she turned Columbus down. However, she changed her mind at the urging of the royal treasurer, Luis de Santangel, who argued that she would live to regret her refusal to support Columbus. Vowing to sell her jewels to pay for the trip, she met with Columbus again and granted his request for three ships to sail west to the Indies in April 1492.

When Columbus returned to Spain in early 1493, Isabella moved quickly to outfit another expedition. She sent him back to the Indies in September with orders to establish a colony, search for gold, and convert the natives. Although she funded two more expeditions for Columbus in 1498 and 1502, she took ever more control of the enterprise. She appointed officials to govern the colonies and established a royal monopoly on trade. In 1503, one year before her death, she put her final stamp on Spain's overseas empire by founding the Board of Trade, which would govern her nation's many colonies in the New World for the next 300 years.

Mary Stockwell

See also: Spanish Empire.

BIBLIOGRAPHY
Liss, Peggy K. *Isabel the Queen: Life and Times.* New York: Oxford University Press, 1992.

ISLAM

> Islam, a monotheistic religion with the world's second-highest number of adherents (more than 1.3 billion, or 20 percent of the world population), was founded by a merchant.

The exact year in which Islam was founded is not clear: it varies from 570 (the presumed birth of Muhammad) to 622 (the first Hijra, when Muhammad and his followers immigrated to Medina from Mecca and from which the Muslims start counting) to 632 (the presumed death of Muhammad).

Muslims call the period before the rise of Islam as one of "ignorance" (*Jaheliya*). The prophet (or messenger, *Rasul*) Muhammad and his wife, Khadija, were both merchants traveling across the Arabian Peninsula and the Fertile Crescent. During one of his travels, Muhammad met a monk who introduced him to monotheism.

Islam originated as a religion of traders. The first followers of Islam were Arab merchants who lived in the holy city of Mecca, along with the other tribes in the Arabian Peninsula.

Soon after Muhammad's death, the Muslim empire emerged as the "Old World's" largest power. Until the thirteenth century, no army could stop the Muslim army in its conquest of new territories and the conversion of their inhabitants to Islam. When a Muslim army conquered an area, the Jews and Christians were allowed to retain their religion (although they remained second-class citizens in Muslim society). Followers of nonmonotheistic faiths had the choice of either converting to Islam, leaving the area under Muslim control, or being killed. Most converted to Islam.

TRADE IN THE MUSLIM EMPIRE

From the seventh to the ninth centuries, Muslims maintained flourishing trade centers. As the empire expanded, so did its trade routes. By the end of the eighth century, Islam ruled areas from the English Channel to India. The fact that the Muslim empire spread well into central Asia gave Muslim merchants control over the spice trade and other trade routes from Europe to Asia.

One of the ways in which Islam was spread to the far corners of the world was through traders who traveled to faraway destinations, farther than any Muslim army could reach at that time. The merchants not only carried goods, but also brought the new religion with them. They proselytized in a peaceful fashion. Thus merchants, rather than soldiers, mainly responsible for the spread of Islam throughout the world.

The Qur'an, the Muslim holy book, is written in Arabic. This common language helped to unite many different ethnic groups under the Muslim empire. It also made possible the easy exchange of knowledge and ideas and the development of an impressive trading economy.

The strength of Muslim rule ushered in a period of peace and stability that enabled increased production. The development of large-scale trade was facilitated by the widespread naval and land routes, which were relatively safe, peace and political stability, and the geographic reach of the empire, which controlled the entire area between the Far East, North Africa (the first black African people to convert to Islam did so before 1050 B.C.E. in the region known today as Senegal), the Mediterranean, and parts of Europe.

The largest part of trade was exporting goods to faraway countries and importing goods from those same countries. The connection to Southeast Asia and the Far East—India, Ceylon (Sri Lanka), the Indian islands (Minicoy, Cannanore, Laccadive, and Amindivi), and China—was conducted in naval routes, from the ports of the Persian (Arabian) Gulf and the ancient routes by way of Afghanistan (Khyber Pass) and Central Asia. The merchants brought with them silk, spices, perfume, wood, porcelain, silver, gold, and jewelry.

As Islam continued fortifying itself and steps were being taken to convert more followers, Muslims became more and more involved in trading. For the Muslim merchants, spices became a key product of the trade industry. Spices were an easy product to trade because they were not bulky, perishable, or breakable and thus could be easily carried over long distances. For these reasons, the actual process of trading probably began with such items. Spices continued to be popular as people, early on, began relying on them to preserve food, improve their health, add taste to food, enhance their personal appearance and hygiene, and perfume their houses.

Furthermore, the characteristically Muslim impact on the spice trade was revolutionary. Before the Muslim conquest, trading had been indirect and was accomplished by local merchants who traded exclusively in their local areas. They were involved in a trade relay of sorts in which the spices were transported from one carrier to another, without any single group making the entire journey itself. When Muslim forces gained control over the trade, however, one of their first innovations was to make this trade direct, wherein Muslims would personally travel the entire length of the trade routes, without relying on intermediaries. This markedly influenced their ability to spread the word of God and Muhammad.

During this period, Muslim merchants reached Russia and took with them goods that originated from as far away as the Scandinavian countries. The merchants reached deep into Africa (before European explorers did so), and from there they brought mainly slaves and gold. The merchants also exported goods from the Muslim empire itself.

The development of vast trading networks, new methods of doing business, and the increased movement of peoples and goods increased the power of the Muslim empire (under the rule of the Abbasid and Umayyad dynasties). Jews were major contributors to the trade throughout the Muslim world and enjoyed, relatively speaking, wide freedom of belief and profession. They were able to establish contacts with people in Europe, especially other Jews, since they had a common language, base of laws, family connections, and mutual trust. This era was a golden age in both Jewish and Muslim history.

THE RISE OF THE OTTOMANS AND TRADE IN THE EMPIRE

The good trade conditions survived the collapse of the Abbasid and Umayyad empires. Muslims continued to conbine trade and religion, finding new methods of trade and converting more people to Islam. One of the tribes that converted to Islam after meeting Muslim merchants was that of the Turks. In the tenth century, the tribes of Oguz accepted Islam. Those tribes joined the Muslim armies and as time passed gained more and more power.

By the sixteenth century, the Ottoman (or as pronounced in Turkish—Ossman) empire was a recognizable force in the Muslim world. In less than 100 years, the Ottoman empire gained control over all Arab lands, forming the largest Muslim empire of the time. The economic view of the Ottoman Empire can be called "Passive Despotism Economy." The central government had limited involvement in the market economy and focused primarily on collecting taxes.

The Ottoman empire was a land empire (rather than a naval empire such as Great Britain), and when the European Christian rivals of the Ottomans founded naval routes to the New World and India, the importance of the Ottoman Empire declined. The empire ceased expanding and therefore lacked new resources, a factor that resulted in high inflation within the Ottoman empire.

The spread of trade in the Ottoman empire brought with it developments in banking that allowed the cashing of checks across state borders. Banking was managed by non-Muslims, since Islam forbids the charging of interest.

The Ottomans maintained good relations, which included trade relations, with the European powers and the capital of the empire, Istanbul, was set half in Europe and half in Asia, and the Ottoman empire looked in both directions. Trade brought many goods from Europe to the Muslim world as well as the reverse (the most famous of these goods is probably coffee, which was introduced to the Europeans by the Turks). Nevertheless, the main basis of the economy changed from trade to that of agriculture and industry.

The Muslim world, however, was introduced to the Industrial Revolution only after it had already taken place in Europe, and the Muslim world was not industrialized for a long period—there are still some areas in the Muslim world that are not industrialized. The fall of the Ottoman empire at the end of World War I brought with it the end of the last of the large Muslim empires. In the period between the two world wars, most

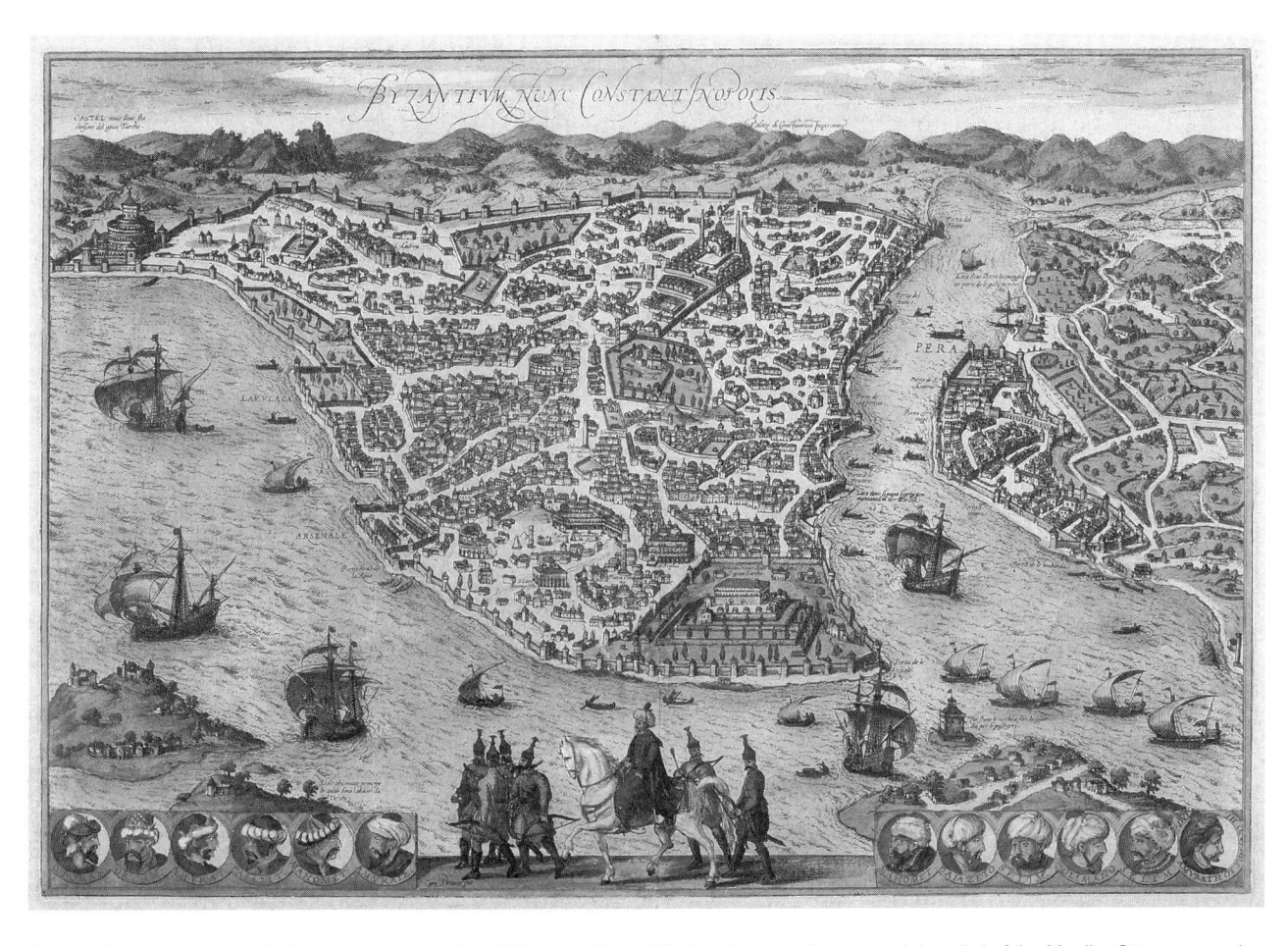

Constantinople (later Istanbul), pictured here in the 1570s, was the political, cultural, and commercial capital of the Muslim Ottoman empire. Located at the crossroads between Europe and Asia, it was for centuries a thriving center of East-West trade.

of the Islamic world, from Africa (including North Africa and sub-Saharan Africa) through Palestine and to Indonesia were under some kind of colonial control by foreign Christians.

After World War II ended, many colonial states achieved independence, among them former members of the Muslim empire. Independence often replaced religion with secular politics in the 1950s, which loosened the common bond that had facilitated trade relations among Muslim countries. There was no single economic system throughout the Muslim world. All known economic theories were practiced in the Muslim world, from capitalism, to communism, to all kinds of socialist arrangements. At first, traditional rulers (with religious justifications) gained power, but soon afterward a wave of socialism swept the Muslim world (especially in the Arab countries). This movement tried to combine Muslim traditions, Arab traditions, socialism, and modernization (not to say Westernization), yet failed in the end to grapple with the challenges of the day.

ISLAMIC NORMS AND REGULATIONS ON TRADE

Inspired by Max Weber thesis, which deals with the contribution of the Protestant ethos to the development of capitalism in Western civilization's famous researchers on Muslim society have tried to establish a thesis that will connect the basic laws of Islam with economic activity.

One of these theses establishes a strong connection between predestiny (*Qadder*) and the volume of economic activity in the Muslim world. According to this thesis, God (Allah) determines the future of every Muslim. In this view, the will of God, not the individual, will determine a person's achievements in this world. The individual has no influence, and no control, over them. If the believer benefits from wealth and richness, it will not be because of his or her efforts, decisions, or actions. It seems that this idea, which has a strong place in the beliefs in Islam, would not have encouraged Muslims to make a special effort in the economic field and in trade. However, this thesis suffers from some inaccuracies, especially with the one that deals with the Muslim theological development in the first centuries of Islam.

Although Islam, like every other religion, can be interpreted in many ways, the Prophet Muhammad was clear when speaking about the importance of property rights. In his farewell pilgrimage, he declared to the assembled masses, "Nothing shall be legitimate to a Muslim which belongs to a fellow Muslim unless it was given freely and willingly." This is a milestone in Islam and therefore any Muslim country is by definition a country that guards the rights of its citizen with regard to private property (this is implied for Muslims only). In Muslim countries, it is common to see a house surrounded by high walls with a heavy door. Behind this door and these walls, women walk around freely without being covered by their veils, and in general this house is considered private property that the government can penetrate only in extreme cases.

Islamic trade values and its inclination toward free trade could be demonstrated in the stories about Muhammad ("Hadith"), which demonstrate that Muhammad turned to the marketplace to determine the just price of commodities. When he heard that his companion Bilal had traded poor-quality dates for high-quality dates, Muhammad advised him that buying and selling at market prices over barter avoided the dangers of overcharging (*ribâ*) inherent in barter. After the caliphs of the early Umayyad dynasty had departed from Muhammad's practices, the reformer Omar II ordered his governors to leave prices to the market with this advice, "God has made land and waters for seeking His bounties. So let traders travel between them without any intervention. How can you intervene between them and their livelihood?"

Islam is usually not restrictive in its trade regulations, and many prohibitions are the product of later interpretations. Not many commodities are prohibited from being traded but include those banned from consumption (such as alcohol, which is forbidden, but could be sold to non-Muslims). Islam does not ban slavery and those nonbelievers who were captured during the wars of Islamic expansion were likely to be enslaved.

Consequently, Muslims were highly active in the slave trade from Africa, at the borders of their empire to the south and west. Muslim traders were responsible for several major routes of the African slave trade. They operated trans-Saharan routes, which passed through the Sahel on their way to Benghazi (in Libya), Cairo, Khartoum (in Sudan), and the western Saharan countries. Slaves were shipped from these destinations to Europe and eastward. In the Horn of Africa and on the eastern shores of the continent, Muslims administered the trade across the Indian Ocean, in which African slaves were shipped to the Arabian Peninsula and to India. Muslims were less involved in the transatlantic slave trade, but Muslim leaders in the Sahel, who were eager to sell humans to the Europeans on the shore, managed to receive a special religious permission, allowing them to wage war against fellow Muslims (thus selling the captives to slavery), who were allegedly "heretic." According to various sources, practices of slavery still exist in Sudan, as well as other Muslim countries.

However, Islam could also be perceived as restrictive in its economic attitude. Islam bans the practice of interest, leaving creditors without much incentive to lend money. In the modern period, a solution to this problem was found in the form of the establishment of Islamic banks, which follow interpretations to the laws of Islam and which allow some arrangements (such as commissions) of lending without "real" interest.

Another limitation is placed on the sale of land. Properties belonging to the Waqf (religious consecration) could not be sold or mortgaged, and the profits from the asset could not be redirected to other means than the original purpose (e.g., if someone donated the property to a school that no longer exists). Following the need to reform the landowning system, the Waqf properties were nationalized, thus releasing them to the market,

Trade in slaves, gold, and salt brought great wealth to the kingdom of Mali, linking the Arab-Muslim civilization of North Africa and the native cultures of sub-Saharan Africa. The ancient city of Timbuktu (seen here in an 1830 engraving) was a hub of trade and Islamic culture. *(Archives Charmet/Bridgeman Art Library)*

by governments in Turkey (1924), Egypt (1952–1957), and other countries.

The early Arabs had a strong commitment to trade and bargaining. The rise of Islam did not change, nor did it seek to change, the centrality of trade and commerce to the Arab way of life. On the contrary, the establishment of commercial law, the expansion of property rights for women, the prohibition of fraud, the call for the establishment of clear standards of weights and measures, and the uncompromising defense of property rights (even while calling for a greater responsibility for alleviating the plight of the poor and needy) pushed the Islamic civilization to the front of the world's economic stage and made the Muslim world the defining force in international trade for over 800 years.

Tamar Gablinger

See also: Buddhism; Christianity; Missionaries; Slavery.

BIBLIOGRAPHY

Akbar, A.S., and H. Donnan, eds. *Islam, Globalization and Postmodernity.* London: Routledge, 1994.

Amin, Galal A. *The Modernisation of Poverty.* Leiden, Netherlands: E.J. Brill, 1974.

Ayubi, Nazih. *Political Islam, Religion and Politics in the Arab World.* London: Routledge, 1991.

Braudel, Fernand. *Civilization and Capitalism, 15th–18th Century: The Perspective of the World,* trans. Siân Reynolds. Berkeley: University of California Press, 1992.

Crone, Patricia. *Meccan Trade and the Rise of Islam.* Princeton: Princeton University Press, 1987.

Hourani, Albert. *A History of the Arab Peoples.* New York: Warner, 1991.

Lewis, Bernard. *The Arabs in History.* 6th ed. New York: Oxford University Press, 1970.

———. *The Political Language of Islam.* Chicago: University of Chicago, 1991.

Lubeck, Paul M. "Islamist Responses to Globalization: Cultural Conflict in Egypt, Algeria, and Malaysia." 2000 (http://escholarship.cdlib.org/ias/crawford/pdf/lu.pdf, accessed August 2003).

Richards, Alan, and John Waterbury. *A Political Economy of the Middle East: State, Class, and Economic Development.* Boulder: Westview, 1990.

Wittek, Paul. *The Rise of the Ottoman Empire.* London: The Royal Asiatic Society, 1971.

IVORY

> Dentine material of elephant, extinct mammoth, hippopotamus, walrus, narwhal, and sperm whale tusks.

Ivory's texture, firmness, and white color was appealing to the carver and consumer alike and was believed to have healing and magical properties. From the archaic to modern periods, ivory was carved into various luxury and semiluxury items.

Ivory of the ancient world derived from African, Indian, and Asian elephants. Egypt, the chief exporter of ivory in the classical period, was supplied with ivory through trade and tribute collection from North Africa through Libya and East Africa by way of the Nile and the Red Sea. During the Hellenistic and Roman periods, Egypt reexported ivory to much of the Greco-Roman world of the Mediterranean through the port of Alexandria. Indian ivory was also imported to the Mediterranean during these periods. Less common was Hippopotamus ivory, which came from the upper Nile and Syria-Palestine.

The ivory trade and production was greatly influenced by the political changes in late antiquity/early Middle Ages. From the late sixth to the mid-tenth centuries, little ivory was worked in Byzantium and the Christian Mediterranean, in general. This "Dark Age" of ivory production occurred because of the extinction of the North African elephant, the Persian and then Arab seizure of Roman African provinces, and the closing of the Red Sea route, which supplied the Mediterranean with Indian ivory. This hiatus in ivory working ended with a major revival in the ivory trade that spanned the middle Byzantine period (from the mid-tenth to the late eleventh/early twelfth centuries). In contrast, ivory was widely used in the medieval Muslim world from Spain to central Asia. Basra was a key market for elephant ivory, which probably came there by sea from Hindustan and Cambodia. As in the classical period, Africa was the largest supplier for the lands of Islam. Since only male Indian elephants bore tusks and they were smaller in size, African ivory was exported to Persia, the Far East, and even India during the Middle Ages.

Trade of walrus, narwhal, sperm whale, and extinct mammoth ("fresh" or petrified) tusks became common by the tenth century throughout much of Eurasia. Ivory of these animals was exported to central Asia and Liao China (916–1125) from arctic and subarctic European Russia and Siberia by way of Rus', Volga Bulgar, and Kyrgyz middlemen. In later centuries, Russia became a key exporter of the so-called fish-teeth, or northern ivory, of various types throughout Eurasia: it has been estimated that over the last 300 years, tusks of at least 45,000 Russian mammoths had

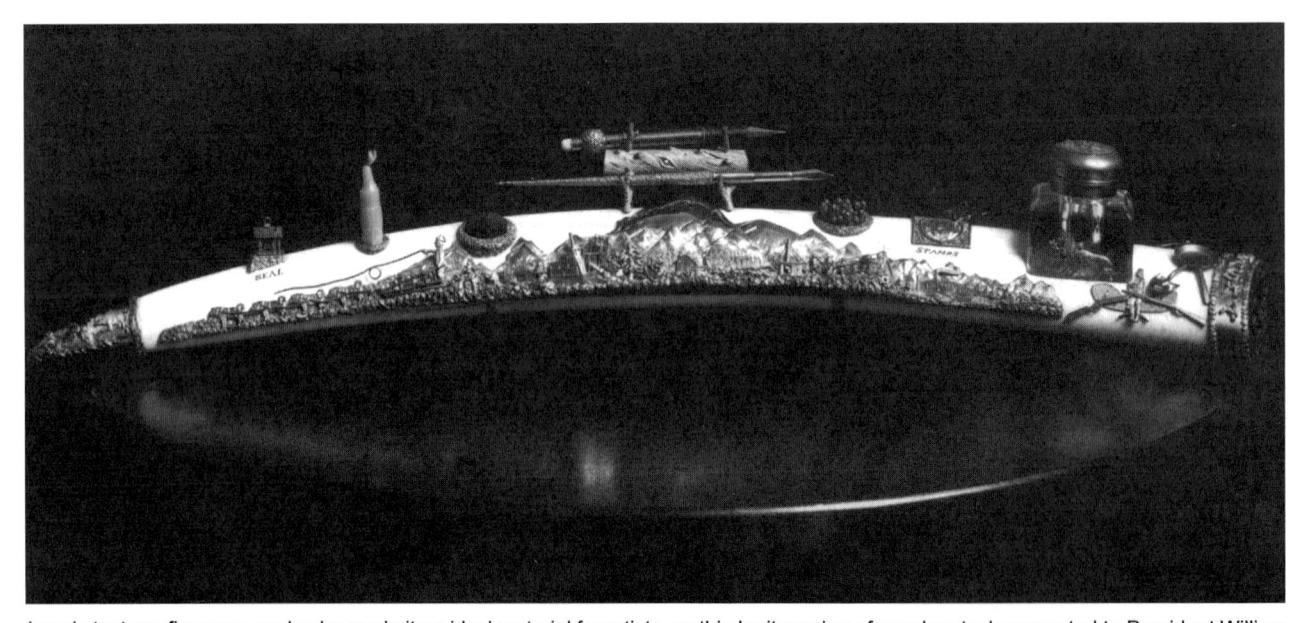

Ivory's texture, firmness, and color made it an ideal material for artists, as this Inuit carving of a walrus tusk presented to President William Taft in the early twentieth century indicates. A major export commodity until the late twentieth century, trade in ivory has fallen into disrepute in recent years because of its devastating effect on elephant herds in Africa, which served as a major source of the substance.
(Library of Congress)

been traded. With the colonization of the North Atlantic by the Vikings at the turn of the eleventh century, Greenland and Canadian walrus ivory became a common import to Scandinavia and western Europe and lasted until the mid-1350s, when the colonies declined and ceased to exist.

Throughout the nineteenth and into the late twentieth century, ivory was derived primarily through the hunting of African elephants. The legal and illegal trade in ivory escalated throughout the 1980s as African elephant herds were decimated due to mass slaughter by poachers. Between 1979 and 1989, an estimated 700,000 elephants were killed for ivory, endangering the elephant populations of Africa.

In early 1989, the United States, Canada, Europe, Australia, and other countries banned the importation of ivory due to pressure from conservation and environmental groups. Later that year, at a meeting of the Convention on International Trade in Endangered Species (CITES), African elephants were added to the endangered species list (Asian elephants had been added in 1975), banning the legal ivory trade in over 140 countries and effectively curbing elephant poaching, though not stopping it completely. A one-time exclusion was granted by CITES to Namibia, Zimbabwe, and Botswana in 1997 to allow one experimental exportation of ivory to Japan, which took place in 1999. CITES members voted to continue the ban in 2004 after Namibia applied for permission to export 2,000 kilograms of ivory annually. Even so, illegal poaching continues in Africa and elephant herds remain endangered.

Roman K. Kovalev

See also: Indian Ocean Trade; Mediterranean Sea; Roman Empire.

BIBLIOGRAPHY

Cutler, Anthony. *The Craft of Ivory: Sources, Techniques, and Uses in the Mediterranean World*, A.D. 200–1400. Washington, DC: Dumbarton Oaks Research Library and Collection, 1985.

Kovalev, Roman K. "'Fish Teeth'—The Ivory of the North: Russia's Medieval Trade of Walrus and Petrified Mammoth Tusks." In *Russian History/Histoire Russe*, ed. R.K. Kovalev and H.M. Sherman. Dearborn, MI: Festschrift for Thomas S. Noonan, 2001.

Krzyszkowska, Olga. *Ivory and Related Materials.* London: Institute of Classical Studies, 1990.

Roesdahl, Else. "L'Ivoire de morse et las Colonies du Groenland." *Proxima Thulé (Ultima Thulé)* 3 (1998): 9–48.

IVORY COAST OF AFRICA

A geographic region on the west African coast and since 1960 an independent republic, Côte d'Ivoire.

The Portuguese named the Ivory Coast in the fifteenth century because of the enormous amounts of ivory used in the area. Like many other European explorers of the fifteenth century, the Portuguese were fascinated by the supposed wealth of Africa. Other European marine forces followed the Portuguese in the search for the treasures of Africa.

This Eurocentric name concentrates on the main export of the region and remained the name of the French colony and later of the independent state of Côte d'Ivoire. Similarly, other regions in West Africa were named "Gold Coast" (the area that consists of contemporary Ghana and was also the British colonial name of the region), "Slave Coast" (an area that includes parts of modern-day Nigeria, as well as Benin and Togo), and "Grain Coast" (contemporary Liberia). Indeed, trade relations with coastal West Africa were set early in the fifteenth century by the Portuguese, and revolved around gold, ivory, and spices. However, from the sixteenth century onward, the chief demand was for slaves.

The area of the Ivory Coast was inhabited by different groups, some of which (notably the Mandé, the Kru, and the Akan) wandered to the area—which was outside the influence of the medieval Mali and Ashanti kingdoms—in search of gold and cola nuts for the trans-Saharan trade, as early as the sixteenth century.

KINGDOMS

Monarchical structures of regimes began to appear by the mid-eighteenth century. Five prominent kingdoms dominated the area of the Ivory Coast. Four kingdoms were founded by Akans: Abron, Baulé, and the Anyi kingdoms of Indénié and Sanwi. The Jola and the Senufo established another kingdom: the Kong kingdom.

The kingdoms' economies were based mainly on agriculture (among the products were maize, plantains, bananas, pineapples, limes, pepper, and cotton), but they also maintained trade relations

Until a late 1999 coup, Côte d'Ivoire was West Africa's most stable and prosperous country, as revealed in this busy 1959 market scene in Agboville. It remains the world's largest exporter of cocoa. *(Library of Congress/Photo Information, Ivory Coast)*

northward, considering themselves the southernmost outreach of the Saharan trade. Unlike major centers of trade, the kingdoms were isolated from influences of northern cultures. However, to the north of the kingdoms, the Hausa converted to Islam as early as the fourteenth or fifteenth century (when Bontuku was supposedly founded), as a result of their connections with the Muslim empires of Sokoto (and earlier, with Timbuktu). The internal parts of the Ivory Coast region were a link between the trade in the Sokoto and Timbuktu areas and the internal, southern kingdoms, especially in cola nuts, but also in gold and other commodities.

The geography of the region of the kingdoms to the south consisted mainly of the dense woods and a treacherous coastline. Consequently, contact with the Europeans before the nineteenth century was also sporadic. In 1687, the French established a mission and a trade station in Assinie, which was the first European settlement in the region. During the seventeenth century, the French traded guns and other goods for gold and ivory. The trade in ivory proved itself profitable. However, the demand for ivory was so high that the population of elephants in the region was decimated and, with it, the trade in ivory.

By the eighteenth century, the French abandoned the outpost in Assinie. Trade in ivory was almost extinguished by the eighteenth century. For the French, the conditions on the coast, including endemic yellow fever in their settlements, prevented the foundation of a permanent settlement, and a decision to desert Assinie was made in 1704, while Grand Bassam was deserted in 1707.

As a result, the Ivory Coast was little affected by the flourishing slave trade of the sixteenth to the eighteenth centuries.

It was only after the slave trade became illegal, in the mid-nineteenth century, that the French decided to colonize Côte d'Ivoire. In 1842, the French signed a treaty with a few coastal groups, which enabled them to control Assinie and Grand Bassam. During the 1850s and 1860s, the French assumed to sign trade treaties with local leaders, sometimes by coercion or deceit, which ensured the French control on the posts and provided for trade privileges, in return for annual payments to the local rulers of the coast area. Despite their unwillingness to adhere to the agreements, the French maintained them to strengthen their control on West Africa, because of the rivalry with the British for control of the region. However, after the Franco-Prussian War (1871), the bankrupted France gave a European merchant, Arthur Verdier, control over the area of Grand Bassam, in the hope of maintaining future control of the area.

The success of economic activity along the coast motivated European interest in the interior, especially along the Niger and the Senegal Rivers. In the case of France, private individuals, like Verdier, were central to the trend and made independent policy decisions without direct intervention from Paris. While expanding his businesses on the coastline, Verdier sent a delegation to explore the Niger River basin in 1887. The French government sent a similar delegation to the interior the same year. The two delegations successfully negotiated treaties (separately) with the dominant groups in the interior and in 1889 joined forces and declared the southern region a French protectorate.

COLONIZATION

In 1893, Côte d'Ivoire was declared a French colony, and the political system was changed from a loose system of administration on different kingdoms into a firmer, authoritarian style of regime. The French encountered difficulties in promoting their sovereignty, because of uprisings by the local population, especially the Boule.

During the second half of the nineteenth century, the settlements developed into small towns: Grand Bassam on the coast, Assinie in the east, and Grand Lahou, Sassandra and Tabu in the west. Grand Bassam in particular became the trade center of the colony, as well as the seat of the administration and judiciary. Modest means of transportation (a train) and dockland were built.

In 1908, the French turned Grand Bassam into the main post of the colony. Abidjan, the present capital of Côte d'Ivoire (in the vicinity of Port Bouet, or Little Bassam), became the starting place for the trains heading for the rail to the palm oil and rubber-producing regions. Rubber and mahogany were exported from the colony, mostly to England. Further investment in the infrastructure was carried out after World War I.

Another main development was economic. By the end of the nineteenth century, the West African export transformed from a system based on slaves to one based on agricultural produce and minerals. The French designated Côte d'Ivoire (along with several other colonies) to provide France with cash crops. In the Ivory Coast, the beginning of the economic transformation was marked by the beginning of the cultivation of coffee (1909) and cocoa (1912), which would later become the chief export product of Côte d'Ivoire. Like the gold mines, coffee plantations were maintained under European control through concessions and merchandise sold to European elements.

In 1932, France united two colonies—Côte d'Ivoire and its northern neighbor, the colony of "Upper Volta" (today the independent republic of Burkina Faso). After World War II, infrastructure and economy developed further, making the colony the most profitable for the French in West Africa. The territory was made part of the French Union in 1946. The northern border of the colony remained unsettled until the French established it in 1947 and separated Upper Volta from Côte d'Ivoire. In 1958, residents of Côte d'Ivoire voted to become an independent republic within the French Community (an organization that links France and its former colonies and which replaced the French Union).

However, while maintaining their control over the population, the French colonial labor policies, and the discrimination of local farmers in favor of European settlers, created bitterness and aggravated the natives, especially small-scale plantation cultivators. A movement for the abolition of colonial labor recruitment policies, the African Agricultural Union, was founded in 1944, and it gradually became an anticolonial movement, although its original goals were to improve conditions under the colonial framework.

The African Agricultural Union transformed itself into the Democratic Party of Côte d'Ivoire. Since those who constituted the founders of the party—the cultivators—have had an interest in maintaining good economic relations with France, even after Côte d'Ivoire was granted independence in 1960, its economy was still very much linked to that of France. Western coffee and cacao conglomerates upheld their control over the country's economy, which became dependent on global prices for the two commodities. The independent Republic of Côte d'Ivoire, under the autocratic leadership of Félix Houphouët-Boigny, began its first steps as one of the richest nations in postindependent sub-Saharan Africa. However, much of the wealth remained in the hands of a relatively small elite group of small bourgeoisie and cultivators, and the administration is plagued with corruption.

Tamar Gablinger

See also: Cacao; Coffee; Slavery.

BIBLIOGRAPHY
Ajayi, J.F. Ade, and Michael Crowder, eds. *History of West Africa.* Vol. 2. New York: Columbia University Press, 1974.
Hopkins, A.G. *An Economic History of West Africa.* New York: Columbia University Press, 1973.
Lynn, Martin. *Commerce and Economic Change in West Africa: The Palm Oil Trade in the Nineteenth Century.* Cambridge: Cambridge University Press, 1997.
Zartman, I. William, and Christopher Delgado, eds. *The Political Economy of Ivory Coast.* New York: Praeger, 1984.
Zolberg, Aristide R. *One-Party Government in the Ivory Coast.* Princeton: Princeton University Press, 1964.

J

JADE

> A historically scarce natural resource of limited normal distribution further enhanced in value when worked or carved into elaborate objects.

Jade is chemically and visually variable within deposits, making it difficult to assign trade goods to their origin. Ancient and modern artisans often imported jade and other greenstones from the same deposits interchangeably. Mineralogists identify jade as nephrite (actinolite or tremolite) or jadeite (which is more complex and variable chemically). Iron contributes to the green color in nephrite and the green or blue color of jadeite. Chrome provides an apple green color in jadeite.

Although true jadeite is quite rare worldwide, nephrite and jadeite mixed with other chemicals are more common. True jadeite occurs in California, Russia, Japan, Burma, and the Motagua River valley of Guatemala. Jadeite mixed with other chemicals is found in the Dominican Republic, Colombia, California, Canada, Corsica, Italy, and New Caledonia. Nephrite, but not jadeite, occurs in China, and there are other nephrite deposits elsewhere, including in Siberia.

Prehistorically in Central America, the Olmec, Mayan, and Costa Rican elite used highly crafted, imported jadeite as jewelry, offerings, and ultimately grave goods to demarcate their high rank. Trade likely took place as gift and ritual exchange to develop and maintain foreign relations, although long-distance traders, perhaps at the behest of the elite, sometimes included jade in their cargos. Jade was likely traded from mines along the Motagua River area of Guatemala. Olmec jade artifacts were traded to the Mayan area and to Costa Rica. Jade was a favored trade good for royalty of the Mayan civilization. The largest Mayan jade object is a nine-pound carved head of the Sun god Kinich Ahau found in a burial tomb at Altun Ha, Belize.

The ancient Chinese regarded jade as a symbol of immortality, wealth, and virtue, valuing it higher than gold or silver. Until recently, most Chinese nephrite was obtained from the Xinjiang region of China. Not until the eighteenth century were other sources used, notably jadeite mines in Burma and nephrite from Siberia. From early use of jade beads in Neolithic burials to more elaborate figurines, zoomorphic pendants, and other objects of later Shang, Zhou, and Han Chinese dynasties, jade was traded over long distances. Foreign trade in jade reached its height during the Tang dynasty (618–907 C.E.), because of military control and improvement of transportation, with the reopening of the Silk Road, which dated to the Han dynasty.

The allure of jade continues because of its scarcity as a resource and difficulty to manufacture. Private companies export jade from British Columbia, Canada, to Asia for manufacture into figurines that are reimported for sale. Collectors have long desired jade artifacts. Antiquities traded both legally and illegally often fetch high prices. The UNESCO Convention on the Means of Prohibiting and Preventing the Illicit Import, Export, and Transfer of Ownership of Cultural Property, which the United States signed in 1982, restricts the import and export of jade.

Heather McKillop

See also: Archaeology; Art; China; Chinese Dynasties; Gold; Illegal Trade; Mayan Civilization; Silk Road; Silver.

BIBLIOGRAPHY

Capon, Edmund. *Art and Archaeology in China*. Melbourne: Macmillan, 1977.

Harrison, Peter D. *The Lords of Tikal.* New York: Thames and Hudson, 1999.

Keverne, Ladislav, ed. *Jade.* New York: Lorenz, 1995.

Lange, Frederick W. *Precolumbian Jade: New Geological and Cultural Interpretations.* Salt Lake City: University of Utah Press, 1993.

Pendergast, David M. *Excavations at Altun Ha, Belize.* Vol. 1. Toronto: Royal Ontario Museum, 1979.

Rawson, Jessica, ed. *The British Museum Book of Chinese Art.* New York: Thames and Hudson, 1996.

Schmidt, Carolyn Woodford. *From Heaven and Earth: Chinese Jade in Context.* Columbus: Columbus Museum of Art, 1998 (http://kaladarshan.arts.ohio-state.edu/exhib/jade/hp/hp.html, accessed September 2002).

Vollmer, John, E.J. Keall, and E. Nagai-Berthrong. *Silk Roads, China Ships.* Toronto: Royal Ontario Museum, 1983.

JEWS

> Jews became important to trade and commerce in early medieval times due to the role they played in facilitating trade relationships between Christian and non-Christian lands.

In antiquity, Jewish Palestine had a strategic location on the trade routes from Egypt and Arabia. The establishment of the monarchy pushed Palestine toward direct participation in external commerce. The rule of King Solomon (ca. 930–ca. 970 B.C.E.) was especially prosperous. His fleet regularly voyaged to Ophir, bringing back gold, silver, rare woods, and ivory. From Lebanon came imports of wood, and from Egypt came linen, chariots, and horses. Palestine's exports to Egypt included spices, balm, myrrh, honey, and almonds. Solomon's alliance with Tyre allowed exports of wheat and oil into Tyre in return for materials and labor used in Solomon's building projects. The political turmoil that followed after Solomon's death caused this prosperous era to come to an end, and after many political upheavals over the next several centuries the Jewish people came to be scattered throughout the known world.

During the time of the Roman empire, Jewish Palestine remained essentially rural, its economic activity consisting of exportation of surplus agricultural products such as wheat, barley, dates, figs, oil, and wine. Imports included Italian furniture, Corinthian candlesticks, and Edomite vinegar. It was during this era that Jews in the many diaspora settlements began to play a larger part in economic activities. Though most lived in poverty, a select few were able to take advantage of the opportunities afforded them. Jews in Alexandria, for example, became major players in trade, controlling exports in papyrus, wheat, and dates. By the second century, diasporic Jews were playing a large part in eastern trade, by both sea and land. They had established themselves in areas such as the Malabar Coast of India and played an important role in the overland caravan silk traffic from China to Europe.

From early medieval times, the Jewish people were important in economic activity because of their ability to travel between Christian and non-Christian lands without arousing suspicion. The enmity between these lands gave Jews the opportunity to serve as middlemen. Charlemagne saw this potential and allowed Jews much freedom during his rule in the eighth century. Jewish merchants of Byzantium were highly involved, with both the East and the West. By the mid-ninth century, Jews in France carried cargoes of slaves, brocades, and furs from France's southern ports to various destinations in eastern Europe. Some went as far as India and China, returning with many Eastern products, including musk, aloe, wood, camphor, and cinnamon. The Jews in Spain, under Muslim rule, experienced what many have termed their "golden age" during this era, participating in all areas of commerce, including trade.

One damaging factor for the Jews in this era of trade was the breakdown of Arab unity. The Christian lands no longer saw the Islamic world as a large threat, and therefore direct trade relations had begun between the two, thereby pushing the Jewish middleman out of the picture. By the eleventh century, heavy competition from Italian merchants forced the Jews out of maritime trade in the Mediterranean. In addition, the onset of the Crusades ushered in an era of increased religious intolerance, bringing an end to Jewish economic freedom.

It was during the Middle Ages that a money economy developed in medieval Europe. The expansion into new territories as a result of the Crusades created a need for a new economic system. The Catholic Church, however, saw usury as morally repulsive, and in 1274 the pope officially condemned the lending of funds for profit. At the same time, the formation of exclusive Christian merchant guilds began to force Jews out of trade. It was the Jews, outside of the church's jurisdiction, who stepped into the necessary role of moneylender. As a result, stereotypes arose of the Jew as ruthless and money-hungry, and people blamed them for economic problems. Several large-scale massacres and expulsions took place during these centuries: Jews were expelled from England in 1290, France in 1306 and 1394, Austria in 1420, and Spain in 1492, among other areas.

During the age of mercantilism, Jews gradually began reassimilating into the economies of western Europe, and by the beginning of the eighteenth century Jews found their economic roles increasing in importance. The Jewish community of Amsterdam serves as an example of this growing importance. Amsterdam Jewry played a large role in Amsterdam's dominance of the trade industry during the seventeenth century. Their commercial ties were numerous. Trade with North Africa provided grain, wax, almonds, figs, and cork. Dutch Jews also maintained offices in German ports, where they traded in colonial products. They were also important in both Asian and New World trade, their main areas of involvement being silken textiles, sugar refining, diamond cutting, and tobacco blending. It was the Amsterdam Jewry's contacts with Cochin that helped the Dutch East India Company to form its monopoly on pepper. Jews also settled in the New World—many of the Jews who were expelled from Portugal in the late fifteenth century found success in Brazil as part of the sugar industry. A number of Jews owned large sugar plantations worked by African slaves and natives. The Portuguese soon expelled them from Brazil, and many went to other New World areas such as the Caribbean islands, continuing sugar production there.

The turbulent history of the Jews continued. Beginning in the early twentieth century, Jews began immigrating in large numbers to the United States, because of both the culture of persecution they experienced in their respective countries and the low cost of travel. Economic conditions in the United States at the time were favorable, and Jews were able to attain success mostly as manual labor. They soon came to constitute the largest and wealthiest Jewish population in the world, providing support to co-religionists in other countries.

The State of Israel was established in 1948 and recognized by many countries. Israel's economy is an advanced market economy. Its imports include grains, crude oil, raw materials, and military equipment. Exports include cut diamonds, high-technology equipment, and agricultural products.

Krystal Hopkins

See also: Religion; Roman Empire; World War II.

BIBLIOGRAPHY
Arkin, Marcus. *Aspects of Jewish Economic History.* Philadelphia: Jewish Publication Society of America, 1975.
Roth, Cecil. *A Bird's-Eye View of Jewish History.* Cincinnati: Union of American Hebrew Congregations, 1935.

JOINT-STOCK COMPANIES

> The need for capital in foreign trade during the age of exploration led to the creation of joint-stock companies.

The growth and expansion of commerce in Europe during the age of exploration and settlement in the New World created problems that required the adaptation of business organizations necessary to meet the developing conditions. The joint-stock company was created to provide the required capital for large-scale enterprises and skilled management.

The discovery of new trade routes and the opening of direct trade by sea between Europe and other parts of the world, mainly in the seventeenth century, led to new problems that merchants had not previously encountered. Foreign trade, along with mining and shipbuilding, posed the biggest problems for businessmen. The opening of all-water trade routes enabled European merchants to make direct contact with markets and raw materials all over the world. However, the enormous trading opportunities resulting from these new territorial discoveries were not taken advantage of by most European merchants. Few were able to "single-handedly" profit from such developments in the new commercial age.

The developing needs of business in foreign trade led to the creation of the joint-stock company. The joint-stock company and its later development, the corporation, were examples of modern business institutions. Joint-stock companies addressed the needs of large-scale business in three ways. First, the new trading opportunities involved more risk of loss than previous ventures. Despite the prospects of greater profits, the potential danger of losing ships at sea along with the threat of piracy required more investors be involved. Few merchants who were able to raise the necessary capital to prepare a ship for a long journey could afford to lose all they had. The joint-stock company addressed this worry by splitting up the capital invested in a trading venture. The total risk of a venture could thus be shared by many stockholders. Second, the need to raise large amounts of capital was met by selling shares of stock. Thousands of Europeans participated by purchasing shares that they could afford to buy and thereby invest in the venture. Third, adequate and unified management, despite ownership of the business being scattered among many stockholders, was achieved by management policies being determined by a majority vote of the shares. The joint-stock company made management a professional function separate from ownership.

Historically, joint-stock companies did not fare very well over the long term. The English South Sea Bubble and the French Mississippi Bubble (both in 1720) were financial disasters that typified the nature of such speculative ventures and subsequently led to restrictions on the privileges of incorporation and slowed the growth of corporate enterprise. The oldest joint-stock company was chartered in 1555 in England to trade with Russia. The Muscovy Company was given a trade monopoly by the Russian tsar and English king. It survived for more than a century, but fell victim to Dutch competition and uncertain conditions in Russia. The most successful joint-stock companies were the East India Companies chartered in England in 1600 and Holland in 1602. The Dutch company was a permanent joint-stock company from the beginning, whereas the English company was organized for single voyages until 1657, when the stock was made permanent. Both companies became the wealthiest of their day. The British East India Company continued to rule until 1858, and until 1833 it had exclusive trading rights in India. Chartered in 1670, the Hudson's Bay Company, which conducted business in Canada, was another prominent joint-stock company organized during the Commercial Revolution. Some others, though far less successful, were the Levant Company, the African Company, the Mines Royal, and the South Sea Company. What enabled many of them to survive was government support rather than corporate investment.

American colonization expanded with the assistance of commercial companies—joint-stock ventures. The London Company and the Plymouth Company were chartered in 1606. The first attempt of the Plymouth Company in what is now Maine was a failure. The London Company's colonization of Jamestown, Virginia, eventually succeeded despite great financial losses to the company. Crown support to trading companies was the primary factor in the growth of the American colonies throughout the seventeenth and eighteenth centuries. With the creation of the United States, the development of big business occurred in the late nineteenth century. Although the United States had many merchants, it had no desire for large joint-stock trading companies. The mechanization of industry and saturation of markets resulting from the post–Civil War Industrial Revolution led to the rise of big business in the American economy.

Although sole proprietorship was the best kind of arrangement for the merchant manufacturer, businessmen who focused on commerce and trade required so much capital that it was necessary for them to find other forms of business organization. The discovery of sixteenth- and seventeenth-century trade routes during the era of the Commercial Revolution resulted in the creation of the joint-stock company. Although joint-stock enterprises represented a spectacular development in the organization of business enterprise in the modern era, they had compiled "a dreary record of failure." The family firm and partnership continued to dominate trade and industry well into the nineteenth century.

Charles F. Howlett

See also: British Empire; Mercantilism; United States.

BIBLIOGRAPHY

Bowden, Witt, Michael Karpovich, and A.P. Usher. *Economic History of Europe since 1750.* New York: American Book, 1937.

Heaton, Herbert. *Economic History of Europe.* New York: Harper, 1948.

Hexter, J.H., Richard Pipes, and Anthony Molho. *Europe Since 1500.* New York: Harper and Row, 1971.

Nettles, Curtis P. "British Mercantilism and the Economic Development of the Thirteen Colonies." *Journal of Economic History* 12 (Spring 1952): 105–141.

Patton, Robert D. *The American Economy.* Chicago: Scott, Foresman, 1953.

JUDAISM

Oldest monotheistic religion that encourages trade and commerce.

Judaism and its normative code of conduct in business had a great impact on trade and commerce, not only within Jewish circles but also on the trade norms in the Christian and Muslim worlds. Jewish commercial values are prominent in modern culture as they were in the ancient world and have a tremendous effect on legal and ethical thought regarding trade.

JEWISH LAW

Jewish religious laws, the Halacha, set a comprehensive and far-reaching normative system regarding trade. The Halacha itself is based on the Torah, and on its later elaborations in the Talmud (the oral tradition), in Maimonides' *Mishnah Torah* (1168), in Joseph Karo's *Shulchan 'aruch* (1565), and in countless legal decisions handed down by Jewish authorities. This set of sources also relies strongly on a common legal tradition and is therefore flexible and changeable with new innovations and practices.

Both the Torah and later sources, such as the Talmud, detail the expected business norms and conduct. The Torah contains (according to Jewish belief) 613 precepts—many of which discuss the required business conduct. The Jewish civil code is described in the Talmud (which explicates the Torah) and contains information on business relationships and ethics, contracts, and disputes.

However, unlike many other religious legal codes, Jewish ruling on business is dynamic, and changes to the rules of conduct are made to apply the Halachic rules to the modern settings. The businessman and the arbitors are expected to go beyond the dry legal requirements and lean toward justice, charity, and righteousness, always following "the way of the pious." Selfishness and adherence to the law in cases of deprivation are recoiled from in Jewish law. Moreover, the separation between the laymen and the religious authorities was not so distinguished in Judaism—most commentators who shaped the legal culture had lay professions.

The Jewish religious and legal culture does not negate business and commerce. Consequently, the acquisition of wealth through legal earnings is viewed positively, so long as the riches are used to assist the poor, the needy, and the stranger. Business ethics, therefore, are an important basis of Jewish legal and cultural traditions, giving clear importance to the relationships between individuals as to the relationships between individuals and God. The righteousness of business conduct is illustrated in many legal cases described in the Talmud.

The Jewish approach to justice and righteousness is also reflected in the treatment of employees. In the biblical period, slavery was legitimate but subject to the direction "You shall not rule over him through rigorous labor." Jewish law details many rights of employees and slaves, including that of limited work hours and timely wages. In the case of slaves, an option to be released was offered every seven years, and the employer was expected to care for the basic needs of the released slave and not release him or her empty-handed. A property owner was expected to take care of and leave part of his yield to the "stranger, the orphan, and the widow." This extrapolates to

Legally and socially confined to ghettoes in eastern Europe, Jewish merchants, like this stationer in Vilna, Russia, in the early twentieth century, operated on the margins of national economies. Poverty and discrimination forced many to immigrate to the United States during this period. *(Library of Congress)*

comprehensive treatment of the stranger in the society.

The Bible contains many references to trade and its principles. Some refer to the ethical conduct expected from the trader and compare it to the conduct of merchants. Others describe the central role of trade in the daily lives of the ancient period. For example, the Bible describes how the Hebrew kingdom sought to increase its influence using trade, including through interactions with foreign peoples such as the Canaanites and the Phoenicians. Under the rule of King Solomon (tenth century B.C.E.), Hebrews invested in continental and maritime trade—between Egypt and Phoenicia, as well as in maritime routes to Arabia and East Africa. However, since the collapse of the kingdoms in the sixth century B.C.E., Jews traded under non-Jewish regimes because of the exile enforced by the conquering regimes of their land that led them to immigrate and carry their merchant culture with them into their exile. Life in the Diaspora shaped many Jewish commercial traditions, as Jewish culture remained dynamic. Above all, Jewish communities, a marginalized minority in a larger gentile population, developed trade relations with other Jewish communities to survive.

Jewish culture possessed several unique characteristics that made it preferable for developing trade relations. Jews maintained trading skills, multilingual knowledge, and important connections. Jewish trader communities were founded in various parts of the world—especially in Europe and in the Middle East. However, their trade skills and the persecution they suffered also brought Jews to relatively remote destinations.

ANTI-SEMITISM

Anti-Semitism played a major role in the choice of many Jews to engage in trade. After the stabilization of the guilds' feudal system in Europe, landowning, membership in craftsmen guilds, as well as many other occupations were prohibited to Jews, leaving trade as one of the only fields from which they were not prohibited. A common principle in the persecution of Jews sometimes became a boycott on trade with Jews or a ban on the entrance of Jews to certain trade guilds and later to associations and unions.

Involvement in money lending, which was banned by the Catholic Church (until the fifteenth century) was relatively widespread. Anti-Semitic accusations of usury were frequent. The anti-Semitic symbol of the Jew as a salesman, banker, or moneylender, as depicted, for example, in William Shakespeare's *The Merchant of Venice*, was popular and remained in the popular culture long after Jews were allowed in work in other occupations. However, in reality most Jews of the Middle Ages were poor and did not engage in money lending or trade.

The involvement in trade also had demographic consequences for the Jewish communities, as Jews settled mainly in places that were trade centers or ports. Like other immigrant diasporas (such as that of the Armenians), the formation of the Jewish Diaspora and the persecution of Jews created wide-reaching trade networks all over Eurasia and later on in the Americas. Jewish trade networks played a major role in the development of commerce. After the expulsion of Jews from Spain and Portugal (1492), Sephardic communities grew in various parts of Europe and under the Ottoman empire, especially in North Africa, Turkey, Palestine, and the Balkans. Those who settled in exile brought with them their trade connections with the Iberian Peninsula as well as other trade centers.

Jews immigrated to the North American colonies in hopes of avoiding the persecution that they encountered in Europe, especially in Spain and Portugal during the sixteenth century. Jews from the Iberian Peninsula were among the first immigrants to the Americas, where they established trade networks reaching from New York to Brazil as early as the late 1640s.

The ability of Jews to trade freely depended on the different attitudes toward them of the regimes under which they lived. While some, like the Ottomans, invited Jews to their territory—realizing that their trade links would benefit the economy—others persecuted Jews and prevented them from engaging in trade. For example, in the late eighteenth century Dutch authorities rejected demands made by Christian diamond merchants to form a diamond merchant's guild that excluded Jews (partly because of the dominance of Jews in the diamond commerce).

EMANCIPATION

The emancipation of Jews in the late eighteenth century (e.g., in the French Revolution) gave them equal rights as citizens, but did not eliminate anti-Semitic prejudice. Jews were targeted as subversive agents opposed to the new collective—the nation. During the nineteenth century, persecution and hatred of Jews became more widespread in Europe and America. The anti-Semitic wave in Europe culminated in the rise to power in 1932 of a racist, anti-Semitic party in Germany, the National Socialist Workers' Party.

The rise to power in Germany of the National Socialists (Nazis), and later of sympathetic regimes in other countries, worsened the situation. One of the first steps was setting limits on choice of profession and prohibition of trade with Jews. Later steps included the Nazi "Final Solution," the plan to annihilate the Jews, which resulted in the murder of 6 million Jews.

However, even in the post-1945 atmosphere Jews are discriminated against, especially in Middle Eastern countries, and their freedom of movement as merchants, among other rights, is hindered.

Tamar Gablinger

See also: Silk Road; Songhay Empire.

BIBLIOGRAPHY

Elon, Menachem, ed. *The Principles of Jewish Law.* Jerusalem: Keter, 1975.

Friedman, Hershey H. "The Impact of Jewish Values on Marketing and Business Practices." *Journal of Macromarketing* 21 (June 2001): 74–80.

Meir, Tamari. *With All Your Possessions: Jewish Ethics and Economic Life.* New York: Free Press, 1987.

de Vries, Barend A. *Champions of the Poor: The Economic Consequences of Judeo-Christian Values.* Washington, DC: Georgetown University Press, 1998.

JUTE

> Made from the fibers of *Corchorus capsularis* and *Corchorus olitorius*, two species of plants that grow throughout India, but flourish in the Ganges and Brahmaputra River Deltas.

Jute has been woven since ancient times into coarse rope, burlap sacks, and, in modern times, as a backing fiber for things such as rugs and linoleum. Both *C. capsularis* and *C. olitorius* grow in wetlands to a height of ten feet. The stems are cut, soaked, beaten, dried, and then spun into useful fibers. Although jute historically has been occasionally mixed with other fibers to make

A main source of fiber and a major export commodity, jute has been grown since ancient times for use in ropes, bags, and rugs. Here, workers manufacture jute coffee bags in Mexico in the early twentieth century. *(Library of Congress)*

paper, its strength is unsuited for the weaving of fine cloth. It remains, however, one of the world's cheapest fibers.

Knowledge of jute was limited to Asian markets until fairly recently. As late as 1792, the British East India Company was still investigating its uses in India for possible export as a substitute for rope and cloth made from hemp (*Cannabis sativa*), but most of the pre-1800 trade was in gunnysacks woven in India. The distribution of jute products followed the extensive Indian Ocean routes into which European colonial powers tapped in the sixteenth and seventeenth centuries. James Watt Jr., however, was instrumental in successfully having jute fibers industrially spun into usable threads in the 1830s in Dundee, Scotland, after which jute manufacturing soared, especially in the production of rugs, industrial sacks, and cordage of all kinds.

By the middle of the nineteenth century, large amounts of raw jute were being imported from India to Britain by British companies, spun and woven into sacks, bailing, and rope in mechanized factories, and then reexported around the world as a finished product. Industrialization of production was slowly introduced into India during British colonial times, but picked up after independence in 1948. The Indian subcontinent, and Bangladesh in particular, still produces most of the world's raw jute. Calcutta is the main distribution center.

Fabio Lopez-Lazaro

See also: British Empire; India.

BIBLIOGRAPHY
Warden, Alexander J. *The Linen Trade, Ancient and Modern.* London: Frank Cass, 1967.

K

KEYNES, JOHN MAYNARD

A leading twentieth-century British economist, who dealt with issues such as deficit spending and balance of payments between nations.

John Maynard Keynes's views on trade and the importance of the balance of trade and payments changed over the course of his career, as manifested in his academic and polemical tracts and policy pronouncements. The two major influences on his views were the Ricardian-Marshallian approach, advocating free trade and comparative advantage, and the Malthusian approach, advocating expansion of "effective demand," which in his view would, in turn, bring about an expansion of world trade. The former approach is reflected in Keynes's *Economic Consequences of the Peace* (1919), in which he advocated free trade as a panacea for the economic ills of Europe following World War I, as he believed that only free trade would lead to economic growth.

Indeed, at the time Keynes pressed for what he called a "free-trade union," within the context of the Treaty of Versailles, that, however, did not materialize. Keynes advocated this as he realized that for Germany to be able to meet reparations payments, it would be necessary to allow German access to European resources so as to enable it to increase productive capacity; and that this could only come about if the treaty allowed the creation of free trade between Germany and the Allies in coal and iron ore. It was only after the consequences of the lack of such an arrangement, and World War II, that a European Coal and Steel Community, which became the cornerstone of the Common Market and European Union, emerged.

At times, however, Keynes was ambivalent regarding the efficacy of free trade, especially when he considered the British situation. Indeed, in a series of polemic articles on "national self sufficiency" in the 1920s, he advocated import tariffs and export subsidies to improve the United Kingdom's balance of trade and payments.

Over the course of the late 1920s and 1930s, his views changed. He adopted the notion of "effective demand," which he attributed to Thomas Robert Malthus, and asserted that international coordination and stimulation of effective demand in the industrial countries would revive their foreign trade and ensure growth of world trade as a whole. He made forceful statements on the issue not only in his major theoretical contribution, *The General Theory of Employment, Interest, and Money* (1936), but also in his policy advice to the British and American governments. For example, in a May 1936 statement, communicated by Henry Wallace, then the secretary of agriculture, to Franklin D. Roosevelt, Keynes said that "if the industrial nations all set to work to increase their domestic demand, they would soon have a revival in their foreign trade without having to worry about it."

Keynes's penultimate approach to the issues appeared in his 1946 *Economic Journal* paper on the problem of the U.S. balance of payments, published posthumously, in which he synthesized the Ricardian-Marshallian and Malthusian-Keynesian approaches. He advocated a policy mix of "classical" and "modern medicine," so as to bring about, in the "long run," a tendency "toward equilibrium," as he put it, and ultimately deal with problems in the balance of trade and balance of payments of the United States and other countries.

Warren Young

See also: World War II.

BIBLIOGRAPHY

Colander, David C., and Harry Landreth, eds. *The Coming of Keynesianism to America: Conversations with the Founders of Keynesian Economics.* Cheltenham, UK: Edward Elgar, 1996.

De Angelis, Massimo. *Keynesianism, Social Conflict and Political Economy.* London: Macmillan, 2000.

Keyes, John Maynard. *The Economic Consequences of the Peace.* London: Macmillan, 1919.

———. *The General Theory of Employment, Interest, and Money.* London: Macmillan, 1936.

———. "The Balance of Payments of the United States." *Economic Journal* 41, no. 222 (June 1946): 172–87.

Skidelsky, Robert. *John Maynard Keynes.* 3 vols. London: Macmillan, 1983–2000.

KHAN, GENGHIS (1162-1229)

A Mongol emperor and military leader who founded the Mongol empire and promoted trade with Europe.

Known for their prowess on the battlefield, the Mongols—led by Genghis Khan, shown here in a fourteenth-century European manuscript—helped consolidate political power in Central Asia, encouraging trade between Europe and Asia. *(The Art Archive/Bodleian Library Oxford/The Bodleian Library)*

Originally named Temuchin and born into a Mongol clan decimated by enemy raiding and premature death, Genghis Khan restored his family's prestige and following by raiding against the Tatars and organizing his growing following to serve as mercenaries for the Jin empire in China. Genghis slowly constructed a great army composed of the various nomadic tribes of the steppe, either by making alliances with them or by conquering them, until in 1206 the Mongols and their vassal tribes named him their "King of Kings" at the Great Council. He then launched attacks against the Jin empire, perfecting techniques of siege warfare against walled cities and accumulating captives, supplies, and intelligence from the world that bordered the steppes.

Although the Mongol campaigns were incredibly ruthless and destructive, the damage was not random or capricious. Resistance by an enemy was met by total annihilation, but surrendering regions were carefully managed, with trade preserved and skilled craftsmen singled out for Mongol control. The Mongols patrolled the Silk Road and used the Kwarezm Shah's inability to control banditry as a pretext for invading his lands and seizing the trade cities of Bukhara and Samarkand as Mongol possessions. In 1223, the Mongols moved northwest into the trade cities of the Rus', capturing Kiev and installing Mongol tax collectors and advisors to the surviving Rus' princes, insisting that the Rus' reform their system of royal inheritance to avoid civil war and ensure order.

Advised by a captured Confucian scholar who became his personal secretary, Genghis oversaw the construction of a Mongol civil service, the maintenance of efficient postal routes (called *yam*) for government messages, and the codification of Mongol law—the Yasa. At his death in 1229, Genghis left his sons the foundations of a great empire stretching from China to eastern Europe. The Mongols, as advised by their great leader, cultivated trade between their subjects, oversaw a sophisticated internal passport system and intelligence-gathering network using Muslim and Chinese merchants, and placed a high value on the safety of the major trade routes from rival nomadic tribes and bandits. Genghis and his successors encouraged the embassies of west Europeans like the Polo family, and the efficient infrastructure of their vast empire cut the transit time from China to the Mediterranean substantially, allowing the flow of both luxury trade goods and less desirable travelers, like the bubonic plague.

Margaret Sankey

See also: Mongol Invasions; Polo, Marco; Silk Road.

BIBLIOGRAPHY

Cleaves, Francis Woodman, ed. *The Secret History of the Mongols.* Cambridge, MA: Harvard University Press, 1982.

Hartog, Leo de. *Genghis Khan: Conqueror of the World.* New York: St. Martin's Press, 1989.

Hoáang, Michel. *Genghis Khan*, trans. Ingrid Cranfield. London: Saqi, 1990.

Marshall, Robert. *Storm from the East: From Ghengis Khan to Khubilai Khan.* Berkeley: University of California Press, 1993.

KHAZAR EMPIRE

A country in southeastern Europe that existed from the 650s until the 960s.

The Khazar empire encompassed a vast land that served as a center for world trade and was regarded as a major political power by its contemporary neighbors. Its inhabitants consisted of diverse ethnic, linguistic, and religious groups. The ruling Khazar tribe, the members of which converted to Judaism in the ninth century, included seminomads, farmers, fishermen, crafters, and merchants. The empire had many workshops throughout the country that manufactured a wide range of products both for internal and external use.

The Khazar empire exercised control over major navigable rivers, including the Volga, Don, Dnieper, and Seversky Donets, and bordered the Caspian and Black Seas. Khazaria's important trading cities included Sarkel on the Don, Khazaran on the Volga (next to the Khazar capital city, Atil), and Tamatarkha (modern-day Tmutorokan) on the Taman peninsula near the Black Sea. A number of caravanserais existed in the empire. Khazaria connected to the north-south Silver Road (which stretched from the Baltic Sea to the Arab caliphate) and to the east-west Silk Road trade routes, which both enjoyed significant commercial traffic. Overland trade routes connected Khazaria with other major Eurasian cities, including Kiev, Baghdad, Gurganj, and Kath in Khwarazm, and Bulgar in Volga Bulgaria. Sea routes linked Khazaria with Constantinople in the Byzantine empire and with port cities in the south Caucasus and Persia.

Those who came to Khazaria to trade included Arabs, Chinese, Ghuzz Turks, Alans, Scandinavian Rus' (Vikings), and Jews called Radhanites. Importers paid a tariff of 10 percent of the value of traded goods to the Khazar king. According to the anonymous tenth-century Persian work *Hudud al-Alam*, maritime customs duties represented the largest source of revenue for the Khazar government. Secondary sources included taxes collected from land traders and tribute collected from subject kings and tribes. Goods imported into Khazaria included candle wax, honey, pottery, silver wares, pendants, weapons, scabbards, fur, and silk and cotton clothing. Notable foreign specialty imports included an ivory elephant chess piece from Asia, a Byzantine bone comb, a Siberian iron hook, Chinese mirrors, Central Asian bronze buckles, and paper from Samarkand in Central Asia. Coins came to Khazaria from the Byzantine empire, China, Persia, and the Abbasid and Umayyad caliphates.

Goods exported from Khazaria to other countries included isinglass (sturgeon glue), fish, pottery, silver and gold wares, jewelry, mirrors, spears, leather belts, and wine stored in amphoras. Khazaria also supplied slaves, cows, and sheep. Several types of furs from Khazaria were known as *khazari* in Arabic countries. Slavic and Finnic tribes in Russia employed Khazarian goods in common use.

Trading activity in Khazaria peaked during the eighth and ninth centuries, after which it declined and was largely superseded by trade through Volga Bulgaria and Kievan Rus'.

Kevin Alan Brook

See also: Goths; Volga Bulgaria.

BIBLIOGRAPHY

Brook, Kevin. *The Jews of Khazaria.* Northvale, NJ: Jason Aronson, 1999.

Noonan, Thomas. "The Khazar Economy." *Archivum Eurasiae Medii Aevi* 9 (1995–1997): 253–318.

KILWA

Ancient African city that operated as a major slave trading port.

Over time, three Kilwas existed on the eastern coast of Africa with the oldest being Kilwa Kisiwani, which was located on a small island off the coast, the twelfth- to nineteenth-century city of Kilwa Kivinje, and Kilwa Masoko of the twentieth century to the present.

The ancient city of Kilwa Kisiwani was the city King Solomon supposedly traded with for gold for his temple. Little archeological evidence remains of ancient Kilwa because of the erosion of the soil caused by the annual monsoons.

The city of Kilwa Kivinje operated as a major slave-trading center. Caravans brought slaves from the Lake Nyasa region to Kilwa. At the height of the slave trade, more than 20,000 slaves a year passed through Kilwa. In addition to slaves, merchants in Kilwa traded gold, silver, and pearls for perfumes, jewelry from India, as well as Arab, Chinese, and Indian pottery. Goods from the interior of Africa that were traded with Arab merchants also included ivory, iron, copper, rhino horns, and coconuts. The inhabitants of Kilwa grew cotton that they traded for goods. Local rulers, of which there were many who were economically linked, levied a tariff on foreign merchants that helped increase their wealth.

From the twelfth century until the beginning of the sixteenth century, an Arab sultan, who encouraged the development of trade with the rest of the Arab world and India, ruled Kilwa. In 1505, the Portuguese arrived at Kilwa and threatened to take the city by force. The Portuguese were intent on controlling the wealth of the city and managed to do so until 1512, when the Arabs liberated Kilwa. The Arab rulers then forced merchants to restrict their trade with other Arab and Indian merchants and prohibited trade with Europeans. The prosperity of the city declined rapidly and was never restored to its former greatness. During the nineteenth century, the French and the Germans vied for power over Kilwa, but by 1840 they had abandoned the region.

The present-day Kilwa operates only as a local market where fruits and vegetables are exchanged. The ruins of the ancient cities attract some tourists to the region, but trade remains minimal.

Cynthia Clark Northrup

See also: Africa.

BIBLIOGRAPHY

Davidson, B. *The Lost Cities of Africa*. Boston: Little, Brown, 1959.
Freeman-Grenville, G.S.P. *The French at Kilwa Island*. London: Oxford University Press, 1965.
Pearson, M.N. *Port Cities and Intruders*. Baltimore: Johns Hopkins University Press, 1998.
Shinnie, M. *Ancient African Kingdoms*. Norwich, UK: Fletcher, 1965.

KIPLING, RUDYARD (1865-1936)

An English novelist and poet who rallied popular support for the British imperial system.

Born in Bombay, India, in 1865, Rudyard Kipling is perhaps best known for his novels about India, notably *The Jungle Books* (1894–1895) and *Kim* (1901). However, Kipling also represented one of the most strident and articulate voices to speak in favor of British colonialism.

The son of a Bombay schoolteacher, Rudyard Kipling spent his early childhood in India but was soon sent to England to receive an education. He graduated from public school in 1882 and returned to India to work first as an assistant editor for the *Civil and Military Gazette* and later as a correspondent for *Pioneer*. It was this journalistic training, learning to write in a compact, economical style, with an emphasis on the short-story medium that provided Kipling with the ability to capture the public imagination. After receiving critical success in England for several poems and stories written while he resided in India, Kipling returned to London in 1889 to pursue his writing full time.

Scholars and critics are in substantial disagreement as to when Kipling's virulent imperialism began, but it is certainly evident in the poem "The English Flag" (1891), as well as in "The Song of the English" (1893), where he writes:

> Fair is our lot—O goodly is our heritage!
> (Humble ye, my people, and be fearful in your mirth!)
> For the Lord our God Most High
> He hath made the deep as dry,
> He hath smote for us a pathway to the ends of all the Earth!

Rudyard Kipling promoted the idea that a benevolent British empire led to global peace, trade, and prosperity in his poetry and stories. *(Library of Congress)*

Throughout the 1890s, Kipling's work increasingly reflected this positive view of British imperialism, culminating in "The White Man's Burden" (1899). This poem, alternately praised and condemned, represented the pinnacle of Kipling's writing on the subject, and its influence extended across the Atlantic to find a welcome audience among those who supported the U.S. capture of the Philippines and other territories from Spain. Although Kipling's verse is laced with warnings to imperial powers on the high costs of colonial aggrandizement, the substance of the work reflects the "glory and the trust of empire" as exemplified by Benjamin Disraeli. The burden of the European, according to Kipling, was to

> Take up the White Man's burden—
> Send forth the best ye breed—
> Go bind your sons to exile
> To serve your captives' need;
> To wait in heavy harness,
> On fluttered folk and wild—
> Your new-caught, sullen peoples,
> Half-devil and half-child.
> And bear the hatred and blame
> of these "silent, sullen peoples"

Kipling's star, and that of the British empire, began to fall in the same year that "White Man's Burden" was published. The Boer War, which began in 1899, had disastrous consequences for Britain. In spite of Britain's victory, the war exposed the weakness of the army, demonstrated the failure of social reforms by the evident ill health of British recruits, and carried an enormous financial price tag. British public opinion began to turn away from the jingoistic sentiment that glorified the empire and Britain's right to rule foreign peoples, and Kipling's popularity suffered. Although his prolificacy did not dissipate, his impact certainly did.

The author of over seventy-five books of prose and poetry, Kipling, for a decade, represented the high point of British imperial sentiment and emerged as its most articulate and forceful spokesman. His influence was great both at home and abroad, and in the case of the United States, at least, his writings were seized on by those in favor of American expansion and used to prop up this side of a bitterly debated policy. Kipling continued to write until his death, and if many of his works retained the vivid, and often spectacular qualities of his earlier work, he was more often than not regarded as the voice of an increasingly anachronistic and naive point of view where foreign affairs were concerned.

Jefferson T. Dillman

See also: British Empire; Imperialism.

BIBLIOGRAPHY

Gross, John J., ed. *Rudyard Kipling: The Man, His Work and His World.* London: Weidenfeld and Nicholson, 1972.

Wilson, Angus. *The Strange Ride of Rudyard Kipling: His Life and Works.* New York: Viking, 1978.

KNIGHTS TEMPLARS

A Christian military order founded after the First Crusade.

Following the successful completion of the First Crusade in the early twelfth century, a Christian religious order of men known as the Poor Fellow-Soldiers of Christ and the Temple of Solomon was founded in 1118 by a French knight named Hugh

562 KNIGHTS TEMPLARS

SUPPLICE DES TEMPLIERS. — Composition et dessin de Ludovic Mouchot.

A major force in the Crusades to conquer the Holy Land for Christianity in the Middle Ages and organizers of an early banking system in Europe, the military order known as the Knights Templar fell into disrepute after the Holy Land was reconquered by the Muslims. Here, Philippe le Bel, the king of France, orders the burning of leading Knights Templar in Paris in 1314.
(Mary Evans Picture Library)

de Payens and several of his companions in Jerusalem to protect the many Christian pilgrims making their way to the Holy Land. Later known as the Knights Templar, or Templars, the men who joined the new order were both soldiers who formed a standing army for the Frankish kingdoms in the Middle East and monks who took vows of poverty, chastity, and obedience. The main headquarters of the Templars was a fortified monastery on the Dome of the Rock in Jerusalem. The order established similar outposts for military training and religious formation at places such as Haifa, Beirut, and Sidon. For 200 years, the Templars defended the roads, guarded the Holy Sepulcher, and participated in the remaining Crusades alongside such leaders as Richard the Lion-Hearted, the Holy Roman emperor Frederick I (Barbarossa), and King Louis IX of France. The Templars also joined the Crusades against the Albigensians in southern France and the Moors in Spain.

The Knights Templar won wide support from the Catholic clergy and people alike for their military power and religious devotion during the Crusades. Bernard of Clairvaux wrote the rule for the order in 1128, while Pope Innocent II placed them under his direct authority in 1139. Kings, noblemen, and merchants granted them profitable estates throughout Europe that included farmland, castles, and livestock. People of every class from the wealthiest to the poorest made donations to the many fortified monasteries or "temples" that the order built in the West. Many Templars never left Europe, but instead spent their lives working on the donated land owned by their order to supply the food, arms, equipment, horses, and clothing needed by the 300 to 500 knights stationed in the Middle East.

ORGANIZATION AND STRUCTURE

The Templars organized themselves into three separate classes known as knights, sergeants, and priests. The knights were drawn from the nobility and wore white robes to distinguish themselves from the other classes. They came to the order already fully trained and equipped for battle. They gave up all their property on entering the order and could only leave if they promised to join another order with more stringent rules. The sergeants were mounted men who were usually drawn from the wealthy middle class. They were each granted two horses on entering the order and wore black or brown robes to distinguish their status. The sergeants were called "brothers" and acted as guards, stewards, or squires for the knights. The priests served as chaplains for the knights and sergeants and were bound to the order for life. They wore green robes and gloves at all times to keep their hands pure for the sacraments. As educated men, the priests also acted as secretaries who kept records and wrote letters on behalf of the order. After the Second Crusade, the Templars were given the right to wear a red cross on their robes.

The order developed an effective military organization that influenced the development of armies in Europe for centuries to come.

The leader of the order was known as the grand master. While his power over his fellow Templars was not absolute, his decisions were rarely questioned. He acted as the commander in chief of the order and was expected to be a fearless military leader. Many of the twenty-three men who served as the grand master of the Templars died in battle or as prisoners of the Muslims. The marshal aided the grand master in battle by acting as the field commander. The seneschal served as the chief officer of the grand master, while the treasurer oversaw the finances of the order. The draper acted as the quartermaster and was responsible for securing and maintaining the weapons, clothing, and equipment. An officer called the turcpoler commanded the light cavalry. The Templars are credited with developing a swifter cavalry than commonly used in medieval European warfare to act as advance scouts, forage for supplies, and pursue fleeing soldiers on the battlefield.

BANKING

Known for their trustworthiness as well as for their courage in battle, the Templars soon developed an early banking system for the Christian West. Many kings and noblemen deposited their wealth in gold, silver, and jewels in the order's castles throughout Europe before heading to the Crusades themselves. King Philip Augustus left the entire French national treasury at the Temple in Paris before embarking on the Third Crusade. Eventually, many noblemen, church officials, and wealthy merchants who were not planning to join the Crusades also left their treasures with the Templars for safekeeping. There could be no better place to hide wealth than in the order's forts with their high thick walls and heavily guarded entrances.

While the Templars were not allowed to charge interest on the wealth deposited in their castles, they were able to charge fees for holding and guarding the treasures. They also made loans and collected fees as part of the transaction. The Templars made their first loan in 1149 when they granted a large sum of money to King Louis VII of France when the national treasury was bankrupt. The most famous Templar loan was made a hundred years later when the grand master of the order agreed to pay 30,000 livres to help ransom King Louis IX from the sultan of Egypt, who had captured the French king in battle. The Templars made even greater profits from their vast holdings in western Europe. Money poured into their temples from fees on their many estates and from the tithes that the pope allowed them to charge. They also ran successful export businesses, with the most profitable one being in England, where they dominated the wool trade.

As long as the Crusades continued, few were willing to question or confront the growing power and wealth of the Templars. But after the fall of Acre in 1291, the Templars and all other military orders gradually returned to Europe, where they were criticized for failing to protect Jerusalem. The Knights Hospitaller found a new role for themselves fighting Muslim pirates on the Mediterranean, while the Teutonic Knights settled along the Baltic Sea and fought the Slavs. The Templars now led by Grand Master Jacques de Molay contemplated returning to their headquarters in Paris and possibly even laying plans for another Crusade. Before the Templars could decide on the best direction for their order, King Philip IV of France decided to destroy them. Desperate for money, the king hoped to wrest control of the order's holdings for himself and his bankrupt nation, as the yearly income of the Templars was four times greater than his own. Philip began a public campaign of slander against the order and accused the Templars of heresy, idolatry, and immorality.

DISPUTES WITH THE CATHOLIC CHURCH

In 1307, King Philip asked Pope Clement V to investigate the Templars. When the pope agreed to begin proceedings against the order, Philip promptly arrested all the Templars in France and sent royal officers to confiscate their holdings. He hoped that Pope Clement would destroy the order throughout all of Europe. Instead, the pope determined that individual Templars would be tried in their own nation, while a council of the Catholic Church would investigate the order as a whole. The Templars were found innocent in England, Ireland, Scotland, Castile, Aragon, and the German kingdoms. They were found guilty only in France and areas under French control, such as Provence and Naples. Many of the French Templars had been brutally tortured into confessing their guilt.

Despite the pressure placed on them by the pope, the members of the church council investigating the Templars declared in December 1311 that the charges against the order were unfounded. Ignoring the decision of his own council, Pope Clement V suppressed the order in the spring of 1312 and declared that he would decide what was to be done with the Templars and their property. Philip in turn ignored the pope's ruling and ordered the execution of Molay and several of the order's high officials. They were burned at the stake in front of the Cathedral of Notre Dame in Paris on March 18, 1314, declaring their innocence against all charges until the end. According to legend, Molay placed a curse on both the king and the pope by declaring that they would both be dead within the year.

While he had destroyed the Templars, King Philip was less successful in winning the order's wealth for himself and his nation. The pope decided to turn the holdings of the Templars over to the Knights Hospitaller. King Philip was able to win a considerable settlement from the Hospitallers by claiming the Templars owed him money. However, his victory was short lived, for he died within the year along with Pope Clement as predicted in the legendary curse of the last grand master of the Templars.

Mary Stockwell

See also: Crusades.

BIBLIOGRAPHY
Robinson, John J. *Dungeon, Fire, and Sword: The Knights Templar in the Crusades.* New York: M. Evans, 1991.

KUSH (CUSH)

> An ancient Nubian kingdom located between the third and the fourth cataract of the Nile River in the upper Sudan.

The kingdom of Kush (called Nubia in the Middle Ages) was the transshipment point for goods exchanged from Central and South Africa to ancient Egyptians and the Arabs throughout the Middle East. Nubia engaged in trade with Egypt and at times the two kingdoms vied for power. The Egyptians called the region "nub," which meant "gold." Nubian merchants from Kush traded gold, ivory, slaves, precious metals, and exotic feathers with the Egyptians. After the Egyptian dynasty weakened in the eighth century B.C.E., the Nubians, which had been a colony of Egypt, attacked Egypt and by 712 B.C.E. ruled the ancient kingdom of the pharaohs. After the Assyrians pushed the Nubians out of Egypt and sacked their capital at Kerma, they established a second capital at Napata in the southern Sudan.

The Nubians lived in relative peace until an assault by a combined Egyptian-Greek force occurred in 591 B.C.E., when the capital of Napata was sacked. The Nubians then moved their capital to Meroë. The new kingdom, located between the fifth and sixth cataracts, combined Egyptian, Greek, and African cultures that lasted for another thousand years. During Alexander the Great's rule of Egypt, the Nubian kingdom coexisted with the Egyptians. Trade continued between Ethiopia and Egypt through the ancient kingdom of Kush. When the Roman empire assumed control over the Mediterranean Sea and Egypt, Julius Caesar sent a Roman legion to capture the kingdom. The Nubian army resisted the Roman army, and a truce was negotiated with Rome.

The prosperity of ancient Nubia had rested on trade as well as on the development of iron processing. The destruction of the soil and the inability to produce enough food for the population weakened the once powerful nation. In 350 C.E., Ethiopia conquered Nubia.

Cynthia Clark Northrup

See also: Egypt, Ancient; Roman Empire.

BIBLIOGRAPHY
Service, Pamela F. *The Ancient African Kingdom of Kush.* New York: Marshall Cavendish, 1998.
Welsby, Derek A. *The Kingdom of Kush: The Napatan and Meroitic Empires.* Princeton: Markus Wiener, 1998.

L

LABOR

Manual work that produces manufactured, handmade, or agricultural products.

Labor, like work, should be seen as a socially constructed category. In spite of the importance of economic and linguistic terms in denoting what constitutes work, the social context and defining worldview are very basic. In this sense, labor and its nature may be seen as affected by social circumstance and the meaning or interpretation of the activity by those concerned. It is, however, important to realize that whereas a distinction can be made between work and nonwork or leisure, labor can be used to cover mental and physical activities undertaken both as leisure and work. But it is also imperative to state that the accomplishment of tasks that labor involves is essentially economic and/or socially useful.

This fact is especially important in the contemporary world, where a difference is often assumed between exertions or activities geared toward economic profit and those driven by other less economic but often more socially useful goals. Therefore, an apt conceptualization of labor may be achieved by extending its boundaries and avoiding the limitations imposed by precision and specificity, since the forms of labor vary across and among cultures and societies. In this case, accounts of traditional societies would reveal the irrelevance of economic or monetary incentives in a cashless economy where social obligations may determine engagement in labor (e.g., kinsmen getting together to help one of them erect a new dwelling unit). Also, even in so-called industrial societies, there often exists a seamless web that embodies together what may be called work and nonwork activities. In other words, both may be embodied in one process (a good example of this can be readily seen in the area of arts or work/leisure of artists).

Moreover, as has been demonstrated in the literature, contemporary motives behind work or labor are a product of both Western civilization and the demands of industry and trade. In this sense, the motivation to work in order to fill time with productive or economic activities is a Western notion that differs from what prevails in traditional societies, where labor may be constricted by immediate needs. But this should not be misconstrued as giving weight to the notion of the lazy native often found in Western accounts, in which the native or those from other cultures are seen as inherently lazy in terms of labor and work involvement. At the same time, this should not be seen as a denial of the difficulty faced by the labor force of so many developing societies in their transformation from nonindustrial to industrial societies. The problems in such cases arise from adjusting to the strict separation between work and leisure, the geographical or spatial specificity of work venues, and the formalization of labor and economic activity in general. Therefore, labor as a concept can be seen as embodied in the rubric of work. The imperative of labor derives essentially from humanity's need to work or indulge in some form of productive or objectively meaningful activity.

Even though a distinction is often made between work and labor, it is obvious that both are intertwined in contemporary life. On one hand, the definition of labor as a bodily activity designed to ensure the survival of the individual in which the results are consumed immediately would confine labor to the activities or work roles of blue-collar workers or manual laborers. On the other hand, work is broadly seen as an activity or effort undertaken with the individual's hands, which gives objectivity to the world. The utility of these definitions seems doubtful both from the point of view of history and even contemporary reality. At the semantic level, one wonders what the difference is between a bodily activity and an activity undertaken with hands. In other words, where does the body end and where does the hand begin independent of the body? Moreover, even the most rudimentary form of labor involves at least a minimum coordination between the brain and the body.

For instance, the simple activity of shoveling sand into a truck cannot be effectively performed unless the brain-body coordination is intact, since efficiency depends on gauging the exact distance between the heap of sand and the truck as well as how to shovel the sand to minimize waste and conserve time. The main idea behind this distinction between labor and work is that what obtained in the preindustrial era or the period of slave labor was labor, whereas what is predominantly done now is work. But even this thinking is historically flawed.

In this sense, in many industrial societies of today's world, many work-related activities generate objects for immediate consumption, whereas in the simple hunting and gathering or traditional society some activities involving labor do not lead to immediate consumption. For example, the process of harvesting crops involves not only getting food for immediate consumption but, more crucially, setting aside something for the next season's planting. It would appear that regardless of the differences that exist in the nature of activity undertaken, the part of anatomy used, or the need the activity serves, the structure of society has changed over time and affected the economic activity of humanity. Basically, what is seen as both labor and work in the previous distinction can be seen as tied up neatly with the question of fulfillment of needs or economic relevance. It is in this sense that an overlaboring of any perceived difference between work and labor can only obfuscate reality. Therefore, labor can be seen rightly as embodied in work, and hence both concepts can be interchangeably and integrally used, especially when there is nothing to be gained from a distinction between the two.

In its contemporary sense, labor may be seen as engaging in a given occupation. However, this raises the problem of how to classify those who, even though they belong to a given occupational category, are not employed as such at the time in question. In this sense, there is the likelihood of separating the occupational status of the individual from his or her practice of that occupation. The use of the concept of labor can be traced historically to the emergence of slavery. The work of slaves or the drudgery of agriculture under the slave system was derogatively referred to as "labor." Even work itself cannot boast of a more dignified origin. Work originally meant manual labor, which is undoubtedly the oldest form of work. Therefore, in medieval times, noblemen were those who were not bothered with work. No wonder the earliest dictionary definition of the word "gentleman" as one who did not have to work to earn a living. According to Keith Grint, *avodah*, the Hebrew word for "work," has the same root as the word *eved*, meaning slavery; the Greeks had the words *pono* (painful activity), *ergon* (military or agricultural task), and *techne* (technique) for work. Therefore, work even in the original sense referred to physical or manual drudgery and was for the less fortunate members of society. In fact, the previous relation makes the attempt to achieve a fine distinction between work and labor all the more pointless. The conceptualization of both labor and work along the lines of physical exertion were products of the eras of slavery and feudalism, when crude agriculture made manual labor unavoidable. But these conceptions were eventually shattered or radicalized by the Industrial Revolution. It was the Industrial Revolution that broke the tradition of landed gentry who depended on the labor of others for survival.

In the understanding of labor, and particularly in the attempt to see why it had a not-too-noble beginning, the ideas of the early philosophers are important. Among these philosophers, Aristotle and Plato were instrumental in defining labor as a vocation for lesser mortals. They disliked the laboring class since they believed that those who are dependent on others cannot be free to partake in political debates. In other words, labor undermined the political process in society.

SLAVERY

One of the earliest places where labor was used was in the area of agriculture. Indigenous agriculture of whatever type relied entirely on human brawn. However, this labor was grossly inefficient in terms of mass production or ability to efficiently produce for the market. In other words, this form of labor was grossly inadequate in terms of meeting the economic demands of trade. This explains why the eras of feudalism in Europe and precolonialism in Africa were characterized by small-scale agriculture and a relatively rudimentary market economy that were severely limited by crude mechanization and lack of a well-defined and ungendered division of labor.

However, in the case of Africa, beyond these constraints the limitation of labor was sometimes seen by external observers as a reflection of laziness. In this case, the picture of the lazy native or local who spends six days in a week drumming and dancing and the seventh for relaxation was created. This notion has its roots in the myth of "tropical abundance." According to the myth, the native African was seen as occupying the naturally rich tropics that were endowed with food crops and fruits that grew in overflowing abundance and within easy reach. Because of this paradise-like environment, the native African saw no challenge in labor.

Related to this notion, though of a later origin, is the idea of describing the labor supply of Africans with the backward bending supply curve in the immediate era of European contact and colonization. In this logic, given the limited wants of the African worker he would return to his village or cease further labor efforts once these needs were met. This idea was used to justify not paying higher wages to the African colonial civil servant, since he would prefer to curtail rather than increase labor even if his wages kept increasing. Therefore, according to this logic, if the wage level increased beyond a certain level, the labor supply would begin to diminish.

Needless to say, both of these notions were the result of a failure to comprehend the dynamics of the African labor process before contemporary times, of early ethnocentric scholarship, and a natural reaction or interpretation of strange sociocultural and economic contexts.

The Industrial Revolution put paid to slavery and slave labor just as the Mechanical Revolution alongside it made human labor unattractive and dear when compared to machines. The legal abolition of the slave trade in Europe and America between 1803 and 1836 brought the final end to this form of exploitative labor, especially after the passage of the Thirteenth Amendment to the U.S. Constitution in 1865. It was first abolished by Denmark in 1803, and Portugal abolished it in 1836. Britain, which could be considered a great slave power, abolished it in 1807. Before the abolitions, slavery had been a great source of labor, and previous civilizations before the Industrial Revolution were more or less built on it.

West Africa was one of the most prominent sources of slave labor. To this end, slaves were taken from almost the whole of West Africa. Slavery is significant in the treatment of labor not because of the great use to which it was put in building civilizations before the Industrial Revolution or its basic obnoxious nature but because of the drudgery it signified for labor. The perception of labor as drudgery, which persisted through the feudal era in Europe and even in the early Industrial Revolution, was a direct result of the degrading use of slaves and labor gangs in those days. A good example of this degradation is the fact that a ton of a product like palm oil that came from the same geographic area had the same coastal price as one slave. In other words, one slave was valued as the equivalent (more or less) of a ton of palm oil. Slave labor was also boosted by the growth of what is called legitimate trade (trade in commodities and other goods apart from humans). The trade increased the demand for slaves within West Africa since export commodities such as palm oil were often produced and transported by slave labor.

It is also crucial to point out that slavery, as a practice, was not a work-induced development per se. It was rather a trade development. In this sense, the trade in human beings was part of the blossoming commerce and mercantile link among Europe, America, and Africa. Therefore, slaves, even though representing a watershed in labor history, were articles of trade. However, the trade in slavery is often distinguished from trade in other commodities. This distinction gave rise to the often-contested concept of legitimate trade—to indicate that one is referring to trade other than slavery. The trade nature of slavery is perhaps vividly captured in the fact that in West Africa, where slavery proliferated in the coastal towns that had the advantage of transportation routes (sea routes), there were prominent slave ports. The trade in slaves was the outcome of previous commercial links among Africa, Europe, and America. Actually, the trade between Africa and Europe goes backs to at least the fifteenth century. The early stages involved the exportation of goods like ivory, pepper, beeswax, and a few slaves. However, the slave trade became dominant in the seventeenth century. This development can be traced to high demand for slave labor in North and South America as well as in the Caribbean. These slaves were needed for the production of sugar, cotton, and tobacco and for the mining of different minerals.

The place of slavery and the slave trade in the evolution of labor as we know it today can be glimpsed from an observation by George Orwell. According to Orwell, civilization founded on slavery lasted for as long as 4,000 years, even though no credit for or record of these slaves exists today. It would be stating the obvious to maintain that civilizations from the Greek to the Egyptian were built on the shoulders of unknown and degraded slaves. The labor that was seen as a derogatory preoccupation for slaves is today the cornerstone of socioeconomic life in the world.

RELIGION AND LABOR

Also instrumental in the development of labor and its rise from the concern of lesser mortals to a noble engagement was religion. Christianity, specifically the Protestant version, was important in the promotion of labor. As has been reported by the sociologist Max Weber, capitalism received a boost from the Calvinists' Protestant ethic, which saw work/labor as a route to salvation or a confirmation of salvation (if one prospers in his or her chosen occupation or vocation). This notion, which gained acceptance as a result of the remarkable progress of the Calvinists in business, elevated labor from a necessary engagement and preserve of largely the less privileged to a moral cum spiritual duty. Accounts regarding the role of religion vary, from the use of classical Christianity to create a compliant slave population, to the use of Christianity as a soothing balm for inequalities (that is, in the sense of the Marxian notion of religion as an opiate of the masses), to the accounts of the connivance between the political authority and religion in perpetrating exploitation (as classically epitomized in France before the revolution in 1789). But the fact remains that Weber's account vividly captures the impact of a brand of religion on development of capital and labor. This fact also holds true in some early Islamic empires, where progress in trade was tied to or seen as a mark of divine favor. Such religious beliefs were basic to the transformation of labor.

Even after Weber, scholars and activists did much to make labor a moral duty for those who claim social responsibility. Thus, starting from Samuel Smile's doctrine of "heaven helps those who help themselves," to T. Carlyle's Gospel of Work (1977) and other proponents of the Victorian work ethic, labor was projected as consistent with if not a sure measurement of morality and spirituality. But fundamental to the church's involvement was the concern with trade. In spite of protestations to the contrary, the church was especially prominent in the seventeenth and eighteenth centuries in areas with flourishing trade and commerce. Religion, as the Calvinists aptly showed, can engender a productive commerce mentality in its adherents. In Africa, for instance, it is axiomatic to state that colonialism was built on the brace of religion and trade. As a matter of fact, religion in most developing regions of the world followed the known routes of trade. It is in this sense that it is often argued that religion was a palliative in securing geographical posts for eventual trading activities by colonial powers. Be that as it may, the religious doctrines are full of exhortations on how to be good merchants and how to cultivate proper commercial productive habits.

In contemporary times, religion has also played a big role in our understanding and appreciation of labor and trade. Thus, modern religion has also anchored on instilling commitment and devotion to labor among faithfuls. This religious duty has been taken to new heights by the Pentecostal churches that preach the gospel of prosperity. For most of these relatively new churches, prosperity in one's calling or occupation is a sure indication of good spiritual living, a brand of gospel that has received a big boost from the labor or work-filled lives of Jesus and other New Testament prophets. Jesus provided what can be considered the ultimate example of the prominence of labor in human life when he shunned the worldly piety of the Pharisees and declared that the Sabbath was made for man and not the other way around.

INDUSTRIAL REVOLUTION

As already mentioned, it was the Industrial Revolution that radicalized the existing conception of labor or manual drudgery. The Industrial Revolution, which occurred in western Europe in the eighteenth century, radically transformed the productive relations of society as well as the meaning and nature of labor.

There is controversy over whether the Industrial Revolution was the same phenomenon as the Mechanical Revolution. The fact is that the Mechanical Revolution and the Industrial Revolution, even though they took place during the same time period and influenced each other, were in essence different. In this sense, the Mechanical Revolution arose out of the development and progress in organized science, which led to new inventions in agriculture and other areas of life. But the Industrial Revolution was more of a social and financial phenomenon. The Industrial Revolution was primarily motivated by the changing nature of trade and commerce brought about by the division of labor. In a sense, the Industrial Revolution put paid to the idea of gang labor, labor as drudgery, and the animalization of human labor—the use of man as a mere work animal (classically illustrated in the plowing of fields by a combination of men and oxen or the use of men as sweating rowers in the galley of a ship). In spite of the difference in nature between the Mechanical Revolution and the Industrial Revolution, the Industrial Revolution was reinforced and even driven by the Mechanical Revolution and the related social process of many people working together under a roof as a work unit or the factory system. In concrete terms, the Industrial Revolution turned the human mind away from the ideas of slave and gang labor to the notions of mechanical power and the machine.

The Industrial Revolution, unlike the Mechanical Revolution that went on regardless of the consequences or changes it might produce, was affected by the constant changes in human and social realities occasioned by the Mechanical Revolution. The difference between the Industrial Revolution and the classic Roman Republic civilization was essentially in the character of labor and trade. The Industrial Revolution radicalized the prevailing conception of the nature and essence of labor. The process was aided by the rise of mass education. Continuous progress inevitably depended on an educated working population. The process was further aided by the spread of religion, which required enlightened adherents who would appreciate and spread the doctrine or belief.

Therefore, the Industrial Revolution discarded the idea of labor as drudgery. The world before the Industrial Revolution was built essentially on the idea that everything depended on the sheer brute effort and muscle of the human being, the muscle of ignorant and exploited human beings. In this situation, humanity in the centuries before the Industrial Revolution was engaged in purely mechanical drudgery or physical labor. Against this background, the Industrial Revolution created a scenario in which human beings were no longer needed as a source of physical power, since what could be done manually by a human being could be done faster and more efficiently by a machine. The human being now began to be seen as the supervisor of the process, who was needed where choice, decisions, and intelligence were required. The human being was now needed as a thinking being and not as a mechanical tool or chattel of the slave era. Hence, while previous civilization was built on cheap and exploited human labor, modern civilization was powered by mechanical devices under the control of men. The Industrial Revolution also necessitated the education of the labor force and the understanding of machines to bring about the industrial efficiency that was the greatest impetus to industrialization from both revolutions. The Mechanical Revolution also facilitated improvements in transportation and in the production (by way of machines) of a larger quantity of goods. These improvements boosted trade and commerce and made trade a large-scale affair responding to the needs of an ever-growing urban population.

The Industrial Revolution also reinforced the emerging factory system of production. Factories per se were the products of the increasing division of labor in society even before the Industrial Revolution. The factory system is the core root of the industrial era and gave birth to the social transformation associated with the industrial era. For Anugwom, the industrial life is a product of the factory system, both as a production and as an organizational principle. Therefore, a highly specialized division of labor as required by mechanization and the factory system is probably the most primary and basic structural feature of industrial society. Weber sees a characteristic factory as organized workshops where nonhuman means of production are fully appropriated by an owner but workers are not, where there is an internal specialization of functions, and where mechanical power and machines that must be tended are used.

Definitely, the factory system benefited from the rise of mechanization. As a matter of fact, steam power provided the initial energy required by the factory. But more crucial for labor was that the factory brought many people together as workers and fostered some level of cooperative interaction among them; in the process, it gave vent to the articulation of common problems and values on which informal groups and later labor unions were built. Equally pertinent is that the factory, machines, and energy would have been unnecessary without a corresponding growth in the nature and volume of trade. Definitely, the two revolutions and the factory changed the face of the production of goods, but these changes were driven by the economic forces of improved trade and large-scale commerce. It is in this sense that the Industrial Revolution was a social and financial response to the era.

MODERN LABOR PROCESS

A critical point of departure in understanding labor in modernity is the idea of labor process. We owe much of what we know about labor process to the insightful contribution of Harry Braverman in *Labor and Monopoly Capital*. In this contribution, Braverman expounds the seminal idea of Karl Marx, that the main area for explaining conflict and control in society is the labor process. In this sense, the labor process refers to the place where commodities (goods) are constructed and developed by a mixture of human labor and raw materials. In other words, the derivation of the finished goods is through systematic utilization of human labor and raw materials. Needless to say, Marx saw the exploitative nature of the labor process under capitalism as a reason for its overthrow through a revolution anchored by the working class.

Braverman's ideas can be seen as a bold attempt to extend the frontiers originally set by Taylorism and the scientific management principles. Like Frederick W. Taylor, Braverman believes that the contemporary labor process is built on the twin poles of control and achievement of maximum effort by workers for minimum reward. Thus, for Braverman the concerns are how to bring to the shop floor or factory the structurally determined cooperatives of managerial control, with the effects of this control on the workers themselves, and how to achieve monopoly capitalism through the dynamic and immanent process of de-skilling and degradation. For Braverman, effective managerial control, which is essential for monopoly capitalism, can be achieved through extending the division of labor. This creates a distinction between the conception and execution of work and contributes to the general de-skilling of the workforce. The target in these efforts is to achieve not only higher productivity, but also a pliable labor force. In effect, Braverman ideally seeks the separation of the labor process from both the worker and the control of the worker.

On the route to monopoly, capitalism, or a trade economy in which money determines the allocation of society's valuables in a cash-and-carry manner, the conditions of work are further deteriorated. Labor is prevented from realizing this by a combination of higher wages and consumer-oriented lifestyles. Equally important in the Braverman scheme are the roles of science and technology, which function as tools of capitalism to replace labor and de-skill labor that is left. This implies that science and technology do not just aid modern production, but also reduce the relevance of labor and at the same time increase the control of management. The end point of the labor process as envisaged by Braverman is that with the aid of science and technology, the delusion of a better life, and the control of a strengthened and stratified management, control is taken from the direct producers (labor) and reinvested after the fragmentation of the labor process, through de-skilling and managerial practice, under the control of management.

In a nutshell, Braverman postulates a new kind of labor process and shop floor reality built from the original ideas of Taylor. In the new situation, the labor process is wrestled away from labor and the control of labor, that is, the interaction between labor and capital cum other factors of production in the workplace is now determined and controlled by management, aided by science and technology, which together through de-skilling reduce the relevance of labor. It is in this process that monopoly capitalism emerges as the dominant order in society.

However, like all ideal conceptions of reality, Braverman's labor process notion fails to take cognizance of the dynamic nature of labor itself, the real meaning and impact of skill, and the consistent if not rapidly transforming contestations between labor and capital in modern society. The fact is that Braverman's conception of early and precapitalist-era labor as skilled is flawed. In other words, skill these days emanates not from the craft conception of those days, but from the ability to manipulate the tools of science and technology. So, even if one concedes that the emergence of science and technology at the workplace displaced the craft laborer, they engendered the emergence of a more adept labor. In a sense, the value of skill and what makes up skill are determined by trade or market realities in modern times. Moreover, skill per se has social and historical connotations that affect what is seen as skilled or otherwise, when, and in what context. But what seals the coffin on Braverman's idea of de-skilling is that if de-skilling were possible as he and Taylor hypothesize, time would have left us with a huge mass of homogeneous de-skilled proletariats. The contrary reality is obvious today.

However, Braverman, in spite of the voluminous criticisms of his ideas in literature, remains an important figure in the evolvement of the labor process and labor itself by implication. Just as Taylor opened our eyes ironically to the need for a well-run organization for production and the imperative of good management, Braverman calls attention to the challenges of technology and extreme managerial control over labor. The ability of labor to survive and grow despite science and technology and even the ever-expanding control of management (in some industries) indicates the central place of human labor in life itself.

LABOR ORGANIZATIONS

Labor developed in the capitalist system of Europe to tackle the challenge of capitalism, as it were. A significant form of this orientation is the concept of laborism. Laborism simply denotes the pursuit of reforms within the existing forms and methods of parliamentary government and collective bargaining. According to Alan Fox, this has been the dominant response of the working class in Britain to the challenges posed by capitalism. Laborism or the adoption of this form of accommodation of capital by labor was born out of two factors. The first was the general rise in real living standards and workers' quality of life. This both diminished the revolutionary impetus and gave hope that capitalism could give more economistic rewards or accommodate such if labor readily articulated a clear position. The success of the trade unions and the readiness of most employers to find accommodation with labor greatly undermined the desire for control of the productive and political processes by labor.

Second and crucial in undermining the revolutionary cause of labor is the generally heterogeneous nature of the working class in many countries of the world. Heterogeneity by implication fragments the working class and makes the formation of the solidarity needed for revolution impossible.

Invariably, labor unions and organizations, while projecting and promoting the interests of labor, grew along the lines of the existing political and economic processes. In spite of projecting an apparently contradictory worldview, labor ironically became structured by the existing framework of society and bureaucratized. This was not as a result of leadership betrayal, whether one thinks along the lines of Robert Michels's oligarchy or Leon Trotsky's scenario. In the former case, the labor union is depicted as being hijacked over time by the powerful members or leaders and in this case is soon enough routinized. In the latter case, Trotsky's thesis suggests that all labor defeats or conversely lack of victory can be ascribed to the existence of traitors in the leadership rank.

The fact is that the modern labor and trade union is more or less a product of the capitalist system. It is in this sense that Grint posits that trade unions are constructed through and reflective of capitalism. He argues that the world of trade unions and the world of employment are not automatically or naturally conducive to class solidarity, but are more likely to boost the sectionalist and sectarian ideologies on which capitalism itself is built. The previous viewpoint, which is seen as more tenable especially in developing countries or nations in transition, gives credence to the earlier postulation by Antonio Gramsci that while trade unions may be socialist subjectively, they are objectively capitalist. In fact, the contemporary history and reality of labor confirms this reality, that even though labor may appear socialist or revolutionary and radical, it is in fact molded and informed by the dominant economic and political order of the society. This fact may equally explain the absence of a clear-cut revolutionary labor movement in contemporary society. However, the aligning of the labor movement with the dominant political and economic process has not reduced its ability to agitate for improving the conditions of life for its weaker members. It has also not deprived it of the strength for confronting inequalities in the system. But the nature of the labor movement as an organized collectivity places a limit on its radical posture. Even in Russia, where unions are seen as radical, the radicalism has been within the context of the prevalent societal reality. This tendency has been greater in the liberal parts of the world like Britain, where the drive is generally toward eform. Even where a political party emerges along the line of labor as in the case of the British Labour Party, the party has been geared toward reformist changes.

The fact is that in spite of the reverse wave or influence of such working-class tendencies as syndicalism, guild socialism, and the Communist Party, they have been swallowed up or grossly marginalized by the preeminent position of laborism. In this sense, laborism has remained the consistent and dominant response of labor to the challenges of capitalism. (However, it would be revealing to see how laborism has remained dominant or what changes labor has witnessed in view of the intensification of capitalism as represented by globalization.)

In spite of this, it seems pertinent to argue that even though the labor movement has a tendency to marginalize radical leadership, the aspirations represented by these radical members are often in consonance with those of the rank-and-file members. Thus, J. Zeitlin argues that trade union organizations are often so structured that radical local leaders are outside the boundary of national leadership, even though they are aligned more with the "real" and "larger" interests of the rank-and-file membership. Even though the nullity of local radical leadership emerging in control of the national leadership can be seen as partially reflective of the inherent oligarchical control of labor, this fact is more a reflection of the political process that is mostly beyond the control of labor. In this case, in spite of the conflicting ideals between labor and capital, labor and capital are equally well aware of the need to maintain the production process. This is a fact that has been reinforced over time by the precarious economic condition of labor and the willingness of marginal members, who incidentally are in the majority, to seek accommodation with capital in order to stave off the threats of immediate privation and hunger. To see the value of this argument, one must understand that the most successful of labor wars with capital have been those tied to the immediate economic needs or conditions of labor, rather than those that hinged on facilitating the enthronement of an ideal political and economic order, with all the adverse consequences of this on labor in the short run.

The control of national labor leadership by the reformist elites is also enabled by the political leader, who see the reformist elites as more pliable and amenable than the radicals. Thus, the state has a stake in the triumph of the reformist elites of labor. The triumph of the reformists ensures the survival of laborism as a labor response and strategy toward capitalism. It is the desire of the state to achieve this end and to work toward the separation of industrial relations from the political process that promotes the collective bargaining practice. Collective bargaining easily becomes an instrument for resolving conflicts in the productive process and achieves the dissociation of conflicts or tension between labor and capital. However, as Grint points out, this should not be conceived to mean that collective bargaining operates autonomous of political interest or exists "within the arena of equal parties" but, rather, that conflicts can be settled or dispersed before they escalate into political movements that may threaten the legitimacy of the state. The lack of collective bargaining seriously erodes laborism and engenders the adoption of more radical cum political tactics by labor. This actually accounts for the near-universalization of collective bargaining —an attempt by capitalism to cover its flanks and watch its back.

Another major shift in the understanding of labor has been its conception as a social reality or a social phenomenon by disciplines other than economic. Thus, from the 1960s a predominantly economic concern like the labor market, for instance, drew the attention of sociologists and economic historians, following the influential work of John Harry Goldthorpe et al., who conducted an extensive interview project among the Vauxhall factory workers in Luton, England. The result of this revealing study of labor was the emergence of the notion of labor segmentation. In other words, the postulation of Goldthorpe et al. drew attention to the need to examine the operation of relevant labor market(s) if one is to have an adequate insight and understanding of the determinants of both the priorities and expectations of workers in any enterprise. These concerns were made all the more apparent by studies by Michael Mann and Robert Martin Blackburn.

The concepts of "dual" and "segmented" labor markets were used to delineate a labor market structure that while appearing objective created subjective opportunities for some groups and denied others the same opportunities. In other words, low-quality employment opportunities or labor involvement were a permanent feature of labor market structures. More crucially, discriminatory recruitment policies were used to ensure that certain categories of employees were likely to fill them, as determined by sex, race, ethnicity, and social class. The inability of, for example, women and ethnic minorities to obtain better jobs did not really derive from their inferior skill or such other objective criteria, but from a discriminatory segmented labor market.

Even though the segmentation of the labor market with the division it creates in labor ranks ultimately enhances the control over labor exercised by the employer, the labor union can still play a role in checking this trend. As a matter of fact, many labor unions and human rights groups have risen to the challenge with the support of the International Labor Organization of the United Nations in fighting this malaise. The fight has been especially successful in the developed regions of the world, where no discriminatory and equal opportunity practices have received the concrete backing of government and other institutions. Apparently, labor segmentation is more of a social response than a phenomenon driven by the demands of trade or market for labor. In this sense, while labor segmentation might help maintain the labor status quo, it works against efficiency and competition in the labor market. In other words, trade demands, while met by labor, are not met to the utmost and most efficient levels.

GLOBALIZATION

The most contemporary challenge to both the nature and form of labor has come from globalization. Globalization, whether seen as an entirely novel process or as a new form of interaction between different nations, should be seen mostly as a trade-related phenomenon. In this sense, the relationship among different nations has been structured through history by the nature of trade among them. Thus, what goes by the name of globalization denotes a radical change in the nature of trade relations among nations. This is a process that has been facilitated by the new wave of capitalism and the role of the Bretton Woods institutions in promoting economic, monetary, and trade ties among nations. Interestingly, a country's profile in the new dispensation has been measured by the volume of trade it attracts and the direct foreign investments coming to it.

Besides trade, a close scrutiny of globalization would reveal that the economic dimension of the process has been fundamental. This economic dimension is linked to the issue of development, whereby development becomes a function of the economic benefits accruing from globalization. However, labor is undoubtedly a major factor in both trade and the general economy. As a result, developments in these areas inevitably affect labor. P. Dawkins and J. Kenyon and Richard B. Freeman and Lawrence F. Katz point out the various ways that globalization has affected labor and the entire work process: income inequality, work fragmentation, dichotomization of the workforce, the casualization of labor, and so on. The concern with the impact of global trade or globalization on labor was further reinforced by the World Bank, which in its 1995 *World Development Report* focused on workers in an integrating world.

The improved international trade expressed in globalization has been built on the notion that

The use of cheap labor in developing countries—as in this Reebok shoe factory in Vietnam—is an important element in the modern international economic phenomenon of globalization. (© Lou Dematteis/The Image Works)

it will ultimately lead to an improvement in the workers' lives. Generally, the idea is that countries will attract new industrial investments and an increasing trade volume that will eventually gain jobs for skilled workers and create new opportunities for labor in general. Labor is expected to collaborate with management to discover new international markets and improved production processes that will engender a high-skill, high-wage route to prosperity. But the reality, it appears, is far from this ideal. Jeremy Brecher and Tim Costello argue that labor is now confronted by an adverse situation, in which the competition for new investment and capital among the developing countries has enabled the multinational companies to institute a regime of low wages and a stable cheap labor force. Even in the advanced nations labor has not fared any better. In these places, there are complaints of unemployment, casualization of labor, crippling of labor unions or collectivities, and the abandonment of labor rights. It would seem that the financial and trade nature of capitalism involved in globalization has put labor in greater peril than ever before. A. Roy sees globalization as simply an effort to reconstitute capitalism that, instead of creating new markets, enables takeovers of existing markets and trade opportunities by a few privileged countries.

In all, globalization and its emphasis on global trade have emasculated labor and weakened the labor union while strengthening capital. While financial capital enjoys an unhindered mobility across national boundaries, labor mobility has been constrained severely. The radicalization of the work process and the relations of production determined nowadays by global trade have created a mass of working-class labor characterized by deaggregation, de-skilling, casualization, and recomposition.

Edlyne E. Anugwom

See also: Slavery.

BIBLIOGRAPHY

Anugwom, E.E. "Sociology, Industrial Sociology and Industrial Life: A Nexus of Necessity in Society." In *Readings in Sociological Studies*, vol. 2, ed. P.C. Onyia, C. Owoh, and P.C. Ezeah. Enugu, Nigeria: Rainbow and ESUT, 2003.

———. *Work, Occupation and Society*. Nsukka, Nigeria: AP, 2002.

Blackburn, Robert Martin, and Michael Mann. *The Working Class in the Labour Market*. London: Palgrave Macmillan, 1979.

Braverman, Harry. *Labor and Monopoly Capital*. New York: Monthly Review Press, 1974.

Brecher, Jeremy, and Tim Costello. *Global Village or Global Pillage: Economic Reconstruction from the Bottom Up*. Boston: South End Press, 1994.

Carlyle, T. "The Mechanical Age." In *Nature and Civilization*, ed. A. Carlyle. Oxford: Oxford University Press, 1977.

Dawkins, P., and J. Kenyon. "Globalisation and Labor Markets: Implications for Australian Public Policy." Research paper, no. 200017. University of Nottingham, Centre for Research on Globalisation and Labor Market, Nottingham, UK, 2000.

Fox, Alan. *History and Heritage: The Social Origins of the British Industrial Relations System*. London: Allen and Unwin, 1985.

Freeman, Richard B., and Lawrence F. Katz, eds. *Differences and Changes in Wage Structures*. Chicago: University of Chicago Press, 1995.

Goldthorpe, John Harry, David Lockwood, Frank Bechhofer, and Jennifer Platt. *The Affluent Worker: Industrial Attitudes and Behaviour*. Cambridge: Cambridge University Press, 1968.

Grint, Keith. *The Sociology of Work*. Cambridge: Polity, 1991.

Mann, Michael. *Worker on the Move*. Cambridge: Cambridge University Press, 1973.

Michels, Robert. *Political Parties: A Sociological Study of the Oligarchical Tendencies of Modern Democracy*. Glencoe, IL: Free Press, 1949.

Orwell, George. *The Penguin Essays of George Orwell*. Harmondsworth, UK: Penguin, 1984.

Roy, A. "Imperialist Globalisation and Labor." *Revolutionary Democracy* 3, no. 2 (September 1997).

Sahlins, Marshall David. *Stone Age Economics*. London: Tavistock, 1972.

Weber, Max. *Theory of Social and Economic Organisation*. New York: Free Press, 1947.

Zeitlin, J. "Trade Unions and Job Control: A Critique of Rank and Filism." Paper presented to the Society of Labour History, Birkbeck College, London, November 27, 1982.

LAISSEZ-FAIRE

An economic policy in which the owners of business and industry allow the rules of competition and the conditions of labor to develop as they naturally evolve without government regulation or intervention.

The term "laissez-faire" originated with the Physiocrats, a group of eighteenth-century French economists led by François Quesnay. They believed in the existence of a natural order in which only agriculture yielded wealth. In view of this, they condemned as inefficient and harmful any interference with industry by a central authority except when it was necessary to break up private monopoly.

The principle of nonintervention of government in economic affairs was refined by Adam Smith. Smith had met the Physiocrats on a visit to France and found his economic beliefs much more akin to their policies than with the interventionist beliefs of English mercantilists. This affinity for the Physiocrats led Smith to construct an economic theory designed to minimize government interference with individual freedom and to devise a methodology that would encourage individualism and a laissez-faire approach to the marketplace. In *On the Wealth of Nations*, he wrote, "The statesman who should attempt to direct private people in what manner they ought to employ their capitals, would not only load himself with a most necessary attention, but assume an authority which could safely be trusted, not only to no single person, but to no council or senate whatever, and which would nowhere be as dangerous as in the hands of a man who had folly and presumption enough to fancy himself fit to exercise it."

This principle of nonintervention of government in economic affairs was given support by many of the classical economists. Economic historians generally accept that these authors constitute a specific identifiable school of thought. According to Phyllis Deane, "[t]hey shared a distinctive framework of economic ideas, shaped by a particular set of axioms and theories and generally characterised by a strong bias toward economic policies favoring economic individualism and laissez-faire."

David Ricardo brought the laissez-faire concept to fruition in the theory of international trade. Ricardo stated explicitly for the first time the law of comparative cash. Using a tightly argued numerical example, Ricardo asserted that two countries with different comparative costs can, through the exchange of freely traded goods, both benefit.

This concrete example of the instinctive belief in Smith's "hidden hand," the greatest benefit to society, which is maximized if each individual economic agent is left to seek his or her own profit, brought about the free-trade era in England. (England became the world's workhouse and therefore imported more foodstuffs.) The free-trade era lasted in England for almost a century. After World War I, economic nationalism brought about the fall of the system in response to protectionist demands.

The laissez-faire concept is still very much in evidence in modern economic academic circles. Economists such as Milton Friedman and George Stigler advocate the market as the central instrument needed to order economic activities.

Robert Koehn

See also: Economics, Classical; Free Trade; Smith, Adam.

BIBLIOGRAPHY
Bannock, G., R.E. Baxter, and R. Rees. *The Penguin Dictionary of Economics*. New York: Penguin, 1982.
Deane, Phyllis. *The Evolution of Economic Ideas*. New York: Cambridge University Press, 1978.

LAW

> Rules of procedure within society that have binding authority.

Trade, the successful exchange of goods and services between related and nonrelated entities, remains the backbone of all economies. The success of this exchange depends on the goods and services available, the needs of the exchanging parties, and the mechanics by which the exchange is to be accomplished. More specifically, trade involves the business of buying and selling commodities, whether goods, services, or species under terms reasonably agreeable to both parties, measured by the balance of risks to rewards in a manner or under a system where there is likelihood it will take place and there is some recourse for failure to complete the transaction.

The history of trade reveals a complicated, tortuous, and often frustrating process whereby this exchange is hampered or enhanced by the often-contradictory demands of politics, personalities, religion, and happenstance. There has always existed a conflict between the simple desires of the trader and the political needs of the body politic. In addition, the various religious experiences of the people involved and the manifestations and needs of the believers have deeply influenced the mechanics of trade. The manifestation of the world of the divine and its strictures on conduct has profoundly affected the terms of the bargain, items to be bargained for, and often whether there would be any bargain at all. Lastly, the variety of objectives among the traders of the world has added a personal, if not necessarily advantageous, touch to trade and its success.

The necessity for rules to ensure reliability and dependability in these transactions no doubt gave rise to the earliest attempts to control and simplify the system of trade. This process of order and control produced rules, guidelines, and penalties that we call law. Law could be tribal agreements, monarchial or imperialistic decrees, parliamentary/congressional laws and codes or international agreements, whether individually promulgated, such as tariffs, quotas, and taxes, or mutually agreed on to regulate international trade as embodied in treaties. This response to an acknowledged need, along with the commensurate political and social needs of society, necessarily gave rise to the ever evolving and increasingly complex national laws and decrees that continue into the present. The evolution of law and its influence on trade is a varied and often counterproductive attempt to balance the subjective needs of the trading system with the more general and pervasive world of politics, personality, and religion.

Any rational discussion of the interaction of law and trade must consider the varied and inconsistent change over time and region that law addresses.

EUROPE, THE UNITED STATES, AND THE MIDDLE EAST TO WORLD WAR II

The earliest surviving complete law code is the Code of Hammurabi (approximately 1750 B.C.E.). Although most of the code is devoted to civil and criminal law, sections 90 to 104 provide strictures and actions for traders as well as set the general tone for trade within Hammurabi's realm. This early Mesopotamian work continued to influence Middle Eastern law until Roman times.

In contrast to the Code of Hammurabi, the nature of the Egyptian pharaonic state does not indicate the use of specific legal codes or enactments until well into the Ptolemaic period (332–30 B.C.E.). Like China, Egypt, until the period of the Roman conquest, lacked any institution similar to a parliament or other legislative body. Rather, the pharaohs made decrees or treaties regarding trade. There are few surviving examples of such treaties or decrees. However, references to an ordered system of trade can be inferred from various preserved Egyptian texts such as *The Story of Sinuhe* and *The Journey of Wen-Amon to Phoenicia*. This situation continued in this manner until Egypt's assimilation into the Roman empire.

The initial and foundational basis of early Rome was the Twelve Tables (ca. 450 B.C.E.). This early example of Roman law did not address trade in any meaningful way; rather, it provided civil and criminal guidance forming the foundation of the Roman state and the Roman notion of the universality of law. Despite Rome's position as the leading trading power in the Mediterranean, there is little specific trade-related information relative to its conduct in the empire other than the standardization of weights, measures, and specie content and the establishment of trading colonies. Although it is clear that Rome was aware at least of the larger trade issues such as the balance of payments (Pliny complained of the balance of trade in India's favor), on the whole, Rome seems to have left trade to the marketplace and the Pax Romana.

In the period after the Roman empire, the broader and more uniform Digest, including the Codex of Justinian (529–34 B.C.E.) based at least partially on the earlier Theodosian Code, was a later attempt by the emperor of the Eastern Roman empire not only to codify Roman law, but also to incorporate the theory and teachings of the legal profession. The code addressed all areas of Roman law, including trade and business that are found in book 1, chapters 5 and 7, and book 2, chapters 4, 5, and 7.

The collapse of the Western Roman empire in 476 C.E. allowed the Catholic Church to slowly become the governmental structure and lawgiver of the core of the Roman empire in Italy. Roman law was soon combined with applicable church law (canon law), producing a Christianized version that would permeate and dominate Europe until the Protestant Reformation.

Probably the most significant aspect of church law in relation to merchants and trade was the biblical prohibition of interest on money borrowed or lent. This aspect of late antiquity through the Middle Ages may be one of the significant factors contributing to the dearth of trade and the insularity of the manor and attendant serfdom. In addition, the notion of charity and almsgiving created an atmosphere that did not favor the accumulation of wealth, at least outside the nobility and the clergy. In this regard, neither trade nor law was particularly relative, as the world was irrelevant in the face of the promise of eternal life that was attainable only on denial of the world and its wealth. Merchants at medieval trade fairs throughout Europe during the Middle Ages did not need governmental or church authority to control the day-to-day terms of trade, as they independently adopted agreements for payment and exchange based on the next fair or meeting.

Trade would always push the boundaries of law, especially in the Middle Ages. The Republic of Venice experienced one of the most peaceful and extensive periods of government from the twelfth to the seventeenth centuries based on a republican form of government that placed trade at the center of state policy. The extensive trading power of Venice continued until the Portuguese maritime explorers discovered a new route to the riches of the East.

The first major national efforts in the Middle Ages that foreshadowed changes in the conduct of trade are found in England. Various sections of the Magna Charta (1215) relate to the standardization of weights and measures used in trade and the disposition and treatment of both foreign and native English traders. A second change that occurred in England about this time concerned the foundations of the English Common Law and the systemized court system that arose in this period, based, at least partly, on the Magna Charta. The English Common Law provided the foundation for the legal system by which England would emerge as the leading trading power in the world.

The final document to guarantee the supremacy of law was the English Bill of Rights of 1689. Although not specifically dealing with trade, it finished the process by which Parliament began to control the king, thus guaranteeing a less erratic and stable legal system. The impact of this process and the elevation of "the rule of law" cannot be overstated in view of the dissemination of Anglo-Saxon influence throughout the world.

The second major influence on the issue of trade and its legal aspects relates to the adoption by most west European states of mercantilism in the seventeenth century. The colonial ventures and empires of the sixteenth, seventeenth, and eighteenth centuries spearheaded the system of trade and economic interchange. The adoption of mercantilism and the regulation of trade between home country and colony would dominate the world of business and commerce well into the nineteenth century. Mercantile theory was based on the assumption that there was a fixed and limited amount of wealth in the world, thus leading both nations and individuals to concentrate on the importance of wealth accumulation, especially gold. Mercantilism fit well into the world of empires and colonies and thus facilitated the economic subjugation of colonies that produced raw goods in exchange for manufactured goods from the home country, which in turn transformed these raw products into additional manufactured goods to be sold back to the colony or any other destination where it could find a market.

Beginning in the mid-1700s, various political and economic writers began to question mercantilism and in the process created and advanced the laissez-faire theory of open markets and open trade. Adam Smith's *Wealth of Nations* (1776) is generally considered the seminal work of what came to be called capitalism. Smith's arguments on creation of wealth, minimal governmental restraint, and the laws of supply and demand are still the foundations of modern capitalism. Capitalism slowly replaced mercantilism, but the colonial and protectionist legacy of the latter lingered well into the twentieth century. Under mercantilism and capitalism, the imposition of tariffs, basically a tax on items produced outside the nation, was and remains the preferred method of protection of the home industry.

The broad acceptance of capitalism in the early 1800s on the strength of the Industrial Revolution produced the greatest and most continuous expansion of trade and economic power in human history. The capitalism of national protectionism only slowly gave way to the capitalism of free trade of the global economy in the latter half of the twentieth century. During this period of mercantilist/capitalistic growth, England and the United States, as well as various other nations, used tariffs and quotas against each other as these two powers came to dominate the international world of commerce in the second half of the twentieth century.

From its earliest inception as a colony of England, the United States was first and foremost a trading nation, although not necessarily to its benefit. Leading up to, and during, the American Revolution, England made various attempts to control both the American colonies and the empire in general through tariffs, quotas, and other trade legislation. The Navigation Laws (1651, 1660, and 1696), Molasses Act (1733), and Sugar Act (1764) were all English attempts to control colonial trade.

To the framers of the U.S. Constitution, commerce was one of the most important considerations after individual liberty and self-government. The newly approved Constitution included, first, the powerful commerce clause that gave the federal government the power to control interstate and international trade and, second, the right to bankruptcy that would give millions the ability to start again.

The decisions of the Supreme Court, newly established under the Constitution, created a long-desired stability in law. Long favoring the right to contract and freedom to engage in business, the Court determined the commercial and trade aspects of the country. The Court's decisions in *Gibbons v. Ogden* (1824) affirmed the national government's supremacy in interstate commerce. During the period from the 1880s through the 1920s, the Court backed up the use of the injunction against strikes. In *Lochner v. New York* (1905), it struck down maximum-hour laws based on what it perceived as prohibitions on "freedom of contract." In *United States v. E.C. Knight Company* (1895), the Court neutralized the Sherman Anti-trust Act, taking an initial stance against antitrust legislation that it later reversed.

In *Bailey v. Drexel Furniture Co.* (1922), it invalidated child labor laws, all directly or indirectly affecting national and international trade. During the period from the late 1930s through the 1970s, the Court reversed or clarified many of its earlier decisions, and through the present, it continues the process of interpreting the Constitution and the commerce clause, attempting a balance between the rights of the states and those of the federal government.

The use of tariffs and quotas by both England and the United States continued to be the main tool to protect national markets. English trade policy from the nineteenth into the first half of the twentieth century revolved around its empire and its integrity. American trade policy after the Civil War reflected its growing economic power and its competition with England and Europe. From the earliest days of the republic, the United States used tariffs to protect itself and its industries from English industrial power. The early tariff debates that emerged from the War of 1812 led to the Tariff of Abominations (1828) and to the high tariffs after the Civil War through the 1920s that eventually led to balance of payment problems and the Great Depression. Beginning with the Reciprocal Trade Agreements Act (1934) and the Neutrality Act (1935), the return of the United States to lower tariffs reflected the need for trade of any nature during the prewar years. Although the use of tariffs continues to the present, the rise of regional and international trade agreements began to erode this most common of trade policies.

Protectionism as national policy determined the extent and rate at which the free-trade theories of Smith and others would advance outside the context of the nation-state. The twentieth century, with the Bolshevik revolution, the rise of international communism, and the Great Depression, shook the world economies to their foundations. A wave of tariffs, trade laws, and other protective legislation during this period seemed to have doomed the free-trade principles of Smith and his like. It is only with the aftermath of World War II, when the United States emerged as the most powerful economic nation in the world, that the issue of free trade began to take hold as the driving force behind the globalization of trade.

ASIA TO WORLD WAR II

The world of Asia north of the Himalayas is the world of China and its emperors. From the earliest dynasties of Xia and Shang through the final years of the Qing dynasty, China maintained a self-centered worldview that determined its future in the world of commerce. The circular and cyclical dynastic phases of Chinese history kept China's eye on itself while it manipulated its surrounding world. Although there were several major codifications of Chinese law, such as the Tang Code (653 C.E.) and the Great Ming Code (1390s), the legal atmosphere of China was primarily one of imperial decrees issued over time according to the imperial policies and whims of the emperor. The foremost concept of Chinese trading policy, as reflected in the decrees, was the centrality of China to all trade and the necessity of acquiescence in this concept by all others.

As the predominant economic country in this part of Asia for the period from the Han dynasty (206 B.C.E.–220 C.E.) to the nineteenth century, China pictured itself as a trading country par excellence, reaching its intellectual and trading heyday under the Song dynasty (960–1279). This dynasty, one of the most expansive in Chinese history, took bold steps in the world of trade outside its borders and inaugurated an era of international maritime trade. One must bear in mind, however, that in the China of this period, it was ritual, not law, that would dictate international diplomacy and trade. China lacked the dominant element of Western jurisprudence: law was a concrete instrument of governance to which all were subject. In the Chinese view, laws were to prevent controversy, while in the West, laws were enacted to solve controversy. It would take the European treaties and their spheres of economic and political influence that developed in the late nineteenth century before China began to understand and integrate the Western concept of law into its trading world. Despite these differences in law and the self-centered concept, the seventeenth and eighteenth centuries allowed China to become the greatest nonindustrial commercial power in the world.

It was with the arrival in force of European nations in the nineteenth century that China's trade policies began to be dictated by various European and American colonial and economic interests. By the end of the nineteenth century, large parts of China had devolved into a series of European spheres of influence that eventually caused the end of the Qing dynasty in 1911. From 1911 through 1949, China's trade policies shifted wildly as it attempted to stabilize its internal convulsions and react to the effects of the two world wars.

By approximately 1600, Japan was finally unified after an uprising that defeated warring feudal leaders. Soon thereafter, the country was closed off from all international contact as the Tokugawa rulers promulgated a national policy of exclusion (1630s), cutting Japan off from virtually the entire the world except Chinese and Dutch merchants through small trading posts in Nagasaki. Not until 1853 and Commodore Matthew Perry's demand for the opening of Japan to foreign trade did Japan end this isolation. Thereafter, Japan, especially during the Meiji period, fervently, vigorously, and energetically embraced the industrial and mercantile world of the West. It can be argued that, as far as Asia is concerned, it was only in Japan that there was a successful incorporation of the Western concepts of law and trade that prevented Western political and economic dominance.

On the Indian subcontinent of Asia, the earliest compilation of laws was the Laws of Manu (1280–880 B.C.E.). Although there were sections dealing with trade, this work was primarily a criminal and civil text. Its importance lies in the fact that it codified the caste system that left an indelible mark on India's life, commercial and otherwise. All subsequent law revolved around this institution. The next major influence on Indian law was the introduction of Islamic law in the sixteenth century. The British victory at Plassey (1757) introduced English Common Law into the country, with its attendant changes. The 200 years of British rule and law would produce the fusion of Indian, Islamic, and British law under which India operates today.

The most significant event in the Middle East was the rise of Islam beginning in the seventh century. Beginning with the solidification of Muhammad's control of Mecca in 630 and Islamic conquests well into the European subcontinent and into the Indian subcontinent, Islamic armies and traders carried with them Islamic law, in the form of the Shari'a. In terms of trade, Islam was one of the most active forces in the world through the seventeenth century. It brought with it the Qur'anic prohibitions of interest, the relationship of profit that is conditioned on the probability of risk, and its concept of corporate entities. These aspects of Islamic commercial law allowed it to achieve early and widespread success but later created conflicts with Western mercantilism and capitalism that remain today.

POST–WORLD WAR II

The shift in emphasis to free trade after World War II began the process of regional and international attempts to bring unity and order to the world trading community. In addition, free trade and globalization of world markets began to exert increasing pressure against national protectionism, treaty preferences, and colonial models of trade and production. The collapse of the British, French, Portuguese, and Belgian empires and the ensuing confusion created additional pressure for change. That change was the driving force for the globalization of world trade. National law began to give way to treaty law as the world economy began to slowly embrace globalization and the interdependent international marketplace.

GATT AND THE WTO

A discussion of post–World War II trade law should begin with a discussion of the General Agreement on Tariffs and Trade (GATT), now incorporated into the World Trade Organization (WTO). At the end of World War II, fifty countries met at the Preparatory Committee of the United Nations Conference on Trade and Employment to negotiate the creation of a new organization to oversee world trade disputes among countries. Like many initiatives after the war, the idea was to reduce the high tariffs and significant protectionism that had grown among countries in the period leading up to the war.

Before the conclusion of these negotiations, twenty-three of the fifty countries met to discuss the more immediate reduction and binding of tariffs. The combination of tariff agreements and rules that these nations agreed to came to be known as the GATT, which went into effect January 1948. GATT was initially only intended as a provisional measure until the creation of the International Trade Organization (ITO). However, as the ITO, although fully negotiated, was never ratified, GATT continued on for another forty-seven years.

During its nearly fifty-year existence as a multilateral trading system governing international trade, GATT achieved its results primarily through two mechanisms: organization rules and trade negotiation rounds. The two critical rules were the most-favored-nation status, whereby any benefit given to one contracting state must be given to all contracting states, and the national treatment rule, whereby imported goods were to be treated the same as their domestically produced counterparts. Besides these two rules, there were additional "rounds" of trade negotiations among the signatory states. It was with these general principles, and through eight different rounds of trade negotiations, that the participating countries came to agree on various reciprocal trade terms. Looking at the entire history of GATT, average tariffs in developed countries fell from an average of 40 percent around World War II to around 4 percent by the early 1990s. Additionally, with some limited exceptions, quotas have been significantly reduced as a means of trade regulation. In 1995, after nearly eight years of negotiations, at the final GATT trade round, known as the Uruguay Round, the framework of the WTO, the successor to GATT, was agreed on.

Unlike GATT, which was provisional and lacked the status of an organization, the WTO is a legal entity. This stronger legal status means the WTO has much greater ability to ensure compliance with its trading rules. Specifically, the WTO has the ability to rule that the laws of certain countries place an illegal restraint on trade. In addition, the WTO has much broader responsibilities than GATT did. While GATT focused on the trade of goods, the WTO encompasses not only trade in goods, but also services and intellectual property rights. Both GATT and the WTO had the effect of transferring the ability of individual nations to determine their own trade policies by the voluntary submission to a body outside the nation, an issue that continues to plague further discussions on world trade especially for the United States.

Although both GATT and the WTO have their detractors, from the perspective of the law and trade these have been significant developments. These entities represent a significant shift away from the use of tariffs and quotas as the primary tools of trading relations. Even more significantly, these two entities brought into existence a previously unknown multilateral trade order that, in the case of the WTO, has the ability to deem illegal the conduct of member states in the realm of trade.

BEYOND GATT AND THE WTO: REGIONAL PACTS

After GATT/WTO, a continuing discussion of post–World War II international trade policy must also mention regional trading agreements. Much of the economic trade literature of this period focuses on free-trade agreements, customs unions, and common markets. Although not an exhaustive list, some of the more significant initiatives are the European Union, the Mercado Comun del Cono Sur (MERCOSUR; Southern Cone Common Market), the North American Free Trade Agreement (NAFTA), and the Association of Southeast Asian Nations Free Trade Area.

While GATT, and subsequently the WTO, sought to encourage the development of trade and the reduction of trade barriers at the global level, Europe was embarking on its own regional initiative with trade. In 1952, six European countries (Belgium, France, West Germany, Italy, Luxembourg, and the Netherlands) founded the European Coal and Steel Community (ECSC) to oversee Europe's postwar industrial rebuilding and to regulate and facilitate the trade of two crucial industrial elements among the members. The ECSC functioned by pooling resources for administration by the respective countries and through a supranational organization. The goal was to gradually eliminate tariffs and other trade restrictions in these traditionally heavy industry sectors.

Although limited to coal and steel, this union represented a new paradigm in European trade and political development. Not only were these states agreeing to coordinate their strategic interest goods, but also they were agreeing to do so though a supranational entity. Even more ambitious than the ECSC's initial undertaking was the idea held by many of the member states that once these barriers to trade were eliminated, the next phase would be the development of a common market among those countries.

Building on the ECSC, in 1957 the same six countries joined together to form the European Economic Community (EEC), an organization intended to move beyond the relatively limited scope of steel and coal issues and toward the creation of a customs union among the members. In 1967, the ECSC, the EEC, and the European Atomic Energy Community merged and were renamed the European Community (EC). Consistent with this notion of a customs union, the idea was that member countries would gradually reduce their quotas, tariffs, and preferences on goods traded among them. Additionally, there was to be the establishment of a common external tariff for goods coming into the EEC from nonmember countries.

Looking strictly to the trade aspects of the EEC, the European states were successful in meeting their objectives. In ten years or less, the EEC achieved two of its primary goals. The first objective was the establishment of a common pricing policy for agricultural goods. Second was the establishment of a common external customs and commercial tariff toward nonmember countries. With the achievement of these two goals among the member states, much of the subsequent efforts of the EEC, and its modern successor organization, the European Union (EU), were carried out through the GATT/WTO trading order. The EEC/EU represented their member states' interests at the different trade rounds, thus creating a far stronger bargaining position as a coalition of states than individually.

Although not created until nearly forty years after the EEC, MERCOSUR represents an effort to increase economic and trade cooperation among members in a manner similar to the European Common Market established by the EEC. The full members to this agreement include Argentina, Brazil, Paraguay, and Uruguay. Negotiations are ongoing with other countries for possible entry; for example, Chile and Bolivia have associate member status.

The origins of this common market idea can be found in the bilateral trade efforts of the full members in the 1970s and 1980s. These efforts culminated with the 1991 signing of the Treaty of Asuncion, which provided a loose blueprint for regional economic integration among members. The practical effect of MERCOSUR has been the creation of a quasi-duty free zone for goods originating among its members. The term "quasi" is appropriate because while many goods carry a zero-percent tariff, several sectors are not covered by this agreement. Furthermore, certain goods are exempted and each state maintains a list of additional goods not covered by the agreement.

MERCOSUR, unlike the EU, does not use any type of supranational entity. Rather, it functions based on intergovernmental structure. The resolution of issues among members is left to discussion among the governments of the respective countries rather than to a central body. The structure can lead to problems in resolving disputes between members over related issues of trade, as there is no entity that can enter a final decision applicable to all parties.

In contrast to the European and South/Central American efforts is NAFTA. Signed in 1992 by Canada, Mexico, and the United States and taking effect in 1994, NAFTA created a free-trade zone among the three signatory countries. NAFTA is exactly what its name implies, a free-trade agreement. In stark contrast to the broader political and social emphasis of the EU, NAFTA focuses on trade with limited discussion of investment. Furthermore, while it has its origins in trade agreements with Canada, NAFTA moved quickly to lower tariffs among Canada, Mexico, and the United States, with fewer sectors and goods excluded from those reductions. The situation reflects the strong debate within the United States concerning the protectionist focus on the exportation of jobs and the issue of standards. The agreement established ten-year, in some cases fifteen-year, periods for the elimination of trade and nontariff barriers. The agreement contains a limited discussion of both the implementation of the agreement and resolution of disputes arising under the agreement.

Furthermore, the agreement leaves unchanged any tariffs that the signatory countries may place on goods from third-party countries.

Among the Southeast Asian countries, recent explosive economic growth brought with it efforts to boost regional trade. The Association of Southeast Asian Nations (ASEAN) is an organization consisting of ten Southeast Asian countries. The organization has a broad mandate to promote socioeconomic progress and regional stability through cooperation in several areas including trade. Although historically an informal political body, in 1992 the then six member nations agreed to create the ASEAN Free Trade Area.

The goal of this free-trade area was the reduction of intraregional tariffs on manufactured goods and agricultural products with an exception for goods identified as sensitive. By 2003, the goals of the area had been largely met by the original six members through the Common Effective Preferential Tariff, which was a list of commodities for which tariffs were to be reduced. The goal of this trade area was encouragement of intra-ASEAN trade, goods with at least 50 percent ASEAN products, as this had been a historically weak area of trade among ASEAN members.

Because of ASEAN's origins primarily as a political rather than economic entity, the use of a supranational authority was not seen as in the EU. ASEAN's limited institutions developed as needed but always relied on the member states to resolve their differences, rather than imposing an authority above the states to handle compliance or disputes.

Further analysis of the interaction of law and trade might include the subtler aspects of the interaction between laws or restrictions enhancing or enlarging the social and political rights of individuals and groups within the wider social realm. Clearly, religious admonitions on theft, murder, and observance of times of worship had ramifications outside their religious framework. These strictures, admonitions, and guidelines produced a moral and political atmosphere that clearly advanced society and its ability to form the solid and dependable structures that allow for trade. The condemnation of usury in early and medieval Christian Europe, along with the Qur'anic strictures against interest, clearly influenced trade. Actions as varied as the elimination of the slave codes enacted before the Civil War in the southern United States and the clear but steady expansion of the suffrage movement in Europe and the United States paved the way for a larger and more diverse population to expand beyond "the economy of scarcity" to the ever widening world of globalization. Issues as diverse as the civil rights legislation enacted in the United States in the last half of the twentieth century, change in immigration policy, and the continued exodus of political refugees to the United States may have inadvertently boosted productivity, allowing the country to maintain or advance its position within the international economy. These events and their interactions await another day.

From the earliest trading societies to the complex and interdependent world of modern commerce, the necessity for rules to simplify and give stability to trade appears obvious. Law has attempted to provide both this simplicity and stability and a framework for future change. While it may be argued that the law could exist without trade, it is inconceivable to imagine meaningful trade without law.

Robert R. Ansiaux and Vincent J. Ansiaux

See also: British Empire; Roman Empire; United States.

BIBLIOGRAPHY

Beaney, William M. *American Constitutional Law: Introductory Essays and Selected Cases.* New York: Prentice Hall, 1954.
Blacksell, Mark. *Post-War Europe: A Political Geography.* Boulder: Westview, 1978.
Cromwell, Oliver, and Joseph S. Roucek. *Caste, Class and Race: A Study in Social Dynamics.* Garden City, NY: Doubleday, 1948.
Declareuil, J. *Rome the Law-Giver.* New York: Knopf, 1926.
Delener, Nejdet. *Strategic Planning and Multinational Trading Blocs.* Westport: Quorum, 1999.
Diegold, William, Jr. *The Schuman Plan: A Study in Economic Cooperation, 1950–1959.* New York: Council on Foreign Relations, 1959.
Fischer, Thomas C., and David Williams. *The United States, the European Union and "Globalization" of World Trade: Allies or Adversaries?* Westport: Quorum, 2000.
Gianaris, Nicholas V. *The North American Free Trade Agreement and the European Union.* Westport: Praeger, 1998.
Haley, John Owen. *Authority Without Power: Law and the Japanese Paradox.* New York: Oxford University Press, 1996.
Hurwitz, Leon, and Robert S. Jordan. *International Organizations: A Comparative Approach.* Westport: Praeger, 1994.
Kelly, J.M. *History of Western Legal Theory.* Oxford: Clarendon, 1992.
Moon, Bruce E. *Dilemmas of International Trade Book.* Boulder: Westview, 2000.
Mote, F.W. *China, 900–1800.* Cambridge, MA: Harvard University Press, 1999.
Pritchard, James B., ed. *The Ancient Near East.* Vol. 1, *An Anthology of Texts and Pictures.* Princeton: Princeton University Press, 1973.
———. *The Ancient Near East.* Vol. 2, *A New Anthology of Texts and Pictures.* Princeton: Princeton University Press, 1975.
Rosenberg, Jerry M. *Encyclopedia of the North American Free Trade Agreement, the New American Community and Latin-American Trade.* Westport: Greenwood, 1995.
Schimmel, Annemarie. *Islam: An Introduction.* New York: SUNY Press, 1999.
Smith, Anthony. "The AFTA-CER Linkage: Forging a New Direction in Relations with ASEAN." *New Zealand International Review* 22 (1997).
Urwin, Defek W. *The Community of Europe: A History of European Integration Since 1945.* London: Longman, 1995.

LEATHER

The processed hide of animals that has had the feathers or fur removed.

People have used leather, in its various stages, since prehistoric times. The skins of animals have been cured through the process of tanning, initially with grease, so that the leather was more pliable. Early items that were made of leather included clothing, shoes, containers, and various forms of shelter. The ancient method of tanning leather was described in Homer's *The Iliad.* Ancient Egyptians, although they preferred linen, used leather for its durability for clothing articles such as gloves. Roman soldiers used leather shirts to protect themselves from the arrows and spears of their enemies. Roman aristocrats wore leather sandals while the rest of the population remained barefoot.

In more recent times, leather was treated with fats. Europeans first used the modern tanning process in 1620, when they adopted the methods used by the Indians in North America. Indians in North America used leather for shelter and clothing. Some tribes developed a technique for painting leather to be used to make clothing for ceremonies and other special occasions.

Leather has been used in a variety of industries over time. The shoemaker, before the advent

Leather has been an important internationally traded commodity since ancient times. Shown here are two 1870s'-era workers in Turkmenistan trampling millet seed into animal skins, which is part of the process of turning rawhide into finished leather. *(Library of Congress)*

of synthetic materials, used leather for footwear. Harness makers used leather as well. Even parchment was manufactured from leather. Before the invention of plastic, leather was used for belts, bags, and carrying straps. Leather jackets, although expensive, were also made, as were leather pants on occasion. During the Middle Ages, leather was used for wall or door coverings. Leather was also used for bookbinding. Leather furniture became popular, especially in the United States in the nineteenth century.

By the eighteenth century, machines were capable of slicing thin layers of leather that could be used to cover hard surfaces. Various stains were used to produce a variety of colors with the most popular being black, brown, and a deep red. Since the mid-1850s, manufacturers have developed artificial leather.

Cynthia Clark Northrup

See also: Animals; Livestock.

BIBLIOGRAPHY
Richardson, Adele. *Leather.* Mankato, MN: Creative Education, 2000.
Sterlacci, Francesca. *Leather Apparel Design.* Albany: Delmar, 1997.

LINEAR B SCRIPT

A Late Bronze Age script used by the Mycenaean Greeks for temporary administrative record keeping.

In form, Linear B is a syllabary that was borrowed from another language, although which language is not known. A syllabary is a writing system that uses a single letter for each syllable in the language. Since the typical language has something like seventy syllables, a syllabary employs more letters than does an alphabet. Linear B is not the world's only syllabary; syllabaries have been devised to write many languages. The Japanese *kana* script, for example, is a syllabary.

Documents in Linear B, written on hardened clay tablets, were first discovered in 1899, and Michael Ventris deciphered the script in 1952. It employs five symbols for vowels, fifty-four for consonant-vowel combinations, and nineteen others for punctuation, numerals, weights, measures, and commodities.

Linear B was used to keep records of the Mycenaean kings from the mid-sixteenth until the twelfth century B.C.E. at such centers as Mycenae, Thebes, Tiryns, and Pylos on the Greek mainland, and briefly at Knossos and Khania on Crete. It records the kings' accounts of equipment, such as chariots, chariot wheels, harnesses, helmets, armlets, spears, and arrows, and of commodities, such as grains, spices, cheese, and fruits. Craftspeople identified in the texts include spinners, weavers, sewers, perfumers, masons, carpenters, shipwrights, bow makers, and bronze and gold workers. Most products of Mycenaean farms and workshops were already known from the archaeological record, which also shows that the most important Mycenaean trade goods were bronze and utility pottery. The Linear B inventories add details about trade of goods (cumin, ivory, and slaves from Lemnos, Knidos, and Miletus) that are not otherwise preserved.

Paul Edson

See also: Communication.

BIBLIOGRAPHY

Chadwick, John. *Linear B and Related Scripts.* Berkeley: University of California Press, 1987.

LINEN

A cloth or yarn made from flax.

Although rough linen has been made occasionally from hemp (*Cannabis sativus*), flax (*Linum usitatissimum*) has always been the primary source for quality linen. The plant's stem fibers are processed into the thread used for weaving linen. History's oldest surviving garment is made of ancient Egyptian linen. Until the rise of cotton production and synthetic materials after the 1880s, linen was the most frequently used natural plant fiber from Europe to Russia and India in the east and Ethiopia in the south, although cotton (*Gossypium*) is more predominant in southerly climates. In colonial America, for example, linen was characteristic of northern areas, while cotton dominated the South.

Native from western Europe to Iran and south to North Africa, wild flax (*L. bienne*) is the most probable ancestor of the cultivated species *L. usitatissimum*. Edible and industrial oils have also been produced from both flax species. *L. bienne* seeds have been found in Middle Eastern archaeological sites dated to 9200–8500 B.C.E., proving the plant's use predates domestication, but by 6000 B.C.E. *L. usitatissimum* seeds are more common in sites in Syria, an indication that they were part of the wheat and barley agricultural complex developing at the same time as irrigation technology. From the Fertile Crescent, cultivation spread westward to the Mediterranean basin and northern Europe, becoming common by the Bronze Age. Though not native to the Nile River valley, flax was farmed there as early as 5000 B.C.E. and became practically the sole wrapping material for mummies. Ancient priests in Judea, Egypt, Greece, and the Fertile Crescent often wore linen garments as a sign of purity.

The eastward spread of flax cultivation lagged behind Western distribution, but archaeological evidence records its cultivation in Pakistan and India by 3000 B.C.E. Throughout the Eurasian landmass, linen cloth has been a staple item of exchange between sedentary peoples and nomads, along with horses, rice, grains, and weapons. This relationship was fraught with periodic crises of demand and supply tied to population migrations and conquests, such as the movement of the Huns, who depended on linen imports for summer clothing in the hot Central Asian steppes.

Flax cultivation flourished in the ancient Western world, whereas silk dominated in China and cotton dominated in India. Though linen production decreased after the fall of the Roman empire, production of Egyptian linen flourished under Muslim rule. Linen elaborately embroidered in silver and gold—called *tiraz*—was a medieval luxury good, particularly when the Fatimids (969–1171) sponsored commerce with Italy. The Ayyubids, however, who ruled Egypt and Syria from 1169 to 1252, turned to bulk flax thread production for export and then focused on sugar exports by the twelfth century. As flax acreage dwindled, medieval west European linens outpaced Egyptian ones. Flemish, Dutch, and northern Italian production attracted merchants seeking the fine linens of Ypres, Ghent, Bruges, Cambrai (hence "cambric"), Verona, Cremona, and Brescia at distribution markets like the famous four annual fairs in Champagne, France, sites of some of the earliest innovative banking. From the fifteenth to the seventeenth centuries, Spain was a major player in the linen trade, with reportedly 16,000 looms operating in Seville, its port with the Americas. To the north, the Hanseatic League's wealth depended on linen, which remained the choice for underclothing and for luxury dress throughout Europe, despite competition from silk. The poor wore wool.

Textiles were the major industry of the medieval and early modern periods and fueled interest in mechanization. As a result of the revocation of the edict of Nantes in 1685—meaning France no longer tolerated Protestants—many skilled linen manufacturers immigrated to England and Ireland, turning both countries into major fine linen producers. The first experimental spinning factory in England dates to 1797, but it took fifteen years to develop an effective system of industrial production. Early industrialization allowed British merchants to compete successfully in the nineteenth century against local manufactures throughout the world. Thereafter, manufacturing became mechanized worldwide, though north European linen dominated markets well into the twentieth century. Ireland, followed by Japan, Russia, and Belgium, remains the world's finest linen producer.

Fabio Lopez-Lazaro

See also: Egypt; Hanseatic League.

BIBLIOGRAPHY

Abu-Lughod, Janet. *Before European Hegemony: The World System A.D. 1250–1350.* New York: Oxford University Press, 1989.

Friedman, John Block, and Kristen Mossler Figg. *Trade, Travel, and Exploration in the Middle Ages: An Encyclopedia.* New York: Garland, 2000.

Warden, Alexander J. *The Linen Trade: Ancient and Modern.* London: Frank Cass, 1967.

Zohary, Daniel, and Maria Hopf. *Domestication of Plants in the Old World: The Origin and Spread of Cultivated Plants in West Asia, Europe, and the Nile Valley.* Oxford: Oxford University Press, 2000.

LIST, GEORG FRIEDRICH (1789-1846)

A German economist, journalist, politician, and promoter, whose arguments in favor of protective tariffs and state-sponsored economic development and against the free-trade doctrines of Adam Smith and David Ricardo, exercised great influence in Germany and the United States.

Born in Reutlingen, Georg Friedrich List pursued a highly successful career in the Württemberg civil service, which culminated in a professorship at the University of Tübingen. His activities as a liberal journalist and politician led to his dismissal from state service in 1818. He became the leader of a national organization lobbying the German states to form a customs union (*Zollverein*). He was charged in 1822 with political offenses, fled abroad, but returned to Württemberg for a brief imprisonment, and immigrated to the United States in 1825. While in the United States, List participated in railroad and other development projects and took part in the debates over American tariff policy. After returning to Germany in 1830, List worked as a freelance journalist promoting railway construction, the expansion of the Zollverein, and German political unification. His book *Das Nationale System der politischen Ökonomie* (1841) was the most important presentation of economic protectionism published in the first half of the nineteenth century. It was read widely in Germany and the United States (where its first English edition appeared in 1856). List committed suicide in Kufstein, in the Austrian Alps, in 1846.

List is an extremely important figure in the history of German economics, whose work influenced national policy from the time of his death until the end of the twentieth century. More clearly than anyone else in his time, he articulated the view that development was the central feature of modern economic life, that the process of economic development could not be entirely deduced from the analysis of free markets tending toward equilibrium as the classical economists assumed, and that successful economic development required active state participation in the economy, not simply an absence of state interference. He saw manufacturing as the key to development and tended to subordinate trade to considerations of industrial expansion, but trade nevertheless played an important role in his thinking. List agreed with the classical economists that restrictions on the free exchange of goods through trade within a marketing area created a less-than-optimal economic situation and retarded capital formation, investment, and expansion. He pointed out, however, that under most real circumstances, differences in current industrial capacity between countries and regions meant that, under conditions of unrestricted trade, areas with high levels of manufacturing capacity, like Britain in the first half of the nineteenth century, would always be able to dominate the markets of areas with less capacity such as Germany and the United States.

The assumption that industrial expansion was the core of economic development meant that less industrialized countries might never be able to create competitive manufacturing sectors and would therefore be condemned to economic underdevelopment as well as to political subordination. The solution to the problem, List argued, was to mark off large geographical areas, the boundaries of which incorporated most of the exchanges that affected most people within the areas. Inside the boundaries, free exchange was to be maintained and state resources were to be used to support the private development of manufacturing capacity and markets for industrial products. At the boundaries, state power was to be employed, mainly through the instrument of tariffs, to impose limits on the entry of manufactured goods from the outside and to ensure that the goods that were imported sold at prices with which domestic producers could compete.

This situation could be created, according to List, either through the establishment of large nation-states such as the United States that would pursue protectionist policies, or through the creation of associations among smaller states in economically coherent regions whose members would agree to a common economic and tariff policy. It was the latter course that List advocated for Germany, through the mechanism of an expanded Zollverein. That the German states might follow the former pattern, that is, unite into a single federal entity like the United States, was something that he contemplated, but it was not the main thrust of his economic writing. Because of his advocacy of regional economic unions, List is considered to be one of the forebears of the thinking that produced the European Community and other regional economic associations in modern times.

Woodruff D. Smith

See also: Free Trade; Ricardo, David; Smith, Adam.

BIBLIOGRAPHY
Henderson, W.O. *Friedrich List: Economist and Visionary 1789–1846.* London: Frank Cass, 1983.

LIVESTOCK

Animals, raised for food or food products, that have often been used as a medium of exchange.

Livestock is one of the oldest forms of exchange used in human history. Sheep, cattle, pigs, and poultry have been domesticated for thousands of years. Early humans used cattle for dairy products such as milk, and poultry for products such as eggs. In early times, a family would have only enough animals to provide for its basic needs, but by the rise of the ancient civilizations of Sumer and Egypt, livestock had become a means of measuring wealth. Animals could be given as gifts, as was often done in the case of a dowry, or used as a means of exchange for other products. Widespread transport of livestock did not occur as in modern times, but animals were transferred from one region to another to be used for a variety of purposes, both as food sources and commodities.

Sheep, raised for their wool, originated in western Asia and by Roman times could be found throughout much of Europe. By the twelfth century, wool had become an important commodity; it was the primary reason for England's enclosure movement (where wealthy landowners enclosed common fields shared with peasants for their own private use) and an important aspect of the English mercantile system.

Pictured here are two men with a herd of cattle in the Sahelian Zone of West Africa in 1973. Livestock represents one of the oldest forms of exchange known to humanity. *(Library of Congress)*

Cattle became important throughout much of Africa, particularly South Africa. When the Dutch established a station in South Africa, they encountered the Xhosa, with whom they traded fresh meat and dairy products for their journey around the Cape of Good Hope en route to India and South Asia. As the Boers (Dutch who settled in South Africa) began raising livestock, the two groups competed for pasture—a competition that resulted in several wars.

Pigs, considered "unclean" animals and hence taboo for adherents of several religions, such as Judaism and Islam, were raised extensively in Europe as a food source. During the Middle Ages, pigs were consumed by the local inhabitants, but their real importance as a food source came with their introduction to the New World. Spaniards routinely left pigs behind in areas where they explored. Since the animals were feral and required no maintenance, the Spanish had an available supply of meat when they returned. Throughout much of American history, the pig was the main source of protein.

The livestock industry developed in the United States during the nineteenth century. The open ranges of the West provided ample grazing land for large herds. Cattle from as far south as Texas were annually driven north to the railheads in Kansas and then shipped alive or, after the invention of the refrigerated boxcar, slaughtered for transport to the meat-packing houses in Chicago. The United States became a major exporter of beef to Europe during the late nineteenth and early twentieth centuries. After the creation of the European Economic Community (now the European Union), increased livestock cultivation within the community reduced, but did not eliminate, the importation of U.S. beef. Of the 1 million tons of beef consumed annually in Great Britain, only 15 tons originate in the United States. Other countries that export a large amount of beef are Canada, Australia, Brazil, and Argentina.

The United States exported livestock to Japan during the late eighteenth century, but before then, the Japanese relied almost exclusively on soybeans and fish for their protein needs. The

Japanese raised cattle primarily for dairy products. As the Japanese economy boomed during the 1960s and 1970s, the Japanese turned to beef as a major source of protein. In 2003, the Japanese imported approximately 150,000 tons of beef from the United States.

In 2003 alone the beef industry earned $175 billion in the United States. One of the major fears of beef producers is the spread of livestock diseases such as bovine spongiform encephalopathy (BSE), more commonly known as mad cow disease. There is evidence that cattle infected with BSE, if consumed by humans, leads to an increased risk of developing the human form of the disease called variant Creutzfeld-Jakob Disease (vCJD), an untreatable and fatal brain disease. One confirmed case in the United States led many countries, such as Japan, Mexico, and several in the European Union, to ban imports of U.S. beef. When mad cow disease was discovered in England in 1996, more than 6 million head of cattle were destroyed to prevent its spread. Cattle become infected by eating feed that contains ground up brains and other soft tissue from other cattle that died of this neurological disease. Since then, most governments have banned this type of feed, but some animals could still be infected by previous exposure to the feed or by leftover feed that was never destroyed.

While sales of beef have been uncertain and at some points declined because of BSE, pork sales have increased. China is the largest producer of pork, raising 430 million hogs in 2002, compared with 52.9 million in the United States. Japan, the largest consumer of U.S. pork, increased its imports of pork to replace beef following the discovery of mad cow disease in the state of Washington in late 2003 and 2004. Mexico and Canada are also importers of U.S. pork, especially as tariffs on the product have been phased out in accordance with the North American Free Trade Agreement.

Cynthia Clark Northrup

See also: Food and Diet.

BIBLIOGRAPHY

Ball, Charles E. *Building the Beef Industry: A Century of Commitment.* Denver: National Cattlemen's Foundation, 1998.

Buglass, Dan. "U.S. Beef Producers Fear for the Future of Their $175 Billion Industry." *The Scotsman,* December 26, 2003 (http://business.scotsman.com/agriculture.cfm?id=1409282003/, accessed January 2004).

Miller, Malinda. "Pork: International Markets Industry Profile." Agricultural Marketing Resource Center, Iowa State University, June 2003 (www.agmrc.org/pork/profiles/porkintlmktprofile.pdf, accessed January 2004).

LUDDITES

Early nineteenth-century English workingmen who destroyed labor-saving machines in an attempt to preserve their jobs.

Hurt by the Industrial Revolution and the Napoleonic Wars, the textile workers of north central England rebelled in the summer of 1811, naming themselves after the fictional leader Ned Ludd. The leaders of the movement were skilled cloth finishers and stocking knitters, craftsmen who had quickly fallen from a position of wealth and respect when the home-based production of luxury items was replaced by factory manufacture and was crippled by the Continental System of the French state, which blocked British imports. The protesters acted by attacking factories at night and breaking the offending machines; they eventually struck factories in Nottingham, Leeds, Halifax, Lancaster, and Yorkshire.

The government, needing factory production at high levels to maintain the war effort, responded by recruiting 4,000 special constables and deploying 12,000 soldiers to the area. Spencer Perceval, the prime minister, also put a bill through Parliament making the destruction of machines a capital offense, despite the protests and speeches of reformers and George G. Byron, better known as Lord Byron. Factory owners also hired armed guards and defended themselves against Luddite attacks. In April 1812, Luddites killed William Horsfall during an attack on his factory, a murder for which more than 100 Luddites were arrested and fourteen were hanged.

The general economic conditions of the period, including food shortages and riots among English workers, exacerbated the problems protested by the Luddites. The government made

Believing that technology threatened their livelihoods, hand loom weavers, known as Luddites, attack machine looms in a textile factory in early nineteenth-century Britain. *(Mary Evans Picture Library)*

mass arrests and indictments and executed major participants, including a twelve-year-old boy, who cried for his mother on the scaffold. With public sympathy dangerously split between the beleaguered workers and the manufacturers, the government compromised by ending Luddite executions and instead deporting their convicted leaders to Australia, where, ironically, there were no machines among the penal colonists.

Luddite protests were aimed at the machines that had replaced their valuable hand labor with cheap and unskilled factory work, but also included resistance to the unsafe and squalid conditions of the early Industrial Revolution. The authorities clearly sided with the factory owners and suppressed the rebellion as a threat to the nation's prosperity. The term "Luddite" survives into the twenty-first century as a description of a person resistant to new technology, such as computers.

Margaret Sankey

See also: Napoleonic Wars.

BIBLIOGRAPHY

Brooke, Alan, and Lesley Kipling. *Liberty or Death: Radicals, Republicans and Luddites, 1793–1823.* Honley, UK: Workers History Publications, 1993.

Dinwiddy, John Rowland. *From Luddism to the First Reform Bill: Reform in England, 1810–1832.* New York: Basil Blackwell, 1986.

Sale, Kirkpatrick. *Rebels Against the Future: The Luddites and Their War on the Industrial Revolution.* Reading, MA: Addison-Wesley, 1995.

GENERAL INDEX

Volume numbers are in boldface.

A

Abbasid caliphate, **1**:1–2, 43, 161, **3**:841
Abbey of Saint Denis, **2**:349
Abdul Ghaffur, **3**:869–870
Abdur Razzak, **1**:138
About the Ocean (Pytheas), **2**:339
Académie des Sciences, **1**:98
Achaemenian empire, **1**:113
Acrophonic principle, **1**:25
Adidas, **2**:324
Adolphus, Gustavus, **2**:438
Adrian IV (pope), **2**:465
Adriatic Sea, **1**:31, 178, **4**:936
Ad valorem tariff, **3**:872
HMS *Adventure*, **1**:230
Adventures of Marco Polo, The (Polo), **2**:343
Advertising
  and consumerism, **1**:225
  early forms of, **1**:3–4
  insecurities of the consumer and, **1**:5
  Internet, **1**:5–6, **2**:532
  and the media, **3**:613
  and motivational research, **1**:226
  objective of, **1**:3
  patriotic themes used in, **1**:4
  Principles of Marketing, **1**:2
  and printing/rotary press, **1**:4
  radio, **1**:5
  slogans/jingles and, **1**:5
  and sports/entertainment, **2**:324–325
  and technology, **1**:6, **3**:889
  television, **1**:5, **2**:469
Aegean Sea, **1**:6–8, 74, 179, 262, **3**:621, 659
Afghanistan, **1**:60, 293, **3**:718, 733, 851
AFL-CIO (American Federation of Labor and Congress of Industrial Organizations), **1**:32–34, **2**:398
Afonso I, **3**:664
Africa
  and art/luxury objects, **1**:67
  Asia, trade relations with, **1**:10
  and aviation, **1**:88

Africa *(continued)*
  Bantu migrations in, **1**:95–96, 160, **2**:486, **3**:648
  and barter system, **1**:100
  Berbers, **1**:104–105
  and British empire, **1**:126–127
  central, **1**:160–163
  and cities/trade, **1**:178
  and Columbian exchange, **1**:193
  contemporary trade profile of, **1**:9–11
  and copper, **1**:232, 233
  and corn, **1**:235
  cowry shells used as currency in, **1**:188, 244–245
  and diamonds, **1**:269, 272
  and diseases, **1**:280
  and donkeys, **1**:288, 289
  Dyula people, **1**:295–296
  Europe, trade relations with, **2**:327–328
  and European empire building, **2**:310, 318
  geographic/demographic profile, **1**:8–9
  Germany, trade relations with, **2**:405
  and Henry the Navigator, **2**:460
  and history of trade, **1**:9
  Islamic societies, trade relations with, **2**:540
  and ivory, **2**:544–545
  Kilwa, **1**:178
  and livestock, **2**:589
  Lomè Convention and, **1**:10, **3**:912
  and Marx (Karl), **3**:610
  and migrations (human), **1**:95–96, 160, **2**:486, **3**:648
  and missionaries, **3**:663–664
  and motion picture industry, **2**:325
  Napoleonic Wars and, **4**:950
  and new imperialism, **2**:494–495, **3**:696
  and Pan-Africanism, **2**:408
  and population issues, **3**:750
  postcolonial era in, **1**:162–163
  poverty in, **1**:9
  Soviet Union, trade relations with, **3**:852–854
  and stocks/stock exchanges, **2**:362; **4**:966

Africa *(continued)*
  West, **4**:964–966
  and World War I, **4**:950
  See also Colonialism; Slavery; *individual countries*
African Agricultural Union, **2**:548
African Economic History (Austen), **1**:9
African National Congress (ANC), **3**:843
Age-segmented marketing, **1**:224
Aghlabid emirate, **3**:743
Agora (marketplace), **1**:10–11, **2**:457; **3**:604
Agreement of Mudros (1918), **1**:264
Agreement on Trade-Related Aspects of Intellectual Property Rights (TRIPS), **1**:214, **2**:467, 521–524, **3**:726, 908, 917
Agriculture
  as Africa's main occupation, **1**:9
  and American Revolution, **1**:34–37
  and Bantu migrations in Africa, **1**:95
  and bioterrorism, **1**:109–110
  in Brazil, **1**:117
  and Carolingian empire, **1**:149
  in China, **1**:165, 184
  and climate, **1**:183–184
  and colonialism, **1**:11–13
  and Columbian exchange, **1**:193
  and Crete/Minoan civilization, **1**:246
  crop rotation, **1**:249–251, **2**:368, 371, **3**:886
  current status of, **1**:17–18
  and fertilizer, **2**:353–354, 436
  and feudalism, **1**:266
  in Germany, **2**:403, **3**:878
  and guano, **2**:436
  and intracontinental European trade, **2**:331
  and irrigation, **2**:536–537, **4**:957
  and Latin American/Caribbean colonies, **3**:845–846
  in Mali, **3**:594–595
  manorialism, **1**:158, 159
  in nineteenth century, **1**:13–14
  overview of, **1**:11
  plantation system and, **4**:932
  and technology, **3**:886–888
  and tin, **3**:900

I-1

Agriculture *(continued)*
    in twentieth century, **1:**14–15
    and warfare impacting/being impacted by trade, **4:**943
    and World War I, **4:**984
    and World War II, **4:**991
    and post–World War II era, **1:**15–17
    See also Legislation: Great Britain: Corn Laws; Legislation: United States: Hawley-Smoot Tariff of 1930
Agwa Gede of Dahomey, **1:**245
Ahmad al-Mans, **3:**806
AIDS (acquired immune deficiency syndrome), **1:**9, 162, **3:**619, **4:**929
Aiken, Howard, **1:**215
Aircraft, **1:**18–20
Air France, **1:**90
Airline industry, **3:**923
Akan people, **2:**545
Akbar (emperor), **3:**679
Alaric (king), **2:**424
Albania, **1:**113, 189, 244
Albert I, **2:**446
Albert II, **2:**446
Albert IV, **2:**446
Albert (prince), **1:**256–257, **2:**351
d'Albuquerque, Alfonso, **3:**622
Alcohol, **2:**365–366, 482–483
Aleppo, **3:**720
Alexander II, **1:**249
Alexander (merchant), **2:**338
Alexander the Great
    and Armenia, **1:**56
    and art/luxury objects, **1:**59
    Black Sea region and, **1:**113
    and coins/coinage, **1:**188
    drugs used by soldiers of, **1:**291
    and exploration/trade, **2:**338
    overview of, **1:**20–21
    and Phoenicians, **3:**738
Alexandria, **1:**21–22, **2:**449, 456–457
Alexius I, **1:**254, 255, **2:**343
Algeria, **1:**10, **2:**384, **3:**853, 926
Algiers Accord (1981), **1:**284
Ali, Muhammad (boxer), **2:**324
Ali, Muhammad (pasha), **3:**698
al-Mans, **3:**806
Almoravid empire, **1:**105, **3:**808
Alphabet
    Aramaic language, **1:**22–23
    Cyrillic, **1:**23
    Etruscan, **1:**24
    Greek, **1:**23–24, 198
    Latin, **1:**24, 198
    Phoenician, **1:**24–26, 198, **3:**738
Alsace-Lorraine, **1:**26–28, **2:**404, 534
Amalasuntha, **2:**423
Amalfi Sea Code, **2:**518
Amazon.com, **1:**216
Amazon rain forest, **4:**978

Amazon River, **1:**28–29
Amazon Steam Navigation Company, **1:**28
Amber, **1:**29–32, 261
Ambergris, **4:**967
Amboyna Incident (1623), **2:**505
American Airlines, **1:**87, 120
American Federation of Labor-Congress of Industrial Organizations (AFL-CIO), **1:**32–34, **2:**398
American Online (AOL), **2:**531, 532
American Overseas Airways, **1:**90
American Pharmaceutical Association, **1:**292
American Sugar Alliance, **1:**18
American Telephone and Telegraph Company (AT&T), **1:**104
Amery, Leopold, **3:**877
Amherst, Jeffrey, **4:**956
Amory Show (1913), **1:**68
Amphetamines, **1:**292, 293
Amphorae, **4:**970
Amr Ibn Al-As (king), **3:**866
Amsterdam, **1:**37–38, 271, **2:**551
Anabaptists, **3:**773
Analects of Confucius, **1:**216
Anarchism, **3:**840
Anasazi people, **1:**235
Anastasius (emperor), **2:**423
Anatolia, **1:**246, 260, **3:**830–831
    See also Ottoman empire
Ancient era. *See* Egypt, ancient; Greece, ancient; Rome, ancient
Andean cultures, boats/canoes/vessels used by, **1:**47
Andrew II, **1:**256
Andrews, Anthony P., **1:**47
Anglican Church, **3:**649, 773, 794
Anglo-Boer War (1899–1902), **2:**494, **3:**843
Anglo-Dutch Wars (1652–1684), **1:**38–39, 103, **2:**447, **4:**947
Anglo-French Cobden-Chevalier Treaty (1860), **1:**14, **2:**425, **3:**770, 875, 878
Anglo-French Treaty of Dover, **1:**39
Angola, **1:**162, 235, **3:**752
Animals
    and bioterrorism, **1:**109, 110
    camels, **1:**39, 47, 144, 145, **3:**806, 919
    and Cook's (James) voyages, **1:**230
    donkeys, **1:**288–289
    and Egypt, **2:**303
    elephants, **1:**40–41, **2:**544–545
    and food/diet, **2:**368
    horses, **1:**39, **2:**303
    and ivory trade, **2:**544–545
    and leather, **2:**584–585
    and livestock, **2:**588–590
    overview of, **1:**39–41
    and transportation/trade, **1:**47, **3:**919–920

Animals *(continued)*
    whales, **3:**710, **4:**967–968
    See also Fur industry/trade
Animistic religions, **3:**778
Annona, **2:**366–367
Anschutz-Kaempfe, Hermann, **1:**209
Anson, George, **3:**598
Anthony, Mark, **1:**56
Anthrax, **1:**109, 110
Anti–Corn Law League, **3:**876
Antioch, **1:**254, 255, **2:**457
Anti-Semitism, **2:**554–555
Antoinette, Marie, **1:**84
Antwerp, **1:**37, 271
Anugwom, E.E., **2:**566
Apartheid, **1:**271, **3:**843
Apollo Belvedere, **1:**60
Appian Way, **1:**41–42
Appleby binder/knotter, **2:**372
Apple Computer, **1:**216
Aqueducts, **3:**886
Arabic language, **1:**198
Arab League, **1:**44
Arabs
    Alexandria captured by, **1:**22
    Baghdad Pact, **1:**228
    and Bantu migrations in Africa, **1:**95–96
    Bedouins, **1:**43, **3:**701
    Calicut, trade relations with, **1:**138, 139
    Carolingian empire, military conflicts with, **1:**151, **3:**645
    China, military conflicts with, **1:**168
    compass and, **1:**209
    and cotton, **1:**241
    and Cyprus, **1:**260
    and Dark Ages, **1:**266
    and dirhams, **1:**273
    and donkeys, **1:**289
    and drugs, **1:**291, 292
    Dyula people, trade relations with the, **1:**295
    and embargoes, **2:**307–308
    and food/diet, **2:**367
    and frankincense/myrrh, **2:**376–377
    Genoa, military conflicts with, **2:**401
    and Goths, **2:**424
    and Indian Ocean trade, **2:**505
    and Israel, **1:**44, **3:**732, 867, 907–908, **4:**953
    and ivory, **2:**544
    kamal used by, **1:**251
    and Kilwa, **2:**560
    kola use by, **1:**296
    and linen, **2:**586
    Mahdali trading family, **1:**178
    Mediterranean Sea vital to, **3:**621
    Middle Ages and, **3:**645
    and migrations (human), **3:**649
    and nationalism, **1:**43–44
    and paper/pulp, **3:**724

Arabs *(continued)*
   and pepper, **3**:729
   and Petra, **3**:736
   and pilgrimages, **3**:740
   and piracy/privateering, **3**:743
   Shirazi dynasty, **1**:178
   and Sicily, **3**:826
   and silk trade/Silk Road to China, **3**:829
   and slavery, **3**:835, **4**:935
   and socialism, **2**:541
   and Songhay empire, **3**:841
   and Southeast Asia, **3**:847–848
   and spice trade, **2**:367, **3**:848, 858, 860
   and terrorism, **3**:892
   and Tunisia, **3**:924–925
   See also Crusades; Islam/Islamic societies; Ottoman empire
Aragon and Castile, the union of, **3**:633–634
Aramaeans, **1**:71
Aramaic language, **1**:22–23
Arawak tribe, **1**:195
Arbitration. *See* Disputes and arbitration, international
Archaeology
   and economic systems, **1**:49–50
   and eighteenth/nineteenth centuries, **1**:64–67
   and formalist trade perspective, **1**:48–49
   and identification of trade goods, **1**:46–47
   and importance of trade, **1**:52
   and long distance/local trade distinctions, **1**:45
   and market forces, **1**:48–49
   and pottery, **3**:754
   and reconstructing trade routes, **1**:47–48
   and role of trade in emergence of ancient civilizations, **1**:50–52
   and shipwrecks, **3**:825–826
   and social role of trade, **1**:46, 48
   and tally sticks, **3**:871–872
   and twentieth century/modernism, **1**:67–68
   and world systems theory, **1**:45
Archer Daniels Midland (ADM), **2**:425
Architecture, **1**:98, 99, **2**:455–457; **3**:639–641
Arden, Elizabeth, **4**:975
Arensberg, Conrad M., **1**:48, 49
Argentina
   and aviation, **1**:90
   Brazil, trade relations with, **1**:53
   currency boards in, **2**:335
   and diasporas, **1**:272
   Falkland Islands/Islas Malvinas War, **1**:128
   fur industry in, **1**:41
   Great Britain, trade relations with, **1**:128

Argentina *(continued)*
   and import-substitution industrialization, **1**:118
   Japan, trade relations with, **1**:53
   and nuts, **3**:707
   overview of, **1**:53–54
   and rice, **1**:17
   and soybeans, **3**:855
   United States, trade relations with, **1**:53
   and warfare impacting/being impacted by trade, **4**:943
Argentinean-Bolivian Agreement, Second, **1**:174
Aristarchus, **1**:21
Aristotle, **1**:20, **3**:617
Arkwright, Richard, **1**:54–55, **2**:452
Armenia, **1**:55–57, 71, 113
Arms/weapons trade
   history of, **4**:960–962
   illegal trade and, **2**:480
   and profits under war conditions, **4**:943–944
   and Soviet Union–African relations, **3**:852–853
   United States and, **4**:951, 983, 985, 987
   and weapons/armament production, **2**:437–439, 475, 477, 478, **4**:988
Arsacid dynasty, **1**:56
Art
   and art dealers, **1**:64
   Baroque style, **1**:62–64, 97–99
   and Crete/Minoan civilization, **3**:659
   and early/classical civilizations, **1**:57–60
   and Egypt, **1**:57, 58, 65–66, **2**:303
   in eighteenth/nineteenth centuries, **1**:64–67
   gold and, **1**:57, 59, 62, **2**:419
   illegal trade in, **2**:481
   and Manchu dynasty, **3**:597
   and Manila galleons, **3**:601
   and migration period/medieval era, **1**:60–61
   and Renaissance period, **1**:61–62
   sculpture, **3**:812–814
   tortoiseshell, **3**:902–903
   and twentieth century/modernism, **1**:67–68
Artavazd II, **1**:56
Artaxias, **1**:56
Arte de Navegar (Cortes), **1**:251
Arte of Navigation (Eden), **1**:251
ASEAN. *See* Association of Southeast Asian Nations
Ashanti empire, **1**:296, **2**:407, **4**:965, 966
Ashikaga Yoshimitsu (shogun), **1**:171
Ashkelon, **1**:255
Ashurbanipal, **3**:699–700
Ashur-uballit (king), **1**:70
Asia
   Africa, trade relations with, **1**:10

Asia *(continued)*
   Association of Southeast Asian Nations, **1**:68–70, **2**:583
   and Atlantic trade route, **1**:77
   Batavia as largest European settlement in, **1**:102
   and cartography, **1**:152
   and cities/trade, **1**:177–178
   and Cold War to regional integration, **2**:298
   and corn, **1**:235
   cowrie shells used as currency in, **1**:244
   and diasporas, **1**:272, 273
   and diseases, **1**:279
   and donkeys, **1**:288–289
   East, **2**:297–298
   Europe, trade relations with, **2**:328–330
   and globalization, **2**:413
   Great Britain, trade relations with, **2**:230, 329
   harbors in, **2**:449–450
   and immigration, **2**:488–489
   and ivory, **2**:545
   and mercantilism, **3**:630
   and migrations (human), **3**:647–648, 651
   and new imperialism, **2**:495–496
   and rice, **3**:792
   and slavery, **3**:835
   Southeast, **3**:847–849
   and tin, **3**:900
   See also China; India; Japan
Asia-Europe Meeting, **1**:69
Asia Pacific Economic Cooperation (APEC), **1**:69, 166
Asiento Agreement (1713), **4**:955
Askia the Great, **2**:406
Askiya people, **3**:841
Assembly-line method, **3**:889, 923
Association of Coffee Producing Countries, **1**:187
Association of French Industry (AIF), **3**:878
Association of Southeast Asian Nations (ASEAN), **1**:68–70, **2**:583
Assyrian empire
   Babylonian empire, military conflicts with, **1**:70–71
   and bioterrorism, **1**:107
   and iron technology, **2**:533
   Nubia, military conflicts with, **2**:564
   overview of, **1**:70–71
   and sculpture, **3**:812
   and tin, **3**:900
   and wool, **4**:979
Astrolabe, **1**:72, **3**:887
Astronomy, **1**:72
Aswan High Dam, **1**:72–74, **3**:697
Atahuallpa (king), **2**:501
Atanassoff, John, **1**:215

Athens, ancient
  Aegean islands, trade relations with, **1:**6
  and bioterrorism, **1:**107
  and Delian League, **1:**74, 266–267, **2:**357, 434, **3:**617
  and food/diet, **3:**714–715
  harbors in, **2:**449
  Mediterranean Sea vital to, **3:**621
  overview of, **1:**74–75
  Persia, military conflicts with, **2:**433–434
  as predominant trading city in Greek world, **1:**177
  and tourism, **3:**904
  and warfare impacting/being impacted by trade, **4:**944
Atkinson, James, **1:**251
Atlantic Charter (1941), **1:**89
Atlantic trade route
  Asia and, **1:**77
  and cities, **1:**179–181
  and colonialism, **1:**79, 82, 181, 191
  defining the, **1:**75
  and exploration/trade, **2:**344
  France and, **1:**81–82
  Genoa and, **2:**402
  Great Britain and, **1:**77, 79, 81
  and gunpowder, **2:**439
  and Hanseatic League, **2:**445
  map of, **1:**76
  and navigation, **3:**689–690
  Netherlands and, **1:**79–81
  Portugal and, **1:**77
  and Royal Niger Company, **3:**801
  and silver, **3:**831–832
  Spain and, **1:**77–79
  and spice trade, **1:**77, 78
  and triangle trade, **3:**923–924
Atomic bomb, **4:**988
AT&T, **2:**325
Attila the Hun, **3:**793
Auction sites, Internet, **1:**216
Auguste, Philippe, **3:**731
Augustus (emperor), **1:**21, **2:**339
Aum Shinrikyo, **1:**109
Aurangzeb (king), **2:**462
Australia
  and Cook's (James) voyages, **1:**230
  and cotton, **1:**17–18
  and diamonds, **1:**271
  and diasporas, **1:**272
  and electricity, **2:**304
  Hamburg, trade relations with, **2:**442
  and missionaries, **3:**665–666
  as a penal colony, **1:**125, 231
Australia's World Exposition (1988), **2:**352
Austria, **1:**86, 248, 264, **3:**818
Austrian school of economists, **1:**211–212
Austro-Hungarian empire, **1:**173, 261
Automobiles
  and combustion engine, **3:**923

Automobiles *(continued)*
  and consumerism, **1:**223–225
  and copper, **1:**233
  and Ford Motor Company, **2:**372–374
  Germany and, **1:**83
  and insurance, **2:**521
  and internal combustion engine, **2:**524–526
  Japan and, **1:**83–84
  and oil/oil industry, **3:**711
  overview of, **1:**82–83
  and technology, **3:**889
  and World War II, **4:**987, 989
Availability approach to provisioning, **3:**771
Aviation
  aircraft, **1:**18–20
  and airline industry, **3:**923
  early flight and trade, **1:**84–85
  and jet age, **1:**90–92
  and September 11th terrorist attacks in the United States, **1:**92
  and sovereignty in a nation's airspace, **1:**85–87
  and technology, **3:**889
  and tourism, **3:**907
  and World War II, **1:**88–90, **4:**987
  world wars, flight between the, **1:**87–88
Ayyubid dynasty, **2:**586
Azerbaijan, **1:**113
Azores, **1:**77, **2:**459
Aztecs
  and archaeology, **1:**48–52
  and Atlantic trade route, **1:**77, 78
  cacao plants in, **1:**172
  and copper, **1:**232
  and empire building, **2:**312
  and gemstones, **2:**395
  and gold, **3:**845
  overview of the, **1:**92–93
  and *pochteca*, **3:**744–745

B

Babeuf, Francois-Noël, **3:**609, 839
Babur (emperor), **3:**678
Babylonian empire
  and architecture, **3:**641
  Assyrian empire, military conflicts with, **1:**70–71
  Egypt, trade relations with, **2:**303
  Hittites, military conflicts with, **2:**463
  overview of, **1:**94–95
  Phoenicians absorbed by, **2:**337
  and tin, **3:**900
  and weights/measures, **4:**962
  and wool, **4:**978–979
Back staff, **1:**251–252
Bacterial agents and bioterrorism, **1:**106
Baghdad Pact, **1:**228

Bagratids dynasty, **1:**56
Bahrain, **2:**503, **3:**732
Bakongo kingdom, **1:**160, **3:**664
Bakunin, Mikhail, **3:**840
Balance-of-payment issues, **1:**203, **3:**771
Balboa, Vasco Núñez de, **2:**345, **3:**594, 722
Baldwin III, **1:**255
Balfour Report (1926), **1:**121
Balloons, hot air, **1:**84–85
Baltic Sea, **1:**30
Bananas, **2:**370, 387
Bangkok Summit (1995), **1:**69
Bangladesh, **3:**791
Baniya merchants, **2:**503, 505
Banks, Joseph, **1:**230, 231
Banks/banking
  and Bardi House of banking, **1:**96–97, **3:**614–615, 728
  Federal Reserve Act of 1913 (U.S.), **4:**1111–1117
  and Florence, **2:**364
  and Genoa, **2:**402
  and Germany, **2:**404
  and gold, **2:**422
  and the Great Depression, **2:**361, 428–429
  Hamburg and, **2:**442
  Hong Kong and, **2:**472
  Industrial Revolution and, **2:**512
  and Islamic societies, **2:**543
  and Knights Templar, **2:**563
  and Medici family, **1:**61, **2:**364–365, **3:**614–615, 646
  Middle Ages and, **3:**646
  and money theories, **3:**672
  overview of, **2:**357–361
  and Radanites, **3:**763–764
  and Roosevelt (Franklin D.), **3:**817
  and Rothschild family, **3:**800–810
  and service-sector expansion, **3:**816
Bantu migrations in Africa, **1:**95–96, 160, **2:**486, **3:**648
Baptista, Pedro, **1:**161
Baptists, **1:**176
Barbados, **2:**316
Barbaricum, **2:**509
Barbary States, **3:**743
Barbon, Nicholas, **2:**519
Barbosa, Duarte, **1:**138
Barca, Hamilcar, **3:**759
Barcelona, **3:**632–633
Bardi House of banking, **1:**96–97, **3:**614, 728
Bardo Treaty (1881), **3:**926
Barnes Foundation, **1:**67
Barons' Crusade, **1:**253–254
Baroque period/style, **1:**62–64, 97–99
Barter system, **1:**99–101, 187, **3:**605
Barth, Heinrich, **1:**277
Bartholomew, Peter, **1:**254

Bartholomew Fair, **2**:355
Batavia, **1**:101–103
Batista, Fulgencio, **1**:259
Battle of Agincourt, **2**:478
Battle of Austerlitz, **4**:948
Battle of the Chernaya River, **1**:249
Battle of Guagamela, **1**:21
Battle of Krak des Chevaliers, **1**:255
Battle of Lake Champlain (1814), **4**:943
Battle of Lake Erie (1813), **4**:942
Battle of Leipzig (1813), **4**:948
Battle of Magenta, **3**:652
Battle of Navarino, **1**:8
Battle of New Orleans (1815), **4**:943
Battle of Plassey (1757), **1**:185, **2**:580, **3**:592, 630
Battle of Poitiers (732), **1**:266
Battle of Talas (751), **1**:168
Battle of Tannenberg (1410), **3**:895
Battle of Thames, **4**:942
Battle of Tondibi (1591), **3**:841
Battle of Trafalgar (1805), **4**:948
Battle of Wagram (1809), **4**:948
Bauxite, **1**:147
Bayer, Adolph von, **2**:506
Bedouins, **1**:43, **3**:701
Beech, Olive, **4**:975
Beef industry, **2**:589–590
Begho, **4**:965
Belgium, **1**:162, 268, **2**:351, 352, 533, **3**:694
Belisarius, **2**:423
Belize, **1**:46–47, 172
Bell, Alexander G., **1**:85, **2**:300, **3**:888
Bell, Henry, **3**:921
Bell Telephone Company, **1**:104
Benedict (saint), **2**:424, **3**:793
Benelux, **3**:694
Benin, **3**:802, **4**:965
Bentham, Jeremy, **2**:535
Benue–Cross River region, **1**:95
Benz, Karl, **2**:524, **3**:711
Berbers, **1**:104–105
Berenice, **1**:105–106
Bering Strait, **1**:192
Berlin Conference (1884–1885), **1**:126, 162, **2**:407, 495
Berlin Decree (1806), Napoleon's, **2**:384, **3**:685, **4**:941, 1069–1070
Berlin Wall, **1**:131
Bernard of Clairvaux, **1**:254–255, **2**:464, 562
Berne Convention for the Protection of Literary and Artistic Works, **2**:467, 523, **3**:727
Bernhard (prince), **1**:120
Bernstein, Edward, **3**:841
Bible, the, **2**:554, **3**:724, 756, 835
Biddle, Nicholas, **2**:360
Bilateral investment treaties (BITs), **1**:283, 285

Bilateral investment treaties (BITs) (*continued*)
  See also Disputes and arbitration, international
Bin Laden, Osama, **2**:541
Biological exchanges and increased human interactions, **1**:192–193
Bioterrorism, **1**:106–110
Bishop, Ron, **1**:46
Bismarck, Otto von, **1**:162, **2**:403
Bissell, George, **3**:710
Bison, **1**:40
Black artists of the twentieth century, **1**:67
Blackburn, Robert M., **2**:573
Black Death, **1**:11, 107–108, 111–112, 192, 278–279, **2**:402, **3**:647
Black Sea, **1**:31, 112–113, 134, 218, **3**:720
Blanc, Louis, **3**:840
Blast furnace, **2**:534
Bleau family, **1**:155
Boats/canoes/vessels used in maritime trade, **1**:47
  See also Ships/shipbuilding
Boccaccio, Giovanni, **1**:97
Boccaccio di Chellino, **1**:97
Boehm-Bawerk, Eugen von, **3**:765
Boeing 707/747 aircraft, **1**:19, 20
Boeing Transport, **1**:88, 92
Boer Wars, **1**:126, **3**:843
Bohemund of Taranto, **1**:254
Boleyn, Ann, **2**:305
Bolivia, **1**:293, **3**:845
Bolshevism, **1**:113–115, 141, 142, **3**:849
Bonaparte, Napoléon
  Alexandria captured by, **1**:22
  and Alsace-Lorraine region, **1**:27
  and Arab nationalism, **1**:44
  and art/luxury objects, **1**:65, 66
  and Berlin/Milan decrees, **2**:384, **3**:685, 686, **4**:941, 1069–1070, 1076–1077
  Continental System imposed by, **1**:38
  Egypt conquered by, **2**:302
  and embargoes, **2**:306
  and Genoa, **2**:402
  Germany dominated by, **2**:403
  and illegal trade, **3**:814
  and insurance, **2**:518
  stock exchanges and, **2**:362
  sugar profits and, **1**:82
  and Venice, **4**:937
  and War of 1812, **4**:942
  See also Napoleonic Wars
Bon Marché, **1**:267–268
Book publishing, **3**:756–757
Book of Roads and Kingdoms (Ibn Khordadbeh), **3**:763
Bootlegged products, **2**:325
Borah, William, **2**:299
Borden, Gail, **2**:372

Borno empire, **4**:965
Bose, Jagadis C., **1**:136
Bose, Satyendra N., **1**:136–137
Bosporus channel/strait, **1**:262–264
Boston Fair, **2**:354–355
Bougainville, Louis-Antoine de, **1**:276
Boulton, Matthew, **1**:55, **3**:862
Bourgeoisie, **1**:115–116, **3**:839
Bourne, William, **1**:251
Bovine spongiform encephalopathy (BSE), **1**:280, **2**:590
Boxer Rebellion, **1**:116, 170, **3**:715
Brancusi, Constantin, **1**:68
Brandt, Willy, **1**:189
Braque, Georges, **1**:67
Braudel, Fernand, **3**:785
Braverman, Harry, **2**:570–571
Brazil
  and agriculture, **1**:18, 117
  and Amazon River area, **1**:28
  Argentina, trade with, **1**:53
  and art/luxury objects, **1**:63
  and aviation, **1**:90
  cacao grown in, **1**:135
  Canada, trade relations with, **1**:118
  cholera in, **1**:173
  and coffee, **1**:186–187
  and cotton, **1**:241
  and diamonds, **1**:270–271
  and diasporas, **1**:272
  and food/diet, **2**:387
  and imperialism/emergence of world economy, **4**:946–947
  iron ore producer, **1**:117
  and medicine, **3**:619
  and missionaries, **3**:662
  and pepper, **3**:730
  and Portugal, **3**:752, 845
  and rice, **1**:17
  and slavery, **3**:835–836, 845
  and soybeans, **3**:855
  and sugar, **3**:868
  United States, trade relations with, **1**:118
  and wood, **4**:977
Brazza, Pierre de, **1**:277
Brecher, Jeremy, **2**:575
Brendan (saint), **2**:341
Breton and Bristol fisherman, **3**:689
Bretton Woods system, **2**:335, 361, 400, 574, **3**:910, **4**:980
Brewer, John, **1**:124
Brezhnev, Leonid, **1**:206
Bribery, **1**:118–120
Bright, John, **1**:237
British Commonwealth, **1**:121–122
  See also Great Britain
British East India Company
  and art, **1**:64
  and Asian-British trade relations, **2**:329

British East India Company *(continued)*
  Calcutta and, **1:**135
  and cartography, **1:**155–157
  charter of, **4:**1011–1012
  and Clive's (Robert) administrative reforms, **1:**186
  as corporate success story, **1:**237–238
  and cotton, **3:**898
  Drake's (Francis) profits used to start, **1:**290
  and drugs, **1:**292
  Elizabeth I helps to start the, **2:**306
  and empire building, **2:**314–316
  and indigo, **2:**506
  as a joint-stock company, **2:**552
  and jute, **2:**556
  and Madras, **3:**592
  and Manchu dynasty, **3:**598
  and Mughal empire, **3:**681, 682
  opium trade and the, **2:**471
  overview of, **1:**122–125
  share selling in the, **2:**361
  and tea, **3:**883–885
  and tourism, **3:**907
British Overseas Airways Corporation (BOAC), **1:**90
British Royal Society, **1:**98
Brock, Thomas, **3:**678
Brockeden, William, **1:**258
Brodie, Neil, **2:**481
Brokaw, Tom, **1:**109
Bronze Age, **1:**32, 232, 260, **3:**886
Brunei, **1:**69, **3:**848
Bruni, Leonardo, **2:**365
Brusa, **3:**720
Brussels Universal and International Exhibition (1958), **2:**351, 352
Bryan, William J., **4:**983
Bubonic plague, **1:**278
  See also Black Death
Buchanan, James, **4:**932
Buckelew, Alvin, **3:**893
Buck-Morss, Susan, **3:**787
Bucur, Martin, **3:**773
Buddhism, **1:**128–130, **3:**740, 776, 830, 847
Bugis people, **1:**130
Bukhara, **3:**708
Bulgaria, **1:**113, 189, 228, 244, **2:**335
Bulow, Heinrich von, **2:**403
Bunau-Varilla, Philippe, **3:**723
Burckhardt, Johann, **3:**736
Bureau Interationaux pour la Protection de la Propriété Intellectuelle, **3:**727
Bureau of International Exhibitions (BIE), **2:**351
Burghers of Calais (Rodin), **3:**678
Burghley, William C., **2:**441
Burial tombs, **1:**47
Burroughs, Peter, **1:**136

Bursa, **3:**719
Bush, George H.W., **1:**131–132, **3:**614, 704
Bush, George W., **1:**109, 131, **3:**619
Bush, Vannevar, **1:**215, **4:**988
Bush-Overby Oil Development Company, **1:**131
Butzer Design Partnership, **3:**678
Byblos, **1:**177, **2:**303
Byrnes, James F., **4:**991
Byron, George G., **2:**590
Byzantine empire
  and art, **1:**61
  and Black Sea region, **1:**113
  and Cyprus, **1:**260
  and Dark Ages, **1:**266
  and Egypt, **1:**219
  fall of the, **1:**220
  and food/diet, **2:**367
  and glass, **2:**410
  and Goths, **2:**423–424
  Italy, trade relations with, **1:**134
  and ivory, **2:**544
  Mediterranean Sea vital to, **3:**621
  Middle Ages and, **3:**643
  overview of, **1:**133–134
  and Sicily, **3:**826
  and silk trade/Silk Road to China, **3:**828–829
  and Tunisia, **3:**924
  and Venice, **1:**134, **4:**935
Byzantium, **1:**61

C

Cable communications, **1:**227
Cabot, John, **1:**77, **2:**305, 344, **3:**859
Cabot, Sebastian, **1:**154
Cabral, Pedro A., **1:**139, 153, **3:**845
Cacao, **1:**135, 172–173, **2:**547, 548, **4:**966
Cadmus, **1:**26
Caesar, Julius, **1:**21, 26, **2:**339, 340, 366–367
Caffa, **3:**720
Cairo, **1:**177–178, **2:**301–302
Calais, **2:**478
Calcutta, **1:**125, 135–137, 185
Calhoun, John C., **1:**241, **4:**941
Calicut, **1:**137–139
California, **2:**320, 420, 526
Calkins, Ernest, **1:**225
Calvin, John, **3:**758, 773, 794
Calvinism, **1:**64, 175–176, **2:**568, **3:**758, 773, 775–777
Calvo Doctrine, **1:**282, 286
Cambodia, **1:**69, 70
Camels, **1:**39, 47, 144, 145, **3:**806, 919
Cameroon, **1:**135
Campbell, John, **4:**956
Canaanites, **1:**25, 198

Canada
  and agriculture, **1:**17
  and automobile production, **1:**83
  and bioterrorism, **1:**108
  Brazil, trade relations with, **1:**118
  and British Commonwealth, **1:**121
  cholera in, **1:**173
  and consumerism, **1:**222
  and copper, **1:**233
  and diamonds, **1:**271
  and diasporas, **1:**272
  and electricity, **2:**304
  and fairs/festivals, **2:**352
  French control over, **2:**382
  Great Britain and, **2:**283
  and livestock, **2:**590
  and outsourcing jobs, **3:**818
  and reciprocity, **3:**769
  sedentary societies in, **1:**49
  and stocks, **2:**362
  and tariffs, **3:**880–881
  and wood, **4:**978
  See also North American Free Trade Agreement
Canal du Midi, **1:**99
Canaries, **1:**77
Cannon, **2:**475, 477, 478, **4:**960
Cantillon, Richard, **4:**958
Canton system, **1:**164, **2:**297, 435, 470, **3:**597
Cape of Good Hope, **2:**310
Cape Verde, **1:**77, **2:**310
Capital I (Marx), **1:**141, **3:**840
Capitalism
  and cities/trade, **1:**179, **2:**357
  Crusades and, **2:**357
  debates on origins/structure/evolution of, **1:**140
  and globalization, **1:**139–140, **2:**413
  Industrial Revolution and, **2:**578–579
  and Keynesian Revolution, **3:**789–790
  and laissez-faire theory, **2:**535, 578, **3:**595, 601
  and Malthus (Thomas), **3:**595
  and market revolution, **3:**601–602
  political economy and invention of, **1:**140–143
  and religion, **3:**774–777
  and Weber (Max), **1:**40, **3:**758, 772, 775–777
Capital transfers and disputes/arbitration, **1:**286–287
Caravans, **1:**144–145, 289, **3:**919
Caravel (ship), **2:**459, **3:**690, 824
Carey, Henry C., **2:**535
Carey, William, **1:**135
Cargill, Inc., **2:**425–427
Caribbean Community (CARICOM), **1:**147

Caribbean Free Trade Association (CARIFTA), **1:**147
Caribbean region, **1:**145–147, **3:**744, **4:**968
  See also Colonies, Latin American/Caribbean
Carnegie, Andrew, **1:**148–149
Carnegie, Hattie, **4:**975
Carnegie Steel Company, **1:**148
Carolingian empire, **1:**149–151, 266, **2:**342, 356, **3:**645
Carson, Rachel, **1:**226
Carson Pirie Scott, **1:**267
Cartels, **1:**151–152
Carthage/Carthaginians
  and exploration/trade, **2:**337
  and harbors, **2:**449
  and Phoenicians, **1:**177, **3:**739
  Rome, military conflicts with, **1:**177, **3:**739, 759–760, 826
  and Sahara Desert/trade, **3:**806
  and Sicily, **2:**434, **3:**826
  and silver, **3:**831
  and Tunisia, **3:**924
Cartier, Jacques, **1:**77, **2:**344
Cartography
  and British East India Company, **1:**155–157
  earliest nautical charts, **1:**153–154
  and France, **1:**155–157
  Mercator's projection, **1:**154–155
  modern nautical charts, **1:**157–158
  oral traditions as basis of first charts, **1:**152
  and Ptolemy of Alexandria, **1:**152–153
  and technology, **3:**887
  in the thirteenth/early fourteenth centuries, **1:**152
Caspian Sea, **3:**710
Cassel, Gustav, **2:**454
Caste system, **2:**461, 462
Castles, **1:**158–160
Cast/pig iron, **2:**533
Castro, Fidel, **1:**259, **2:**308, 350
Catalog-based businesses, **1:**224–225, 268
Catherine II, **1:**65, 263, 272
Catholic Church
  and the Black Death, **1:**112
  and Carolingian empire, **1:**149
  and communism, **3:**778
  and copyrights, **1:**234
  Counter Reformation in the, **3:**794
  and Dark Ages, **1:**265, 266
  and diminished institutional control, **3:**777
  Frederick II, military conflicts with, **2:**466
  and Fugger family, **2:**388
  and gold, **2:**420
  and Goths, **2:**424
  Hundred Years' War and, **2:**475

Catholic Church *(continued)*
  and indulgences, **4:**1007–1008
  and insurance, **2:**518
  and Knights Templar, **2:**562, 563–564
  and Latin American/Caribbean colonies, **3:**846
  and law, **2:**577–578
  and Manila, **3:**599, 601
  Middle Ages and, **3:**646
  overview, **3:**792–793
  and perfume, **3:**731
  and political-economic institutions, **3:**779
  and Protestant Reformation, **3:**649, 756, 771–774, 794
  and Roman empire, **3:**793, 795, 797
  schism between Eastern Orthodox/Roman Catholic, **1:**252, 255
  Second Vatican Council, **3:**794
  and usury, **2:**551, **3:**793, **4:**996–997, 1000–1001
  and Venice, **4:**935
  and wine, **4:**970
  See also Christianity; Crusades
Cato the Censor, **1:**60, **3:**760
Cattle, **2:**589, 590
Caventou, Joseph-Bienaimé, **4:**977
Cecil, Robert, **2:**441
Cedar (Lebanese), **3:**737
Celebrities and advertising, **1:**5, **2:**324–325
Cell phones, **1:**199, 216
Celts, **1:**60, **2:**331
Centennial International Exhibition (1876), **4:**972
Centers for Disease Control and Prevention (CDC), **1:**109
Central America, **1:**46–52, 77, 78, **2:**549, **3:**611–612
  See also Aztecs; Colonies, Latin American/Caribbean; Latin America
Central Pacific Railroad, **3:**767
Ceramics for the Archaeologist (Shepard), **1:**46
Certaine Errors in Navigation (Wright), **1:**155
Ceylon, **2:**314, **3:**884
Cézanne, Paul, **1:**68
Chain stores, **3:**605
Chaldeans, **1:**251
Chamberlain, Joseph, **1:**127, **3:**876–877
Chamberlain, Neville, **3:**877
Chamberlin, Edward H., **1:**211
Champagne fairs, **2:**349, 354, 587, **3:**605, 646
Champlain, Samuel de, **1:**81
"Charge of the Light Brigade, The" (Tennyson), **1:**248
Chariot, horse-drawn, **2:**463
Charlemagne (king), **1:**26, 149, 150, 158, 266, **2:**342, **3:**793, 799, **4:**960

Charles I, **1:**237, **2:**359, **3:**594, 634, 826
Charles II, **1:**38, 39, 237, 238, **2:**359, 519, **3:**693
Charles IV, **3:**637
Charles V, **2:**365, 446, 475, 478
Charles VI, **2:**447
Charles VII, **2:**447, 478
Charles of Burgundy, **1:**27
Charles the Bald, **1:**151
Charnock, Job, **1:**135
Chartalists, **3:**672
Charts. *See* Cartography
Chase, Stuart, **1:**226
Château de Versailles, **1:**99
Chatterjee, Bankim C., **1:**137
Chatterjee, Sharat C., **1:**137
Chaucer, Geoffrey, **1:**72
Chavin people, **2:**499
Chemical weapons, **1:**106, 108
Chert (flint), **1:**46, 49
Chesapeake, **4:**941, 949
Chiang Kaishek, **2:**435, **3:**823
Chicago, **1:**181–182
Chicago Daily Tribune, **4:**988
Chicago Exposition (1893), **2:**351
Chicago Fire (1871), **2:**519
Chicago School of economists, **1:**213
Chicago system of grain exportation, **1:**14, **2:**425
Childhood and consumerism, **1:**227
Child labor, **1:**224, **3:**898
Children's Crusade, **1:**256
Chile, **1:**233, **2:**388
China
  agriculture in, **1:**165, 184
  Arabs, military conflicts with, **1:**168
  and arms sales, **3:**853
  and art/luxury objects, **1:**60, 61, 65, **3:**601
  and Asian-British trade relations, **2:**330
  and barter system, **1:**100
  Boxer Rebellion, **1:**116, 170, **3:**715
  and bribery, **1:**120
  and British East India Company, **1:**124
  and Buddhism, **1:**128–130, **3:**740, 776, 830, 847
  Bugis people and, **1:**130
  Calicut, trade relations with, **1:**138–139
  and Canton system, **1:**164, **2:**297, 435, 470, **3:**597
  and cities/trade, **1:**178, 182
  and coins/coinage, **1:**171
  and Cold War, **1:**189
  and communism, **1:**164–165
  compass and, **1:**209
  and Confucianism, **1:**163–164, 166, 169, **2:**309, **3:**654–655, 776
  Confucius, **1:**216–218
  and consumerism, **3:**657
  and copper, **1:**233

China *(continued)*
    and cotton, **1**:241–242
    decline of imperial, **1**:169–170
    and diasporas, **1**:272, 273
    and discovery/exploration, **1**:275
    and diseases, **1**:279
    and drugs, **1**:290–292
    dynasties in, **1**:166–170
    and empire building, **2**:309
    and exploration/trade, **2**:340, 341–342
    and fairs/festivals, **2**:348
    fertilizer used in, **2**:353
    and food/diet, **2**:388
    France, military conflicts with, **2**:473
    France, trade relations with, **1**:116
    and fur trade, **1**:41
    geographical overview, **1**:163, 184
    Germany, trade relations with, **1**:116
    and glass, **2**:410
    and globalization, **2**:415
    and gold, **2**:420
    and grain, **2**:426
    Great Britain, trade relations with, **1**:116, 164, 169, **2**:297, 435
    Great Leap Forward, **1**:165
    Han Chinese, **1**:163
    Han dynasty, **1**:163, 166, 168, 170, 209, **2**:367, 580, **4**:945
    Hangzhou, **1**:178
    and immigration, **2**:488–489
    India, trade relations with, **3**:847
    Industrial Revolution and, **2**:512, 513
    and insurance, **2**:518
    and iron technology, **2**:533
    and irrigation, **2**:537
    and ivory, **2**:545
    and jade, **2**:549
    Japan, military conflicts with, **1**:116, **2**:432, 473, 474
    Japan, trade relations with, **1**:165, 170–172, 190
    and law, **2**:580–581
    and livestock, **2**:590
    and market reform, **2**:298
    and migrations (human), **3**:650, 651
    Ming dynasty, **1**:164, 169–171; **3**:653–658, 830, 832
    and missionaries, **3**:663
    and modernization in the 1970s, **1**:165–166
    Mongols, military conflicts with the, **3**:674, 675
    and most-favored-nation status, **1**:166
    and multinational corporations, **1**:240
    Netherlands, trade relations with, **2**:297
    and new imperialism, **2**:495–496, **3**:696
    and nuts, **3**:707
    and oases, **3**:708
    and oil/oil industry, **3**:710
    and open door notes, **3**:715

China *(continued)*
    paper currency used in, **1**:101
    and paper/pulp, **3**:724
    People's Commune movement, **1**:165
    People's Republic of China, **1**:164–165, 189, 244
    and pirated entertainment, **2**:468
    and population growth, **2**:426
    Portugal, military conflicts with, **3**:655, 657
    and pottery, **2**:512, **3**:601, 657, 754–755
    Qing dynasty, **1**:164, 169, 171, **2**:469–473, 580, **3**:596–598, 821
    Qin to the Qing dynasty, trade from the, **1**:163–164
    Republican era, **1**:164
    and rice, **1**:17, **3**:791
    Russian empire, trade relations with, **1**:116
    and severe acute respiratory syndrome, **3**:619
    Shang dynasty, **1**:163
    Shanghai, **3**:821–823
    and silver, **3**:832
    Sino-Japanese Wars, **1**:116, **2**:473
    Song dynasty, **1**:163, 168–171, 178, **2**:297, 580
    and Soviet Union, **1**:165, **3**:850
    and soybeans, **3**:854, 855
    and spice trade, **2**:367
    Surat, trade relations with, **3**:870
    Tang dynasty, **1**:163, 168, 170, **2**:549, **3**:764
    and tea, **3**:883, 884
    and textile trade, **3**:657
    and Tiananmen Square demonstration, **1**:190
    tribute system in, **1**:168–169
    United States, trade relations with, **1**:116, 165, 166, 190
    West, trade relations with the, **1**:189–190
    Yuan dynasty, **1**:163, 169, 170, **3**:821
    Zhou dynasty, **1**:163, 217
    See also Hong Kong; Opium Wars; Silk trade/Silk Road to China; Treaty of Nanjing
Chinsurah, **1**:136
Chocolate, **1**:135, 172–173, **3**:612
Chola empire, **3**:847
Cholera, **1**:173–174
Christianity
    Alexandria and, **1**:22
    in the Alsace-Lorraine region, **1**:26
    ambiguous/contradictory positions on trade/wealth, **3**:777
    and banks/banking, **2**:358
    and Berenice, **1**:106
    Bible, the, **2**:554, **3**:724, 756, 835
    and colonialism, **1**:175–176
    and exploration/trade, **2**:341

Christianity *(continued)*
    and frankincense/myrrh, **2**:377
    and Goths, **2**:423
    and Islam/Islamic societies, **2**:541
    and Kongo kingdom, **1**:161
    and labor, **2**:568, 569
    and Manila, **3**:599
    Middle Ages and, **3**:645
    and Milan, **3**:651
    and missionaries, **3**:661–667
    Netherlands and, **1**:175–176
    and Petra, **3**:736
    and pilgrimages, **3**:740
    and political-economic institutions, **3**:778
    as a proselytizing religion, **1**:174
    and Reformation, **3**:649
    and salt, **3**:810
    and socialism, **3**:840
    and Southeast Asia, **3**:848
    Vikings convert to, **2**:342
    See also Catholic Church; Crusades
Christie's, **3**:814
Chronometer, **1**:157, **3**:690–691
Chrysler Corporation, **1**:83
Churchill, Winston, **1**:227–228
Circulationists, **1**:140
Circus Maximus, **2**:323
Cities
    and Atlantic trade route, **1**:179–181
    and capitalism, **1**:179, **2**:357
    and Crete/Minoan civilization, **3**:659
    and Dark Ages, **1**:265
    and diseases, **1**:278
    and Eurasian trade in thirteenth and fourteenth centuries, **1**:177–178
    European, early modern, **1**:179
    fortified, **1**:159–160, **2**:437, 439, **3**:599
    and Hanseatic League, **2**:444
    and Industrial Revolution, **1**:181–182
    and Islam/Islamic societies, **1**:178–179
    and marketplaces, **1**:176
    and Mediterranean Sea region, **1**:176–177
    Middle Ages and, **3**:646–647
    and new imperialism, **1**:182
    and Sumerian civilization, **1**:291
    trade playing a key role in the earliest, **1**:176
    twentieth-century trade and, **1**:182–183
Civil Aeronautics Board (CAB), **1**:88
Civilian Conservation Corps, **3**:817; **4**:978
Civilization and Capitalism, 15th–18th Century (Braudel), **3**:788
Civil-law countries, **3**:917
Civil War, U.S. (1860–1865), **1**:14, 108, **3**:602, 603, 832, 901, **4**:933, 943
Claremont, **3**:887, 921
Clark, J.M., **1**:211

Clark, William, **1**:276, **4**:1066–1067
Classical economists, **1**:211, **2**:299–300, 587–588
Class of Civilizations, The (Huntington), **2**:417
Claudius, Appius, **1**:41
Claudius (emperor), **2**:327
Claudius II, **2**:423
Clausewitz, Carl von, **4**:948
Clay, Henry, **1**:241, **3**:603, **4**:932, 941
Clement III (pope), **1**:255
Clement IV (pope), **3**:826
Clement V (pope), **2**:563, 564
Cleopatra, **1**:56
Clerk, Dugald, **2**:524
Cleveland, Grover, **2**:420, **3**:770, 879
Climate, **1**:183–185
Clinton, Bill, **1**:132, **3**:614, 704
Clipper ships, **3**:690
Clive, Robert, **1**:124, 185–186, 238, **3**:592, 819, 820
CNN, **2**:417
Coal, **2**:404
Cobden, Richard, **1**:236, 237, **3**:876
Coca-Cola, **2**:324, 418
Cocaine, **1**:293
Coca leaf, **1**:291–292
Cochrane, William, **1**:12
Cocks, Richard, **4**:1015–1016
Cocoa processing, **1**:173, **4**:966
Coconuts, **3**:707
Code of Hammurabi, **2**:463, 517–518, 577, **4**:993–995
Coffee, **1**:99, 186–187, **2**:370, 547
Cohen, Lizabeth, **1**:225
Cohen, Warren, **2**:418
Coins/coinage
  barter used before, **1**:187
  Byzantine empire and, **1**:133
  and Carolingian empire, **1**:149
  in China, **1**:171
  and dirhams, **1**:273–274
  and food/diet, **2**:366
  Greece and, **1**:101, 188
  in Lydia, **1**:187–188
  and Ming dynasty, **3**:657
  and North American colonies, **1**:101
  and Renaissance period, **3**:784
  Rome and, **1**:188
  in Spain, **1**:188
  in United States, **1**:188
  and Vikings, **4**:938
Colaeus, **2**:337
Colbert, Jean-Baptiste, **1**:64, **3**:627, 628, 877, **4**:1032
Cold War
  and agriculture, **1**:16
  and American ideals, **4**:934
  and Asian regional integration, **2**:298
  and aviation, **1**:90

Cold War *(continued)*
  and bioterrorism, **1**:108
  consumerism as winner of, **1**:220
  and foreign aid, **2**:375
  and Japanese-U.S. trade relations, **4**:927
  and Mediterranean Sea region, **3**:621
  overview of, **1**:187–190
  and trade impacting/being impacted by, **4**:953, 990
Cole, G.D.H., **3**:840
Collection of Plans of Ports, etc., in the East Indies (Dalrymple), **1**:157
Collective bargaining, **2**:573
Collins, Greenville, **1**:156
Colombia, **1**:90, 135, 187, 293, **2**:387, **3**:722–723, 922
Colonialism
  in the Baroque period, **1**:99
  and barter system, **1**:101
  and British language, **1**:199
  Calcutta controlled by Great Britain, **1**:135–137
  characteristics of, **2**:491–493
  and cities/trade, **1**:180, 182
  and corporations, **1**:238
  demise of, **1**:192
  and diasporas, **1**:273
  and discovery/exploration, **1**:277
  and disputes/arbitration, **1**:281
  and drugs, **1**:292
  and empire building, **2**:317
  and Equatorial Africa, **1**:161–162
  and European-African relations, **1**:9
  and food/diet, **2**:369
  and France, **1**:191, **2**:383–384, 547–548, **3**:547–548
  and fur trade, **1**:40, 81–82
  and Germany, **2**:405
  and Great Britain, **1**:124–127, 191, **2**:407–408
  and immigration, **2**:489–491
  and imperialism/emergence of a world economy, **4**:946–947
  and Kipling (Rudyard), **2**:560–561
  Lomè Convention, **1**:10
  and missionaries, **3**:664–665
  and the Netherlands, **1**:191
  and new imperialism, **1**:191–192
  and Phoenicians, **3**:738–739
  and slavery, **1**:191
  and Spain, **1**:190–191
  See also British East India Company; Colonies; Dutch East India Company; Empire building; Hong Kong; Imperialism, the new; Mercantilism; Slavery
Colonies, Latin American/Caribbean
  and agriculture, **1**:12, **3**:845–846
  and Atlantic trade route, **1**:78–82
  Catholic Church and, **3**:846

Colonies, Latin American/Caribbean *(continued)*
  and Christianity, **1**:175–176
  and coffee, **1**:186
  Columbus explores the, **1**:195
  Cuba and Spain, **1**:258–259
  and diseases, **1**:193
  and empire building, **2**:316
  and exploration/trade, **2**:345
  France and, **2**:383, 440
  and imperial competition, **3**:857
  and indentured servants, **2**:501–503
  and Isabella I, **2**:538
  and mercantilism, **3**:625
  overview of, **3**:845–846
  piracy/privateers in, **1**:79
  politics and regional/international trade, **1**:146–147
  and rum, **3**:804
  Saint Domingue and, **2**:384
  and silver, **3**:831–832, 845
  and slavery, **1**:12, 146, **3**:836
  and sugar, **3**:868
  and tortoiseshell, **3**:903
Colonies, North American
  and advertising, **1**:4
  and agriculture, **1**:11–13
  and Anglo-Dutch Wars, **1**:38–39
  and arms/weapons trade, **4**:961
  and art/luxury objects, **1**:67
  and Atlantic trade route, **1**:81–82
  and banks/banking, **2**:360
  and Canada ceded to British empire, **2**:383
  and coins/coinage, **1**:101
  and Continental Congress, **4**:931
  Declaration of Independence, **4**:931
  and exploration/trade, **2**:345
  France and, **2**:382–384
  and glass, **2**:410
  harbors in, **2**:450–451
  and hemp, **2**:457
  and indentured servants, **2**:501–503
  Industrial Revolution and, **2**:512, 513
  and insurance, **2**:519
  and iron technology, **2**:533
  and Jewish people/Judaism, **2**:555
  and joint-stock companies, **2**:552
  and Louisiana territory, **2**:383, 384
  and migrations (human), **3**:650
  and molasses, **3**:670
  Navigation Acts (British) and, **3**:629–630, 693
  overview of, **4**:930–931
  and Protestantism, **3**:758–759
  Revolutionary War, **1**:34–38, 81, **2**:317
  and rum, **3**:803–804
  and salt, **3**:811
  and silk trade, **3**:829
  and Stamp Act of 1765 (British), **4**:1043–1047

Colonies, North American *(continued)*
   and Tea Act of 1773 (British), **4:**1047–1049
   and tobacco, **3:**900–901
   and Wars for Empire, **4:**954–956
Colt revolver, **2:**351
Columbian exchange, **1:**77, 192–193, **3:**845
Columbus, Christopher
   and agriculture, **1:**11
   and chocolate, **1:**173
   and discovery/exploration, **1:**275, **2:**344
   and food/diet, **2:**369
   and imperialism/emergence of world economy, **4:**946
   and Isabella I, **2:**538
   and journal of first voyage, **4:**1001–1003
   overview of, **1:**194–195
   and pepper, **3:**729–730
   and the quadrant, **3:**761
   and spice trade, **3:**860
   and sugar, **3:**669–670
   trade route discovery as goal of, **1:**146
Columbus Quincentennial Exposition (1992), **2:**352–353
Comacchio, **4:**935
Combination acts (British), **1:**195–196
Combustion engine, internal, **2:**524–526, **3:**865, 923
Comet, **3:**921
Comintern, **1:**196–197
Commerce Department, U.S., **2:**352, 529–530
Commodity Credit Corporation, **1:**15
Commodity inconvertibility and communist systems, **1:**204
Common Law, English, **2:**578, 580
Commons, John, **4:**959
Commonwealth of Independent States, **3:**851
Commonwealth of Nations, **1:**122
Communication
   collapse of, **4:**934
   and consumerism, **1:**225, 227
   cuneiform, **1:**259–260, **2:**365, **3:**724
   Gothic script, **1:**24
   hieroglyphic symbols, **1:**25, 198, **3:**658, 659
   industrialization and, **2:**515
   linear A/B script, **1:**198, **2:**585–586, **3:**658, 659, 684
   and the media, **3:**613–614
   and modern communications, **1:**199
   Pony Express, **3:**747–748
   printing press, **1:**4, 161, 233, **3:**756–758
   service sector and revolution in, **3:**817–818
   Shanghai and, **3:**823
   and technology, **3:**888

Communication *(continued)*
   telegraph, **1:**119, **2:**515, **3:**726, 888, 890–891
   telephone, **1:**199, 233, **3:**891–892
   and written languages, **1:**197–199
   See also Alphabet
Communism
   and aversion to trade, **1:**202
   balance of payments and, **1:**203
   and bribery, **1:**119–120
   Catholic Church and, **3:**778
   and central planning, **1:**204–205
   and classical communist political thought, **1:**200
   and Comintern, **1:**196–197
   commercial polices and, **1:**203
   and the *Communist Manifesto,* **2:**321, **3:**785, 840, **4:**1097–1102
   and disputes/arbitration, **1:**281–282
   employment and, **1:**205
   and Engels (Friedrich), **1:**200, **2:**321, **3:**609, 840, **4:**1089–1091
   export pricing/exchange rates and, **1:**202
   and globalization, **2:**414–415
   goals for, economic, **1:**206–208
   Guangzhou and, **2:**435
   and incentive factors, **1:**206
   long-term agreements and, **1:**202
   and Marshall Plan, **1:**16, **3:**607
   and monopolistic competition, **1:**200–201
   ownership rights and, **1:**204
   People's Republic of China comes to power, **1:**164–165, 189, 244
   and pricing, **1:**205–206
   and resource inconvertibility, **1:**203–204
   theory at work, **1:**200
   and trade between blocs, **1:**207
   and United States, **1:**227–228, **4:**952
   See also Marx, Karl; Cold War; Soviet Union, the former
Communist Manifesto (Marx and Engels), **2:**321, **3:**785, 840, **4:**1097–1102
Compania de Navigacao e Commercio do Amazonas, **1:**28
Comparative advantage, **1:**207–208, **3:**652, 749, 790
Comparative cash, the law of, **2:**576
Compass, **1:**208–209, **3:**668–669, 887
Competition
   definition of, **1:**210
   economic meaning of, **1:**210–212
   and electricity, **2:**304–305
   and energy technology/markets, **2:**319
   and Engels (Friedrich), **2:**321
   monopolistic, **1:**200–201, 211; **2:**304–305, 319
   regulations and, **1:**212

Competition *(continued)*
   schools of thought/paradigms pertaining to, **1:**213
   and trade, **1:**213–215
Computers, **1:**199, 215–216, 227, 233, **3:**817, 889, 892
Comstock Lode (silver), **3:**832–833
Condition of the Working Class in England, The (Engels), **2:**321
Conditions of Agricultural Growth (Boserup), **3:**750
Conference on European Security (SEC), **2:**362
Conference on the Illicit Trade in Small Arms and Light Weapons in All Its Aspects (2001), **2:**480
Confucianism, **1:**163–164, 166, 169, **2:**309, **3:**654–655, 776
Confucius, **1:**168, 216–218
Congo, **1:**162
Congo River system, **1:**160, 277
Congress of Industrial Organizations (CIO), **1:**32–34, **4:**991
Congress of Vienna (1815), **2:**448, **3:**694
Conquistadors, Spanish, **1:**78, 93, 176, **2:**344, 501, **3:**599, 749
Conrad III, **1:**255, **2:**464, 465
Constantine (emperor), **1:**218, **3:**651
Constantinople, **1:**39, 61, 133, 134, 179, 218–220, **3:**719, 720
Constitution, U.S., **2:**567, 579, **3:**878–879
Constitution (USS), **4:**942
Consumerism
   and China, **3:**657
   and consumer rights movement, **1:**226
   critiques of, **1:**225–227
   and department stores, **1:**269
   fragmented character of the new, **1:**227
   and globalization, **2:**418
   as an ideology, **1:**220–222
   and labor, **1:**224–225
   and uniform consumption styles, **2:**418
   and variations in consumer societies, **1:**222–224
Consumer price index (CPI), **2:**516
Container ships, **3:**691
Containment, **1:**227–228, **3:**607, **4:**943, 952, 991
Content Scrambling System, **2:**468
Contestability theory and competition policy, **1:**213
Continental Grain, **2:**425
Continental System, **1:**38, 229, **3:**685–687
Continental System (Heckscher), **2:**455
Contractus, Herman, **1:**72
Contribution to the Critique of Political Economy, A (Marx), **1:**141
Convention on the Border Extension of Hong Kong with the Qing (1898), **2:**473

Convention of Commerce and Navigation between Her Britannic Majesty and the Sultan of the Ottoman Empire (1838), **1:**263
Convention of Constantinople (1888), **4:**1103–1105
Convention on the Means of Prohibiting and Preventing the Illicit Import, Export, and Transfer of Ownership of Cultural Property (1982), **2:**549
Convention of the Rights and Duties of States (1933), **1:**282
Convention on Stolen or Illegally Exported Cultural Objects (1995), **2:**481
Cook, James, **1:**67, 125, 157, 229–231, 276
Coolidge, Calvin, **1:**15, **4:**975
Coolidge, Grace, **4:**972
Copals, **1:**29
Copper, **1:**231–233, 260, **2:**303
Copyrights, **1:**233–234
Corn, **1:**17, 234–236, **2:**369
Coronado, Francisco, **3:**845
Corporations, **1:**237–240, **2:**324, **3:**627, 682–683
Cortés, Hernán, **1:**193, **3:**845
Costa Rica, **2:**387
Costco, **3:**606
Costello, Tim, **2:**575
Cost-of-living indices, **2:**516
Coston, Martha, **4:**975
Cost-pull inflation, **2:**516–517
Côte d'Ivoire, **2:**547–548
Cotton
 and current status of global trade, **1:**17–18
 and Egypt, **2:**302, **4:**932
 and Industrial Revolution, **2:**511–513
 and nineteenth-century trade, **1:**13–14
 overview of, **1:**240–242
 and post–World War II trade, **1:**15–17
 and slavery, **4:**932
 and spinning frame, **1:**54–55
 and twentieth-century trade, **1:**14–15
 and warfare impacting/being impacted by trade, **4:**943
Cotton gin, **1:**241, 242–243, **3:**888, **4:**969, 979
Council of Economic Advisers, **4:**992
Council for Mutual Economic Assistance (CMEA), **1:**189, 207, 228, 243–244, **3:**850–851
Council of Trent (1545–1563), **3:**794
Country Club Plaza, **3:**605
Cournot, Antoine-Augustin, **1:**211
Court cases
 Bailey vs. Drexel Furniture (1922), **2:**579
 Gibbons vs. Ogden (1824), **2:**579
 Lochner vs. New York (1905), **2:**579
 Muller vs. Oregon (1908), **4:**973

Court cases *(continued)*
 United States vs. E. C. Knight Company (1895), **2:**579
Cowries, **1:**188, 244–245, **2:**486
Credit systems, **1:**224, **2:**357–358, 362, **3:**817
 See also Usury
Crete/Minoan civilization
 agriculture and, **1:**246
 and art, **1:**58–59
 decline of, **1:**6
 earliest settlements, **1:**246, **3:**658–659
 Egypt, trade relations with, **1:**246–247, **2:**303, 336
 and food/diet, **3:**714
 geographical overview of, **1:**245
 and gold, **2:**419
 Greece, trade relations with, **1:**247
 and immigration, **2:**484
 late history of, **3:**659
 and pottery, **1:**246, **3:**658, 754
 and silver, **3:**831
Creutzfeld Jakob disease (CJD), **2:**590
Crimean War (1854–1856), **1:**14, 247–249, 261, 264
Critique of the Gotha Programme (Marx), **2:**535
Crompton, Samuel, **2:**452
Cromwell, Oliver, **1:**38, **3:**629, 692
Crop rotation, **1:**249–251, **2:**368, 371, **3:**886
Crosby, Alfred, **1:**192
Crossick, Geoffrey, **1:**269
Cross-staff, **1:**251–252, **3:**689, 887
Crusades
 and Armenia, **1:**56
 and art, **1:**61
 and biological exchanges, **1:**192
 and capitalism, **2:**357
 Catholic Church's dominance and the, **1:**252
 Children's Crusade, **1:**256
 and Constantinople, **1:**220
 and Danube River, **1:**261
 and drugs, **1:**290
 effects of the, **1:**256
 Fifth Crusade, **1:**256
 First (Paupers and Barons) Crusade, **1:**253–254
 and food/diet, **2:**368
 Fourth Crusade, **1:**255
 and indigo, **2:**506
 and missionaries, **3:**661
 and pepper, **3:**729
 and Petra, **3:**736
 reasons for fighting in the, **1:**252–253
 Second Crusade, **1:**254–255
 and silk trade/Silk Road to China, **3:**793
 Sixth Crusade, **1:**256
 and spice trade, **2:**368, **3:**858

Crusades *(continued)*
 and Templar Knights, **2:**561–564
 Third Crusade, **1:**255
 Urban II initiating the, **4:**995–996
 and Venice, **1:**178, 255, **4:**936
Crystal Palace, **1:**256–258, **2:**351
Cuba
 and American Revolution, **1:**36
 Cold War and, **1:**189
 and Council for Mutual Economic Assistance, **1:**244
 and Cuban missile crisis, **1:**189
 and embargoes, **2:**308
 and fairs/festivals, **2:**350
 and guilds, **3:**637–638
 and new imperialism, **2:**497
 overview of, **1:**258–259
 and Soviet Union, **1:**259, **3:**851
 Spanish-American War, **1:**147, 259, **3:**599, 722–723
 and tobacco, **1:**258
Culpepper, Thomas, **4:**1022–1024
Cultural objects, illegal trade in, **2:**480
Culture and globalization, **2:**416–419
Cumulative causation process, **3:**771
Cuneiform, **1:**259–260, **2:**365, **3:**724
Curaçao, **1:**147
Currencies, trade in national, **2:**481–482
Currency and market revolution in the 1830s and 1840s, **1:**101
Currency boards, **2:**335, 422
Currency convertibility and communist systems, **1:**203–204
Curtis, Glen, **1:**85
Curtis, Penelope, **3:**676
Cushite people, **2:**486
Cuzco, **2:**500, 501
Cyclades, **1:**6
Cyprus, **1:**231, 260, **2:**303, 402, **3:**720
Cyrillic alphabet, **1:**23
Cyrus (king), **1:**95, **2:**433
Czechoslovakia, **1:**189, 244, **3:**607–608

D

Dagobert I, **2:**349
Dahomey kingdom, **4:**965
Daimler, Gottlieb, **2:**524
Daimler, Wilhelm, **3:**711
Dalai Lama, **1:**273
Dalí, Salvador, **1:**68
d'Almeida, Francisco, **3:**593
Dalyrmple, Alexander, **1:**157
Daninos, Adrian, **1:**73
Danish East India Company, **1:**135
Danube River, **1:**31, 249, 261–262
Darby, Abraham, **2:**533
Dardanelles channel/strait, **1:**262–264
Darius I, **2:**338, **3:**866
Darius III, **1:**21

Dark Ages
  Arabs and the, **1**:266
  Byzantine empire and the, **1**:266
  Catholic Church in the, **1**:256, 266
  and cities, **1**:265
  and exploration/trade, **2**:340–343
  overview of, **2**:264–266
  and Radanites, **3**:763
Darwin, Charles, **3**:596, 696
Daschle, Tom, **1**:109
Das Kapital (Marx), **2**:321
Das Nationale System der politischen Ökonomie (List), **2**:587
Datini, Francesco, **1**:61, **3**:647
Davidson, Paul, **3**:771
Davies, Arthur, **1**:68
Davis, John, **1**:251–252, **2**:441
Davis Quadrant, **1**:252, **3**:761, 762
Dawes Plan (1924), **2**:299
Dawkins, P., **2**:574
Day, Francis, **3**:592
Deane, Phyllis, **1**:115
"Death in Arcadia," **1**:230
De Beers diamond cartel, **1**:271, **2**:395
Decameron (Boccaccio), **1**:97
Decius (emperor), **2**:423
Declaration of Independence (U.S.), **4**:931
Defense Department, U.S., **2**:530
Defoe, Daniel, **1**:294
Deforestation, **4**:978
Degas, Edgar, **1**:66
de Gaulle, Charles, **3**:854
DeGolyer, Everette L., **1**:82
de Klerk, F.W., **3**:843
de la Casa, Bartholomew, **1**:77
de la Rua, Fernando, **1**:53
Delian League, **1**:74, 266–267, **2**:357, 434, **3**:617
Dell Computer, **1**:216
Delphi, Oracle at, **3**:903–904
Delta Airlines, **1**:87
Demand-pull inflation, **2**:516, 517
Democracy defined by consumerism, **1**:221–222, 226
Democracy defined by the market, **3**:603
Deng Xiaoping, **1**:189, **2**:298, 435, **3**:821, 823
Denmark
  and Calcutta, **1**:135
  and Caribbean region, **1**:146
  and cartography, **1**:157
  and Continental System, **3**:687
  and fur trade, **1**:41
  and Hanseatic League, **2**:444–445
  and Mughal empire, **3**:681
  and Ottoman empire, **3**:721
  and slavery, **2**:567
Department stores, **1**:267–269, **3**:605

Depression, Great
  and agriculture, **1**:15
  and automobiles, **1**:83
  and banks/banking, **2**:361, 428–429
  causes of, **2**:427–429
  and consumerism, **1**:225
  Cuban economy hurt by, **1**:259
  and dictatorships, **4**:933
  and General Agreement on Tariffs and Trade, **2**:396
  and General Electric Company, **2**:398
  and gold, **2**:334, 420, 421
  and Hawley-Smoot Tariff, **2**:454
  industrial output and, **2**:427, 428
  and intracontinental European trade, **2**:332
  and isolationist polices of U.S., **4**:985
  and Keynes (John M.), **1**:143, **2**:400
  map of, **2**:430
  and Netherlands, **3**:694
  and oil/oil industry, **3**:711
  and patents, **3**:726
  and Roosevelt (Franklin D.), New Deal, **2**:429
  and service sector, **3**:817
  and South Africa, **3**:843
  and Soviet Union, **1**:142
  and tariffs, **3**:880
  and telephones, **3**:891
  and unions, **1**:32
  and wood, **4**:978
Derain, André, **1**:67
Deregulation of energy markets, **2**:319–320
Descent from the Cross, The, **1**:63
Deserts and the climate, **1**:184
  See also Sahara Desert/trade
Desiderius, Peter, **1**:254
De Spieghel der Zeevaert (Waghenaer), **1**:155
Developing countries
  and agriculture, **1**:18
  fertilizer used in, **2**:354
  and foreign aid, **2**:375, 376
  and globalization, **2**:414
  and grain, **2**:426
  industrialization and, **2**:515
  and Integrated Framework, **4**:981
  and Marx (Karl), **3**:610
  and missionaries, **3**:666
  and United Nations, **4**:928
  and wood, **4**:978
  See also Imperialism, the new
Dexter, Harry, **3**:789
Dialectical materialism, **3**:840
Diamonds, **1**:269–272, **2**:395, 494, **3**:842, **4**:943–944, 962–963
Dias, Bartolomeu, **1**:153, 154, **2**:369, **3**:593, 783, 859
Diasporas, **1**:272–273, **2**:462, 550, 554, 555
Diesel, Rudolf, **2**:524

Diesel engines, **2**:524
Diet. *See* Food/diet
Diet of Worms (521), **3**:773
Dillon, Douglas, **2**:397
Dilmun, **3**:642
Dingler, Jules, **3**:722
Dinocrates, **1**:21
Diocletian (emperor), **3**:793
Diogenes, **2**:339–340
Dionysius Exiguus, **2**:424
Dirhams, **1**:273–274
Dirigibles, **1**:18–19, 85, 88
Discobolus (Myron), **3**:812
Discourse of the Commonweal of this Realm England (Smith), **3**:875
Discovery and exploration, **1**:274–278, **2**:305–306
  See also Exploration and trade
Disease, spread of, **1**:193, 278–280, **3**:617–619, 722, 723, 749, 845
  See also Black Death
Disputes and arbitration, international
  and bilateral investment treaties/NAFTA, **1**:285
  Calvo Doctrine, **1**:282
  and capital transfers, **1**:286–287
  communism and, **1**:281–282
  expropriation of property, **1**:286
  extraterritoriality and, **1**:281
  and friendship/commerce and navigation treaties, **1**:282
  Geneva Convention (1927), **1**:282–283
  International Center for the Settlement of Investment Disputes, **1**:283–284
  jurisprudence and, **1**:287
  in the Middle Ages, **1**:281
  and minimum standard treatment, **1**:286
  and most-favored-nation status, **1**:286
  and national treatment obligations, **1**:285
  New York Convention (1958), **1**:283
  origins of investment arbitration, **1**:280
  and performance requirements, **1**:286
  Renaissance/age of empire and, **1**:281
  UN Commission on International Trade Law, **1**:284
  after World War II, **1**:283
Djenne, **1**: 295, **4**:965
Dobb, Maurice, **1**:140
Documents
  Berlin Decree (1906), Napoléon's, **4**:1069–1070
  British East India Company's charter, **4**:1011–1012
  British trade decay, Thomas Roe's speech on, **4**:1024–1026
  Code of Hammurabi, **4**:993–995
  Columbus (Christopher) and journal of first voyage, **4**:1001–1003

Documents *(continued)*
  Communist Manifesto, **4:**1097–1102
  Dutch East India Company's charter, **4:**1016–1022
  Economic Consequences of the Peace, **4:**1117–1124
  English-Japanese trading relations, Richard Cocks's journal on, **4:**1015–1016
  Enterprise for the Americas Initiative, **4:**1164–1167
  Essay on the Principle of Population, **4:**1063–1066
  exchange, the workings of an, **4:**1027–1029
  Federal Reserve Act, U.S., **4:**1111–1117
  free trade, Edwin Sandys's report on, **4:**1012–1015
  free trade, Frederick Engels on, **4:**1089–1090
  free trade, Merchant Adventurers' views on, **4:**1033–1035
  French Community, Constitution of the, **4:**1152–1157
  General Agreement on Tariffs and Trade, **4:**1144–1152
  Hoover's (Herbert) response to Franklin D. Roosevelt over Hawley-Smoot Tariff, **4:**1131–1135
  indulgences and Johann Tetzel, **4:**1007–1008
  iron law of wages, David Ricardo's, **4:**1083–1084
  Lewis and Clark expedition and Thomas Jefferson, **4:**1066–1067
  Louisiana Purchase, **4:**1067–1069
  Marx's (Karl) speech to Democratic Association of Brussels, **4:**1090–1097
  mercantilism, Jean-Baptiste Colbert on, **4:**1032
  Milan Decree (1807), Napoléon's, **4:**1076–1077
  Navigation Acts of 1651 and 1660, British, **4:**1029–1032
  Neutrality Act of 1935, U.S., **4:**1135–1137
  Nye Committee Report, **4:**1138–1144
  Observations on the Effects of the Corn Laws, **4:**1078–1083
  open door notes, **4:**1106–1107
  Panama Canal Treaty of 1903, **4:**1107–1111
  Panama Canal Treaty of 1977, **4:**1157–1162
  Pegolotti's merchant handbook, **4:**997–1000
  Raleigh (Walter), charter to, **4:**1008–1011

Documents *(continued)*
  Reagan's (Ronald) speech to British House of Commons, **4:**1162–1164
  Roosevelt (Franklin D.) and the Hawley-Smoot Tariff, **4:**1126–1131
  Royal Niger Company contract, **4:**1102–1103
  St. Louis Missouri Fur Company and Thomas James, **4:**1077–1078
  slave trade and Great Britain, **4:**1070–1076, 1087–1089
  Stamp Act of 1765, British, **4:**1043–1047
  Statute of Westminster, **4:**1124–1126
  Suez Canal, Convention Respecting the Free Navigation of the, **4:**1103–1105
  Sugar Act of 1764, British, **4:**1039–1043
  Tea Act of 1773, British, **4:**1047–1049
  Treaty of Nanjing, **3:** 884, 717, **4:**949, 1084–1087
  Treaty of Paris (1763), **4:**1035–1039
  Treaty of Tordesillas, **4:**1003–1007
  Treaty of Utrecht, **4:**1032–1033
  Urban II and the Crusades, **4:**995–996
  on usury, **4:**996–997, 1000–1001, 1022–1024
  Wealth of Nations, The, **4:**1049–1063
  World Trade Organization, **4:**1167–1174
Dodson, Joseph, **2:**520
Dog sleds, **1:**47
Doha Round (2002), **1:**10, **3:**894, 909, 911
Dollarization process, **2:**422
Dominican Republic, **1:**135, 147
Dom Pedro II, **1:**28
Donkeys, **1:**288–289
Dorian tribes, **3:**659
Douglas, Aaron, **1:**67
Drachman, Virginia, **4:**975–976
Drake, Edwin, **3:**710
Drake, Francis
  and circumnavigating the globe, **1:**289–290, **3:**859
  and Elizabeth I, **2:**290, 306, 359
  and Hakluyt (Richard), **2:**441
  and mercantilism, **3:**624–625
  overview of, **1:**289–290
  and piracy/privateering, **1:**124, **2:**420, **3:**845
Drugs, **1:**290–293, **2:**471, **3:**597, 717–718, 822
  See also Opium Wars
Dual labor markets, **2:**573
Dubrovnik, **3:**719, 721, 765–766, **4:**937
Duchamp, Marcel, **1:**68
Duhalde, Eduardo, **1:**53
Dukakis, Michael, **1:**131
Dumping commodities on international market, **1:**203
Dupleix, Joseph, **1:**239, **3:**819

Dürer, Albrecht, **1:**62
Duryea, Charles, **2:**524
Duryea, J. Frank, **2:**524
Dutch, the. *See* Netherlands
Dutch East India Company
  Amsterdam and, **1:**37
  and art, **1:**64
  and Baroque economic theorists, **1:**99
  Batavia as administrative capital of, **1:**101–103
  charter of, **4:**1016–1022
  and cities/trade, **1:**179, 180
  corruption and decline of, **1:**228
  and empire building, **2:**314
  and indigo, **2:**506
  as a joint-stock company, **2:**552
  share selling in the, **2:**361
  and South Africa, **3:**842
  and spice trade, **3:**860
  success of, **1:**80, 228
Dutch Swedish War (1657), **4:**947
Dutch Trading Company, **1:**38
Dutch West India Company, **1:**80
Dyes, **1:**13, 56, **2:**404, 506–507, **3:**898
Dyula people, **1:**295–296

E

Earhart, Amelia, **1:**88
Earthlink, **2:**531, 532
East African Common Market, **1:**10
East India Company, **1:**37, 65, 118, 275
Ecclesiastical movements impacting the political economy, **3:**779
E-commerce, **1:**216, **2:**530–532, **3:**606–607
Economic Commission for Latin America and the Caribbean, **1:**118
Economic Community of West African States (ECOWAS), **1:**10, **3:**914, **4:**966
Economic Consequences of the Peace, The (Keynes), **2:**298–299, 557, **4:**1117–1124
Economic Cooperation Administration (ECA), **3:**608
Economic History of Sweden (Heckscher), **2:**455
Economic Journal, **2:**557
Economics, classical, **2:**299–300
Economic systems, archaeological studies of, **1:**49–50
Ecuador, **1:**63, 135, **2:**387
Eden-Reyneval Treaty (1786), **2:**385
Edgeworth, Francis, **1:**211
Edison, Thomas A., **2:**300–301, 398, **3:**711, 726, 888
Edison Electric Illuminating Company, **2:**301, 398
Edo kingdom (Africa), **4:**965
Edomite people, **3:**734–735

Edo period (Japan), **1**:171, **2**:439
Education, mandatory, **1**:224
Edward I, **2**:476
Edward II, **2**:476
Edward III, **1**:97, **2**:475–477, **3**:615
Edward VI, **2**:305
Effective competition, **1**:211
Effective demand, **2**:557
"Effect of Foreign Trade on the Distribution of Income" (Heckscher), **2**:454
Egypt
  Aswan High Dam, **1**:72–74
  Baghdad Pact, **1**:228
  Cairo, **1**:177–178, **2**:301–302
  and Great Britain, **1**:127, **2**:302
  and Islam's emergence, **2**:301–302
  and Israel, **2**:302, **3**:853
  nationalism, center of Arab, **1**:44
  as weak actor in global trade, **2**:302
  See also Suez Canal
Egypt, ancient
  and African imports, **1**:10
  Alexandria, **1**:21–22
  and art/luxury objects, **1**:57, 58, 65–66, **2**:203
  Babylonian empire, trade relations with, **2**:303
  and barter system, **1**:100–101
  Berenice, **1**:105–106
  and Byzantine empire, **1**:219
  and cities/trade, **1**:177–178
  and copper, **1**:231, 232
  and cotton, **1**:241, **3**:898
  Crete, trade relations with, **1**:246–247, **2**:303, 336
  and diseases, **1**:278
  and drugs, **1**:290, 291
  and exploration/trade, **2**:336
  fertilizer used in, **2**:353
  and frankincense/myrrh, **2**:376
  and gemstones, **2**:395
  and glass, **2**:410
  and gold, **2**:419
  Greece, trade relations with, **2**:304
  and hieroglyphic symbols, **1**:25, 198
  Hittites, military conflicts with, **2**:463–464
  Hykso people and, **3**:703
  and immigration, **2**:483, 484
  and irrigation, **2**:536–537
  and law, **2**:577
  and leather, **2**:584
  and linen, **2**:586, **3**:896
  and livestock, **2**:588
  and medicine, **3**:616
  Mogadishu, trade relations with, **3**:668–669
  monuments in, **3**:677
  Nubia, military conflicts with, **2**:564

Egypt, ancient *(continued)*
  and perfume, **3**:730
  Phoenicians, trade relations with, **2**:303, 304
  and pottery, **3**:754
  Rome, trade relations with, **2**:304, 309
  and sculpture, **3**:812
  and spice trade, **3**:860
  and technology, **3**:885, 886
  time periods (six) of, **2**:302–303
  and trade/expansion, **2**:303–304
  and transportation/trade, **3**:919
  and warfare impacting/being impacted by trade, **4**:943
  and weights/measures, **4**:962, 963
  and wood, **4**:977
  and wool, **4**:978–979
Einstein, Albert, **1**:137, **4**:988
Eisenhower, Dwight D., **2**:398, **3**:923, **4**:989
Elcano, Juan Sebastian, **3**:859
Electric industry, **2**:301
Electricity, **1**:233, **2**:304–305, **3**:888
Electronic Numerical Integrator and Calculator, **1**:215
Elephants, **1**:40–41, **2**:544–545
Elizabeth I
  and Anglican Church, **3**:649
  and British East India Company, **1**:123, 237
  and Drake (Francis), **1**:290, **2**:290, 306, 359
  overview of, **2**:305–306
  and piracy/privateering, **3**:845
  and salt, **3**:810–811
  and weights/measures, **4**:963
Elizabeth II, **1**:121
Elizabeth of Russia (tsarina), **1**:65, **3**:818, 820
Elliot, Charles, **2**:471
Elliot, George, **2**:471
Ely, Eugene, **1**:85
Embargoes, **2**:306–308, **3**:687, **4**:941, 949
Emeralds, **2**:394–395
Empire building
  ancient empires, **2**:309
  British and the French, **1**:24–27, **2**:314–318, 382–385
  European, early, **2**:310–314
  Germany, **2**:403–406
  imperial/colonial wars and, **1**:125, **4**:953–957
  Netherlands, **1**:294, **2**:314, 316
  nineteenth-century and the new imperialism, **2**:318–319
  overview of, **2**:308
  Portugal, **2**:310–312
  Spain, **2**:314, **3**:856
Employment and communist systems, **1**:205
  See also Labor, **1**:240

Encomienda system, **3**:625
HMS *Endeavour*, **1**:230
Endogenous money approach, **3**:674
Energy technology/markets, **2**:319–321
Engels, Friedrich, **1**:200, **2**:321, **3**:609, 840, **4**:1089–1090
England. *See* British East India Company; Great Britain
England's Treasure by Foreign Trade (Mun), **2**:321–322
"English Flag, The" (Kipling), **2**:560
English Pilot (Seller), **1**:156
English Pilot (Thornton), **1**:156
English Quadrant, **1**:252
Enlightenment, age of, **3**:661, 677
Enlil-nirari (king), **1**:70
Enterprise for the Americas Initiative, **1**:131, **4**:1164–1167
Enterprise resource planning (ERP), **3**:874
"Enterprising Women: 250 Years of American Business," **4**:974–976
Enterprising Women: 250 Years of American Business (Drachman), **4**:975–976
Entertainment
  ancient and medieval eras, **2**:322–324
  and fairs/festivals, **3**:816
  and gambling, **2**:325–326
  and gaming industry, **2**:325
  and Hollywood, **2**:325, 467–469
  and malls, **3**:606
  in the nineteenth century, **2**:324
  spectator sports, **2**:324–325
Environment, concern about the
  consumerism and, **1**:226
  energy technologies/markets and, **2**:319
  fertilizers and, **3**:354
  internal combustion engine and, **3**:526
  paper production and, **3**:726
  United Nations and, **4**:929
  whales and, **4**:967–968
  World Trade Organization and, **3**:915
Equal Employment Opportunity Commission, **4**:974
Equatorial Africa, **1**:160–163
Eric the Red, **2**:342
Erie Canal, **1**:14, 181, **3**:811
Essay on the External Corn Trade (Torrens), **1**:208
Essay on the Influence of a Low Price of Corn on the Profits of Stock (Ricardo), **2**:535
Essay on Nautical Surveying (Dalrymple), **1**:157
Essay on the Principle of Population (Malthus), **3**:595, **4**:1063–1066
Essays on Some Unsettled Questions of Political Economy (Mill), **3**:652
Este dynasty, **1**:62
Estonia, **2**:335
Ethiopia, **1**:244, **2**:564, **3**:853
Etruscans, **1**:24, **2**:326–327

Euboea, **1:**6
Eudoxus, **2:**338
Eugenius III (pope), **1:**254
Eunuchs, **3:**653–654
Euphrates River, **3:**732, 921, **4:**957, 977
    See also Mesopotamian civilization
Eurasia and cities/trade, **1:**177–178
Europe
    and advertising, **1:**4
    Africa, trade relations with, **2:**327–328
    and African structural adjustment programs, **1:**10
    and agriculture, **1:**15, 16–17
    and archaeology, **1:**52
    Argentina, trade relations with, **1:**53
    arms trade and, **2:**480
    and art/luxury objects, **1:**62, 63–68
    Asia, trade relations with, **2:**328–330
    Asia-Europe Meeting, **1:**69
    and automobile production, **1:**83
    and aviation, **1:**85, 91–92
    and Bardi House of banking, **1:**96–97
    and barter system, **1:**100
    and bribery, **1:**120
    China, trade relations with, **1:**169
    chocolate introduced into, **1:**173
    and cities/trade, **1:**177–179
    and coffee, **1:**186
    and coins/coinage, **1:**188
    and Columbian exchange, **1:**193
    compass and, **1:**209
    and computers, **1:**216
    and consumerism, **1:**222
    and corn, **1:**235
    crop rotation in, **1:**249
    Cyprus, trade relations with, **1:**260
    and diasporas, **1:**273
    and dirhams, **1:**274
    and disputes/arbitration, **1:**281
    and drugs, **1:**292
    and empire building, **2:**310–314
    and exploration/trade, **1:**277, **2:**343–345
    feudalism in, **2:**356–357
    and food/diet, **2:**387–388, **3:**858
    and free trade interlude, **3:**694
    and fur industry, **1:**41
    and globalization, **2:**413
    and gunpowder, **2:**438
    and Hapsburg family, **2:**446–448
    harbors in, **2:**451
    and immigration, **2:**486–487
    and Indian Ocean trade, **2:**505–506
    and intracontinental trade, **2:**331–332
    Islamic societies, trade relations with, **2:**541
    and Khazar empire, **2:**559
    and linen, **2:**586–587
    Lomè Convention, **1:**10, **3:**912
    and Manchu dynasty, **3:**598

Europe *(continued)*
    Marshall Plan for, **1:**16, 90, 228, **2:**375, **3:**607–608, **4:**952
    and Medici family, **1:**61, **2:**364–365, **3:**614–615, 646
    and motion picture industry, **2:**325
    and multinational corporations, **1:**240
    and paper/pulp, **3:**724–725
    Rome's fall impacting, **3:**799
    and ships/shipbuilding, **1:**47
    and Soviet Union, **1:**115, **3:**850–851
    stock exchanges in, **2:**362
    and tariffs, **3:**877–878
    and tobacco, **3:**901
    and transportation/trade, **3:**920–921
    See also Black Death; Colonialism; Colonies, Latin American/Caribbean; Colonies, North American; Crusades; Dark Ages; Imperialism, the new; Middle Ages; Missionaries; Slavery; *individual countries*
European Coal and Steel Community (ECSC), **2:**582
European Convention on International Commercial Arbitration (1961), **1:**283
European Economic Community (EEC), **2:**582, **3:**913, **4:**973
European Union (EU)
    and Alsace-Lorraine region, **1:**28
    China, trade relations with, **1:**166
    competition policy in the, **1:**212, 214–215
    expansion of, **2:**334
    and livestock, **2:**589
    Maastricht Treaty and creation of, **2:**332
    map of, **2:**333
    and multinational corporations, **1:**240
    and nuts, **3:**707
    overview of, **3:**913
    and South Africa, **3:**844
Evans, Arthur, **1:**246, **3:**658
Evolution, theory of, **3:**696
Evolutionary socialism, **3:**841
Exchange, the workings of an, **4:**1027–1029
Exchange rates, **1:**202, **2:**334–335, 481
Exchange Systems in Prehistory (Renfrew), **1:**49
Exchange value of a commodity, **3:**609–610
Exploration and trade
    China and, **2:**340, 341–342
    Dark and Middle Ages, **2:**340–343
    and discovery/exploration, **1:**274–278, **2:**305–306
    Egypt, ancient, **2:**336
    European age of, **1:**277, **2:**343–345
    Genoa, **2:**402
    Greeks and Hellenistic empires, **2:**337–339

Exploration and trade *(continued)*
    overview, **2:**335–336
    Phoenicians and Carthaginians, **2:**336–337
    Rome, ancient, **2:**339–340
Explosives/gunpowder, **2:**437–439, 477, 478
Export duties, **3:**875
Export-oriented industrialization (EOI), **2:**516
Export processing zones (EPZs), **3:**683
Expropriation of property and disputes/arbitration, **1:**286
Extraterritoriality, **1:**281, **2:**346–347
Exxon, **3:**711

F

F. David and Company, **1:**56
Fabianism, **3:**840–841
Factor endowment theory of international trade, **2:**454–455
Fairs, international trade
    Champagne fairs, **2:**349, 354, 587, **3:**605
    definition of, **2:**348
    economic changes and, **2:**349–350
    and entertainment, **3:**816
    history/beginnings of, **2:**348–352
    Middle Ages and, **2:**349, **3:**645–646
    participation difficulties with, **2:**351
    present situation, **2:**350
    and tourism, **3:**906
    War World II, expositions since, **2:**352–353
    and women, **4:**972
Faleiro, Ruy, **3:**594
Falkland Islands/Islas Malvinas War, **1:**128
Falling Rocket (Whistler), **1:**65
Family Compact (1761), **3:**820
Farah, Nuruddin, **3:**852
Fast food and globalization, **2:**418
Fatimid dynasty, **1:**22, **2:**586
Federal Deposit Insurance Corporation, **2:**361, **3:**817
Federal Housing Administration (FHA), **1:**225
Federal Reserve Bank, **2:**360, 429, 481, **3:**816, **4:**1111–1117
FedEx, **1:**20, 91, **3:**923
Fees and financial transactions, **2:**357, 358
Fenollosa, Ernest, **1:**66
Ferdinand, Franz (archduke), **2:**448, **4:**982–983
Ferdinand I, **2:**446, 448, **3:**827
Ferdinand V, **1:**62, 195, **2:**344, 369
Ferguson, Adam, **3:**603
Fertilizer, **2:**353–354, 436
Festivals/fairs, medieval, **2:**354–356
Feudalism, **1:**266, **2:**356–357

GENERAL INDEX

Feurbach, Ludwig, **3:**609
Fiber optics, **1:**227, **3:**892
Fichte, Johann G., **1:**200
Ficklin, Benjamin, **3:**748
Fifty-three Stages of the Tokaido (Hiroshige), **1:**65
Filipino-American War, **3:**599
Financial institutions
  banks, **2:**357–361
  credit agencies, **2:**362
  GE Capital, **2:**398
  and globalization, **2:**414
  insurance companies, **2:**362
  international banks, **2:**361
  savings and loans, **2:**362
  stock exchanges, **2:**361–362
  See also International Monetary Fund; World Bank
Finland, **1:**41, 233, **2:**482–483, **4:**974
Firdawsi, **2:**409
Fire insurance, **2:**519
Fire of London (1666), Great, **2:**519
Fireworks at Ryogoku (Hiroshige), **1:**65
Fiscal-military state, **1:**124
Fisher, Irving, **3:**765
Flanders, **2:**475
Flannery, Kent, **1:**46
Flax, **2:**363–364, 586–587
Fleming, J. M., **2:**400
Flemish people, **2:**349
Flint, James, **3:**598
Flood insurance, **2:**521
Florence, **1:**96–97, **2:**364–365, **3:**614–615, 720
Fluitschip, **3:**627
Food and Agriculture Organization (FAO), **2:**427
Food/diet
  in ancient era, **2:**365–367
  bananas, **2:**370, 387
  cacao, **1:**35, 172–173, **2:**547, 548
  and Columbian exchange, **3:**845
  corn, **1:**234–236, **2:**369
  and Europeans, **2:**387–388, **3:**858
  fruits, **2:**387–388
  and government assistance, **2:**366–367
  grain, **2:**425–427
  and Industrial Revolution, **2:**371–372
  in the Middle Ages, **2:**367–368
  in modern era, **2:**368–371
  and nutritional deficiencies/mass production, **2:**372
  nuts, **3:**706–707
  olive oil, **2:**366, 434
  olives, **3:**713–715
  potatoes, **1:**237, **2:**300, 369–371, **3:**753–754
  and processing foods, **1:**16
  rice, **1:**13, 17, 110, 184, **3:**791–792
  and single-food crops, **2:**371

Food/diet *(continued)*
  soybeans, **3:**854–855
  See also Agriculture; Spice Islands/trade
Ford, Gerald R., **1:**131
Ford, Henry, **1:**82, 83, 223, 239, **2:**524–525, **3:**711, 889, 923, **4:**989
Ford Motor Company, **1:**82, 239, 240, **2:**372–374, **4:**989
Foreign aid, **2:**374–376
Forests and climate, **1:**184–185
Formalist trade perspective, **1:**48–49
Fortified towns/cities, **1:**159–160, **2:**437, 439, **3:**599
Forums as central marketplaces, **1:**11
Fourier, Charles, **3:**609, 840
Fox, Alan, **2:**571
France
  and Aegean Sea, **1:**7
  and agriculture, **1:**12, 18
  and Alsace-Lorraine region, **1:**26–28
  and American Revolution, **1:**35–36
  Anglo-French Treaty of Dover, **1:**39
  and art/luxury objects, **1:**62, 64–67
  and Atlantic trade route, **1:**81–82
  and aviation, **1:**84, 86, 87, 90
  in the Baroque period, **1:**97–99
  Batavia occupied by, **1:**103
  and bioterrorism, **1:**108
  British competition as a constant, **2:**383–384
  Canada and, **2:**38
  and Caribbean region, **1:**146
  and cartography, **1:**155–157
  China, military conflicts with, **2:**473
  China, trade relations with, **1:**116
  cocoa processing factories in, **1:**173
  and colonialism, **1:**191, **2:**382–384, 440, **3:**547–548
  and Continental System, **1:**38, 229, **3:**685–687
  and corporations, **1:**238–239
  and cotton, **1:**241
  and Crusades, **1:**253
  and Dardanelles channel, **1:**264
  department stores in, **1:**267–268
  and diasporas, **1:**272
  and discovery/exploration, **1:**275–277
  and electricity, **2:**304
  and embargoes, **2:**306–307
  and empire building, **2:**316, 318, 319, 382–385
  and Equatorial Africa, **1:**161, 162
  and exploration/trade, **2:**344, 345
  and fairs/festivals, **2:**350, 351
  feudalism in, **2:**356
  French Community, Constitution of the, **4:**1152–1157
  and French Mississippi Bubble, **2:**552
  French Revolution, **1:**7, 84, **2:**385–387, **3:**785–787, 794

France *(continued)*
  and fur trade/industry, **1:**40, 81–82
  and Genoa, **2:**402
  Germany, military conflicts with, **2:**403–404
  and glass, **2:**410
  and guilds, **3:**632
  and gunpowder, **2:**437
  India, trading relations with, **1:**123
  and indigo, **2:**506
  and insurance, **2:**518
  and iron technology, **2:**534
  and Ivory Coast, **2:**546–548
  and Knights Templar, **2:**563–564
  and Madras, **3:**592
  and Mali, **3:**595
  and mercantilism, **3:**627–629
  Middle Ages and, **3:**646
  and Mogadishu, **3:**668
  monuments in, **3:**678
  and Mughal empire, **3:**681, 682
  and Nantes Edict, **2:**587
  and navigation, **3:**690
  and new imperialism, **3:**695, 696
  and oases, **3:**708
  and Ottoman empire, **3:**720, 721
  and Panama Canal, **3:**722, 922
  and perfume, **3:**731
  and piracy/privateers, **1:**79
  Ragusa, military conflicts with, **3:**766
  and sculpture, **3:**813–814
  and Shanghai, **3:**822
  and Southeast Asia, **3:**848–849
  Soviet Union, trade relations with, **1:**115
  stock exchanges in, **2:**361
  and tariffs, **3:**877–878
  and tortoiseshell, **3:**902–903
  and tourism, **3:**907
  and transportation/trade, **3:**922
  and Tunisia, **3:**926
  United States, trade relations with, **2:**385
  and warfare impacting/being impacted by trade, **4:**945–946
  and weapons/armament production, **4:**960
  and weights/measures, **4:**964
  and wine, **4:**970
  See also Bonaparte, Napoléon; Napoleonic Wars; Seven Years' War; *individual wars/battles*
Francis I, **1:**62, **2:**447, **3:**634, 800, 813
Francis II, **2:**447–448
Franciscan missionaries, **3:**777
Francisco de Orellana, **1:**28
Franco-British Exhibition (1908), **4:**972
Franco-German Annals (Marx), **2:**321
Franco-Prussian Treaty (1871), **2:**405
Franco-Prussian War (1870–1871), **1:**28, **2:**547

Frank, André G., **1:**140
Frank, Thomas, **1:**226
Frankincense, **2:**376–377
Franklin, Benjamin, **2:**377–379, 519
Frederick I, **1:**26, 255, **2:**442, 464–465, **3:**651
Frederick II of Germany, **1:**256, **2:**465, 466, **3:**826, 895
Frederick II of Prussia, **1:**256, **2:**379–380, **3:**819–820
Frederick III, **2:**446
Free-floating currency rates, **2:**335
Freeman, Richard B., **2:**574
Freemasonry, **2:**381–382
Free trade
 ASEAN Free Trade Area, **1:**69
 and Engels (Frederick), **4:**1089–1090
 European free trade interlude, **3:**694
 French Revolution and, **2:**385
 Great Britain and, **3:**769, 876
 imperialism, **2:**493
 Islam/Islamic societies and, **2:**542–543, **3:**776
 and Keynes (John M.), **2:**557
 and Malthus (Thomas), **3:**595
 and Marx (Karl), **4:**1090–1097
 and the media, **3:**614
 Merchant Adventurers' views on, **4:**1033–1035
 and Mill (John S.), **3:**653
 and open door notes, **3:**715–716
 overview of, **2:**380–381
 and Protestantism, **3:**758, 759
 and regional trade organizations, **3:**911–913
 and religion, **3:**776
 Sandys's (Edwin) report on, **4:**1012–1015
 and Smith (Adam), **3:**838, 876
 and South Africa, **3:**846
French and Indian War. *See* Seven Years' War
French East India Company, **1:**238 239, **2:**385
Friedman, Milton, **2:**576
Friendship, commerce, and navigation treaties (FCNs), **1:**282
Frisians, **4:**938, 970
Frobisher, Martin, **2:**306
Fruits, **2:**387–388
Fugger family, **2:**388–389
Fulbe people, **4:**965
Fulton, Robert, **3:**824, 887, 921
Funan, **3:**847
Fundamentalism, **2:**541–542
Fungal agents and bioterrorism, **1:**109–110
Furet, Francois, **3:**785
Fur industry/trade
 and archaeology, **1:**51
 and corporations, **1:**238

Fur industry/trade *(continued)*
 exchange medium, fur as an, **1:**188
 and exploration/trade, **2:**345
 and forty-unit, **3:**899
 France and, **1:**40, 81–82
 and missionaries, **3:**662
 and overhunting, **1:**40
 St. Louis Missouri Fur Company and Thomas James, **4:**1077–1078
 in twentieth and twenty-first centuries, **1:**41
 as vital to North American colonies, **2:**389
Furneaux, Tobias, **1:**230
Futa Jalo kingdom, **4:**965

G

Gabbaccia, Donna, **2:**418
Gabon, **1:**162
Gades, **3:**738
Galbraith, John K., **3:**789
Galerius (emperor), **3:**793
Galleon, **3:**690
Gallipoli, **1:**262–264
Gallus, Aelius, **2:**340
Galveston, **2:**451
da Gama, Vasco
 and Calicut, **1:**138, 139
 Cape of Good Hope rounded by, **1:**77, **3:**593, 751, 866
 and cartography, **1:**153
 compass and, **1:**209
 and empire building, **2:**310–312
 and India, **2:**344, **3:**626
 and Mediterranean's decline as a link between Europe and the East, **3:**783
Game theoretic tools, **1:**212
Gaming industry, **1:**216, **2:**325–326, 532
Gandära art, **1:**59–60
Gandhi, Mohandas, **2:**391–393, 462, **3:**811–812
Ganges River, **1:**137
Garamantian empire, **2:**393–394
Garamantian Road, **3:**806
Garibaldi, Giuseppe, **3:**827
Garrick, David, **1:**230
Gascony, **2:**475–476
Gates, Bill, **3:**889–890
GATT. *See* General Agreement on Tariffs and Trade
Gaztambide-Geigel, Antonio, **1:**145
GE Capital, **2:**398
Gemstones, **2:**394–395
General Agreement on Tariffs and Trade (GATT)
 AFL-CIO and, **1:**34
 Bush (George H.W.) administration and, **1:**131

General Agreement on Tariffs and Trade (GATT) *(continued)*
 Cold War and, **1:**189
 and competition, **1:**214
 excerpts from, **4:**1144–1152
 founding principles of, **3:**875
 and globalization, **2:**413
 and intellectual property, **2:**523
 and Japanese-U.S. trade relations, **4:**927
 law's evolution and the, **2:**581–582
 meetings (eight major), **2:**397–398
 and multinational corporations, **1:**240
 and Netherlands, **3:**694
 origins of, **2:**396–397, **3:**880
 overview of, **3:**881–882, 908–909
 and reciprocity, **3:**770
 Truman administration and, **1:**16
 World Trade Organization incorporated into, **4:**981
General Agreement on Trade in Services (GATS), **3:**882
General Electric Company, **2:**301, 398–399
General Motors Corporation, **1:**82, 240, **2:**373
General store, **3:**605
General Theory of Employment, Interest, and Money (Keynes), **1:**143, **2:**399–400, 557
Geneva Convention (1927), **1:**282–283
Geneva Phonograms Convention, **2:**467
Geneva Protocol (1925), **1:**108
Genghis Khan, **2:**536, 558, **3:**674–675, **4:**945
Genoa, **2:**401–402, **3:**719–721, 858
Genoa and Seville Expositions (1992), **2:**348
George III, **1:**230
Georgia, **1:**113
Germany and the Industrial Revolution (Veblen), **3:**879
Germany/Germanic people
 Africa, trade relations with, **2:**405
 and agriculture, **1:**17, **2:**403, **3:**878
 and Alsace-Lorraine region, **1:**26–28
 Anglo-French Treaty of Dover, **1:**39
 and automobiles, **1:**83–84, **4:**987
 and aviation, **1:**19, 85–88, 90
 and banks/banking, **2:**404
 and bioterrorism, **1:**108
 China, trade relations with, **1:**116
 and classical economics, **2:**300
 and Cold War, **1:**189
 and colonialism, **2:**405
 and copper, **1:**232
 Council for Mutual Economic Assistance, **1:**244
 and Crusades, **1:**253, 255
 Danube River and, **1:**261
 department stores in, **1:**268, 269

Germany/Germanic people *(continued)*
   and disputes/arbitration, **1:**285
   and dyes, **3:**898
   East and West, trade relations between, **1:**189
   and empire building, **2:**403–406
   and fairs/festivals, **2:**350, 354, 355
   fertilizer used in, **2:**353
   France, military conflicts with, **2:**403–404
   Gothic script, **1:**24
   Hamburg, **2:**441–443
   Hohenstaufen empire, **2:**464–466
   and immigration, **2:**489
   and insurance, **2:**518
   and intracontinental European trade, **2:**331
   and iron technology, **2:**534
   Italy, military alliance with, **4:**986
   and Jewish people/Judaism, **2:**555
   and Kilwa, **2:**560
   Middle Ages and, **3:**643, 645
   and migrations (human), **3:**649
   and monuments, **3:**676, 678
   and NAFTA, **3:**704
   and new imperialism, **3:**696
   and pirated entertainment, **2:**468
   and Poland, **3:**849
   and railroads, **3:**768
   reunification of, **1:**131
   and Russian Revolution, **3:**805
   and ships/shipbuilding, **3:**824
   South America, trade relations with, **1:**128
   Soviet Union, military conflicts with, **3:**849
   Soviet Union, trade relations with, **1:**115
   and tariffs, **3:**878
   and technology, **3:**888
   United States, trade relations with, **4:**987
   and weapons/armament production, **4:**961
   and World War I, **4:**950–951
   World War I, punishment after, **1:**87, 261, **2:**298–299, 361, 405–406, 557, **4:**984
   See also Prussia; *individual wars/battles*
Gerristz, Hessel, **1:**155, 156
Getica (Jordanes), **2:**423
Ghaffur, Abdul, **3:**869–870
Ghana
   ancient, **2:**406
   Berbers and, **1:**105
   and cacao, **1:**135
   and cocoa production, **4:**966
   and colonialism, **2:**407–408
   and Dyula people, **1:**295
   and European's arrival, **2:**406–407
   and gold, **2:**310, 406–407, 419
   and independent/modern, **2:**408

Ghana *(continued)*
   and Mandé-speaking people/Islamized court culture, **4:**965
   Soviet Union, trade relations with, **3:**854
Ghaznavids, **2:**409
Ghibellines (family), **2:**465–466
Ghiberti, Lorenzo, **1:**62
Ghorids, **2:**409
Ghose, Sri Aurobindo, **1:**137
Giddens, Anthony, **2:**411
Giffard, Henri, **1:**85
Gilbert, Humphrey, **2:**306
Gilded age (1869–1877), **1:**67
Gilgamesh Epic, **1:**95, 260
Giotto (artist), **1:**97
Glasgow International Exhibition (1888), **4:**972
Glass, **2:**410
Globalization
   capitalism and, **1:**139–140, **2:**413
   and convergence of sensory/life experiences, **2:**417–419
   definition of, **2:**410, 411, 413
   Industrial Revolution and, **2:**512–514
   and labor, **2:**415–416, 574–575
   map of, **2:**412
   origins of, **2:**411
   and post–World War II order, **2:**413–414
   sovereignty of nation-states and, **2:**416–417
   twentieth century, last quarter of the, **2:**414–415
Gobelin tapestry workshop, **1:**64, 99
Gobi Desert, **1:**289
Goddard, Mary K., **4:**975
Godfrey of Bouillon, **1:**253, 254
Godin de Lepinay, Adolphe, **3:**722
Goethals, George W., **3:**723
Gold
   and African (West) empires, **4:**965
   in ancient world, **2:**419
   and art/luxury objects, **1:**57, 59, 62
   and Ashanti goldfields, **4:**966
   and Atlantic trade route, **1:**77, 79, 81
   and Aztecs, **3:**845
   and coins/coinage, **1:**188
   and Dyula people, **1:**296
   and exchange rates, **2:**334–335
   and Florence (city), **2:**364, 419
   and Ghana, **2:**310, 406–407, 419
   and Indian Ocean trade, **1:**9
   and International Monetary Fund, **2:**527
   Kilwa and, **1:**178
   and Latin American/Caribbean colonies, **3:**845
   and new imperialism, **2:**494–495
   and price fluctuations, **2:**420
   and Sahara Desert/trade, **3:**807–808
   and South Africa, **3:**842–843
   standard, **2:**334, 420–422

Gold Coast, **2:**406–407
Golden Triangle, **3:**717–718
Goldie, George, **2:**318
Goldthorpe, John H., **2:**573
Gompers, Samuel, **1:**32
Gomulka, Wladyslaw, **1:**189
Gonsalves, Ralph E., **1:**146
Goodyear, **2:**351
Gorbachev, Mikhail, **1:**206, **3:**851
Gore, Al, **3:**613–614
Gospel of Wealth, The (Carnegie), **1:**148
Gospel of Work (Carlyle), **2:**568
Gothic script, **1:**24
Goths, **2:**422–425, **3:**826
Gould, Jay, **3:**726
Gournay, Vincent de, **2:**385
Graham, Alexander G., **1:**103–104
Grain, **2:**368, 425–427
   See also specific types
Gramsci, Antonio, **2:**572
Grants, **2:**374
Graphicacy, **1:**155, 156
Grasslands and climate, **1:**184
Graves and archaeology, **1:**47
Gray, Elisha, **1:**104
Great Atlantic and Pacific Tea Company, **3:**605
Great Breakthrough and Its Causes, The (Simon), **3:**750
Great Britain
   and abolition of slavery, **2:**567
   and Aegean Sea, **1:**7
   and agriculture, **1:**12–14
   Amazon River and, **1:**28
   and American Revolution, **1:**34–38
   Anglo-French Treaty of Dover, **1:**39
   Argentina, trade relations with, **1:**128
   and art/luxury objects, **1:**64, 67
   Asia, trade relations with, **2:**230, 329
   and Atlantic trade route, **1:**81
   and Australia, **1:**125
   and aviation, **1:**85, 86, 88–90
   and banks/banking, **2:**359
   in the Baroque period, **1:**97–99
   and barter system, **1:**101
   Batavia occupied by, **1:**103
   and bioterrorism, **1:**108
   Boers, military conflicts with the, **1:**126, **3:**843
   and bribery, **1:**118
   British Commonwealth, **1:**121–122
   Calcutta, control of, **1:**135–137
   and Caribbean region, **1:**146, 147
   China, trade relations with, **1:**116, 164, 169, **2:**297, 435
   cholera in, **1:**173–174
   and cities/trade, **1:**180, 181
   cocoa-processing factories in, **1:**173
   and colonialism, **1:**124–127, 191, **2:**407–408, **3:**857

GENERAL INDEX   I-19

Great Britain *(continued)*
and comparative advantage, **1**:208
and Continental System, **1**:38, 229, **3**:685–687
and copper, **1**:232, 233
and copyrights, **1**:233–234
and corporations, **1**:237–239
and cotton, **1**:241
and Crystal Palace, **1**:256–258, **2**:351
and Dardanelles channel, **1**:263–264
and decaying trade relations, **4**:1024–1026
department stores in, **1**:268, 269
and diasporas, **1**:272
and discovery/exploration, **1**:276
and Egypt, **1**:127, **2**:302
and embargoes, **2**:306–307
and empire building, **1**:124–127, **2**:317–319
England's Treasure by Foreign Trade (Mun), **2**:321–322
and Equatorial Africa, **1**:161
and exploration/trade, **2**:344
and Fabianism, **3**:841
and fairs/festivals, **2**:350, 351, 354–355
fertilizer used in, **2**:353
and food/diet, **2**:372
and free trade, **3**:769, 876
French competition as a constant, **2**:383–384
and General Agreement on Tariffs and Trade, **2**:397
and Genoa, **2**:402
and Ghana, **2**:407
and gold, **2**:420, 421
and grain, **2**:425
and guilds, **3**:636–637
and hemp, **2**:457
and Hinduism, **2**:462
and immigration, **2**:488
Industrial Revolution and, **2**:509–514
and insurance, **2**:518–520
and iron technology, **2**:533
Japan, trade relations with, **4**:1015–1016
and joint-stock companies, **2**:552
and Keynes (John M.), **2**:557
and law, **2**:578, 580, **3**:632
and linen, **2**:587
and livestock, **2**:588
and Manchu dynasty, **3**:597
and Manila, **3**:599
and medicine, **3**:618–619
and Melaka, **3**:623
and mercantilism, **3**:628–630
and migrations (human), **3**:649–650
and Ming dynasty, **3**:657
and Mogadishu, **3**:668
and navigation, **3**:690
and new imperialism, **2**:493, 494, **3**:695–696
and oil/oil industry, **3**:713

Great Britain *(continued)*
Orders in Council of 1804/1806, **1**:13, **2**:384, **4**:941, 942
Ottoman empire, trade relations with, **1**:237
and paper/pulp, **3**:725–726
and patents, **3**:726
Persia, trade relations with, **1**:237
and Persian Gulf, **3**:732
and pilgrimages, **3**:742–743
and piracy/privateering, **1**:79, **3**:624–625, 744
Portugal, alliance with, **1**:128
and pottery, **3**:755
and Protestantism, **3**:759
and railroads, **3**:767, 922
Reagan's (Ronald) speech to British House of Commons, **4**:1162–1164
Russia, trade relations with, **1**:237
and salt, **3**:810–812
and sculpture, **3**:814
Shanghai, trade relations with, **3**:822
and ships/shipbuilding, **3**:824
and Sicily, **3**:827
and silk trade, **3**:829, 897
and slavery, **1**:12, **2**:567
South America, trade relations with, **1**:127–128
and South Seas Bubble in 1720, **1**:125, **2**:552
Soviet Union, trade relations with, **1**:115
Spanish Armada defeated by, **2**:306
and spice trade, **3**:859
stock exchanges in, **2**:361
and Suez Canal, **4**:950, 1103–1105
and Surat, **3**:869
and tally sticks, **3**:872
and tariffs, **3**:875–877
telegraph and, **3**:891
and tobacco, **3**:901
and tourism, **3**:905
and trademarks, **3**:917
and transaction costs, **3**:918
and transportation/trade, **3**:922
unions in, **2**:572
and Vikings, **4**:938
and warfare impacting/being impacted by trade, **4**:945–946
and *Wealth of Nations* (Smith), **4**:1049–1063
and weapons/armament production, **4**:960
and weights/measures, **4**:964
and women, **4**:973
and wool, **3**:896, **4**:979
See also British Commonwealth; British East India Company; British Overseas Airways Corporation (BOAC), British Royal Society; Opium Wars; Seven Years' War; *individual wars/battles*

Great Britain's Coasting Pilot (Collins), **1**:156
Greater East Asia Co-Prosperity Sphere, **2**:431–432
Great Exhibition of the Industry and Works of all Nations (1851), **1**:66, 256–258, **3**:906
Great Ming Code, **2**:580
Great Pyramid at Giza, **3**:676
Greece, **1**:7–8, 113, **2**:402, **3**:607, 814
Greece, ancient
and Aegean Sea, **1**:6
agora (marketplace) in, **1**:10–11, **2**:457, **3**:604
alphabet used in, **1**:23–24, 198
and amber, **1**:30, 31
and architecture, **2**:455–457
Armenia ruled by, **1**:56
and art/luxury objects, **1**:58–60
and bioterrorism, **1**:107
and Black Sea region, **1**:113
and cartography, **1**:152
Celts, trade relations with the, **2**:331
and cities/trade, **1**:177
city-states in, **2**:433–434
coins/coinage in, **1**:101, 188
and copper, **1**:232
Crete, trade relations with, **1**:247
and diasporas, **1**:272
and drugs, **1**:291
Egypt, trade relations with, **2**:304
and entertainment, **2**:322–323
and exploration/trade, **2**:337–339
and fairs/festivals, **2**:349
and food/diet, **2**:366, **3**:714
and gemstones, **2**:395
and gold, **2**:419
and immigration, **2**:484–485
and insurance, **2**:518
linear B script and, **2**:585–586
and marketplaces, **1**:10–11, **2**:457, **3**:604
and medicine, **3**:616–617
Mediterranean Sea vital to, **3**:621
and Mycenaean civilization, **1**:6, 198, **3**:648, 683–684, 831
Nubia, military conflicts with, **2**:564
and pepper, **3**:729
and perfume, **3**:730
Persia, military conflicts with, **2**:433–434
and Petra, **3**:735–736
and Phoenicians, **1**:26, **3**:738, 739
and pottery, **3**:754
and sculpture, **3**:812–814
and ships/shipbuilding, **3**:823
and Sicily, **3**:826
and silver, **3**:831
and slavery, **3**:835
Spain, trade relations with, **2**:337
and technology, **3**:886
and tin, **3**:900
and tourism, **3**:903–904

Greece, ancient *(continued)*
    and transportation/trade, 3:919–920
    and weights/measures, 4:963
    and wine, 4:970
    and women, 4:971
    and wood, 4:977
    and wool, 4:979
    See also Athens, ancient
Green, William, 1:33
Greene, Catherine, 1:242
Greenland, 2:342, 4:938
Green Peace, 4:968
Green Revolution, 2:354, 3:792
Gregory VII (pope), 3:632, 793
Gregory X (pope), 3:745
Gregory XIII (pope), 3:814
Gregory XVI (pope), 1:66
Gregory the Illuminator, 1:56
Grenville, George, 3:693
Grijalva, Juan de, 3:845
Grint, Keith, 2:566, 573
Gross domestic product (GDP), 2:413, 3:673
Gruinard Island, 1:108
Gründrisse, The (Marx), 1:141
Guadeloupe, 2:316
Guangzhou, 1:164, 2:297, 434–435
Guano, 2:436
Guatemala, 1:47, 63, 151, 187, 2:549
Gudea (king), 1:58
Guelfs (family), 2:465–466
Guide to the Holy Land (Würzburg), 3:905
Guilds, merchant
    Aragon/Castile, the union of, 3:633–634
    and British inroads into Spanish America, 3:636–637
    decline of, 3:638–639
    development projects and, 3:637–638
    evolution of, 3:631
    and intracontinental European trade, 2:331
    and Ordenanzas of 1737, 3:637
    and Seville, 3:634–635
    and slavery, 3:635–638
    Spain and, 3:632–639
Guild socialism, 3:840
Guizot, Francois, 3:609
Gulf Wars, 1:109, 131, 3:732–733
Gunpowder, 2:437–439, 4:960
Gutenberg, Johannes, 1:233, 3:724, 756
Gutenberg Galaxy (McLuhan), 2:411
Guyana, 1:147
Gwinn, William, 3:747
Gyrocompass, 1:209

H

Hadley Quadrant, 1:252, 3:761, 762
Hadrian (emperor), 3:795
Haida people, 1:47

Haiti, 1:82, 146, 147, 2:316, 440
Hajj, 3:741–742
Hakluyt, Richard, 2:441
Haley, Catherine M., 3:833, 834
Halley, Edmund, 2:519–520, 3:761
Hamburg, 2:441–443
Hamilton, Alexander, 1:36, 2:360, 3:602, 764, 4:931
Hammurabi (ruler), 1:58, 94
Han Chinese, 1:163
Handler, Ruth, 4:975
Han dynasty, 1:163, 166, 168, 170, 209, 2:367, 580, 4:945
Hangzhou, 1:178
Hanigalbat, 1:71
Hannibal, 1:107, 3:759–760
Hanno, 1:152, 2:337
Hannover Fair, 2:350
Hanseatic League
    and Champagne fairs, 2:349
    decline of, 2:358, 442, 445–446
    early years of, 2:443–445, 3:632
    and fairs/festivals, 2:355
    and grain, 2:368
    and immigration, 2:487
    and insurance, 2:518
    and intracontinental European trade, 2:331
    and linen, 2:587
    Middle Ages and, 3:647
    and Novgorod, 3:705
    and Renaissance period, 3:783
    and salt, 3:810
    and ships/shipbuilding, 3:823–824
    and Thirty Years' War, 2:403
    and wool, 3:896
Hapsburg family, 2:446–448
Harappan civilization, 2:508
Harbors, 3:448–451, 659
Hargreaves, James, 2:452
Harlem Renaissance, 1:67
Harney, George, 2:321
Harrington, John, 3:726
Harrison, John, 1:157
Harrison, William H., 4:942
Harrods, 1:267, 268
Harvard School of economists, 1:213
Haslam, Bob, 3:748
Hastings, Warren, 1:136
Hatshepsut (queen), 2:336
Haupt, Georges, 3:787
Hausaland kingdom, 4:965
Hausa people, 1:9, 2:546
Hawaiian Islands, 1:230, 3:666, 769, 868–869
Hawke, Edward, 3:820
Hawkins, John, 1:289, 2:441, 3:624
Hawley, Willis, 3:613
Hawley-Smoot Tariff (U.S.) of 1930, 2:452–454
    See also under Legislation

Hay, John, 3:715, 723
Hay–Bunau-Varilla Treaty (1903), 3:723
Hay-Herran Treaty (1903), 3:723, 922
Haynes, Elwood, 2:524
Headrick, Daniel R., 3:921
Health and Human Services, U.S. Department of, 1:109
Health insurance, 2:520
Heckscher, Eli F., 2:454–455
Heckscher-Olin model of international trade, 2:454–455
Heian kingdom, 2:297
Heilbroner, Robert, 4:959
Hellenic Steam Navigation Company, 1:8
Hellenistic style, 1:59, 2:455–457
Helsinki Final Act (1975), 1:189
Helsinki Women Business Leaders Summit (2002), 4:974
Hemp, 1:290–291, 2:457–458
Hennu, 2:336
Henri, Robert, 1:68
Henrique (bishop), 1:161
Henry and Sealy Fourdrinier, 3:725
Henry II, 1:255
Henry IV, 2:464, 3:755
Henry V, 2:478
Henry VI, 2:465, 477, 3:726
Henry VII, 1:97
Henry VIII, 2:305, 3:649, 773, 794
Henry the Lion, 2:465
Henry the Navigator
    compass and, 1:209
    and empire building, 2:310
    and exploration/trade, 2:343–344
    and navigation, 2:369, 3:729
    overview of, 2:459–460
    and Polo (Marco), 3:747
    and sugar, 3:867–868
Henry the Proud, 2:464
Herat, 3:708
Herodotus, 1:26, 94, 188, 2:337, 506, 3:806
Heroin, 1:292, 293, 2:480, 3:717
Herophilus, 1:21
Herran, Tomas, 3:723
Hesiod, 1:291
Hess, Moses, 2:321, 3:609
Hester, Thomas, 3:612
Hick, John, 2:400
Hidden Persuaders (Packard), 1:226
Hides/skins, sale of, 1:39–40
    See also Fur industry/trade
Hieroglyphic symbols, 1:25, 198, 3:658, 659
Highway systems, 3:768, 923
Hill, Carla, 1:131
Himlico (king), 2:337
Hinduism, 2:460–463, 3:776, 779
Hipparchus of Bithynia, 1:72
Hippocrates, 1:291, 3:617

Hiram (king), **1**:176–177
Hiroshige, Ando, **1**:65, 66
Hitler, Adolf, **1**:261, **2**:361, **3**:814, **4**:951, 987
Hitt, Peter, **2**:533
Hittite people/empire, **1**:70, 71, 94, **2**:463–464, 533
HIV (human immunodeficiency virus), **1**:9, **4**:929
Ho Chi Minh, **2**:384
Hoffman, Paul G., **3**:608
Hobson, H.C., **3**:840
Hochheim Market, **2**:355
Hohenstaufen empire, **2**:464–466
Hohenzollern, Albrecht von, **3**:895
Hokusai, Katsushika, **1**:65, 66
Holladay, Benjamin, **3**:748
Hollander beater, **3**:725
Hollywood, **2**:325, 467–469
Home ownership, growth in suburban, **1**:225
Homer, **1**:231
Hong Kong
 and agriculture, **1**:165
 and decline of British influence, **2**:474
 founding of, **2**:469–473
 and fur trade, **1**:41
 harbors and, **2**:450
 and Kowloon under British control, **2**:473–474
 and Opium Wars/Treaty of Nanjing, **1**:127, **2**:298, 469–472
 and textile industry, **3**:899
Honorius (emperor), **2**:424
Hooghly River, **1**:135, 137
Hoover, Herbert, **2**:299, 453, **4**:985, 990, 1131–1135
Horizontalist approach to money, **3**:672
Horses, **1**:39, **2**:303
Horsfall, William, **2**:590
Hospitaller Knights, **2**:358, 563, 564, **3**:793
Hot air balloons, **1**:84–85
Houphouët-Boigny, Félix, **2**:548
Houtman, Cornelis de, **3**:859
Houtman, Frederik de, **3**:859
Howe, Elias, **3**:833
Hudad al-Alam (anonymous), **2**:559
Hudson, Henry, **1**:77, **2**:344
Hudson's Bay Company, **1**:238, **2**:552, **3**:662
Hughes, Howard, **1**:88
Hull, Cordell, **3**:880
Hull construction, **3**:690, 691
Humanitarian causes, **3**:696
Hume, David, **2**:299, 421, **3**:838, 876
Hume, Joseph, **1**:196
Hundred Years' War, **1**:27 **1**:97, **2**:437, 475–478, **4**:945
Hungary, **1**:244, 268, **2**:415

Huns, **2**:423, **3**:793
Hunt, Walter, **3**:833
Huskisson, William, **1**:196
Hussein, Saddam, **1**:109, 131, **3**:732, 733
Huygens, Christiaan, **2**:524
Hyde, Anne, **2**:359
Hykso people, **3**:703

I

Ibn Batuta, **1**:137
Ibn Khordadbeh, **3**:763
Iceland, **4**:938
Il Corbaccio (Boccaccio), **1**:97
Iliad, The (Homer), **2**:584, **3**:616, 684, 730
Illegal trade
 alcohol and tobacco, **2**:482
 arms/weapons, **2**:480
 and bribery, **1**:118–120
 cultural objects, **2**:480, 549
 and Ming dynasty, **3**:655–657
 sculpture, **3**:814
 state institutions and, **2**:481–482
 and terrorism, **3**:894
Immigration
 and Asia under imperialism, **2**:488–489
 Bantu migrations in Africa, **1**:95–96, 160, **2**:486, **3**:648
 Boers and the Great Trek, **3**:842
 and consumerism, **1**:221, 224
 culture/customs/new ideas spread through, **2**:483
 and early empires, **2**:484
 and Europe, **2**:486–487
 Germany and, **2**:489
 and Greece and Rome, **2**:484–485
 mass human migrations, **3**:647–651
 mercantilism and European migration, **2**:487–488
 and Nantes Edict, **2**:587
 and Portugal, **3**:752
 and Silk Road to China, **2**:485–486
 and South Africa, **3**:846
 United States and, **2**:489–490
Imperialism, the new
 Africa and, **2**:494–495, **3**:696
 Americas and, **2**:496–497
 Asia and, **2**:495–496
 characteristics of, **2**:493–494
 China and, **3**:696
 cities and, **1**:182
 conclusions/summary, **2**:498
 costs of, **2**:497–498
 debate over cause of, **3**:695
 India and, **2**:495
 Japan and, **2**:496, 497
 old imperialism, characteristics of the, **2**:491–493
 Ottoman empire and, **2**:495
 and Royal Niger Company, **3**:803

Import quotas, **3**:703
Import-substitution industrialization (ISI), **1**:118, **2**:516
I.M. Singer and Company, **3**:833
Incas
 and archaeology, **1**:48, 50
 and Atlantic trade route, **1**:77, 78
 class system and the, **2**:500–501
 and copper, **1**:232
 and drugs, **1**:290, 292
 and empire building, **2**:312
 and food/diet, **2**:369
 origins of, **2**:499–500
 Spain, military conflicts with, **2**:501
Incentive factors and communist systems, **1**:206
Income, per capita, **2**:414
Indentured servants, **2**:501–503
India
 and agriculture, **1**:17
 Alexander the Great, attack of, **1**:21
 Armenia, trade with, **1**:56
 and art/luxury objects, **1**:59–60, 64
 and aviation, **1**:85, 90
 and Berenice, **1**:106
 Calcutta, **1**:125, 135–137
 Calicut, **1**:137–139
 China, trade relations with, **3**:847
 climate in, **1**:184
 Clive's (Robert) combat/administrative efforts in, **1**:185–186
 and corn, **1**:235
 corporate dominance over, **1**:237–239
 and cotton, **1**:241
 and diamonds, **1**:269–271
 and diasporas, **1**:272, 273
 and diseases, **1**:278, 279
 France, trade relations with, **1**:123
 and Gandhi (Mohandas), **2**:391–393, **3**:811–812
 and grain, **2**:427
 and Hinduism, **2**:460–463
 and independence, **1**:127
 Indian National Congress, **2**:392
 and Indian Ocean trade, **2**:503, 505
 Industrial Revolution and, **2**:513
 and ivory, **2**:544–545
 and jute, **2**:556
 and law, **2**:580
 Madras, **3**:592
 and Manchu dynasty, **3**:597
 and mercantilism, **3**:630
 Mesopotamia, trade relations with, **3**:642
 and migrations (human), **3**:651
 and new imperialism, **2**:495
 and nuts, **3**:707
 opium use/trade and, **2**:471
 and outsourcing jobs, **3**:818
 and pepper, **3**:730

India *(continued)*
   and pilgrimages, **3**:742
   and pirated entertainment, **2**:468
   Portugal, trade relations with, **1**:123
   and railroads, **3**:767, 768, 922
   and salt, **3**:811–812
   Seven Years' War and, **3**:820
   and silk, **3**:897
   socioreligious reform movement in, **1**:137
   and spice trade, **2**:367
   Surat, **3**:869–870
   and tariffs, **3**:877
   telegraph and, **3**:891
   and weights/measures, **4**:962
   See also British East India Company; Dutch East India Company; Mughal empire
Indian Ocean trade
   and cities/trade, **1**:178
   and Equatorial Africa, **1**:161
   Europeans arrival and the, **2**:505–506
   and exploration/trade, **2**:338
   and frankincense/myrrh, **2**:377
   and gold, **1**:9
   Islamic societies and, **2**:543
   and jute, **2**:556
   map of, **2**:504
   monsoon winds and, **2**:338
   and Persian Gulf, **3**:732
   and piracy/privateering, **3**:743
   ports in, **2**:503, 505
   and slavery, **1**:9, **2**:543
Indigo, **1**:13, 56, **2**:506–507
Individualism and religious values, **3**:776, 780–781
Indonesia
   Bugis people, **1**:130
   cacao grown in, **1**:135
   and coconut oil, **3**:707
   and coffee, **1**:187
   Dutch culture influenced by, **1**:294
   and France, **2**:384
   and pepper, **3**:730
   and rice, **3**:791
   and spice trade, **3**:860
   and wood, **3**:848, **4**:978
Indulgences, selling of, **4**:1007–1008
Indus River, **2**:338, 507–509, **4**:957
Industrial Revolution
   and bourgeois ethos, **1**:115
   and British-Chinese trade, **1**:169
   and capitalism, **2**:578–579
   and cartography, **1**:158
   and cities, **1**:181–182
   and communication, **2**:515
   and copper, **1**:232–233
   and corporations, **1**:239
   cotton/porcelain industries and, **2**:511–512

India *(continued)*
   debate over causes of, **2**:510–511
   and empire building, **2**:318
   and energy technology/markets, **2**:319
   and Engels (Friedrich), **2**:321
   and European-Africa trade relations, **2**:328
   and food/diet, **2**:371–372
   global economy and, **2**:512–514
   innovation and the, **2**:509–510
   and iron technology, **2**:533–534
   and Islamic societies, **2**:541
   and labor, **2**:567, 569–570
   and navigation, **3**:691
   overview of, **3**:788–789
   and steam engines, **2**:332, **3**:863
   and tariffs, **3**:876, 878
   and textile industry, **3**:898
   and water, **4**:958
   and weapons/armament production, **4**:961
   and women, **4**:971–972
Infant industry argument, **3**:764–765, 769, 879
Inflation, **2**:516–517, **3**:672, 673–674
Influence of Sea Power upon History (Mahan), **3**:722
Innocent II (pope), **2**:562
Innocent III (pope), **1**:255, **3**:793
Innocent IV (pope), **2**:343
Inoculations, **1**:279
Inquisition, the, **2**:538
Installment payments, **1**:224
Insurance, **2**:362, 517–521
Integrated Framework (IF), **4**:981
Intellectual property, **2**:467–468, 521–524, **3**:726–728
Intellectual Property Protection Memorandum (1992), **1**:166
Inter-American Convention on International Commercial Arbitration (1975), **1**:283
Inter-American Development Bank, **1**:132
Interest rates, **1**:53, **3**:672–673
Internal combustion engine, **2**:524–526, **3**:865, 923
International African Association, **1**:277
International Air Navigation Conference (1910), **1**:86
International Air Transport Association (IATA), **1**:89–90, 92
International Bank for Reconstruction and Development (IBRD), **2**:375
   See also World Bank
International Business Machines (IBM), **1**:199, 216
International Center for the Settlement of Investment Disputes (ICSID), **1**:283–284, 287, **4**:980

International Civil Aviation Organization (ICAO), **1**:89, 90, 92
International Coffee Agreement, **1**:187
International Commission for Air Navigation, **1**:87
International Conference of American States (1889/1933), **1**:282
International Conference on Civil Aviation (1944), **1**:89
International Convention for the Protection of Performers, Producers of Phonograms, and Broadcasting Organizations, **2**:524
International Development Association (IDA), **4**:980
International Exhibition on Inventions (1873), **3**:727
International Finance Corporation (IFC), **4**:980
International Labor Organization (ILO), **2**:573
International Monetary Clearing Unit (IMCU), **3**:771
International Monetary Fund (IMF)
   Africa and, **1**:10, 162–163
   Argentina and, **1**:53
   and Bush (George H.W.), **1**:132
   China and, **1**:165
   and exchange rates, **2**:335
   and Ghana, **2**:408
   and globalization, **1**:140
   and gold, **2**:422
   and Japanese-U.S. trade relations, **4**:927
   liberalization process, **1**:10, 143
   origins of, **2**:361
   overview of, **2**:526–528
   and special drawing rights, **2**:527
International Opium Convention in Shanghai (1909), **1**:293
International Pepper Community, **3**:730
International Rice Research Institute, **3**:792
International Spring Gift Fair, **2**:350
International Trade Commission (ITC), **2**:528–530
International Trade Organization (ITO), **2**:396, **3**:880, 908, **4**:981
International Whaling Commission (IWC), **4**:967–968
Internet
   advertising on, **1**:5–6
   e-commerce, **1**:216, **2**:530–532, **3**:606–607
   origins of, **2**:530
   and piracy, **2**:467
   and service sector, **3**:817
   and stock trading, **2**:530–531
   and technology, **3**:889–890
   telephones and, **3**:892
Interpol, **2**:480, 481

Iran, **1**:284, 293, **3**:732
Iraq, **1**:109, 131, **3**:732
Ireland, **1**:122, **2**:587, **3**:650, 661, 818, 819, 897
Irish Potato Famine (1846–1848), **1**:237, **2**:300, 371, **3**:754
Iron Law of Wages (Ricardo), **2**:535–536, **4**:1083–1084
Iron ore, **1**:117
Iron technology, **2**:463, 464, 533–534, **3**:865–866, 886
Iroquois tribe, **4**:954
Irrigation, **2**:536–537, **4**:957
Isabella I, **1**:62, 194–195, **2**:344, 369, 537–538
Islam/Islamic societies
   Abbasid caliphate, **1**:1–2, 43, 161, **3**:841
   Africa, trade relations with, **2**:540
   and African (West) empires, **4**:965
   and ambiguous/contradictory positions on trade/wealth, **3**:777
   and Arabic language, **1**:198
   and the astrolabe, **1**:72
   Berbers converted to, **1**:104–105
   Christians' colonial control over, **2**:541
   and cities/trade, **1**:178–179
   and coffee, **1**:186–187
   emergence of, **1**:43
   and exploration/trade, **2**:341
   and free markets, **2**:542–543, **3**:776
   and glass, **2**:410
   and Hinduism, **2**:462
   and law, **2**:542–543, 580–581
   and missionaries, **3**:660
   and Mogadishu, **3**:668
   origins of Islamic religion, **2**:539
   overview of, **2**:539–540
   and pilgrimages, **3**:741–742
   and political-economic institutions, **3**:778
   radicalized economy and, **2**:541–542
   Russia, trade relations with, **2**:540
   and Sahara Desert/trade, **3**:807–808, **4**:964–965
   and silk trade/Silk Road to China, **3**:830
   and sugar, **3**:867
   and tortoiseshell, **3**:902
   and warfare impacting/being impacted by trade, **4**:945
   See also Arabs; Crusades; Ottoman empire
IS-LM-BP framework, **2**:400
Ismail (viceroy), **3**:867
Isolationism, American, **4**:985–987
Israel
   and Arabs, **1**:44, **3**:732, 867, 907–908, **4**:953
   and diamonds, **1**:271
   and Egypt, **2**:302, **3**:853
   and embargoes, **2**:307–308

Israel *(continued)*
   establishment/recognition of, **2**:551
   and Phoenicians, **1**:25
   See also Jewish people/Judaism
Istanbul, **1**:179, 218, 263
Italy
   and art/luxury objects, **1**:61–62
   Battle of Magenta, **3**:652
   Byzantine empire, trade relations with, **1**:134
   Carolingian empire, trade relations with, **1**:150
   and cartography, **1**:153
   and diamonds, **1**:271
   and diasporas, **1**:273
   and food/diet, **3**:715
   Germany, military alliance with, **4**:986
   and insurance, **2**:518
   and new imperialism, **3**:696
   and paper/pulp, **3**:724
   and sculpture, **3**:814
   and tortoiseshell, **3**:902
Ivory, **2**:544–545
Ivory Coast, **1**:135, **2**:545–548, **4**:966

J

Jackson, Andrew, **2**:360, **3**:602, 603, **4**:932, 943
Jacquard loom, **1**:258
Jade, **1**:46, **2**:549
Jagger, Charles S., **3**:678
Jakarta, **1**:101–103
Jalal-ud-Din Muhammad (emperor), **3**:679
Jamaica, **1**:147, **2**:316
James, Thomas, **4**:1077–1078
James I, **3**:629, 633, 681, 755
James II, **2**:359, 383, **3**:693
Jamestown, **2**:345, 410, 552, **3**:900–901
Jansenist movement, **3**:773
Japan
   and African structural adjustment programs, **1**:10
   and agriculture, **1**:17
   and Amazon River region, **1**:28–29
   Argentina, trade relations with, **1**:53
   and art/luxury objects, **1**:63, 65, 66
   and automobiles, **1**:83–84, **4**:987
   and aviation, **1**:90
   and bioterrorism, **1**:108, 109
   China, military conflicts with, **1**:116, **2**:432, 473, 474
   China, trade relations with, **1**:165, 170–172, 190
   and consumerism, **1**:222
   and copper, **1**:233
   Edo period, **1**:171, **2**:439
   and embargoes, **2**:308
   and empire building, **2**:319
   and GATT, **3**:882

Japan *(continued)*
   and globalization, **2**:413, 419
   Great Britain, trade relations with, **4**:1015–1016
   and Greater East Asia Co-Prosperity Sphere, **2**:431–432
   and gunpowder, **2**:439
   and Hamburg, **2**:442
   and Heian kingdom, **2**:297
   Industrial Revolution and, **2**:513–514
   and integration of regional economies, **2**:298
   Korean War helping economy of, **2**:298
   and law, **2**:580
   and livestock, **2**:589–590
   and Manila, **3**:600
   and Melaka, **3**:623
   and migrations (human), **3**:650–651
   and Ming dynasty, **3**:656
   and missionaries, **3**:663
   and multinational corporations, **1**:240
   and NAFTA, **3**:704
   and new imperialism, **2**:496, 497, **3**:696
   and oil/oil industry, **3**:711, 713
   and piracy/privateering, **2**:297, 468
   and Shanghai, **3**:823
   and Southeast Asia, **3**:848
   and tariffs, **3**:880–881
   and technology, **3**:888
   Treaty of Shimonoseki, **1**:66
   United States, trade relations with, **4**:927–928, 987
   and warfare impacting/being impacted by trade, **4**:951–952
   and weights/measures, **4**:964
   West, trade relations with the, **2**:298
Jaumain, Serge, **1**:269
Jay Treaty (1794), **2**:387
J.D. Power and Associates, **1**:216, **2**:531
Jefferson, Thomas, **2**:306, 360, 384, **3**:602, **4**:931, 949, 1066–1067
Jenkinson, Anthony, **2**:306
Jenner, Edward, **3**:618–619
Jerrold, Douglass, **1**:257
Jerusalem, **1**:254, 256, **2**:466, **3**:699, 742, 904
Jerwan Aqueduct, **3**:699
Jesuit missionaries, **3**:661–664, 666, 777
Jet planes, **1**:19–20, 90–92
Jevons, William, **1**:211
Jewish people/Judaism
   Alexandria, life in, **1**:22
   in Amsterdam, **2**:551
   anti-Semitism, **2**:554–555
   Aramaic language spoken by, **1**:22, 23
   Babylonian empire's enslavement of, **1**:95
   and banks/banking, **2**:358
   and Berenice, **1**:106

Jewish people/Judaism *(continued)*
 and copper, **1:**232
 dispersal of, **1:**272, **2:**550, 554, 555
 and food/diet, **2:**366
 and gemstones, **2:**395
 and Goths, **2:**424
 and immigration, **2:**483
 Islamic societies, trade relations with, **2:**540
 and law, **2:**553
 and moneylending, **2:**551
 and pilgrimages, **3:**740
 and Radanite merchants, **3:**763–764
 Solomon's rule, **2:**550
 and terrorism, **3:**892
 and transaction costs, **3:**918
 turbulent history of, **2:**551
 and World War II, **4:**987
 See also Israel
Jiang Zemin, **3:**823
Joan of Arc, **2:**478
John II, **2:**344, 477
John Phioloponus of Alexandria, **1:**72
John of Utynam, **3:**726
Joint-stock companies, **2:**551–553
Jones, Lois M., **1:**67
Jordanes, **2:**423
Jorden, Edward, **1:**233
José, A., **1:**161
Josef, Franz, **2:**448
Journey to Mongolia (Würzburg), **3:**905
Journey through Wales (Würzburg), **3:**905
Journey of Wen-Amon to Phoenicia, **2:**577
Julius II, **3:**813
Jungle Books (Kipling), **2:**560
Jurisprudence and disputes/arbitration, **1:**287
Justinian Code, **2:**577
Jute, **2:**555–556
Jutland peninsula, **1:**30

K

Kaiser, Henry, **4:**989
Kalahari Desert, **1:**8
Kandinsky, Wassily, **1:**68
Kanem empire, **4:**965
Kangxi (emperor), **1:**171, **2:**435
Kant, Immanuel, **3:**785
Karlowitz Treaty (1699), **3:**718
Kassite people, **1:**94
Katanga people, **1:**160
Katz, Lawrence, **2:**574
Kaunitz, Wenzel, **3:**818
Kautsky, Karl, **1:**200
Kazakhstan, **1:**233
Kazan Khanate, **4:**940
Kellogg-Briand Peace Pact (1928), **4:**985
Kennan, George, **1:**228, **3:**607, **4:**952

Kennedy, David M., **4:**988
Kennedy, John F., **1:**189, **2:**397, **3:**846
Kenya, **1:**127
Kenyon, J., **2:**574
Kerensky, Alexander, **1:**142, **3:**787
Kerosene, **3:**710–711
Key, Francis S., **4:**943
Keynes, John M., **1:**142–143, 210, **2:**298–299, 399–400, 557, **3:**789–790, 877
Khazar empire, **2:**559, **3:**701, 764, **4:**939
Khmer people, **3:**847
Khoisan people, **3:**842
Khrushchev, Nikita, **3:**850
Kiel Canal, **4:**958
Kilwa, **1:**178, **2:**559–560
Kim (Kipling), **2:**560
Kindleberger, Charles, **3:**789
King George's War (1739–1748), **2:**447, **3:**818, **4:**955
King William's War (1690–1697), **4:**954
Kipling, Rudyard, **2:**560–561
Kirchner, Ernst L., **1:**67
Kittim, **3:**738
KLM Royal Dutch Airlines, **1:**92
K-Mart, **1:**226–227
Knight, Frank, **1:**211, 212
Knights and the Crusades, Orders of, **1:**254
 See also Hospitaller Knights; Templar Knights; Teutonic Knights
Knossos palace, **1:**246
Knowles, George O., **4:**967
Knowles, Jane, **4:**974
Koh-i-Noor diamond, **1:**258, 270
Kola, **1:**296
Kong, **1:**296, **4:**965
Kongo kingdom, **1:**160, 161
Königsberg fair, **2:**350
Konrad IV, **1:**26
Köppen, Wladimir, **1:**183
Koprulu, Mehmed, **1:**263
Korea, **1:**84, 129, 273, **2:**297
Korea, South, **1:**120, 165, **2:**298, 413, 527
Korean War (1950–1953), **1:**16, 108, 165, **2:**298, 307, **3:**850
Kornilov, Lavr, **3:**787
Koryo kingdom, **2:**297
Kosovo conflict, **1:**262
Kowloon, **2:**473–474
Kruger, Paul, **3:**843
Kru people, **2:**545
Kuala Lumpur Declaration (1971), **1:**69
Kublai Khan, **1:**169, **2:**343, **3:**745, 858
Kufor, John, **2:**408
Kush, **2:**564
Kuwait, **1:**131, 283, **2:**307, **3:**732
Kwarezm empire, **2:**558

L

Labor
 and consumerism, **1:**224–225
 economic and/or socially useful conceptualizations of, **2:**565–566
 and globalization, **2:**415–417, 574–575
 and Industrial Revolution, **2:**567, 569–570
 laborism, **2:**571
 Luddites and, **2:**590–591
 and Marx (Karl), **3:**609–610
 modern labor processes, **2:**570–571
 and multinational corporations, **1:**240
 Netherlands and, **1:**294
 organizations, **2:**571–573
 outsourcing jobs, **3:**818
 and Panama Canal, **3:**723–724
 and religion, **2:**568–569
 slavery, **2:**567–568
 and textile industry, **3:**898–899
 Wealth of Nations and, **4:**958
 and women, **4:**971–974
 and World War II, **4:**991
 See also Unions
Labor and Monopoly Capital (Braverman), **2:**570
Laclau, Ernesto, **1:**140
Lagos, **2:**459
Lahri-Bandar, **2:**503, 509
Laissez-faire, **2:**535, 575–576, 578, **3:**595, 601
Lake Nasser, **1:**73
Lake Texcoco, **1:**93
Lane, Fitzhugh, **1:**67
La Neptune francais, **1:**156, 157
Laocoon, **1:**60
Laos, **1:**69, 293
Laspeyres price index, **2:**516
Lassalle, Ferdinand, **2:**535
Las Vegas, **2:**325
Latécoère, Pierre, **1:**87
Latin alphabet, **1:**24, 198
Latin America
 and arms/weapons trade, **4:**962
 and art/luxury objects, **1:**63
 and aviation, **1:**88
 cacao plants in, **1:**172
 cholera in, **1:**174
 decolonization struggles in, **4:**952
 and disputes/arbitration, **1:**282
 and dollarization process, **2:**422
 and drugs, **1:**291, 292
 and Enterprise for the Americas Initiative, **1:**131, **4:**1164–1167
 and globalization, **2:**414
 and guilds, **3:**635, 638
 harbors in, **2:**451
 and immigration, **2:**490
 and independence movements, **3:**638, 752

Latin America *(continued)*
  and missionaries, **3:**661–662
  and movie industry, **2:**325
  and narcoterrorism, **3:**894
  and new imperialism, **2:**496–497
  and pilgrimages, **3:**742
  and population issues, **3:**749
  and reciprocity, **3:**769
  See also Colonies, Latin American/Caribbean; South America; *individual countries*
Law
  Asia, before World War II, **2:**580–581
  Code of Hammurabi, **2:**463, 517–518, 577, **4:**993–995
  comparative cash, law of, **2:**576
  and conflict between desires of trader and political needs of state, **2:**576–577
  Europe/United States/Middle East before World War II, **2:**577–579
  evolution of, **2:**577
  and GATT/WTO, **2:**581–582
  and Great Britain, **3:**632
  Islam/Islamic societies and, **2:**542–543, 580–581
  Jewish religious, **2:**553
  maritime, **3:**632
  and Middle Ages, **2:**578, **3:**646
  and Mongols, **2:**558
  and Ottoman empire, **3:**721
  regional pacts, **2:**582–584
  trademark, **3:**916–917
  See also Legislation; Tariffs
Law, John, **2:**361–362
Law of Value (Engels), **2:**321
Laws of Manu, **2:**580
Lawyers, **3:**815, 816
Layard, Austin H., **3:**699
Lazzerini family, **3:**814
League of Nations, **1:**293, **2:**405, 432, **4:**928, 984
Leather, **2:**584–585
Lebanon, **1:**25, 45
Lectures (Toynbee), **3:**788
Legazpi, Miguel López de, **3:**599
Leger, Fernand, **1:**68
Legislation
  France
    Berlin Decree of 1806, **2:**384, **3:**685, **4:**941, 1069–1070
    Fontainebleau Decree of 1810, **3:**686
    Méline Tariff of 1892, **3:**878
    Milan Decree of 1807, **3:**686, **4:**941, 1076–1077
    Rambouillet Decree of 1810, **3:**686
    Saint Cloud Decree of 1810, **3:**687
    Warsaw Decree of 1807, **3:**686

Legislation *(continued)*
  Germany
    Samoan Subsidy Bill of 1879, **2:**405
    Tariff Act of 1879, **2:**404
  Great Britain
    Abolition of the Slave Trade Act of 1807, **4:**1070–1076
    Act for the Better Government of India, 1858, **1:**124
    Act for the More Effectual Suppression of the Slave Trade, 1843, **4:**1087–1089
    Bill of Rights of 1689, **2:**578
    Combination acts of 1799/1800, **1:**195–196
    Corn Laws, **1:**14, 236–237, **2:**300, 425, **3:**790, 791, 875, **4:**1078–1083
    Currency Act, **2:**360
    East India Stock Dividend Redemption Act of 1874, **1:**124
    Hat Act of 1732, **3:**693
    India Act of 1784, **1:**124
    Iron Act of 1750, **3:**693
    London Declaration of 1950, **1:**122
    Marine Insurance Act of 1906, **2:**519
    Metropolitan Fire Brigade Act of 1865, **2:**519
    Molasses Act of 1733, **2:**579, **3:**629
    National Health Service Act, **2:**520
    Navigation Acts of 1651 and 1660, **1:**12, 34, 38, 81, **2:**579, **3:**628–631, 692–694, 816, 839, 901, **4:**930, 1029–1032
    Orders in Council of 1804 and 1806, **1:**13, **2:**384, **4:**941, 942
    Regulating Act of 1773, **3:**630
    Stamp Act of 1765, **1:**180, **4:**1043–1047
    Staple Act of 1663, **1:**12
    Statute of Anne of 1710, **1:**234
    Statute of Westminster of 1931, **4:**1124–1126
    Sugar Act of 1764, **2:**579, **3:**693, **4:**1039–1043
    Tariff Reform Act of 1903, **1:**127
    Tea Act of 1773, **1:**238, **4:**1047–1049
    Wool Act of 1699, **3:**693, 896
  Japan
    Law to Protect and Regulate Trade, 1934, **3:**880
  South Africa
    Indians Relief Act of 1914, **2:**391
  Spain
    Free Trade Act of 1778, **3:**636–637
    Ordenanzas of 1737, **3:**637
  United States
    Agricultural Adjustment Act (AAA) of 1933, **1:**15
    Agricultural Trade Development and Assistance Act of 1954, **1:**16

Legislation
  United States *(continued)*
    Airmail Act of 1925, **1:**87
    Articles of Confederation of 1781, **3:**878
    Celler-Kefauver Act of 1950, **1:**212
    Chinese Exclusion Act of 1882, **3:**650
    Civil Aeronautics Act of 1938, **1:**88
    Civil Rights Act of 1964, **4:**974
    Clayton Antitrust Act of 1914, **1:**212
    Communications Act of 1984, **2:**467
    Compromise Tariff Act of 1833, **1:**241, **4:**980
    Copyright Act of 1976, **1:**234, **2:**467
    Desert Act, **2:**537
    Digital Millennium Copyright Act, **2:**467
    Dingley Tariff Act of 1897, **3:**879
    Embargo Act of 1807, **3:**687, **4:**941, 949
    Emergency Price Control Act of 1945, **1:**16
    Emergency Tariff Act of 1921, **2:**453
    Employment Act of 1946, **4:**992
    Fair Labor Standards Act of 1938, **4:**974
    Federal Agricultural Improvement and Reform Act of 1996, **1:**18
    Federal Aid Highway Act of 1956, **3:**923
    Federal Energy Policy Act of 1992, **2:**304
    Federal Reserve Act of 1913, **2:**360, **4:**1111–1117
    Food and Agricultural Act of 1965, **1:**16
    Food and Agricultural Act of 1977, **1:**17
    Fordney-McCumber Tariff of 1922, **2:**453
    Foreign Corrupt Practices Act of 1977, **1:**120
    Fulbright-Hays Act of 1961, **2:**352
    GI Bill of Rights, **1:**225, **4:**991–992
    Greek-Turkish Act of 1947, **3:**607
    Guano Island Act of 1856, **2:**436
    Hawley-Smoot Tariff of 1930, **1:**15, 34, **2:**429, 452–454, **3:**613, 880, 910, **4:**984, 985, 1126–1135
    Homestead Act of 1862, **2:**537
    Japanese Exclusion Act of 1924, **2:**432
    Jones Act of 1914, **2:**496
    Kelly Foreign Air Mail Act of 1928, **1:**88
    Lacey Act of 1894, **1:**40
    Lend-Lease Act, 1941, **1:**16, **4:**987
    Macon's Bill No. 2 of 1811, **3:**687

Legislation
    United States (continued)
        Neutrality Act of 1935, **2**:579, **4**:1135–1137
        Neutrality Act of 1937, **4**:985
        No Electronic Theft Act, **2**:467
        Nonintercourse Act, 1809, **2**:307, **3**:687, **4**:941
        Payne-Aldrich Tariff of 1901, **2**:453
        Reciprocal Trade Agreements Act of 1934, **2**:429, 579
        Robinson-Patman Act of 1936, **1**:212
        Selective Service Act, **4**:987
        Sherman Antitrust Act of 1890, **1**:212
        Sixteenth Amendment, **3**:816, **4**:984
        Steagall Amendment, **1**:16
        Taft-Hartley Act, **4**:991
        Tariff of Abominations, 1828, **2**:579, **3**:879
        Tariff Act of 1930, **3**:880
        Tariff Acts of 1828 and 1832, **1**:241, **4**:980
        Timber and Stone Act, **2**:537
        Trade Act of 1974, **2**:528, **3**:882
        Trade and Competitiveness Act of 1988, **2**:529
        Wagner Act of 1935, **1**:32
        Welfare Reform Act of 1996, **1**:143
        Wilson-Gorman Tariff of 1894, **1**:258
Leif Ericsson, **2**:342
Leipzig fair, **2**:350
Leisure time and consumerism, **1**:223–225
Lemon, Alaina, **2**:481
Lenin, Vladimir I., **1**:113, 114–115, 142, 196, **3**:787, 805, 849
Lenoir, J.J. Étienne, **2**:524
Leo I (pope), **3**:793
Leo III (pope), **1**:266, **3**:840
Leo IX (pope), **3**:793
Leo X (pope), **3**:772
Leonardo da Vinci, **1**:84
Leopold II, **1**:162, 277
Leopold of Austria, **1**:256
Lerner, Abba P., **3**:672
Lerner, Max, **1**:82
Les Demoiselles d'Avignon (Picasso), **1**:67
Lesseps, Ferdinand de, **3**:722, 866, 921
Lesser Antilles, **1**:146
Levant Company, **1**:237, 290
Levin, Frances, **2**:482
Levittown, **1**:225
Lewis, John L., **4**:991
Lewis, Meriwether, **1**:276
Lewis and Clark expedition, **4**:1066–1067
Lexus and the Olive Tree, The (Friedman), **2**:411
Libya, **1**:283, **2**:303, **3**:853

Life insurance, **2**:519–520
Life of Saint Louis (Joinville), **3**:905
Light bulb, **3**:888
Lighthouses, **3**:691
Ligurian people, **2**:401
Limann, Hilla, **2**:408
Lin, Maya, **3**:676
Lincoln, Abraham, **3**:603, **4**:933
Lindbergh, Charles, **1**:88
Linear A/B script, **1**:198, **2**:585–586, **3**:658, 659, 684
Linen, **2**:586–587, **3**:896–897
Linseed oil, **2**:363, 364, 586
Lin Zexu, **2**:435, **3**:717, 821–822, **4**:949
List, Friedrich, **3**:879
List, Georg F., **2**:535, 587–588
Liverpool, **1**:181
Livestock, **2**:588–590
Livingstone, David, **1**:161, 277, **3**:665, 696
Living wage, **1**:224
Livonian Knights, **3**:706
Llonque Yupanqui (king), **2**:500
Lloyd, Edward, **2**:518
Lloyd's of London, **3**:816
Locke, Alain, **1**:67
Locke, John, **3**:602, 603
Lockheed Martin, **1**:120
Lombard insurers, **2**:518–519
Lomè Convention, **1**:10, **3**:912
London, **1**:173, 268, **2**:326, 519, **3**:647
London Company, **1**:4, **2**:552
London Straits Convention (1841), **1**:264
Long, Russell, **3**:882
Longbow, English, **2**:475, 477, 478
Lopez de Sequeira, Dom Diego, **3**:622
Los Angeles, **1**:182–183, **2**:490
Lothair II, **2**:464
Louis VII, **2**:357
Louis IX, **1**:256, **2**:563, **3**:632
Louis XIII, **2**:438
Louis XIV
    and Anglo-Dutch War of 1672, **1**:39
    and architecture, **1**:99
    and art, **1**:65
    and corporations, **1**:238–239, **3**:627
    and insurance, **2**:518
    and King William's War, **4**:954
    and middle class, **1**:64
    Reformation and, **3**:773
    and scientific/technical developments, **1**:98
    and sculpture, **3**:813–814
Louis XVI, **1**:84
Louisiana Purchase (1803), **3**:846, **4**:931–932, 1067–1069
Louis the Pious, **1**:151
Lozi, **1**:160
Luanda kingdom, **1**:160, 161, 244
Luba kingdom, **1**:160
Lübeck, **2**:443–445

Luberas (baron), **3**:734
Lucas, Elizabeth, **1**:13
Luddites, **2**:590–591
Lüderitz, F.E., **2**:405
Lufthansa, **1**:19, 90
Lugard, Frederick, **3**:803
Lukasiewicz, Ignacy, **3**:710
Lukens, Rebecca, **4**:975
Luminists, **1**:67
Lusitania, **3**:824, **4**:951, 983–984
Luther, Martin, **3**:772–773, 775–776, 794
Lutyens, Edwin, **3**:676, 677
Lydia, **1**:101, 187–188
Lyotard, Jean-Francois, **3**:785
Lysergic acid diethylamide (LSD), **1**:292

M

Maassen, Georg, **2**:403
Maastricht Treaty (1992), **2**:332
Macartney, Earl G., **2**:471
MacDonald, Ramsay, **3**:877
Macdonough, Thomas, **4**:943
Macedonia, **1**:101
Machiavelli, Niccolò, **2**:365
Mackenzie, Murdoch, **1**:157
Mackinnon, William, **3**:803
Macon, Nathaniel, **4**:942
Macrovision, **2**:468
Macy's, **1**:267
Madagascar, **1**:8
Madeira, **1**:77, **2**:459
Madison, James, **1**:36, **4**:931, 942
Madras, **3**:592
Madrid Convention for the International Registration of Marks, **2**:467, **3**:917
Madrid Protocol, **3**:917
Magan, **1**:58
Magellan, Ferdinand, **1**:154, 209, **3**:593–594, 600, 848, 859
Magna Charta, **2**:578
Magyar, László, **1**:161
Magyars, **1**:151, 158, 266, **3**:645
Mahayana Buddhism, **1**:129
Mahdali family, **1**:178
Mahmud (king), **2**:409
Mail order business, **1**:224–225, 268, **3**:606
Mail service and early aviation, **1**:85–88
USS *Maine*, **3**:865
Majors, Alexander, **3**:747
Malacca. *See* Melaka.
Malaria, **1**:280, **3**:619, 722, 723, **4**:977
Malaysia, **1**:69, 135, **3**:730, **4**:978
Maldives, **1**:244
Mali empire, **2**:310, 406, 419, **3**:594–595, 841, **4**:965
Malinowski, Bronislaw, **1**:46
Malleus Malificarum, **3**:756
Malls, shopping, **1**:226–227, **3**:606

Malta, 3:738
Malthus, Thomas R., 1:115, 237, 2:300, 557, 3:595–596, 750, 775
Mamluk empire, 1:43
Mammoths, 2:545
Manchester, 1:181
Manchu dynasty (1644–1911), 1:164, 169, 171, 2:469–473, 580, 3:596–598, 821
  see also Qing dynasty
Mandela, Nelson, 3:843–844
Mandé people, 2:545, 4:965
Mandeville, John, 2:441
Manet, Edouard, 1:66
Manhattan Project, 4:988
Manila, 3:598–601, 634–635
Mann, M., 2:573
Manorialism, 1:158, 159
Mansa Musa (king), 2:406, 420, 3:594, 742, 808
Mansa Uli (king), 2:406
al-Mansur (sultan), 3:708
Manuel I, 2:358, 3:593, 626
Manufacturing jobs, 3:819
Mao Zedong, 1:165, 189, 3:823
Maps. *See* Cartography
Marconi, Guglielmo, 3:726
Marcos, Ferdinand, 3:600
Marginal propensity to consume (MPC), 3:770–771
Maria Theresa of Austria, 2:447, 3:818
Marib, 2:340
Marijuana, 1:293
Marine artists, 1:67
Marine insurance, 2:518–519
Mariner's Compass Rectified (Wakely), 1:251
Mariners Mirrour, 1:155
Maritime law, 3:632
Marius, Gaius, 2:327
Marius, John, 4:1027–1029
Market economy switch and increase in service sector, 3:816
Marketing techniques, 1:224, 2:324–325
Marketplaces, 1:10–11, 48, 176, 2:457, 3:604–606, 705
Market power/efficiency paradigms and competition policy, 1:213
Market revolution, 1:101, 3:601–602
Marshall, Alfred, 1:143, 3:789
Marshall, George C., 3:607
Marshall, John, 3:602
Marshall Field's, 1:267
Marshall Islands, 1:152
Marshall Plan, 1:16, 90, 228, 2:375, 3:607–608, 4:952
Marsh harvester, 2:371
Martel, Charles, 1:150, 266, 2:342
Martinique, 2:316

Marx, Karl
  and Bolshevism, 1:113
  and bourgeoisie economists, 1:115
  and capitalism, 1:141
  and competition, 1:210
  and Democratic Association of Brussels speech, 4:1090–1097
  and Engels (Friedrich), 2:321
  and labor theory of value, 3:609–610
  overview of, 3:609
  and religion, 3:778–779
  and surplus value, 3:610
  and trade relations, 1:200
Marxism, 1:142, 3:840–841
Mary II, 1:39, 2:359, 3:592
Mary of Egypt, 1:175
Mass production systems, 1:223, 3:816, 889, 923
Matisse, Henri, 1:67
Matsuoka Yosuke, 2:431
Maximilian I, 2:446
Mayan civilization, 1:46–52, 172, 2:549, 3:611–612
Mayer, Arno, 1:142, 3:785
Mbeki, Thabo, 3:844
Mbundu, 1:160
McCormick reaper, 1:258, 2:351, 371
McDonald's, 1:240, 2:418
McGonigal, Mary, 3:834
MCI, 3:892
McKillop, Heather, 3:612
McKinley, William, 1:116, 188, 3:715, 879
McLuhan, Marshall, 2:411, 417
McNeill, John R., 3:698
McNulty, Paul, 1:210
McPherson, C.B., 1:222
Meade, James, 2:400
Meany, George, 1:34
Mecca, 1:289, 3:709
Mechanical Revolution, 2:569–570
Medean empire, 1:55–56, 71, 94, 3:730
Media outlets, 2:417–418, 3:613–614
Medical profession, 3:815, 816
Medici family, 1:61, 2:364–365, 3:0, 614–615, 646
Medicine, 3:616–619
Medieval Minuscule, 1:24
Mediterranean Sea region
  and art, 1:58
  and cartography, 1:153
  and cities, 1:176–177
  civilizations in, 3:621
  and copper, 1:231, 232
  Cyprus, 1:231, 260
  and Dardanelles channel, 1:262
  as declining link between Europe and the East, 3:783
  and diseases, 1:279
  and frankincense/myrrh, 2:377
  geography and climate in, 3:620–621

Mediterranean Sea region *(continued)*
  and guilds, 3:631–632
  harbors in, 2:448–449
  and immigration, 2:484
  and migrations (human), 3:648
  and navigation, 3:668–669
  Nile River and, 3:697
  and Ottoman empire, 3:720
  and pilgrimages, 3:741
  and piracy/privateering, 3:743
  and ships/shipbuilding, 3:823
  and tourism, 3:907
Mehemet Ali (ruler), 3:921
Mehmed II, 1:263, 3:719–720
Mehmed IV, 3:718
Meiji (emperor), 1:172
Melaka, 1:154, 197–198, 2:449, 3:622–623, 848
Melanesia, 1:67
Menem, Carlos, 1:53
Mensura Astrolai (Contractus), 1:72
Mercado Comun dell Cono Sur (MERCOSUR), 2:582–583, 3:914
Mercantilism
  and agriculture, 1:12
  and Baroque economic theorists, 1:99
  Colbert (Jean-Baptiste) on, 4:1032
  and empire building, 4:956
  fall of, 3:769
  France and, 3:627–629
  general concepts of, 3:623–624
  Great Britain and, 3:628–630
  and Heckscher (Eli), 2:455
  and immigration, 2:487–488
  and law, 2:578
  and market revolution, 3:601–602
  and migrations in Europe, 2:487–488
  Netherlands and, 3:626–627
  Philippines and, 3:625–626
  Portugal and, 3:626
  Renaissance period and, 1:281
  Spain and, 3:624–626
  and tariffs, 3:875, 876
  world, 3:630–631
  See also Colonialism; Colonies
Mercantilism (Heckscher), 2:455
Mercator, Gerardus, 1:154
Mercator's projection, 1:154–155
Merchant Adventurers, 4:1033–1035
Merchant class, rising wealth of the, 1:61, 64, 67
Merchant of Venice (Shakespeare), 2:554
Merchant ships, U.S., 1:16
Merck, 1:292
Merck, George, 1:108
Mesopotamian civilization
  and archaeology, 1:47
  and architecture, 3:639–641
  and art/luxury objects, 1:57, 58
  Assyrian empire conquering, 1:70–71

Mesopotamian civilization *(continued)*
  and cuneiform, **1**:259–260
  and drugs, **1**:291
  and fairs/festivals, **2**:348
  fertilizer used in, **2**:353
  India, trade relations with, **3**:642
  and Indian Ocean trade, **2**:503
  and iron technology, **2**:533
  and irrigation, **2**:536
  and sculpture, **3**:812
  and technology, **3**:886
  and trade connecting the East to the West, **3**:641–643
  See also Babylonian empire; Sumerian civilization
Messenian War (640 B.C.E.), **4**:944
Methylenedioxy methamphetamine (MDMA), **1**:292
Metric system, **4**:964
Metropolitan Medical Response System (MMRS), **1**:109
Metternich, Klemens, **2**:403
Mexico
  and aviation, **1**:90
  and cacao plants, **1**:135, 172
  and cities, **1**:180
  and coffee, **1**:187
  and corn, **1**:235
  and diseases, **1**:193, 279
  and electricity, **2**:304
  and gold, **3**:845
  and guilds, **3**:635, 637
  and import-substitution industrialization, **1**:118
  and livestock, **2**:590
  and Manila, **3**:599, 601, 634–635
  and missionaries, **3**:667
  and population issues, **3**:749
  and silver, **3**:845
  and soybeans, **3**:855
  See also North American Free Trade Agreement
Mfungu people, **3**:665
Miami, immigration and, **2**:490
Michel, Robert, **2**:572
Michelangelo, **1**:60, 61
Microsoft, **1**:215, 216, **3**:889
Middle Ages
  and art, **1**:60–61
  and deforestation, **4**:978
  disputes/arbitration in, **1**:281
  early, **3**:643, 645
  and entertainment, **2**:324
  and exploration/trade, **2**:340–343
  and fairs/festivals, **2**:349, 354–356, **3**:645–646
  feudalism in, **2**:356–357
  and food/diet, **2**:367–368
  and glass, **2**:410
  and gold, **2**:419–420

Middle Ages *(continued)*
  high, **3**:645–647
  and insurance, **2**:518
  and iron technology, **2**:533
  late, **3**:647
  and law, **2**:578, **3**:646
  and leather, **2**:585
  map of, **3**:644
  and marketplaces, **3**:605
  and medicine, **3**:618
  money economy developed in, **2**:550–551
  and piracy/privateering, **3**:743
  and service sector, **3**:815
  and tourism, **3**:904–905
  and transportation/trade, **3**:920–921
Middle class, **1**:61, 64, 67
Middle East
  and agriculture, **1**:16
  Aramaic language spoken in, **1**:23
  and barter system, **1**:100
  and bribery, **1**:118–119
  and British empire, **1**:127
  and diasporas, **1**:272
  and drugs, **1**:290
  and empire building, **2**:319
  and gemstones, **2**:395
  and movie industry, **2**:325
  and stock exchanges, **2**:362
  and urban revolution, **1**:176
  and women, **4**:971
  See also Arabs; Islam/Islamic societies; Ottoman empire
Migration, human, **3**:647–651
  See also Slavery
Milan, **3**:651–652
Milan Decree (1807), Napoléon's, **4**:941, 1076–1077
Military-industrial complex, **2**:398–399, **4**:988
Mill, James, **2**:535, **3**:653
Mill, John S., **2**:299, 535, **3**:652–653, 764–765
Miltiades, **2**:433
Ming dynasty, **1**:164, 169–171, **3**:653–658, 830, 832
Minoan civilization. *See* Crete
Minot, Charles, **3**:890–891
Miscegenation and Columbian exchange, **1**:193
Mishnah Torah (Maimonides), **2**:553
Missionaries
  Africa and, **3**:663–665
  Americas and, **3**:661–662
  Asia and, **3**:663
  definition of, **3**:659
  interdependence between commerce and, **3**:660–661
  and new imperialism, **3**:696
  and Oceania/Pacific islands, **3**:665–666

Missionaries *(continued)*
  as opposition to regime/market forces, **3**:667
  socialization mechanisms and, **3**:666–667
Mississippi River, **2**:383
Mitanni, **1**:70, 71
Mobil, **3**:711
Moche people, **2**:499
Modernity at Large (Appadurai), **2**:417
Modern World System (Wallerstein), **3**:788
Mogadishu, **3**:668–669
Mohammad and Charlemagne (Pirenne), **3**:621
Molasses, **3**:669–670
Molay, Jacques de, **2**:563
Moldavia, **3**:720
Moldova, **1**:113
Molotov Plan (1947), **3**:850
Molotov-Ribbentrop Treaty (1939), **3**:849
Mondrian, Piet, **1**:68
Monet, Claude, **1**:66
Monetarists, **3**:672
Monetary History from 1914 to 1925 (Heckscher), **2**:455
Money, **2**:550–551, **3**:670–674
Mongols
  and Armenia, **1**:56
  and exploration/trade, **2**:343
  and Genghis Khan, **2**:558
  Ghaznavids, military conflicts with, **2**:409
  and horses, **1**:39
  invasions of the, **3**:674–676
  and irrigation, **2**:536
  and law, **2**:558
  and Ming dynasty, **3**:654
  and Novgorod, **3**:706
  and population issues, **3**:749
  and silk trade/Silk Road to China, **2**:558, **3**:649, 675
  and Volga Bulgaria, **4**:940
  and warfare impacting/being impacted by trade, **4**:945
  world trade encouraged by, **1**:169
Monopolistic competition, **1**:200–201, 211, **2**:304–305, 319
Mon people, **3**:847
Monroe Doctrine, **3**:716
Monsoon winds, Indian Ocean and, **2**:338
Montague, Mary W., **1**:279, **3**:618
Montcalm, Louis Joseph de, **4**:956
Montevideo, **1**:173
Montgomery Ward, **3**:606
Montreal Exposition (1967), **2**:352
Montreux Convention (1936), **1**:264
Monuments, **3**:676–678
Moore, Basil J., **3**:672
Moravian craftsmanship, **2**:410

Morgan, Henry, **1**:38–39
Morgan, J.P., **1**:67, 148, **2**:301
Morocco, **3**:918, **4**:965
Morphine, **1**:292
Morris, Robert, **1**:36
Morris, William, **1**:66
Morse, F.B., **3**:888, 890
Moscow, **3**:706
Most-favored-nation status (MFN)
　Anglo-French Cobden-Chevalier Treaty, **2**:425
　and Bosporus/Dardanelles channels, **1**:263
　China and, **1**:166, 298
　communism and, **1**:203
　definition of, **1**:286, **3**:872, 875
　and disputes/arbitration, **1**:286
　and French-U.S. trade relations, **2**:385
　and Hong Kong, **2**:472
　and reciprocity, **3**:770
　and World Trade Organization, **4**:981
Mother Teresa, **1**:175
Motion Picture Association (MPA), **2**:467, 468
Motion Picture Association of America (MPAA), **2**:467, 468
Motion picture industry, **2**:325, 467–469
Motivational research and consumerism, **1**:226
Mountains and climate, **1**:185
Mozambique, **1**:235, **3**:752
M. Sarkies and Sons, **1**:56
Mughal empire
　and art, **1**:64
　demise and subjugation of, **2**:325, **3**:682
　and domestic trade, **3**:679
　and emeralds, **2**:395
　and gold, **2**:420
　and Hinduism, **2**:462
　map of, **3**:680
　and mercantilism, **3**:630
　Netherlands and, **3**:681, 682
　overland trade and, **3**:678–679
　and overseas trade, **3**:679, 681
Muhammad (prophet), **2**:539, 542–543, **3**:709
Mule (weaving device), **2**:452
Mulroney, Brian, **3**:704
Multilateral Investment Guarantee Agency (MIGA), **4**:980
Multinational corporations/enterprises, **1**:239–249, **3**:682–683
Mun, Thomas, **2**:321–322, **3**:628
Mundell, Robert, **2**:400
Murad II, **3**:719
Murano, **2**:410
Murra, John, **1**:48
Murray's Handbook for Travellers in Central Italy, **3**:814

Muscat, **2**:503
Muscovy Company, **1**:123, 237, **2**:552
Museum of Modern Art, **1**:67
Music industry, **2**:325
Muslims. *See* Arabs, Islam/Islamic societies
Mussolini, Benito, **3**:678, **4**:986
Musson, Matthijs, **1**:64
Mutual aid societies, **2**:518
Mutual Security Administration, U.S., **3**:608
Myanmar, **1**:69, **4**:978
Mycenaean civilization, **1**:6, 198, **3**:648, 683–684, 831
Myrdal, Gunnar, **3**:771
Myrrh, **2**:376–377

N

Nabataean people, **3**:735
Nabopolassar (king), **1**:94
Nader, Ralph, **1**:226
NAFTA. *See* North American Free Trade Agreement
Najraf oasis, **3**:708
Namath, Joe, and endorsements, **2**:324
Namban art, **1**:63
Namibia, **1**:271
Nantes Edict (1685), **2**:587
Naples, **1**:96–97
Napoléon III, **1**:247, 249, **2**:404, **3**:652
Napoleonic Wars (1803–1815)
　and Aegean sailors, **1**:7
　and agriculture, **1**:13, 14
　and aviation, **1**:84
　Batavia and, **1**:103
　and Continental System, **1**:38, 229, **3**:685–687
　Hamburg conquered by, **2**:442
　and Manila, **3**:601
　and Milan, **3**:651–652
　overview of, **4**:947–950
　and Spain, **3**:846
　and technology, **4**:948
　trade issues central to, **2**:384
　United States and, **3**:687, **4**:932, 948–949
　War of 1812 and, **4**:941–943
Naramsin (ruler), **1**:58
Narcoterrorism, **3**:894
Narses, **2**:423
Nash, Gary B., **4**:954
Nasmyth, James, **2**:534
Nasser, Gamal A., **1**:73, 228, **3**:867
National Aeronautics and Space Administration (NASA), **1**:199
National Africa Company, **3**:802
National Labor Relations Board (NLRB), **1**:32

Native Americans
　and archaeology, **1**:47, 52
　barter system used by, **1**:101
　bioterrorism used on, **1**:108
　and empire building, **4**:954–956
　and exploration/trade, **2**:345
　and food/diet, **2**:369
　France, trade relations with, **1**:81
　fur industry/trade, **2**:389
　and gemstones, **2**:395
　and Internet gambling, **2**:532
　and leather, **2**:584
　and missionaries, **3**:662
　as nomads, **3**:701
　and Pony Express, **3**:748
　and population issues, **3**:749
　and slavery, **3**:835
　and smallpox, **3**:618
　unrest/agitation toward United States, **4**:932
　and War of 1812, **4**:942
Nautical cartography charts. *See* Cartography
Naval warfare and gunpowder, **2**:439
Navigation
　and astrolabe, **1**:72
　and Atlantic trade route, **3**:689–690
　and chronometer, **1**:157, **3**:690–691
　and compass, **1**:208–209, **3**:668–669, 887
　contemporary, **3**:691–692
　and cross-staff, **1**:251–252, **3**:689, 887
　and Henry the Navigator, **2**:369, **3**:729
　in the nineteenth century, **3**:691
　and octant, **3**:761
　and quadrant, **3**:689, 690, 761–762
　and Renaissance period, **3**:784
　rise of modern, **3**:668–669
　and sextant, **3**:690, 761
　and technology, **3**:887
　and trade winds, **3**:915–916
　See also Cartography
Navigium (Lucian), **3**:794
Nazis, **2**:555, **3**:678, **4**:951, 986
Ndogo, **1**:160
Nearchus, **2**:338
Nebuchadnezzar II, **1**:94, **3**:641
Necho II, **2**:337, **3**:866
Neckam, Alexander, **1**:209
Need, Samuel, **1**:54, 55
Negritos people, **3**:847
Nelson, Donald, **4**:991
Neoclassical economists, **3**:671, 672
Nero (emperor), **3**:793
Nestle, **1**:240
Netherlands
　and agriculture, **1**:18
　Amsterdam, **1**:37–38
　and arms/weapons trade, **4**:961
　and art/luxury objects, **1**:63–65, 67
　and Atlantic trade route, **1**:79–81

Netherlands *(continued)*
  and aviation, **1:**92
  and banks/banking, **2:**358–359
  and bribery, **1:**120
  Bugis people and, **1:**130
  and Caribbean region, **1:**147
  and cartography, **1:**155–156
  China, trade relations with, **2:**297
  and Christianity, **1:**175–176
  and colonialism, **1:**191
  and cotton, **1:**241
  department stores in, **1:**268
  and discovery/exploration, **1:**275–276
  and drugs, **1:**293
  and embargoes, **2:**308
  and empire building, **1:**294, **2:**314, 316
  and Equatorial Africa, **1:**161
  and exploration/trade, **2:**344
  and food/diet, **2:**371
  and fur trade, **1:**40
  and gold, **2:**420
  and grain, **2:**425
  and gunpowder, **2:**438–439
  and immigration, **2:**483, 487–488
  and imperialism/emergence of world economy, **4:**947
  and Indian Ocean trade, **2:**505
  Indonesian culture influencing the, **1:**294
  and insurance, **2:**518
  and labor relations, **1:**294
  and Madras, **3:**592
  and Manchu dynasty, **3:**597
  and Melaka, **3:**623
  and mercantilism, **3:**626–627
  and Ming dynasty, **3:**657
  molasses and, **3:**670
  and Mughal empire, **3:**681, 682
  and navigation, **3:**690
  and Ottoman empire, **3:**721
  overview of, **3:**694–695
  and paper/pulp, **3:**725
  and piracy/privateers, **1:**79
  and Renaissance period, **3:**783
  Russia, trade relations with, **3:**733
  and spice trade, **2:**367, 369, **3:**859
  stock exchanges in, **2:**361
  and Surat, **3:**869
  and unions, **1:**295, **3:**694
  and women, **4:**971
  See also Dutch East India Company; Dutch Swedish War (1657); Dutch Trading Company, Dutch West India Company; *individual wars/battles*
Neutron activation analysis (NAA), **1:**46
Nevsky, Alexander, **3:**706, 895
New Amsterdam, **1:**180
New classical economists, **2:**400
Newcomen, Thomas, **3:**862

New Deal, **1:**15, 32, 140, 143, **2:**429, **3:**789, 817, **4:**991
New England colonies, **1:**81, **2:**345, **3:**670, 804
New Guinea, **2:**405
New Orleans, **2:**450–451
New Practical Navigator, The (Moore), **3:**761
New Principles of Political Economy (Rae), **3:**764
New Rhenish Gazette, **2:**321
Newspapers, **1:**4, **3:**613
Newton, Isaac, **3:**603, 761
New York, **1:**180, 271, **2:**326
New York Convention on the Recognition and Enforcement of Foreign Arbitral Awards (1958), **1:**283
New York Stock Exchange, **2:**362
New York Tribune, **1:**104
New Zealand, **1:**121, 230, 231, **3:**666, 877
New Zealand Centennial Exhibition (1939), **4:**972
Ngbandi, **1:**160
Nicaea, **1:**254
Nicaragua, **2:**497
Nicholas I, **1:**249
Nicholas II, **3:**787, 805
Nicholas V (pope), **2:**370
Nigeria, **1:**10, 135, **3:**801–803, **4:**966
Niger River, **1:**295, 296, **2:**547
Nightingale, Florence, **1:**249
Nike, **2:**324
Nike of Samothrace, **3:**812
Nile River, **1:**73–74, 106, **2:**339–340, 586, **3:**696–698, **4:**957
Niles Register, **3:**613
Nimrod, **3:**699
Ninety-Five Theses (Luther), **1:**4, **3:**773
Nineveh, **3:**699–700
Nixon, Richard M., **1:**120, 131, **2:**527
Nkrumah, Kwame, **2:**408, **3:**610
Nomads, **2:**367, **3:**701–703
Nontariff barriers (NTBs), **3:**703–704
Nonviolent civil disobedience, **2:**391–393
Noriega, Manuel, **3:**846
North America, **1:**10, 41, 52, 193
  See also Canada; Colonies, North American; United States
North American Free Trade Agreement (NAFTA)
  and AFL-CIO, **1:**34
  and Bush (George H.W.), **1:**132–133
  and corporations, **1:**240
  and disputes/arbitration, **1:**284, 285, 287
  and imbalance between parties involved, **3:**705
  law's evolution and, **2:**583
  and liberalization process, **1:**143
  and the media, **3:**613–614
  negotiation and ratification of, **3:**704

North American Free Trade Agreement (NAFTA) *(continued)*
  overview of, **3:**914
  and soybeans, **3:**855
North Atlantic Treaty Organization (NATO), **1:**228
North Sea, **1:**30
Northwest Airlines, **1:**87, 92
North West Company, **1:**238
Norway, **1:**233, **3:**871, 872
Not Like Us (Pells), **2:**418–419
Novgorod, **3:**705–706, **4:**939
Nubia, **2:**303, 564
Nuclear power/weapons, **4:**988
Nunes, Pedro, **1:**154
Nurredin (king), **1:**255
Nuts, **3:**706–707
Nyamwezi, **1:**161
Nye, Gerald, **4:**985
Nyon Conference (1937), **3:**744

O

Oases, **3:**708–709
Observations on the Effects of the Corn Laws (Malthus), **4:**1078–1083
Observations on the Report of the Committee of Ways and Means (List), **3:**879
Obsidian, **1:**46, 48–51, 57
Oceanic island chains, **1:**66–67
Octant, **3:**761
Octavian, **1:**21
Oda Nobunaga, **2:**439
Odovacar (king), **2:**423
Odyssey (Homer), **3:**684, 730
Ohlin, Bertil, **2:**455
Oil/oil industry
  and alternatives to internal combustion engine, **2:**526
  and Arab people's increasing trade power, **1:**44–45
  and combustion engine, **3:**865
  and disputes/arbitration, **1:**283
  and embargoes, **2:**307–308
  and empire building, **2:**319
  and energy technology/markets, **2:**320
  and foreign aid, **2:**375–376
  and kerosene, **3:**710–711
  and Latin American/Caribbean colonies, **1:**147
  and Mediterranean Sea region, **3:**621
  and Persian Gulf, **3:**732–733
  before the twentieth century, **3:**710–711
  in the twentieth century, **3:**711, 713
  and Venezuela, **1:**128, **3:**713, 846
Oil palm, **3:**707
Okinawa Ocean Exposition (1975), **2:**352
Old and New World, first exchanges between, **1:**192
Olds, Ransom E., **2:**524

Olivares, Gaspar de, **1**:97
Olive oil, **2**:366, 434
Olives, **3**:713–715
Olmec people, **1**:49–50, 172, **2**:549
Olympics, the, **3**:904
Omai, or a Trip around the World (Garrick), **1**:230
Oman, **3**:642–643
Omar II, **2**:543
On Authority (Engels), **2**:321
One-line stores, **3**:605
"On the Importance of Railroads to Sweden's Economic Development" (Heckscher), **2**:454
On War (Clausewitz), **4**:948
Open door notes, **3**:715–716, **4**:1106–1107
Opium use/trade, **1**:290–292, **2**:471, **3**:597, 717–718, 822
Opium Wars
  and British East India Company, **1**:124
  Canton system ended by, **2**:435
  Hong Kong and, **1**:127, **2**:298, 469–472
  Industrial Revolution and, **2**:513
  and Manchu dynasty, **3**:598
  and most-favored-nation status, **2**:298
  and Qing dynasty, **1**:164
  and Shanghai, **3**:821–822
  silver drain to China as reason for, **3**:716–717
  and steamships, **3**:865
  and Treaty of Wangxia, **2**:496
  as turning point in China/world trade history, **1**:169–170, **4**:944, 949–950
Oppenheimer, Ernest, **2**:395
Oranges, **2**:387
Organization for Economic Cooperation and Development (OECD), **1**:214, 293, **2**:298, 414
Organization for Economic Cooperation and Development Convention on Combating Bribery of Foreign Public Officials in International Business Transactions, **1**:120
Organization for European Economic Cooperation (OEEC), **3**:608
Organization of the Petroleum Exporting Countries (OPEC), **1**:84, 152, **2**:375, **3**:713, 732, 846
Orhan (sultan), **1**:262
Oribe, Furuta, **1**:63
Origin of the Family, Private Property, and the State (Engels), **2**:321
Origin of Species (Darwin), **3**:596
Origins of the State and Civilization (Service), **1**:49
Orinoco River, **1**:235
Orontid family, **1**:56
Orwell, George, **2**:568
Ostia, **2**:449
Ostrogoths, **2**:423–424

Ottawa Conference (1932), **3**:877
Otto, Nikolaus A., **2**:524
Otto I, **2**:403
Otto IV, **2**:465
Ottoman empire
  and Aegean Sea, **1**:7
  Arab nationalism and weakening of, **1**:44
  Armenia ruled by, **1**:56
  Black Sea region controlled by, **1**:113
  and cities/trade, **1**:179
  and coffee, **1**:186
  and conquest, **3**:719–720
  Constantinople captured by, **1**:220
  Crimean War, **1**:14, 247–249, 261, 264
  and Dardanelles channel, **1**:262–264
  and drugs, **1**:293
  Egypt conquered by, **2**:302
  and extraterritoriality, **2**:346–347
  and foreign traders, **3**:720–721
  Great Britain, trade relations with, **1**:237
  Greece declares independence from, **1**:7–8
  and gunpowder, **2**:437, 439
  Jewish people, trade relations with, **2**:555
  and law, **3**:721
  and Mediterranean Sea region, **3**:720
  and new imperialism, **2**:495
  and Nile River, **3**:698
  Ragusa, trade relations with, **3**:765
  trade and international policy of, **2**:540–541, **3**:718–719
  and Tunisia, **3**:925–926
  and Venice, **1**:179, **3**:721, **4**:937
Outlines of American Political Economy (List), **3**:879
Outlines of a Critique of Political Economy (Engels), **2**:321
Outsourcing jobs, **3**:818
Ovambo people, **1**:161
Overnight package services, **3**:923
Owen, Robert, **3**:840
Ownership rights and communist systems, **1**:204
Ownership *vs.* wealth, **4**:959
Oxfam, **1**:187
Oxygen isotope analysis of human bones, **1**:46–47, 51
Oyo kingdom, **4**:965

P

Paasche price index, **2**:516
Pacific Ocean, **2**:345
Packard, Vance, **1**:226
Paekche kingdom (350–668), **2**:297
Paiute War (1860), **3**:748
Pakistan, **1**:122, 241, 285, 293
Palast, Greg, **2**:414
Pan-Africanism, **2**:408

Panama, **2**:497, **3**:846
Panama Canal
  and aviation, **1**:88
  and medicine, **3**:619
  overview of, **3**:722–724
  and superships, **3**:691
  Treaty of 1903, **4**:1107–1111
  Treaty of 1977, **4**:1157–1162
  United States and, **3**:722–726, 922–923
Pan American Airways, **1**:88
Pan-American Exposition (1901), **2**:352, **3**:906
Paper currency, **1**:101
Paper and pulp, **3**:724–726
Papua New Guinea, **1**:135
Parameswara (prince), **3**:622
Paris Air Show, **2**:350
Paris Convention for the Protection of Industrial Property (1883), **3**:727
Paris Convention for Protection of Industry Property (1967), **2**:467, 524
Paris Exposition (1855), **2**:351
Paris Exposition Universelle (1867), **1**:66
Paris Peace Conference (1919), **1**:86, 87
Park, Mungo, **1**:277
Parthians, **2**:340
Patent Cooperation Treaty, **2**:467
Patents, **2**:522–525, **3**:619, 726–728
Patriotic themes and advertising, **1**:4
Patterson, Robert P., **4**:990–991
Paul III (pope), **3**:814
Paupers Crusade, **1**:253
Paxton, Joseph, **1**:257
Payens, Hugh de, **2**:561–562
Peace of the Amiens (1802), **2**:384
Peace of Beijing treaty, **1**:116
Peace of Noteborg (1323), **3**:706
Pearl Harbor, **4**:951, 987, 988–989
Pearson, Harry W., **1**:48, 49
Peel, Robert, **1**:237, **3**:876
Pegolotti, Francesco B., **1**:97, **3**:728, **4**:997–1000
Peisistratus, **1**:11
Pellagra, **1**:235
Peloponnesian War (433–404 B.C.E.), **4**:944
Pennsylvania Railroad, **1**:148
Pennsylvania Rock Oil Company, **3**:710
Pentecostal Church, **3**:667
Penty, A.J., **3**:840
People's Republic of China (PRC), **1**:164–165, 189, 244
Pepin I, **1**:149–150
Pepper, **1**:138, 219, **2**:369, **3**:699, 728–730
Pepperrell, William, **4**:955
PepsiCo, **1**:240, **2**:324
Père, Charles Le, **3**:866
Perfect competition model, **1**:210–211
Performance requirements and disputes/arbitration, **1**:286
Perfume, **3**:730–731

Pergamon, 2:457
Periplus Maris Erythraei, 1:106
Perkin, William, 3:898
Perot, Ross, 3:613–614
Perry, Matthew C., 1:66, 2:496, 580
Perry, Oliver H., 4:942
Persia
  and Abbasid caliphate, 1:1, 2
  Achaemenian empire, 1:113
  Alexander the Great's conquest of, 1:20–21
  Aramaic language spoken in, 1:22
  Armenia ruled by, 1:55–56
  and Babylonian empire, 1:94, 95
  and coins/coinage, 1:101
  and Dark Ages, 1:266
  and Delian League, 1:266–267
  Egypt, trade relations with, 2:303
  Egypt conquered by, 2:304
  and gemstones, 2:395
  Great Britain, trade relations with, 1:237
  Greece, military conflicts with, 2:433–434
  Indus River and, 2:508, 509
  and oil/oil industry, 3:710
  and perfume, 3:730
  and Phoenicians, 3:738
Persian Gulf Wars, 1:109, 3:732–733, 131
Peru
  and corn, 1:235
  and diseases, 1:174, 193, 279
  and drugs, 1:293
  and guano, 2:436
  and guilds, 3:635
  and Manila, 3:601
  and maritime resources, 1:49
  silver from, 1:180
Pessen, Edward, 4:959
Pesticides, 1:226
Peter (apostle), 3:792
Peter III, 3:820, 826
Peter the Great, 1:64, 3:733–734
Peter the Hermit, 1:253
Petra, 3:734–736
Petty, William, 4:958
Phaedo (Socrates), 3:621
Pharmaceutical industry, 1:292, 3:889
Pheidon (king), 3:672
Philadelphia Centennial (1976), 2:352
Philanthropic Society, 1:196
Philip II, 1:62, 79, 255, 2:434, 446, 3:601, 626
Philip IV, 1:97, 2:358, 476, 563, 564
Philip VI, 2:475
Philippines
  and ASEAN, 1:69
  and aviation, 1:90
  and coconut oil, 3:707
  Manila, 3:598–601
  and mercantilism, 3:625–626

Philippines *(continued)*
  and missionaries, 3:667
  and new imperialism, 2:496
  and wood, 4:978
Philo, 1:21
Phoenicia/Phoenicians
  alphabet and, 1:24–26, 198, 3:738
  and art/luxury objects, 1:58
  Carthage and, 1:177, 3:739
  and cities/trade, 1:176–177
  and colonialism, 3:738–739
  and copper, 1:231–232
  culture and religion of, 3:737–738
  decline and fall of, 3:738
  as a dominant power, 3:737
  Egypt, trade relations with, 2:303, 304
  and exploration/trade, 2:336–337
  and food/diet, 2:366
  and glass, 2:410
  and immigration, 2:483, 484
  origins of, 3:736–737
  and Sahara Desert/trade, 3:806
  and ships/shipbuilding, 1:47, 3:823
  and Sicily, 3:826
  and Tunisia, 3:924
  and wine, 4:970
  and wood, 4:977
Physiocratic School, 1:141, 2:385, 575, 576, 3:838
Picart, Jean-Michel, 1:64
Picasso, Pablo, 1:67, 68
Pictorial images, licensing/selling, 1:225
Pigs, 2:589, 590
Pike, Zebulon, 1:276
Pilgrimages, 3:740–743, 806
Pilgrims, 3:649, 756, 4:930
Pinckney, Eliza L., 4:975
Pinkham, Lydia, 4:975
Piracy/privateering
  ancient and medieval history of, 3:743
  and Anglo-Dutch Wars, 1:38–39
  and Atlantic trade route, 1:79
  and Berenice, 1:106
  and British-Spanish animosity, 3:624–625
  golden age of, 3:744
  Great Britain and, 1:124, 2:420, 3:314, 845
  and intellectual property, 2:467–468
  Japan and, 2:297
  Latin American/Caribbean colonies and, 3:845
  Mesopotamia and, 3:642
  and Ming dynasty, 3:655–657
  in modern times, 3:744
  Tunisia and, 3:925–926
Piraeus, 1:177
Pisa, 3:632
Pitt, William, 1:195, 196, 2:471, 3:820, 4:956

Pitts mechanical thresher, 2:371
Pius VI (pope), 1:66
Pizarro, Francisco, 1:108, 193, 2:501
Place, Francis, 1:196
Plague, 1:133, 3:617–618, 749
Plantation system and slavery, 3:837, 4:932
Plastics, 3:713
PlayStation, 1:216, 2:325
Plea for a Theory in Economic History (Heckscher), 2:455
Pliny the Elder, 2:377, 3:795
Plows and oxen, 2:368, 3:886
Plymouth Company, 2:552
Pochteca merchants, 3:744–745
Poland, 1:189, 273, 2:415, 3:778, 849, 4:987
Polanyi, Karl, 1:48, 49
Political Discourses (Hume), 2:299
Political economy and the invention of capitalism, 1:140–143
Politics, The (Aristotle), 3:785
Pollution, 3:726
Polo, Maffeo, 3:745
Polo, Marco, 1:169, 177, 2:343, 3:675, 710, 745–747, 858–859
Polo, Niccolò, 3:745
Polybius, 2:339
Polynesians, 1:67, 2:345
Pompey the Great, 2:339, 3:743
Pony Express, 3:747–748
Population, 2:426, 3:595, 749–750, 4:1063–1066
Porcelain, 2:511, 512, 3:601, 657
Porter, Bernard, 3:695
Portolan charts, 1:153, 155
Ports of trade model of exotic trade, 1:49
Portugal
  and art, 1:63, 65
  and Atlantic trade route, 1:77, 78
  and Brazil, 3:752, 845
  Bugis people and, 1:130
  Calicut, trade relations with, 1:138, 139
  and cartography, 1:153–155
  China, military conflicts with, 3:655, 657
  and cities/trade, 1:178, 179–180
  compass and, 1:209
  and Continental System, 3:687
  and cowry shells, 1:245
  and diamonds, 1:270, 271
  and discovery/exploration, 1:275
  and drugs, 1:292
  and empire building, 2:310–312
  and Equatorial Africa, 1:161
  and exploration/trade, 2:343–345
  and Ghana, 2:406–407
  Great Britain, alliance with, 1:128
  and Guangzhou, 2:435
  and gunpowder, 2:439

Portugal *(continued)*
   and Hinduism, **2:**462
   and immigration, **3:**752
   and imperialism/emergence of world economy, **4:**946–947
   India, trading relations with, **1:**123
   and insurance, **2:**518
   kamal, used by, **1:**251
   and Kilwa, **1:**178, **2:**560
   and Manila, **3:**599, 600
   and Melaka, **3:**622–623
   and mercantilism, **3:**626
   and Ming dynasty, **3:**655, 657
   and missionaries, **3:**661–664
   and Mogadishu, **3:**668
   and Mughal empire, **3:**681, 682
   and navigation, **3:**689
   and Ottoman empire, **3:**719
   overview of, **3:**750–752
   and pepper, **3:**729
   and Renaissance period, **3:**783
   and salt, **3:**811
   and ships/shipbuilding, **3:**824
   and silver, **3:**832
   and South America, **3:**845
   and Southeast Asia, **3:**848
   and spice trade, **2:**367, 369, **3:**859, 860
   and sugar, **3:**669, 867–868
   and Surat, **3:**869
   and *Wealth of Nations,* **4:**1049–1063
   and wood, **4:**977
   See also Henry the Navigator
Post, Willey, **1:**88
Potatoes, **1:**237, **2:**300, 369–371, **3:**753–754
Potato famine, Irish (1846–1848), **1:**14, 237, **2:**300, 371, **3:**754
Potosí, **1:**180
Pottery
   and archaeology, **1:**46
   as art, **1:**57
   Athens and, **1:**74
   Berenice and, **1:**106
   and China, **2:**512, **3:**601, 657, 754–755
   and Crete/Minoan civilization, **1:**246, **3:**658, 754
   Etruscans, **2:**327
   Industrial Revolution and, **2:**511–513
   made by two methods, **3:**754
   manufactured, **3:**756
   and Negritos, **3:**847
   and shipwrecks, **3:**825
   and Wedgwood (Josiah), **1:**65
   and weights/measures, **4:**962
Pottinger, Henry, **2:**471–472
Poultry products, **1:**18
Poverty, **1:**9, **2:**414, **4:**959
Practica della Mercatura (Pegolotti), **1:**97, **3:**728, **4:** 997–1000
Predestination, **3:**776

Preferential tariffs, **3:**872
Prehistoric technology, **3:**885–886
Premdas, R.R., **1:**146
Price, Barbara, **1:**51
Pricing, electricity and real-time, **2:**305
Pricing and communist systems, **1:**205–206
Principal Navigations, Voyages and Discoveries of the English Nation (Hakluyt), **2:**441, **3:**905
Principles of Marketing (Kotler & Armstrong), **1:**2
Principles of Political Economy (Malthus), **3:**596
Principles of Political Economy (Mill), **2:**299, **3:**652, 653, 764–765
Principles of Political Economy and Taxation (Ricardo), **1:**141, 208, **2:**535, **3:**790
Principles of Population (Malthus), **2:**535
Printing, advent of, **1:**62
Printing press, **1:**4, 161, 233, **3:**756–758
Process of Creative Destruction, The (Schumpeter), **1:**212
Productionists, **1:**140
Prohibitive tariff, **3:**873
Proletariat, **3:**839
Property insurance, **2:**520–521
Protectionism, **1:**18, **2:**380–381, 452–454, 579, 587, **3:**769–770
   See also Tariffs
Protestant ethic, **2:**568
Protestant Ethic and the Spirit of Capitalism, The (Weber), **1:**140, **3:**758, 772, 775
Protestantism, **1:**175–176, **3:**649, 756, 758–759, 771–777, 794
Protocol on Arbitration Clauses (1923), **1:**282
Proudhon, Pierre-Joseph, **3:**840
Prussia
   Baroque period and, **1:**98–99
   and cholera, **1:**173
   and Dardanelles channel, **1:**264
   Frederick II and, **2:**379–380, **3:**819–820
   and Ottoman empire, **3:**721
   Russia, military conflicts with, **2:**379
   Russia, trade relations with, **3:**733
   and Seven Years' War, **2:**403, **3:**818
Ptolemy II, **1:**105
Ptolemy of Alexandria, **1:**152–153, 155, **2:**339
Puerto Rico, **1:**146, 147, **3:**637
Punic Wars (264–241 B.C.E.), **1:**177, **3:**739, 759–760, 826
Puritans, **3:**649, 756, **4:**930
Pytheas, **2:**338–339

Q

Qaddafi, Muammar, **1:**283, **3:**853
Qin dynasty, **1:**163, 170

Qin Shihuang (emperor), **2:**435
Qianlong (emperor), **2:**435, **3:**597
Qing dynasty, **1:**164, 169, 171, **2:**469–473, 580, **3:**596–598, 821
   See also Manchu dynasty
Quadrant, **3:**689, 690, 761–762
Quakers, **1:**176
Quesnay, Francois, **1:**141, **2:**575
Quinine, **1:**280, **3:**619, **4:**977
Qur'an, **1:**43, **2:**539, 541, 581

R

Radanite merchants, **3:**763–764
Radio, **1:**5, 225, **2:**515, **3:**613
Radio Corporation of America, **2:**398, **3:**726
Rae, John, **3:**764–765
Raffles, Stanford, **2:**489
Ragusan merchants, **3:**719, 721, 765–766, **4:**937
Railroads
   Britain and, **3:**922
   Germany and, **2:**404, 405
   India and, **3:**922
   and iron technology, **2:**534
   origins of, **3:**888
   overview of, **3:**767–768
   and telegraph, **3:**890–891
   and transportation revolution, **3:**602, 603
Raimondi, Marcantonio, **1:**62, 63
Raleigh, Walter, **2:**306, 441, **4:**1008–1011
Ramses II, **2:**463, 464
Ramses V, **1:**278
Raphael, **1:**62
Raschèr, Andrea, **2:**481
Rassemblement Démocratique Africain, **1:**296
Rathje, William, **1:**50
Rationality, roots of, **3:**775
Ravenscroft, George, **2:**410
Rawlings, Jerry, **2:**408
Raymond of Toulouse, **1:**253, 254
Readings in Theory of International Trade (Heckscher), **2:**454
Reagan, Ronald, **1:**131, 143, **2:**399, **4:**1162–1164
Real-time pricing, **2:**305
Reciprocity, **1:**48, 49, **3:**769–770
Recording Industry Association of America, **2:**325
Redemption system, **2:**503
Reden, Fryderyk von, **2:**534
Redistribution, **1:**48, **3:**770–771
Red Sea, **1:**105–106, **2:**544, **3:**643, 729
Reed, Walter, **3:**619
Reents-Budet, Doric, **1:**46
Reformation, Protestant, **3:**649, 756, 771–774, 794

Regional trading agreements/ organizations, 2:582–584, 588, 3:911–915
Regulations and competition, 1:212
Reid, Thomas, 3:603
Reinel, Jorge, 1:154
Religion
  and art, 1:63
  and capitalism, 3:774–777
  as a construction of social reality, 3:774
  and diasporas, 1:273
  and individualism, 3:776, 780–781
  and labor, 2:568–569
  Phoenicians and, 3:737
  and pilgrimages, 3:740–743
  and political-economic institutions, 3:777–780
  as a regulator of trade, 3:780
  and tourism, 3:903, 904–905
  See also specific religions
Remade in Japan (Tobin), 2:419
Renaissance period
  and art, 1:61–62
  commercial life changed during the, 3:784
  and disputes/arbitration, 1:281
  expansion during the, 3:782–784
  and Milan, 3:651
  and modern world trade system, 3:781–782
  and monuments, 3:677
  and printing press, 3:756
  and sculpture, 3:813
  and tourism, 3:905
  and warfare, 3:784
Renfrew, Colin, 1:49
Report on Manufactures (Hamilton), 3:764
HMS *Resolution*, 1:230
Resource inconvertibility and communist systems, 1:203–204
Retail stores, 1:226–227, 269, 3:606
Revisionism, 3:841
Revolutionary War, U.S., 1:34–38, 81, 2:317
Revolutions
  Industrial Revolution, 3:788–789
  Keynesian Revolution, 3:789–790
  in knowledge and science, 3:788
  Russian Revolution, 3:787–788
  social, 3:785
Reynald of Chantillon (prince), 1:255
Reyneval, Conrad de, 2:385
Rhodes, Cecil, 1:162, 271, 2:395, 494, 3:803, 843
Rhodesia, 1:162
Ribeiro, Diogo, 1:154
Ricardian-Marshallian approach, 2:557
Ricardo, David
  and comparative advantage, 1:208, 2:300, 3:652

Ricardo, David *(continued)*
  and Corn Laws (British), 1:237
  and iron law of wages, 2:535–536, 4:1083–1084
  and Keynes (John M.), 3:789
  and laissez-faire, 2:576
  and Marx (Karl), 1:115
  overview of, 3:790–791
  and tariffs, 3:876
Rice, 1:13, 17, 110, 184, 3:791–792
Rich and poor, gaps between, 2:414
Richard I, 1:255
Richard II, 2:477, 3:628, 692
Richelieu, Cardinal, 1:97
Richthofen, Ferdinand von, 2:328
Rig Vedic civilization, 2:508
Robert, Nicholas-Louis, 3:725
Robertson, Roland, 2:411
Rochambeau, Comte de, 1:36
Rockefeller, John D., 3:710
Roe, Thomas, 3:681, 4:1024–1026
Roger I, 3:826
Roger II, 3:826
Rolfe, John, 1:12, 3:901
Romania, 1:113, 244, 3:710
Rome, ancient
  advertising in, 1:4
  and Aegean Sea, 1:7
  and agriculture, 1:11
  and amber, 1:30, 131
  Appian Way, 1:41–42
  and art/luxury objects, 1:60
  and Berenice, 1:106
  and Black Sea region, 1:113
  Carthage, military conflicts with, 1:177, 3:739, 759–760, 826
  and cartography, 1:152
  and Catholic Church, 3:793, 795, 797
  Celts, trade relations with, 2:331
  and cities/trade, 1:177
  and coins/coinage, 1:101, 188
  Constantinople and, 1:218–220
  and copper, 1:231, 232
  Danube River and, 1:261–262
  and drugs, 1:291
  Egypt, trade relations with, 2:304, 309
  and empire building, 2:309
  and entertainment, 2:323
  Etruscans dominated by, 2:327
  and exploration/trade, 2:339–340
  and fairs/festivals, 2:349
  fall of, 3:799
  and food/diet, 2:366, 367, 3:714, 715
  forums as central marketplaces in, 1:11
  and frankincense/myrrh, 2:377
  Garamantian empire, trade relations with, 2:393
  and gemstones, 2:395
  and glass, 2:410
  and gold, 2:419

Rome, ancient *(continued)*
  and Goths, 2:423
  and governance/trade, 3:795, 797
  harbors in, 2:449
  and immigration, 2:483–486
  and income of merchants, 3:794–795
  and Latin language, 1:24, 198
  and law, 2:577
  and livestock, 2:588
  map of, 3:796
  and medicine, 3:618
  Mediterranean Sea vital to, 3:621
  Middle Ages and, 3:643, 645
  and Milan, 3:651
  Nubia, military conflicts with, 2:564
  and perfume, 3:730
  and Petra, 3:736
  and piracy/privateering, 3:743
  plague in, 3:617–618
  and population issues, 3:749
  and Sahara Desert/trade, 3:806–807
  and salt, 3:810
  and sculpture, 3:813
  and ships/shipbuilding, 3:823
  and silk trade/Silk Road to China, 3:829, 897
  and silver, 3:831
  and slavery, 3:835
  and technology, 3:886
  trading networks in, 3:798–799
  and transportation/trade, 3:920
  and Tunisia, 3:924
  types of trade movement, 3:797–798
  and warfare impacting/being impacted by trade, 4:944
  and weights/measures, 4:963
  and wine, 4:970
  and wood, 4:977
  and wool, 3:896, 4:979
Rome Convention, 2:524
Rom people, 3:701
Roosevelt, Franklin D.
  and agriculture, 1:15
  and aviation, 3:889
  and banks/banking, 3:817
  and competition, 1:212
  and Hawley-Smoot Tariff (U.S.) of 1930, 4:1126–1134
  and Keynes (John M.), 1:143, 2:557, 3:789
  and New Deal, 2:429, 4:933
  and tariffs, 3:880
Roque, Jean de la, 1:186
Rotary press, 1:4
Rothschild family, 3:800–801
Roubiliac, Louis-Francois, 3:677
Roy, A., 2:575
Roy, Rammohun, 1:137
Royal African Company, 1:12, 81, 125
Royal Geographical Society (RGS), 1:277

Royal Niger Company, **3:**801–803, **4:**1102–1103
Rubies, **2:**394
Rudolf I, **1:**27
Rudolf II, **2:**446
Ruhr, **2:**534
Rum, **3:**803–804
Rumeli Hisari fortress, **3:**719
Rural Electrification Agency, **3:**891
Rurik (prince), **3:**705
Rus principalities, **2:**558, **4:**970
Russell, John, **2:**321
Russell, Majors and Waddell, **3:**747, 748
Russell, William H., **3:**747
Russia
  and Black Sea region, **1:**113
  and bribery, **1:**120
  China, trade relations with, **1:**166
  economic problems in, **1:**53
  fur industry, **1:**41
  and oil/oil industry, **3:**713
  and pirated entertainment, **2:**468
  unions in, **2:**572
  See also Soviet Union, the former
Russian empire
  and Aegean Sea, **1:**7
  and art/luxury objects, **1:**64–65
  in the Baroque period, **1:**98–99
  and Black Sea region, **1:**113
  and Bolshevism, **1:**113–114
  and cartography, **1:**157
  China, trade relations with, **1:**116
  cholera in, **1:**173
  climate in, **1:**185
  and Continental System, **3:**687
  and copper, **1:**233
  Crimean War, **1:**14, 247–249, 261, 264
  Cyrillic alphabet spoken in, **1:**23
  and Dardanelles channel, **1:**264
  and dirhams, **1:**274
  furs used as a medium of exchange in, **1:**188
  Great Britain, trade relations with, **1:**237
  and hemp, **2:**457
  Islamic societies, trade relations with, **2:**540
  and ivory, **2:**545
  Netherlands, trade relations with, **3:**733
  and new imperialism, **3:**696
  and Peter the Great, **3:**733–734
  Prussia, military conflicts with, **2:**379
  Prussia, trade relations with, **3:**733
  and tally-sticks, **3:**871, 872
  and Vikings, **4:**938
Russian Revolution, **1:**197, 282, **3:**787–788, 805, **4:**983
Ruyter, Michael de, **1:**38

S

Sa'adian people, **3:**841
Saami people, **3:**701
Safavid empire, **1:**43, 179
Sahagun, Bernadino de, **1:**48
Sahara Desert/trade, **1:**8, 9, 105, **3:**708, 806–810, **4:**964–965
Sahel area in Africa, **1:**8
Saint Croix, **1:**146
Saint Domingue, **2:**383, 440, **3:**384
Saint Francis of Assisi, **1:**175
Saint John, **1:**146
Saint-Simon, Comte de, **3:**609, 809
Saint Thomas, **1:**146
Saladin (king), **1:**255
Salazar, Antonio, **3:**752
Salinas de Gortari, Carlos, **1:**132, **3:**704
Salmon, Robert, **1:**67
Salt, **1:**105, 178, **2:**370–371, **3:**810–812, **4:**936
SALT (Strategic Arms Limitation Treaty) negotiations, **1:**131
Saltykov, Peter S., **3:**734
Samaritaine, **1:**267
Samoa, **2:**496
Samory Touré, **1:**296
Samothrace, **1:**6
Sam's Club, **3:**606
Samuelson, Paul, **2:**455
Sanders, William T., **1:**51
Sandys, Edwin, **4:**1012–1015
San Francisco, **1:**182
Sansovino, Andrea, **1:**62
Santley, Robert, **1:**51
Santo Domingo, **1:**147
Sapphires, **2:**394
Saracens, **1:**266
Sardinia, **1:**248
Sargon II, **3:**812
Sarmatians, **1:**113
Satellite technology, **1:**199
Saudi Arabia, **3:**708, 709, 711, 713, 733
S.S. Savannah, **3:**921
Savary de Brèves, Francois, **3:**925
Savery, Thomas, **3:**862
Savings and loan associations, **2:**362
Savonarola, **2:**365
Say, Jean-Baptiste, **2:**299
Say's Law of Markets, **1:**143, **3:**789
Scandinavia, **2:**304
Schlebecker, John T., **1:**13
Schliemann, Heinrich, **3:**684, 905
Schools, commercialization of, **1:**227
Schumpeter, Joseph, **1:**212
Science and industrialization, **2:**515
Scientific exploration, **1:**275–277
Scientific socialism, **3:**840–841
Scipio, Publius C., **3:**760
Scofield, Levi T., **3:**678

Scotland, **2:**304, 359, 556, **3:**833
Scott, Winfield, **4:**943
Sculpture, **1:**59–60, **3:**812–814
Scylax, **2:**338
Scythians, **1:**113
Sea of Marmara, **1:**218
Sea Peoples, **3:**648, 659, 737, 743, 886
Sears, Richard, **1:**224
Sears, Roebuck and Company, **3:**605, 606
Seattle World's Fair (1962), **2:**352
Second Treatise of Government (Locke), **3:**785
Securities and Exchange Commission (SEC), **1:**120
Sedentary societies and archaeological studies, **1:**49–50
Seed-planting drill, **2:**371
Segmented markets, **1:**225–227, **2:**573
Selden, George, **2:**524
Seleucid family, **1:**56
Selfridges, **1:**267
Self-service stores, **1:**225
Selim I, **3:**720
Seljuk Turks. *See* Turks
Semyenov, F.N., **3:**710
Sen, Amartya, **3:**771
Seneca Oil Company, **3:**710
Senegal, **3:**707
Senegal Company, **2:**385
Senegambia kingdom, **4:**965
Sennacherib (king), **3:**699
Sepoy Mutiny (1857), **3:**592
September 11th terrorist attacks in the United States, **1:**92, 109, **3:**733, 893, 907, 923, **4:**966
Septuagint (bible translation), **1:**21
Serampore, **1:**135–136
Serbia, **4:**983
Service sector, **3:**815–818
Seurat, Georges, **1:**68
Seven Years' War (1751–1763)
  and British dominance around the world, **2:**383
  conclusion of, **3:**820–821
  and corporations, **1:**238
  and empire building, **1:**125, **2:**317
  and English language, **1:**199
  and guilds, **3:**636
  and imperialism/emergence of world economy, **4:**947
  Maria Theresa, and start of, **2:**447
  origins of, **3:**818–820
  overview of, **4:**955–956
  Prussia emerges as leading European power after, **2:**403
Severe acute respiratory syndrome (SARS), **1:**280, **3:**619, 908
Seville, **3:**634–635
Sewing machine, **3:**833–834
Sextant, **3:**690, 761

Sforzas family, **3**:651
Shafer, Harry, **3**:612
Shah' Alam II, **3**:682
Shaka (ruler), **3**:842
Shalmaneser I, **1**:71
Shamshi-Adad V, **1**:71
Shang dynasty (1766–1122 B.C.E.), **1**:163
Shanghai, **1**:182, **3**:821–823
Shaw, George B., **3**:841
Shell, **1**:240
Shiba Kokan, **1**:65
Ships/shipbuilding
  caravel, **2**:459, **3**:690, 824
  and Henry the Navigator, **2**:459
  and Indian Ocean trade, **2**:506
  and navigation, **3**:690–692
  Netherlands and, **3**:627
  and Renaissance period, **3**:784
  and shipping/trade centers, **3**:823–826
  and shipwrecks, **3**:825–826
  steamships, **1**:28, **3**:602, 690–691, 824, 863–864, 887–888, 921
  and technology, **3**:824–825, 887
  and wood, **4**:976–977
  and World War II, **4**:989
Shirazi dynasty, **1**:178
Shopping centers, **3**:605
Shulchan 'aruch (Karo), **2**:553
Sicily, **2**:434, **3**:826–827
Sidon, **2**:448–449, **3**:736–737
Siemens, **1**:240
Sigismund of Hapsburg (duke), **1**:27
Signal Success, A (Coston), **4**:975
Sijilmasa, **3**:807
Silent Spring (Carson), **1**:226
Silk trade/Silk Road to China
  and aviation, **1**:84
  and Buddhism, **1**:129
  Byzantine empire and, **1**:133
  and caravans, **1**:144
  Chang Chi'en opening up the, **2**:340
  and Confucian attitudes, **1**:168
  and Constantinople, **1**:218–219
  and Crusades, **3**:793
  and donkeys, **1**:289
  and gunpowder, **2**:437
  and immigration, **2**:485–486
  and Manila, **3**:601
  and Marco Polo, **3**:745–746
  and Mongols, **2**:558, **3**:649, 675
  nomads and, **2**:367, **3**:702
  and oases, **3**:708
  and Ottoman empire, **3**:719, 720
  overview of, **3**:827–830, 897
  Rome and, **1**:60
  silk worms, **1**:39, **3**:827–828
Silla kingdom (350–918), **2**:297
Silliman, Benjamin, Jr., **3**:710

Silver
  and Atlantic trade route, **1**:79
  Bolivia/Mexico and, **3**:845
  China and, **1**:169, **3**:656–657, 832
  and cities/trade, **1**:180
  and coins/coinage, **1**:188
  and colonialism, **1**:190
  and empire building, **2**:312–313
  first major source of mined, **3**:830–831
  gold and abandonment of, **2**:421
  Latin American/Caribbean colonies and, **3**:831–832, 845
  and Manila, **3**:601
  and Mughal empire, **3**:681
  and Opium Wars, **3**:716–717
  and Ottoman empire, **1**:179
  and Renaissance period, **3**:783–784
  United States and, **2**:420, **3**:832–833
  Vikings and, **4**:939
Sims, William, **4**:984
Sinchi Roca (king), **2**:500
Singapore, **1**:69, 166, **2**:449–450, 489, **3**:848
Singapore Summit Declaration (1992), **1**:69
Singer, Isaac, **3**:833–834
Singer Manufacturing Company, **3**:833–834
Singer Sewing Machine, **1**:224
Singleton, John, **2**:481
Sino-French War (1884–1885), **2**:473
Sino-Japanese Wars, **1**:116, **2**:473
Sismondi, Jean, **3**:609
Sixtus IV, **3**:813
Slavery
  abolition of, **2**:567, **3**:836, **4**:1070–1076, 1087–1089
  and agriculture, **1**:12, 13
  Arabs and, **3**:835, **4**:935
  and archaeology, **1**:52
  Asia and, **3**:835
  Asiento Agreement, **4**:955
  and Atlantic trade route, **1**:77–79, 81
  Babylonian empire and, **1**:95
  in the Baroque period, **1**:99
  Brazil and, **3**:835–836, 845
  British empire and, **1**:126
  and cities/trade, **1**:181
  and colonialism, **1**:191
  and Columbian exchange, **1**:77, 192–193, **3**:845
  and cotton, **1**:241, 242, **3**:898
  and Cuba, **1**:258
  and diamonds, **1**:271
  and empire building, **2**:313, 316, 317
  Equatorial Africa and, **1**:161–162
  European-African trade relations, **1**:9, **2**:328

Slavery *(continued)*
  and food/diet, **2**:369, 370
  and Genoa, **2**:402
  and Ghana, **2**:407
  and guilds, **3**:635–638
  and Haiti, **2**:440
  and Henry the Navigator, **2**:460
  Indian Ocean trade and, **1**:9
  Industrial Revolution and, **2**:510, 512
  Islamic societies and, **2**:543
  and Jewish people/Judaism, **1**:95, **2**:553
  and Kilwa, **2**:559–560
  labor conceptualizations and, **2**:567–568
  in Latin America, **3**:625
  Latin American/Caribbean colonies and, **1**:12, 146, **3**:836
  and mercantilism, **3**:625, 630
  overview of, **3**:834–836, **4**:932–933, 965–966
  and plantation system, **3**:837
  and Protestantism, **3**:759
  Quakers/Baptists speak out against, **1**:176
  and Ragusa, **3**:765
  religion legitimizing, **3**:778
  and rum, **3**:803–804
  Sahara Desert/trade and, **1**:9, **3**:808, 809
  Saint Domingue and, **2**:384
  and salt, **3**:811
  and service sector, **3**:816
  and South Africa, **3**:842
  and South American–British trade relations, **1**:127–128
  and triangle trade, **3**:924
  Venice and, **4**:935
  and warfare impacting/being impacted by trade, **4**:944
Slogans, advertising, **1**:5
Smallpox, **1**:106, 108, 193, 279, **3**:617, 618–619, 845
Smelting and iron technology, **2**:533
Smith, Adam
  and colonialism, **4**:947
  and comparative advantage, **1**:208
  and competition, **1**:214
  and Corn Laws (British), **1**:237
  and Keynes (John M.), **3**:789
  and market revolution, **3**:603
  and Marx (Karl), **1**:115
  and nonintervention of government, **2**:576
  and religion, **3**:775
  See also *Wealth of Nations, The*
Smith, George, **3**:699
Smithsonian Institution, **2**:351, 352
Smoot, Reed, **3**:613
Smuggling, **2**:313–314, **3**:629, 687
Socialism, **1**:141–142, **2**:541, **3**:610, 839–841

Socialism: Utopian and Scientific (Engels), **2**:321
Social revolutions, **3**:785
Social role of trade, **1**:46, 48
Social welfare insurance, **2**:520
Society for the Encouragement of Arts, Commerce, and Manufacturers, **2**:452
Sokoto caliphate, **4**:965
Solis, Juan, **1**:154
Solomon (king), **2**:337, 366, 550, 554, **3**:737
Solon of Athens, **2**:366, **3**:714–715
Soltow, Lee, **4**:959
Solzhenitsyn, Alexander, **3**:785
Somalia, **3**:668–669
Song dynasty, **1**:163, 168–171, 178, **2**:297, 580
Songhay empire, **1**:295, **2**:310, 406, **3**:808, 841, **4**:965
"Song of the English, The" (Kipling), **2**:560
Sorel, Georges, **3**:840
Sotheby's, **3**:814
South Africa
  and apartheid system, **3**:843
  Boer War, **1**:126
  and bribery, **1**:119
  and Commonwealth of Nations, **1**:122
  contemporary trade profile of, **1**:10
  and diasporas, **1**:272
  and embargoes, **2**:308
  and fur trade, **3**:846
  and Gandhi (Mohandas), **2**:391
  and gold/diamonds, **1**:271, **2**:395, 420, **3**:842–843
  Khoisan people, **3**:842
  and Mandela (Nelson), **3**:843–844
  stock exchanges in, **2**:362
South America
  and Atlantic trade route, **1**:77, 78
  cacao grown in, **1**:135
  and corn, **1**:235
  geographical overview of, **3**:845
  Germany, trade relations with, **1**:128
  Great Britain, trade relations with, **1**:127–128
  and Portugal, **3**:845
  postcolonial, **3**:846
  and Spanish America, **3**:845–846
  and tortoiseshell, **3**:903
  United States, trade relations with, **1**:128
  and wood, **4**:977
  See also Colonies, Latin American/Caribbean; Latin America
South China Sea, **3**:744
Southern African Development Community, **3**:844
Sovereignty and airspace, **1**:85–87, 89
Sovereignty of nation-states and globalization, **2**:416–417

Soviet Union, the former
  Africa, trade relations with, **3**:852–854
  and agriculture, **1**:16, 17
  and alcoholic beverages, **2**:483
  Armenia ruled by, **1**:56
  and arms/weapons trade, **4**:962
  and aviation, **1**:19, 20, 87, 90
  and bioterrorism, **1**:108–109
  and Black Sea region, **1**:113
  and Bolshevism, **1**:114–115
  and China, **1**:165, **3**:850
  and Cold War, **1**:187–190
  collapse of, **1**:131
  and containment policy of United States, **1**:227–228
  Council for Mutual Economic Assistance, **1**:189, 207, 228, 243–244, **3**:850–851
  and Cuba, **1**:259, **3**:851
  currency controls in, **2**:481
  Danube River and, **1**:262
  department stores in, **1**:268
  and diamonds, **1**:271
  and diasporas, **1**:272
  early period of, **3**:849–850
  and Eastern Europe, **3**:850–851
  and embargoes, **2**:308
  and empire building, **2**:319
  Europe, trade relations with, **1**:115
  Germany, military conflicts with, **3**:849
  and globalization, **2**:414–415
  and intracontinental European trade, **2**:332
  and Marshall Plan, **3**:607
  and Mediterranean Sea region, **3**:621
  and oil/oil industry, **3**:711
  and political economy/invention of capitalism, **1**:142
  United States, trade relations with, **1**:115, 189, **4**:986
  and world economy, **3**:851
  See also Communism; Russia; Russian empire; Russian Revolution
Soybeans, **3**:854–855
Spain
  and agriculture, **1**:12
  and Amazon River, **1**:28
  and American Revolution, **1**:36
  Armada defeated by Great Britain, **2**:306
  and art/luxury objects, **1**:62, 63
  and Atlantic trade route, **1**:77–79
  and Aztecs, **1**:93
  and banks/banking, **2**:358
  in the Baroque period, **1**:97
  and bioterrorism, **1**:108
  and Caribbean region, **1**:146, 147
  and cartography, **1**:154
  and cities/trade, **1**:179–180
  and coins/coinage, **1**:188

Spain *(continued)*
  and colonialism, **1**:190–191, **3**:857
  and Columbian exchange, **1**:193
  and Columbus (Christopher), **1**:194–195
  compass and, **1**:209
  and conquistadors, **1**:78, 93, 176
  and corn, **1**:235
  and cotton, **1**:241
  Cuba as colony of, **1**:258–259
  and decline of the empire, **3**:856–857
  and discovery/exploration, **1**:275
  and diseases, **1**:279
  Drake's (Francis) attacks on, **1**:289
  and empire building, **2**:312–314, **3**:856
  and exploration/trade, **2**:344
  and fairs/festivals, **2**:352–353
  and food/diet, **2**:387
  and Fugger family, **2**:388–389
  and gold, **2**:420
  and Goths, **2**:424
  Great Britain, military conflicts with, **2**:306
  Greeks, trade relations with, **2**:337
  and guilds, **3**:632–639
  Hundred Years' War and, **2**:478
  and immigration, **2**:487
  and imperialism/emergence of world economy, **4**:946
  Incas, military conflicts with the, **2**:501
  and indigo, **2**:506
  and iron technology, **2**:533
  and linen, **2**:587
  and Manila, **3**:599–601
  and mercantilism, **3**:624–626
  and Ming dynasty, **3**:657
  and missionaries, **3**:661
  and Napoleonic Wars, **3**:846
  and navigation, **3**:689, 690
  and Phoenicians, **3**:738
  and piracy/privateering, **3**:624–625
  and Renaissance period, **3**:783–784
  and Sicily, **3**:826–827
  and silver, **3**:831–832
  and slavery, **1**:78
  and spice trade, **2**:369, **3**:859
  and sugar, **3**:867
  and tortoiseshell, **3**:902
  and wool, **4**:979
  See also Colonies, Latin American/Caribbean; *individual wars/battles*
Spanish-American War (1898), **1**:147, 259, **3**:599, 722–723
Sparta, **1**:74, 266–267, **2**:433, 434, **4**:944
Special drawing rights (SDRs), **2**:527
Specie-flow mechanism, **2**:421
Spectator sports, **2**:324–325
Spence, Michael, **1**:50–51
Spending (consumer) and the Great Depression, **2**:428
Sperry, Elmer, **1**:209

Spice Islands/trade
   and Arabs, **2:**367, **3:**848, 858, 860
   and Atlantic trade route, **1:**77, 78
   and cities, **1:**178
   and Constantinople, **1:**219
   and Crusades, **3:**858, **2:**368
   and Drake (Francis), **1:**290
   and Indian Ocean trade, **2:**505
   influential nature of, **2:**368–369
   Islamic societies and, **2:**540
   and Manchu dynasty, **3:**597
   and Manila, **3:**599
   and Melaka, **2:**449, **3:**622
   and Nineveh, **3:**699
   overview of, **3:**860–861
   Portugal/Netherlands impacting the, **2:**367
   Rome's fall impacting, **3:**799
   spice route (on water), **3:**858–860
Spinning frame, **1:**54–55
Spinning jenny, **2:**452
Spinoza, Baruch, **3:**609
Sponsler, Mary A., **3:**833, 834
Sporades, Northern, **1:**6
Sports, **2:**324–325, **3:**907
Sprenkle, Case, **2:**481
Sprint, **3:**892
Srivijaya empire, **3:**847, 861
Stalin, Joseph, **1:**113–115, 141–142, 244, 272, **3:**607, 849, **4:**986, 989
Standard of living, **3:**749
Standard Oil, **1:**239
Standing Buddha, **1:**60
Stanley, Henry M., **1:**162, 277
Starcraft, **2:**325
Statue of Liberty, **3:**677
Statute of Westminster (1931), **1:**121, **4:**1124–1126
Steam engine, **2:**332, 509, 534, **3:**862–863, 887, 921–922
Steamships, **1:**28, 261, **3:**602, 690–691, 824, 863–864, 887–888, 921
Steel, **3:**865–866
Stephenson, George, **3:**767, 888, 922
Stevens, John F., **3:**723
Stigler, George, **1:**210, 211, **2:**576
Stiglitz, Joseph, **2:**413
Stilicho, **2:**424
Stimson, Henry L., **4:**989, 990
St. Louis Missouri Fur Company, **4:**1077–1078
Stoas, **2:**457
Stocks/stock exchanges
   and Ashanti goldfields, **4:**966
   Depression, the Great, **2:**427–428
   Hamburg and, **2:**442
   and the Internet, **2:**530–531
   and joint-stock companies, **2:**551–553
   overview of, **2:**361–362
   and service sector, **3:**816–817

Story of Sinuhe, The, **2:**577
Strait of Magellan, **3:**594
Strange, Marty, **1:**18
Strozzi family, **2:**438
Structural Impediment Initiative (1989), **4:**927–928
Strutt, Jebediah, **1:**54, 55
Stuckofen, **2:**533
Sturm, James, **4:**959
Submarines, **3:**824, 825
Suburbs and single-household homes, **1:**225
Sudan, **1:**105, 245, **4:**965
Sudden Shower at Atake (Hiroshige), **1:**65
Suez Canal
   and African ports losing importance, **2:**494
   and bankruptcy problems for Egypt, **2:**302
   British control over, **1:**127
   Convention of Constantinople and, **4:**1103–1105
   East-West trade and shipbuilding impacted by, **3:**921
   and Indian-European relations, **1:**126
   and Mediterranean Sea gaining importance, **3:**621
   overview of, **3:**866–867
   and steamships, **3:**824
   and superships, **3:**691
   and warfare impacting/being impacted by trade, **4:**950
   and water's role in international trade, **4:**958
Sugar
   and American Sugar Alliance, **1:**18
   in the Americas, **3:**868–869
   and Baroque states, **1:**99
   biggest food product, **2:**370
   in the Caribbean region, **1:**12, 146, 147
   and colonialism, **1:**191
   and Cuba, **1:**258–259
   in Eastern Hemisphere, **3:**867–868
   and empire building, **2:**316–317
   France and, **1:**82
   Great Britain and, **1:**125, **4:**1039–1043
   Industrial Revolution and, **2:**510, 512
   molasses as by-product of, **3:**669–670
   Portugal and, **1:**78
   and rum, **3:**804
   and Saint Domingue, **2:**383
   and slavery, **2:**370
   and Southeast Asia, **3:**848
Suleiman the Magnificent, **2:**306, **3:**599, 720
Sulla, Lucius C., **2:**327
Sumerian civilization
   and architecture, **3:**641
   and copper, **1:**231
   and cuneiform, **1:**259–260, **2:**365, **3:**724
   and drugs, **1:**290, 291

Sumerian civilization *(continued)*
   and food/diet, **2:**365–366
   and glass, **2:**410
   and immigration, **2:**484
   and Indian Ocean trade, **2:**503
   and livestock, **2:**588
   and medicine, **3:**616
   merchants and, **1:**57
   and paper/pulp, **3:**724
   and tin, **3:**900
   and transportation/trade, **3:**919
Summerville, Isabella, **3:**834
Sundiata (king), **2:**406
Sunni Ali (king), **3:**841
Sun Yatsen, **2:**435, **3:**598
Superships, **3:**691, 825
Supreme Court, U.S., **1:**15, **2:**579, **3:**602
Surat, **3:**869–870
Suriname, **1:**147
Surplus value, theory of, **3:**610
Swahili people, **1:**161
Sweden, **1:**233, **2:**482, **3:**687, 706, 721, 871, **4:**961
Sweet potatoes, **3:**753–754
Sweezy, Paul, **1:**140
Swidden cultivation, **1:**184
Switzerland, **1:**173
Syllabaries, **2:**585
Symphony in White No. II: The Little White Girl (Whistler), **1:**66
Syndicalism, **3:**840
Synopsis of Capital (Engels), **2:**321
Synthetic drugs, **1:**292–293
Synthetic textiles, **3:**898
Syphilis, **1:**193
Syria, **1:**25, 58, 59, 71, 145, **2:**303, 340, 586

T

Tableau Oeconomique (Quesnay), **1:**141
Tacitus (emperor), **2:**423
Taft, William H., **2:**528
Tagore, Rabindranath, **1:**137
Tag tallies, **3:**872
Tahiti, **1:**230
Taino people, **2:**440
Taiwan, **1:**110, 120, 166, **2:**413
Taliban, **2:**541
Talleyrand, Charles, **2:**385
Tally-sticks, **3:**871–872
Talmud, **2:**553
Talonen, Tarja, **4:**974
Taney, Roger B., **3:**602
Tang Code, **2:**580
Tang dynasty, **1:**163, 168, 170, **2:**549, **3:**764
Tarascan people, **3:**745
Tariffs
   Europe and, **3:**877–878
   France and, **3:**877–878

Tariffs (continued)
  and General Agreement on Tariffs and Trade, **3:**881–882
  governmental motivations for, **3:**872–873
  Great Britain and, **2:**579, **3:**875–877
  and International Trade Commission, **2:**528–530
  Japan and, **3:**880–881
  and Keynes (John M.), **2:**557
  and Khazar empire, **2:**559
  and List (Georg), **2:**587–588
  and the media, **3:**613–614
  and multinational enterprises, **3:**683
  Navigation Acts (British) and, **3:**692
  nominal and effective rates, **3:**873–874
  and nontariff barriers, **3:**703–704
  and oil/oil industry, **3:**710–711, 713
  and reciprocity, **3:**769–770
  three basic types of, **3:**875
  as trade barriers, **3:**872
  United States and, **2:**579, **3:**716, 878–880
  War of 1812 and, **4:**943
  and wool, **4:**979–980
  World War I and, **4:**984
  See also General Agreement on Tariffs and Trade; Legislation: United States: Hawley-Smoot Tariff of 1930; Most-favored-nation status
Tariq ibn-Ziyad, **2:**424
Tartars, **1:**107, 111, 278, **4:**940
Taubman, George D.G., **3:**801–803
Tawney, R.H., **3:**758
Taylor, Frederick W., **2:**570
Tea, **1:**99, 238, **2:**315, 367, **3:**597, 821, 883–885
Technology, **1:**68, 98, **3:**885–890, **4:**948, 961
Tecumseh, **4:**932, 942
Teixeira, Pedro, **1:**28
Teleconferencing, **3:**923
Telegraph, **1:**199, **2:**515, **3:**726, 888, 890–891
Telemarketing industry, **3:**892
Telephone, **1:**199, 233, **3:**891–892
Television, **1:**5, 225, **2:**468–469
Temperance movements, **2:**482
Templar Knights, **2:**357–358, 381, 561–564, **3:**741, 793
Tenochtitlán, **1:**48, 92–93
Teotihuacán, **1:**47, 50, 51–52
Terrorism, **1:**106–110, **3:**892–894, 907, 923
  See also September 11th terrorist attacks in the United States
Tertullian, **3:**795
Tetzel, Johann, **4:**1007–1008
Teutonic Knights, **2:**381, 443–445, 563, **3:**706, 894–895
Texaco, **3:**711

Texas Centennial (1937), **3:**906
Textiles, **2:**404, **3:**657, 896–899
  See also Cotton; Silk trade/Silk Road to China
Thackeray, William M., **1:**141
Thailand, **1:**17, 69, 293, **3:**730, 791, 848
Thales, **1:**30
Thames School of cartography, **1:**156–157
Thásos, **1:**6
Theater, attending the, **2:**326
Thebes, **1:**291
Theodoric the Great, **2:**423
Theodosian Code, **2:**577, **3:**797
Theodosius I, **1:**22
Theophrastus, **2:**376
Theravada Buddhism, **1:**129
Thera volcano eruption, **1:**6
Thirty Years' War (1618–1648), **1:**98, **2:**403, 439, 447
Thomson-Houston Company, **2:**398
Thornton, John, **1:**156
Thucydides, **3:**617
Thutmose III, **2:**336
Tiananmen Square, **1:**190
Tibetan diaspora, **1:**273
Tigranes the Great, **1:**56
Tigris River, **3:**732, 921, **4:**957, 977
  See also Mesopotamian civilization
Timber/sorochok unit, **3:**899
Timber trade, **4:**935
Timbuktu, **2:**406, **3:**594, 809, 810, **4:**965
Timbuktu-Gao-Djenne triangle, **1:**295–296
Tin, **2:**337, **3:**899–900
Tiridates II, **1:**56
Titanic, **2:**419
Tiwanaku people, **2:**499
Tobacco
  and advertising/marketing techniques, **1:**5, **2:**324
  and American colonies, **1:**12, **3:**900–901
  Baroque states and, **1:**99
  and corporations, **1:**238
  and crop rotation, **1:**250
  and Cuba, **1:**258
  France and, **1:**35–36
  illegal trade in, **2:**482
  negative image of, **1:**293
  prohibition of, England's, **3:**629
  and United States, **3:**902
de Tocqueville, Alexis, **3:**905
Tokugawa Iemitsu (shogun), **1:**171
Tokugawa Ieyasu (shogun), **2:**439
Tomich, Dale, **1:**140
Topa (king), **2:**500
Torah, **2:**553
Torrens, Robert, **1:**208, **2:**300, **3:**652, 876
Torrianis family, **3:**651
Tortoiseshell, **3:**902–903

Toulouse-Lautrec, Henri de, **1:**66
Tourism, **2:**418, **3:**815, 816, 903–907
Toyota, **1:**240
Toyotomi Hideyoshi, **2:**439
Trade and Market in the Early Empires (Polanyi, Arensberg, and Pearson), **1:**48
Trademarks, **3:**916–917
Trade organizations, **3:**908
  See also World Trade Organization; *specific organizations*
Trade-Related Investments Measures, **1:**214
Trade winds, **3:**915–916
Trading companies, overseas, **1:**124
  See also British East India Company; Dutch East India Company
Tragan (emperor), **1:**11, **3:**866
Transaction costs, **3:**917–919
Transistors, **1:**215
Transit duties, **3:**875
Transportation and trade, **1:**41–42, **3:**602–603, 919–923
Trans-World Air (TWA), **1:**90
Travel literature, **3:**905
Travels of Marco Polo, The (Polo), **3:**746, 859
Treatise on Maritime Surveying (Mackenzie), **1:**157
Treaty of Aix-la-Chapelle (1748), **2:**447, **3:**818, **4:**955
Treaty of Alcócavas (1479), **3:**783
Treaty of Amity and Cooperation in Southeast Asia (1976), **1:**69
Treaty of Beijing (1860), **2:**472
Treaty of Breda (1667), **1:**38
Treaty of Commerce and Navigation between the United States and the Ottoman empire (1830), **1:**263
Treaty of Dardanelles (1809), **1:**263
Treaty of Ghent (1814), **4:**932, 943
Treaty of Guadalupe-Hidalgo (1848), **4:**933
Treaty of Hubertusburg (1763), **3:**818, 820
Treaty of Hünkar Iskelesi (1833), **1:**263
Treaty of Lausanne (1923), **1:**264
Treaty of Maastricht (1992), **3:**913–914
Treaty of Meuthen (1703), **3:**752
Treaty of Nanjing (1842), **1:**127, 169–170, 292, **2:**298, 435, 472, **3:**598, 717, 822, 884, **4:**949, 1084–1087
Treaty of Nvarsag (536), **1:**56
Treaty of Paris (1763), **3:**693, 818, 820, **4:**956, 1035–1039
Treaty of Paris (1783), **2:**383
Treaty of Paris (1856), **1:**249, 261, 264
Treaty of Rastatt (1714), **4:**954
Treaty of Rome (1957), **3:**913, **4:**973
Treaty of Ryswick (1697), **2:**440, **4:**954
Treaty of Saint Petersburg (1762), **3:**820

Treaty of Sèvres (1920), **1:**264
Treaty of Shimonoseki (1854), **1:**66
Treaty of Tianjin (1858), **2:**472
Treaty of Tilsit (1807), **3:**687
Treaty of Tordesillas (1494), **3:**845, **4:**1003–1007
Treaty of Utrecht (1713), **2:**383, **4:**954, 1032–1033
Treaty of Versailles (1871), **2:**404
Treaty of Versailles (1919), **1:**87, 261, **2:**298–299, 361, 405–406, **4:**933, 951, 984
Treaty of Wangxia (1844), **2:**496
Treaty of Westminster (1755), **3:**819
Triangle trade, **3:**923–924
Tribute and trade linked in rise of ancient empires, **1:**51, 168–169
Trinidad and Tobago, **1:**147, 195
Triumphant Democracy (Carnegie), **1:**148
Trojan War, **1:**6
Trotsky, Leon, **1:**142, **2:**572, **4:**986
Truman, Harry S, **1:**16, 228, **3:**607, **4:**990, 991
Tuareg people, **4:**965
Tukulti-Ninurta (king), **1:**71
Tull, Jethro, **2:**371
Tunis, **3:**720
Tunisia, **3:**924–926
Turé, Muhammad, **3:**841
Turgot, Anne, **3:**838
Turgot, Jacques, **2:**385
Turkey, **1:**113, 264, **2:**405, **3:**707
Turks, **1:**7, 44, 56, 186, **2:**343, 409
  See also Crusades; Ottoman empire
Turner, Frederick J., **3:**602
Turpan, **3:**708
Turquoise, **2:**395
Tuwat oasis, **3:**708, 807
Twelve Tables, **2:**577
Typhus epidemic, **1:**180
Tyre, **1:**176–177

U

uBid, **1:**216
Ukraine, **1:**113
Umayyad caliphate, **1:**1
Underwood, Oscar, **2:**528
UNESCO (United Nations Educational, Scientific and Cultural Organization), **2:**480, 549
Unicode Consortium, **1:**24
Unilever, **1:**240
Union Pacific Railroad, **3:**767
Unions
  AFL-CIO, **1:**32–34, **2:**398
  and Combination Acts (British), **1:**195–196
  General Electric Company and, **2:**398
  Japan and, **1:**84

Unions *(continued)*
  and multinational corporations, **1:**240
  Netherlands and, **1:**295, **3:**694
  overview of, **2:**571–573
  World War II and, **4:**991
  See also Guilds, merchant; Hanseatic League
United Gold Coast Convention (UGCC), **2:**408
United Kingdom. *See* Great Britain
United Mine Workers, **4:**991
United Nations
  arms trade and, **2:**480
  and aviation, **1:**89
  and coffee, **1:**187
  Commission on International Trade Law, **1:**284, 287
  Conference on Trade and Development, **1:**285, **2:**376, **3:**908, 911, **4:**929
  and drug policy, **1:**293
  and economic agencies/programs, **4:**928–929
  Economic and Social Council, **4:**929
  and embargoes, **2:**307
  Environment Program, **4:**929
  General Assembly, **4:**928–929
  and illegal trade, **2:**481
  and jade, **2:**549
  Millennium Summit (2000), **4:**929
  and Mogadishu, **3:**668
  origins of, **4:**928
  and Persian Gulf, **3:**732–733
  Security Council, **4:**928
  and South Africa, **3:**843
  and World Bank, **4:**980
United Parcel Service (UPS), **1:**91, **3:**923
United States
  abolition of slavery in, **2:**567
  and agriculture, **1:**13–18
  aircraft production, **1:**19
  Argentina, trade relations with, **1:**53
  and arms/weapons trade, **2:**480, **4:**961
  and art/luxury objects, **1:**67–68
  and automobile production, **1:**83
  and aviation, **1:**19, 85, 87–92
  and banks/banking, **2:**360–361
  and bioterrorism, **1:**108–110
  Brazil, trade relations with, **1:**118
  and bribery, **1:**120
  British Orders in Council of 1804 and 1806, **1:**13, **2:**384
  Caribbean region, colonial possessions in, **1:**146
  and cartography, **1:**157
  China, trade relations with, **1:**116, 165, 166, 190
  Civil War, **1:**14, 108, **3:**602, 603, 901, **4:**933, 943
  cocoa-processing factories in, **1:**173

United States *(continued)*
  and coffee, **1:**187
  coins/coinage in, **1:**188
  and Cold War, **1:**187–190
  and competition policy, **1:**212, 214–215
  computer use in, **1:**216
  Constitutional Convention in 1781, **4:**931
  and consumerism, **1:**221–224, 226–227
  and containment policy, **1:**227–228, **3:**607, **4:**943, 952, 991
  and copper, **1:**233
  and copyrights, **1:**233, 234
  and corn, **1:**235–236
  and corporations, **1:**239
  and cotton, **1:**241, 242–243, **3:**898
  crop rotation in, **1:**250
  and Cuban missile crisis, **1:**189
  and Dardanelles channel, **1:**263
  department stores in, **1:**268
  and diasporas, **1:**272, 273
  and disputes/arbitration, **1:**284
  and drugs, **1:**293
  early republic in, **4:**931–932
  and electricity, **2:**304
  and embargoes, **2:**306–308, **4:**932
  and empire building, **2:**318
  and English language as dominant common language, **1:**199
  and Equatorial Africa's mineral resources, **1:**162
  and fairs/festivals, **2:**350–353
  fertilizer used in, **2:**353
  and food/diet, **2:**387, 388
  and foreign aid, **2:**375
  France, trade relations with, **2:**385
  and GATT, **3:**882
  Germany, trade relations with, **4:**987
  and Gilded age, **1:**67
  and globalization, **1:**140, **2:**413, 416, 418
  and gold, **2:**420, 421
  and guano, **2:**436
  and Gulf Wars, **1:**109, 131
  and hemp, **2:**457–458
  and immigration, **2:**489–490
  and imperial competition, **3:**857
  and insurance, **2:**519, 520
  and irrigation, **2:**537
  Japan, trade relations with, **4:**927–928, 987
  and law, **2:**579
  and livestock, **2:**589–590
  Louisiana Purchase, **3:**846, **4:**931–932, 1067–1069
  and Manila, **3:**599–600
  and market revolution, **1:**101, **3:**602
  and medicine, **3:**619
  and Mediterranean Sea region, **3:**621
  and migrations (human), **3:**650–651
  and Mogadishu, **3:**668

United States *(continued)*
  monuments in, **3:**676
  and multinational enterprises, **3:**682–683
  and Napoleonic Wars, **3:**687, **4:**932, 948–949
  and new imperialism, **2:**496, 497, **3:**696
  and nuts, **3:**707
  and oil/oil industry, **3:**710–711, 713
  and open door notes, **3:**715–716
  and Panama Canal, **3:**722–726, 922–923
  and paper/pulp, **3:**725–726
  and perfume, **3:**731
  and Persian Gulf, **3:**733
  and pottery, **3:**755
  and Protestantism, **3:**759
  and railroads, **3:**767, 922
  and reciprocity, **3:**769–770
  and regional trade organizations, **3:**913
  Revolutionary War, **1:**34–38, 81, **2:**317
  and rise to world power, **4:**933–934
  and Russian Revolution, **3:**805
  September 11th terrorist attacks in, **1:**92, 109, **3:**733, 893, 907, 923, **4:**966
  and Shanghai, **3:**822
  and ships/shipbuilding, **3:**824
  and silver, **3:**832–833
  and slavery, **2:**567, **4:**932–933
  South America, trade relations with, **1:**128
  and Southeast Asia, **3:**848
  Soviet Union, trade relations with, **1:**115, 189, **4:**986
  and soybeans, **3:**854, 855
  and Spain's decline, **3:**857
  stock exchanges in, **2:**362
  and tariffs, **3:**877, 878–880
  and technology, **3:**888–890
  and textile industry, **3:**898
  and tobacco, **3:**902
  and tourism, **3:**905–906
  and trademarks, **3:**917
  and transportation/trade, **3:**602 603, 922
  and warfare impacting/being impacted by trade, **4:**952
  and weapons/armament production, **4:**961
  and whales, **4:**967
  and women, **4:**973–974
  and wood, **4:**978
  and wool, **4:**979–980
  See also Colonies, North American; North American Free Trade Agreement; *individual wars/battles*
Universal Automatic Computer (UNIVAC), **1:**215
Universal Copyright Convention, **2:**467
University of Alexandria, **1:**22
University of Calcutta, **1:**136
University of Pennsylvania, **1:**215
University of Philippines, **3:**600

Unsafe at Any Speed (Nader), **1:**226
Upper Volta, **2:**547
Urartians, **1:**55
Urban II (pope), **1:**252, **2:**343, **3:**793, **4:**995–996
Urban revolution in the Middle East, **1:**176
  See also Cities
Uruk period, **1:**57
U.S. Agency for International Development, **4:**952
U.S. Army Chemical Warfare Service, **1:**108
U.S. Information Agency (USIA), **2:**352, 353
U.S. Steel, **1:**239
Use value of a commodity, **3:**609–610
Usury, **2:**358, 551, 583, **3:**793, **4:**996–997, 1000–1001, 1022–1024
Uttmann, Barbara, **4:**971
Uzbekistan, **3:**708

V

Valens (emperor), **2:**423
Van Buren, Martin, **4:**932
Vandals, **2:**424, **3:**826
Vanderbilt, Cornelius, **1:**67, **3:**726
Vanek, Jaroslav, **2:**455
van Gogh, Vincent, **1:**68
Varaginians, **2:**342
Veblen, Thorstein, **3:**879, **4:**959
Venezuela, **1:**128, 195, 271, **3:**713, 846
Venice
  and Aegean Sea, **1:**7
  and art/luxury objects, **1:**62
  and banks/banking, **2:**358
  and Black Death, **1:**107
  and Byzantine empire, **1:**134, **4:**935
  Carolingian empire, trade relations with, **1:**151
  and Catholic Church, **4:**935
  Comacchio, military conflicts with, **4:**935
  compass and, **1:**209
  and cotton, **1:**241
  and Crusades, **1:**178, 255, **4:**936
  and Dardanelles channel, **1:**263
  and exploration/trade, **2:**343
  and gemstones, **2:**395
  Genoa and, **2:**402, **4:**937
  and glass, **2:**410
  and Hanseatic League, **3:**647
  as the hinge of Europe, **1:**178
  and insurance, **2:**518
  and interregional transit trade, **4:**937
  and intracontinental European trade, **2:**331
  Middle East and, **3:**645
  and Ottoman empire, **1:**179, **3:**721, **4:**937
  Ragusa, military conflicts with, **3:**765, 766

Venice *(continued)*
  resources needed in, **4:**935–937
  and salt, **1:**178, **3:**810
  and service sector, **3:**815
  and silk trade, **1:**219
  and spice trade, **1:**77, **3:**858
Ventris, Michael, **2:**585, **3:**684
Verdier, Arthur, **2:**547
Vernatt, Philip, **1:**233
Verrazano, Giovanni da, **2:**344, 382
Vesconte, Petru, **1:**152
Vespucci, Amerigo, **1:**154
Vevey, M.D., **1:**135
Victoria (queen), **1:**257, **2:**351
Videoconferencing, **3:**892
Video games, **3:**817
Vietnam
  and ASEAN, **1:**69
  and coffee, **1:**187
  and Cold War, **1:**189
  and Council for Mutual Economic Assistance, **1:**244
  France and, **2:**384
  and rice, **1:**17, **3:**791
  and wood, **4:**978
Vietnam Veterans' Memorial, **3:**676
Vietnam War, **3:**651
Vike-Freiberga, Vaira, **4:**974
Vikings
  and art/luxury objects, **1:**60–61
  and Black Sea region, **1:**113
  boats/canoes/vessels used by, **1:**47
  Carolingian empire, military conflicts with, **1:**151, **3:**645
  and Christianity, **2:**342
  and Dark Ages, **1:**266
  and dirhams, **1:**274
  and evolution from raiders to traders, **3:**645
  and exploration/trade, **2:**342
  and immigration, **2:**487
  and intracontinental European trade, **2:**331
  Old and New World, first exchanges between, **1:**192
  overview of, **4:**938–939
  and piracy/privateering, **3:**743
  and ships/shipbuilding, **3:**823
Villard, Henry, **2:**398
Villiers, George, **1:**97
Viner, J., **3:**758
Vingboon, Johannes, **1:**155, 156
Viracocha (king), **2:**500
Viral agents and bioterrorism, **1:**106
Virginia colony, **1:**12, **2:**345
Virginia Company, **1:**238
Virginia Slims Tennis Circuit, **2:**324
Viscontis family, **3:**651
Visigoths, **2:**424
Vitoria, Francisco de, **1:**282

Vivekenanda, **1:**137
Vladimir-Suzdal, **4:**939
Vlaminck, Maurice de, **1:**67
Volga Bulgaria, **4:**939–940
Voltaire, **2:**379
Voluntary exports restraints (VERs), **3:**703
Vora, Virji, **3:**869

W

Waddell, William B., **3:**747
Wages, **1:**224, **2:**414, 535–536, **3:**673, 794–795, 898, **4:**1083–1084
Waghenaer, Lucas J., **1:**155
Waldemar IV, **2:**444–445
Walker, C.J., **4:**975
Walker, William, **2:**497
Wallace, Henry, **2:**557
Wallenstein, Albrecht von, **2:**438
Wallerstein, Immanuel, **1:**45, **3:**695, 786
Wal-Mart, **1:**226–227, 269, **3:**606
Walrasian model, **3:**671
Walruses, **2:**545
Walsingham, Francis, **2:**441
Walters, Mary E., **3:**834
Waltz, Kenneth, **2:**416
Wampum, **1:**101
Wangara people, **1:**295
Wang Zhi, **3:**656
Wanli (emperor), **3:**657
Warcraft, **2:**325
Warfare
  in antiquity, **4:**944–945
  empire building as reason for, **4:**953–957
  gunpowder/explosives enter into, **2:**437–439, 477, 478
  and imperialism/emergence of world economy, **4:**946–947
  Napoleonic Wars, **4:**947–950
  and post-1945 era, **4:**952–953
  trade impacting/being impacted by, **4:**943–944
  World War I and its aftermath, **4:**950–951
  World Wars, trade between the, **4:**951–952
  See also Arms/weapons trade; *individual wars/battles*
War of 1812, **1:**14, 239, **3:**879, **4:**932, 941–943
War of Austrian Succession (1744–1748), **2:**447, **3:**818, **4:**955
War of Chioggia (1378–1380), **3:**810
War of the Grand Alliance (1688–1697), **2:**447
War of the League of Augsburg (1689–1697), **1:**98, **2:**383, **4:**954
War of the Schmalkaldic League, **3:**773

War of Spanish Succession (1702–1711), **1:**98, **2:**383, **3:**857, **4:**954–955
Washington, Augustine, **2:**533
Washington, George, **4:**931
Washington Conference (1921), **3:**744
Washington Naval Conference (1921), **2:**432
Water, **4:**957–958
Water frame, **1:**54–55, **2:**452
Watergate scandal, **1:**120
Watson, Charles, **1:**185
Watson, Thomas, **1:**104
Watt, James, **1:**55, **2:**509, 534, **3:**862–863, 921
Watt, James, Jr., **2:**556
Watteau, Jean-Antoine, **1:**65
Wealth, **4:**958–960
Wealth of Nations, The (Smith)
  "capitalism" term never used in, **1:**141
  and competition, **1:**210
  excerpts of, **4:**1049–1063
  and laissez-faire, **2:**535, 578
  and market revolution, **3:**601–602
  overview of, **3:**838–839
  and productivity, **3:**631
  and state direction *vs.* market forces, **2:**299, 578
  and tariffs, **3:**876
  and wealth, **4:**958
  See also Smith, Adam
Weapons/armament. *See* Arms/weapons trade
Weather contrasted with climate, **1:**185
Webb, Beatrice, **3:**841
Webb, Sidney, **3:**841
Weber, Max, **1:**140, **2:**542, **3:**758, 775
Wedgwood, Josiah, **1:**65, **2:**510
Weights and measures, **4:**962–964
Weimar Republic, **3:**878
Weiss, Linda, **2:**414
Welsh immigrants, **3:**650
West Africa Conference (1884), **1:**192
West Edmonton Mall, **3:**606
Western Union Telegraph Company, **3:**890, 891
West India Company, **1:**228
West Indies. *See* Caribbean region; Colonies, Latin American/Caribbean
Westinghouse, George, **2:**301
Westinghouse Corporation, **2:**398
Whales, **3:**710, **4:**967–968
"What Is Enlightenment" (Kant), **3:**785
Wheat, **1:**15, 17, 110, 219, **2:**367, 371–372
Wheeled vehicles, early forms of, **3:**919
Whistler, James A.M., **1:**65, 66
White, Christine, **1:**46, 51
Whiteley's, **1:**268
"White Man's Burden, The" (Kipling), **2:**561
Whitman, Meg, **4:**975

Whitney, Eli, **1:**241, 242, **3:**888, **4:**969, 979
Wickard, Claude, **1:**16
Wielbark culture, **2:**423
Wilberforce, William, **1:**196
Wild Cane Cay, **1:**48
William I, **2:**404
William I of Orange, **1:**38
William II, **2:**383, **3:**592
William III, **1:**135, **2:**359, **3:**694
William III of Orange, **1:**39
William IV, **1:**136
Williams, Eric, **2:**510
Wilson, Woodrow, **1:**86, **2:**453, **4:**933, 984, 986
Wine, **2:**366, 434, **4:**969–970
Winston Cup, NASCAR, **2:**324
Winton, Alexander, **2:**524
Wittenborg, Johann, **2:**445
Wolfe, James, **3:**820, **4:**956
Wolff, Edward, **4:**959
Wolf furnace, **2:**533
Woll, Matthew, **1:**33
Women
  in ancient/medieval times, **4:**971
  and fairs/festivals, **4:**972
  and present happenings, **4:**974–976
  in the United States, **4:**973–974
  and World War II, **4:**972–973, 989
Women's Christian Temperance Union (WCTU), **2:**482
Women's World Fair (1925), **4:**972
Wood, **3:**848, **4:**976–978
Woodblock prints, **1:**65
Wood pulp and paper, **3:**725–726
Wool, **2:**588, **3:**896, **4:**978–980
Workable competition, concept of, **1:**211
World Bank
  Africa and, **1:**10, 163
  and Bush (George H.W.), **1:**132
  and globalization, **2:**574
  and gold, **2:**422
  and liberalization process, **1:**10, 143
  origins of, **2:**361
  overview of, **4:**980–981
WorldCom, **3:**892
World Development Report (1995), **2:**574
World Economic and Monetary Conference (1934), **3:**877
World Exposition at Vancouver (1986), **2:**352
World Food Council, **1:**17
World Health Organization (WHO), **1:**22, 173
World Intellectual Property Organization (WIPO), **2:**467, 523, **3:**727, 917
World Investment Report (2003), **1:**285
World Monuments Fund, **3:**676
World's Columbian Exposition (1893), **4:**972

World-systems theory, **1:**45, **3:**695, 786
World Trade Organization (WTO)
   Africa and, **1:**10
   agreement establishing the, **4:**1167–1174
   and AIDS, **1:**140, **3:**619
   Caribbean region and, **1:**147
   China and, **1:**166
   and competition policy, **1:**214
   and consensus agreements, **3:**911
   and dispute resolution, **3:**909–910, **4:**982
   and environmental protection, **3:**915
   GATT and, **4:**981
   goal of, **3:**908, 910
   law's evolution and the, **2:**581–582
   and liberalization policies, **1:**143, **3:**909
   and the media, **3:**614
   and multinational corporations, **1:**240
   and national treatment obligations, **1:**285
   Netherlands and, **3:**694
   and patents, **3:**619, 726
   and regional trade organizations, **3:**911–915
   Trade-Related Intellectual Property Rights and, **2:**521, 523
World War I
   advertising during and after, **1:**4
   and agriculture, **1:**14
   and aviation, **1:**86–87
   and banks/banking, **2:**361
   beginning of, **4:**982–983
   bioterrorism used during, **1:**108
   consumerism as ultimate victor after, **1:**220
   and Cuban sugar boom, **1:**259
   and Dardanelles channel, **1:**264
   Germany punished after, **1:**87, 261, **2:**298–299, 361, 405–406, 557, **4:**984
   and gold, **2:**420
   and grain, **2:**525
   legacy of, **4:**984–985, 989–990
   and monuments, **3:**676, 678
   and Netherlands, **3:**694
   and new imperialism, **3:**696
   and Nye Committee, **4:**985, 1138–1144
   and Russian Revolution, **3:**805
   and ships/shipbuilding, **3:**824
   and tariffs, **3:**877, 879–880
   and trade impacting/being impacted by, **4:**950–951, 983–985
   and unions, **1:**32
   U.S. entry into, **4:**933

World War II
   and agriculture, **1:**15–17, **4:**991
   and Arab nationalism, **1:**44
   automobile production impacted by, **1:**83
   and aviation, **1:**88–90, **4:**987
   and Congo's mineral resources, **1:**162
   consumerism as ultimate victor after, **1:**220
   economic aspects of U.S. entry into, **4:**987–991
   and empire building, **2:**319
   and foreign aid, **2:**374–375
   and General Electric Company, **2:**398–399
   and Genoa, **2:**402
   and globalization, **2:**413–414
   and Hamburg, **2:**442
   and hemp, **2:**458
   and internal combustion engine, **2:**525–526
   and intracontinental European trade, **2:**332
   and isolationist policies of United States, **4:**985–987
   and Manila, **3:**599–600
   and migrations (human), **3:**651
   and Milan, **3:**652
   and oases, **3:**709
   and oil/oil industry, **3:**711
   and Pearl Harbor attack, **4:**951, 987, 988–989
   and ships/shipbuilding, **3:**824–825
   and South American–British trade relations, **1:**128
   and Southeast Asia, **3:**848
   and technology, **3:**889
   and time/men/matériel, **4:**988
   trade impacting/being impacted by, **4:**951–952, 989–990
   and unions, **1:**34
   U.S. entry into, **4:**933
   and weapons/armament production, **4:**961
   and women, **4:**972–973
Wray, L. Randall, **2:**422, **3:**672, 674
Wright, Edward, **1:**155
Wright, Ichabod, **1:**54
Wright brothers, **1:**85
Written languages, rise of, **1:**197–199
   See also Alphabet
Wrought iron, **2:**533

WTO. *See* World Trade Organization
Wu Di (emperor), **2:**340

X

XBox, **1:**216, **2:**325, **3:**817
X-ray fluorescence (XRF), **1:**46
Xerxes (king), **2:**434
Xhosa people, **3:**665
Xuanzang, **2:**342

Y

Yahoo, **1:**216, **2:**531
Yasa Code, **2:**558
Yellow fever, **3:**619, 722, 723
Yemen, **2:**377
Yom Kippur War, **2:**307
Yoruba people, **1:**9, **4:**965
Young Plan (1929), **2:**299
Yuan dynasty, **1:**163, 169, 170, **3:**821
Yugoslavia, **1:**244, **3:**853

Z

Zahir-ud-Din Muhammad (emperor), **3:**678
Zambia, **1:**233
Zanzibar, **1:**244, 245
Zapata Off-Shore Company, **1:**131
Zapata Petroleum Corporation, **1:**131
Zayandeh River, **1:**179
Zeitlin, J., **2:**572
Zengi (sultan), **1:**254
Zeppelin, Ferdinand von, **1:**85, 87
Zeppelins, **1:**18–19, 85, 88
Zeravshan River, **3:**708
Zhang Qian, **2:**340, 485
Zheng He, **1:**169, 275, **3:**654, 655
Zhou dynasty, **1:**163, 217
Zhu Rongji, **3:**823
Zhu Wan, **3:**656
Zhu Yuanzhang, **3:**653
Zieber, George, **3:**833
Zimbabwe, **1:**96
Zimba people, **1:**178
Zionists, **1:**44
Zola, Emile, **1:**66
Zixi (empress), **1:**116
Zulu nation, **3:**842
Zwingli, Ulrich, **3:**773

BIOGRAPHICAL INDEX

Volume numbers are in boldface.

A

Abdul Ghaffur, **3**:869–870
Abdur Razzak, **1**:138
Adolphus, Gustavus, **2**:438
Adrian IV (pope), **2**:465
Afonso I, **3**:664
Agwa Gede of Dahomey, **1**:245
Ahmad al-Mans, **3**:806
Aiken, Howard, **1**:215
Akbar (emperor), **3**:679
Alaric (king), **2**:424
Albert I, **2**:446
Albert II, **2**:446
Albert IV, **2**:446
Albert (prince), **1**:256–257, **2**:351
d'Albuquerque, Alfonso, **3**:622
Alexander II, **1**:249
Alexander (merchant), **2**:338
Alexander the Great
  and Armenia, **1**:56
  and art/luxury objects, **1**:59
  Black Sea region and, **1**:113
  and coins/coinage, **1**:188
  drugs used by soldiers of, **1**:291
  and exploration/trade, **2**:338
  overview of, **1**:20–21
  and Phoenicians, **3**:738
Alexius I, **1**:254, 255, **2**:343
Ali, Muhammad (boxer), **2**:324
Ali, Muhammad (pasha), **3**:698
al-Mans, **3**:806
Amalasuntha, **2**:423
Amery, Leopold, **3**:877
Amherst, Jeffrey, **4**:956
Amr Ibn Al-As (king), **3**:866
Anastasius (emperor), **2**:423
Andrew II, **1**:256
Andrews, Anthony P., **1**:47
Anschutz-Kaempfe, Hermann, **1**:209
Anson, George, **3**:598
Anthony, Mark, **1**:56
Antoinette, Marie, **1**:84
Anugwom, E. E., **2**:566

Arden, Elizabeth, **4**:975
Arensberg, Conrad M., **1**:48, 49
Aristarchus, **1**:21
Aristotle, **1**:20, **3**:617
Arkwright, Richard, **1**:54–55, **2**:452
Artavazd II, **1**:56
Artaxias, **1**:56
Ashikaga Yoshimitsu (shogun), **1**:171
Ashurbanipal, **3**:699–700
Ashur-uballit (king), **1**:70
Askia the Great, **2**:406
Atahuallpa (king), **2**:501
Atanassoff, John, **1**:215
Atkinson, James, **1**:251
Attila the Hun, **3**:793
Auguste, Philippe, **3**:731
Augustus (emperor), **1**:21, **2**:339
Aurangzeb (king), **2**:462

B

Babeuf, Francois-Noël, **3**:609, 839
Babur (emperor), **3**:678
Bakunin, Mikhail, **3**:840
Balboa, Vasco Núñez de, **2**:345, **3**:594, 722
Baldwin III, **1**:255
Banks, Joseph, **1**:230, 231
Baptista, Pedro, **1**:161
Barbon, Nicholas, **2**:519
Barbosa, Duarte, **1**:138
Barca, Hamilcar, **3**:759
Barth, Heinrich, **1**:277
Bartholomew, Peter, **1**:254
Batista, Fulgencio, **1**:259
Bayer, Adolph von, **2**:506
Beech, Olive, **4**:975
Belisarius, **2**:423
Bell, Alexander G., **1**:85, **2**:300, **3**:888
Bell, Henry, **3**:921
Benedict (saint), **2**:424, **3**:793
Bentham, Jeremy, **2**:535
Benz, Karl, **2**:524, **3**:711
Bernard of Clairvaux, **1**:254–255, **2**:464, 562
Bernhard (prince), **1**:120
Bernstein, Edward, **3**:841
Biddle, Nicholas, **2**:360

Bin Laden, Osama, **2**:541
Bishop, Ron, **1**:46
Bismarck, Otto von, **1**:162, **2**:403
Bissell, George, **3**:710
Blackburn, Robert M., **2**:573
Blanc, Louis, **3**:840
Bleau family, **1**:155
Boccaccio, Giovanni, **1**:97
Boccaccio di Chellino, **1**:97
Boehm-Bawerk, Eugen von, **3**:765
Bohemund of Taranto, **1**:254
Boleyn, Ann, **2**:305
Bonaparte, Napoléon
  Alexandria captured by, **1**:22
  and Alsace-Lorraine region, **1**:27
  and Arab nationalism, **1**:44
  and art/luxury objects, **1**:65, 66
  and Berlin/Milan decrees, **2**:384, **3**:685, 686, **4**:941, 1069–1070, 1076–1077
  Continental System imposed by, **1**:38
  Egypt conquered by, **2**:302
  and embargoes, **2**:306
  and Genoa, **2**:402
  Germany dominated by, **2**:403
  and illegal trade, **3**:814
  and insurance, **2**:518
  stock exchanges and, **2**:362
  sugar profits and, **1**:82
  and Venice, **4**:937
  and War of 1812, **4**:942
Borah, William, **2**:299
Borden, Gail, **2**:372
Bose, Jagadis C., **1**:136
Bose, Satyendra N., **1**:136–137
Bougainville, Louis-Antoine de, **1**:276
Boulton, Matthew, **1**:55, **3**:862
Bourne, William, **1**:251
Brancusi, Constantin, **1**:68
Brandt, Willy, **1**:189
Braque, Georges, **1**:67
Braudel, Fernand, **3**:785
Braverman, Harry, **2**:570–571
Brazza, Pierre de, **1**:277
Brecher, Jeremy, **2**:575
Brendan (saint), **2**:341
Brewer, John, **1**:124

BIOGRAPHICAL INDEX

Brezhnev, Leonid, **1**:206
Bright, John, **1**:237
Brock, Thomas, **3**:678
Brockeden, William, **1**:258
Brodie, Neil, **2**:481
Brokaw, Tom, **1**:109
Bruni, Leonardo, **2**:365
Bryan, William J., **4**:983
Buchanan, James, **4**:932
Buckelew, Alvin, **3**:893
Buck-Morss, Susan, **3**:787
Bucur, Martin, **3**:773
Bulow, Heinrich von, **2**:403
Bunau-Varilla, Philippe, **3**:723
Burckhardt, Johann, **3**:736
Burghley, William C., **2**:441
Burroughs, Peter, **1**:136
Bush, George H. W., **1**:131–132, **3**:614, 704
Bush, George W., **1**:109, 131, **3**:619
Bush, Vannevar, **1**:215, **4**:988
Byrnes, James F., **4**:991
Byron, George G., **2**:590

C

Cabot, John, **1**:77, **2**:305, 344, **3**:859
Cabot, Sebastian, **1**:154
Cabral, Pedro A., **1**:139, 153, **3**:845
Cadmus, **1**:26
Caesar, Julius, **1**:21, 26, **2**:339, 340, 366–367
Calhoun, John C., **1**:241, **4**:941
Calkins, Ernest, **1**:225
Calvin, Jean, **3**:794
Calvin, John, **3**:758, 773
Campbell, John, **4**:956
Cantillon, Richard, **4**:958
Carey, Henry C., **2**:535
Carey, William, **1**:135
Carson, Rachel, **1**:226
Cartier, Jacques, **1**:77, **2**:344
Cassel, Gustav, **2**:454
Castro, Fidel, **1**:259, **2**:308, 350
Catherine II, **1**:65, 263, 272
Cato the Censor, **1**:60, **3**:760
Caventou, Joseph-Bienaimé, **4**:977
Cecil, Robert, **2**:441
Cézanne, Paul, **1**:68
Chamberlain, Joseph, **1**:127, **3**:876–877
Chamberlain, Neville, **3**:877
Chamberlin, Edward H., **1**:211
Champlain, Samuel de, **1**:81
Charlemagne (king), **1**:26, 149, 150, 158, 266, **2**:342, **3**:793, 799, **4**:960
Charles I, **1**:237, **2**:359, **3**:594, 634, 826
Charles II, **1**:38, 39, 237, 238, **2**:359, 519, **3**:693
Charles IV, **3**:637
Charles V, **2**:365, 446, 475, 478
Charles VI, **2**:447
Charles VII, **2**:447, 478

Charles of Burgundy, **1**:27
Charles the Bald, **1**:151
Charnock, Job, **1**:135
Chase, Stuart, **1**:226
Chatterjee, Bankim C., **1**:137
Chatterjee, Sharat C., **1**:137
Chaucer, Geoffrey, **1**:72
Chiang Kaishek, **2**:435, **3**:823
Churchill, Winston, **1**:227–228
Clark, J. M., **1**:211
Clark, William, **1**:276, **4**:1066–1067
Claudius, Appius, **1**:41
Claudius (emperor), **2**:327
Claudius II, **2**:423
Clausewitz, Carl von, **4**:948
Clay, Henry, **1**:241, **3**:603, **4**:932, 941
Clement III (pope), **1**:255
Clement IV (pope), **3**:826
Clement V (pope), **2**:563, 564
Cleopatra, **1**:56
Clerk, Dugald, **2**:524
Cleveland, Grover, **2**:420, **3**:770, 879
Clinton, Bill, **1**:132, **3**:614, 704
Clive, Robert, **1**:124, 185–186, 238, **3**:592, 819, 820
Cobden, Richard, **1**:236, 237, **3**:876
Cochrane, William, **1**:12
Cocks, Richard, **4**:1015–1016
Cohen, Lizabeth, **1**:225
Cohen, Warren, **2**:418
Colaeus, **2**:337
Colbert, Jean-Baptiste, **1**:64, **3**:627, 628, 877, **4**:1032
Cole, G. D. H., **3**:840
Collins, Greenville, **1**:156
Columbus, Christopher
 and agriculture, **1**:11
 and chocolate, **1**:173
 and discovery/exploration, **1**:275, **2**:344
 and food/diet, **2**:369
 and imperialism/emergence of world economy, **4**:946
 and Isabella I, **2**:538
 and journal of first voyage, **4**:1001–1003
 overview of, **1**:194–195
 and pepper, **3**:729–730
 and the quadrant, **3**:761
 and spice trade, **3**:860
 and sugar, **3**:669–670
 trade route discovery as goal of, **1**:146
Commons, John, **4**:959
Confucius, **1**:168, 216–218
Conrad III, **1**:255, **2**:464, 465
Constantine (emperor), **1**:218, **3**:651
Contractus, Herman, **1**:72
Cook, James, **1**:67, 125, 157, 229–231, 276
Coolidge, Calvin, **1**:15, **4**:975
Coolidge, Grace, **4**:972
Coronado, Francisco, **3**:845
Cortés, Hernán, **1**:193, **3**:845

Costello, Tim, **2**:575
Coston, Martha, **4**:975
Cournot, Antoine-Augustin, **1**:211
Crompton, Samuel, **2**:452
Cromwell, Oliver, **1**:38, **3**:629, 692
Crosby, Alfred, **1**:192
Crossick, Geoffrey, **1**:269
Culpepper, Thomas, **4**:1022–1024
Curtis, Glen, **1**:85
Curtis, Penelope, **3**:676
Cyrus (king), **1**:95, **2**:433

D

Dagobert I, **2**:349
Daimler, Gottlieb, **2**:524
Daimler, Wilhelm, **3**:711
Dalai Lama, **1**:273
Dalí, Salvador, **1**:68
d'Almeida, Francisco, **3**:593
Dalyrmple, Alexander, **1**:157
Daninos, Adrian, **1**:73
Darby, Abraham, **2**:533
Darius I, **2**:338, **3**:866
Darius III, **1**:21
Darwin, Charles, **3**:596, 696
Daschle, Tom, **1**:109
Datini, Francesco, **1**:61, **3**:647
Davidson, Paul, **3**:771
Davies, Arthur, **1**:68
Davis, John, **1**:251–252, **2**:441
Dawkins, P., **2**:574
Day, Francis, **3**:592
Deane, Phyllis, **1**:115
Decius (emperor), **2**:423
Defoe, Daniel, **1**:294
Degas, Edgar, **1**:66
de Gaulle, Charles, **3**:854
DeGolyer, Everette L., **1**:82
de Klerk, F. W., **3**:843
de la Casa, Bartholomew, **1**:77
de la Rua, Fernando, **1**:53
Deng Xiaoping, **1**:189, **2**:298, 435, **3**:821, 823
Derain, André, **1**:67
Desiderius, Peter, **1**:254
Dexter, Harry, **3**:789
Dias, Bartolomeu, **1**:153, 154, **2**:369, **3**:593, 783, 859
Diesel, Rudolf, **2**:524
Dillon, Douglas, **2**:397
Dingler, Jules, **3**:722
Dinocrates, **1**:21
Diocletian (emperor), **3**:793
Diogenes, **2**:339–340
Dionysius Exiguus, **2**:424
Dobb, Maurice, **1**:140
Dodson, Joseph, **2**:520
Dom Pedro II, **1**:28
Douglas, Aaron, **1**:67
Drachman, Virginia, **4**:975–976

Drake, Edwin, **3**:710
Drake, Francis
  and circumnavigating the globe, **1**:289–290, **3**:859
  and Elizabeth I, **2**:290, 306, 359
  and Hakluyt (Richard), **2**:441
  and mercantilism, **3**:624–625
  overview of, **1**:289–290
  and piracy/privateering, **1**:124, **2**:420, **3**:845
Duchamp, Marcel, **1**:68
Duhalde, Eduardo, **1**:53
Dukakis, Michael, **1**:131
Dupleix, Joseph, **1**:239, **3**:819
Dürer, Albrecht, **1**:62
Duryea, Charles, **2**:524
Duryea, J. Frank, **2**:524

E

Earhart, Amelia, **1**:88
Edison, Thomas A., **2**:300–301, 398, **3**:711, 726, 888
Edward I, **2**:476
Edward II, **2**:476
Edward III, **1**:97, **2**:475–477, **3**:615
Edward VI, **2**:305
Einstein, Albert, **1**:137, **4**:988
Eisenhower, Dwight D., **2**:398, **3**:923, **4**:989
Elcano, Juan Sebastian, **3**:859
Elizabeth I
  and Anglican Church, **3**:649
  and British East India Company, **1**:123, 237
  and Drake (Francis), **1**:290, **2**:290, 306, 359
  overview of, **2**:305–306
  and piracy/privateering, **3**:845
  and salt, **3**:810–811
  and weights/measures, **4**:963
Elizabeth II, **1**:121
Elizabeth of Russia (tsarina), **1**:65, **3**:818, 820
Elliot, Charles, **2**:471
Elliot, George, **2**:471
Ely, Eugene, **1**:85
Engels, Friedrich, **1**:200, **2**:321, **3**:609, 840, **4**:1089–1090
Enlil-nirari (king), **1**:70
Eric the Red, **2**:342
Euclid, **1**:21
Eudoxus, **2**:338
Eugenius III (pope), **1**:254
Evans, Arthur, **1**:246, **3**:658

F

Faleiro, Ruy, **3**:594
Farah, Nuruddin, **3**:852
Fenollosa, Ernest, **1**:66

Ferdinand, Franz (archduke), **2**:448, **4**:982–983
Ferdinand I, **2**:446, 448, **3**:827
Ferdinand V, **1**:62, 195, **2**:344, 369
Ferguson, Adam, **3**:603
Feurbach, Ludwig, **3**:609
Fichte, Johann G., **1**:200
Ficklin, Benjamin, **3**:748
Firdawsi, **2**:409
Fisher, Irving, **3**:765
Flannery, Kent, **1**:46
Fleming, J. M., **2**:400
Flint, James, **3**:598
Ford, Gerald R., **1**:131
Ford, Henry, **1**:82, 83, 223, 239, **2**:524–525, **3**:711, 889, 923, **4**:989
Fourier, Charles, **3**:609, 840
Fox, Alan, **2**:571
Francisco de Orellana, **1**:28
Francis I, **1**:62, **2**:447, **3**:634, 800, 813
Francis II, **2**:447–448
Frank, André G., **1**:140
Frank, Thomas, **1**:226
Franklin, Benjamin, **2**:377–379, 519
Frederick I, **1**:26, 255, **2**:442, 464–465, **3**:651
Frederick III, **2**:446
Frederick II of Germany, **1**:256, **2**:465, 466, **3**:826, 895
Frederick II of Prussia, **1**:256, **2**:379–380, **3**:819–820
Freeman, Richard B., **2**:574
Friedman, Milton, **2**:576
Frobisher, Martin, **2**:306
Fugger family, **2**:388–389
Fulton, Robert, **3**:824, 887, 921
Furet, Francois, **3**:785
Furneaux, Tobias, **1**:230

G

Gabbaccia, Donna, **2**:418
Galbraith, John K., **3**:789
Galerius (emperor), **3**:793
Gallus, Aelius, **2**:340
da Gama, Vasco
  and Calicut, **1**:138, 139
  Cape of Good Hope rounded by, **1**:77, **3**:593, 751, 866
  and cartography, **1**:153
  compass and, **1**:209
  and empire building, **2**:310–312
  and India, **2**:344, **3**:626
  and Mediterranean's decline as a link between Europe/the East, **3**:783
Gandhi, Mohandas, **2**:391–393, 462, **3**:811–812
Garibaldi, Giuseppe, **3**:827
Garrick, David, **1**:230
Gates, Bill, **3**:889–890
Gaztambide-Geigel, Antonio, **1**:145

Genghis Khan, **2**:536, 558, **3**:674–675, **4**:945
George III, **1**:230
Gerristz, Hessel, **1**:155, 156
Ghaffur, Abdul, **3**:869–870
Ghibellines (family), **2**:465–466
Ghiberti, Lorenzo, **1**:62
Ghose, Sri Aurobindo, **1**:137
Giddens, Anthony, **2**:411
Giffard, Henri, **1**:85
Gilbert, Humphrey, **2**:306
Giotto, **1**:97
Goddard, Mary K., **4**:975
Godfrey of Bouillon, **1**:253, 254
Godin de Lepinay, Adolphe, **3**:722
Goethals, George W., **3**:723
Goldie, George, **2**:318
Goldthorpe, John H., **2**:573
Gompers, Samuel, **1**:32
Gomulka, Wladyslaw, **1**:189
Gonsalves, Ralph E., **1**:146
Gorbachev, Mikhail, **1**:206, **3**:851
Gore, Al, **3**:613–614
Gould, Jay, **3**:726
Gournay, Vincent de, **2**:385
Graham, Alexander G., **1**:103–104
Gramsci, Antonio, **2**:572
Gray, Elisha, **1**:104
Green, William, **1**:33
Greene, Catherine, **1**:242
Gregory the Illuminator, **1**:56
Gregory VII (pope), **3**:632, 793
Gregory XIII (pope), **3**:814
Gregory X (pope), **3**:745
Gregory XVI (pope), **1**:66
Grenville, George, **3**:693
Grijalva, Juan de, **3**:845
Grint, Keith, **2**:566, 573
Gudea (king), **1**:58
Guelfs (family), **2**:465–466
Guizot, Francois, **3**:609
Gutenberg, Johannes, **1**:233, **3**:724, 756
Gwinn, William, **3**:747

H

Hadrian (emperor), **3**:795
Hakluyt, Richard, **2**:441
Haley, Catherine M., **3**:833, 834
Halley, Edmund, **2**:519–520, **3**:761
Hamilton, Alexander, **1**:36, **2**:360, **3**:602, 764, **4**:931
Hammurabi (ruler), **1**:58, 94
Handler, Ruth, **4**:975
Hannibal, **1**:107, **3**:759–760
Hanno, **1**:152, **2**:337
Hapsburg family, **2**:446–448
Hargreaves, James, **2**:452
Harney, George, **2**:321
Harrington, John, **3**:726
Harrison, John, **1**:157

BIOGRAPHICAL INDEX

Harrison, William H., **4:**942
Haslam, Bob, **3:**748
Hastings, Warren, **1:**136
Hatshepsut, **2:**336
Haupt, Georges, **3:**787
Hawke, Edward, **3:**820
Hawkins, John, **1:**289, **2:**441, **3:**624
Hawley, Willis, **3:**613
Hay, John, **3:**715, 723
Haynes, Elwood, **2:**524
Headrick, Daniel R., **3:**921
Heckscher, Eli F., **2:**454–455
Heilbroner, Robert, **4:**959
Hennu, **2:**336
Henri, Robert, **1:**68
Henrique (bishop), **1:**161
Henry II, **1:**255
Henry IV, **2:**464, **3:**755
Henry V, **2:**478
Henry VI, **2:**465, 477, **3:**726
Henry VII, **1:**97
Henry VIII, **2:**305, **3:**649, 773, 794
Henry the Lion, **2:**465
Henry the Navigator
    compass and, **1:**209
    and empire building, **2:**310
    and exploration/trade, **2:**343–344
    and navigation, **2:**369, **3:**729
    overview of, **2:**459–460
    and Polo (Marco), **3:**747
    and sugar, **3:**867–868
Henry the Proud, **2:**464
Herodotus, **1:**26, 94, 188, **2:**337, 506, **3:**806
Herophilus, **1:**21
Herran, Tomas, **3:**723
Hesiod, **1:**291
Hess, Moses, **2:**321, **3:**609
Hester, Thomas, **3:**612
Hick, John, **2:**400
Hill, Carla, **1:**131
Himlico (king), **2:**337
Hipparchus of Bithynia, **1:**72
Hippocrates, **1:**291, **3:**617
Hiram (king), **1:**176–177
Hiroshige, Ando, **1:**65, 66
Hitler, Adolf, **1:**261, **2:**361, **3:**814, **4:**951, 987
Hitt, Peter, **2:**533
Ho Chi Minh, **2:**384
Hobson, H. C., **3:**840
Hoffman, Paul G., **3:**608
Hohenzollern, Albrecht von, **3:**895
Hokusai, Katsushika, **1:**65, 66
Holladay, Benjamin, **3:**748
Homer, **1:**231
Honorius (emperor), **2:**424
Hoover, Herbert, **2:**299, 453, **4:**985, 990, 1131–1135
Horsfall, William, **2:**590
Houphouët-Boigny, Félix, **2:**548
Houtman, Cornelis de, **3:**859

Houtman, Frederik de, **3:**859
Howe, Elias, **3:**833
Hsüang-tsang, **2:**342
Hudson, Henry, **1:**77, **2:**344
Hughes, Howard, **1:**88
Hull, Cordell, **3:**880
Hume, David, **2:**299, 421, **3:**838, 876
Hume, Joseph, **1:**196
Hunt, Walter, **3:**833
Huskisson, William, **1:**196
Hussein, Saddam, **1:**109, 131, **3:**732, 733
Huygens, Christiaan, **2:**524
Hyde, Anne, **2:**359

I

Ibn Batuta, **1:**137
Ibn Khordadbeh, **3:**763
Innocent II (pope), **2:**562
Innocent III (pope), **1:**255, **3:**793
Innocent IV (pope), **2:**343
Isabella I, **1:**62, 194–195, **2:**344, 369, 537–538
Ismail (viceroy), **3:**867

J

Jackson, Andrew, **2:**360, **3:**602, 603, **4:**932, 943
Jagger, Charles S., **3:**678
Jalal-ud-Din Muhammad (emperor), **3:**679
James, Thomas, **4:**1077–1078
James I, **3:**629, 633, 681, 755
James II, **2:**359, 383, **3:**693
Jaumain, Serge, **1:**269
Jefferson, Thomas, **2:**306, 360, 384, **3:**602, **4:**931, 949, 1066–1067
Jenkinson, Anthony, **2:**306
Jenner, Edward, **3:**618–619
Jerrold, Douglass, **1:**257
Jevons, William, **1:**211
Jiang Zemin, **3:**823
Joan of Arc, **2:**478
John II, **2:**344, 477
John of Utynam, **3:**726
John Phioloponus of Alexandria, **1:**72
Jones, Lois M., **1:**67
Jordanes, **2:**423
Jorden, Edward, **1:**233
José, A., **1:**161
Josef, Franz, **2:**448
Julius II, **3:**813

K

Kaiser, Henry, **4:**989
Kandinsky, Wassily, **1:**68
Kangxi (emperor), **1:**171, **2:**435
Kant, Immanuel, **3:**785
Katz, Lawrence, **2:**574
Kaunitz, Wenzel, **3:**818

Kautsky, Karl, **1:**200
Kennan, George, **1:**228, **3:**607, **4:**952
Kennedy, David M., **4:**988
Kennedy, John F., **1:**189, **2:**397, **3:**846
Kenyon, J., **2:**574
Kerensky, Alexander, **1:**142, **3:**787
Key, Francis C., **4:**943
Keynes, John M., **1:**142–143, 210, **2:**298–299, 399–400, 557, **3:**789–790, 877
Khrushchev, Nikita, **3:**850
Kindleberger, Charles, **3:**789
Kipling, Rudyard, **2:**560–561
Kirchner, Ernst L., **1:**67
Knight, Frank, **1:**211, 212
Knowles, George O., **4:**967
Knowles, Jane, **4:**974
Konrad IV, **1:**26
Köppen, Wladimir, **1:**183
Koprulu, Mehmed, **1:**263
Kornilov, Lavr, **3:**787
Kruger, Paul, **3:**843
Kublai Khan, **1:**169, **2:**343, **3:**745, 858
Kufor, John, **2:**408

L

Laclau, Ernesto, **1:**140
Lane, Fitzhugh, **1:**67
Lassalle, Ferdinand, **2:**535
Latécoère, Pierre, **1:**87
Law, John, **2:**361–362
Layard, Austin H., **3:**699
Lazzerini family, **3:**814
Legazpi, Miguel Lopez de, **3:**599
Leger, Fernand, **1:**68
Leif Ericsson, **2:**342
Lemon, Alaina, **2:**481
Lenin, Vladimir I., **1:**113, 114–115, 142, 196, **3:**787, 805, 849
Lenoir, J. J. Étienne, **2:**524
Leo I (pope), **3:**793
Leo III (pope), **1:**266, **3:**840
Leo IX (pope), **3:**793
Leo X (pope), **3:**772
Leonardo da Vinci, **1:**84
Leopold II, **1:**162, 277
Leopold of Austria, **1:**256
Lerner, Abba P., **3:**672
Lerner, Max, **1:**82
Lesseps, Ferdinand de, **3:**722, 866, 921
Levin, Frances, **2:**482
Lewis, John L., **4:**991
Lewis, Meriwether, **1:**276
Limann, Hilla, **2:**408
Lin, Maya, **3:**676
Lincoln, Abraham, **3:**603, **4:**933
Lindbergh, Charles, **1:**88
Lin Zexu, **2:**435, **3:**717, 821–822, **4:**949
List, Friedrich, **3:**879
List, Georg F., **2:**535, 587–588

Livingstone, David, **1:**161, 277, **3:**665, 696
Llonque Yupanqui (king), **2:**500
Lloyd, Edward, **2:**518
Locke, Alain, **1:**67
Locke, John, **3:**602, 603
Long, Russell, **3:**882
Lopez de Sequeira, Dom Diego, **3:**622
Lothair II, **2:**464
Louis VII, **2:**357
Louis XIII, **2:**438
Louis IX, **1:**256, **2:**563, **3:**632
Louis XIV
  and Anglo-Dutch War of 1672, **1:**39
  and architecture, **1:**99
  and art, **1:**65
  and corporations, **1:**238–239, **3:**627
  and insurance, **2:**518
  and King William's War, **4:**954
  and middle class, **1:**64
  Reformation and, **3:**773
  and scientific/technical developments, **1:**98
  and sculpture, **3:**813–814
Louis XVI, **1:**84
Louis the Pious, **1:**151
Luberas (baron), **3:**734
Lucas, Elizabeth, **1:**13
Lüderitz, F. E., **2:**405
Lugard, Frederick, **3:**803
Lukasiewicz, Ignacy, **3:**710
Lukens, Rebecca, **4:**975
Luther, Martin, **3:**772–773, 775–776, 794
Lutyens, Edwin, **3:**676, 677
Lyotard, Jean-Francois, **3:**785

M

Maassen, Georg, **2:**403
Macartney, Earl G., **2:**471
MacDonald, Ramsay, **3:**877
Macdonough, Thomas, **4:**943
Machiavelli, Niccolò, **2:**365
Mackenzie, Murdoch, **1:**157
Mackinnon, William, **3:**803
Macon, Nathaniel, **4:**942
Madison, James, **1:**36, **4:**931, 942
Magellan, Ferdinand, **1:**154, 209, **3:**593–594, 600, 848, 859
Magyar, László, **1:**161
Mahdali family, **1:**178
Mahmud (king), **2:**409
Majors, Alexander, **3:**747
Malinowski, Bronislaw, **1:**46
Malthus, Thomas R., **1:**115, 237, **2:**300, 557, **3:**595–596, 750, 775
Mandela, Nelson, **3:**843–844
Mandeville, John, **2:**441
Manet, Edouard, **1:**66
Mann, M., **2:**573
Mansa Musa (king), **2:**406, 420, **3:**594, 742, 808

Mansa Uli (king), **2:**406
al-Mansur (sultan), **3:**708
Manuel I, **2:**358, **3:**593, 626
Mao Zedong, **1:**165, 189, **3:**823
Marconi, Guglielmo, **3:**726
Marcos, Ferdinand, **3:**600
Maria Theresa of Austria, **2:**447, **3:**818
Marius, Gaius, **2:**327
Marius, John, **4:**1027–1029
Marshall, Alfred, **1:**143, **3:**789
Marshall, George C., **3:**607
Marshall, John, **3:**602
Martel, Charles, **1:**150, 266, **2:**342
Marx, Karl
  and Bolshevism, **1:**113
  and bourgeoisie economists, **1:**115
  and capitalism, **1:**141
  and competition, **1:**210
  and Democratic Association of Brussels' speech, **4:**1090–1097
  and Engels (Friedrich), **2:**321
  and labor theory of value, **3:**609–610
  overview of, **3:**609
  and religion, **3:**778–779
  and surplus value, **3:**610
  and trade relations, **1:**200
Mary II, **1:**39, **2:**359, **3:**592
Mary of Egypt, **1:**175
Matisse, Henri, **1:**67
Matsuoka Yosuke, **2:**431
Maximilian I, **2:**446
Mayer, Arno, **1:**142, **3:**785
Mbeki, Thabo, **3:**844
McGonigal, Mary, **3:**834
McKillop, Heather, **3:**612
McKinley, William, **1:**116, 188, **3:**715, 879
McLuhan, Marshall, **2:**411, 417
McNeill, John R., **3:**698
McNulty, Paul, **1:**210
McPherson, C. B., **1:**222
Meade, James, **2:**400
Meany, George, **1:**34
Medici family, **1:**61, **2:**364–365, **3:**0, 614–615, 646
Mehemet Ali (ruler), **3:**921
Mehmed II, **1:**263, **3:**719–720
Mehmed IV, **3:**718
Meiji (emperor), **1:**172
Menem, Carlos, **1:**53
Mercator, Gerardus, **1:**154
Merck, George, **1:**108
Metternich, Klemens, **2:**403
Michel, Robert, **2:**572
Michelangelo, **1:**60, 61
Mill, James, **2:**535, **3:**653
Mill, John S., **2:**299, 535, **3:**652–653, 764–765
Miltiades, **2:**433
Minot, Charles, **3:**890–891
Molay, Jacques de, **2:**563

Mondrian, Piet, **1:**68
Monet, Claude, **1:**66
Montague, Mary W., **1:**279, **3:**618
Montcalm, Louis Joseph de, **4:**956
Moore, Basil J., **3:**672
Morgan, Henry, **1:**38–39
Morgan, J. P., **1:**67, 148, **2:**301
Morris, Robert, **1:**36
Morris, William, **1:**66
Morse, F. B., **3:**888, 890
Mother Teresa, **1:**175
Muhammad (prophet), **2:**539, 542–543, **3:**709
Mulroney, Brian, **3:**704
Mun, Thomas, **2:**321–322, **3:**628
Mundell, Robert, **2:**400
Murad II, **3:**719
Murra, John, **1:**48
Mussolini, Benito, **3:**678, **4:**986
Musson, Matthijs, **1:**64
Myrdal, Gunnar, **3:**771

N

Nabopolassar (king), **1:**94
Nader, Ralph, **1:**226
Namath, Joe, **2:**324
Napoléon III, **1:**247, 249, **2:**404, **3:**652
Naramsin (ruler), **1:**58
Narses, **2:**423
Nash, Gary B., **4:**954
Nasmyth, James, **2:**534
Nasser, Gamal A., **1:**73, 228, **3:**867
Nearchus, **2:**338
Nebuchadnezzar II, **1:**94, **3:**641
Necho II, **2:**337, **3:**866
Neckam, Alexander, **1:**209
Need, Samuel, **1:**54, 55
Nelson, Donald, **4:**991
Nero (emperor), **3:**793
Nevsky, Alexander, **3:**706, 895
Newcomen, Thomas, **3:**862
Newton, Isaac, **3:**603, 761
Nicholas I, **1:**249
Nicholas II, **3:**787, 805
Nicholas V (pope), **2:**370
Nightingale, Florence, **1:**249
Nimrod, **3:**699
Nixon, Richard M., **1:**120, 131, **2:**527
Nkrumah, Kwame, **2:**408, **3:**610
Nobunaga, Oda, **2:**439
Noriega, Manuel, **3:**846
Nunes, Pedro, **1:**154
Nurredin (king), **1:**255
Nye, Gerald, **4:**985

O

Octavian, **1:**21
Odovacar (king), **2:**423

BIOGRAPHICAL INDEX

Ohlin, Bertil, **2**:455
Olds, Ransom E., **2**:524
Olivares, Gaspar de, **1**:97
Omar II, **2**:543
Oppenheimer, Ernest, **2**:395
Orhan (sultan), **1**:262
Oribe, Furuta, **1**:63
Orontid family, **1**:56
Orwell, George, **2**:568
Otto, Nikolaus A., **2**:524
Otto I, **2**:403
Otto IV, **2**:465
Owen, Robert, **3**:840

P

Packard, Vance, **1**:226
Palast, Greg, **2**:414
Parameswara (prince), **3**:622
Park, Mungo, **1**:277
Patterson, Robert P., **4**:990–991
Paul III (pope), **3**:814
Paxton, Joseph, **1**:257
Payens, Hugh de, **2**:561–562
Pearson, Harry W., **1**:48, 49
Peel, Robert, **1**:237, **3**:876
Pegolotti, Francesco B., **1**:97, **3**:728, **4**:997–1000
Peisistratus, **1**:11
Penty, A. J., **3**:840
Pepin I, **1**:149–150
Pepperrell, William, **4**:955
Père, Charles Le, **3**:866
Perkin, William, **3**:898
Perot, Ross, **3**:613–614
Perry, Matthew C., **1**:66, **2**:496, 580
Perry, Oliver H., **4**:942
Pessen, Edward, **4**:959
Peter (apostle), **3**:792
Peter III, **3**:820, 826
Peter the Great, **1**:64, **3**:733–734
Peter the Hermit, **1**:253
Petty, William, **4**:958
Pheidon (king), **3**:672
Philip II, **1**:62, 79, 255, **2**:434, 446, **3**:601, 626
Philip IV, **1**:97, **2**:358, 476, 563, 564
Philip VI, **2**:475
Picart, Jean-Michel, **1**:64
Picasso, Pablo, **1**:67, 68
Pike, Zebulon, **1**:276
Pinckney, Eliza L., **4**:975
Pinkham, Lydia, **4**:975
Pitt, William, **1**:195, 196, **2**:471, **3**:820, **4**:956
Pius VI (pope), **1**:66
Pizarro, Francisco, **1**:108, 193, **2**:501
Place, Francis, **1**:196
Pliny the Elder, **2**:377, **3**:795
Polanyi, Karl, **1**:48, 49
Polo, Maffeo, **3**:745

Polo, Marco, **1**:169, 177, **2**:343, **3**:675, 710, 745–747, 858–859
Polo, Niccolò, **3**:745
Polybius, **2**:339
Pompey the Great, **2**:339, **3**:743
Porter, Bernard, **3**:695
Post, Willey, **1**:88
Pottinger, Henry, **2**:471–472
Premdas, R. R., **1**:146
Price, Barbara, **1**:51
Proudhon, Pierre-Joseph, **3**:840
Ptolemy II, **1**:105
Ptolemy of Alexandria, **1**:152–153, 155, **2**:339
Pytheas, **2**:338–339

Q

Qaddafi, Muammar, **1**:283, **3**:853
Qianlong (emperor), **2**:435, **3**:597
Qin Shihuang (emperor), **2**:435
Quesnay, Francois, **1**:141, **2**:575

R

Rae, John, **3**:764–765
Raffles, Stanford, **2**:489
Raimondi, Marcantonio, **1**:62, 63
Raleigh, Walter, **2**:306, 441, **4**:1008–1011
Ramses II, **2**:463, 464
Ramses V, **1**:278
Raphael, **1**:62
Raschèr, Andrea, **2**:481
Rathje, William, **1**:50
Ravenscroft, George, **2**:410
Rawlings, Jerry, **2**:408
Raymond of Toulouse, **1**:253, 254
Reagan, Ronald, **1**:131, 143, **2**:399, **4**:1162–1164
Reden, Fryderyk von, **2**:534
Reed, Walt, **3**:619
Reents-Budet, Dorie, **1**:46
Reid, Thomas, **3**:603
Reinel, Jorge, **1**:154
Renfrew, Colin, **1**:49
Reynald of Chantillon (prince), **1**:255
Reyneval, Conrad de, **2**:385
Rhodes, Cecil, **1**:162, 271, **2**:395, 494, **3**:803, 843
Ribeiro, Diogo, **1**:154
Ricardo, David
   and comparative advantage, **1**:208, **2**:300, **3**:652
   and Corn Laws (British), **1**:237
   and iron law of wages, **2**:535–536, **4**:1083–1084
   and Keynes (John M.), **3**:789
   and laissez-faire, **2**:576
   and Marx (Karl), **1**:115
   overview of, **3**:790–791
   and tariffs, **3**:876

Richard I, **1**:255
Richard II, **2**:477, **3**:628, 692
Richelieu, Cardinal, **1**:97
Richthofen, Ferdinand von, **2**:328
Robert, Nicholas-Louis, **3**:725
Robertson, Roland, **2**:411
Rochambeau, Comte de, **1**:36
Rockefeller, John D., **3**:710
Roe, Thomas, **3**:681, **4**:1024–1026
Roger I, **3**:826
Roger II, **3**:826
Rolfe, John, **1**:12, **3**:901
Roosevelt, Franklin D.
   and agriculture, **1**:15
   and aviation, **3**:889
   and banks/banking, **3**:817
   and competition, **1**:212
   and Hawley-Smoot Tariff (US) of 1930, **4**:1126–1134
   and Keynes (John M.), **1**:143, **2**:557, **3**:789
   and New Deal, **2**:429, **4**:933
   and tariffs, **3**:880
Roque, Jean de la, **1**:186
Rothschild family, **3**:800–801
Roubiliac, Louis-Francois, **3**:677
Roy, A., **2**:575
Roy, Rammohun, **1**:137
Rudolf I, **1**:27
Rudolf II, **2**:446
Rurik (prince), **3**:705
Russell, John, **2**:321
Russell, Majors and Waddell, **3**:747, 748
Russell, William H., **3**:747
Ruyter, Michael de, **1**:38

S

Sahagun, Bernadino de, **1**:48
Saint Francis of Assisi, **1**:175
Saint John, **1**:146
Saint-Simon, Comte de, **3**:609, 840
Saint Thomas, **1**:146
Saladin (king), **1**:255
Salazar, Antonio, **3**:752
Salinas de Gortari, Carlos, **1**:132, **3**:704
Salmon, Robert, **1**:67
Saltykov, Peter S., **3**:734
Samory Touré, **1**:296
Samuelson, Paul, **2**:455
Sanders, William T., **1**:51
Sandys, Edwin, **4**:1012–1015
Sansovino, Andrea, **1**:62
Santley, Robert, **1**:51
Sargon II, **3**:812
Savary de Brèves, Francois, **3**:925
Savery, Thomas, **3**:862
Savonarola, **2**:365
Say, Jean-Baptiste, **2**:299
Schlebecker, John T., **1**:13
Schliemann, Heinrich, **3**:684, 905

BIOGRAPHICAL INDEX   I-51

Schumpeter, Joseph, **1**:212
Scipio, Publius C., **3**:760
Scofield, Levi T., **3**:678
Scott, Winfield, **4**:943
Scylax, **2**:338
Sears, Richard, **1**:224
Selden, George, **2**:524
Seleucid family, **1**:56
Selim I, **3**:720
Semyenov, F. N., **3**:710
Sen, Amartya, **3**:771
Sennacherib (king), **3**:699
Seurat, Georges, **1**:68
Sforzas family, **3**:651
Shafer, Harry, **3**:612
Shah' Alam II, **3**:682
Shaka (ruler), **3**:842
Shalmaneser I, **1**:71
Shamshi-Adad V, **1**:71
Shaw, George B., **3**:841
Shiba Kokan, **1**:65
Sigismund of Habsburg (duke), **1**:27
Silliman, Benjamin, Jr., **3**:710
Simon (saint), **3**:840
Sims, William, **4**:984
Sinchi Roca (king), **2**:500
Singer, Isaac, **3**:833–834
Singleton, John, **2**:481
Sismondi, Jean, **3**:609
Sixtus IV, **3**:813
Smith, Adam
  and colonialism, **4**:947
  and comparative advantage, **1**:208
  and competition, **1**:214
  and Corn Laws (British), **1**:237
  and Keynes (John M.), **3**:789
  and market revolution, **3**:603
  and Marx (Karl), **1**:115
  and nonintervention of government, **2**:576
  and religion, **3**:775
Smith, George, **3**:699
Smoot, Reed, **3**:613
Solis, Juan, **1**:154
Solomon (king), **2**:337, 366, 550, 554, **3**:737
Solon of Athens, **2**:366, **3**:714–715
Soltow, Lee, **4**:959
Solzhenitsyn, Alexander, **3**:785
Sorel, Georges, **3**:840
Spence, Michael, **1**:50–51
Sperry, Elmer, **1**:209
Spinoza, Baruch, **3**:609
Sponsler, Mary A., **3**:833, 834
Sprenkle, Case, **2**:481
Stalin, Joseph, **1**:113–115, 141–142, 244, 272, **3**:607, 849, **4**:986, 989
Stanley, Henry M., **1**:162, 277
Stephenson, George, **3**:767, 888, 922
Stevens, John F., **3**:723
Stigler, George, **1**:210, 211, **2**:576

Stiglitz, Joseph, **2**:413
Stilicho, **2**:424
Stimson, Henry L., **4**:989, 990
Strange, Marty, **1**:18
Strozzi family, **2**:438
Strutt, Jebediah, **1**:54, 55
Sturm, James, **4**:959
Suleiman the Magnificent, **2**:306, **3**:599, 720
Sulla, Lucius C., **2**:327
Summerville, Isabella, **3**:834
Sun Yatsen, **2**:435, **3**:598
Sundiata (king), **2**:406
Sunni Ali (king), **3**:841
Sweezy, Paul, **1**:140

T

Tacitus (emperor), **2**:423
Taft, William H., **2**:528
Tagore, Rabindranath, **1**:137
Talonen, Tarja, **4**:974
Talleyrand, Charles, **2**:385
Taney, Roger B., **3**:602
Tariq ibn-Ziyad, **2**:424
Taubman, George D. G., **3**:801–803
Tawney, R. H., **3**:758
Taylor, Frederick W., **2**:570
Tecumseh, **4**:932, 942
Teixeira, Pedro, **1**:28
Tertullian, **3**:795
Tetzel, Johann, **4**:1007–1008
Thackeray, William M., **1**:141
Thales, **1**:30
Theodoric the Great, **2**:423
Theodosius I, **1**:22
Theophrastus, **2**:376
Thornton, John, **1**:156
Thucydides, **3**:617
Thutmose III, **2**:336
Tigranes the Great, **1**:56
Tiridates II, **1**:56
de Tocqueville, Alexis, **3**:905
Tokugawa Iemitsu (shogun), **1**:171
Tokugawa Ieyasu (shogun), **2**:439
Tomich, Dale, **1**:140
Topa (king), **2**:500
Torrens, Robert, **1**:208, **2**:300, **3**:652, 876
Torrianis family, **3**:651
Toulouse-Lautrec, Henri de, **1**:66
Toyotomi Hideyoshi, **2**:439
Tragan (emperor), **1**:11, **3**:866
Trotsky, Leon, **1**:142, **2**:572, **4**:986
Truman, Harry S., **1**:16, 228, **3**:607, **4**:990, 991
Tukulti-Ninurta (king), **1**:71
Tull, Jethro, **2**:371
Turé, Muhammad, **3**:841
Turgot, Anne, **3**:838
Turgot, Jacques, **2**:385
Turner, Frederick J., **3**:602

U

Underwood, Oscar, **2**:528
Urban II (pope), **1**:252, **2**:343, **3**:793, **4**:995–996
Uttmann, Barbara, **4**:971

V

Valens (emperor), **2**:423
Van Buren, Martin, **4**:932
Vanderbilt, Cornelius, **1**:67, **3**:726
Vanek, Jaroslav, **2**:455
van Gogh, Vincent, **1**:68
Veblen, Thorstein, **3**:879, **4**:959
Ventris, Michael, **2**:585, **3**:684
Verdier, Arthur, **2**:547
Vernatt, Philip, **1**:233
Verrazano, Giovanni da, **2**:344, 382
Vesconte, Petru, **1**:152
Vespucci, Amerigo, **1**:154
Vevey, M. D., **1**:135
Victoria (queen), **1**:257, **2**:351
Vike-Freiberga, Vaira, **4**:974
Villard, Henry, **2**:398
Villiers, George, **1**:97
Viner, J., **3**:758
Vingboon, Johannes, **1**:155, 156
Viracocha (king), **2**:500
Viscontis family, **3**:651
Vitoria, Francisco de, **1**:282
Vivekenanda, **1**:137
Vladimir-Suzdal, **4**:939
Vlaminck, Maurice de, **1**:67
Vora, Virji, **3**:869

W

Waddell, William B., **3**:747
Waghenaer, Lucas J., **1**:155
Waldemar IV, **2**:444, 445
Walker, C. J., **4**:975
Walker, William, **2**:497
Wallace, Henry, **2**:557
Wallenstein, Albrecht von, **2**:438
Wallerstein, Immanuel, **1**:45, **3**:695, 786
Walsingham, Francis, **2**:441
Walters, Mary E., **3**:834
Waltz, Kenneth, **2**:416
Wang Zhi, **3**:656
Wanli (emperor), **3**:657
Washington, Augustine, **2**:533
Washington, George, **4**:931
Watson, Charles, **1**:185
Watson, Thomas, **1**:104
Watt, James, **1**:55, **2**:509, 534, **3**:862–863, 921
Watt, James, Jr., **2**:556
Watteau, Jean-Antoine, **1**:65
Webb, Beatrice, **3**:841
Webb, Sidney, **3**:841

Weber, Max, **1**:140, **2**:542, **3**:758, 775
Wedgwood, Josiah, **1**:65, **2**:510
Weiss, Linda, **2**:414
Westinghouse, George, **2**:301
Whistler, James A. M., **1**:65, 66
White, Christine, **1**:46, 51
Whitman, Meg, **4**:975
Whitney, Eli, **1**:241, 242, **3**:888, **4**:969, 979
Wickard, Claude, **1**:16
Wilberforce, William, **1**:196
William I, **2**:404
William II, **2**:383, **3**:592
William III, **1**:135, **2**:359, **3**:694
William IV, **1**:136
William I of Orange, **1**:38
William III of Orange, **1**:39

Williams, Eric, **2**:510
Wilson, Woodrow, **1**:86, **2**:453, **4**:933, 984, 986
Winton, Alexander, **2**:524
Wittenborg, Johann, **2**:445
Wolfe, James, **3**:820, **4**:956
Wolff, Edward, **4**:959
Woll, Matthew, **1**:33
Wray, L. Randall, **2**:422, **3**:672, 674
Wright, Edward, **1**:155
Wright, Ichabod, **1**:54
Wright brothers, **1**:85
Wu Di (emperor), **2**:340

X

Xerxes (king), **2**:434

Z

Zahir-ud-Din Muhammad (emperor), **3**:678
Zeitlin, J., **2**:572
Zengi (sultan), **1**:254
Zeppelin, Ferdinand von, **1**:85, 87
Zhang Qian, **2**:340, 485
Zheng He, **1**:169, 275, **3**:654, 655
Zhu Rongji, **3**:823
Zhu Wan, **3**:656
Zhu Yuanzhang, **3**:653
Zieber, George, **3**:833
Zixi (empress), **1**:116
Zola, Emile, **1**:66
Zwingli, Ulrich, **3**:773

GEOGRAPHICAL INDEX

Volume numbers are in boldface.

A

Adriatic Sea, **1**:31, 178, **4**:936
Aegean Sea, **1**:6–8, 74, 179, 262, **3**:621, 659
Afghanistan, **1**:60, 293, **3**:718, 733, 851
Africa
   and art/luxury objects, **1**:67
   Asia, trade relations with, **1**:10
   and aviation, **1**:88
   Bantu migrations in, **1**:95–96, 160, **2**:486, **3**:648
   and barter system, **1**:100
   Berbers, **1**:104–105
   and British empire, **1**:126–127
   central, **1**:160–163
   and cities/trade, **1**:178
   and Columbian exchange, **1**:193
   contemporary trade profile of, **1**:9–11
   and copper, **1**:232, 233
   and corn, **1**:235
   cowry shells used as currency in, **1**:188, 244–245
   and diamonds, **1**:269, 272
   and diseases, **1**:280
   and donkeys, **1**:288, 289
   Dyula people, **1**:295–296
   Europe, trade relations with, **2**:327–328
   and European empire building, **2**:310, 318
   geographic/demographic profile, **1**:8–9
   Germany, trade relations with, **2**:405
   and Henry the Navigator, **2**:460
   and history of trade, **1**:9
   Islamic societies, trade relations with, **2**:540
   and ivory, **2**:544–545
   Kilwa, **1**:178
   and livestock, **2**:589
   Lomè Convention and, **1**:10, **3**:912
   and Marx (Karl), **3**:610
   and migrations (human), **1**:95–96, 160, **2**:486, **3**:648
   and missionaries, **3**:663–664
   and motion picture industry, **2**:325

Africa *(continued)*
   Napoleonic Wars and, **4**:950
   and new imperialism, **2**:494–495, **3**:696
   and Pan-Africanism, **2**:408
   and population issues, **3**:750
   postcolonial era in, **1**:162–163
   poverty in, **1**:9
   Soviet Union, trade relations with, **3**:852–854
   and stocks/stock exchanges, **2**:362, **4**:966
   West, **4**:964–966
   and World War I, **4**:950
   See also individual countries
Albania, **1**:113, 189, 244
Aleppo, **3**:720
Alexandria, **1**:21–22, **2**:449, 456–457
Algeria, **1**:10, **2**:384, **3**:853, 926
Alsace-Lorraine, **1**:26–28, **2**:404, 534
Amazon rain forest, **4**:978
Amazon River, **1**:28–29
Amsterdam, **1**:37–38, 271, **2**:551
Anatolia, **1**:246, 260, **3**:830–831
   See also Ottoman empire
Angola, **1**:162, 235, **3**:752
Antioch, **1**:254, 255, **2**:457
Antwerp, **1**:37, 271
Aragon and Castile, the union of, **3**:633–634
Argentina
   and aviation, **1**:90
   Brazil, trade relations with, **1**:53
   currency boards in, **2**:335
   and diasporas, **1**:272
   Falkland Islands/Islas Malvinas War, **1**:128
   fur industry in, **1**:41
   Great Britain, trade relations with, **1**:128
   and import-substitution industrialization, **1**:118
   Japan, trade relations with, **1**:53
   and nuts, **3**:707
   overview of, **1**:53–54
   and rice, **1**:17
   and soybeans, **3**:855
   United States, trade relations with, **1**:53
   and warfare impacting/being impacted by trade, **4**:943

Armenia, **1**:55–57, 71, 113
Ashkelon, **1**:255
Asia
   Africa, trade relations with, **1**:10
   Association of Southeast Asian Nations, **1**:68–70, **2**:583
   and Atlantic trade route, **1**:77
   Batavia as largest European settlement in, **1**:102
   and cartography, **1**:152
   and cities/trade, **1**:177–178
   and Cold War to regional integration, **2**:298
   and corn, **1**:235
   cowrie shells used as currency in, **1**:244
   and diasporas, **1**:272, 273
   and diseases, **1**:279
   and donkeys, **1**:288–289
   East, **2**:297–298
   Europe, trade relations with, **2**:328–330
   and globalization, **2**:413
   Great Britain, trade relations with, **2**:230, 329
   harbors in, **2**:449–450
   and immigration, **2**:488–489
   and ivory, **2**:545
   and mercantilism, **3**:630
   and migrations (human), **3**:647–648, 651
   and new imperialism, **2**:495–496
   and rice, **3**:792
   and slavery, **3**:835
   Southeast, **3**:847–849
   and tin, **3**:900
   See also China; India; Japan
Athens, ancient
   Aegean islands, trade relations with, **1**:6
   and bioterrorism, **1**:107
   and Delian League, **1**:74, 266–267, **2**:357, 434, **3**:617
   and food/diet, **3**:714–715
   harbors in, **2**:449
   Mediterranean Sea vital to, **3**:621
   overview of, **1**:74–75
   Persia, military conflicts with, **2**:433–434
   as predominant trading city in Greek world, **1**:177

Athens, ancient *(continued)*
  and tourism, **3:**904
  and warfare impacting/being impacted by trade, **4:**944
Australia
  and Cook's (James) voyages, **1:**230
  and cotton, **1:**17–18
  and diamonds, **1:**271
  and diasporas, **1:**272
  and electricity, **2:**304
  Hamburg, trade relations with, **2:**442
  and missionaries, **3:**665–666
  as a penal colony, **1:**125, 231
Austria, **1:**86, 248, 264, **3:**818
Azerbaijan, **1:**113
Azores, **1:**77, **2:**459

B

Babylonian empire
  and architecture, **3:**641
  Assyrian empire, military conflicts with, **1:**70–71
  Egypt, trade relations with, **2:**303
  Hittites, military conflicts with, **2:**463
  overview of, **1:**94–95
  Phoenicians absorbed by, **2:**337
  and tin, **3:**900
  and weights/measures, **4:**962
  and wool, **4:**978–979
Baltic Sea, **1:**30
Bangladesh, **3:**791
Barbados, **2:**316
Barbaricum, **2:**509
Barcelona, **3:**632–633
Batavia, **1:**101–103
Begho, **4:**965
Belgium, **1:**162, 268, **2:**351, 352, 533, **3:**694
Belize, **1:**46–47, 172
Benin, **3:**802, **4:**965
Benue–Cross River region, **1:**95
Berenice, **1:**105–106
Bering Strait, **1:**192
Black Sea, **1:**31, 112–113, 134, 218, **3:**720
Bolivia, **1:**293, **3:**845
Bosporus channel/strait, **1:**262–264
Brazil
  and agriculture, **1:**18, 117
  and Amazon River area, **1:**28
  Argentina, trade with, **1:**53
  and art/luxury objects, **1:**63
  and aviation, **1:**90
  cacao grown in, **1:**135
  Canada, trade relations with, **1:**118
  cholera in, **1:**173
  and coffee, **1:**186–187
  and cotton, **1:**241
  and diamonds, **1:**270–271
  and diasporas, **1:**272
  and food/diet, **2:**387

Brazil *(continued)*
  and imperialism/emergence of world economy, **4:**946–947
  iron ore producer, **1:**117
  and medicine, **3:**619
  and missionaries, **3:**662
  and pepper, **3:**730
  and Portugal, **3:**752, 845
  and rice, **1:**17
  and slavery, **3:**835–836, 845
  and soybeans, **3:**855
  and sugar, **3:**868
  United States, trade relations with, **1:**118
  and wood, **4:**977
Brunei, **1:**69, **3:**848
Brusa, **3:**720
Bukhara, **3:**708
Bulgaria, **1:**113, 189, 228, 244, **2:**335
Burma, **1:**293
Bursa, **3:**719
Byblos, **1:**177, **2:**303
Byzantine empire
  and art, **1:**61
  and Black Sea region, **1:**113
  and Cyprus, **1:**260
  and Dark Ages, **1:**266
  and Egypt, **1:**219
  fall of the, **1:**220
  and food/diet, **2:**367
  and glass, **2:**410
  and Goths, **2:**423–424
  Italy, trade relations with, **1:**134
  and ivory, **2:**544
  Mediterranean Sea vital to, **3:**621
  Middle Ages and, **3:**643
  overview of, **1:**133–134
  and Sicily, **3:**826
  and silk trade/Silk Road to China, **3:**828–829
  and Tunisia, **3:**924
  and Venice, **1:**134, **4:**935
Byzantium, **1:**61

C

Caffa, **3:**720
Cairo, **1:**177–178, **2:**301–302
Calais, **2:**478
Calcutta, **1:**125, 135–137, 185
Calicut, **1:**137–139
California, **2:**320, 420, 526
Cambodia, **1:**69, 70
Cameroon, **1:**135
Canada
  and agriculture, **1:**17
  and automobile production, **1:**83
  and bioterrorism, **1:**108
  Brazil, trade relations with, **1:**118
  and British Commonwealth, **1:**121
  cholera in, **1:**173

Canada *(continued)*
  and consumerism, **1:**222
  and copper, **1:**233
  and diamonds, **1:**271
  and diasporas, **1:**272
  and electricity, **2:**304
  and fairs/festivals, **2:**352
  French control over, **2:**382
  Great Britain and, **2:**283
  and livestock, **2:**590
  and outsourcing jobs, **3:**818
  and reciprocity, **3:**769
  sedentary societies in, **1:**49
  and stocks, **2:**362
  and tariffs, **3:**880–881
  and wood, **4:**978
Cape of Good Hope, **2:**310
Cape Verde, **1:**77, **2:**310
Caribbean region, **1:**145–147, **3:**744, **4:**968
  See also Colonies, Latin American/Caribbean
Carthage/Carthaginians
  and exploration/trade, **2:**337
  and harbors, **2:**449
  and Phoenicians, **1:**177, **3:**739
  Rome, military conflicts with, **1:**177, **3:**739, 759–760, 826
  and Sahara Desert/trade, **3:**806
  and Sicily, **2:**434, **3:**826
  and silver, **3:**831
  and Tunisia, **3:**924
Caspian Sea, **3:**710
Central America, **1:**46–52, 77, 78, **2:**549, **3:**611–612
  See also Colonies, Latin American/Caribbean; Latin America
Ceylon, **2:**314, **3:**884
Chicago, **1:**181–182
Chile, **1:**233, **2:**388
China
  agriculture in, **1:**165, 184
  Arabs, military conflicts with, **1:**168
  and arms sales, **3:**853
  and art/luxury objects, **1:**60, 61, 65, **3:**601
  and Asian-British trade relations, **2:**330
  and barter system, **1:**100
  Boxer Rebellion, **1:**116, 170, **3:**715
  and bribery, **1:**120
  and British East India Company, **1:**124
  and Buddhism, **1:**128–130, **3:**740, 776, 830, 847
  Bugis people and, **1:**130
  Calicut, trade relations with, **1:**138–139
  and Canton system, **1:**164, **2:**297, 435, 470, **3:**597
  and cities/trade, **1:**178, 182
  and coins/coinage, **1:**171
  and Cold War, **1:**189
  and communism, **1:**164–165

China *(continued)*
  compass and, **1:**209
  and Confucianism, **1:**163–164, 166, 169, **2:**309, **3:**654–655, 776
  Confucius, **1:**216–218
  and consumerism, **3:**657
  and copper, **1:**233
  and cotton, **1:**241–242
  decline of imperial, **1:**169–170
  and diasporas, **1:**272, 273
  and discovery/exploration, **1:**275
  and diseases, **1:**279
  and drugs, **1:**290–292
  dynasties in, **1:**166–170
  and empire building, **2:**309
  and exploration/trade, **2:**340, 341–342
  and fairs/festivals, **2:**348
  fertilizer used in, **2:**353
  and food/diet, **2:**388
  France, military conflicts with, **2:**473
  France, trade relations with, **1:**116
  and fur trade, **1:**41
  geographical overview, **1:**163, 184
  Germany, trade relations with, **1:**116
  and glass, **2:**410
  and globalization, **2:**415
  and gold, **2:**420
  and grain, **2:**426
  Great Britain, trade relations with, **1:**116, 164, 169, **2:**297, 435
  Great Leap Forward, **1:**165
  Han Chinese, **1:**163
  Han dynasty, **1:**163, 166, 168, 170, 209, **2:**367, 580, **4:**945
  Hangzhou, **1:**178
  and immigration, **2:**488–489
  India, trade relations with, **3:**847
  Industrial Revolution and, **2:**512, 513
  and insurance, **2:**518
  and iron technology, **2:**533
  and irrigation, **2:**537
  and ivory, **2:**545
  and jade, **2:**549
  Japan, military conflicts with, **1:**116, **2:**432, 473, 474
  Japan, trade relations with, **1:**165, 170–172, 190
  and law, **2:**580–581
  and livestock, **2:**590
  and market reform, **2:**298
  and migrations (human), **3:**650, 651
  Ming dynasty, **1:**164, 169–171, **3:**653–658, 830, 832
  and missionaries, **3:**663
  and modernization in the 1970s, **1:**165–166
  Mongols, military conflicts with the, **3:**674, 675
  and most-favored-nation status, **1:**166
  and multinational corporations, **1:**240

China *(continued)*
  Netherlands, trade relations with, **2:**297
  and new imperialism, **2:**495–496, **3:**696
  and nuts, **3:**707
  and oases, **3:**708
  and oil/oil industry, **3:**710
  and open door notes, **3:**715
  paper currency used in, **1:**101
  and paper/pulp, **3:**724
  People's Commune movement, **1:**165
  People's Republic of China, **1:**164–165, 189, 244
  and pirated entertainment, **2:**468
  and population growth, **2:**426
  Portugal, military conflicts with, **3:**655, 657
  and pottery, **2:**512, **3:**601, 657, 754–755
  Qin to the Qing dynasty, trade from the, **1:**163–164
  Qing dynasty, **1:**164, 169, 171, **2:**469–473, 580, **3:**596–598, 821
  Republican era, **1:**164
  and rice, **1:**17, **3:**791
  Russian empire, trade relations with, **1:**116
  and severe acute respiratory syndrome, **3:**619
  Shang dynasty, **1:**163
  Shanghai, **3:**821–823
  and silver, **3:**832
  Sino-Japanese Wars, **1:**116, **2:**473
  Song dynasty, **1:**163, 168–171, 178, **2:**297, 580
  and Soviet Union, **1:**165, **3:**850
  and soybeans, **3:**854, 855
  and spice trade, **2:**367
  Surat, trade relations with, **3:**870
  Tang dynasty, **1:**163, 168, 170, **2:**549, **3:**764
  and tea, **3:**883, 884
  and textile trade, **3:**657
  and Tiananmen Square demonstration, **1:**190
  tribute system in, **1:**168–169
  United States, trade relations with, **1:**116, 165, 166, 190
  West, trade relations with the, **1:**189–190
  Yuan dynasty, **1:**163, 169, 170, **3:**821
  Zhou dynasty, **1:**163, 217
  See also Hong Kong; Manchu dynasty
Chinsurah, **1:**136
Colombia, **1:**90, 135, 187, 293, **2:**387, **3:**722–723, 922
Colonies, Latin American/Caribbean
  and agriculture, **1:**12, **3:**845–846
  and Atlantic trade route, **1:**78–82
  Catholic Church and, **3:**846
  and Christianity, **1:**175–176
  and coffee, **1:**186
  Columbus explores the, **1:**195
  Cuba and Spain, **1:**258–259

Colonies, Latin American/Caribbean *(continued)*
  and diseases, **1:**193
  and empire building, **2:**316
  and exploration/trade, **2:**345
  France and, **2:**383, 440
  and imperial competition, **3:**857
  and indentured servants, **2:**501–503
  and Isabella I, **2:**538
  and mercantilism, **3:**625
  overview of, **3:**845–846
  piracy/privateers in, **1:**79
  politics and regional/international trade, **1:**146–147
  and rum, **3:**804
  Saint Domingue and, **2:**384
  and silver, **3:**831–832, 845
  and slavery, **1:**12, 146, **3:**836
  and sugar, **3:**868
  and tortoiseshell, **3:**903
Colonies, North American
  and advertising, **1:**4
  and agriculture, **1:**11–13
  and Anglo-Dutch Wars, **1:**38–39
  and arms/weapons trade, **4:**961
  and art/luxury objects, **1:**67
  and Atlantic trade route, **1:**81–82
  and banks/banking, **2:**360
  and Canada ceded to British empire, **2:**383
  and coins/coinage, **1:**101
  and Continental Congress, **4:**931
  Declaration of Independence, **4:**931
  and exploration/trade, **2:**345
  France and, **2:**382–384
  and glass, **2:**410
  harbors in, **2:**450–451
  and hemp, **2:**457
  and indentured servants, **2:**501–503
  Industrial Revolution and, **2:**512, 513
  and insurance, **2:**519
  and iron technology, **2:**533
  and Jewish people/Judaism, **2:**555
  and joint-stock companies, **2:**552
  and Louisiana territory, **2:**383, 384
  and migrations (human), **3:**650
  and molasses, **3:**670
  Navigation Acts (British) and, **3:**629–630, 693
  overview of, **4:**930–931
  and Protestantism, **3:**758–759
  Revolutionary War, **1:**34–38, 81, **2:**317
  and rum, **3:**803–804
  and salt, **3:**811
  and silk trade, **3:**829
  and Stamp Act of 1765 (British), **4:**1043–1047
  and Tea Act of 1773 (British), **4:**1047–1049
  and tobacco, **3:**900–901
  and Wars for Empire, **4:**954–956

Comacchio, **4:**935
Congo, **1:**162
Congo River system, **1:**160, 277
Constantinople, **1:**39, 61, 133, 134, 179, 218–220, **3:**719, 720
Costa Rica, **2:**387
Côte d'Ivoire, **2:**547–548
Crete/Minoan civilization
 agriculture and, **1:**246
 and art, **1:**58–59
 decline of, **1:**6
 earliest settlements, **1:**246, **3:**658–659
 Egypt, trade relations with, **1:**246–247, **2:**303, 336
 and food/diet, **3:**714
 geographical overview of, **1:**245
 and gold, **2:**419
 Greece, trade relations with, **1:**247
 and immigration, **2:**484
 late history of, **3:**659
 and pottery, **1:**246, **3:**658, 754
 and silver, **3:**831
Cuba
 and American Revolution, **1:**36
 Cold War and, **1:**189
 and Council for Mutual Economic Assistance, **1:**244
 and Cuban missile crisis, **1:**189
 and embargoes, **2:**308
 and fairs/festivals, **2:**350
 and guilds, **3:**637–638
 and new imperialism, **2:**497
 overview of, **1:**258–259
 and Soviet Union, **1:**259, **3:**851
 Spanish-American War, **1:**147, 259, **3:**599, 722–723
 and tobacco, **1:**258
Curacao, **1:**147
Cuzco, **2:**500, 501
Cyclades, **1:**6
Cyprus, **1:**231, 260, **2:**303, 402, **3:**720
Czechoslovakia, **1:**189, 244, **3:**607–608

D

Dardanelles channel/strait, **1:**262–264
Denmark
 and Calcutta, **1:**135
 and Caribbean region, **1:**146
 and cartography, **1:**157
 and Continental System, **3:**687
 and fur trade, **1:**41
 and Hanseatic League, **2:**444–445
 and Mughal empire, **3:**681
 and Ottoman empire, **3:**721
 and slavery, **2:**567
Dilmun, **3:**642
Djenne, **1:** 295, **4:**965
Dubrovnik, **3:**719, 721, 765–766, **4:**937

E

Ecuador, **1:**63, 135, **2:**387
Egypt
 Aswan High Dam, **1:**72–74
 Baghdad Pact, **1:**228
 Cairo, **1:**177–178, **2:**301–302
 and Great Britain, **1:**127, **2:**302
 and Islam's emergence, **2:**301–302
 and Israel, **2:**302, **3:**853
 nationalism, center of Arab, **1:**44
 as weak actor in global trade, **2:**302
 See also Suez Canal
Egypt, ancient
 and African imports, **1:**10
 Alexandria, **1:**21–22
 and art/luxury objects, **1:**57, 58, 65–66, **2:**203
 Babylonian empire, trade relations with, **2:**303
 and barter system, **1:**100–101
 Berenice, **1:**105–106
 and Byzantine empire, **1:**219
 and cities/trade, **1:**177–178
 and copper, **1:**231, 232
 and cotton, **1:**241, **3:**898
 Crete, trade relations with, **1:**246–247, **2:**303, 336
 and diseases, **1:**278
 and drugs, **1:**290, 291
 and exploration/trade, **2:**336
 fertilizer used in, **2:**353
 and frankincense/myrrh, **2:**376
 and gemstones, **2:**395
 and glass, **2:**410
 and gold, **2:**419
 Greece, trade relations with, **2:**304
 and hieroglyphic symbols, **1:**25, 198
 Hittites, military conflicts with, **2:**463–464
 Hykso people and, **3:**703
 and immigration, **2:**483, 484
 and irrigation, **2:**536–537
 and law, **2:**577
 and leather, **2:**584
 and linen, **2:**586, **3:**896
 and livestock, **2:**588
 and medicine, **3:**616
 Mogadishu, trade relations with, **3:**668–669
 monuments in, **3:**677
 Nubia, military conflicts with, **2:**564
 and perfume, **3:**730
 Phoenicians, trade relations with, **2:**303, 304
 and pottery, **3:**754
 Rome, trade relations with, **2:**304, 309
 and sculpture, **3:**812
 and spice trade, **3:**860
 and technology, **3:**885, 886

Egypt, ancient *(continued)*
 time periods (six) of, **2:**302–303
 and trade/expansion, **2:**303–304
 and transportation/trade, **3:**919
 and warfare impacting/being impacted by trade, **4:**943
 and weights/measures, **4:**962, 963
 and wood, **4:**977
 and wool, **4:**978–979
England. *See* Great Britain
Estonia, **2:**335
Ethiopia, **1:**244, **2:**564, **3:**853
Euboea, **1:**6
Euphrates River, **3:**732, 921, **4:**957, 977
 See also Mesopotamian civilization
Eurasia and cities/trade, **1:**177–178
Europe
 and advertising, **1:**4
 Africa, trade relations with, **2:**327–328
 and African structural adjustment programs, **1:**10
 and agriculture, **1:**15, 16–17
 and archaeology, **1:**52
 Argentina, trade relations with, **1:**53
 arms trade and, **2:**480
 and art/luxury objects, **1:**62, 63–68
 Asia, trade relations with, **2:**328–330
 Asia-Europe Meeting, **1:**69
 and automobile production, **1:**83
 and aviation, **1:**85, 91–92
 and Bardi House of banking, **1:**96–97
 and barter system, **1:**100
 and bribery, **1:**120
 China, trade relations with, **1:**169
 chocolate introduced into, **1:**173
 and cities/trade, **1:**177–179
 and coffee, **1:**186
 and coins/coinage, **1:**188
 and Columbian exchange, **1:**193
 compass and, **1:**209
 and computers, **1:**216
 and consumerism, **1:**222
 and corn, **1:**235
 crop rotation in, **1:**249
 Cyprus, trade relations with, **1:**260
 and diasporas, **1:**273
 and dirhams, **1:**274
 and disputes/arbitration, **1:**281
 and drugs, **1:**292
 and empire building, **2:**310–314
 and exploration/trade, **1:**277, **2:**343–345
 feudalism in, **2:**356–357
 and food/diet, **2:**387–388, **3:**858
 and free trade interlude, **3:**694
 and fur industry, **1:**41
 and globalization, **2:**413
 and gunpowder, **2:**438
 and Hapsburg family, **2:**446–448
 harbors in, **2:**451
 and immigration, **2:**486–487

Europe *(continued)*
  and Indian Ocean trade, **2:**505–506
  and intracontinental trade, **2:**331–332
  Islamic societies, trade relations with, **2:**541
  and Khazar empire, **2:**559
  and linen, **2:**586–587
  Lomè Convention, **1:**10, **3:**912
  and Manchu dynasty, **3:**598
  Marshall Plan for, **1:**16, 90, 228, **2:**375, **3:**607–608, **4:**952
  and Medici family, **1:**61, **2:**364–365, **3:**614–615, 646
  and motion picture industry, **2:**325
  and multinational corporations, **1:**240
  and paper/pulp, **3:**724–725
  Rome's fall impacting, **3:**799
  and ships/shipbuilding, **1:**47
  and Soviet Union, **1:**115, **3:**850–851
  stock exchanges in, **2:**362
  and tariffs, **3:**877–878
  and tobacco, **3:**901
  and transportation/trade, **3:**920–921
  See also individual countries
European Union (EU)
  and Alsace-Lorraine region, **1:**28
  China, trade relations with, **1:**166
  competition policy in the, **1:**212, 214–215
  expansion of, **2:**334
  and livestock, **2:**589
  Maastricht Treaty and creation of, **2:**332
  map of, **2:**333
  and multinational corporations, **1:**240
  and nuts, **3:**707
  overview of, **3:**913
  and South Africa, **3:**844

F

Finland, **1:**41, 233, **2:**482–483, **4:**974
Flanders, **2:**475
Florence, **1:**96–97, **2:**364–365, **3:**614–615, 720
France
  and Aegean Sea, **1:**7
  and agriculture, **1:**12, 18
  and Alsace-Lorraine region, **1:**26–28
  and American Revolution, **1:**35–36
  Anglo-French Treaty of Dover, **1:**39
  and art/luxury objects, **1:**62, 64–67
  and Atlantic trade route, **1:**81–82
  and aviation, **1:**84, 86, 87, 90
  in the Baroque period, **1:**97–99
  Batavia occupied by, **1:**103
  and bioterrorism, **1:**108
  British competition as a constant, **2:**383–384
  Canada and, **2:**38
  and Caribbean region, **1:**146
  and cartography, **1:**155–157

France *(continued)*
  China, military conflicts with, **2:**473
  China, trade relations with, **1:**116
  cocoa processing factories in, **1:**173
  and colonialism, **1:**191, **2:**382–384, 440, **3:**547–548
  and Continental System, **1:**38, 229, **3:**685–687
  and corporations, **1:**238–239
  and cotton, **1:**241
  and Crusades, **1:**253
  and Dardanelles channel, **1:**264
  department stores in, **1:**267–268
  and diasporas, **1:**272
  and discovery/exploration, **1:**275–277
  and electricity, **2:**304
  and embargoes, **2:**306–307
  and empire building, **2:**316, 318, 319, 382–385
  and Equatorial Africa, **1:**161, 162
  and exploration/trade, **2:**344, 345
  and fairs/festivals, **2:**350, 351
  feudalism in, **2:**356
  French Community, Constitution of the, **4:**1152–1157
  and French Mississippi Bubble, **2:**552
  French Revolution, **1:**7, 84, **2:**385–387, **3:**785–787, 794
  and fur trade/industry, **1:**40, 81–82
  and Genoa, **2:**402
  Germany, military conflicts with, **2:**403–404
  and glass, **2:**410
  and guilds, **3:**632
  and gunpowder, **2:**437
  India, trading relations with, **1:**123
  and indigo, **2:**506
  and insurance, **2:**518
  and iron technology, **2:**534
  and Ivory Coast, **2:**546–548
  and Knights Templar, **2:**563–564
  and Madras, **3:**592
  and Mali, **3:**595
  and mercantilism, **3:**627–629
  Middle Ages and, **3:**646
  and Mogadishu, **3:**668
  monuments in, **3:**678
  and Mughal empire, **3:**681, 682
  and Nantes Edict, **2:**587
  and navigation, **3:**690
  and new imperialism, **3:**695, 696
  and oases, **3:**708
  and Ottoman empire, **3:**720, 721
  and Panama Canal, **3:**722, 922
  and perfume, **3:**731
  and piracy/privateers, **1:**79
  Ragusa, military conflicts with, **3:**766
  and sculpture, **3:**813–814
  and Shanghai, **3:**822
  and Southeast Asia, **3:**848–849

France *(continued)*
  Soviet Union, trade relations with, **1:**115
  stock exchanges in, **2:**361
  and tariffs, **3:**877–878
  and tortoiseshell, **3:**902–903
  and tourism, **3:**907
  and transportation/trade, **3:**922
  and Tunisia, **3:**926
  United States, trade relations with, **2:**385
  and warfare impacting/being impacted by trade, **4:**945–946
  and weapons/armament production, **4:**960
  and weights/measures, **4:**964
  and wine, **4:**970
Funan, **3:**847

G

Gabon, **1:**162
Gades, **3:**738
Gallipoli, **1:**262–264
Galveston, **2:**451
Ganges River, **1:**137
Gascony, **2:**475–476
Genoa, **2:**401–402, **3:**719–721, 858
Georgia, **1:**113
Germany/Germanic people
  Africa, trade relations with, **2:**405
  and agriculture, **1:**17, **2:**403, **3:**878
  and Alsace-Lorraine region, **1:**26–28
  Anglo-French Treaty of Dover, **1:**39
  and automobiles, **1:**83–84, **4:**987
  and aviation, **1:**19, 85–88, 90
  and banks/banking, **2:**404
  and bioterrorism, **1:**108
  China, trade relations with, **1:**116
  and classical economics, **2:**300
  and Cold War, **1:**189
  and colonialism, **2:**405
  and copper, **1:**232
  Council for Mutual Economic Assistance, **1:**244
  and Crusades, **1:**253, 255
  Danube River and, **1:**261
  department stores in, **1:**268, 269
  and disputes/arbitration, **1:**285
  and dyes, **3:**898
  East and West, trade relations between, **1:**189
  and empire building, **2:**403–406
  and fairs/festivals, **2:**350, 354, 355
  fertilizer used in, **2:**353
  France, military conflicts with, **2:**403–404
  Gothic script, **1:**24
  Hamburg, **2:**441–443
  Hohenstaufen empire, **2:**464–466
  and immigration, **2:**489
  and insurance, **2:**518

Germany/Germanic people *(continued)*
   and intracontinental European trade, **2:**331
   and iron technology, **2:**534
   Italy, military alliance with, **4:**986
   and Jewish people/Judaism, **2:**555
   and Kilwa, **2:**560
   Middle Ages and, **3:**643, 645
   and migrations (human), **3:**649
   and monuments, **3:**676, 678
   and NAFTA, **3:**704
   and new imperialism, **3:**696
   and pirated entertainment, **2:**468
   and Poland, **3:**849
   and railroads, **3:**768
   reunification of, **1:**131
   and Russian Revolution, **3:**805
   and ships/shipbuilding, **3:**824
   South America, trade relations with, **1:**128
   Soviet Union, military conflicts with, **3:**849
   Soviet Union, trade relations with, **1:**115
   and tariffs, **3:**878
   and technology, **3:**888
   United States, trade relations with, **4:**987
   and weapons/armament production, **4:**961
   and World War I, **4:**950–951
   World War I, punishment after, **1:**87, 261, **2:**298–299, 361, 405–406, 557, **4:**984
   See also Prussia
Ghana
   ancient, **2:**406
   Berbers and, **1:**105
   and cacao, **1:**135
   and cocoa production, **4:**966
   and colonialism, **2:**407–408
   and Dyula people, **1:**295
   and European's arrival, **2:**406–407
   and gold, **2:**310, 406–407, 419
   and independent/modern, **2:**408
   and Mandé-speaking people/Islamized court culture, **4:**965
   Soviet Union, trade relations with, **3:**854
Gobi Desert, **1:**289
Gold Coast, **2:**406–407
Golden Triangle, **3:**717–718
Great Britain
   and abolition of slavery, **2:**567
   and Aegean Sea, **1:**7
   and agriculture, **1:**12–14
   Amazon River and, **1:**28
   and American Revolution, **1:**34–38
   Anglo-French Treaty of Dover, **1:**39
   Argentina, trade relations with, **1:**128
   and art/luxury objects, **1:**64, 67
   Asia, trade relations with, **2:**230, 329
   and Atlantic trade route, **1:**81
   and Australia, **1:**125

Great Britain *(continued)*
   and aviation, **1:**85, 86, 88–90
   and banks/banking, **2:**359
   in the Baroque period, **1:**97–99
   and barter system, **1:**101
   Batavia occupied by, **1:**103
   and bioterrorism, **1:**108
   Boers, military conflicts with the, **1:**126, **3:**843
   and bribery, **1:**118
   British Commonwealth, **1:**121–122
   Calcutta, control of, **1:**135–137
   and Caribbean region, **1:**146, 147
   China, trade relations with, **1:**116, 164, 169, **2:**297, 435
   cholera in, **1:**173–174
   and cities/trade, **1:**180, 181
   cocoa processing factories in, **1:**173
   and colonialism, **1:**124–127, 191, **2:**407–408, **3:**857
   and comparative advantage, **1:**208
   and Continental System, **1:**38, 229, **3:**685–687
   and copper, **1:**232, 233
   and copyrights, **1:**233–234
   and corporations, **1:**237–239
   and cotton, **1:**241
   and Crystal Palace, **1:**256–258, **2:**351
   and Dardanelles channel, **1:**263–264
   and decaying trade relations, **4:**1024–1026
   department stores in, **1:**268, 269
   and diasporas, **1:**272
   and discovery/exploration, **1:**276
   and Egypt, **1:**127, **2:**302
   and embargoes, **2:**306–307
   and empire building, **1:**124–127, **2:**317–319
   England's Treasure by Foreign Trade, **2:**321–322
   and Equatorial Africa, **1:**161
   and exploration/trade, **2:**344
   and Fabianism, **3:**841
   and fairs/festivals, **2:**350, 351, 354–355
   fertilizer used in, **2:**353
   and food/diet, **2:**372
   and free trade, **3:**769, 876
   French competition as a constant, **2:**383–384
   and General Agreement on Tariffs and Trade, **2:**397
   and Genoa, **2:**402
   and Ghana, **2:**407
   and gold, **2:**420, 421
   and grain, **2:**425
   and guilds, **3:**636–637
   and hemp, **2:**457
   and Hinduism, **2:**462
   and immigration, **2:**488
   Industrial Revolution and, **2:**509–514

Great Britain *(continued)*
   and insurance, **2:**518–520
   and iron technology, **2:**533
   Japan, trade relations with, **4:**1015–1016
   and joint-stock companies, **2:**552
   and Keynes (John M.), **2:**557
   and law, **2:**578, 580, **3:**632
   and linen, **2:**587
   and livestock, **2:**588
   and Manchu dynasty, **3:**597
   and Manila, **3:**599
   and medicine, **3:**618–619
   and Melaka, **3:**623
   and mercantilism, **3:**628–630
   and migrations (human), **3:**649–650
   and Ming dynasty, **3:**657
   and Mogadishu, **3:**668
   and navigation, **3:**690
   and new imperialism, **2:**493, 494, **3:**695–696
   and oil/oil industry, **3:**713
   Orders in Council of 1804/1806, **1:**13, **2:**384, **4:**941, 942
   Ottoman empire, trade relations with, **1:**237
   and paper/pulp, **3:**725–726
   and patents, **3:**726
   Persia, trade relations with, **1:**237
   and Persian Gulf, **3:**732
   and pilgrimages, **3:**742–743
   and piracy/privateering, **1:**79, **3:**624–625, 744
   Portugal, alliance with, **1:**128
   and pottery, **3:**755
   and Protestantism, **3:**759
   and railroads, **3:**767, 922
   Reagan's (Ronald) speech to British House of Commons, **4:**1162–1164
   Russia, trade relations with, **1:**237
   and salt, **3:**810–812
   and sculpture, **3:**814
   Shanghai, trade relations with, **3:**822
   and ships/shipbuilding, **3:**824
   and Sicily, **3:**827
   and silk trade, **3:**829, 897
   and slavery, **1:**12, **2:**567
   South America, trade relations with, **1:**127–128
   and South Seas Bubble in 1720, **1:**125, **2:**552
   Soviet Union, trade relations with, **1:**115
   Spanish Armada defeated by, **2:**306
   and spice trade, **3:**859
   stock exchanges in, **2:**361
   and Suez Canal, **4:**950, 1103–1105
   and Surat, **3:**869
   and tally sticks, **3:**872
   and tariffs, **3:**875–877
   telegraph and, **3:**891
   and tobacco, **3:**901

Great Britain *(continued)*
  and tourism, 3:905
  and trademarks, 3:917
  and transaction costs, 3:918
  and transportation/trade, 3:922
  unions in, 2:572
  and Vikings, 4:938
  and warfare impacting/being impacted by trade, 4:945–946
  and *Wealth of Nations,* 4:1049–1063
  and weapons/armament production, 4:960
  and weights/measures, 4:964
  and women, 4:973
  and wool, 3:896, 4:979
Greece, 1:7–8, 113, 2:402, 3:607, 814
Greece, ancient
  and Aegean Sea, 1:6
  agora (marketplace) in, 1:10–11, 2:457, 3:604
  alphabet used in, 1:23–24, 198
  and amber, 1:30, 31
  and architecture, 2:455–457
  Armenia ruled by, 1:56
  and art/luxury objects, 1:58–60
  and bioterrorism, 1:107
  and Black Sea region, 1:113
  and cartography, 1:152
  Celts, trade relations with the, 2:331
  and cities/trade, 1:177
  city-states in, 2:433–434
  coins/coinage in, 1:101, 188
  and copper, 1:232
  Crete, trade relations with, 1:247
  and diasporas, 1:272
  and drugs, 1:291
  Egypt, trade relations with, 2:304
  and entertainment, 2:322–323
  and exploration/trade, 2:337–339
  and fairs/festivals, 2:349
  and food/diet, 2:366, 3:714
  and gemstones, 2:395
  and gold, 2:419
  and immigration, 2:484–485
  and insurance, 2:518
  linear B script and, 2:585–586
  and marketplaces, 1:10–11, 2:457, 3:604
  and medicine, 3:616–617
  Mediterranean Sea vital to, 3:621
  and Mycenaean civilization, 1:6, 198, 3:648, 683–684, 831
  Nubia, military conflicts with, 2:564
  and pepper, 3:729
  and perfume, 3:730
  Persia, military conflicts with, 2:433–434
  and Petra, 3:735–736
  and Phoenicians, 1:26, 3:738, 739
  and pottery, 3:754
  and sculpture, 3:812–814
  and ships/shipbuilding, 3:823

Greece, ancient *(continued)*
  and Sicily, 3:826
  and silver, 3:831
  and slavery, 3:835
  Spain, trade relations with, 2:337
  and technology, 3:886
  and tin, 3:900
  and tourism, 3:903–904
  and transportation/trade, 3:919–920
  and weights/measures, 4:963
  and wine, 4:970
  and women, 4:971
  and wood, 4:977
  and wool, 4:979
  See also Athens, ancient
Greenland, 2:342, 4:938
Gruinard Island, 1:108
Guadeloupe, 2:316
Guangzhou, 1:164, 2:297, 434–435
Guatemala, 1:47, 63, 151, 187, 2:549
Guyana, 1:147

H

Haiti, 1:82, 146, 147, 2:316, 440
Hamburg, 2:441–443
Hangzhou, 1:178
Hanigalbat, 1:71
Hawaiian Islands, 1:230, 3:666, 769, 868–869
Herat, 3:708
Hollywood, 2:325, 467–469
Hong Kong
  and agriculture, 1:165
  and decline of British influence, 2:474
  founding of, 2:469–473
  and fur trade, 1:41
  harbors and, 2:450
  and Kowloon under British control, 2:473–474
  and Opium Wars/Treaty of Nanjing, 1:127, 2:298, 469–472
  and textile industry, 3:899
Hooghly River, 1:135, 137
Hungary, 1:244, 268, 2:415

I

Iceland, 4:938
India
  and agriculture, 1:17
  Alexander the Great attacks, 1:21
  Armenia, trade with, 1:56
  and art/luxury objects, 1:59–60, 64
  and aviation, 1:85, 90
  and Berenice, 1:106
  Calcutta, 1:125, 135–137
  Calicut, 1:137–139
  China, trade relations with, 3:847
  climate in, 1:184

India *(continued)*
  Clive's (Robert) combat/administrative efforts in, 1:185–186
  and corn, 1:235
  corporate dominance over, 1:237–239
  and cotton, 1:241
  and diamonds, 1:269–271
  and diasporas, 1:272, 273
  and diseases, 1:278, 279
  France, trade relations with, 1:123
  and Gandhi (Mohandas), 2:391–393, 3:811–812
  and grain, 2:427
  and Hinduism, 2:460–463
  and independence, 1:127
  Indian National Congress, 2:392
  and Indian Ocean trade, 2:503, 505
  Industrial Revolution and, 2:513
  and ivory, 2:544–545
  and jute, 2:556
  and law, 2:580
  Madras, 3:592
  and Manchu dynasty, 3:597
  and mercantilism, 3:630
  Mesopotamia, trade relations with, 3:642
  and migrations (human), 3:651
  and new imperialism, 2:495
  and nuts, 3:707
  opium use/trade and, 2:471
  and outsourcing jobs, 3:818
  and pepper, 3:730
  and pilgrimages, 3:742
  and pirated entertainment, 2:468
  Portugal, trade relations with, 1:123
  and railroads, 3:767, 768, 922
  and salt, 3:811–812
  Seven Years War and, 3:820
  and silk, 3:897
  socioreligious reform movement in, 1:137
  and spice trade, 2:367
  Surat, 3:869–870
  and tariffs, 3:877
  telegraph and, 3:891
  and weights/measures, 4:962
  See also Mughal empire
Indian Ocean trade
  and cities/trade, 1:178
  and Equatorial Africa, 1:161
  Europeans arrival and the, 2:505–506
  and exploration/trade, 2:338
  and frankincense/myrrh, 2:377
  and gold, 1:9
  Islamic societies and, 2:543
  and jute, 2:556
  map of, 2:504
  monsoon winds and, 2:338
  and Persian Gulf, 3:732
  and piracy/privateering, 3:743
  ports in, 2:503, 505
  and slavery, 1:9, 2:543

Indonesia
  Bugis people, **1**:130
  cacao grown in, **1**:135
  and coconut oil, **3**:707
  and coffee, **1**:187
  Dutch culture influenced by, **1**:294
  and France, **2**:384
  and pepper, **3**:730
  and rice, **3**:791
  and spice trade, **3**:860
  and wood, **3**:848, **4**:978
Indus River, **2**:338, 507–509, **4**:957
Iran, **1**:284, 293, **3**:732
Iraq, **1**:109, 131, **3**:732
Ireland, **1**:122, **2**:587, **3**:650, 661, 818, 819, 897
Israel
  and Arabs, **1**:44, **3**:732, 867, 907–908, **4**:953
  and diamonds, **1**:271
  and Egypt, **2**:302, **3**:853
  and embargoes, **2**:307–308
  establishment/recognition of, **2**:551
  and Phoenicians, **1**:25
Istanbul, **1**:179, 218, 263
Italy
  and art/luxury objects, **1**:61–62
  Battle of Magenta, **3**:652
  Byzantine empire, trade relations with, **1**:134
  Carolingian empire, trade relations with, **1**:150
  and cartography, **1**:153
  and diamonds, **1**:271
  and diasporas, **1**:273
  and food/diet, **3**:715
  Germany, military alliance with, **4**:986
  and insurance, **2**:518
  and new imperialism, **3**:696
  and paper/pulp, **3**:724
  and sculpture, **3**:814
  and tortoiseshell, **3**:902
Ivory Coast, **1**:135, **2**:545–548, **4**:966

J

Jakarta, **1**:101–103
Jamaica, **1**:147, **2**:316
Jamestown, **2**:345, 410, 552, **3**:900–901
Japan
  and African structural adjustment programs, **1**:10
  and agriculture, **1**:17
  and Amazon River region, **1**:28–29
  Argentina, trade relations with, **1**:53
  and art/luxury objects, **1**:63, 65, 66
  and automobiles, **1**:83–84, **4**:987
  and aviation, **1**:90
  and bioterrorism, **1**:108, 109
  China, military conflicts with, **1**:116, **2**:432, 473, 474

Japan (*continued*)
  China, trade relations with, **1**:165, 170–172, 190
  and consumerism, **1**:222
  and copper, **1**:233
  Edo period, **1**:171, **2**:439
  and embargoes, **2**:308
  and empire building, **2**:319
  and GATT, **3**:882
  and globalization, **2**:413, 419
  Great Britain, trade relations with, **4**:1015–1016
  and Greater East Asia Co-Prosperity Sphere, **2**:431–432
  and gunpowder, **2**:439
  and Hamburg, **2**:442
  and Heian kingdom, **2**:297
  Industrial Revolution and, **2**:513–514
  and integration of regional economies, **2**:298
  Korean War helping economy of, **2**:298
  and law, **2**:580
  and livestock, **2**:589–590
  and Manila, **3**:600
  and Melaka, **3**:623
  and migrations (human), **3**:650–651
  and Ming dynasty, **3**:656
  and missionaries, **3**:663
  and multinational corporations, **1**:240
  and NAFTA, **3**:704
  and new imperialism, **2**:496, 497, **3**:696
  and oil/oil industry, **3**:711, 713
  and piracy/privateering, **2**:297, 468
  and Shanghai, **3**:823
  and Southeast Asia, **3**:848
  and tariffs, **3**:880–881
  and technology, **3**:888
  Treaty of Shimonoseki, **1**:66
  United States, trade relations with, **4**:927–928, 987
  and warfare impacting/being impacted by trade, **4**:951–952
  and weights/measures, **4**:964
  West, trade relations with the, **2**:298
Jerusalem, **1**:254, 256, **2**:466, **3**:699, 742, 904

K

Kalahari Desert, **1**:8
Kenya, **1**:127
Kilwa, **1**:178, **2**:559–560
Kittim, **3**:738
Kong, **4**:965
Korea, **1**:84, 129, 273, **2**:297
Korea, South, **1**:120, 165, **2**:298, 413, 527
Kowloon, **2**:473–474
Kush, **2**:564
Kuwait, **1**:131, 283, **2**:307, **3**:732

L

Lagos, **2**:459
Lahri-Bandar, **2**:503, 509
Lake Nasser, **1**:73
Lake Texcoco, **1**:93
Laos, **1**:69, 293
Las Vegas, **2**:325
Latin America
  and arms/weapons trade, **4**:962
  and art/luxury objects, **1**:63
  and aviation, **1**:88
  cacao plants in, **1**:172
  cholera in, **1**:174
  decolonization struggles in, **4**:952
  and disputes/arbitration, **1**:282
  and dollarization process, **2**:422
  and drugs, **1**:291, 292
  and Enterprise for the Americas Initiative, **1**:131, **4**:1164–1167
  and globalization, **2**:414
  and guilds, **3**:635, 638
  harbors in, **2**:451
  and immigration, **2**:490
  and independence movements, **3**:638, 752
  and missionaries, **3**:661–662
  and movie industry, **2**:325
  and narcoterrorism, **3**:894
  and new imperialism, **2**:496–497
  and pilgrimages, **3**:742
  and population issues, **3**:749
  and reciprocity, **3**:769
  See also Colonies, Latin American/Caribbean; South America; *individual countries*
Lebanon, **1**:25, 45
Lesser Antilles, **1**:146
Libya, **1**:283, **2**:303, **3**:853
Liverpool, **1**:181
London, **1**:173, 268, **2**:326, 519, **3**:647
Los Angeles, **1**:182–183, **2**:490
Lozi, **1**:160
Lübeck, **2**:443–445
Lydia, **1**:101, 187–188

M

Macedonia, **1**:101
Madagascar, **1**:8
Madeira, **1**:77, **2**:459
Madras, **3**:592
Magan, **1**:58
Malacca. *See* Melaka
Malaysia, **1**:69, 135, **3**:730, **4**:978
Maldives, **1**:244
Malta, **3**:738
Manila, **3**:598–601, 634–635
Marib, **2**:340
Marshall Islands, **1**:152

GEOGRAPHICAL INDEX   I-61

Martinique, 2:316
Mbundu, 1:160
Mecca, 1:289, 3:709
Mediterranean Sea region
   and art, 1:58
   and cartography, 1:153
   and cities, 1:176–177
   civilizations in, 3:621
   and copper, 1:231, 232
   Cyprus, 1:231, 260
   and Dardanelles channel, 1:262
   as declining link between Europe/the East, 3:783
   and diseases, 1:279
   and frankincense/myrrh, 2:377
   geography and climate in, 3:620–621
   and guilds, 3:631–632
   harbors in, 2:448–449
   and immigration, 2:484
   and migrations (human), 3:648
   and navigation, 3:668–669
   Nile River and, 3:697
   and Ottoman empire, 3:720
   and pilgrimages, 3:741
   and piracy/privateering, 3:743
   and ships/shipbuilding, 3:823
   and tourism, 3:907
Melaka, 1:154, 197–198, 2:449, 3:622–623, 848
Melanesia, 1:67
Mesopotamian civilization
   and archaeology, 1:47
   and architecture, 3:639–641
   and art/luxury objects, 1:57, 58
   Assyrian empire conquering, 1:70–71
   and cuneiform, 1:259–260
   and drugs, 1:291
   and fairs/festivals, 2:348
   fertilizer used in, 2:353
   India, trade relations with, 3:642
   and Indian Ocean trade, 2:503
   and iron technology, 2:533
   and irrigation, 2:536
   and sculpture, 3:812
   and technology, 3:886
   and trade connecting the East to the West, 3:641–643
   See also Babylonian empire; Sumerian civilization
Mexico
   and aviation, 1:90
   and cacao plants, 1:135, 172
   and cities, 1:180
   and coffee, 1:187
   and corn, 1:235
   and diseases, 1:193, 279
   and electricity, 2:304
   and gold, 3:845
   and guilds, 3:635, 637
   and import-substitution

Mexico *(continued)*
   industrialization, 1:118
   and livestock, 2:590
   and Manila, 3:599, 601, 634–635
   and missionaries, 3:667
   and population issues, 3:749
   and silver, 3:845
   and soybeans, 3:855
Miami, 2:490
Middle East
   and agriculture, 1:16
   Aramaic language spoken in, 1:23
   and barter system, 1:100
   and bribery, 1:118–119
   and British empire, 1:127
   and diasporas, 1:272
   and drugs, 1:290
   and empire building, 2:319
   and gemstones, 2:395
   and movie industry, 2:325
   and stock exchanges, 2:362
   and urban revolution, 1:176
   and women, 4:971
   See also Ottoman empire
Milan, 3:651–652
Mississippi River, 2:383
Mitanni, 1:70, 71
Mogadishu, 3:668–669
Moldavia, 3:720
Moldova, 1:113
Montevideo, 1:173
Morocco, 3:918, 4:965
Moscow, 3:706
Mozambique, 1:235, 3:752
Mughal empire
   and art, 1:64
   demise and subjugation of, 2:325, 3:682
   and domestic trade, 3:679
   and emeralds, 2:395
   and gold, 2:420
   and Hinduism, 2:462
   map of, 3:680
   and mercantilism, 3:630
   Netherlands and, 3:681, 682
   overland trade and, 3:678–679
   and overseas trade, 3:679, 681
Murano, 2:410
Muscat, 2:503
Myanmar, 1:69, 4:978

N

Najraf oasis, 3:708
Namibia, 1:271
Naples, 1:96–97
Ndogo, 1:160
Netherlands
   and Aegean Sea, 1:7
   and agriculture, 1:18
   Amsterdam, 1:37–38

Netherlands *(continued)*
   and arms/weapons trade, 4:961
   and art/luxury objects, 1:63–65, 67
   and Atlantic trade route, 1:79–81
   and aviation, 1:92
   and banks/banking, 2:358–359
   and bribery, 1:120
   Bugis people and, 1:130
   and Caribbean region, 1:147
   and cartography, 1:155–156
   China, trade relations with, 2:297
   and Christianity, 1:175–176
   and colonialism, 1:191
   and cotton, 1:241
   department stores in, 1:268
   and discovery/exploration, 1:275–276
   and drugs, 1:293
   and embargoes, 2:308
   and empire building, 1:294, 2:314, 316
   and Equatorial Africa, 1:161
   and exploration/trade, 2:344
   and food/diet, 2:371
   and fur trade, 1:40
   and gold, 2:420
   and grain, 2:425
   and gunpowder, 2:438–439
   and immigration, 2:483, 487–488
   and imperialism/emergence of world economy, 4:947
   and Indian Ocean trade, 2:505
   Indonesian culture influencing the, 1:294
   and insurance, 2:518
   and labor relations, 1:294
   and Madras, 3:592
   and Manchu dynasty, 3:597
   and Melaka, 3:623
   and mercantilism, 3:626–627
   and Ming dynasty, 3:657
   molasses and, 3:670
   and Mughal empire, 3:681, 682
   and navigation, 3:690
   and Ottoman empire, 3:721
   overview of, 3:694–695
   and paper/pulp, 3:725
   and piracy/privateers, 1:79
   and Renaissance period, 3:783
   Russia, trade relations with, 3:733
   and spice trade, 2:367, 369, 3:859
   stock exchanges in, 2:361
   and Surat, 3:869
   and unions, 1:295, 3:694
   and women, 4:971
New Amsterdam, 1:180
New England colonies, 1:81, 2:345, 3:670, 804
New Guinea, 2:405
New Orleans, 2:450–451
New York, 1:180, 271, 2:326
New Zealand, 1:121, 230, 231, 3:666, 877
Ngbandi, 1:160

Nicaea, **1**:254
Nicaragua, **2**:497
Nigeria, **1**:10, 135, **3**:801–803, **4**:966
Niger River, **1**:295, 296, **2**:547
Nile River, **1**:73–74, 106, **2**:339–340, 586, **3**:696–698, **4**:957
Nineveh, **3**:699–700
North America, **1**:10, 41, 52, 193
  See also Canada; Colonies, North American; United States
North Sea, **1**:30
Norway, **1**:233, **3**:871, 872
Novgorod, **3**:705–706, **4**:939
Nubia, **2**:303, 564
Nyamwezi, **1**:161

O

Oceanic island chains, **1**:66–67
Oman, **3**:642–643
Orinoco River, **1**:235
Ostia, **2**:449
Ottoman empire
  and Aegean Sea, **1**:7
  Arab nationalism and weakening of, **1**:44
  Armenia ruled by, **1**:56
  Black Sea region controlled by, **1**:113
  and cities/trade, **1**:179
  and coffee, **1**:186
  and conquest, **3**:719–720
  Constantinople captured by, **1**:220
  Crimean War, **1**:14, 247–249, 261, 264
  and Dardanelles channel, **1**:262–264
  and drugs, **1**:293
  Egypt conquered by, **2**:302
  and extraterritoriality, **2**:346–347
  and foreign traders, **3**:720–721
  Great Britain, trade relations with, **1**:237
  Greece declares independence from, **1**:7–8
  and gunpowder, **2**:437, 439
  Jewish people, trade relations with, **2**:555
  and law, **3**:721
  and Mediterranean Sea region, **3**:720
  and new imperialism, **2**:495
  and Nile River, **3**:698
  Ragusa, trade relations with, **3**:765
  trade and international policy of, **2**:540–541, **3**:718–719
  and Tunisia, **3**:925–926
  and Venice, **1**:179, **3**:721, **4**:937

P

Pacific Ocean, **2**:345
Pakistan, **1**:122, 241, 285, 293
Panama, **2**:497, **3**:846
Panama Canal
  and aviation, **1**:88
  and medicine, **3**:619

Panama Canal (*continued*)
  overview of, **3**:722–724
  and superships, **3**:691
  Treaty of 1903, **4**:1107–1111
  Treaty of 1977, **4**:1157–1162
  United States and, **3**:722–726, 922–923
  and water's role in international trade, **4**:958
Papua New Guinea, **1**:135
Paris, **3**:678
Pearl Harbor, **4**:951, 987, 988–989
People's Republic of China (PRC), **1**:164–165, 189, 244
Pergamon, **2**:457
Persia
  and Abbasid caliphate, **1**:1, 2
  Achaemenian empire, **1**:113
  Alexander the Great's conquest of, **1**:20–21
  Aramaic language spoken in, **1**:22
  Armenia ruled by, **1**:55–56
  and Babylonian empire, **1**:94, 95
  and coins/coinage, **1**:101
  and Dark Ages, **1**:266
  and Delian League, **1**:266–267
  Egypt, trade relations with, **2**:303
  Egypt conquered by, **2**:304
  and gemstones, **2**:395
  Great Britain, trade relations with, **1**:237
  Greece, military conflicts with, **2**:433–434
  Indus River and, **2**:508, 509
  and oil/oil industry, **3**:710
  and perfume, **3**:730
  and Phoenicians, **3**:738
Peru
  and corn, **1**:235
  and diseases, **1**:174, 193, 279
  and drugs, **1**:293
  and guano, **2**:436
  and guilds, **3**:635
  and Manila, **3**:601
  and maritime resources, **1**:49
  silver from, **1**:180
Petra, **3**:734–736
Philippines
  and ASEAN, **1**:69
  and aviation, **1**:90
  and coconut oil, **3**:707
  Manila, **3**:598–601
  and mercantilism, **3**:625–626
  and missionaries, **3**:667
  and new imperialism, **2**:496
  and wood, **4**:978
Phoenicia/Phoenicians
  alphabet and, **1**:24–26, 198, **3**:738
  and art/luxury objects, **1**:58
  Carthage and, **1**:177, **3**:739
  and cities/trade, **1**:176–177
  and colonialism, **3**:738–739
  and copper, **1**:231–232

Phoenicia/Phoenicians (*continued*)
  culture and religion of, **3**:737–738
  decline and fall of, **3**:738
  as a dominant power, **3**:737
  Egypt, trade relations with, **2**:303, 304
  and exploration/trade, **2**:336–337
  and food/diet, **2**:366
  and glass, **2**:410
  and immigration, **2**:483, 484
  origins of, **3**:736–737
  and Sahara Desert/trade, **3**:806
  and ships/shipbuilding, **1**:47, **3**:823
  and Sicily, **3**:826
  and Tunisia, **3**:924
  and wine, **4**:970
  and wood, **4**:977
Piraeus, **1**:177
Pisa, **3**:632
Poland, **1**:189, 273, **2**:415, **3**:778, 849, **4**:987
Portugal
  and art, **1**:63, 65
  and Atlantic trade route, **1**:77, 78
  and Brazil, **3**:752, 845
  Bugis people and, **1**:130
  Calicut, trade relations with, **1**:138, 139
  and cartography, **1**:153–155
  China, military conflicts with, **3**:655, 657
  and cities/trade, **1**:178, 179–180
  compass and, **1**:209
  and Continental System, **3**:687
  and cowry shells, **1**:245
  and diamonds, **1**:270, 271
  and discovery/exploration, **1**:275
  and drugs, **1**:292
  and empire building, **2**:310–312
  and Equatorial Africa, **1**:161
  and exploration/trade, **2**:343–345
  and Ghana, **2**:406–407
  Great Britain, alliance with, **1**:128
  and Guangzhou, **2**:435
  and gunpowder, **2**:439
  and Hinduism, **2**:462
  and immigration, **3**:752
  and imperialism/emergence of world economy, **4**:946–947
  India, trading relations with, **1**:123
  and insurance, **2**:518
  kamal used by, **1**:251
  and Kilwa, **1**:178, **2**:560
  and Manila, **3**:599, 600
  and Melaka, **3**:622–623
  and mercantilism, **3**:626
  and Ming dynasty, **3**:655, 657
  and missionaries, **3**:661–664
  and Mogadishu, **3**:668
  and Mughal empire, **3**:681, 682
  and navigation, **3**:689
  and Ottoman empire, **3**:719
  overview of, **3**:750–752
  and pepper, **3**:729

GEOGRAPHICAL INDEX   I-63

Portugal *(continued)*
    and Renaissance period, **3:**783
    and salt, **3:**811
    and ships/shipbuilding, **3:**824
    and silver, **3:**832
    and South America, **3:**845
    and Southeast Asia, **3:**848
    and spice trade, **2:**367, 369, **3:**859, 860
    and sugar, **3:**669, 867–868
    and Surat, **3:**869
    and *Wealth of Nations*, **4:**1049–1063
    and wood, **4:**977
Potosí, **1:**180
Prussia
    Baroque period and, **1:**98–99
    and cholera, **1:**173
    and Dardanelles channel, **1:**264
    Frederick II and, **2:**379–380, **3:**819–820
    and Ottoman empire, **3:**721
    Russia, military conflicts with, **2:**379
    Russia, trade relations with, **3:**733
    and Seven Years War, **2:**403, **3:**818
Puerto Rico, **1:**146, 147, **3:**637

R

Red Sea, **1:**105–106, **2:**544, **3:**643, 729
Rhodesia, **1:**162
Romania, **1:**113, 244, **3:**710
Rome, ancient
    advertising in, **1:**4
    and Aegean Sea, **1:**7
    and agriculture, **1:**11
    and amber, **1:**30, 131
    Appian Way, **1:**41–42
    and art/luxury objects, **1:**60
    and Berenice, **1:**106
    and Black Sea region, **1:**113
    Carthage, military conflicts with, **1:**177, **3:**739, 759–760, 826
    and cartography, **1:**152
    and Catholic Church, **3:**793, 795, 797
    Celts, trade relations with, **2:**331
    and cities/trade, **1:**177
    and coins/coinage, **1:**101, 188
    Constantinople and, **1:**218–220
    and copper, **1:**231, 232
    Danube River and, **1:**261–262
    and drugs, **1:**291
    Egypt, trade relations with, **2:**304, 309
    and empire building, **2:**309
    and entertainment, **2:**323
    Etruscans dominated by, **2:**327
    and exploration/trade, **2:**339–340
    and fairs/festivals, **2:**349
    fall of, **3:**799
    and food/diet, **2:**366, 367, **3:**714, 715
    forums as central marketplaces in, **1:**11
    and frankincense/myrrh, **2:**377

Rome, ancient *(continued)*
    Garamantian empire, trade relations with, **2:**393
    and gemstones, **2:**395
    and glass, **2:**410
    and gold, **2:**419
    and Goths, **2:**423
    and governance/trade, **3:**795, 797
    harbors in, **2:**449
    and immigration, **2:**483–486
    and income of merchants, **3:**794–795
    and Latin language, **1:**24, 198
    and law, **2:**577
    and livestock, **2:**588
    map of, **3:**796
    and medicine, **3:**618
    Mediterranean Sea vital to, **3:**621
    Middle Ages and, **3:**643, 645
    and Milan, **3:**651
    Nubia, military conflicts with, **2:**564
    and perfume, **3:**730
    and Petra, **3:**736
    and piracy/privateering, **3:**743
    plague in, **3:**617–618
    and population issues, **3:**749
    and Sahara Desert/trade, **3:**806–807
    and salt, **3:**810
    and sculpture, **3:**813
    and ships/shipbuilding, **3:**823
    and silk trade/Silk Road to China, **3:**829, 897
    and silver, **3:**831
    and slavery, **3:**835
    and technology, **3:**886
    trading networks in, **3:**798–799
    and transportation/trade, **3:**920
    and Tunisia, **3:**924
    types of trade movement, **3:**797–798
    and warfare impacting/being impacted by trade, **4:**944
    and weights/measures, **4:**963
    and wine, **4:**970
    and wood, **4:**977
    and wool, **3:**896, **4:**979
Ruhr, **2:**534
Russia
    and Black Sea region, **1:**113
    and bribery, **1:**120
    China, trade relations with, **1:**166
    economic problems in, **1:**53
    fur industry, **1:**41
    and oil/oil industry, **3:**713
    and pirated entertainment, **2:**468
    unions in, **2:**572
    See also Soviet Union, the former
Russian empire
    and Aegean Sea, **1:**7
    and art/luxury objects, **1:**64–65
    in the Baroque period, **1:**98–99
    and Black Sea region, **1:**113

Russian empire *(continued)*
    and Bolshevism, **1:**113–114
    and cartography, **1:**157
    China, trade relations with, **1:**116
    cholera in, **1:**173
    climate in the, **1:**185
    and Continental System, **3:**687
    and copper, **1:**233
    Crimean War, **1:**14, 247–249, 261, 264
    Cyrillic alphabet spoken in, **1:**23
    and Dardanelles channel, **1:**264
    and dirhams, **1:**274
    furs used as a medium of exchange in, **1:**188
    Great Britain, trade relations with, **1:**237
    and hemp, **2:**457
    Islamic societies, trade relations with, **2:**540
    and ivory, **2:**545
    Netherlands, trade relations with, **3:**733
    and new imperialism, **3:**696
    and Peter the Great, **3:**733–734
    Prussia, military conflicts with, **2:**379
    Prussia, trade relations with, **3:**733
    and tally sticks, **3:**871, 872
    and Vikings, **4:**938

S

Sahara Desert/trade, **1:**8, 9, 105, **3:**708, 806–810, **4:**964–965
Sahel area in Africa, **1:**8
Saint Croix, **1:**146
Saint Domingue, **2:**383, 440, **3:**384
Samoa, **2:**496
Samothrace, **1:**6
San Francisco, **1:**182
Santo Domingo, **1:**147
Sardinia, **1:**248
Saudi Arabia, **3:**708, 709, 711, 713, 733
Scandinavia, **2:**304
Scotland, **2:**304, 359, 556, **3:**833
Sea of Marmara, **1:**218
Senegal, **3:**707
Serampore, **1:**135 136
Serbia, **4:**983
Seville, **3:**634–635
Shanghai, **1:**182, **3:**821–823
Sicily, **2:**434, **3:**826–827
Sidon, **2:**448–449, **3:**736–737
Sijilmasa, **3:**807
Singapore, **1:**69, 166, **2:**449–450, 489, **3:**848
Somalia, **3:**668–669
South Africa
    and apartheid system, **3:**843
    Boer War, **1:**126
    and bribery, **1:**119
    and Commonwealth of Nations, **1:**122
    contemporary trade profile of, **1:**10
    and diasporas, **1:**272

South Africa *(continued)*
  and embargoes, **2:**308
  and fur trade, **3:**846
  and Gandhi (Mohandas), **2:**391
  and gold/diamonds, **1:**271, **2:**395, 420, **3:**842–843
  Khoisan people, **3:**842
  and Mandela (Nelson), **3:**843–844
  stock exchanges in, **2:**362
South America
  and Atlantic trade route, **1:**77, 78
  cacao grown in, **1:**135
  and corn, **1:**235
  geographical overview of, **3:**845
  Germany, trade relations with, **1:**128
  Great Britain, trade relations with, **1:**127–128
  and Portugal, **3:**845
  postcolonial, **3:**846
  and Spanish America, **3:**845–846
  and tortoiseshell, **3:**903
  United States, trade relations with, **1:**128
  and wood, **4:**977
  See also Colonies, Latin American/Caribbean; Latin America
South China Sea, **3:**744
Soviet Union, the former
  Africa, trade relations with, **3:**852–854
  and agriculture, **1:**16, 17
  and alcoholic beverages, **2:**483
  Armenia ruled by, **1:**56
  and arms/weapons trade, **4:**962
  and aviation, **1:**19, 20, 87, 90
  and bioterrorism, **1:**108–109
  and Black Sea region, **1:**113
  and Bolshevism, **1:**114–115
  and China, **1:**165, **3:**850
  and Cold War, **1:**187–190
  collapse of, **1:**131
  and containment policy of U.S., **1:**227–228
  Council for Mutual Economic Assistance, **1:**189, 207, 228, 243–244, **3:**850–851
  and Cuba, **1:**259, **3:**851
  currency controls in, **2:**481
  Danube River and, **1:**262
  department stores in, **1:**268
  and diamonds, **1:**271
  and diasporas, **1:**272
  early period of, **3:**849–850
  and Eastern Europe, **3:**850–851
  and embargoes, **2:**308
  and empire building, **2:**319
  Europe, trade relations with, **1:**115
  Germany, military conflicts with, **3:**849
  and globalization, **2:**414–415
  and intracontinental European trade, **2:**332
  and Marshall Plan, **3:**607

Soviet Union, the former *(continued)*
  and Mediterranean Sea region, **3:**621
  and oil/oil industry, **3:**711
  and political economy/invention of capitalism, **1:**142
  United States, trade relations with, **1:**115, 189, **4:**986
  and world economy, **3:**851
  See also Russia/Russian *listings*
Spain
  and agriculture, **1:**12
  and Amazon River, **1:**28
  and American Revolution, **1:**36
  Armada defeated by Great Britain, **2:**306
  and art/luxury objects, **1:**62, 63
  and Atlantic trade route, **1:**77–79
  and Aztecs, **1:**93
  and banks/banking, **2:**358
  in the Baroque period, **1:**97
  and bioterrorism, **1:**108
  and Caribbean region, **1:**146, 147
  and cartography, **1:**154
  and cities/trade, **1:**179–180
  and coins/coinage, **1:**188
  and colonialism, **1:**190–191, **3:**857
  and Columbian exchange, **1:**193
  and Columbus (Christopher), **1:**194–195
  compass and, **1:**209
  and conquistadors, **1:**78, 93, 176
  and corn, **1:**235
  and cotton, **1:**241
  Cuba as colony of, **1:**258–259
  and decline of the empire, **3:**856–857
  and discovery/exploration, **1:**275
  and diseases, **1:**279
  Drake's (Francis) attacks on, **1:**289
  and empire building, **2:**312–314, **3:**856
  and exploration/trade, **2:**344
  and fairs/festivals, **2:**352–353
  and food/diet, **2:**387
  and Fugger family, **2:**388–389
  and gold, **2:**420
  and Goths, **2:**424
  Great Britain, military conflicts with, **2:**306
  Greeks, trade relations with, **2:**337
  and guilds, **3:**632–639
  Hundred Years' War and, **2:**478
  and immigration, **2:**487
  and imperialism/emergence of world economy, **4:**946
  Incas, military conflicts with the, **2:**501
  and indigo, **2:**506
  and iron technology, **2:**533
  and linen, **2:**587
  and Manila, **3:**599–601
  and mercantilism, **3:**624–626
  and Ming dynasty, **3:**657
  and missionaries, **3:**661
  and Napoleonic Wars, **3:**846

Spain *(continued)*
  and navigation, **3:**689, 690
  and Phoenicians, **3:**738
  and piracy/privateering, **3:**624–625
  and Renaissance period, **3:**783–784
  and Sicily, **3:**826–827
  and silver, **3:**831–832
  and slavery, **1:**78
  and spice trade, **2:**369, **3:**859
  and sugar, **3:**867
  and tortoiseshell, **3:**902
  and wool, **4:**979
  See also Colonies, Latin American/Caribbean
Sparta, **1:**74, 266–267, **2:**433, 434, **4:**944
Spice Islands/trade
  and Arabs, **2:**367, **3:**848, 858, 860
  and Atlantic trade route, **1:**77, 78
  and cities, **1:**178
  and Constantinople, **1:**219
  and Crusades, **3:**858, **2:**368
  and Drake (Francis), **1:**290
  and Indian Ocean trade, **2:**505
  influential nature of, **2:**368–369
  Islamic societies and, **2:**540
  and Manchu dynasty, **3:**597
  and Manila, **3:**599
  and Melaka, **2:**449, **3:**622
  and Nineveh, **3:**699
  overview of, **3:**860–861
  Portugal/Netherlands impacting the, **2:**367
  Rome's fall impacting, **3:**799
  spice route (on water), **3:**858–860
Sporades, Northern, **1:**6
Sri Lanka, **3:**730
Strait of Magellan, **3:**594
Sudan, **1:**105, 245, **4:**965
Suez Canal
  and African ports losing importance, **2:**494
  and bankruptcy problems for Egypt, **2:**302
  British control over, **1:**127
  Convention of Constantinople and, **4:**1103–1105
  East-West trade and shipbuilding impacted by, **3:**921
  and Indian-European relations, **1:**126
  and Mediterranean Sea gaining importance, **3:**621
  overview of, **3:**866–867
  and steamships, **3:**824
  and superships, **3:**691
  and warfare impacting/being impacted by trade, **4:**950
  and water's role in international trade, **4:**958
Sumerian civilization
  and architecture, **3:**641

Sumerian civilization (continued)
    and copper, **1:**231
    and cuneiform, **1:**259–260, **2:**365, **3:**724
    and drugs, **1:**290, 291
    and food/diet, **2:**365–366
    and glass, **2:**410
    and immigration, **2:**484
    and Indian Ocean trade, **2:**503
    and livestock, **2:**588
    and medicine, **3:**616
    merchants and, **1:**57
    and paper/pulp, **3:**724
    and tin, **3:**900
    and transportation/trade, **3:**919
Surat, **3:**869–870
Suriname, **1:**147
Sweden, **1:**233, **2:**482, **3:**687, 706, 721, 871, **4:**961
Switzerland, **1:**173
Syria, **1:**25, 58, 59, 71, 145, **2:**303, 340, 586

T

Tahiti, **1:**230
Taiwan, **1:**110, 120, 166, **2:**413
Tenochtitlán, **1:**48, 92–93
Teotihuacán, **1:**47, 50, 51–52
Thailand, **1:**17, 69, 293, **3:**730, 791, 848
Thásos, **1:**6
Thebes, **1:**291
Tiananmen Square, **1:**190
Tigris River, **3:**732, 921, **4:**957, 977
    See also Mesopotamian civilization
Timbuktu, **2:**406, **3:**594, 809, 810, **4:**965
Trinidad and Tobago, **1:**147, 195
Tunis, **3:**720
Tunisia, **3:**924–926
Turkey, **1:**113, 264, **2:**405, **3:**707
    See also Ottoman empire
Turpan, **3:**708
Tuwat oasis, **3:**708
Tyre, **1:**176–177

U

Ukraine, **1:**113
United Kingdom. *See* Great Britain
United States
    abolition of slavery in, **2:**567
    and agriculture, **1:**13–18
    aircraft production, **1:**19
    Argentina, trade relations with, **1:**53
    and arms/weapons trade, **2:**480, **4:**961
    and art/luxury objects, **1:**67–68
    and automobile production, **1:**83
    and aviation, **1:**19, 85, 87–92
    and banks/banking, **2:**360–361
    and bioterrorism, **1:**108–110
    Brazil, trade relations with, **1:**118
    and bribery, **1:**120

United States (continued)
    British Orders in Council of 1804/1806, **1:**13, **2:**384
    Caribbean region, colonial possessions in, **1:**146
    and cartography, **1:**157
    China, trade relations with, **1:**116, 165, 166, 190
    Civil War, **1:**14, 108, **3:**602, 603, 901, **4:**933, 943
    cocoa processing factories in, **1:**173
    and coffee, **1:**187
    coins/coinage in, **1:**188
    and Cold War, **1:**187–190
    and competition policy, **1:**212, 214–215
    computer use in, **1:**216
    Constitutional Convention in 1781, **4:**931
    and consumerism, **1:**221–224, 226–227
    and containment policy, **1:**227–228, **3:**607, **4:**943, 952, 991
    and copper, **1:**233
    and copyrights, **1:**233, 234
    and corn, **1:**235–236
    and corporations, **1:**239
    and cotton, **1:**241, 242–243, **3:**898
    crop rotation in, **1:**250
    and Cuban missile crisis, **1:**189
    and Dardanelles channel, **1:**263
    department stores in, **1:**268
    and diasporas, **1:**272, 273
    and disputes/arbitration, **1:**284
    and drugs, **1:**293
    early republic in, **4:**931–932
    and electricity, **2:**304
    and embargoes, **2:**306–308, **4:**932
    and empire building, **2:**318
    and English language as dominant common language, **1:**199
    and Equatorial Africa's mineral resources, **1:**162
    and fairs/festivals, **2:**350–353
    fertilizer used in, **2:**353
    and food/diet, **2:**387, 388
    and foreign aid, **2:**375
    France, trade relations with, **2:**385
    and GATT, **3:**882
    Germany, trade relations with, **4:**987
    and Gilded age, **1:**67
    and globalization, **1:**140, **2:**413, 416, 418
    and gold, **2:**420, 421
    and guano, **2:**436
    and Gulf Wars, **1:**109, 131
    and hemp, **2:**457–458
    and immigration, **2:**489–490
    and imperial competition, **3:**857
    and insurance, **2:**519, 520
    and irrigation, **2:**537
    Japan, trade relations with, **4:**927–928, 987
    and law, **2:**579

United States (continued)
    and livestock, **2:**589–590
    Louisiana Purchase, **3:**846, **4:**931–932, 1067–1069
    and Manila, **3:**599–600
    and market revolution, **1:**101, **3:**602
    and medicine, **3:**619
    and Mediterranean Sea region, **3:**621
    and migrations (human), **3:**650–651
    and Mogadishu, **3:**668
    monuments in, **3:**676
    and multinational enterprises, **3:**682–683
    and Napoleonic Wars, **3:**687, **4:**932, 948–949
    and new imperialism, **2:**496, 497, **3:**696
    and nuts, **3:**707
    and oil/oil industry, **3:**710–711, 713
    and open door notes, **3:**715–716
    and Panama Canal, **3:**722–726, 922–923
    and paper/pulp, **3:**725–726
    and perfume, **3:**731
    and Persian Gulf, **3:**733
    and pottery, **3:**755
    and Protestantism, **3:**759
    and railroads, **3:**767, 922
    and reciprocity, **3:**769–770
    and regional trade organizations, **3:**913
    Revolutionary War, **1:**34–38, 81, **2:**317
    and rise to world power, **4:**933–934
    and Russian Revolution, **3:**805
    September 11th terrorist attacks in, **1:**92, 109, **3:**733, 893, 907, 923, **4:**966
    and Shanghai, **3:**822
    and ships/shipbuilding, **3:**824
    and silver, **3:**832–833
    and slavery, **2:**567, **4:**932–933
    South America, trade relations with, **1:**128
    and Southeast Asia, **3:**848
    Soviet Union, trade relations with, **1:**115, 189, **4:**986
    and soybeans, **3:**854, 855
    and Spain's decline, **3:**857
    stock exchanges in, **2:**362
    and tariffs, **3:**877, 878–880
    and technology, **3:**888–890
    and textile industry, **3:**898
    and tobacco, **3:**902
    and tourism, **3:**905–906
    and trademarks, **3:**917
    and transportation/trade, **3:**602–603, 922
    and warfare impacting/being impacted by trade, **4:**952
    and weapons/armament production, **4:**961
    and whales, **4:**967
    and women, **4:**973–974
    and wood, **4:**978

United States *(continued)*
  and wool, **4:**979–980
  See also Colonies, North American
Upper Volta, **2:**547
Uzbekistan, **3:**708

V

Venezuela, **1:**128, 195, 271, **3:**713, 846
Venice
  and Aegean Sea, **1:**7
  and art/luxury objects, **1:**62
  and banks/banking, **2:**358
  and Black Death, **1:**107
  and Byzantine empire, **1:**134, **4:**935
  Carolingian empire, trade relations with, **1:**151
  and Catholic Church, **4:**935
  Comacchio, military conflicts with, **4:**935
  compass and, **1:**209
  and cotton, **1:**241
  and Crusades, **1:**178, 255, **4:**936
  and Dardanelles channel, **1:**263
  and exploration/trade, **2:**343

Venice *(continued)*
  and gemstones, **2:**395
  Genoa and, **2:**402, **4:**937
  and glass, **2:**410
  and Hanseatic League, **3:**647
  as the hinge of Europe, **1:**178
  and insurance, **2:**518
  and interregional transit trade, **4:**937
  and intracontinental European trade, **2:**331
  Middle East and, **3:**645
  and Ottoman empire, **1:**179, **3:**721, **4:**937
  Ragusa, military conflicts with, **3:**765, 766
  resources needed in, **4:**935–937
  and salt, **1:**178, **3:**810
  and service sector, **3:**815
  and silk trade, **1:**219
  and spice trade, **1:**77, **3:**858
Vietnam
  and ASEAN, **1:**69
  and coffee, **1:**187
  and Cold War, **1:**189

Vietnam *(continued)*
  and Council for Mutual Economic Assistance, **1:**244
  France and, **2:**384
  and rice, **1:**17, **3:**791
  and wood, **4:**978
Virginia colony, **1:**12, **2:**345
Volga Bulgaria, **4:**939–940

W

Weimar Republic, **3:**878
Wild Cane Cay, **1:**48

Y

Yemen, **2:**377
Yugoslavia, **1:**244, **3:**853

Z

Zambia, **1:**233
Zanzibar, **1:**244, 245
Zeravshan River, **3:**708
Zimbabwe, **1:**96